Some Kind of Justice

Some Kind of Justice

The ICTY's Impact in Bosnia and Serbia

DIANE ORENTLICHER

OXFORD
UNIVERSITY PRESS

OXFORD
UNIVERSITY PRESS

Oxford University Press is a department of the University of Oxford. It furthers the University's objective of excellence in research, scholarship, and education by publishing worldwide. Oxford is a registered trademark of Oxford University Press in the UK and certain other countries.

Published in the United States of America by Oxford University Press
198 Madison Avenue, New York, NY 10016, United States of America.

First issued as an Oxford University Press paperback, 2020
ISBN 9780190090258

Library of Congress Cataloging-in-Publication Data
Names: Orentlicher, Diane, author.
Title: Some kind of justice : the ICTY's impact in Bosnia and Serbia / Diane Orentlicher.
Description: New York : Oxford University Press, 2018. | Includes bibliographical references and index.
Identifiers: LCCN 2017048647 | ISBN 9780190882273 ((hardback) : alk. paper)
Subjects: LCSH: International Tribunal for the Prosecution of Persons Responsible for Serious Violations of International Humanitarian Law Committed in the Territory of the Former Yugoslavia since 1991. | War crime trials—Yugoslavia. | War crime trials—Serbia. | War crime trials—Bosnia and Herzegovina.
Classification: LCC KZ1203.A12 O74 2018 | DDC 341.6/90268—dc23
LC record available at https://lccn.loc.gov/2017048647

Note to Readers

This publication is designed to provide accurate and authoritative information in regard to the subject matter covered. It is based upon sources believed to be accurate and reliable and is intended to be current as of the time it was written. It is sold with the understanding that the publisher is not engaged in rendering legal, accounting, or other professional services. If legal advice or other expert assistance is required, the services of a competent professional person should be sought. Also, to confirm that the information has not been affected or changed by recent developments, traditional legal research techniques should be used, including checking primary sources where appropriate.

(Based on the Declaration of Principles jointly adopted by a Committee of the American Bar Association and a Committee of Publishers and Associations.)

You may order this or any other Oxford University Press publication
by visiting the Oxford University Press website at www.oup.com.

For Mort

CONTENTS

PREFACE AND ACKNOWLEDGMENTS

In periodic trips to the former Yugoslavia during and after the 1990s conflicts accompanying its implosion, I saw how urgently victims of wartime atrocities yearned for justice, investing soaring hopes in the International Criminal Tribunal for the former Yugoslavia (ICTY) in The Hague. Across the first dozen years of the Tribunal's working life, I was in frequent contact with Bosnian and Serbian advocates who sought to bolster its work by, for example, ensuring the ICTY gained custody of those it had indicted. Thus I had ample grounds to believe global efforts to support the Tribunal were in line with the aspirations of survivors and of local citizens who championed their calls for justice. Even so, once the ICTY successfully addressed early, fundamental challenges to its work, it seemed crucially important to take a deeper look at how citizens of the former Yugoslavia were experiencing Hague justice.

I approached Aryeh Neier, then president of the Open Society Institute (OSI), with an idea I hoped OSI would support: researching and reporting on the Tribunal's impact in Bosnia, where the vast majority of atrocities prosecuted before the ICTY occurred, and Serbia, whose wartime leader plunged the region into calamitous conflict. Aryeh readily agreed, and convened a meeting of leading human rights experts to advise me on the project's design. Other members of what is now known as the Open Society Foundations (OSF), including Beka Vučo, Laura Silber, Kelly Askin, and Jim Goldston, provided invaluable suggestions and guidance.

This was the beginning of myriad forms of support by OSI/OSF for the larger project culminating in *Some Kind of Justice*. OSI funded research visits to Bosnia-Herzegovina and Serbia in 2006, 2007, and 2009; the Open Society Justice Initiative published the reports resulting from this fieldwork in 2008 (Serbia) and 2010 (Bosnia), the latter in collaboration with the International Center for Transitional Justice. When I returned to this inquiry several years later, Emily Martinez, director of OSF's Human Rights Initiative, agreed to fund research visits to Bosnia and Serbia in 2012 and in 2014.

The Open Society Fund Serbia (OSF Serbia) and Open Society Fund Bosnia and Herzegovina (OSF BiH) provided indispensable guidance and assistance in organizing hundreds of interviews in Serbia and Bosnia. Despite pressing claims on their attention (both organizations are centrally involved in addressing a raft of consequential challenges in their countries), their leaders and staff could not have been more generous with their time, expertise, insights, and wisdom. I owe a special debt to Jadranka Jelinčić, executive director of OSF Serbia, and Dobrila Govedarica, executive director of OSF BiH, both of whom marshaled the resources of their offices and staff to support my work while offering wise counsel and insights about their countries' experience of Hague justice. Mervan Miraščija, OSF BiH's Law Program Coordinator, and Mihajlo Čolak of OSF Serbia, provided countless forms of support during all of my research visits. During my 2014 research visit to Bosnia, I was ably assisted as well by Nermina Mujčić, then a Project Assistant at OSF BiH. Irfan Hatić drove me across the lengths and breadths of Bosnia, logging long days as well as miles in good cheer. Haris Imamović provided compassionate companionship as well as able translation services.

This book draws upon a rich body of cross-disciplinary research to illuminate the impact of the ICTY in Bosnia and Serbia and explain dynamics behind the Tribunal's changing impact across more than two decades. But if its assessment is informed by myriad sources and perspectives, whenever possible I have structured its account with the words of those I interviewed in Bosnia and Serbia. Although I am acutely aware I cannot speak for any Bosnian or Serbian citizens, I wanted to let those I interviewed speak for themselves to the extent possible in a book they did not write.

During research visits, I sought interviews with sources with diverse perspectives, ranging from survivors of wartime atrocities to individuals who have played key roles in developments this book explores, such as judges and prosecutors in Bosnian and Serbian war crimes institutions. Some whom I interviewed generously shared additional source materials, such as the results of public opinion surveys they administered, along with invaluable insights into their significance. The contributions of many Bosnian and Serbian citizens whom I interviewed are "acknowledged" throughout *Some Kind of Justice*. Yet three individuals merit special thanks here: along with Mervan Miraščija, whom I have already mentioned, Ivan Jovanović and Bogdan Ivanišević have been endlessly generous with their time and insights, not only during research visits but whenever I had a question. I am also grateful to Refik Hodžić and Nina Bang-Jensen for invaluable suggestions and contacts in advance of several research visits.

I am most grateful, as well, to judges, prosecutors, outreach officers, and other ICTY personnel who shared their time and insights during interviews in The Hague, Bosnia, and Serbia. Like the contributions of Bosnians and Serbians whom I interviewed, theirs are recognized in relevant portions of this book. Here, I wish to add a special thanks to Kevin Hughes for helping me arrange interviews at the ICTY in May 2015, patiently answering follow-up questions for the next two years, and providing invaluable perspectives on developments chronicled in this book.

As any full-time academic knows, a project like this cannot be undertaken without the support of her institution. The dean of the Washington College of Law of American University, Camille Nelson, and former dean Claudio Grossman generously supported this effort through summer research grants, funding for a research visit to The Hague, research assistants, course releases and, mercifully arriving in the final stages of this project, a sabbatical leave. Bill Ryan, International Law Librarian at the Pence Law Library, provided outstanding assistance at every phase of this project.

An extraordinary group of students at the Washington College of Law provided able research assistance across the years of this project, helping me prepare for each field trip; remain abreast of developments in the practice of the ICTY and the literature about it, as well as developments in Bosnia and Serbia; and finalize the manuscript. Some have, in the time since I began this work, emerged as noted experts in their own right. I am indebted to Mona Adabi, Stephanie Alves, Neha Baht, Sonja Balić, Kaitlin Bruno, Peter Chapman, Chris Davis, Christian de Vos, Chase Dunn, Lyndsay Gorton, Rahma Hussein, Kimi Johnson, Alanna Kennedy, Manuela Londoño, Andrew Maki, Katherine Marshall, Natasha Mikha, Elizabeth Raulston, Steven Everett Simpson, Christopher Tansey, and Chang Zhou.

I am also more grateful than I can say to colleagues who devoted precious time to reviewing draft chapters and answering a multitude of questions that came into focus as I finalized *Some Kind of Justice*. Special thanks are owed to Nina Bang-Jensen, Kurt Bassuener, Belinda Cooper, Shireen Fisher, Howard Goldman, Matias Hellman, Mort Halperin, Edin Hodzić, Kevin Hughes, Bogdan Ivanišević, Ivan Jovanović, Sandra Orlović, Ivana Nizich, Bill Stuebner, Alex Whiting, Clint Williamson, Timothy William Waters, and Eric Witte. While comments on earlier drafts helped avert a number of mistakes, any that remain are, of course, my own.

The person to whom I owe the largest debt of gratitude is my husband, Mort Halperin, who has taken this journey with me, literally and in every other meaningful sense. Mort did not need to be convinced of the importance of this endeavor: as a senior official in the Clinton administration, he made singular contributions to alleviating the suffering of victims of ethnic violence in Bosnia and Kosovo. But his support was nonetheless extraordinary. Mort accompanied me to Bosnia during one of my research visits despite looming deadlines on two of his own books (he completed both in our hotel room in Sarajevo while I traveled across Bosnia for interviews). Other members of my family, including David Orentlicher, John Orentlicher, Mark Halperin, Karen Avrich, and David Halperin, provided sage advice and support. Peter Hartmann, then traveling in Europe after graduating college, enthusiastically embraced this project when he visited Sarajevo during one of my research visits. Gary Halperin; Roseanne McCabe; and Madelyn, Megan and Hannah Halperin were endlessly understanding when book deadlines intruded on family visits, and provided welcome cheer when I emerged from long stretches at my computer. James Halperin, born in January 2017, brought indescribable joy during the final months of writing.

ABBREVIATIONS

AFBiH	Armed Forces of Bosnia and Herzegovina
BCS	Bosnian/Croatian/Serbian
BIA	Security Information Agency (Serbia)
BiH	Bosnia and Herzegovina
BIRN	Balkan Investigative Reporting Network
BWCC	Bosnian War Crimes Chamber
DOS	Democratic Opposition of Serbia
DPA	Dayton Peace Agreement
EU	European Union
FRY	Federal Republic of Yugoslavia
HLC	Humanitarian Law Center
HVO	Hrvatsko Vijeće Obrane (Croat Defense Council)
ICC	International Criminal Court
ICJ	International Court of Justice
ICT	international criminal tribunal
ICTR	International Criminal Tribunal for Rwanda
ICTY	International Criminal Tribunal for the former Yugoslavia
IFOR	Implementation Force (NATO)
IMT	International Military Tribunal
IWPR	Institute for War and Peace Reporting
JNA	Jugoslovenska Narodna Armija (Yugoslav National Army)
KLA	Kosovo Liberation Army
MICT	Mechanism for International Criminal Tribunals
MUP	Ministarstvo Unutrašnjih Poslova (Ministry of the Interior, Serbia)
NATO	North Atlantic Treaty Organization
NGO	Nongovernmental Organization
OHR	Office of the High Representative
OSCE	Organization for Security and Co-operation in Europe
OTP	Office of the Prosecutor (ICTY)
OWCP	Office of the War Crimes Prosecutor (Serbia)
PIC	Peace Implementation Council
POBiH	Prosecutor's Office of Bosnia and Herzegovina
RFL/RL	Radio Free Europe/Radio Liberty
RS	Republika Srpska
SAA	Stabilisation and Association Agreement

SaM	Serbia and Montenegro
SDA	Stranka Demokratske Akcije (Party for Democratic Action)
SDS	Srpska Demokratska Stranka (Serb Democratic Party)
SDWC	Special Department for War Crimes (Bosnia)
SFOR	Stabilization Force (NATO)
SFRY	Socialist Federal Republic of Yugoslavia
SNS	Srpska Napredna Stranka (Serb Progressive Party)
SNSD	Alliance of Independent Social Democrats
SPS	Socijalistička Partija Srbija (Socialist Party of Serbia)
SRS	Srpska Radikalna Stranka (Serbian Radical Party)
SWCC	Serbian War Crimes Chamber
UNDP	United Nations Development Programme
VJ	Vojska Jugoslavije (Army of Yugoslavia)
VRS	Vojska Republike Srpske (Army of Republika Srpska)
YIHR	Youth Initiative for Human Rights
WCIS	War Crimes Investigation Service (Serbia)

1

Introduction

As Yugoslav states endured lacerating horrors in the early 1990s, the UN Security Council answered urgent pleas for rescue with plainly inadequate measures, at grievous cost to communities in crisis. In this setting, it was easy to dismiss its decision to create a court in the mold of Nuremberg as another futile gesture; indeed, many did.

Yet it was arresting to see Council members reach for higher ground, summoning the conscience of humanity to justify what was, quite literally, an exceptional measure. As the Council prepared to create the International Criminal Tribunal for the former Yugoslavia (ICTY), Madeleine Albright, then U.S. ambassador to the United Nations, evoked a hallowed symbol: "There is an echo in this Chamber today. The Nuremberg Principles have been reaffirmed." Of the ethnic violence then claiming countless lives, Albright said:

> We cannot ignore the human toll.... Bold tyrants and fearful minorities are watching to see whether ethnic cleansing is a policy the world will tolerate.... [O]ur answers must be a resounding "no".[1]

In that moment, no one could foresee the Tribunal's impact on the near horizon (though Council members assuredly knew it would do nothing to stop the carnage

[1] Provisional Verbatim Record, U.N. SCOR, 3,175th mtg. at 12–13, U.N. Doc. S/PV.3175 (Feb. 22, 1993). The indented language is that of then U.S. secretary of state Warren Christopher, whom Ambassador Albright quoted in her intervention.

Some Kind of Justice. Diane Orentlicher.
© Diane Orentlicher 2018. Published 2018 by Oxford University Press.

underway), much less its reverberations across an unexpectedly long lifetime. Within a few years, the ICTY's global influence had become clear enough: Unexpectedly, the Tribunal was the leading edge in a new era of global justice. Its very existence inspired governments to create war crimes tribunals in other countries and an International Criminal Court (ICC) with wider remit, and catalyzed national efforts to prosecute atrocities committed beyond states' borders. Before long, moreover, ICTY judges were recasting the laws of war, whose core tenets had remained largely settled for half a century.

Of these developments, much has been written. Yet for over a decade after the ICTY was launched, scholars paid scant attention to its impact on those most affected by its work: citizens of former Yugoslav states.[2] In this setting, about a dozen years after the Tribunal began operating I undertook field research in Bosnia and Herzegovina ("Bosnia"), whose citizens suffered the highest levels of wartime atrocities, and Serbia, whose former leader, Slobodan Milošević, brought the region to ruinous conflict, to see how local communities were experiencing Hague justice. Even as I wrote the studies reporting my findings,[3] I knew there was much more to say about the Tribunal's local impact[4] than the study format allowed, and planned to delve deeper straight away. But circumstances intervened. I was invited to serve in the Obama administration, where I worked on international and transitional justice issues and atrocity prevention. The resulting delay in starting this book profoundly transformed its nature and conclusions.

The Tribunal's impact in Bosnia and Serbia had changed markedly since my earlier studies, often in the direction of setbacks where I had previously charted progress, and continued to evolve as I wrote this book. The intervening years also brought a welcome development—a burgeoning scholarly interest in the local effects of international criminal tribunals (ICTs).[5] While the latter has enriched this book, it

---

[2] One of the earliest accounts of local perspectives was by a journalist, who explored victims' perceptions of the ICTY and a tribunal created by the Security Council in November 1994, the International Criminal Tribunal for Rwanda (ICTR). ELIZABETH NEUFFER, THE KEY TO MY NEIGHBOR'S HOUSE: SEEKING JUSTICE IN BOSNIA AND RWANDA (2001). An important 2004 publication includes several chapters that address perceptions of the ICTY and ICTR by local communities. MY NEIGHBOR, MY ENEMY: JUSTICE AND COMMUNITY IN THE AFTERMATH OF MASS ATROCITY (Eric Stover & Harvey M. Weinstein eds., 2004). Other comparatively early efforts to explore discrete aspects of the ICTY's local impact include James Meernik, *Justice and Peace? How the International Criminal Tribunal Affects Societal Peace in Bosnia*, 42 J. PEACE RES. 271 (2005); Rachel Kerr, *The Road from Dayton to Brussels? The International Criminal Tribunal for the Former Yugoslavia and the Politics of War Crimes in Bosnia*, 14 EUR. SECURITY 319 (2005).

[3] DIANE F. ORENTLICHER, OPEN SOCIETY JUSTICE INITIATIVE, SHRINKING THE SPACE FOR DENIAL: THE IMPACT OF THE ICTY IN SERBIA (2008); DIANE F. ORENTLICHER, OPEN SOCIETY JUSTICE INITIATIVE & INTERNATIONAL CENTER FOR TRANSITIONAL JUSTICE, THAT SOMEONE GUILTY BE PUNISHED: THE IMPACT OF THE ICTY IN BOSNIA (2010).

[4] Throughout this book I use the phrase "local impact" as shorthand for the effects of an international tribunal in a country directly affected by its work. More commonly, when scholars of international and transitional justice focus on "local" communities, they use the term in its ordinary sense and for an important reason—to emphasize that justice interventions are experienced differently at local and national levels. See, e.g., Laura J. Arriaza & Naomi Roht-Arriaza, *Weaving a Braid of Histories: Local Post-Armed Conflict Initiatives in Guatemala, in* LOCALIZING TRANSITIONAL JUSTICE: INTERVENTIONS AND PRIORITIES AFTER MASS VIOLENCE 205 (Rosalind Shaw et al. eds., 2010).

[5] See, e.g., LARA J. NETTELFIELD, COURTING DEMOCRACY IN BOSNIA AND HERZEGOVINA: THE HAGUE TRIBUNAL'S IMPACT IN A POSTWAR STATE (2010); JANINE NATALYA CLARK, INTERNATIONAL

would be an understatement to say the first made it challenging to complete *Some Kind of Justice*. Writing it was like riding a wave in a churning sea as I tried to paint the ocean beneath me. Chapters I thought I had completed had to be massively rewritten—*repeatedly*—to reflect far-reaching changes in Bosnia, Serbia, and The Hague. However challenging, this was deeply instructive, throwing into high relief the dynamic nature of an ICT's impact, key factors underlying shifts in its local influence, and the interplay among them.

The ICTY's longevity made for an exceptionally rich case study of these dynamics: Where the trial of major Nazi war criminals in Nuremberg lasted only a year, the ICTY's formal life ran nearly a quarter century.[6]

TAKING ITS SHAPE FROM THE SHORE IT MEETS

A theme running through *Some Kind of Justice* is that, while the ICTY has had a palpable impact in Bosnia and Serbia, the nature of its influence has been shaped in no small part by each country's political, social, and economic landscape. (To write about how local conditions shape a tribunal's "local impact" makes for awkward prose, but highlights a fundamental point.) As Zora Neale Hurston wrote of love, the Hague Tribunal is not like a stone that does the same thing to everything it touches. Like the sea, "it's a moving thing," taking "its shape from the shore it meets, and it's different with every shore."[7] While illuminating, Hurston's metaphor takes us only so far here: another leitmotif of this book is that, to a heightened degree in post-conflict countries like Bosnia and Serbia, the shores themselves are "moving things" during decades of volatile transition.

As both the Bosnian and Serbian experiences demonstrate, the context that matters here is wider and more complex than the balance of power constellations long seen as crucial in shaping countries' homegrown approaches to retrospective justice.[8] Situational factors ranging from elite discourses to daily struggles to make ends meet have shaped and reshaped citizens' *cognitive landscapes*,[9] a phrase I use here to capture the interlocking ways political developments in a country and region;

TRIALS AND RECONCILIATION: ASSESSING THE IMPACT OF THE INTERNATIONAL CRIMINAL TRIBUNAL FOR THE FORMER YUGOSLAVIA (2014); SANJA KUTNJAK IVKOVIĆ & JOHN HAGAN, RECLAIMING JUSTICE: THE INTERNATIONAL TRIBUNAL FOR THE FORMER YUGOSLAVIA AND LOCAL COURTS (2011); Marko Milanović, *The Impact of the ICTY on the Former Yugoslavia: An Anticipatory Postmortem*, 110 AM. J. INT'L L. 233 (2016).

[6] The ICTY will close at the end of 2017. But its remaining functions will be transferred to the Mechanism for International Criminal Tribunals (MICT), which has already assumed many of them.

[7] More precisely, Hurston wrote in dialect: "Love is lak de sea. It's uh movin' thing, but still and all, it takes its shape from de shore it meets, and it's different with every shore." ZORA NEALE HURSTON, THEIR EYES WERE WATCHING GOD 191 (Modern Classics 2013 ed., Harper Perennial) (1937).

[8] *See, e.g.*, SAMUEL P. HUNTINGTON, THE THIRD WAVE: DEMOCRATIZATION IN THE LATE TWENTIETH CENTURY 215–18 (1991) (noting there is greater scope for trials of human rights violations committed by a recent regime following its wholesale defeat than after a transition entailing significant continuity with that regime).

[9] I borrow this phrase from Sanja Kutnjak Ivković and John Hagan, who used it to connote how "the structural landscape of [a] country's current national circumstance determines its localized attitudes toward the ICTY." KUTNAK IVKOVIĆ & HAGAN, *supra* note 5, at 53. These authors, in turn, were influenced by the work of Robert Sampson and Dawn Bartusch. *See id.*

everyday conditions, including economic circumstances; dominant elite discourses and local community perspectives; as well as the local reverberations of citizens' initiatives, shape a society's engagement with an ICT.

Adding another layer of complexity, the actions of third parties—in particular, states that have backed the ICTY and inter-governmental organizations such as the European Union and North Atlantic Treaty Organization (NATO)—have at times significantly influenced developments in Bosnia and Serbia. On occasion, the Hague Tribunal and the governments that back it have altered domestic politics in ways that profoundly influence local experiences of Hague justice. For example, a wave of arrests of ICTY fugitives by NATO forces in Bosnia beginning in July 1997 encouraged many who had fled murderous violence to return to their homes—an outcome widely considered a dividend of international justice.[10]

Reflecting the crucial importance of context to this book's inquiry, the chapters in Part One (Chapters 2 and 3) explore contextual conditions that have loomed large in Bosnian and Serbian citizens' cognitive landscapes. Both chapters pay close attention to the role of external actors in shaping those conditions, as well as the downstream impact of their actions and policies on citizens' experience of Hague justice.

BENCHMARKS FOR ASSESSING IMPACT

At the threshold of this book's inquiry is a question of metrics: By what criteria should the domestic impact of an ICT be evaluated? In the literature of impact assessment it has been common to derive relevant benchmarks from claims about an ICT's goals and functions put forth (1) in instruments formally creating a tribunal, such as Security Council resolutions launching the ICTY; (2) by tribunal leaders; and (3) by scholars who have developed arguments in support of international justice.[11] In keeping with the aim of this inquiry—to illuminate Bosnian and Serbian citizens' experience of Hague justice—this book takes a different approach, deriving benchmarks from the expectations of Bosnians and Serbians. During interviews in Bosnia and Serbia I asked individuals who had welcomed the creation of the ICTY, *why* did you support it—what did you expect it to achieve? Particularly at a time of robust debate about the goals of ICTs,[12] it seemed important to understand the priorities of those who have the deepest investment in their work.

The chapters in Part Two describe the richly layered answers these questions elicited. Chapter 4 explores the expectations of Bosnians, whose country experienced the highest levels of wartime atrocities committed in the 1990s' Yugoslav wars. For reasons that follow from the nature of the conflict in Bosnia, this chapter focuses in particular, though not exclusively, on Bosniak (Muslim) victims' expectations:[13]

---

[10] *See* Chapter 2.

[11] *See, e.g.*, Leslie Vinjamuri, *Deterrence, Democracy, and the Pursuit of International Justice*, 24 ETHICS & INT'L AFF. 191, 192 (2010).

[12] *See infra* notes 19-22 and accompanying text.

[13] The nature of the conflict in Bosnia was such that few Bosniaks were spared grave harm. Many Bosnians nonetheless recognize meaningful distinctions among survivors. For example, Sarajevans often referred in interviews to Bosnians who were detained in concentration camps and/or sexually enslaved, or whose relatives were murdered in acts of ethnic cleansing, as "the victims" of wartime atrocities. Yet those who lived in Sarajevo during the war were also

Although all three of Bosnia's major ethnic groups—Bosniaks, Croats, and Serbs—committed and were victimized by vicious crimes, Bosniaks endured the vast majority, culminating in the 1995 genocide in Srebrenica.[14] For that reason, Bosniaks have long supported the ICTY's work at significantly higher levels than members of other ethnic groups.[15]

The kind of justice survivors sought is multilayered, but at its heart is what some of my interlocutors called "justice for its own sake," a phrase they used to distinguish the inherent value of prosecutions from their presumed social effects. For many who survived haunting crimes, retributive justice is elemental: victims interviewed for this study emphatically believe those responsible for wartime atrocities deserve to be prosecuted and punished in just proportion to the gravity of their crimes. Many Bosnians also embrace what scholars call the *expressive function* of criminal trials and punishment: they crave a clarion affirmation, by a court representing the conscience of humanity and enforcing its basic code, that what happened to them was profoundly wrong.[16] For some, the moral satisfaction derived from Hague justice answers a deeply personal need. For others, the Tribunal's expressive function serves a wider aim. Tarik Jusić evoked the latter when he praised a then-recent judgment convicting Stanislav Galić for his role commanding Serbs who laid siege to Sarajevo, saying the judgment "re-established the basic preconditions for society as such. It cannot be that someone bombs you for four years and it's fine. . . . It's a re-establishing of basic, underlying values of civilization and society."[17]

Another bundle of expectations was of paramount importance to Serbians who embraced the ICTY: as elucidated in Chapter 5, many hoped and believed that, by judicially authenticating the core facts of wartime atrocities, the ICTY would dispel widespread denial about the nature and scope of violence instigated by Serbia's wartime government, forge a shared understanding of the region's immediate past, foster acknowledgment and unequivocal condemnation of wartime atrocities by government leaders and citizens alike, and thereby lay a necessary foundation for reconstituting shattered bonds of civic community across the region's major ethnic groups. In short, they hoped that, if it took a distant court to expose the malevolence of the Milošević regime, its work would catalyze a far-reaching process of

---

targets of war crimes: for three-and-one-half years they were besieged by Serb snipers in violation of international humanitarian law.

[14] According to the most reliable source of information about wartime casualties, the Research and Documentation Center (Sarajevo), approximately 83 percent of Bosnian civilians killed and missing during the 1990s conflict were Bosniak. As explained later, this does not necessarily mean all were victims of war crimes, but nonetheless provides a rough proxy for victimization. *See* Chapter 7.

[15] In Chapter 6, I describe fluctuating patterns of support for the ICTY among Bosnia's three major ethnic groups.

[16] In some iterations retributivism "closely resembles" expressive justifications of punishment, as retribution is seen "as an *expressive defeat* that reasserts moral truth against the wrongdoer's devaluation of the victim." David Luban, *Fairness to Rightness: Jurisdiction, Legality, and the Legitimacy of International Criminal Law*, in THE PHILOSOPHY OF INTERNATIONAL LAW 569, 576–77 (Samantha Besson & John Tasioulas eds., 2010). More commonly, retributivism and expressivism are seen as distinct justifications. *See, e.g.*, MARK A. DRUMBL, ATROCITY, PUNISHMENT, AND INTERNATIONAL LAW 173 (2007). I address these conceptions in Chapter 4.

[17] Interview with Tarik Jusić, then Program Director, Mediacentar Sarajevo, in Sarajevo, Bosn. & Herz. (Dec. 6, 2006).

national reckoning and repair. In the meantime, some saw Serbian cooperation with the ICTY, particularly by arresting fugitives and dispatching them to The Hague, as a litmus test of moral leadership during the country's political transition. Many Bosnians had similar expectations, as explained in Chapter 4.

Claims put forth in Security Council resolutions and by Tribunal officials shaped many citizens' expectations in Bosnia and Serbia. Inspired in part by far-reaching claims of diplomats and ICTY leaders, many "attributed all these *amazing* powers to the court, like 'it will . . . establish the whole truth about [the] conflict'"[18] and foster reconciliation. Inevitably, many would be gravely disappointed in the reality of Hague justice. *Some Kind of Justice* thus offers a cautionary tale about the perils of raising unrealistic expectations of international justice.

If the claims of diplomats and court officials influenced early expectations, Bosnians and Serbians later developed a new benchmark of ICTY "success" in the light of experience. Many now count as one of the Tribunal's signal achievements its role in catalyzing domestic war crimes prosecutions, a function no one anticipated when the ICTY was launched.

ASSESSING IMPACT: RECURRING QUESTIONS

Building from the benchmarks for "success" set forth in Part Two, Parts Three to Five (Chapters 6 through 10) assess the ICTY's evolving impact in three spheres: (1) Bosnians' experience of ICTY trials, focusing in particular on the extent to which the Tribunal satisfied victims' desire for justice (Chapter 6); (2) acknowledgment of and remorse for crimes committed in the 1990s on the part of citizens and political leaders in Serbia and Bosnia (Chapters 7 and 8); and (3) domestic war crimes prosecutions (Chapters 9 and 10). Inevitably, a great deal of the analysis in these chapters reflects idiosyncratic aspects of two countries' engagement with the ICTY. Even so, the Bosnian and Serbian experiences have wider relevance for two overlapping issues.

One set of questions concerns the writ of ICTs: What goals should be assigned to them, and how should we prioritize among them? The proliferation since 1993 of Nuremberg-styled tribunals, each of which has faced and failed a raft of challenges, has invited attention to the "goal-related problems" of ICTs.[19] Putting the case starkly, Mirjan Damaška argued in 2008 "that current views on the objectives of [ICTs] are in disarray," generating "curable weaknesses" in their work.[20] A foundational problem, Damaška averred, is the overabundance and ambitious sweep of goals ascribed to ICTs, whose fulfillment in whole would be a "truly gargantuan" feat.[21] Damaška's diagnosis is now widely shared, yet we remain far from consensus about appropriate

---

[18] Interview with Marijana Toma, then Deputy Director, Humanitarian Law Center, in Belgrade, Serb. (June 10, 2014).

[19] Mirjan Damaška, *What Is the Point of International Criminal Justice?*, 83 CHI.-KENT L. REV. 330, 330 (2008).

[20] *Id.*

[21] *Id.* at 331. Damaška cites nine examples of goals ICTs have assigned to themselves, ranging from objectives commonly attributed to criminal punishment in national settings to aims, such as producing a "reliable historical record" and ending an ongoing conflict, that are "far removed from the normal concerns of national criminal justice." *Id.*

aims of global justice.[22] Though it is not the task of this book to prescribe an agenda for all ICTs, *Some Kind of Justice* illuminates goals the Hague Tribunal was inherently well-suited to advance, as well as those for which it was not.

The experiences explored here raise an overlapping but distinct set of questions: Under what circumstances and in what ways can a tribunal created outside the social and political will of a nation advance the aims of transitional justice? While it has not been defined consistently, *transitional justice* is widely used to connote measures a society undertakes to address *its own* legacy of wholesale violations of fundamental rights, including domestic trials, truth commissions, reparations programs, and institutional reforms.[23] Yet a recurring theme in interviews with Bosnians and Serbians was that the ICTY would serve as an "instrument of transitional justice,"[24] or at least help advance domestic processes of retrospective justice.

To note this begs the question, what did these individuals believe the nature and goals of transitional justice to be? While they expressed a range of views, several core assumptions loomed large in interviews: transitional justice measures address a legacy of human rights failures with a view to (1) acknowledging and discharging a country's moral debt, (2) advancing its transformation *toward* a state whose government and society are firmly committed to moral precepts previously breached wholesale,[25] (3) establishing robust protections against future depredations, while

---

[22] For example some scholars endorse the expressive function of ICTs as a paramount justification for their labors or as a guiding principle for specific aspects of their work, such as case selection, *see, e.g.*, Robert D. Sloane, *The Expressive Capacity of Punishment: The Limits of the National Law Analogy and the Potential of International Criminal Law*, 43 STAN. J. INT'L L. 39 (2007); Margaret M. deGuzman, *Choosing to Prosecute: Expressive Selection at the International Criminal Court*, 33 MICH. J. INT'L L. 265 (2012), while others hold that prevention of international crimes should be the primary aim of an ICT. *See, e.g.*, Stuart Ford, *A Hierarchy of the Goals of International Criminal Courts*, 27 MINN. J. INT'L L. ___ (forthcoming 2017).

[23] *See, e.g.*, U.N. Secretary-General, *The Rule of Law and Transitional Justice in Conflict and Post-Conflict Societies*, ¶ 8 U.N. Doc. S/2004/616 (Aug. 23, 2004) (defining *transitional justice* as "the full range of processes and mechanisms associated with a society's attempts to come to terms with a legacy of large-scale past abuses, in order to ensure accountability, serve justice and achieve reconciliation"); Jemima García-Godos & Chandra Lekha Sriram, *Introduction* to TRANSITIONAL JUSTICE AND PEACEBUILDING ON THE GROUND: VICTIMS AND COMBATANTS 1, 2 (Chandra Lekha Sriram et al. eds., 2013) (defining *transitional justice* as "a broad set of practices that emerged from efforts by countries in transition from authoritarianism and conflict to address past abuses").

[24] While the quoted phrase succinctly captures this theme as it arose in interviews, the direct source is David Tolbert & Aleksandar Kontić, *The International Criminal Tribunal for the Former Yugoslavia: Transitional Justice, the Transfer of Cases to National Courts, and Lessons for the ICC*, *in* THE EMERGING PRACTICE OF THE INTERNATIONAL CRIMINAL COURT 135, 135 (Carsten Stahn & Göran Sluiter eds., 2009). Like many whom I interviewed in Bosnia and Serbia, scholars and other commentators have often implicitly treated ICTs as transitional justice measures. *See, e.g.*, Kim C. Priemel & Alexa Stiller, *Introduction* to REASSESSING THE NUREMBERG MILITARY TRIBUNALS: TRANSITIONAL JUSTICE, TRIAL NARRATIVES, AND HISTORIOGRAPHY 1, 3–4 (Kim C. Priemel & Alexa Stiller eds., 2014); Matias Hellman, *Challenges and Limitations of Outreach: From the ICTY to the ICC*, *in* CONTESTED JUSTICE: THE POLITICS AND PRACTICE OF INTERNATIONAL CRIMINAL COURT INTERVENTIONS 251, 254 (Christian de Vos et al. eds., 2015). Some have explicitly defined *transitional justice* to include trials before ICTs. For example Ruti Teitel has defined *transitional justice* as "the conception of justice associated with periods of political change, characterized by legal responses to confront the wrongdoings of repressive predecessor regimes," and has identified postwar prosecutions by Allied countries as the first historical phase of transitional justice. Ruti G. Teitel, *Transitional Justice Genealogy*, 16 HARV. HUM. RTS. J. 69, 69–70 (2003).

[25] In line with the views of a number of Serbians and Bosnians interviewed for this study, Ruti Teitel has emphasized the transformative aims of transitional justice measures, which transcend while

(4) providing redress to those who were harmed by past violations, a goal that also instantiates a government's commitment to normative change.

SATISFYING AND DISAPPOINTING THE EXPECTATIONS OF VICTIMS

Reflecting the central importance for many Bosnians of "justice for its own sake," the assessment portion of this book begins (in Chapter 6) by exploring the degree to which their expectations have been met, as well as reasons for their disappointments in, and satisfaction with, Hague justice. Four overarching themes emerge from this assessment.

First, while contextual factors are crucial to virtually every dimension of the ICTY's local impact, victims' satisfaction has to a considerable extent turned on the Tribunal's performance. Second, while profoundly gratified by aspects of the ICTY's work, Bosnian victims are deeply disappointed in many others: sentences are too short, proceedings take too long, judges have allowed some defendants to transform their trials into theaters of the absurd, suspects who bear prime responsibility for wholesale brutality are acquitted on incomprehensible grounds, and on and on. Third, problematic aspects of the ICTY's performance for which no one but the Tribunal is responsible account for many of these frustrations. While this is implicit in the first two points, I want to emphasize the degree to which avoidable shortcomings account for many Bosnians' disappointment in Hague justice.

To a striking degree, Bosnian critiques have been echoed by international legal experts, who have put forth a raft of viable suggestions for improving the delivery of international justice. To its credit, the ICTY responded to a number of performance-related concerns by, for example, adopting measures to streamline trials. Even so, Chapter 6 highlights a pressing need to improve key aspects of ICTs' work, offering lessons particularly relevant to the ICC, the only criminal tribunal with a potentially global remit.

Finally, and perhaps remarkably in light of the litany of discontents described in Chapter 6, many (perhaps most) Bosniaks—who, as noted, account for the great majority of Bosnian victims—as well as other Bosnians remain deeply grateful the Tribunal was created. Some of its fiercest Bosnian critics still count the ICTY as "the best thing that happened to the people of the former Yugoslavia since 1991," when ethnic conflict erupted.[26] What this tells us about the appropriate aims of ICTs is important: they *can* meet a need, incomparably important to many survivors of monstrous crimes,[27] for "some kind of justice."[28]

---

still advancing "traditional corrective aims" of measures such as reparations. RUTI G. TEITEL, TRANSITIONAL JUSTICE 147 (2000).

[26] Refik Hodžić, *Accepting a Difficult Truth: ICTY Is Not Our Court*, BALKAN INSIGHT (Mar. 6, 2013).

[27] I do not want to make a generalized claim about the importance of criminal justice to all victims of atrocities. As previously noted, there was and is a strong demand for criminal justice among Bosniaks.

[28] As one of my interlocutors in Bosnia observed, after experiencing "terrible things many times over, . . . people [in Bosnia] don't expect perfect justice but they want some kind of justice." Interview with Asta Zinbo, then Director, Civil Society Initiatives Program, International Commission on Missing Persons, in Sarajevo, Bosn. & Herz. (Dec. 6, 2006). One of my interlocutors in Serbia used the same words to capture the expectations of Serbians who

It also suggests one respect in which the ICTY served as "an instrument of transitional justice": it provided moral satisfaction to many victims. As Pablo de Greiff has emphasized, a key aim of transitional justice measures is to answer victims' demand for "recognition of the fact that they have been harmed"[29] and *wronged*, "which is possible only by appealing to norms."[30] As we shall see, many victims value the ICTY's work above all because it recognized and condemned the harms they suffered as grave breaches of universal law.

SOCIAL TRANSFORMATION: DISPELLING DENIAL AND FOSTERING ACKNOWLEDGMENT

As the Tribunal's formal life drew to an end, discourses of denial were on the rise in both Bosnia and Serbia. Bosnian Serb leaders in particular brazenly challenged facts and legal conclusions established in ICTY judgments, while leaders in both countries celebrated convicted war criminals as national heroes.[31] In this setting, the Tribunal's longtime supporters in both countries were acutely aware it had not had a transformative effect, as they once expected, in fostering acknowledgment and advancing normative change.

As elucidated in Chapter 7, a rich body of social science research helps us understand why credibly establishing facts (as the ICTY assuredly did) is no guarantee people will accept them. In many societies emerging from wholesale violence, denialism is abetted by psychological dynamics that operate in the most prosaic spheres of human endeavor—in particular, a human propensity to discredit information that challenges our (collective) self-esteem, our habitual reliance on trusted sources to interpret reality, and our resistance to information at odds with established beliefs. All of these dynamics were at play in post-Milošević Serbia and postwar Bosnia. Many citizens have been loath to believe information implicating their ethnic community in crimes of singular depravity, wartime narratives molded many citizens' beliefs about wartime atrocities and remain influential today, and the ICTY is anything but a trusted source of information among those most disposed toward denialism in the first place. For most citizens, evidence adduced in The Hague is mediated by political

---

mobilized in support of the ICTY. Interview with Maja Mičić, then Director, Youth Initiative for Human Rights, in Belgrade, Serb. (June 11, 2014) (noting that she and other Serbian advocates promoted the Tribunal "as something that would bring some kind of justice").

[29] Pablo de Greiff, *Report of the Special Rapporteur on the Promotion of Truth, Justice, Reparation and Guarantees of Non-Recurrence*, ¶ 2, U.N. Doc. A/HRC/21/46 (Aug. 9, 2012). De Greiff considers this a "mediate" aim of transitional justice, by which he means an aim a transitional justice measure can reasonably be supposed to advance, even if fully achieving it requires other steps.

[30] *Id.* The quoted language does not exhaust De Greiff's account of recognition as a goal of transitional justice, but most nearly captures a value articulated by many of my Bosnian interlocutors. De Greiff also emphasizes the importance of recognizing victims' "status as *rights bearers*, and, ultimately, as co-participants in a common political project—that is, *as citizens*." Pablo de Greiff, *Some Thoughts on the Development and Present State of Transitional Justice*, 5 ZEITSCHRIFT FÜR MENSCHENRECHTE (J. HUM. RTS.) 98, 114 (2011) [hereinafter *Thoughts on Transitional Justice*] (emphasis in original). Of course, an ICT cannot advance victims' inclusion in the common political project of citizenship the way national measures and institutions alone can do.

[31] These developments and other points noted in this section are explored in Chapters 7 (Serbia) and 8 (Bosnia).

elites and other influential sources, many of whom have the motive and means to discredit Tribunal judgments.

To be clear, I am not suggesting ICTs are incapable of advancing acknowledgment of grievous wrongs when a country emerges from lawless violence. In fact, both Serbia and Bosnia saw palpable progress in this sphere in the early years of this century, when the political environment in each country was relatively auspicious. Many Serbians and Bosnians are convinced (and, in this belief, convincing) that the ICTY was a key factor behind this development. Yet recent years have seen growing denialism in a wider context of resurgent nationalism.

In light of the dynamics underlying denialism explored in Chapters 7 (Serbia) and 8 (Bosnia), a key takeaway of both chapters is that it is misguided and counterproductive to *ascribe* to ICTs aims that sound in social transformation. Doing so raises hopes almost sure to be disappointed among those who already have suffered enough, at least in the absence of far-reaching changes in other spheres.[32]

Ascribing "*amazing* powers"[33] to an ICT also risks diverting political leaders' and citizens' attention and energy from the hard work they must undertake to reconstitute and deepen their society's moral commitments and social fabric. Edin Hodžić evoked the misplaced expectations of many Bosnians when he reflected, "We thought here in Bosnia . . . that the judicial paradigm would do everything, would do the job of dealing with the past—that some good things will emerge from the trials on their own, and trials will have a positive impact on other activities."[34] Svjetlana Nedimović, too, recognized the perilously seductive appeal of believing a war crimes tribunal can successfully address a multitude of social and political challenges: "Disillusionment with the Hague Tribunal was not just a problem of the Hague Tribunal. It was also the problem of how we understood what it was going to do for us. Courts do not set political reality right."[35]

CATALYZING DOMESTIC PROSECUTIONS

By all accounts, the ICTY's most tangible, and perhaps enduring, impact in Bosnia and Serbia was its role catalyzing domestic prosecutions. As elaborated in Chapter 9, it did so intentionally in Bosnia, though hardly for enlightened reasons: under mounting pressure to complete their work, ICTY leaders devised a "completion strategy," a key component of which was transferring some of the Tribunal's cases to local courts. They envisioned sending most of these cases to Bosnia, and thus focused on strengthening its courts. Concerned about the state of Bosnia's judiciary,

---

[32] As already intimated, particularly when backed by influential governments and institutions, the ICTY's work has at times itself positively influenced political developments in Bosnia and Serbia. Dejan Anastasijević has noted, for example, that by "physically removing some of the worst criminals," the ICTY provided Serbia a viable chance to chart a new path forward when the Milošević regime collapsed, a contribution "usually neglected by experts." Interview with Dejan Anastasijević, Journalist, in Belgrade, Serb. (Nov. 20, 2006).

[33] Interview with Marijana Toma, then Deputy Director, Humanitarian Law Center, in Belgrade, Serb. (June 10, 2014).

[34] Interview with Edin Hodžić, Director, Public Law Program, Center for Social Research Analitika, in Sarajevo, Bosn. & Herz. (Sept. 11, 2014). Hodžić added: "I don't think that, you know, that was proven in subsequent years."

[35] Interview with Svjetlana Nedimović, Activist, in Sarajevo, Bosn. & Herz. (Sept. 18, 2014).

ICTY officers collaborated with the Office of the High Representative and Bosnian lawyers to launch state-of-the-art war crimes institutions in Sarajevo.

Although the ICTY made no comparable effort in Serbia, the government in Belgrade created a dedicated war crimes chamber and prosecutor's office in 2003. Despite its marginal role in launching these institutions, the Hague Tribunal provided crucial impetus. How this came about is a fascinating and important case study of the dynamics underlying an ICT's positive relationship with national courts. Much to its credit, the ICTY Office of the Prosecutor (OTP) recognized and seized the opportunities that emerged in Serbia as well as Bosnia, developing a partnership with local war crimes prosecutors and bolstering their capacity. In doing so, it helped advance what many consider an overarching goal of transitional justice—strengthening the rule of law[36] in societies previously governed through the arbitrary exercise of power.

Like other developments chronicled in this book, the emergence of domestic war crimes institutions tells us something important about the contributions an ICT is well-suited to make, while highlighting specific measures and contextual factors crucial to their success. Capacity-building programs developed by the OTP should be of particular interest to the ICC, whose leadership has long grappled with the question of how to focus on the Court's core mandate of prosecuting masterminds of mass atrocities while maximizing its potential to catalyze domestic prosecutions. As elucidated in Chapters 9 and 10, the ICTY steered clear of a risk ICC officials have insisted they must avoid—becoming a development institution. But the OTP made creative use of the contributions it could offer to advance domestic capacity, while third parties underwrote and played the lead role in implementing a host of initiatives.

Yet progress in this sphere is fragile. Both Serbia's and Bosnia's war crimes institutions have been subject to intense pressure, and with visible effects. At times, external actors have played a critical role in alleviating those threats; at other times, they have failed to use the significant influence they possess to address them. The latter is regrettable. While external actors can never do the work of local leaders, citizens, and institutions, their support can make the crucial difference when domestic reforms and reformists are threatened.

It is now abundantly clear such support may be necessary far longer than most governments and institutions are generally disposed to provide it. For if we have learned anything from experience, it is that, for countries that have seen the depths of human degradation, the project of moral, political, and institutional repair is the work of generations. Indeed, it never ends.

---

[36] See De Greiff, *Thoughts on Transitional Justice, supra* note 30, at 115. In De Greiff's framework, strengthening the democratic rule of law, which establishes "social relations mediated by means of *rights*," is a "final" aim of transitional justice. *Id.* at 115-116 (emphasis in original).

PART ONE

The Landscape of Justice

*Overview of the ICTY's Relationship
with Bosnia and Serbia*

2

Forged in War

Bosnia's Relationship with the ICTY

Scholars have long recognized that context matters deeply to the design and success of transitional justice initiatives,[1] while contesting crucial details—when, for example, countries that have descended into the darkest abyss can benefit from criminal trials, whether fragile countries can prosecute those responsible for mass atrocities without provoking a backlash, and whether it is wise for external actors to press newly restored democracies to pursue retrospective justice. The advent of global justice in the 1990s layered onto these debates a question of particular importance to this inquiry: Under what conditions can an international criminal tribunal (ICT) advance aims long associated with home-grown measures of retrospective justice, such as strengthening the rule of law and preventing future atrocities?[2] Does it make sense to launch an ICT to address wartime atrocities before the guns are silenced?

---

[1] *See, e.g.*, Ruti Teitel, *Transitional Justice Genealogy*, 16 Harv. Hum. Rts. J. 69, 76 (2003); Laurel E. Fletcher et al., *Context, Timing and the Dynamics of Transitional Justice: A Historical Perspective*, 31 Hum. Rts. Q. 163, 209 (2009). For a recent inquiry into contextual factors that influence transitional justice trajectories, see International Center for Transitional Justice, Justice Mosaics: How Context Shapes Transitional Justice in Fractured Societies (Roger Duthie & Paul Seils eds., 2017).

[2] An article published in 2003/2004 crystalized this question. At a time when ICTs had become central to human rights advocacy, Jack Snyder and Leslie Vinjamuri challenged the premise of these efforts, arguing "Justice does not lead; it follows." Jack Snyder & Leslie Vinjamuri, *Trials and Errors: Principle and Pragmatism in Strategies of International Justice*, 28 Int'l Sec. 5, 6 (2003– 2004). If the goal is to prevent atrocities, they argued, a stable political order is a precondition for successful justice efforts. Other scholars have critiqued this critique. *See, e.g.*, Kathryn Sikkink

No ICT raises these issues more starkly than the ICTY, created in the crucible of vicious conflict in 1993. As well, Bosnia offers a rich case study of how external actors can help *shape* a local context in ways that enlarge or contract the potential impact of an ICT. As this chapter elucidates, decisions of states and international organizations during and in the immediate aftermath of war have had a lasting impact on Bosnians' experience of Hague justice.

I. CREATING A COURT IN THE CRUCIBLE OF WAR

What happens during war shapes what happens afterward.
                                    —LARA NETTELFIELD & SARAH WAGNER[3]

Inevitably, Bosnians' initial views of the ICTY were shaped by conditions surrounding its creation. Yet they influenced Bosnian perceptions in unexpected as well as predictable ways. To explain, it is necessary first to recall the circumstances that gave rise to the Tribunal.

In 1991, two constituent republics of the country then called the Socialist Federal Republic of Yugoslavia (SFRY), Slovenia and Croatia, declared their independence in the face of rising and virulent Serb nationalism under the leadership of Slobodan Milošević, after first declaring they would remain in Yugoslavia if it became a looser confederation. The government in Belgrade responded by dispatching the Yugoslav army, triggering the first armed conflicts surrounding the breakup of the SFRY.[4] In contrast to the wartime leaders of Slovenia and Croatia,[5] the government of Bosnia— then led by Alija Izetbegović—had scant wish to secede. Quite the opposite: it desperately hoped to avoid Yugoslavia's disintegration.[6]

& Carrie Booth Walling, Errors about Trials: The Emergence and Impact of the Justice Cascade, presented at the Princeton International Relations Faculty Colloquium (Mar. 27, 2006).

[3] LARA J. NETTELFIELD & SARAH E. WAGNER, SREBRENICA IN THE AFTERMATH OF GENOCIDE 5 (2014).

[4] *See* BOGDAN DENITCH, ETHNIC NATIONALISM: THE TRAGIC DEATH OF YUGOSLAVIA 125 (1994).

[5] The decision of the Yugoslav republic of Slovenia to declare its independence from the SFRY, formalized by the Slovene parliament on June 25, 1991, triggered a ten-day war between Yugoslav and Slovene forces. With only a small minority of ethnic Serbs in Slovenia (roughly 2.5 percent of the republic's population), the government in Belgrade offered minimal resistance to its secession. Indeed, Allan Little and Laura Silber characterize the conflict with Slovene forces as a "phony war," and write that Serbian leader Slobodan Milošević and Slovene leader Milan Kučan "had, between them, agreed [upon] Slovenia's departure from the federation." LAURA SILBER & ALLAN LITTLE, YUGOSLAVIA: DEATH OF A NATION 166 (1995). The 1991 declaration of independence by Croatia, which had a more substantial Serb population (over 12 percent in 1991), triggered a longer and more intensive war between Yugoslav and Croatian forces.

[6] As Misha Glenny has written, "The last thing the [Bosnian] Muslims . . . were demanding at that time was independence." Misha Glenny, *Yugoslavia: The Great Fall*, N.Y. REV. BOOKS (Mar. 23, 1995). Bosnia's wartime president, Alija Izetbegović, feared Croatia's secession would leave multiethnic Bosnia vulnerable to the territorial aspirations of both Serbia and Croatia. MISHA GLENNY, THE FALL OF YUGOSLAVIA: THE THIRD BALKAN WAR 163 (3d ed. 1996). *See also* TIM JUDAH, THE SERBS 201 (3d ed. 2009). According to a 1991 census, 43.5 percent of Bosnia's population were Muslims (Bosniaks), 31.2 percent were Serbs, 17.4 percent were Croats, 5.5 percent identified as Yugoslav, and 2.4 percent identified themselves as "other." Report Submitted by Bosnia and Herzegovina Pursuant to Article 25, Paragraph 1 of the Framework Convention for the Protection of National Minorities, ¶ 4, Council of Europe, ACFC/SR 001 (2004), https://www.coe.int/t/dghl/monitoring/minorities/3_FCNMdocs/PDF_1st_SR_BiH_en.pdf.

Many Bosnian citizens, too, dreaded the prospect of seceding from Yugoslavia. Elmina Kulašić described a common perspective this way:

In Bosnia, people really did feel the centralized structure of Yugoslavia, and it did benefit them. I mean today when you talk to, even to some people of my generation, if they listen to their parents when they talk to them, they always talk about the stability, the comfortable life, because people had a job, they could afford a place, they could afford to go to a vacation once a year. . . . [F]or ordinary citizens, it was a stable system.[7]

Even as conflict raged in neighboring Croatia, Kulašić's parents, like many Bosnians of their generation, could hardly contemplate war in Bosnia. "It was," Kulašić recalled, "just sort of like Yugoslavia was their answer, and you just look forward. They never really believed that a war would erupt."[8]

The "centralized structure of Yugoslavia"[9] on which many Bosnians counted was already collapsing under the stress of Belgrade's nationalist agenda. In 1990, Serbian writer Dobrica Ćosić, an ardent supporter of Milošević, anointed Radovan Karadžić to lead Serb nationalists in Bosnia and provided crucial guidance to his protégé.[10] By 1991, Serbia's State Security Service was organizing Serb paramilitary forces that would commit grievous atrocities in Bosnia and Serbia.[11]

Only when it became clear that recognition of Slovenian and Croatian independence by other states was inevitable did Izetbegović seek independence for Bosnia, believing it would fare better as an independent country than as a republic within a rump Yugoslavia, now dominated by the bellicose president of Serbia, Slobodan Milošević.[12] Following a referendum, widely boycotted by Serbs, in which voters opted overwhelmingly for independence, Karadžić declared a Bosnian Serb Republic on March 27, 1992.[13] (On January 9, 1992, a date that would later loom large in Serb

---

[7] Interview with Elmina Kulašić, Transitional Justice, Accountability and Remembrance, in Sarajevo, Bosn. & Herz. (Sept. 13, 2014).

[8] Id.

[9] Id.

[10] JULIAN BORGER, THE BUTCHER'S TRAIL: HOW THE SEARCH FOR BALKAN WAR CRIMINALS BECAME THE WORLD'S MOST SUCCESSFUL MANHUNT 261 (2016). Ćosić served as president of the FRY in 1992–1993.

[11] See SABRINA P. RAMET, THE THREE YUGOSLAVIAS: STATE-BUILDING AND LEGITIMATION, 1918–2005, at 414 (2006); Prosecutor v. Stanišić et al., Case No. IT-03-69-T, Trial Judgment (Int'l Crim. Trib. for the Former Yugoslavia May 30, 2013). The trial judgment in the Stanišić case found that Serbian institutions had provided extensive support to murderous Serb paramilitaries in Bosnia and Croatia but nonetheless acquitted the defedants. The defendants' acquittal was reversed on appeal, Prosecutor v. Stanišić et al., Case No. IT-03-69-A, Appeal Judgment (Int'l Crim. Trib. for the Former Yugoslavia Dec. 9, 2015), and a retrial of the two suspects began on June 13, 2017. See Marlise Simons, Retrial Begins for 2 Serbs at U.N. War Crimes Tribunal, N.Y. TIMES (June 13, 2017).

[12] Diane F. Orentlicher, Separation Anxiety: International Responses to Ethno-Separatist Claims, 23 YALE J. INT'L L. 1, 65 (1998); GLENNY, supra note 6, at 164. The other alternative confronting Bosnian authorities was to acquiesce in Bosnia's division between Serbia and Croatia, as their respective leaders had proposed between themselves. See GLENNY, supra note 6, at 143.

[13] NOEL MALCOLM, BOSNIA: A SHORT HISTORY 231–32 (1994). In holding a referendum, Bosnia dutifully complied with a process established by the European Community (EC) for recognizing its independence. Although many Serbs boycotted the poll, almost 63 percent of the electorate

nationalist provocations, Karadžić had vowed no one would separate Bosnia from Yugoslavia; any effort to do so would result in an independent Serb entity.[14]) By then, Karadžić had stockpiled weapons dispatched "in a constant flow" from Belgrade.[15] The European Community's recognition of Bosnia's independence on April 6, 1992, intended to ensure its security, instead marked a lethal watershed: That day, Bosnian Serb rebels fired shots on peaceful demonstrators from a hotel in Sarajevo, which was widely (though not altogether accurately) seen as the start of Bosnia's three-and-one-half year ethnic conflict.[16] Throughout the war, Belgrade provided crucial forms of support to the Bosnian Serb rebels.[17]

These circumstances—alternately described in many interviews as "Serb aggression" or "Serbian aggression"—gave shape to the justice Bosnians hoped the Hague Tribunal would provide. Many hoped the ICTY would establish in clarion terms who were the "aggressors" in the ferocious war that consumed Bosnia for more than three years.[18] But the reason many Bosniaks "desparately need[ed] justice"[19] in the first place—a theme I develop in Chapter 4—is that they endured grievous harms on a staggering scale.

The territory of the new "state" Karadžić proclaimed, Republika Srpska, would be defined through the war's signature crime, "ethnic cleansing"[20]—atrocities committed against non-Serbs to secure exclusive Serb control of territory claimed

voted for independence. *See* Marc Weller, *The International Response to the Dissolution of the Socialist Federal Republic of Yugoslavia*, 86 AM. J. INT'L L. 569, 593 (1992).

[14] *See* Gordana Knežević, *A Day of Reckoning for Bosnia?*, RFE/RL (Jan. 9, 2017); *Dodik Confirms Bosnian Serb Entity Referendum on Sept 25*, HINA CROATIAN NEWS AGENCY (Aug. 11, 2016). Tim Judah describes the January 9, 1992, declaration as a "final threat," as Bosnian Serb leader Radovan Karadžić had explained his party would begin building the new republic's institutions only if "the Croats or Muslims try to separate from Yugoslavia or if they are recognised." JUDAH, *supra* note 6, at 202. In most other accounts, the January 9 declaration is described as a declaration of the Serb Republic. *See, e.g.*, RAMET, *supra* note 11, at 417.

[15] BORGER, *supra* note 10, at 263. From the outset of its formal existence, the Bosnian Serb army (VRS) enjoyed "a massive heavy arms advantage," Kurt Bassuener, A Durable Oligarchy: Bosnia and Herzegovina's False Postwar Democratic Transition 7 (unpublished draft on file with author) [hereinafter Durable Oligarchy], because the Yugoslav National Army (JNA) transferred its Bosnian troops, weapons, officers, and equipment to the VRS in May 1992. *See Prosecutor v. Tadić*, Case No. IT-94-1-A, Appeal Judgment, 63 n.180 (Int'l Crim. Trib. for the Former Yugoslavia July 15, 1999).

[16] *See* JUDAH, *supra* note 6, at 202–03. Bosnia's independence was recognized by the United States on April 7, 1992. *See* David Binder, *U.S. Recognizes 3 Yugoslav Republics as Independent*, N.Y. TIMES (Apr. 8, 1992). Bosnia was admitted to the United Nations on May 22, 1992.

[17] For example, as already noted, Serbia's State Security Service (known by its Serbian acronym DB) organized Serb paramilitary units that operated in Bosnia and Croatia. In addition, the DB provided training, financing, and supplies to those forces. *See Prosecutor v. Stanišić et al.*, Case No. IT-03-69-T, Trial Judgment (Int'l Crim. Trib. for the Former Yugoslavia May 30, 2013).

[18] Aleksandra Letić, a civil society leader based in Republika Srpska, described the early hopes of many Bosniaks this way: "From the early beginning," Bosniaks "were counting very much on the ICTY," hoping the Tribunal would, in effect, say "yes, the major victims of the war in B-H were the Bosniaks, and really stating that, yes, the crimes committed in Bosnia were the result of an aggression." Interview with Aleksandra Letić, Secretary-General, Helsinki Committee for Human Rights in Republika Srpska, in Sarajevo, Bosn. & Herz. (Sept. 8, 2014).

[19] Interview with Mirsad Tokača, President, Research and Documentation Center (Sarajevo), in Sarajevo, Bosn. & Herz. (Dec. 6, 2006).

[20] SILBER & LITTLE, *supra* note 5, at 245. Within months, Serb forces had gained control of roughly two-thirds of Bosnian territory. *Id.* at 256.

by Serbs. Laura Silber and Allan Little describe the early months of ethnic cleansing:

> Humiliation, terror and mental cruelty were almost universally deployed [by Bosnian Serbs]. Captured men . . . were . . . told that their wives had been raped and then killed, that their children were dead. They were forced, on pain of death, to perform atrocities against each other—mutilation, physical and sexual, and, even, mutual killing. They were forced to dig mass graves and collect and bury the bodies of their families and neighbors. Sometimes, those on grave detail would themselves be killed and thrown on top of the bodies they had just delivered.[21]

For Elmina Kulašić, like thousands of other Bosniak citizens, "literally overnight, everything was taken away." Her family was dispatched to a camp in Kozarac.[22] Kulašić, who was seven at the time, described their experience:

> The younger generation, they would ask me, 'Well, can you define a concentration camp?' Well, if you're starved, you hear beatings, screams, you know that your uncle was taken out and tortured, and you can't move, and you know fear is all around you, that's concentration camp, and that's exactly what happened.[23]

Four months into the war, journalists Roy Gutman, Penny Marshall, and Ed Vulliamy discovered camps in northwest Bosnia whose emaciated captives evoked the skeletal survivors of Nazi concentration camps.[24] Their accounts galvanized global attention, and prompted local Serbs to close one of the camps, Omarska, within days.[25] But it would take over three years for external actors to take robust action to end the atrocities. In the meantime, the United Nations Security Council adopted a blizzard of resolutions irresolutely addressing the Bosnian crisis.[26] In February 1993, the Council adopted still another resolution, deciding in principle that an international tribunal would be established to judge those responsible for atrocities then underway.[27]

---

[21] *Id.* at 245.

[22] Interview with Elmina Kulašić, Transitional Justice, Accountability and Remembrance, in Sarajevo, Bosn. & Herz. (Sept. 13, 2014).

[23] *Id.*

[24] *See, e.g.,* Roy Gutman, *Serbs Have Slain Over 1,000 in 2 Bosnia Camps, Ex-prisoners Say,* NEWSDAY (Aug. 2, 1992); Roy Gutman, *Serbian Guards Executed Prisoners, Survivor Says,* NEWSDAY (Aug. 5, 1992); Ed Vulliamy, *Shame of Camp Omarska,* GUARDIAN (Aug. 7, 1992). David Scheffer describes the impact of these press reports as "[t]he public turning point" in addressing Bosnia. DAVID SCHEFFER, ALL THE MISSING SOULS: A PERSONAL HISTORY OF THE WAR CRIMES TRIBUNALS 15 (2012).

[25] *See Bosnia 1992: The Omarska Camp,* AL JAZEERA (May 10, 2017).

[26] *See* Thomas G. Weiss, *Collective Spinelessness: U.N. Actions in the Former Yugoslavia, in* THE WORLD AND YUGOSLAVIA'S WARS 59, 59–96 (Richard H. Ullman ed., 1996). The gap between Security Council resolutions addressing the Bosnia conflict and effective responses prompted a commander of UN peace operations in Bosnia to say, "I don't read the . . . resolutions anymore because they don't help me. There is a fantastic gap between the resolutions of the Security Council, the will to execute those resolutions and the means available to commanders." Roger Cohen, *Dispute Grows Over U.N.'s Troops in Bosnia,* N.Y. TIMES (Jan. 20, 1994).

[27] The resolution decided a tribunal for the former Yugoslavia "shall be established" and requested the UN Secretary-General to prepare a report on "all aspects of this matter, including specific proposals." S.C. Res. 808, ¶¶ 1–2 (Feb. 22, 1993).

Soon after, as Bosnian Serb forces laid merciless siege to several towns, the Council adopted two resolutions declaring six of them, including the Bosnian capital Sarajevo, "safe areas."[28] At first, the Council made no provision for the towns' safety other than authorizing (but not ensuring) the deployment of a small number of UN monitors.[29] Even after the Council approved the use of military force to protect them,[30] the "safe areas" remained sites of extreme peril. One, Srebrenica, would see genocidal violence two years after the Council demanded it be "free from any armed attack or any other hostile act."[31] The second "safe area" resolution was adopted less than three weeks before the Council formally created the ICTY on May 25, 1993.[32]

Set against these developments, the decision to launch a wartime tribunal was widely derided outside Bosnia as a "fig leaf" for the United Nations' failure to staunch the slaughter of Bosnian Muslims then underway.[33] Thus it came as something of a surprise to discover while researching this book that the Council's action evoked rather different reactions among many Bosnians.

A. Reactions to the Council's Action

The predominantly Muslim government led by Alija Izetbegović welcomed the Tribunal's creation, if warily, but was more cautious than optimistic about its prospects. Damir Arnaut, who served in the cabinet of the Bosniak member of the presidency when I interviewed him in 2009, recalled that the wartime government "was very much in favor of the Tribunal" when it was created.[34] But, he said, its establishment "was not on the top of [the government's] agenda" in 1993.[35] Its highest

---

[28] S.C. Res. 819, ¶ 1 (Apr. 16, 1993) (declaring Srebrenica a "safe area" that shall be free from armed attack) and S.C. Res. 824, ¶ 3 (May 6, 1993) (declaring Sarajevo, Tuzla, Goražde, Žepa, Bihać, as well as Srebrenica "safe areas" that shall be free from armed attacks).

[29] S.C. Res. 824, ¶ 6 (May 6, 1993) (authorizing the "strengthening" of the UN Protection Force in Bosnia by an additional fifty military observers, apparently to be spread among the six besieged towns).

[30] S.C. Res. 836, ¶¶ 5, 9–10 (June 4, 1993).

[31] S.C. Res. 819, ¶ 1 (Apr. 16, 1993).

[32] SC Res. 827 (May 25, 1993).

[33] The metaphor is widely used to characterize the Council's action. See, e.g., Peter Malcontent, Introduction to FACING THE PAST: AMENDING HISTORICAL INJUSTICES THROUGH INSTRUMENTS OF TRANSITIONAL JUSTICE 6 (Peter Malcontent ed., 2016); ISABELLE WESSELINGH & ARNAUD VAULERIN, RAW MEMORY: PRIJEDOR, LABORATORY OF ETHNIC CLEANSING 114–15 (2005); PIERRE HAZAN, JUSTICE IN A TIME OF WAR: THE TRUE STORY BEHIND THE INTERNATIONAL CRIMINAL TRIBUNAL FOR THE FORMER YUGOSLAVIA 41 (2004); JOHN HAGAN, JUSTICE IN THE BALKANS: PROSECUTING WAR CRIMES IN THE HAGUE TRIBUNAL 60 (2003); ARYEH NEIER, WAR CRIMES: BRUTALITY, GENOCIDE, TERROR AND THE STRUGGLE FOR JUSTICE 112 (1998). This metaphor obscures the complexity of motivations that led to the ICTY's creation. Madeleine Albright, then U.S. ambassador to the United Nations, forcefully advocated for its creation because she believed victims of mass rapes and other atrocities deserved justice. See SCHEFFER, supra note 24, at 65. Even so, she expressed relatively low expectations when the Security Council voted to establish the ICTY in May 1993. Answering the "skeptics . . . who deride this Tribunal as being powerless because the suspects may avoid arrest," Albright said the ICTY would "issue indictments whether or not suspects can be taken into custody." U.N. SCOR, 47th Sess., 3217th mtg. at 13, U.N. Doc. S/PV.3217 (May 25, 1993).

[34] Interview with Damir Arnaut, then Advisor for Legal-Constitutional Affairs, Cabinet of Haris Silajžić, in Sarajevo, Bosn. & Herz. (July 16, 2009).

[35] Id.

priority then was lifting the siege of Sarajevo, and many feared the decision to launch a tribunal "was a way to skirt [this] issue."[36]

Indeed, throughout the war, the government's foreign minister and ambassador to the United Nations, Muhamed Sacirbey, implored the Security Council to take "resolute action" to end the slaughter then underway and, failing that, to modify the arms embargo it had imposed on the former Yugoslavia in September 1991[37] so that Bosnians could properly defend themselves.[38] In telling contrast, in numerous Security Council deliberations about Bosnia during the war, Ambassador Sacirbey spoke about the ICTY only occasionally, typically in passing.[39]

Sacirbey evoked his government's ambivalence when the Council adopted a resolution in February 1993 deciding in principle to create a tribunal. Describing it as "maybe the one U.N. resolution that in the long term will define the peace in our country," Sacirbey nonetheless cautioned: "we shouldn't kid ourselves" into believing the measure would deter Serb aggression.[40] (Twenty years later, Sacirbey rued the Council's creation of the Tribunal as "a sordid affair of insincerity," undertaken "largely as a rationalization to avoid engaging Slobodan Milošević's sponsored assault upon Bosnia & Herzegovina."[41])

Despite the inauspicious context in which the ICTY was launched, the Council's action was extoled by international human rights advocates, who believed atrocities then underway warranted a tribunal in the mold of Nuremberg. Western organizations and governments had led international calls for such a court, though a Yugoslav journalist, Mirko Klarin, is believed to have been the first to call for one as the SFRY moved toward war in 1991,[42] and a UN Commission of Experts, established in

---

[36] *Id.*

[37] S.C. Res. 713, ¶ 6 (Sept. 25, 1991).

[38] *See, e.g.*, U.N. SCOR, 48th Sess., 3336th mtg. at 13, U.N. Doc. S/PV.3336 (Feb. 14, 1994) ("It is clear to us that the arms embargo imposed by resolution 713 (1991) does not apply to the Government of the Republic of Bosnia and Herzegovina. We are a country under attack from a much better-armed aggressor bent on territorial conquest and genocide. It is clear that the aggression continues and that the Council still has not fully confronted the aggressor."). *See also* U.N. SCOR, 48th Sess., 3367th mtg. at 4–5, U.N. Doc. S/PV.3367 (Apr. 21, 1994); U.N. SCOR, 48th Sess., 3370th mtg. at 40–41, U.N. Doc. S/PV.3370 (Apr. 27, 1994); U.N. SCOR, 49th Sess., 3454th mtg. at 36–37, U.N. Doc. S/PV.3454 (Nov. 9, 1994); U.N. SCOR, 47th Sess., 3247th mtg. at 2, U.N. Doc. S/PV.3247 (June 29, 1993) (choosing between diplomacy, which is not working, and self-defense, Bosnia should be allowed to exercise its right to self-defense).

[39] *See generally* U.N. SCOR, 47th Sess., 3175th mtg. at 2, U.N. Doc. S/PV.3175 (Feb. 22, 1993) (present, but silent); U.N. SCOR, 47th Sess., 3217th mtg. at 2, U.N. Doc. S/PV.3217 (May 25, 1993) (same); U.N. SCOR, 47th Sess., 3269th mtg. at 15, U.N. Doc. S/PV.3269 (Aug. 24, 1993) (saying it was reprehensible that only two women out of a total of twenty-three candidates had been forwarded to the General Assembly for selection as judges for the war crimes tribunal).

[40] Julia Preston, *U.N. Creates Tribunal to Try War Crimes in Yugoslav Warfare*, Wash. Post (Feb. 23, 1993).

[41] Muhamed Sacirbey, *International Criminal Tribunal Born as Bastard?*, World Post (May 30, 2013).

[42] Mirko Klarin, *Nuremberg Now!*, Borba (May 16, 1991), *reprinted in* ICTY, The Path to The Hague: Selected Documents on the Origins of the ICTY 43 (2001). One of the earliest government calls for an international court came from Germany's minister of foreign affairs, who said "[a]n international court of criminal justice has to be created." Dr. Klaus Kinkel, Address at the London Conference, Aug. 26, 1992, *reprinted in* ICTY, The Path to The Hague *supra*, at 49. Another early call for prosecutions came from then acting U.S. secretary of state Laurence Eagleburger. In a statement delivered on December 16, 1992, Eagleburger said the

October 1992, also expressed support for a tribunal.[43] Aryeh Neier, who led Human Rights Watch (HRW) at the time, describes the New York-based organization's role this way:

> Seeking a commensurate response to the crimes we documented, we called on the United Nations Security Council to establish a tribunal to bring to justice those responsible, and we named ten Serbian and Bosnian Serb political, military, and militia leaders against whom we had collected sufficient evidence to warrant their investigation for committing war crimes.[44]

Although scarcely the sole crime associated with ethnic cleansing, reports of mass rape, used as a weapon of war, galvanized a global women's movement, which issued similar calls for accountability.[45] Indeed, women's human rights advocates provided crucial impetus to the creation of the ICTY.[46]

Understandably, the Hague Tribunal is widely perceived as an artifact of global politics and advocacy.[47] Yet this obscures the powerful demand for justice among many Bosnian survivors and the key role some of them played in preparing the ground for a legal reckoning. Bosnian women's organizations began documenting wartime rapes with a view to securing justice as early as 1992. Rape survivors, including Nusreta Sivac and Jadranka Cigelj, started collecting testimonies of other victims in Croatia, to which they fled after their release from the Omarska camp in August 1992.[48] Sivac, a former judge, recalls that, when she and some fifty-six other

---

U.S. government "believes it is time for the international community to begin identifying individuals who may have to answer for having committed crimes against humanity," and proceeded to name candidates for "any trial proceedings that may occur." Laurence Eagleburger, The Need to Respond to War Crimes in the Former Yugoslavia, presented at the International Conference on the former Yugoslavia, Geneva, *reprinted in* ICTY, THE PATH TO THE HAGUE, *supra*, at 67–69.

[43] In an interim report, the commission noted that creation of a tribunal by the UN Security Council "would be consistent with the direction of its work." Interim Report of the Commission of Experts Established Pursuant to Security Council Resolution 780 (1992), ¶ 74, U.N. Doc. S/25274, Annex I (Feb. 10, 1993).

[44] NEIER, *supra* note 33, at 124.

[45] *See* Janet Halley, *Rape at Rome: Feminist Interventions in the Criminalization of Sex-Related Violence in Positive International Criminal Law*, 30 MICH. J. INT'L L. 1, 12–13 (2008).

[46] *See* JULIE MERTUS & OLJA HOČEVAR VAN WELY, WOMEN'S PARTICIPATION IN THE INTERNATIONAL CRIMINAL TRIBUNAL FOR THE FORMER YUGOSLAVIA (ICTY): TRANSITIONAL JUSTICE FOR BOSNIA AND HERZEGOVINA, at vii (July 2004); GABRIELA MISCHKOWSKI & GORANA MLINAREVIĆ, MEDICA MONDIALE, "... AND THAT IT DOES NOT HAPPEN TO ANYONE ANYWHERE IN THE WORLD": THE TROUBLE WITH RAPE TRIALS—VIEWS OF WITNESSES, PROSECUTORS AND JUDGES ON PROSECUTING SEXUALISED VIOLENCE DURING THE WAR IN THE FORMER YUGOSLAVIA 5 (2009). In its resolution creating the Tribunal, the Security Council expressed "once again its great alarm" at ongoing reports of grave violations of international humanitarian law, "including reports of mass killings, massive, organized and systematic detention and rape of women." S.C. Res. 827, preamble (May 25, 1993).

[47] In a departure from what many consider good practice, Bosnians were not consulted about the possibility of establishing a Tribunal. *See* Sanja Kutnjak Ivković, *Justice by the International Criminal Tribunal for the Former Yugoslavia*, 37 STAN. J. INT'L L. 255, 291 (2001).

[48] *See* Aida Čerkez, *Bosnian Woman Helped Make Rape a War Crime*, ASSOCIATED PRESS (Mar. 8, 2013). The wartime government had begun documenting atrocities as early as 1992, setting up a Commission for Gathering Facts on War Crimes. Its work was later taken over by the nongovernmental Research and Documentation Center, led by the same person who was secretary of the

women were released, they began to talk about prosecuting Omarska guards notorious for rape.[49] Soon after the ICTY was created, Bosnian women's organizations called for the Tribunal "to focus specifically and intensely on these types of crimes."[50]

Amnesty International describes the interplay between Bosnian women's organizations and international advocates this way:

> In 1992 women's organizations in BiH and Croatia reported the occurrence of rape in Bosnia and Herzegovina on a massive scale. Following such reports human rights organizations, women's organizations and other civil society actors worldwide campaigned for the establishment of an international tribunal which would prosecute all allegations of rape and other war crimes which took place in the context of the conflicts in the former Yugoslavia.[51]

My first set of interviews for this study came thirteen years after the Security Council's decision to create the Tribunal, too late reliably to capture Bosnians' contemporaneous reactions. What many recalled in interviews, however, is that "Bosnians had big hopes, major expectations from the fact that the Hague Tribunal was established."[52] Bosniaks, who suffered the lion's share of atrocities in the 1990s' war, "were

---

governmental commission. *See* Dženana Halimović, *Bosnian Researcher Counts War Dead, and Faces Threats for His Methods*, RFE/RL (Nov. 21, 2008).

[49] This recollection was shared with Miki Jačević who, at my request, asked Sivac and other Bosnian sources about their contemporaneous reactions to the ICTY's creation. Email from Miki Jačević, Vice Chair, Initiative for Inclusive Security, to Diane Orentlicher (Nov. 24, 2015).

[50] *Id.* Jačević served as a translator at the U.N. World Conference on Human Rights in Vienna, which "many of the Bosnian women's groups" attended. *Id.* The quote by Jačević in the text relates to this conference, which took place in June 1993—just weeks after the ICTY was created. The declaration adopted at the end of the conference called for prosecution of those responsible for "systematic rape" and other atrocities:

> The World Conference on Human Rights expresses its dismay at massive violations of human rights especially in the form of genocide, "ethnic cleansing" and systematic rape of women in war situations, creating mass exodus of refugees and displaced persons. While strongly condemning such abhorrent practices it reiterates the call that perpetrators of such crimes be punished and such practices immediately stopped.

Vienna Declaration and Programme of Action, ¶ 28 (June 25, 1993).

[51] AMNESTY INTERNATIONAL, BOSNIA AND HERZEGOVINA: "WHOSE JUSTICE?": THE WOMEN OF BOSNIA AND HERZEGOVINA ARE STILL WAITING 8 (2009). Mertus and Hočevar van Wely similarly attribute the ICTY's existence "in large part to the efforts of local and international women human rights advocates." MERTUS & HOČEVAR VAN WELY, *supra* note 46, at vii.

A news report published soon after the Bosnian war ended indicated that Bosnian organizations were actively engaged in the ICTY's efforts to prosecute crimes of sexual violence: "Counseling and aid groups have spent the past weeks organizing their patient records for investigators and asking alleged victims [of rape] if they would be willing to testify in court." *Investigators Compile Mass Rape Allegations*, USA TODAY (Feb. 14, 1996). Reflecting on these efforts, Jasna Bakšić Muftić, then leader of the Sarajevo chapter of the Union of Women's Associations of Bosnia, noted: "This could be the first time in history that women are coming forward right after a war to talk about rape. It could be a very important milestone for war crime prosecutors." *Id.*

[52] Interview with Emsuda Mujagić, President, Srcem do Mira, in Kozarac, Bosn. & Herz. (July 23, 2009). I believe Mujagić was describing Bosniak responses in particular. In similar terms, Fadil Budnjo told me victims had "great, great expectations of international justice." Interview with Fadil Budnjo, President, Association of Families of Killed and Missing from Foča and Kalinovik, in Ilidža, Bosn. & Herz. (July 24, 2009). I do not discount the possibility that some sources who

counting very much on the ICTY . . . from the early beginning,"[53] and would over-whelmingly support it in the years to come.[54]

Over time, as later chapters explore, Bosnians' early expectations would prove to have been gravely inflated, and the gap between hope and experience would diminish their sense of justice. Nusreta Sivac made the point this way in 2014: "People who survived all these atrocities, all this misery, all this torture, probably had *major* illusions and expectations about the ICTY."[55] (Even so, when asked if, in light of their frustrations with the ICTY's performance, they now thought it was a mistake to have created the Tribunal, virtually every Bosniak whom I interviewed emphatically answered along these lines: "No! Without the ICTY we would not have received justice."[56])

I have often wondered why Bosniaks, still under siege and largely abandoned to their fate by the UN Security Council, would enthusiastically welcome its decision to create a court. When I put this question to Emir Hodžić he replied: "It was like, well, finally justice."[57] Hodžić suggested the Council's action also stirred hopes that "the international community would help and . . . get involved"[58] in ending the conflict then in full rage. Smail Čekić had a somewhat different account. He recalled that, when the ICTY was created, many Bosnians' "expectation was . . . that the aggressor states . . . will stop or at least reduce their aggression-related activities simply for the fact that they are now aware of such a UN-organized international tribunal."[59] Former Hague prosecutor Dan Saxon explains Bosniak reactions this way: "Although the Bosnian Muslim population had hoped for a military intervention by the West that never came, the ICTY was seen as a second best but still positive action."[60] In short,

---

shared memories of contemporaneous reactions were recalling views that emerged in the early post-Dayton period, when many Bosnians focused on the Tribunal for the first time. Writing seventeen years after the ICTY's creation, Refik Hodžić, a Bosniak from Prijedor, recalled that most victims at first had little understanding of the Tribunal. Hodžić nonetheless quotes one victim saying she was "very happy when ICTY was established." Refik Hodžić, *Living the Legacy of Mass Atrocities: Victims' Perspectives on War Crimes Trials*, 8 J. INT'L CRIM. JUST. 113, 119 n.12 (2010).

[53] Interview with Aleksandra Letić, Secretary-General, Helsinki Committee for Human Rights in Republika Srpska, in Sarajevo, Bosn. & Herz. (Sept. 8, 2014).

[54] *See* Stuart Ford, *A Social Psychology Model of the Perceived Legitimacy of International Criminal Courts: Implications for the Success of Transitional Justice Mechanisms*, 45 VAND. J. TRANSNAT'L L. 405, 416–17 (2012).

[55] Interview with Nusreta Sivac, Former Judge, in Prijedor, Bosn. & Herz. (Sept. 16, 2014).

[56] *See* Chapter 6. *See also* JANINE NATALYA CLARK, INTERNATIONAL TRIALS AND RECONCILIATION: ASSESSING THE IMPACT OF THE INTERNATIONAL CRIMINAL TRIBUNAL FOR THE FORMER YUGOSLAVIA 59 (2014). Many Bosnian Serbs also told me it was right to have created the ICTY, though many also said they strongly disapproved of the way it operated.

[57] Interview with Emir Hodžić, Jer Me Se Tiče, in Sarajevo, Bosn. & Herz. (Sept. 13, 2014).

[58] *Id.*

[59] Interview with Smail Čekić, Professor of History and Director, Institute for Research of Crimes against Humanity and International Law, University of Sarajevo, in Sarajevo, Bosn. & Herz. (July 16, 2009).

[60] Dan Saxon, *Exporting Justice: Perceptions of the ICTY Among the Serbian, Croatian, and Muslim Communities in the Former Yugoslavia*, 4 J. HUM. RTS. 559, 563 (2005). Saxon cites as his source for this view Aleksandar Kontić, a longtime member of the ICTY prosecutor's office. *See also* JELENA SUBOTIĆ, HIJACKED JUSTICE: DEALING WITH THE PAST IN THE BALKANS 129 (2009) ("For the Bosniac majority . . . the [ICTY's] establishment . . . was seen as a welcome development, as the next best thing in the absence of an international military intervention to stop the Bosnian bloodshed").

the very fact that robust measures were then off the table led some Bosnians to redirect their hopes, at least in part, toward the Tribunal.[61]

Cultural perspectives may have played a part as well. As Jasna Bakšić Muftić explained, the political culture forged during Yugoslavia's communist past disposed Bosnians to expect strong institutions to take care of their needs. The Communist party, she said, cultivated a sense among Yugoslav citizens "that someone, another, is responsible for them, for the future, for solving all the problems."[62] When Bosnians' own government could not protect them from grave harm, she suggested, many redirected their expectations to an "international institution, believing 'only [the] international community [can] help us."[63]

Whatever combination of factors shaped their responses, the establishment of the ICTY "meant a lot to victims," Edin Hodžić recalled. And if subsequent experience tempered once-soaring hopes, some Bosniaks' spirits were lifted at a time of unremitting misery.[64]

Generalizations can, of course, be perilous. A key risk here would be to suggest all Bosniaks enthusiastically embraced the ICTY when they learned of its creation. Ivana Nizich, who investigated atrocities throughout the war, recalls that while some survivors were eager to advance prosecutions as early as 1992, most were overwhelmingly preoccupied with urgent concerns: "'I don't know where my husband is, I don't know where my house is, I've got my kids missing'—it was very existential concerns at that point."[65] In addition, Nizich recalled, those who were documenting sexual violence with a view to future prosecutions tended to be "well educated" women who were "connected to the West." While these women embraced international justice, rural survivors of scant means repeatedly expressed a variation of the sentiment, "we're just left behind."[66]

With appropriate caveats, then, a key point to be made here is that Bosniaks were not simply passive objects of international decision-making. Local actors prepared the way for accountability as early as 1992 and became active participants in the global effort to ensure justice once the ICTY was launched the following year.

---

[61] During the period the ICTY was launched, Bosnians took other measures to halt attacks against them. Two months before the Council formally created the Tribunal, the predominantly Bosniak government instituted proceedings against the FRY before the International Court of Justice (ICJ), alleging the respondent was responsible for genocide in Bosnia. The Bosnian government asked the ICJ to issue the equivalent of an urgent injunction, preventing the FRY from taking further steps to support genocidal violence.

[62] Interview with Jasna Bakšić Muftić, Professor, Faculty of Law, University of Sarajevo, in Sarajevo, Bosn. & Herz. (Sept. 17, 2014). The Communist Party of Yugoslavia was renamed the League of Communists of Yugoslavia in 1952, and held its last party congress in 1990. Professor Bakšić Muftić used the phrase "Communist party" to refer to "the political leader of the whole society . . . during the Communist time."

[63] Id.

[64] Interview with Edin Hodžić, Director, Public Law Program, Center for Social Research Analitika, in Sarajevo, Bosn. & Herz. (Sept. 11, 2014).

[65] Interview with Ivana Nizich, Former Investigator, Human Rights Watch; Former Military Analyst, Office of the Prosecutor, ICTY, in Washington, D.C., United States (Apr. 28, 2017). More generally, Nizich recalled, while the conflict was underway she would often hear comments from Bosnians to the effect, "You Americans are doing nothing and the Europeans are having conferences. And we're dying." Id.

[66] Id.

If Bosniaks overwhelmingly supported the new Tribunal, Bosnian Serb rebels had much the opposite view. Like their sponsors in Belgrade, whose defiance of the ICTY is explored in Chapter 3,[67] they bitterly opposed the Tribunal. Their opposition was foregone: although Bosniak and Croat combatants were also implicated in war crimes, the overwhelming majority were committed by Serb forces, and Serbs believed they would be the principal focus of prosecutions.[68] (It should be emphasized, however, that some of the Tribunal's most staunch supporters in Bosnia have been ethnic Serbs, whose perspectives loom large in this book.)

As for Bosnians of Croat ethnicity, it is difficult to find references to their contemporaneous reactions in the vast literature on the ICTY,[69] and most of my Bosnian interlocutors were hard-pressed to recall how they responded.[70] But Bill Stuebner, who was in Bosnia and in frequent contact with Bosnian Croats throughout the war, believes "90 percent of Bosnian Croats were not even aware" the Security Council created the Tribunal, as "they had other things on their mind" at the time.[71] Indeed, by the time the Security Council resolved to create the ICTY, Bosnian Croat forces were ramping up a military campaign to create an ethnically homogeneous Croat statelet in Bosnia, "Herceg-Bosna," which they hoped would become part of Croatia. Consumed with this effort, Ivana Nizich recalled, Bosnian Croat military leaders couldn't "care less about the Tribunal."[72]

To the extent they thought about the new Tribunal, Bosnian Croats would have had grounds for ambivalence. On the one hand, ethnic Croats were early victims of Serb atrocities, which were later prosecuted in The Hague.[73] Perhaps for this reason,

---

[67] See also Isabelle Delpla, In the Midst of Injustice: The ICTY from the Perspective of Some Victim Associations, in THE NEW BOSNIAN MOSAIC: IDENTITIES, MEMORIES AND MORAL CLAIMS IN A POST-WAR SOCIETY 211, 214 (Xavier Bougarel et al. eds., 2007).

[68] In an assessment completed in early 1995, the U.S. Central Intelligence Agency attributed 90 percent of atrocities committed in Bosnia to ethnic Serbs. See Roger Cohen, C.I.A. Report on Bosnia Blames Serbs for 90% of the War Crimes, N.Y. TIMES (Mar. 8, 1995). At times, the Security Council had condemned in particular the conduct of Bosnian Serbs, presumably heightening Serbs' belief that a war crimes tribunal created by the Council would focus on Serb atrocities. See, e.g., S.C. Res. 819, preambular ¶¶ 6–10; op. ¶ 2 (Apr. 16, 1993); S.C. Res. 820, op. ¶ 11 (Apr. 17, 1993).

[69] One of my research assistants at the Washington College of Law, Alanna Kennedy, reviewed transcripts of Security Council meetings in which the ICTY was discussed from the early 1990s through the early 2000s. She reported that, although representatives of Croatia periodically attended these sessions, they either did not make statements or made remarks that did not touch upon the ICTY.

[70] An exception is Štefica Galić, whose contemporaneous reaction is described in Chapter 4. As that account makes clear, Galić is exceptional in many respects.

[71] Telephone interview with William Stuebner (May 25, 2017). During the Bosnian war Stueber helped arrange humanitarian assistance on behalf of the U.S. government. Ivana Nizich, who was in a predominantly Croat region of Bosnia as a researcher for Human Rights Watch when the ICTY was created, acknowledged she was hard-pressed to remember contemporaneous Bosnian Croat reactions. But, in line with Stuebner's recollection, Nizich said: "I don't think they had much of a reaction." Interview with Ivana Nizich, Former Investigator, Human Rights Watch; Former Military Analyst, Office of the Prosecutor, ICTY, in Washington, D.C., United States (Apr. 28, 2017).

[72] Interview with Ivana Nizich, Former Investigator, Human Rights Watch; Former Military Analyst, Office of the Prosecutor, ICTY, in Washington, D.C., United States (Apr. 28, 2017).

[73] See, e.g., Prosecutor v. Mrkšić et al., Case No. IT-95-13/1-T, Trial Judgment (Int'l Crim. Trib. for the Former Yugoslavia Sept. 27, 2007) (war crimes in Vukovar, Croatia, in 1991); Prosecutor v. Strugar, Case No. IT-01-42-T, Trial Judgment (Int'l Crim. Trib. for the Former Yugoslavia Jan. 31, 2005) (war crimes in Dubrovnik, Croatia, in 1991).

the wartime government of Croatia, with which Bosnian Croats were aligned, officially supported the Security Council's decision to launch a tribunal (although it turned against the ICTY when it brought charges against Croats).[74] On the other hand, at the precise moment the Council launched the Tribunal, Bosnian Croats had recently committed atrocities against Bosnian Muslims in Central Bosnia, also eventually prosecuted in The Hague.[75] Even so, Stuebner notes, Bosnian Croats—like Croatian officials who supported them—were unlikely to have contemplated Croats being prosecuted in The Hague. Acting in the context of what they considered "a defensive war,"[76] they did not consider their actions war crimes.

B. The Wartime Court: Early Indictments of Low-Level Perpetrators

> *A great expectation was . . . created by the ICTY that . . . everyone will get their day in court.*
>
> —Thomas Osorio[77]

Almost every aspect of the Tribunal's wartime years (the period from its creation until the end of 1995, when the Dayton Peace Agreement finally ended the Bosnian conflict) seemed to vindicate the skeptics. Judges were not in place until six months after the ICTY was formally created by the Security Council.[78] It would take fourteen months to identify a candidate for Prosecutor who would enjoy the support of a fractious Security Council *and* remain on the job more than a few days, the length of the first Prosecutor's tenure.[79] In July 1994, the ICTY received a desperately

---

[74] *See Sanadar in a Letter to Ban Ki-moon: Seriously Examine All Aspects of the Hague Tribunal's Work*, Jutarnji (Sept. 29, 2007) (in letter to then UN secretary-general Ban Ki-moon, then prime minister of Croatia Ivo Sanadar recalled Croatia was "one of the founders of the Hague Tribunal and a solid supporter" of the two Security Council resolutions establishing the Tribunal); Jelena Stojanović, EU Political Conditionality and Domestic Politics: Cooperation with the International Criminal Tribunal for the Former Yugoslavia in Croatia and Serbia 199 (2009) (unpublished Ph.D. dissertation, Central European University) (on file with author) (Croatia's position toward the ICTY "changed from . . . very positive when the Tribunal began its work to a very hostile and uneasy relationship towards 1999"; "Once the Tribunal started indicting Croats from 1995 onwards, especially for the actions that represented defense of Croatia from the aggressors, Croatia became very negative towards the ICTY").

[75] *See, e.g.*, Prosecutor v. Blaškić, Case No. IT-95-14-T, Trial Judgment (Int'l Crim. Trib. for the Former Yugoslavia Mar. 3, 2000) (war crimes in Vitez, Bosnia, in 1993); Prosecutor v. Kordić et al., Case No. IT-19-14/2-T, Trial Judgment (Int'l Crim. Trib. for the Former Yugoslavia Feb. 26, 2001) (war crimes in Central Bosnia in 1992–1993; Prosecutor v. Prlić et al., Case No. IT-04-74-T, Trial Judgment (Int'l Crim. Trib. for the Former Yugoslavia May 29, 2013) (war crimes in Central Bosnia in 1992–1994). The conflict between Bosniak and Croat forces in Bosnia ended in March 1994 in accordance with the U.S.-brokered Washington Agreement, which also established the Federation of Bosnia and Herzegovina.

[76] Telephone interview with William Stuebner (May 25, 2017).

[77] Interview with Thomas Osorio, then Chief Technical Advisor, Rule of Law, UNDP, in Sarajevo, Bosn. & Herz. (Sept. 8, 2014).

[78] The lead sentence of a wire service account of the Tribunal's opening captured the world's low expectations: "The first war crimes tribunal since World War II opened today amid doubt that it had enough documented proof or power to punish those guilty of atrocities in former Yugoslavia." *War-Crimes Tribunal Opens Inquiry on Yugoslav Fighting*, N.Y. Times (Nov. 18, 1993).

[79] Venezuela's attorney general, Ramon Escovar-Salom, was appointed Prosecutor but soon withdrew so that he could accept another appointment in Venezuela. *See* Paul Lewis, *South*

needed boost when the Council appointed renowned South African jurist Richard Goldstone, instantly bolstering the Tribunal's credibility.[80]

While the ICTY would later amass a rich archive of atrocity, in its early years investigators struggled to gather evidence in a theater of ongoing conflict, a challenge for which there was no playbook from postwar prosecutions in Nuremberg and Tokyo.[81] With the conflict underway, investigators were largely blocked from Serb-controlled areas of Bosnia, at that time roughly two-thirds of the country.[82]

Establishing a financially secure foundation for its work was another mountain the Tribunal had to climb. Goldstone, all but technically the ICTY's first Prosecutor, devoted much of his tenure to global diplomacy aimed at securing adequate funding, while his staff sought to identify suspects with respect to whom there was a reasonable prospect of issuing an indictment and, even more challenging, gaining custody. These dual preoccupations were closely linked: in his memoir, Goldstone explains why the Office of the Prosecutor (OTP) issued its first indictment against Dragan Nikolić, whom Goldstone characterized as "a comparatively low-level" suspect. Going into his first budget meeting at UN headquarters soon after taking up his post, Goldstone had "been informed ahead of time that at least one indictment had to be issued before the . . . meeting in order to demonstrate that the system was working and that the tribunal was worthy of financial support."[83] With the Tribunal starved for cash, the OTP indicted Nikolić because "he was the only person against whom we had sufficient evidence to justify an indictment" at that time.[84]

Goldstone's explanation begs the question, Why did his office have "sufficient evidence" against Nikolić and not other, more notorious, individuals? A significant part

---

African Is to Prosecute Balkan War Crimes; A Yearlong Search, Complicated by Slavic Alliances, N.Y. TIMES (July 9, 1994). The ICTY website indicates Escovar-Salom never took up his position. *See Office of the Prosecutor,* INT'L CRIM. TRIB. FOR THE FORMER YUGOSLAVIA, http://www.icty. org/sid/287 (last visited Dec. 7, 2017). Goldstone, who was appointed Prosecutor after Escovar-Salom withdrew, recalls that his predecessor announced he was resigning his third day on the job. Richard Goldstone, 20 Years Later: Reflections on International Justice from the First Chief Prosecutor of the International Criminal Tribunal for the former Yugoslavia (ICTY), Remarks at the Washington College of Law, American University (Feb. 5, 2014). The Security Council approved Goldstone's appointment unanimously on July 8, 1994. For an account of the internal wrangling that prevented a consensus until then, see NIKOLAS M. RAJKOVIĆ, THE POLITICS OF INTERNATIONAL LAW AND COMPLIANCE: SERBIA, CROATIA AND THE HAGUE TRIBUNAL 49–51 (2012).

[80] *See* RAJKOVIĆ, *supra* note 79, at 51.

[81] Goldstone's first visit to Sarajevo as Prosecutor was "unforgettable because of the problems and danger associated" with visiting a city "under vicious siege." RICHARD J. GOLDSTONE, FOR HUMANITY: REFLECTIONS OF A WAR CRIMES INVESTIGATOR 94 (2000). While it was difficult to conduct investigations in Bosnia during the war, the fledgling tribunal received evidence from other sources, of which the most important was the Commission of Experts established by the UN Security Council before it launched the ICTY. *See* M. Cherif Bassiouni, *The United Nations Commission of Experts Established Pursuant to Security Council Resolution 780 (1992),* 88 AM. J. INT'L L. 784, 792 (1994).

[82] Interview with Alan Tieger, then Senior Trial Attorney, Office of the Prosecutor, ICTY, in The Hague, Neth. (May 26, 2015). As noted later, however, investigators were allowed limited access to mass grave sites in Republika Srpska early on.

[83] GOLDSTONE, *supra* note 81, at 105.

[84] *Id.* at 105–06. Although indicted in November 1994, Nikolić eluded arrest until April 20, 2000. *See* INT'L CRIB. TRIB. FOR THE FORMER YUGOSLAVIA, CASE INFORMATION SHEET, http://www. icty.org/x/cases/dragan_nikolic/cis/en/cis_nikolic_dragan.pdf (last visited Dec. 7, 2017).

of the answer is that it is easier to build a strong case against direct perpetrators than masterminds of mass atrocity, who are often physically removed from crime scenes. In the specific case of Nikolić, moreover, the OTP seized an opportunity: Much of the evidence supporting his indictment came from a former guard at a camp where Nikolić murdered, tortured, and illegally detained Muslim prisoners, who provided information after fleeing the region.[85]

The same pressures and constraints that prompted the OTP to indict Nikolić also led Goldstone to issue his second indictment against another low-level suspect, Dušan Tadić. Goldstone saw an opportunity when German authorities arrested Tadić, whom refugees from Prijedor recognized in Germany, in February 1994. The OTP immediately indicted Tadić. Two months later Germany transferred him to The Hague, where he was the first person tried before the ICTY. In this way a truly sadistic yet unexceptional participant in Bosnia's organized violence became the vehicle for the ICTY's early, pathbreaking, jurisprudence.[86]

While financial and other pressures go a long way toward explaining the OTP's early indictments, they were not the only factors.[87] In the early years of the Tribunal, its investigators, many of whom had no previous exposure to the former Yugoslavia,[88] exercised substantial autonomy in shaping their priorities, producing investigations that did not add up to an overarching prosecutorial strategy.[89]

---

[85] The *New York Times* published a series of articles based on this source's account in August 1994. *See* Roger Cohen, *Tribunal Charges Serbian Camp Commander with War Crimes*, N.Y. Times (Nov. 8, 1994). Nikolić eventually pleaded guilty before the ICTY. *See* Int'l Crim. Trib. for the Former Yugoslavia, Statements of Guilt, http://www.icty.org/sid/217 (last visited Dec. 7, 2017).

[86] For example, a jurisdictional ruling in the *Tadić* case established that war crimes could be committed in the context of a non-international armed conflict as well as an interstate conflict. Prosecutor v. Tadić, Case No. IT-94-1-AR72, Decision on Defence Motion for Interlocutory Appeal on Jurisdiction, ¶¶ 96–137 (Int'l Crim. Trib. for the Former Yugoslavia Oct. 2, 1995).

[87] Among them, for awhile the OTP had "no strategic plan" for its work, according to a former member of its staff. Interview with Ivana Nizich, Former Investigator, Human Rights Watch; Former Military Analyst, Office of the Prosecutor, ICTY, in Washington, D.C., United States (Apr. 28, 2017).

[88] This had a deleterious effect on early investigations. On one occasion, an OTP team sought to recruit a potential insider witness, who served in the Yugoslav National Army (JNA) as a high-ranking military intelligence official. When it became clear that two members of the team did not know "KOS" was the operational intelligence and counter-intelligence arm of the JNA, the potential witness cut the meeting short. A former military analyst who was part of the team interpreted his reaction as, "If you expect me to risk my neck and act as an informant, essentially, . . . and you don't even have the decency to send professional investigators here, . . . we're done." *Id.*

[89] The OTP's Investigation Division was responsible for directing investigations until the ICTY's third Prosecutor, Carla del Ponte, put investigations under the direction of senior trial attorneys, who provided much-needed guidance. Bill Stuebner, who worked in the OTP in June 1994–February 1996 and May 1996–August 1997, recalls that before then, many of the OTP's investigators and attorneys saw the previously-noted indictment of Dragan Nikolić as a "green light to focus on the low-hanging fruit, resulting in many indictments the OTP should never have brought and thereby clogging up the docket." Comments by William Stuebner on draft chapter (provided June 21, 2017). ICTY prosecutors would later acknowledge some of their early indictments were weak, though they attributed this to pressure from judges who were "impatient with the pace of indictments and deteriorating public confidence." Charles Trueheart, *War Crimes Tribunal Gathers Momentum; 4 Trials Underway for Atrocities in Bosnia, But Top Figures Remain at Large*, Wash. Post (Mar. 3, 1998).

Another often-cited explanation for the ICTY's early indictments of low-level suspects is that Goldstone initially pursued a pyramid theory of prosecution: the OTP would first target comparatively low-level suspects, whose prosecution would produce evidence establishing the responsibility of their superiors; prosecutors would follow evidentiary leads upward until they reached the top.[90] By July 1995, Goldstone changed course, leapfrogging over lower and mid-level suspects to indict Bosnian Serb wartime leaders Radovan Karadžić and Ratko Mladić.[91] But Goldstone would leave office in 1996 without indicting Slobodan Milošević, widely seen as bearing lead responsibility for ruinous violence in the former Yugoslavia.

Some saw political calculation behind Goldstone's restraint,[92] a suggestion he has adamantly denied: "There was no political motivation all," he insisted. "We stated many times that we were looking into the top leaders across the board."[93] Indeed, Goldstone has consistently maintained the OTP followed the evidence wherever it led; it simply did not have sufficient evidence to indict Milošević during his tenure.[94]

Whatever the reasons for its early focus on low-level perpetrators, some Bosnians blame the Tribunal for the long-term costs this exacted. Mirsad Tokača, who directs a war crimes documentation center in Sarajevo, believes ICTY success should be measured in part by whether the Tribunal convicts those who were "most respon-sible . . ., ideologically, politically, militarily" for the 1990s bloodbath.[95] Thus he faults the Tribunal for "wast[ing] time" on "very small, very, very small fishes who were in fact political or military executors."[96]

To be sure, the ICTY's early indictments provided satisfaction to many victims, particularly once suspects were apprehended and tried. Yet the Prosecutor's early

---

[90] *See* Antonio Cassese, *The ICTY: A Living and Vital Reality*, 2 J. INT'L CRIM. JUST. 585, 586 (2004); William A. Schabas, *Selecting Situations and Cases*, *in* THE LAW AND PRACTICE OF THE INTERNATIONAL CRIMINAL COURT 376 (Carsten Stahn ed., 2015). About a decade after the International Criminal Court began operating, its Prosecutor effectively endorsed this approach. While her office had previously targeted those "most responsible" for atrocities, it would now sometimes pursue a "strategy of gradually building upwards," prosecuting "a limited number of mid- and high-level perpetrators in order to ultimately have a reasonable prospect of conviction for the most responsible." Int'l Crim. Ct., *Strategic Plan June 2012–2015* (Oct. 11, 2013), https://www.icc-cpi.int/iccdocs/otp/OTP-Strategic-Plan-2013.pdf.

[91] As noted below, the initial indictments came on the heels of the Srebrenica genocide, though they had been in preparation for some time.

[92] *See* Jane Perlez, *War Crimes Tribunal on Bosnia Is Hampered by Basic Problems*, N.Y. TIMES (Jan. 28, 1996).

[93] *See, e.g.*, Michelle Nicholasen, *What About Milošević?*, FRONTLINE (undated).

[94] There is no reason to doubt the OTP lacked sufficient evidence to bring charges against Milošević during Goldstone's tenure. According to Bill Stuebner, a large part of the problem was that governments that possessed relevant information did not share it with the OTP before the late 1990s. Comments by William Stuebner on draft chapter (provided June 21, 2017). *See also* HAZAN, *supra* note 33, at 67. Nor, however, did the OTP commit significant resources toward developing evidence against Milošević until 1999, the year Goldstone's immediate successor, Louise Arbour, finally indicted Milošević. According to a former military analyst for the ICTY, while the "OTP had a group of analysts devoted to working up the chains of civilian and military leadership, . . . investigators and prosecutors were not assigned to this effort [i.e., investigating Milošević] until the very late 1990s." E-mail from Ivana Nizich to Diane Orentlicher (Aug. 14, 2017).

[95] Interview with Mirsad Tokača, President, Research and Documentation Center (Sarajevo), in Sarajevo, Bosn. & Herz. (Sept. 11, 2014).

[96] *Id.*

focus on direct perpetrators raised expectations that would prove impossible to fulfill. As a former OTP employee put it, "a great expectation was . . . created by the
ICTY that . . . everyone will get their day in court."[97] Regrettably, the Tribunal had
no communications strategy in place to manage victims' expectations.[98] Not surprisingly, many Bosnians were profoundly disappointed when they realized the Tribunal
would leave untouched thousands of perpetrators with direct responsibility for wartime atrocities—the men who tortured them and killed their siblings, spouses, and
children.[99]

Of course, no prosecutorial or communications strategy could fully satisfy those
who survived Bosnia's bloodbath. At a time when top ICTY officials were working
assiduously to meet daunting challenges, moreover, the notion that they should
manage soaring expectations would have seemed anomalous. In retrospect, however, the Tribunal's experience highlights the central importance of developing a
principled and viable prosecutorial strategy in circumstances of finite resources and
massive crimes, and effectively communicating that strategy from the outset.

C. Justice and Peace: Preventing Amnesty at Dayton

When the Security Council created the ICTY in the midst of war, it justified doing
so on the legally necessary ground that its action would help restore peace and security.[100] In reality, diplomats working to end the conflict feared a tribunal would
thwart their efforts.[101] The "peace vs. justice" dilemma surfaced repeatedly during
the Tribunal's early years.

In March 1994, senior U.S. officials who supported the Tribunal repelled a "strong
push" by other members of the five-member Bosnia Contact Group, set up in 1993
to coordinate peacemaking efforts, to grant several wartime leaders amnesty "as
bait for their cooperation in the sputtering peace talks."[102] Reservations about the

---

[97] Interview with Thomas Osorio, then Chief Technical Advisor, Rule of Law, UNDP, in Sarajevo,
Bosn. & Herz. (Sept. 8, 2014). *See also* Refik Hodžić, *A Long Road Yet to Reconciliation: The
Impact of the ICTY on Reconciliation and Victims' Perceptions of Criminal Justice*, *in* Assessing
the Legacy of the ICTY 115, 118 (Richard H. Steinberg ed., 2011) ("With the arrest of some
direct perpetrators, a belief grew among the victims that the crimes committed against them
would not go unpunished").

[98] Soon after taking office the Prosecutor said his office would, while targeting those who ordered
the crimes, make "all efforts . . . to ensure that those who executed such orders" are indicted as
well. Richard J. Goldstone, *The International Tribunal for the Former Yugoslavia: A Case Study in
Security Council Action*, 6 Duke J. Comp & Int'l L. 5, 7 (1995). Goldstone nonetheless affirmed
that those indicted should not include "people at the bottom of the ladder of command." *Id.* at 8.

[99] *See* Chapter 6.

[100] Creating the ICTY was a Chapter VII enforcement measure taken to restore "international peace
and security" and was justified in part on this ground. *See* S.C. Res. 827, preambular ¶ 6 (May
25, 1993).

[101] *See* Gary J. Bass, Opinion, *Settling with the Enemy; The Dicey Politics of Negotiating Peace in
the Balkans with Accused War Criminals*, Wash. Post (Oct. 29, 1995) (describing opposition
by Europeans to the idea of the ICTY on the ground "that pursuing this sort of justice would
interfere with peace-making further down the road"); Carla Anne Robbins, *Balkan Judgments;
World Again Confronts Moral Issues Involved in War-Crimes Trials; Some Feel U.N. Delays Peace
in Former Yugoslavia by Pursuing Atrocities*, Wall Street J. (July 13, 1993).

[102] Scheffer, *supra* note 24, at 19. *See also* John Shattuck, Freedom on Fire: Human Rights
Wars & America's Response 141 (2003).

Tribunal hardly subsided as its work got underway, and Goldstone worked tirelessly to counter diplomats' attraction to the idea of offering immunity to suspected war criminals as an inducement for a peace agreement.[103] The specter of such an offer was inescapable: for a time the chief negotiator on behalf of Bosnian Serbs was Radovan Karadžić, a prime target for prosecution in The Hague.[104]

A massacre that would surpass all others brought this issue to a head. For several days in July 1995, Bosnian Serb forces systematically executed some 8,000 Muslim males who, with their families, had been living in the eastern Bosnian "safe area" of Srebrenica. The final operation, later judged a genocide by both the ICTY and the International Court of Justice, began on July 11, 1995. On July 25, 1995, Goldstone issued an indictment charging wartime Bosnian Serb leaders Radovan Karadžić and Ratko Mladić with genocide and other crimes. The indictment did not cover the July 1995 massacre, which the prosecution had not yet had time to investigate. But it is widely believed Goldstone rushed out an indictment already in the works to ensure a swift response to Srebrenica.[105] While much of the world welcomed the long-awaited indictment, then UN Secretary-General Boutros Boutros-Ghali later told Goldstone that, had the Prosecutor consulted him in advance, he would have advised against indicting Karadžić "before peace had been brokered in Bosnia."[106]

Although long authorized to use military force to protect Srebrenica and other so-called "safe areas," NATO and, even more, the United Nations had been reluctant to do so.[107] But Srebrenica, followed by another massacre in downtown Sarajevo, finally led NATO to use unprecedented firepower against Bosnian Serb forces in late August 1995.[108] NATO's action, along with the crushing effects of international sanctions against Serbia and a decisive Croatian offensive against Serb forces in the Croatian-Serb war, brought Serb leaders to the negotiating table, now under the leadership of

---

[103] *See* Jonathan S. Landay, *Opening the Docket: Trials of a War Tribunal*, CHRISTIAN SCI. MONITOR (Nov. 16, 1994).

[104] The Bosnian Serbs' military chief, Ratko Mladić, was also routinely engaged by European diplomats. *See* SARA DAREHSHORI, HUMAN RIGHTS WATCH, SELLING JUSTICE SHORT: WHY ACCOUNTABILITY MATTERS FOR PEACE 25 (2009). Later, the ICTY Prosecutor (by then, Louise Arbour) would confront a similar challenge. Her concern that Slobodan Milošević would escape prosecution through an offer of amnesty was a key factor behind her decision to indict Milošević during NATO's 1999 intervention, which aimed to end Serbian atrocities in Kosovo. *See* DIANE F. ORENTLICHER, OPEN SOCIETY JUSTICE INITIATIVE, SHRINKING THE SPACE FOR DENIAL: THE IMPACT OF THE ICTY IN SERBIA 28 (2008).

[105] *See* HAZAN, *supra* note 33, at 66.

[106] GOLDSTONE, *supra* note 81, at 103.

[107] A Security Council resolution adopted in June 1993 authorized the UN Protection Force in Bosnia and UN Member States to use force to protect civilians in "safe areas." S.C. Res. 836, ¶¶ 5, 9 (June 4, 1993). Pursuant to the so-called "dual key" arrangement, however, military force was not used to protect the "safe areas" unless both NATO and the UN Secretary-General agreed to do so. Then Secretary-General Boutros Boutros-Ghali was long reluctant to approve force. *See* Craig R. Whitney, *Conflict in the Balkans; The Policy; NATO Gives U.N. Officials Veto on Air Strikes in Bosnia*, N.Y. TIMES (July 26, 1995).

[108] Coming soon after Srebrenica, the August 1995 shelling of the Markale marketplace in Sarajevo was the proverbial last straw prompting NATO's response. *See* GARY JONATHAN BASS, STAY THE HAND OF VENGEANCE: THE POLITICS OF WAR CRIMES TRIBUNALS 231 (2000).

U.S. mediators.[109] After years of inconclusive negotiations, this time the Serbs were ready to negotiate seriously.

Less than four months after the Srebrenica massacre, peace talks led by U.S. mediator Richard Holbrooke got underway at the Wright Patterson Air Force Base outside Dayton, Ohio. In the lead-up to Dayton, U.S. officials were divided about whether Karadžić and Mladić, now ICTY indictees, could participate. At Holbrooke's insistence, the Clinton administration determined it would deal with the Bosnian Serbs principally through Serbian president Slobodan Milošević (though it did not rule out meeting with the indictees in the region, and U.S. representatives did so in September 1995).[110] Milošević, who would later face charges himself, was the lead representative of Bosnian Serbs in Dayton. If the indictment of Karadžić had an impact on prospects for peace, it was the opposite of what some diplomats feared: with peace talks scheduled a few short months after Srebrenica, Bosnia's president, Alija Izetbegović, was loath to attend any meetings at which Karadžić was present.[111]

But the Tribunal faced another challenge at Dayton, again grounded in a perceived trade-off between justice and peace: there appeared to be a real risk negotiators would offer amnesty in exchange for peace.[112] At the beginning of the Dayton talks, the ICTY sent Madeleine Albright, then U.S. ambassador to the United Nations, a letter asking the United States to include in the peace accords a requirement that indicted war criminals be surrendered to the Tribunal.[113] Soon after, Goldstone issued a second set of indictments against Karadžić and Mladić, this time charging them with genocide in relation to Srebrenica. With these and other high-profile indictments in the headlines, it would have been difficult but not impossible for diplomats to neutralize the charges.[114]

The Bosnian delegation wanted the Dayton accords to include detailed obligations concerning ICTY indictees, with a robust mandate for their arrest by the NATO Implementation Force (IFOR) to be deployed in Bosnia.[115] Holbrooke was sympathetic but could not persuade a reluctant White House in light of Pentagon opposition. Still haunted by the deaths of eighteen U.S. soldiers during an operation to

---

[109] See Steven L. Burg, *Intervention in Internal Conflict: The Case of Bosnia* 18 (2004), http://drum.lib.umd.edu/bitstream/handle/1903/7935/burg.pdf;jsessionid=8C66769F97F76E2CFE34231F9E8D45D9?sequence=1.

[110] BASS, *supra* note 108, at 232–38.

[111] According to Richard Goldstone, Bosnia's wartime UN ambassador and foreign minister, Mohammed Sacirbey, confirmed that Izetbegović would not have come to Dayton if Karadžić were there. GOLDSTONE, *supra* note 81, at 103.

[112] BASS, *supra* note 108, at 242–43.

[113] See Stephen Engelberg, *Panel Seeks U.S. Pledge on Bosnia War Criminals*, N.Y. TIMES (Nov. 3, 1995).

[114] Goldstone denies he deliberately issued the second indictments during the peace talks but concedes he speeded up their preparation "[w]hen it was announced that the Dayton talks were to take place." GOLDSTONE, *supra* note 81, at 108. Goldstone's deputy, Graham Blewitt, has said the indictments were timed to make it more difficult for the negotiators to dispose of the Tribunal at Dayton. BASS, *supra* note 108, at 244. Just before he issued the Srebrenica indictments, Goldstone also issued his first set of indictments against Serbian officers in relation to a large massacre in Croatia, which took place in Vukovar in November 1991. Prosecutor v. Mrkšić et al., Case No. IT-95-13a, Indictment (Int'l Crim. Trib. for the Former Yugoslavia Oct. 26, 1995). *See also* Roger Cohen, *Tribunal Indicts 3 Serbia Officers; Hague Inquiry Moves Closer to Belgrade's Leadership*, N.Y. TIMES (Nov. 10, 1995).

[115] BASS, *supra* note 108, at 241.

arrest a Somali warlord in October 1993, the Clinton administration was unwilling to expose U.S. troops to what it saw as a perilous effort to arrest fugitives.[116] A compromise was reached that would, as the following section explains, prove fateful for victims' experience of Hague justice: IFOR would be authorized but not required to arrest ICTY suspects.[117]

II. THE AFTERMATH OF WAR

With the conclusion of the Dayton accords, Bosniaks in particular had high hopes, not only for the restoration of peace but also for justice.[118] In particular, with the deployment of 60,000 NATO troops empowered to arrest ICTY fugitives, many expected the Hague Tribunal's arrest warrants to be quickly answered. Many also "expected[,] . . . the ICTY would bring about changes in Bosnia-Herzegovina"[119] that transcend the writ of judicial process. Both hopes would be disappointed.

A. IFOR's Policy of Avoidance

> *The procedure for arresting people still has to be invented. . . . [A]nyone who has the expectations that there will be convictions soon is an idiot.*
>
> —FRITS KALSHOVEN[120]

> *The whole peace process rests on this issue: going in there and arresting those wanted for war crimes. There will not be a better moment than right now.*
>
> —ROBERT FROWICK[121]

In the early years of post-Dayton peace, Bosnian Serbs indicted by the ICTY would be arrested, if at all, only by IFOR or its successor, the NATO Stabilization Force (SFOR).[122] The predominantly Bosniak authorities in Sarajevo were more than willing to arrest indictees, as they demonstrated when they had the opportunity: just months after the Dayton accords were signed, they arrested two Muslim suspects, Hazim Delić and Esad Landžo, soon after they were indicted by the ICTY[123] and

---

[116] *See id.* at 239–40.

[117] RICHARD HOLBROOKE, TO END A WAR 217 (1998). In a small victory for the ICTY, parties to the agreement signed on to cooperate fully with the Tribunal, including by arresting those whom it had indicted. General Framework Agreement for Peace in Bosnia-Herzegovina, Annex IA, art. 10, Nov. 21, 1995. States were already required to cooperate with the Tribunal pursuant to the resolution establishing it. S.C. Res. 827, ¶ 4 (1993). But this was the first time Milošević acknowledged such a duty—and the last. *See* Chapter 3.

[118] *E.g.*, interview with Sevima Sali-Terzić, Senior Legal Counsel, Constitutional Court of BiH, in Sarajevo, Bosn. & Herz. (Sept. 9, 2014).

[119] Interview with Emir Hodžić, Jer Me Se Tiče, in Sarajevo, Bosn. & Herz. (Sept. 13, 2014).

[120] *War-Crimes Tribunal Opens Inquiry on Yugoslav Fighting*, N.Y. TIMES (Nov. 18, 1993) (quoting Frits Kalshoven, former chairman of commission of experts established by the UN Security Council to investigate war crimes in the former Yugoslavia).

[121] Anthony Lewis, Column, *Seize the Day*, N.Y. TIMES (Nov. 22, 1996) (quoting Robert Frowick, then head of the Organization for Security and Co-operation in Europe Mission to Bosnia).

[122] IFOR operated for a year and was succeeded by SFOR. *See* William W. Croach, *IFOR Becomes SFOR*, SFOR INFORMER ONLINE (Jan. 8, 1997).

[123] *See* Press Release, ICTY, Hazim Delić and Esad Landžo Have Been Transferred to the Tribunal and Will Enter a Plea on 18 June 1996 (June 13, 1996). In his first annual report after the Dayton

quickly transferred them to The Hague.[124] But the government in Sarajevo was rarely in a position to arrest Serb suspects, who enjoyed protection in Bosnia's predominantly Serb entity, Republika Srpska (RS), as well as in Serbia.[125] After praising the Sarajevo-based authorities' record of cooperation in his August 1996 report to the UN General Assembly and Security Council, then ICTY president Antonio Cassese described the RS record this way:

> On the other end of the spectrum, Republika Srpska has failed to execute any of the scores of arrest warrants which have been addressed to it, or to explain its inability or failure to do so, as required by the Tribunal's rules. More troubling is the fact that two indictees—Radovan Karadžić and Ratko Mladić—who have each been twice indicted by the Tribunal, inter alia, for genocide, not only have not been arrested but have remained (or still remain, in the case of Mladić) in official positions, contrary to the express terms of the Dayton Accord. The only cooperation of Republika Srpska with the Tribunal evinced to date has been allowing Tribunal investigators access to sites, notably mass grave sites. At the same time, however, there are numerous media reports that such sites have been emptied of corpses or otherwise tampered with, which would constitute destruction of evidence.[126]

---

accord entered into force, then ICTY president Antonio Cassese noted that, among the countries of the former Yugoslavia, "The Republic of Bosnia and Herzegovina"—more particularly, the authorities in the Federation—"has been by far the most cooperative party." ICTY President, *Report of the International Tribunal for the Prosecution of Serious Violations of International Humanitarian Law Committed in the Territory of the Former Yugoslavia Since 1991*, ¶ 167, U.N. Doc. A/51/292-S/1996/665 (Aug. 16, 1996) [hereinafter *Third Annual Report*].

[124] *Bosnia Extradites 2 to Tribunal*, N.Y. Times (June 14, 1996). As described in Chapter 10, Federation authorities previously provoked a crisis when they arrested two Serb generals whom they suspected of war crimes but who had not been indicted by the ICTY. The Tribunal helped defuse the crisis by seeking the Serbs' provisional arrest and transfer to The Hague for questioning.

[125] By the end of 1997, thirteen U.S. lawmakers asserted in a letter that five RS towns were harboring "as many as a dozen" ICTY fugitives. R. Jeffrey Smith, *U.S. Likely to Send Aid to Serbs Despite Criticism on War Criminals*, Wash. Post (Dec. 16, 1997). In the same letter, the lawmakers wrote that the "vast majority of 52 Serb indictees continue to live comfortably" in RS. *Id.* In its second annual report, covering mid-1994 to mid-1995, the ICTY described cooperation from Sarajevo as "excellent" and cooperation with Pale—then the headquarters of Bosnian Serbs—as "poor." ICTY President, *Report of the International Tribunal for the Prosecution of Serious Violations of International Humanitarian Law Committed in the Territory of the Former Yugoslavia Since 1991*, ¶ 50, U.N. Doc. A/50/365-S/1995/728 (Aug. 23, 1995) [hereinafter *Second Annual Report*]. The report noted that the prosecutor and foreign minister of the Republic of Bosnia and Herzegovina signed a memorandum of understanding concerning cooperation with the ICTY in December 1994. *Id.* ¶ 51. According to former ICTY Prosecutor Carla del Ponte, the first time Bosnian Serbs arrested a fugitive was in 2007. Even then, the principal work in identifying the fugitive was done in Belgrade. Carla del Ponte with Chuck Sudetić, Madame Prosecutor: Confrontations with Humanity's Worst Criminals and the Culture of Impunity 359 (2009). Several Bosnian Serb indictees previously surrendered voluntarily, typically under pressure to do so. *See id. supra*, at 316–18; Colin Soloway, *2 War Crimes Suspects Surrender; Bosnian Serbs Said to Enforce "Ethnic Cleansing,"* Wash. Post (Feb. 15, 1998).

[126] *Third Annual Report, supra* note 123, ¶ 168.

The following year, Cassese reported that RS authorities "flatly deny all cooperation in delivering indictees."[127] Their defiance was officially conveyed in a letter to the UN Security Council dated January 2, 1997, from then RS president (later ICTY defendant) Biljana Plavšić: "The present position of Republika Srpska is that we are unwilling to hand over Dr. Karadžić and General Mladić for trial in The Hague as we believe that any such trial now falls outside the scope of the Tribunal's constitutional framework."[128]

Thus in the first year of peace it fell to IFOR, which operated under the command of a U.S. military officer, to arrest ICTY suspects if they were to be transferred to The Hague. Although IFOR had ample authority to do so, U.S. policy dictated that it avoid this task, particularly when it came to high-profile fugitives,[129] and other force-contributing countries were also reticent.[130] NATO's official policy was that IFOR would arrest ICTY suspects if its personnel encountered them while carrying out their duties but would not actively search for fugitives.[131] In practice, IFOR went out of its way to avoid arresting suspects, waving Karadžić and other suspects through NATO checkpoints.[132] A U.S. official explained IFOR's policy this way: "We will take these people into custody if they surrender to us, preferably with their hands up over their heads, or maybe if they're turned in by someone else." But, he said, "I can't imagine it would happen any other way . . . [W]e have a much bigger mission in Bosnia."[133]

Svjetlana Nedimović, who served as an interpreter for NATO forces in Bosnia, was at pains not to divulge details but told me "a lot was done in order *not* to capture,

---

[127] ICTY President, *Report of the International Tribunal for the Prosecution of Serious Violations of International Humanitarian Law Committed in the Territory of the Former Yugoslavia Since 1991*, ¶184, U.N. Doc. A/52/375-S/1997/729 (Sept. 18, 1997).

[128] *Id.* ¶ 185. Despite Plavšić's stance, the U.S. government sought to bolster her leadership during this period. *See* R. Jeffrey Smith, *U.S. Likely to Send Aid to Serbs Despite Criticism on War Criminals*, WASH. POST (Dec. 16, 1997); Mike O'Connor, *West Fears Bosnia Funds Aid Hard-Line Serbs*, N.Y. TIMES (Feb. 16, 1998).

[129] John Shattuck, who served as the State Department's senior human rights official, writes that IFOR troops arrested "four low-level people indicted by the tribunal who were 'encountered' during routine peacekeeping activities" but would not arrest high-profile suspects. SHATTUCK, *supra* note 102, at 216.

[130] *See* BORGER, *supra* note 10, at 4–5.

[131] *See* North Atlantic Treaty Organization, Press Release: IFOR Assistance to the International Tribunal (Feb. 14, 1996), http://www.nato.int/docu/pr/1996/p96-026e.htm. Even then, IFOR would arrest "encountered" ICTY suspects only "if the tactical situation permits." Michael Scharf, *The Tools for Enforcing International Criminal Justice in the New Millennium: Lessons from the Yugoslav Tribunal*, 4 DEPAUL L. REV. 925, 951 (2000) (quoting Press Briefing in U.S. Newswire on July 10, 1997, by National Security Advisor Berger on Bosnia).

[132] *See* Colin Soloway & Stephen J. Hedges, *How Not to Catch a War Criminal*, U.S. NEWS & WORLD REP. (Dec. 9, 1996). After the Dayton peace agreement was concluded, Karadžić reportedly was considering surrendering until U.S. officials assured one of his key advisors that the Clinton administration would not risk the safety of U.S. troops by having them arrest war criminals. *Id.; see also* BORGER, *supra* note 10, at 13–16.

[133] Philip Shenon, *G.I.'s in Bosnia Shun Hunt for War-Crime Suspects*, N.Y. TIMES (Mar. 2, 1996) (quoting unnamed "Defense Department official involved in Bosnian Policy"). John Shattuck describes IFOR's practice this way: IFOR's mandate "left indicted war criminals free to roam through Bosnia without fear of being hunted down by international troops. . . . [T]he U.S. commanders of IFOR were going out of their way to keep their troops from coming into contact with war criminals or appearing to assist the tribunal in its investigative work." SHATTUCK, *supra* note 102, at 213.

not to arrest people." IFOR troops made sure "they were nowhere to be seen when [ICTY suspects] were passing through."[134] It required considerable determination not to arrest suspects; as Nedimović noted, "you don't hide without being found" in Bosnia,[135] a country roughly the size of West Virginia.[136]

As noted, the policy of avoidance was driven in part by the specter of Somalia, where eighteen U.S. soldiers were killed in an ambush while trying to arrest a Somali warlord in October 1993.[137] But it also reflected NATO countries' concern that arresting indicted war criminals could derail the fragile peace. The perceived tension between peace and justice now shaped IFOR-contributing countries' approach to peace implementation. Once again, Holbrooke had a different view than the one that prevailed. He considered arresting Karadžić to be one of "the most impor- tant . . . things necessary to achieve" Dayton's goals.[138] By his lights, "Karadžić at large was certain to mean Dayton deferred or defeated."[139]

During the first year of peace, Karadžić reportedly was "deeply anxious about his future."[140] But "as the months went by after NATO's arrival, with no sign that the alliance had any interest in making arrests,"[141] he regained his characteristic swagger, venturing from his redoubt in Pale to the RS capital in Banja Luka, "breez[ing] past SFOR troops, including an American patrol."[142]

The destabilizing effect of his impunity soon became clear. In September 1997, the *New York Times* reported: "By refusing to arrest Karadžić and deliver him to The Hague, the NATO forces have enabled him to remain the shadow commander and mafia king of the Bosnian Serb republic from his mountain home in Pale."[143] Assured of impunity, Karadžić was able to "rebuild his position" in Bosnia,[144] rallying nationalist Serbs and opposing interethnic cooperation.[145] As de facto leader of the

---

[134] Interview with Svjetlana Nedimović, Activist, in Sarajevo, Bosn. & Herz. (Sept. 18, 2014).

[135] *Id.*

[136] Bosnia is approximately 51.2 square kilometers.

[137] HOLBROOKE, *supra* note 117, at 217. The United States was not the only NATO-contributing country that harbored such concerns. As Julian Borger recounts, after losing forty-five soldiers in Bosnia during the war, "Paris did not want to lose any more lives in a 'misunderstanding' with Karadžić's bodyguards." BORGER, *supra* note 10, at 21.

[138] HOLBROOKE, *supra* note 117, at 338. Against Holbrooke's claim, Bill Stuebner recalls that the State Department showed no interest in following up on an informed source's tip that Karadžić was visiting his mother in Montenegro every month during this period. Comments by William Stuebner on draft chapter (provided June 21, 2017).

[139] HOLBROOKE, *supra* note 117, at 338.

[140] BORGER, *supra* note 10, at 14.

[141] *Id.* at 15.

[142] *Id.*

[143] Elizabeth Rubin, *The Enemy of Our Enemy*, N.Y. TIMES MAG. (Sept. 14, 1997). *See also* Edward Cody, *Karadžić Faces New Pressures; Allies Bolster Efforts to Push Bosnian Serb from Power*, WASH. POST (Aug. 14, 1997) (more than a year after Karadžić was forced to resign the Bosnian Serb presidency, he "has remained the dominant force behind Serb resistance to the Dayton peace accord").

[144] Rubin, *supra* note 143. *See also* John Pomfret, *Persevering Power Pair; Despite Vows to Rid Bosnia of Them, Mladić, Karadžić Still Lead Serbs*, WASH. POST (Feb. 12, 1996); BORGER, *supra* note 10, at 5.

[145] Following his belated arrest and transfer to The Hague, Karadžić maintained that in mid-1996 he reached an agreement with representatives of the United States that, if he withdrew from public life, he would be immune from prosecution in The Hague. The late Richard Holbrooke denied the claim, insisting "no one in the U.S. government ever promised anything, nor made a deal

predominantly Serb entity in Bosnia, Republika Srpska (RS), Karadžić "ran [it] more in the fashion of a large criminal organization than a political unit."[146] Under his leadership, Karadžić's political party continued to obstruct the return of Bosniaks and Croats to their prewar homes.[147] A U.S. military commander would later acknowledge, "we missed an opportunity to break up the old leadership structure" of Bosnian Serbs.[148] Beyond the impact of well-known fugitives like Karadžić, the International Crisis Group wrote five years after Dayton, "the continued presence in positions of some prominence [in Republika Srpska] of so many people suspected of grave crimes remains a major obstacle to peace building."[149]

John Shattuck, the State Department's top human rights official during the Dayton negotiations and post-Dayton period, assessed the costs of NATO's policy of avoidance this way:

> [T]he cost of early inaction on war criminal arrests after Dayton was high. Although peace has come slowly to Bosnia, it would have come sooner if the international community, led by the United States, had moved early and decisively against war criminals. Many political hardliners were able to stay in power at all levels of government, and moderates were forced back for years on all sides. Corruption and organized crime flourished among the same groups that had led the campaigns of ethnic expulsion that sparked the war. Refugees were more hesitant to return to their homes in the years following Dayton when they knew that the war criminals who had expelled them were still at large.[150]

That Karadžić was an ICTY fugitive and therefore unable formally to hold office[151] nonetheless served to marginalize him.[152] Yet in myriad ways, as Human Rights Watch wrote, "ongoing concerns about continuing ethnic divisions in Bosnia can be traced back, in part, to the early failure to purge the Republika Srpska of leaders implicated in war crimes."[153]

---

of any sort with Karadžić." Marlise Simons, *Study Backs Bosnian Serb's Claim of Immunity*, N.Y. TIMES (Mar. 21, 2009). The ICTY determined that any alleged undertaking between Karadžić and Holbrooke would not affect the Tribunal's jurisdiction. Prosecutor v. Karadžić, Case No. IT-95-5/18-PT, Decision on the Accused's Holbrooke Agreement Motion (Int'l Crim. Trib. for the Former Yugoslavia July 8, 2009).

[146] ADIS MERDŽANOVIĆ, DEMOCRACY BY DECREE: PROSPECTS AND LIMITS OF IMPOSED CONSOCIATIONAL DEMOCRACY IN BOSNIA AND HERZEGOVINA 234 (2015).

[147] BORGER, *supra* note 10, at 268.

[148] *Id.* at 16.

[149] INTERNATIONAL CRISIS GROUP, ICG BALKAN REP. 103, WAR CRIMINALS IN BOSNIA'S REPUBLIKA SRPSKA: WHO ARE THE PEOPLE IN YOUR NEIGHBOURHOOD?, at iv (2000).

[150] SHATTUCK, *supra* note 102, at 218. In February 1998, the *New York Times* reported that only about 3,000 of the estimated 560,000 Muslims and Croats expelled during the war had been allowed to return to areas controlled by Serbs. O'Connor, *supra* note 128.

[151] The Constitution of Bosnia, adopted as part of the Dayton agreement, bars from public office individuals indicted by the ICTY who have not complied with an order to appear before the Tribunal. CONSTITUTION OF BOSNIA AND HERZEGOVINA, art. IX, § 1 (Dec. 14, 1995).

[152] Even so, Karadžić continued to lead the Serb Democratic Party (SDS) and the RS presidency until late July 1996, when he stepped down following negotiations with Richard Holbrooke. *See* MERDŽANOVIĆ, *supra* note 146, at 235; BORGER, *supra* note 10, at 267.

[153] DAREHSHORI, *supra* note 104, at 56.

NATO's failure to arrest Karadžić is, of course, a lost opportunity only if it was feasible to arrest him. By most accounts, it was.[154] In July 1996, General William Nash, who commanded U.S. troops in Bosnia, said he could arrest war criminals if mandated to do so.[155] That same year, a White House official assessed it was "eminently feasible . . . to track down war criminals in Bosnia."[156] After all, as Julian Borger notes, NATO forces deployed in Bosnia "faced no real military opposition."[157]

From the perspective of Bosnians who had been buoyed by the ICTY's indictment of Karadžić and Mladić in 1995, the two wartime leaders' extended impunity cast a long shadow, deeply compromising their experience of justice. When I visited Bosnia in late 2006, both men were still at large more than eleven years after they were first indicted. By then, more than sixty suspects were in custody in The Hague, and the ICTY was generally seen as a viable war crimes court. Nonetheless, I heard repeatedly that the enduring impunity of Karadžić and Mladić risked overwhelming all of the ICTY's achievements. Jasna Bakšić Muftić summed up what I heard from many: the ICTY has done "so many good things but they're in the shadow of Karadžić and Mladić." [158] Because the two had escaped justice for so long, she said, "many ordinary people can't see the good things the ICTY has done."[159] Many realized the Tribunal bore no fault for the extended impunity of Karadžić and Mladić. Even so, as Jasminka Džumhur noted in 2007, if the ICTY were to close its doors without obtaining custody of its top suspects, this would "reflect on the whole work of the Hague Tribunal. People will forget all other prosecutions."[160]

The belated arrest of Karadžić in 2008[161] and Mladić in 2011,[162] both in Serbia, averted this failure but did not expunge the costs of their protracted freedom. Journalist Nidžara Ahmetašević captured the emotional toll on survivors as she described many Bosniaks' immediate reaction to the arrest of Karadžić:

> People were very happy and at the same time very sad. In the first moment people were on the streets celebrating. In the second moment, when reality hit them, people became really sad because they had to wait so long. There were many who cried that day, because, okay, it was so easy to do that [yet] he was free all that time. So it was very mixed.[163]

---

[154] It was generally believed it was riskier to arrest Mladić, who was thought to be heavily guarded. See BORGER, supra note 10, at 71.

[155] See Raymond Bonner, Bosnia Election Campaign Postponed over Karadžić Issue, N.Y. TIMES (July 16, 1996). See also RADHA KUMAR, DIVIDE AND FAIL?: BOSNIA IN THE ANNALS OF PARTITION 122 (1997).

[156] BORGER, supra note 10, at 7 (describing views of Richard Gelbard).

[157] Id. at 3. See also id. at 320.

[158] Interview with Sevima Sali-Terzić, Senior Legal Counsel, Constitutional Court of BiH, in Sarajevo, Bosn. & Herz. (Nov. 30, 2006).

[159] Id.

[160] Interview with Jasminka Džumhur, then National Legal Officer, Office of the UN High Commissioner for Human Rights, in Sarajevo, Bosn. & Herz. (June 11, 2007).

[161] See Dan Bilefsky, Karadžić Arrest Is Big Step for a Land Tired of Being Europe's Pariah, N.Y. TIMES (July 23, 2008).

[162] See Colum Lynch, Mladić's Capture Removes 16-Year "Stain," WASH. POST (May 27, 2011); Dan Bilefsky & Doreen Carvajal, Serb Ex-general Accused of Massacre Is Captured, N.Y. TIMES (May 27, 2011).

[163] Interview with Nidžara Ahmetašević, then Editor, BIRN in BiH, in Sarajevo, Bosn. & Herz. (July 13, 2009).

Bosniaks also experienced the arrest of Mladić three years later with mixed emotions. Had Mladić lived out his days without facing trial, his impunity would have ranked as one of the ICTY's foremost failures, if not defined the Tribunal itself as a failed experiment in global justice. Yet in the eyes of many victims, his belated arrest some sixteen years after he was first indicted came too late to count as the high-water mark in their experience of justice. Instead, many saw Mladić's arrest as they might the end of a calamitous storm—infinitely preferable to its continuation, yet incapable of reversing the devastation it had caused.

For many, Mladić's arrest revived suspicions triggered by Karadžić's arrest three years earlier: Serbia had successful played the international community for too long, and far too easily. Elmina Kulašić told me Mladić's capture was widely seen as confirming what "people are constantly saying [about ICTY fugitives]: 'They are hiding in Serbia, and how hard is it to find them?'"[164] As I elaborate in Chapter 3, Serbia's aspiration to join the European Union (EU), which required full cooperation with the ICTY as a precondition to Serbian accession, provided crucial incentive for Mladić's arrest in Serbia, like that of Karadžić three years earlier. In light of this, Kulašić said, Mladić's 2011 arrest affirmed a pervasive "narrative that Serbia was keeping [ICTY fugitives] in their pockets, so whenever they needed something to pull out to get ahead [in the EU accession process], they did it."[165]

To be sure, many Bosnians celebrated the opening of Mladić's trial in May 2012.[166] Kada Hotić, who lost her husband, son, and brothers in the Srebrenica genocide, expressed what was surely a widespread reaction: "For all those years this monster was hidden by Serbia and they knew where he was. Now they are handing him over to justice. Well, better late than never."[167] As described in Chapter 6, moreover, many survivors exulted in Mladić's November 2017 trial verdict and life sentence.

If there were any upsides to the timing of the arrests of Karadžić and Mladić, they would go something like this: by the time the two were arrested, they had become all but irrelevant in Bosnia, and their arrests therefore did not provoke a significant backlash among Bosnian Serbs. When I interviewed Aleksandra Letić in 2014, she evoked an alternative scenario had the two been arrested ten years earlier. At that time, their political party was still in power in RS, and its leaders "would definitely make a political circus out of their" (counterfactual) arrests. But, Letić noted, "they're not in power right now."[168] As well, from the perspective of Hague prosecutors, there were advantages to prosecuting Karadžić and Mladić late in the Tribunal's life. By the

---

[164] Interview with Elmina Kulašić, Transitional Justice, Accountability and Remembrance, in Sarajevo, Bosn. & Herz. (Sept. 13, 2014).

[165] *Id.* Kulašić believes, as well, that Bosniaks' enduring mistrust of the EU "because of its political stand during the war," when the European Community "did not intervene to end the war," translated into a wary response to its role in securing the arrest of Mladić and other fugitives. She indicated, as well, that many Bosnians believe "the EU was turning a blind eye" to the imperatives of justice beyond checking the box on Serbia's satisfaction of EU "conditionalities." *Id.*

[166] Interview with Jasna Bakšić Muftić, Professor, Faculty of Law, University of Sarajevo, in Sarajevo, Bosn. & Herz. (Sept. 17, 2014).

[167] Alix Kroeger, *Mladić Arrest: Anger and Relief in Bosnia*, BBC NEWS (May 26, 2011).

[168] Interview with Aleksandra Letić, Secretary-General, Helsinki Committee for Human Rights in Republika Srpska, in Sarajevo, Bosn. & Herz. (Sept. 8, 2014). The Serb Democratic Party lost its place as the dominant party in RS in 2006 parliamentary elections, which brought the Alliance of Independent Social Democrats to power.

time the two faced trial, ICTY prosecutors were steeped in the intricacies of evidence adduced from years of trials in The Hague, and could readily counter false claims of defense witnesses.[169] But for victims, this provided scant solace: hardly any Bosnians were following trial proceedings anymore.[170]

Many believe the protracted freedom of Mladić and Karadžić exacted a toll that transcends the costs of justice delayed. "In the beginning," Sevima Sali-Terzić reflected when I interviewed her in late 2006, "it was possible to have improvements with justice." With Karadžić and Mladić still at large more than a decade after Dayton, she wondered if "it's too late. Our ethnic relations are terrible. . . . Too much time was given to those who began the war to be in power after the war . . . to pretend that we have working ethnic relations."[171] When I revisited this question with Sali-Teržić in 2014, when both Karadžić and Mladić were in The Hague, I asked if she thought the defendants' verdicts might redeem what she considered the ICTY's failures. Her own verdict was unambiguous: "It's too late." After all, she explained, young Serbs celebrate both men as "heroes."[172] As Karadžić's trial came to an end, Refik Hodžić similarly doubted the Tribunal's verdict would have a significant impact. Despite being "fair, impartial and reasonably comprehensive," Hodžić wrote, "the trial came far too late to catalyze a genuine reckoning" in Bosnia. By then, "the momentum for a genuine break with the poisonous fruits of Karadžić's efforts had dissipated."[173]

Beyond what many see as a lost opportunity to jump-start Bosnia's social reconstruction, the extended impunity of Karadžić and Mladić undermined public confidence in the ICTY. The Tribunal does not have its own gendarme, and thus depends on governments and, for a time, NATO forces deployed in Bosnia, to do so. But even sophisticated Bosnian lawyers like Sevima Sali-Teržić saw NATO's timidity as the Hague's failure. When I asked her whom she faulted for the long-running failure to arrest suspects, Sali-Teržić replied: "It's the [ICTY] Prosecutor's office. I mean they had all the things, they had resources, they had everything they needed, and they couldn't find Karadžić for so many years, and then suddenly they found him."[174]

B. The OTP Forces NATO's Hand

The confluence of several developments in the late 1990s, each involving leadership changes, brought NATO's policy of avoidance to an end[175] and improved the ICTY's

---

[169] Interview with Alan Tieger, then Senior Trial Attorney, Office of the Prosecutor, ICTY, in The Hague, Neth. (May 26, 2015). *See also* Alex Whiting, *In International Criminal Law, Justice Delayed Can Be Justice Delivered*, 50 HARV. INT'L L.J. 323, 326 (2009).

[170] Interview with Edin Hodžić, Director, Public Law Program, Center for Social Research Analitika, in Sarajevo, Bosn. & Herz. (Sept. 11, 2014); interview with Jasna Bakšić Muftić, Professor, Faculty of Law, University of Sarajevo, in Sarajevo, Bosn. & Herz. (Sept. 17, 2014).

[171] Interview with Sevima Sali-Terzić, Senior Legal Counsel, Constitutional Court of BiH, in Sarajevo, Bosn. & Herz. (Nov. 30, 2006).

[172] Interview with Sevima Sali-Terzić, Senior Legal Counsel, Constitutional Court of BiH, in Sarajevo, Bosn. & Herz. (Sept. 9, 2014).

[173] Refik Hodžić, *Karadžić's Trial Ends, But His Legacy Lives On*, INTERNATIONAL CENTER FOR TRANSITIONAL JUSTICE (Oct. 8, 2014).

[174] Interview with Sevima Sali-Terzić, Senior Legal Counsel, Constitutional Court of BiH, in Sarajevo, Bosn. & Herz. (Sept. 9, 2014).

[175] Several NATO countries developed a plan to arrest Karadžić in 1997 but were betrayed by a French army major who tipped the fugitive off. *See* BORGER, *supra* note 10, at 16–21.

standing in the eyes of Bosnian citizens. First, Goldstone's immediate successor, Louise Arbour, devised a new strategy for arresting fugitives. In her words, there was "a change of attitude in the OTP" rooted in the notion "that we had to make our own luck. We had to start taking some initiatives."[176] A key element of Arbour's initiative was the use of sealed indictments. By harnessing the element of surprise, the OTP could "seize the agenda and make [arrests] happen."[177]

Arbour's team developed a sting operation in collaboration with Jacques Klein, who headed the UN Transitional Authority for Eastern Slavonia, Croatia, known by the acronym UNTAES. Klein and Clint Williamson, then working in the OTP, crafted a plan to lure Slavko Dokmanović, then under sealed indictment for his role in a massacre in Vukovar, Croatia, to Klein's office in Eastern Slavonia in June 1997 (Dokmanović, who was living in Serbia, believed he and Klein were going to discuss compensation for his unsold house).[178] Dokmanović was arrested shortly after the vehicle in which he was riding crossed into Croatia, and was flown to The Hague on a plane under Klein's command.[179] Beyond its immediate success, the joint ICTY-UNTAES operation, carried out by an intrepid UN unit, shamed the more powerful NATO force. IFOR's successor, SFOR,[180] began arresting ICTY indictees in July 1997.[181]

A second, crucially important, factor behind SFOR's newly robust approach entailed leadership changes in key Western countries. The new U.K. government of Prime Minister Tony Blair, who assumed office in early May 1997, vowed to pursue an "ethical foreign policy."[182] Among other manifestations, the government pledged it would track down war crimes suspects in Bosnia. On July 10, 1997, British forces mounted a watershed operation in Prijedor, arresting Milan Kovačević and killing Simo Drljača when the latter resisted arrest.

Developments in Washington contributed, as well, to SFOR's new approach. In November 1996, Bill Clinton was re-elected president of the United States. Reluctant to risk U.S. casualties in advance of elections, the White House now was willing to authorize arrest operations.[183] Crucially, too, Clinton appointed Madeleine Albright, who favored robust implementation of Dayton's war crimes commitments, to be his second-term secretary of state.[184] The July 1997 SFOR arrests, coupled with Albright's blunt diplomacy with Croatian leader Franjo Tuđman backed by a threat to cancel a $30 million loan to Croatia, led to the surrender of ten Bosnian Croat suspects to the Hague Tribunal on October 6, 1997.[185]

---

[176] *Louise Arbour—Farewell Interview*, IWPR (Aug. 30–Sept. 5, 1999).

[177] HAGAN, *supra* note 33, at 100 (quoting Louise Arbour).

[178] See Prosecutor v. Mrkšić et al., Case No. IT-95-13a-PT, Decision on the Motion for Release by the Accused Slavko Dokmanović 3-II (Int'l Crim. Trib. for the Former Yugoslavia Oct. 22, 1997).

[179] *Serb War Crimes Suspect Held*, ASSOCIATED PRESS (June 28, 1997); HAGAN, *supra* note 33, at 103; email from Clint Williamson to Diane Orentlicher (Aug. 29, 2017).

[180] SFOR operated for eight years beginning in December 1996.

[181] Charles Trueheart, *Tribunal Turnaround; Recent Arrest, Surrender of Bosnian War Crimes Suspects Improve Court's Prospects for '98 Budget Increase*, WASH. POST (Oct. 20, 1997).

[182] See *Robin Cook's Speech on the Government's Ethical Foreign Policy*, GUARDIAN (May 12, 1997).

[183] See BORGER, *supra* note 10, at 5–6, 8.

[184] In addition, General Wesley Clark, who supported a robust approach to arrests, became NATO's Supreme Commander in 1997. See *id.* at 159.

[185] Trueheart, *supra* note 181; Charles Trueheart, *War Crimes Tribunal Gathers Momentum*, WASH. POST (Mar. 3, 1998); ICTY President, *Report of the International Tribunal for the Prosecution of*

The months following the Prijedor operation saw further SFOR arrests. While American and Dutch SFOR soldiers arrested some fugitives,[186] the British continued to lead the way.[187] Ultimately, according to NATO's website, SFOR "brought 39 war-crimes suspects to the [ICTY]."[188]

Although not widely recognized, the newly-empowered SFOR bolstered the ICTY's work in another way. Beginning in December 1997, it undertook search-and-seizure operations, capturing and turning over to the ICTY a trove of military records and other documents.[189] These operations yielded vital evidence not only for ICTY prosecutions, but also for domestic war crimes prosecutions in former Yugoslav states.[190] In larger perspective, many Bosnians regard the Tribunal's archive as the most compelling hedge against future denial.[191]

SFOR's new approach contributed to several "voluntary surrenders" by Bosnian Serb suspects in February and March 1998.[192] An additional factor was the then-recent

---

Serious Violations of International Humanitarian Law Committed in the Territory of the Former Yugoslavia Since 1991, ¶113, U.N. Doc. A/53/219-S/1998/737 (Aug. 10, 1998) [hereinafter *Fifth Annual Report*].

[186] Colin Soloway, *Dutch Troops Capture 2 Croat War Crimes Suspects; Pre-dawn Raid Angers Villagers but Draws Praise from Western Governments as Warning to Other Fugitives*, WASH. POST (Dec. 19, 1997); Trueheart, *War Crimes Tribunal Gathers Momentum, supra* note 185. It took some time for the new approach to take hold; months after the July 1997 operation, the *Washington Post* reported that NATO forces were still reluctant to arrest fugitives. John Pomfret & Lee Hockstader, *In Bosnia, a War Crimes Impasse; NATO Differences with U.N. Tribunal Mean Few Are Arrested*, WASH. POST. (Dec. 9, 1997). But the ICTY's 1998 report to the United Nations reflected a significant turnaround in SFOR's approach:

> In December, SFOR forces apprehended two further accused, Vlatko Kupreškić and Anto Furundžija in Prijedor. In January 1998, Goran Jelisić was arrested by SFOR troops in Bijeljina; in March, Dragoljub Kunarac voluntarily surrendered to SFOR forces near Foča; in April, Miroslav Kvočka and Mladen Radić were apprehended in Prijedor by SFOR and Zoran Žigić was taken into custody by ICTY investigators and SFOR troops in Banja Luka; in May, Miroslav Kos was arrested by SFOR troops in Banja Luka; and in June, Milorad Krnojelac, who was charged in a sealed indictment, was arrested by SFOR forces in Foča.

Fifth Annual Report, supra note 185, ¶ 114. The January 1998 arrest of Jelisić was the first by U.S. forces. *See* BORGER, *supra* note 10, at 91.

[187] A year and a half after the Kovačević/Drljača operation, the *New York Times* reported, "the British military has aggressively pursued suspects in western Bosnia. Eleven suspects have been arrested in the British sector; another was killed in a shootout with peacekeepers." Philip Shenon, *War Crimes Suspects Seen as Living Openly in Bosnia*, N.Y. TIMES (Dec. 13, 1999). By that time only three fugitives had been arrested in the American zone. Although many of the most notorious suspects were known to be living in the French zone of Bosnia, the French contingent's first forcible arrest took place in late December 1999. *See* BORGER, *supra* note 10, at 210. Although French forces transferred a fugitive to The Hague in March 1998, the suspect took the initiative, contacting French officers to arrange his own surrender. *See id.* at 205.

[188] North Atlantic Treaty Organization, Peace Support Operations in Bosnia and Herzegovina, http://www.nato.int/cps/en/natolive/topics_52122.htm (last visited Dec. 7, 2017).

[189] Interview with Bob Reid, Chief of Operations, Office of the Prosecutor, ICTY, in The Hague, Neth. (May 28, 2015). According to Bill Stuebner, it was mostly British forces who undertook these operations. Comment by William Stuebner on draft chapter (provided June 21, 2017).

[190] See Chapters 9 and 10.

[191] See Chapters 7 and 8. As elucidated in these chapters, however, denialism was on the rise in both Serbia and Bosnia as the Tribunal wrapped up its work.

[192] According to the *Washington Post*, the surrender of Milorad Tadić and Milan Simić on February 14, 1998, was "the first of Serb war crimes suspects." Colin Soloway, *2 War Crimes Suspects*

elevation of Milorad Dodik to the position of prime minister of Republika Srpska.[193] Although Dodik would later become a radically destabilizing nationalist, at that time he positioned himself as a moderate who sought to "bolster ties to the West by cooperating with the tribunal."[194] The first two Bosnian Serb surrenders came less than a week after Dodik pledged his new government would "do everything it could to encourage suspects to surrender" to the ICTY.[195]

It is difficult to imagine a more clear-cut example of how a change in the nature of external actors' engagement—coupled, to be sure, with political developments in Bosnia—can produce dramatic effects on the ground. SFOR's new approach not only sent defendants to The Hague, but also helped foster an environment in which the Tribunal's work could have a tangible impact on peoples' daily lives. The previously mentioned July 1997 arrest operation, in which Simo Drljača was killed, had palpable effects in Prijedor. Drljača had "personally obstruct[ed] the return of refugees and displaced persons" to Prijedor after the war "by giving weapons to the local [Serb] population so that it could threaten anyone who came back."[196] Along with other factors, the July operation inspired many Bosniaks to return to Prijedor. Political scientist Robert Belloni explains:

> The July 1997 events had a profound impact. Following SFOR's overdue activism, [wartime Prijedor leader] Milomir Stakić, fearing the possibility that ICTY had issued a secret indictment for his arrest, went "on permanent vacation". Instead of the feared backlash against international peacekeepers, local authorities switched allegiance from the hard line wartime leader Radovan Karadžić to the more moderate leadership of Biljana Plavšić . . . These changes gave Bosniak potential returnees a sufficient sense of security seriously to consider returning.[197]

Surrender, WASH. POST (Feb. 15, 1998). Their surrender capped more than a year of negotiations between the ICTY and the suspects' attorney. Id.

[193] Dodik became RS prime minister for the first time in late January 1998. See MERDŽANOVIĆ, supra note 146, at 265.

[194] Trueheart, War Crimes Tribunal Gathers Momentum, supra note 185. Dodik allowed the ICTY to open an office in Banja Luka, the capital of Republika Srpska. Id.

[195] Soloway, supra note 192. See also MERDŽANOVIĆ, supra note 146, at 266.

[196] WESSELINGH & VAULERIN, supra note 33, at 93 (citing Human Rights Watch reporting). According to Julian Borger, IFOR "strongly suspected" that Drljača, acting in concert with another individual who would later be prosecuted in The Hague, was responsible for blowing up the houses of some 100 Bosniak refugees who were preparing to return to their prewar homes in late 1996. BORGER, supra note 10, at 48–49.

[197] ROBERTO BELLONI, STATE BUILDING AND INTERNATIONAL INTERVENTION IN BOSNIA 137 (2007). For a more in-depth account of the factors that combined to produce a surge in returnees to Prijedor, see DIANE F. ORENTLICHER, OPEN SOCIETY JUSTICE INITIATIVE & INTERNATIONAL CENTER FOR TRANSITIONAL JUSTICE, THAT SOMEONE GUILTY BE PUNISHED: THE IMPACT OF THE ICTY IN BOSNIA 79–85 (2010). In its 2004 World Report, Human Rights Watch explained the confluence of factors that inspired minority returns and their patterns over time this way:

> The large-scale return of refugee and displaced Bosnian minorities began only in 2000, after the Office of the High Representative (OHR) in Bosnia . . . introduced well-devised property legislation and international agencies took a more robust approach toward local officials who had obstructed returns. The breakthrough also resulted from a series of arrests between 1998 and 2000 of persons indicted for war crimes by the [ICTY]. While the number of minority returns was 41,000 both in 1998 and 1999, in 2000 the number

The following spring, some 10,000 Bosniaks returned to Kozarac, and others returned to the city of Prijedor.[198] In the view of the International Crisis Group, "The lesson is clear: the removal of suspects indicted for war crimes . . . has a ripple effect."[199]

In short, NATO's newly robust approach was the leading edge of a turnaround in the ICTY's fortunes, with palpable effects on the ground. But it also had unintended consequences: with the arrests of mid-level suspects, Karadžić would no longer breeze past NATO checkpoints.[200] Mladić, who reportedly lived in a bunker in the eastern Bosnian municipality of Han Pijesak after Dayton, sought shelter in Serbia in July 1997.[201] With their impunity in Bosnia breached, many other war criminals fled to Serbia, beyond the remit of SFOR's enforcement jurisdiction.[202] It would take concerted Western efforts more than another decade to secure the arrests of all ICTY fugitives in Serbia.[203]

III. POSTWAR POLITICAL CONTEXT: DAYTON'S LEGACY

The governance structures adopted in Dayton further compromised Bosnians' experience of Hague justice. As elaborated below, those structures hardened Bosnia's ethnic divisions and laid the foundation for a thoroughly dysfunctional state.[204] This, as well as fateful decisions by key international actors, have radically constricted the space in which justice measures *could* facilitate wider processes of social repair in Bosnia.

A. Architecture of Division and Dysfunction

> *Then they designed our state constitution in Dayton . . . This is, you see, sort of a global experiment. . . . We are fully aware that we are cheated, that Bosnia and Herzegovina cannot function as a normal state.*
>
> —KADA HOTIĆ[205]

---

rose to 67,500, in 2001 to 92,000, and in 2002 reached a peak with 102,000 returns. In the first eight months in 2003, some 34,100 minorities returned. In comparison to the same period in the previous year, the figure represents a 50 percent drop. Rather than suggesting a dramatic aggravation of the conditions for return, however, the decrease reflects the narrowing of the pool of persons willing to return, eight or more years after they had fled their homes.

Bogdan Ivanišević, *Legacy of War: Minority Returns in the Balkans, in* HUMAN RIGHTS WATCH, 2004 WORLD REPORT 354–55 (2004).

[198] BELLONI, *supra* note 197, at 138.

[199] INTERNATIONAL CRISIS GROUP, ICG BOSNIA PROJECT REP. 33, MINORITY RETURN OR MASS RELOCATION? 39 (May 14, 1998).

[200] See BORGER, *supra* note 10, at 83. The deployment of a large number of U.S. agents around the same time as the first SFOR arrests amplified this effect. *See id.*

[201] See id. at 83, 283.

[202] See *Bosnian Serb Official Admits Helping Srebrenica Fugitives*, BALKAN TRANSITIONAL JUST. (Nov. 13, 2015) (witness in trial of Ratko Mladić described order from his commander to provide false identification cards to former members of a Bosnian Serb army unit so they could escape possible prosecution). According to Julian Borger, by 2000 "almost every likely suspect in the British zone in western Bosnia either had been arrested or had fled to Serbia." BORGER, *supra* note 10, at 67.

[203] Those efforts are described in Chapter 3.

[204] A Google search on November 7, 2015, using the terms "Bosnia + dysfunctional" identified 257,000 entries.

[205] Interview with Kada Hotić, Vice President, Mothers of Srebrenica and Žepa Enclaves, in Sarajevo, Bosn. & Herz. (Sept. 18, 2014).

> *Dayton has been a poor foundation for peace-building because it institutionalized unresolved conflict, ethnic division, and fragmentation at the heart of the Bosnian state.*
>
> —GERARD TOAL AND CARL T. DAHLMAN[206]

The peace agreement finalized in Dayton and signed in Paris, formally called the General Framework Agreement for Peace in Bosnia and Herzegovina but more widely known as the Dayton Peace Agreement (DPA), adopted a model, *consociationalism*, that enjoyed significant scholarly support. Consociationalism generally connotes a power-sharing arrangement, typically instituted in divided societies, in which representatives of every major ethnic, religious, or other relevant group participate in national decision-making institutions on matters of common concern, while each group exercises significant autonomous authority on matters of particular concern to the group.[207] In this way, governance structures are designed to prevent violence in societies racked by ethnic, religious, and other significant divisions. But as Ian Shapiro warned, consociational arrangements can also reify ethnic divisions and exacerbate the very "malady [they were] allegedly designed to treat."[208] His warning proved prescient for Bosnia, which has aptly been called "a Frankenstein form of state emerging from a transitional settlement in which consociationalism plays a central role."[209]

To be sure, despite Dayton's flawed governance structures, Bosnia saw notable improvements in nation-building and interethnic relations during the early years of the twenty-first century.[210] Not coincidentally, the same period saw significant progress in addressing wartime atrocities.[211] As will be seen, however, progress during this period was due in no small part to the forward-leaning policies of two successive High Representatives. Without this or any other meaningful restraint in subsequent years, Dayton's governance structures have facilitated "the never-ending political crisis of the Bosnian state."[212]

---

[206] GERARD TOAL & CARL T. DAHLMAN, BOSNIA REMADE: ETHNIC CLEANSING AND ITS REVERSAL 310 (2011)

[207] On consociational arrangements generally, see ARENDT LIJPHART, DEMOCRACY IN PLURAL SOCIETIES (1977); Arendt Lijphart, *Consociational Democracy*, 4 WORLD POL. 207 (1969).

[208] IAN SHAPIRO, DEMOCRACY'S PLACE 102 (1996).

[209] Kris Brown & Fionnuala Ní Aoláin, *Through the Looking Glass: Transitional Justice Futures Through the Lens of Nationalism, Feminism and Transformative Change*, 9 INT'L J. TRANSITIONAL JUST. 127, 132 (2014). *See also* Florian Bieber & Sören Keil, *Power Sharing Revisited: Lessons Learned in the Balkans?*, 34 REV. CENT. & EAST EUR. L. 337, 357 (2009); Nidžara Ahmetašević, *Bosnia's Elites Are "Ignoring the New Reality"*, BALKAN INSIGHT (Mar. 3, 2015) (Bosnian sociologist describes harmful long-term impact of Dayton's geography of division).

[210] *See* KURT BASSUENER & BODO WEBER, DEMOCRATIZATION POLICY COUNCIL, "ARE WE THERE YET?"; INTERNATIONAL IMPATIENCE VS. A LONG-TERM STRATEGY FOR A VIABLE BOSNIA 3 (2010) [hereinafter BASSUENER & WEBER, ARE WE THERE YET?]; *Bosnia and Herzegovina: A Hostage to Dayton?*, AL JAZEERA (Dec. 14, 2015).

[211] *See* Chapters 8 and 9.

[212] Dejan Guzina & Branka Marijan, *Local Uses of International Criminal Justice in Bosnia-Herzegovina: Transcending Divisions or Building Parallel Worlds?*, 7 STUD. SOC. JUST. 245, 248 (2013).

1. Ethnic Entities

As representatives of Bosnia's principal ethnic groups gathered in Dayton to negotiate peace, the Bosniak delegation hoped the final accord would establish a reintegrated state.[213] The DPA instead established two largely autonomous entities within a nominally unified state. The arrangement was enshrined in the Constitution of Bosnia and Herzegovina, which was set forth in Annex 4 of the agreement. Forty-nine percent of Bosnia's territory was assigned to the predominantly Serb and largely self-governing Republika Srpska (RS)[214] and 51 percent to the Federation of Bosnia and Herzegovina ("Federation"), an amalgam of cantons largely inhabited by Bosniaks and Croats, with Serbs, Jews, and others constituting minorities.[215] The inter-entity boundaries largely followed the war's frontline.[216]

In exchange for substantial autonomy within Bosnia, Bosnian Serbs' lead representative in Dayton, Slobodan Milošević,[217] accepted in principle what Bosnian Serbs had fought for years to prevent—an independent, multiethnic Bosnian state with its capital in Sarajevo. At first, Bosnian Serbs "hated Dayton, . . . because it forced them to let go of a dream of a separate state."[218] Later, they would vigorously defend it: the accord left Bosnia's state-level powers weak, and RS leaders have fiercely opposed successive efforts to strengthen national institutions.[219] (So, too, has the principal

---

[213] *See* Joanne McEvoy, Power Sharing Executives: Governing in Bosnia, Macedonia, and Northern Ireland 109 (2015).

[214] Early in the war, Bosnian Serbs gained control of more than two-thirds of Bosnia, which they held through much of the war. But a major Croatian-Bosnian offensive launched in August 1995 left Serbs in control of less than 50 percent of Bosnian territory within weeks. *See* Ivo H. Daalder, *Decision to Intervene: How the War in Bosnia Ended* (Dec. 1, 1998), https://www.brookings.edu/articles/decision-to-intervene-how-the-war-in-bosnia-ended/ (last visited Dec. 7, 2017).

[215] The Federation is divided into ten cantons, six with a Bosniak majority and four in which Croats are numerically predominant. In two (Central Bosnia canton and Herzegovina-Neretva canton), the smaller of these two ethnic groups comprises a large minority. The parties at Dayton were unable to reach agreement on the location of the Inter-Entity Boundary Line in the northern town of Brčko, and instead agreed this would be resolved through separate arbitration. DPA, Annex 2, art. V. The arbitration resulted in an autonomous District of Brčko under the control of neither entity. Brčko has emerged as one of the most successful areas of Bosnia, with more highly functioning multiethnic institutions than other Bosnian cities. *See* Adam Moore, Peacebuilding in Practice: Local Experience in Two Bosnian Towns 162–63 (2013).

[216] Merdžanović, *supra* note 146, at 135. As one writer put it, the internal administrative boundaries drawn in Dayton "followed the contours of some of the worst crimes committed during the war's horrific duration." Jasmin Mujanović, *War and Pieces*, New Am. Wkly. (Nov. 19, 2015).

[217] The senior Bosnian Serb representative in Dayton was Momčilo Krajišnik, who had not yet been indicted by the ICTY. The top U.S. negotiator in Dayton, Richard Holbrooke, did not want to deal with the Bosnian Serb leadership, and Milošević "saw no reason to disappoint" him—that is, he was willing to lead the Serb delegation in Dayton. Ivo H. Daalder, Getting to Dayton: The Making of America's Bosnia Policy 128 (2000). In August 1995, Bosnian Serbs agreed Milošević could sign a peace agreement on their behalf. *Id.*

[218] Denis Džidić, *Paddy Ashdown Laments Bosnia's "Lost Opportunities,"* Balkan Transitional Just. (Nov. 6, 2015). In Ashdown's words, many Croats "did not like Dayton and still don't since they were forced to let go of a dream of [a Bosnian Croat state of] Herceg-Bosna." *Id.*

[219] Joanne McEvoy describes the three main ethnic groups' attitudes toward such efforts this way: "The transfer of competences to the state level is favored by the Bosniak community, mostly accepted by Bosnian Croats (provided their group retains equality with the other two), but opposed fiercely by the Bosnian Serbs." McEvoy, *supra* note 213, at 110.

Bosnian Croat-led political party, which under the leadership of Dragan Čović has pressed for a third Bosnian entity for Croats.[220])

Many Bosniaks were initially "thrilled with Dayton because it stopped the war."[221] Even so, many saw Dayton's recognition of RS as an unconscionable capitulation to Serb aggression. Deepening their sense of injustice, Dayton assigned to RS the site of Bosnian Serbs' most infamous crime, Srebrenica.

As implemented, the DPA deepened Bosniak concerns. Although the accord in principle assured Bosnians displaced by ethnic cleansing the right to return home, Serb obstruction has meant that, in reality, large swaths of RS embody Bosnian Serbs' wartime aim: a Serb mini-state.[222] In the words of Nusreta Sivac, "for now, [it appears] the crime paid off."[223] Although Radovan Karadžić was awaiting judgment when I interviewed Sivac, a source of considerable satisfaction (Sivac testified at Karadžić's trial), she noted a painful "paradox": "His concept, his project, Republika Srpska is alive. . . . The creator is held responsible, but the deed remains, the actual work is still in existence. And unfortunately it's even called the same name he called it, Republika Srpska."[224]

In myriad other ways, the ethnic map drawn in Dayton has compromised victims' experience of justice. The ethnic segregation enshrined in the DPA obstructs the kind of everyday, multilayered interactions that can advance mutual empathy and acknowledgment.[225] And for victims of ethnic cleansing, justice is inextricably linked to acknowledgment.[226]

2. Entity Voting and Minority Veto

Other features of the power-sharing arrangement imposed in the DPA have facilitated political paralysis and thwarted local efforts to address wartime atrocities. Pursuant to the "entity voting" mechanism, for example, decisions by both chambers of the state-level parliament should not be taken unless at least one-third of the members

---

[220] See Eleanor Rose, *Bosniaks Slap Down Calls for Bosnian Croat Entity*, Balkan Insight (Jan. 30, 2017).

[221] Džidić, *supra* note 218 (quoting Paddy Ashdown).

[222] According to the 2013 census, approximately 82 percent of Republika Srpska's residents are ethnic Serbs. Agency for Statistics of Bosn. & Herz., Census of Population, Households and Dwellings in Bosnia and Herzegovina 54 (2013). Returns of minorities to some predominantly Croat and Bosniak areas have also been difficult, *see* Carl Dahlman & Gearóid Ó Tuathail, *Broken Bosnia: The Localized Geopolitics of Displacement and Return in Two Bosnian Places*, 95 Annals Ass'n Am. Geographers 644, 645 (2005), while the Bosniak SDA party has passively discouraged Bosniak returns to Republika Srpska, apparently fearing the loss of key voting blocs in the Federation. Bassuener, Durable Oligarchy, *supra* note 15, at 23.

[223] Interview with Nusreta Sivac, Former Judge, in Prijedor, Bosn. & Herz. (Sept. 16, 2014).

[224] *Id.* I heard similar sentiments in other interviews. For example, Emir Hodžić described many Bosniaks' frustration with the ICTY in part on the basis that "the crimes have been rewarded, because you *do* have segregation, you *do* have separate territory." Interview with Emir Hodžić, Jer Me Se Tiče, in Sarajevo, Bosn. & Herz. (Sept. 13, 2014). *See also* Refik Hodžić, *Karadžić's Trial Ends, But His Legacy Lives On*, International Center for Transitional Justice (Oct. 8, 2014) (the author, a Bosniak from Prijedor, felt "an overwhelming sense of defeat" in listening to Karadžić during his trial in The Hague; his "sense of resignation [came] from living in the reality where Karadžić's poisonous contribution to Bosnian history lives on").

[225] As noted in Chapter 8, social science research conducted in Bosnia and elsewhere indicates that physical proximity is likely to increase ethnic groups' readiness to acknowledge harm inflicted on others.

[226] See Chapters 4 and 8.

from each entity votes in support of it. In addition, delegates representing each group have veto power, which can be used when a majority of a group's elected delegates believes a proposed decision is "destructive of a vital interest" of that group.[227] Similarly, the Dayton constitution establishes a three-person presidency comprising one Bosniak, one Croat, and one Serb,[228] any one of whom can exercise a veto to protect his or her constituency's "vital interests."[229] Andrew MacDowall echoed the views of many Bosnians when he characterized the governance structure imposed in the DPA as "both intolerably unjust and mind-bogglingly unwieldy."[230]

With a weak central government and tense relations among Bosnia's recently warring parties, the defining feature of political decision-making processes in the early post-Dayton period was paralysis.[231] In response, the Peace Implementation Council (PIC), an international body devised in Dayton to guide the peace process in Bosnia,[232] enhanced the authority of the High Representative, a position created in Dayton to coordinate implementation of the DPA's civilian provisions. As elaborated in the next section, for a while successive High Representatives were able to surmount obstacles to state-building posed by recalcitrant political leaders. For over a decade, however, the High Representative has lacked the support he needs from the PIC and other key actors to meet rising nationalist threats.

3. The High Representative

The High Representative heads an international governing structure, the Office of the High Representative (OHR), responsible for implementing the civilian provisions of the DPA and coordinating international organizations that have operated in Bosnia since the war.[233] The OHR was initially envisaged as a transitional structure with

---

[227] DPA, Annex 4 (Constitution of Bosnia and Herzegovina), art. IV(3)(f). The entity voting mechanism is prescribed in *id.* art. IV(3)(d).

[228] The members of the presidency must not only belong to one of the three "constituent peoples," but must be "from" specified entities. For example, the Serb member of the presidency must be from Republika Srpska. *Id.* art. V chapeau.

[229] *Id.* art. V(2)(d). For discussion of further complexities in the operation of this veto power, including a procedure for overcoming a minority veto, see McEvoy, *supra* note 213, at 112. Among the challenges presented by the constitution adopted in Dayton, its exclusion of individuals who do not belong to one of the three principal "constituent peoples"—Serbs, Bosniaks, and Croats—from being elected to the presidency or House of Peoples of Bosnia has been judged a violation of the European Convention on Human Rights, which is also part of the Constitution. Sejdić & Finći v. Bosnia & Herzegovina, App. Nos. 27996/06 & 34836/06, Eur. Ct. H.R. (2009). The country has been unable to reach an agreement that would enable it to implement the European court's ruling. *See* Kenan Efendić, *Bosnia Solves "Croat Question" at Sejdić-Finći's Expense*, Balkan Insight (Mar. 29, 2013).

[230] Andrew MacDowall, *Dayton Ain't Going Nowhere*, Foreign Pol'y (Dec. 12, 2015).

[231] *See* Christopher Bennett, *Bosnia's High Representatives: Never-Ending Story*, Balkan Insight (Nov. 20, 2015).

[232] Ivo Daalder, who helped coordinate U.S. policy on DPA implementation, has described the PIC as "a large, unwieldy body of key countries and international organizations . . . whose steering committee . . . would both appoint and be chaired by" the High Representative. Daalder, *supra* note 217, at 156. As of September 2017, seven men have served as High Representative. From 2002 to 2011, four successive High Representatives were dual hatted, serving simultaneously as the High Representative and the European Union Special Representative. *See* Erwan Lagadec, Transatlantic Relations in the 21st Century: Europe, America, and the Rise of the Rest 135 (2012).

[233] DPA, Annex 10. The mandate of the High Representative was affirmed by the UN Security Council immediately after conclusion of the DPA. S.C. Res. 1031, ¶¶ 26–29 (Dec. 15, 1995).

a weak coordination mandate[234] that could be withdrawn as Bosnia stabilized. In the face of Bosnia's perennial political crises, however, its writ has repeatedly been extended.

After two years of "systematic obstructionism"[235] by Bosnian leaders, the PIC augmented the High Representative's authority. In December 1997, it agreed he had executive authority to ensure compliance with Dayton through what came to be known as the "Bonn powers."[236] These included removing individuals from public office "who are found by the High Representative to be in violation of legal commitments made under the Peace Agreement or the terms for its implementation"[237] and even imposing laws himself.[238]

For the next several years, successive High Representatives used their Bonn powers to achieve significant reforms, advancing Bosnia's capacity to function as a self-governing, integrated state. Of particular relevance to this study, Wolfgang Petritsch, the third High Representative, imposed a law establishing the Court of Bosnia and Herzegovina (Court of BiH) in the context of wider efforts to develop state-level institutions, hoping the structures he established or cajoled Bosnian leaders to create would lead to local ownership in a maturing democracy.[239] His immediate successor, Lord Paddy Ashdown (who also represented the European Union), made even greater use of the Bonn powers to advance an ambitious reform agenda.[240] During Ashdown's tenure, the mandate of the Court of BiH was expanded to include prosecuting war crimes.[241] Ashdown, who supported robust cooperation with the ICTY,[242] used his Bonn powers to weaken support networks that enabled

---

[234] *See* Claudio Cordone, *Bosnia and Herzegovina: The Creeping Protectorate, in* HONORING HUMAN RIGHTS UNDER INTERNATIONAL MANDATES: LESSONS FROM BOSNIA, KOSOVO AND EAST TIMOR 63 (Alice H. Henkin ed., 2003); Christopher Bennett, *Bosnia's High Representatives: Never-Ending Story,* BALKAN INSIGHT (Nov. 20, 2015). Despite the generally weak mandate conferred in the DPA, critics have faulted Annex 10 for granting the High Representative authority to issue binding interpretations of his powers under that annex. *See* Tim Banning, *The "Bonn Powers" of the High Representative in Bosnia Herzegovina: Tracing a Legal Figment,* 6 GOETTINGEN J. INT'L L. 259, 264–65 (2014).

[235] Bennett, *supra* note 234.

[236] PIC, *Bosnia and Herzegovina 1998: Self-Sustaining Structures,* art. XI(2) (Dec. 10, 1997) [hereinafter *PIC Decision on Bonn Powers*]. This was not the first time the PIC had enhanced the High Representative's powers. For example, in 1997 the PIC Steering Board "declared that the High Representative has the right to curtail or suspend any media network or programme whose output is in persistent and blatant contravention of either the spirit or letter of the Peace Agreement." PIC, *Political Declaration from Ministerial Meeting of the Steering Board of the Peace Implementation Council,* ¶ 70 (May 30, 1997).

[237] *PIC Decision on Bonn Powers, supra* note 236, art. XI (2)(c).

[238] The PIC Decision on Bonn Powers did not explicitly grant the High Representative authority to impose laws, but instead welcomed his "intention to use his final authority in theatre . . . to facilitate the resolution of difficulties by making binding decisions, as he judges necessary" on a range of issues, including "interim measures to take effect when parties are unable to reach agreement." *Id.* art. XI(2)(b).

[239] *See* Bennett, *supra* note 234. Although Petritsch used the Bonn powers aggressively, his core philosophy was that Bosnians should assume responsibility for governance, an "approach that would imply gradually reducing the use of the Bonn powers." MERDŽANOVIĆ, *supra* note 146, at 228.

[240] Bennett, *supra* note 234; MERDŽANOVIĆ, *supra* note 146, at 228.

[241] *See* Chapter 9.

[242] See MERDŽANOVIĆ, *supra* note 146, at 301.

ICTY fugitives to remain at large,[243] and established a commission to establish the truth concerning Srebrenica after RS authorities issued a report wildly at odds with well-known facts.[244]

Inevitably, the exercise of Bonn powers was vigorously challenged by RS authorities in particular.[245] Even so, for several years local leaders largely accepted (and often welcomed) their use.[246] As Petritsch observed, "When uneasy decisions [were] concerned, the governing parties [relied] on the High Representative to take them."[247] Kurt Bassuener, who served as a strategist for then High Representative Paddy Ashdown, recalls that most major reforms and institutions established during Ashdown's tenure were *not* imposed; even so, the Bonn powers provided necessary incentive for inter-entity agreement to those initiatives.[248] In this setting, the OHR was the principal "motor driving Bosnia forward"[249] during the tenures of Petritsch and Ashdown—the most productive period of state-building in Bosnia's post-Dayton history.

While recognizing progress achieved through the Bonn powers, external actors grew increasingly concerned about their long-term use[250] (a concern shared, in

---

[243] According to Adis Merdžanović, 103 of 345 uses of the Bonn powers between May 2002, when Ashdown became High Representative, and the end of 2004 concerned ICTY cooperation and prosecuting war crimes. *Id.* Joanne McEvoy writes that Ashdown "removed a host of officials, particularly in the RS, for obstructing the work of the [ICTY], with eighty-five such decisions taken in 2004." McEvoy, *supra* note 213, at 125.

[244] This development is discussed in Chapter 8.

[245] The first constitutional challenge to the exercise of the High Representative's Bonn powers came from eleven parliamentarians, who in 2000 lodged a challenge before the Constitutional Court of Bosnia and Herzegovina when the High Representative imposed a law creating a border service for the country after the Parliamentary Assembly failed to adopt one. The court upheld the constitutionality of that law. *See* Rebecca Everly, *Assessing the Accountability of the High Representative, in* Deconstructing the Reconstruction: Human Rights and Rule of Law in Postwar Bosnia and Herzegovina 103 (Dina Francesca Haynes ed., 2008).

[246] *See* Merdžanović, *supra* note 146, at 273–74.

[247] *Id.* at 273 (quoting Wolfgang Petritsch). In similar terms, the sixth High Representative noted that, whenever local politicians "had to deal with difficult situations, they asked the High Representative to intervene so as to accept the responsibility for negative consequences." *Id.* at 334.

[248] Comment by Kurt Bassuener on draft chapter (provided Aug. 5, 2017).

[249] International Crisis Group, Eur. Rep. 198, Bosnia's Incomplete Transition: Between Dayton and Europe 11 (2009) [hereinafter International Crisis Group, Bosnia's Incomplete Transition].

[250] A March 2005 assessment by the Council of Europe's Venice Commission, whose principal focus was the need for far-reaching reform of the Dayton constitution, captured both views. On the one hand, the commission noted:

> The power of the High Representative to enact legislation . . . provides a safety valve making it possible to adopt urgently required legal texts. It also seems a fair assessment to state that . . . decisions of the High Representative . . . were responsible for much of the progress made by BiH hitherto and were a necessary basis for the implementation of the reforms bringing the country closer to European standards.

European Commission for Democracy Through Law (Venice Comm'n), *Opinion on the Constitutional Situation in Bosnia and Herzegovina and the Powers of the High Representative* ¶ 87, Doc. No. CDL-AD (2005) 004 (Mar. 11, 2005). And yet, the Commission continued, the High Representative's exercise of broad legislative power "is fundamentally incompatible with the democratic character of the state and the sovereignty of BiH," and its indefinite use risked creating a "dependency culture incompatible with the future development of BiH." *Id.* ¶ 90. Later that year, the Enlargement Commissioner of the European Union (EU) expressed similar

fact, by those who wielded them[251]). By the end of 2005, the prevailing view among Western governments was that "the state-building process had been enormously successful."[252] In consequence, they believed Bosnia was ready to begin transitioning from international governance to EU membership.[253] Hoping to spur Bosnia to meet EU accession criteria at a quickened pace, the PIC set in motion plans to wind down the OHR.[254] In June 2006, PIC's Steering Board decided in principle to close the OHR one year later.[255]

Among other considerations, the PIC board hoped national elections slated for October 1, 2006, would bring into office leaders "responsible for ensuring effective government in the interests of all BiH citizens."[256] Instead, the divisive campaign surrounding those elections, following on the failure of a constitutional reform package in April 2006, marked the beginning of "a downward spiral of political stagnation and mounting nationalist rhetoric."[257] Fatefully, that same year saw the elevation of Milorad Dodik, leader of the Alliance of Independent Social Democrats (SNSD), to the position of RS prime minister.[258] Hailed as a moderate alternative to

---

concerns and urged local political elites to take greater ownership of Bosnia's reform agenda. *See* McEvoy, *supra* note 213, at 134. Although framed in terms of enlightened principle, Western countries' desire to wind down their engagement in Bosnia also reflected a shift in priorities after the terrorist attacks of September 11, 2001.

[251] For example, while noting the Bonn powers enabled the OHR to address crucial issues when all other avenues had been exhausted, then High Representative Petritsch recognized their use enabled "the 'dependency syndrome.'" Wolfgang Petritsch, Opinion, *The Future of Bosnia Lies with Its People*, WALL STREET J. EUR. (Sept. 17, 1999).

[252] Bassuener, Durable Oligarchy, *supra* note 15, at 27.

[253] *See* BASSUENER & WEBER, ARE WE THERE YET?, *supra* note 210, at 19. During this period, the United States initiated what would be a continuous effort until relatively recently—trying to persuade Bosnian political leader to reach agreement on constitutional reforms. *See* MERDŽANOVIĆ, *supra* note 146, at 322 et seq. That the Dayton constitution needed radical revision seemed clear to most: even the chief architect of the DPA, Richard Holbrooke, is said to have seen the Bosnian constitution as a transitional one that would be revised once peace took hold. *See* Vedrana Maglajlija, *Bosnia and Herzegovina: A Hostage to Dayton?*, AL JAZEERA (Dec. 14, 2015). But with diametrically opposed visions of the Bosnian state, key political elites have used the constitution's cumbersome procedures to thwart constitutional change. *See* McEvoy, *supra* note 213, at 132 et seq. Joanne McEvoy summarizes the three major ethnic groups' fundamental visions this way:

> Bosniaks see the entity structure as a reward for ethnic cleansing and want to create a new constitution based on a unitary state. Bosnian Serbs resist any attempt to erode the authority of the RS and have, on occasion, called for a referendum on independence. Bosnian Croats want to at least retain equal power to protect their group rights, and they occasionally make calls for the creation of their own entity.

Id. at 132.

[254] INTERNATIONAL CRISIS GROUP, BOSNIA'S INCOMPLETE TRANSITION, *supra* note 249, at i. In line with this plan, during his final year as High Representative Lord Ashdown prepared for a transfer of authority to local structures, drastically reducing the OHR's staff and refraining from using Bonn powers by late 2005. Bennett, *supra* note 234.

[255] PIC Steering Board, *Communique: Towards Ownership: From Peace Implementation Toward Euro-Atlantic Integration* (June 23, 2006).

[256] *Id.*

[257] MOORE, *supra* note 215, at 160. *See also* MacDowall, *supra* note 230 (characterizing the decade since 2006 as a "decade of stasis and rising nationalist rhetoric").

[258] Dodik previously served as premier of RS upon appointment in 1998 by Biljana Plavšić, then RS president. Srećko Latal, *Milorad Dodik: From Pro-US Moderate to Bosnian-Serb Separatist*, BALKAN INSIGHT (Sept. 14, 2016).

nationalist Bosnian Serb leaders responsible for mass atrocities when he assumed the same post in 1998, Dodik relied on "radical rhetoric, playing on Bosnian Serb nationalist emotions and threatening the secession of RS from Bosnia" to win the 2006 poll.[259] Elected president of RS in 2010 and again in 2014, Dodik has grown increasingly strident and disruptive.[260] Of particular relevance to this study, he has revived nationalist discourses of the 1990s, rejected key facts established by the ICTY,[261] and celebrated individuals convicted in The Hague as heroes.

The poll that brought Dodik back to power also saw the election of Haris Silajdžić to the Bosniak seat of the three-person state presidency. Silajdžić, who served as Bosnia's prime minister for much of the 1990s war, has called for Dayton to be revised to eliminate the autonomous Serb entity in favor of a centralized state.[262] Against these claims (asserted, not for the first time, during constitutional reform talks in 2006), Dodik has threatened an RS referendum on independence should proposals to abolish the Serb entity or diminish its autonomy succeed.[263] In this setting, although Bosnian Serbs initially opposed Dayton's political outcome, they became its most staunch defenders. Meanwhile, some Bosnian Croat leaders have sought to enhance Bosnian Croats' political status, seeking a predominantly Croat "third entity" within Bosnia.[264] The opposing aspirations of Serb, Bosniak, and Croat leaders have hardly been conducive to interethnic reconciliation, a process many Bosnians hoped the ICTY would foster.[265]

In the past, calls for Serb secession might have led the High Representative to take robust measures, including removal of RS leaders from office. Now, key European states made it clear they did not want the High Representative to confront Dodik.[266] Dodik reportedly drew two lessons: First, nationalist rhetoric is far more likely to win elections than, say, acknowledging Serb atrocities and expressing remorse for them. Second, Dodik could advance nationalist positions without risking his removal through use of the Bonn powers.[267]

---

[259] *Id.* Dodik became RS prime minister in March 2006 when the SDS-led government collapsed. From that position he campaigned on a stridently nationalist platform in the October 2006 elections. In Adis Merdžanović's assessment, the failure of the U.S.-backed "April package" of constitutional reform in 2006 provided Dodik "all the cover he needed" to initiate a nationalist agenda. MERDŽANOVIĆ, *supra* note 146, at 323.

[260] *See* Eldar Sarajlić, *Bosnian Elections and Recurring Ethnonationalisms: The Ghost of the Nation State*, 2 J. ETHNOPOLITICS & MINORITY ISSUES EUR. 66, 77 (2010).

[261] *See, e.g.*, *Dodik: There Was No Genocide in Srebrenica*, TANJUG (July 11, 2016). These points are developed further in Chapter 8.

[262] *See* INTERNATIONAL CRISIS GROUP, BOSNIA'S INCOMPLETE TRANSITION, *supra* note 249, at 1–2. In short, the vote was a "sure recipe for paralysis." *Id.* at 2 n.10.

[263] *See* MERDŽANOVIĆ, *supra* note 146, at 329; Maja Zuvela, *Biggest Serb Party in Bosnia Threatens 2018 Secession*, REUTERS (Apr. 25, 2015). While Dodik's secessionist threats are framed as a response to efforts to strengthen state institutions, many analysts attribute them to electoral calculations, including a felt need to divert attention from deteriorating economic conditions, as well as allegations of personal corruption. *See, e.g.*, Srećko Latal, *Bosniaks Try to Halt Bosnian Serb Referendum*, BALKAN TRANSITIONAL JUST. (Oct. 2, 2015); Nedim Dervisbegović, *Bosnia's Dodik Still Loud and Defiant—But Maybe Nervous Too*, RFE/RL (Jan. 14, 2013).

[264] *See* Daria Sito-Sučić, *Separatist Forces May Slow Bosnia's EU Progress: Envoy*, REUTERS (Dec. 13, 2016); McEVOY, *supra* note 213, at 132.

[265] *See* Chapter 4.

[266] *See* MERDŽANOVIĆ, *supra* note 146, at 329.

[267] *See id.* at 329–30.

In line with the views of analysts outside Bosnia, Elmina Kulašić described the long-term impact of developments in 2006 this way: "And it's really after 2006 that things started going downhill in a sense, and that the OHR *really* started slipping back when it comes to checking, and implementing, really implementing the Dayton agreement."[268] Freed from the prospect of a robust response, "the politicians [in Bosnia] are really fighting back and using nationalistic rhetoric and nationalism to fulfill their political goals."[269]

As 2006 drew to an end, it was painfully clear Western conditions for devolving governance to Bosnians were far from the prevailing reality. In February 2007, the PIC decided to reverse its previous decision to wind down the OHR by late June 2007,[270] and subsequent plans to end the institution have been derailed by Bosnia's ever-deepening governance crisis. In contrast to Petritsch and Ashdown, however, more recent occupants of the office have rarely used the Bonn powers to overcome political obstruction and revitalize the project of state-building.[271] While several developments account for this, one, which came to a head in 2007, merits brief mention because of its enduring impact.

After unsuccessfully pressing Bosnian parties to satisfy relevant standards for signing a Stabilisation and Association Agreement (SAA), a key step toward EU membership, in October 2007 then High Representative Miroslav Lajčák imposed the first of what were intended to be a series of measures to overcome Bosnian paralysis.[272] Dodik responded by threatening to pull his party's members out of state government, and the RS National Assembly warned of "unavoidable" consequences if state institutions tried to outvote one of the entities.[273] Lajčák issued a face-saving interpretation of his edict; Bosnia initialed the SAA the following day.[274] Many saw this as a capitulation to Dodik, a death blow to the OHR's standing in Bosnia,[275] and the de facto end of the Bonn powers[276]—or, more precisely, the end of their use to drive reform rather than merely avert a looming crisis.[277] More generally, continuous

---

[268] Interview with Elmina Kulašić, Transitional Justice, Accountability and Remembrance, in Sarajevo, Bosn. & Herz. (Sept. 13, 2014).

[269] *Id.* For similar views, see Kurt Bassuener & Bodo Weber, *Balkan Tango: The EU's Disjointed Policies Compound Bosnia's Paralysis*, 2 IP GLOBAL EDITION 19, 19 (2010) [hereinafter Bassuener & Weber, *Balkan Tango*].

[270] *See* Christopher Bennett, *Western Powerlessness Strengthens Bosnian Serb Leader*, BALKAN TRANSITIONAL JUST. (Oct. 12, 2016). In February 2008, the PIC decided the OHR would remain open until Bosnia had achieved five objectives and satisfied two conditions, one of which was "full compliance with the Dayton Peace Agreement." Office of the High Representative, Declaration by the Steering Board of the Peace Implementation Council (Feb. 27, 2008).

[271] *See* Bennett, *supra* note 270 (reporting the Bonn powers were used by High Representatives Westendorp, Petritsch, and Ashdown a total of 777 times between December 1997 and January 2006, but only 181 times by their three successors in the years since).

[272] INTERNATIONAL CRISIS GROUP, BOSNIA'S INCOMPLETE TRANSITION, *supra* note 249, at 12.

[273] *Id.* at 13.

[274] *Id.* The PIC Steering Board initially backed Lajčák but then softened its position, asking him to find a way to back down. *See id.*; MERDŽANOVIĆ, *supra* note 146, at 335–37. According to Kurt Bassuener, Lajčák contributed to the latter, in part by failing to press aggressively for support. Comment on draft chapter by Kurt Bassuener (provided Aug. 5, 2017).

[275] INTERNATIONAL CRISIS GROUP, BOSNIA'S INCOMPLETE TRANSITION, *supra* note 249, at 13–14.

[276] MERDŽANOVIĆ, *supra* note 146, at 337–38.

[277] *See* Bassuener, Durable Oligarchy, *supra* note 15, at 30.

debate within the PIC about closing down the OHR has weakened the office and, correspondingly, strengthened Dodik's hand.[278]

Indirectly, the OHR's waning authority might have reinforced citizens' loss of faith in the ICTY—which, to be sure, was more directly attributable to the court's performance.[279] Kulašić believes that, during the OHR's most robust years, public support for that institution "meant also support for [other] international institutions," including the ICTY, which were seen as "sort of above Bosnia, . . . like higher power, and . . . they trusted it."[280] Conversely, when "the OHR started being questioned," Bosnians were more inclined to "question[] everything that was international."[281]

A failed U.S.-EU effort at constitutional reform in 2009 reportedly persuaded Dodik his strategy of continuous confrontation was wearing down international actors, who would abide challenges to OHR authority.[282] By 2010, the reform agenda had "stalled or even reversed," and the EU integration process "ground to a halt."[283] (Nevertheless, the EU would subsequently greenlight Bosnia's accession process despite the country's failure to meet specified preconditions).[284] Defying a ruling of the state-level Constitutional Court as well as Western pleas, in September 2016 Dodik held a referendum in which RS residents voted overwhelmingly to celebrate January 9, a date associated with Bosnian Serbs' declaration of intent to establish an ethnically pure state, as the Serb entity's national holiday.[285] With Bosnia suffering "a complete breakdown of [its] political and governmental structures,"[286] the country was, by 2016, routinely described as a country in crisis, with "unprecedented discussion of the prospect of a return to war."[287]

The West has done little to stop, much less reverse, Bosnia's downward spiral.[288] There are, of course, principled as well as pragmatic reasons to be skeptical of externally-imposed governance.[289] But many Bosnians believe the West simply lost

---

[278] INTERNATIONAL CRISIS GROUP, EUR. BRIEFING 57, BOSNIA'S DUAL CRISIS 11 (2009).

[279] See Chapter 6 for discussion of aspects of the Tribunal's performance that diminished Bosnians' confidence.

[280] Interview with Elmina Kulašić, Transitional Justice, Accountability and Remembrance, in Sarajevo, Bosn. & Herz. (Sept. 13, 2014).

[281] Id.

[282] Bassuener & Weber, Balkan Tango, supra note 269, at 21; Bennett, supra note 270. The impact of this failed effort on Bosnia's war crimes institutions is described in Chapter 9.

[283] Bassuener & Weber, Balkan Tango, supra note 269, at 19.

[284] See Srećko Latal, Crisis-Wracked Bosnia Approaches Tipping Point, BALKAN INSIGHT (June 9, 2016).

[285] See Rose, supra note 220; Bosnian Serbs Keep Holiday in a Vote Assailed as Illegal, N.Y. TIMES (Sept. 26, 2016). Western states were divided on the question whether the High Representative should use his Bonn powers to block the referendum. Ultimately, the PIC "agreed on a lukewarm communiqué, which merely 'urged' the RS authorities not to hold the referendum." Srećko Latal, Divided West Leaves Bosnia's "Governor" Exposed, BALKAN INSIGHT (Aug. 31, 2016).

[286] Latal, supra note 284.

[287] Id. Among those I interviewed who voiced this fear, Aleksandar Trifunović said he was "pretty sure that we [will] have a new war" relatively soon. Interview with Aleksandar Trifunović, Editor, BUKA, in Banja Luka, Bosn. & Herz. (Sept. 15, 2014).

[288] See Kurt Bassuener, Bosnia's Fragile Stability Masks a Downward Spiral, BALKAN INSIGHT (Oct. 28, 2015).

[289] Several are discussed in Nicolas Lemay-Hébert, Coerced Transitions in Timor-Leste and Kosovo: Managing Competing Objectives of Institution-Building and Local Empowerment, 19 DEMOCRATIZATION 465 (2012).

interest in Bosnia, "redirect[ing] its energy into other conflicts," even as Dayton left the country a "semi-protectorate."[290] In this setting, Emir Hodžić observed, "people are just flabbergasted" the international community has allowed "somebody [as] destructive, and obviously dangerous" as Dodik to become "so powerful" when it possesses tools that could curb destructive conduct.[291]

If some are dismayed, most Bosnians long ago lost hope of effective international action. Like Aleksandar Trifunović, they do not "have any kind of dreams of what [the] international community can do" to stop Bosnia's downward spiral. Instead, they are "pretty sure [the] international community want[s] to find [an] exit strategy" from Bosnia.[292] Some wondered whether it was "too late" in any event for effective action by external actors,[293] whom many Bosnians see as largely ineffectual. A frequent visitor to the region, Ivana Nizich characterizes a common perception of international actors (at least among Sarajevans) this way: "All you internationals have been here for over 20 years collecting your salaries and per diems, but Bosnia remains dysfunctional and divided. If you are not willing to revise or get rid of Dayton and rectify the partition of this country, it's time for you all to leave."[294]

Whatever its causes, Bosnia's deepening crisis has diminished Bosnians' assessments of the ICTY. Like many whom I interviewed in 2014, Emir Hodžić said:

> If we're looking from the perspective of this overall context, the political situation and economic situation in Bosnia Herzegovina *has never been worse. And it's 2014.* So you can understand a lot of resentment from the people on the ground. A lot. And that *is*, you know, directed sometimes at ICTY.[295]

IV. CONCLUDING OBSERVATIONS

How Bosnians experience the ICTY has been shaped by myriad factors, which have hardly been stable over time. While the Tribunal's own performance has been crucial to many Bosnians' experience of justice, contextual factors have played a key role as well. As this chapter has elucidated, the actions and inactions of global actors and institutions have significantly shaped the context in which Tribunal "impact" unfolds.

For example, NATO forces' initial reluctance to arrest ICTY suspects not only delayed trials of individuals who bear lead responsibility for wartime atrocities, but also allowed those same individuals to reconstitute positions of influence and roil interethnic relations in postwar Bosnia. Conversely, their belated arrests of Hague suspects had a constructive ripple effect: Along with other developments, the

---

[290] Nidžara Ahmetašević, *Bosnia's Unending War*, NEW YORKER, Nov. 4, 2015.

[291] Interview with Emir Hodžić, Jer Me Se Tiče, in Sarajevo, Bosn. & Herz. (Sept. 13, 2014).

[292] Interview with Aleksandar Trifunović, Editor, BUKA, in Banja Luka, Bosn. & Herz. (Sept. 15, 2014).

[293] Interview with Svjetlana Nedimović, Activist, in Sarajevo, Bosn. & Herz. (Sept. 18, 2014).

[294] Interview with Ivana Nizich, Former Investigator, Human Rights Watch; Former Military Analyst, Office of the Prosecutor, ICTY, in Washington, DC, United States (Apr. 28, 2017).

[295] Interview with Emir Hodžić, Jer Me Se Tiče, in Sarajevo, Bosn. & Herz. (Sept. 13, 2014). (The emphasis reflects Mr. Hodžić's emphasis during my interview with him.) I develop this point in Chapter 8.

removal of spoilers fostered conditions in which many who had been forced to flee their homes now believed it safe to return. In the view of many Bosnians and others, this was a direct dividend of the ICTY's work.[296]

Regrettably, the governance structure imposed in Dayton has, combined with other factors, condemned many survivors to an unstable and increasingly hostile environment—a far cry from the social repair many thought the ICTY would help foster. The provocations abetted by DPA structures could be kept in check only with robust international engagement, as happened for a time in the early 2000s. Without a sustained commitment, however, hard-won progress gave way to a "constantly deepening crisis."[297] As I explore in Chapter 8, a growing sense of hopelessness about their country's prospects—economic, social, and political—has deeply compromised many Bosnians' experience of justice.

---

[296] As previously noted, the rate of returns later declined. *See supra* note 197. In July 2017, Dodik provoked international condemnation by characterizing Bosniak residents in RS as "occupation forces." *See Dodik Threats to Returnees Elicit Strong Criticism*, HINA CROATIAN NEWS AGENCY (July 17, 2017).

[297] Latal, *supra* note 284.

3

Coerced Cooperation

Serbia's Relationship with the ICTY

Haunting images of wartime brutality, gruesomely broadcast in the daily media, galvanized global attention in the 1990s but seemed distant to many Serbians. Describing their experience of grievous harms accompanying the implosion of Yugoslavia,[1] Srđan Bogosavljević told me: "It was all somehow out of Serbia."[2] Yet far from being a remote bystander, Serbia instigated ruinous violence, and organized and underwrote Serb paramilitary forces that carried out atrocities in Bosnia and Croatia. Later, its own forces committed war crimes in Kosovo. At the time of his death in March 2006, Serbia's wartime leader, Slobodan Milošević, was on trial in The Hague on charges encompassing the whole "bloody sweep of the Yugoslav war."[3]

---

[1] At the time the ICTY was created, Serbia was the dominant republic of the Federal Republic of Yugoslavia (FRY), composed of the only two republics that had not yet separated from the six-republic Socialist Federal Republic of Yugoslavia (SFRY, or "former Yugoslavia"), Serbia and Montenegro. In February 2003, the FRY became a confederal state, renamed Serbia and Montenegro (SaM). In June 2006, Montenegro became independent, as a result of which Serbia, too, became a state rather than the dominant republic within a state. This chapter generally uses the designation applicable during the period it addresses.

[2] Interview with Srđan Bogosavljević, General Manager, Strategic Marketing, in Belgrade, Serb. (Nov. 21, 2006). There were some incidents of ethnic violence in Serbia in the early 1990s, but with one exception (in the case against Vojislav Šešelj) they did not lead to charges in The Hague. *See* Eric Gordy, Guilt, Responsibility and Denial: The Past at Stake in Post-Milošević Serbia 10 (2013).

[3] Timothy William Waters, *Preface* to The Milošević Trial: An Autopsy, at xv, xv (Timothy William Waters ed., 2013). Although Milošević did not live to see judgment, evidence introduced in

Serbian society has, moreover, been profoundly affected by Serbia's wartime policies and its crucial role protecting and subsidizing fugitives from Hague justice long after the 1990s wars ended. For eleven weeks in 1999, Serbia was at war with the North Atlantic Treaty Organization (NATO), which intervened to halt Serb atrocities then underway in Kosovo. Until Serbia arrested the last ICTY fugitive in July 2011,[4] its relationship with Western countries and international organizations was defined in significant part by its cooperation with the Tribunal. Even after a democratically-elected government succeeded the Milošević regime, U.S. aid, then seen as vital to Serbia's economy, was linked to cooperation with the Hague Tribunal. More important since 2005, the European Union (EU) conditioned Serbian accession on its "full cooperation with the ICTY."[5]

This chapter provides an overview of Serbia's relationship with the ICTY, focusing on the evolving nature and dynamics of Serbian cooperation. It thus provides a foundation for later chapters on Serbia while elucidating key dimensions of the Tribunal's impact. With respect to the latter, the most obvious effect of Western conditionality is that it induced Serbia to send fugitives to The Hague, however grudgingly. Indeed, and importantly, conditionality was *essential* to this outcome. The importance of this should not be lost: without transfers secured by conditionality, the Tribunal would have been judged an abject failure by victims of Serb atrocities.

In the view of Serbian citizens who support the ICTY, these transfers had broader salutary effects that are often overlooked. In particular, spoilers were removed from Serbia's political scene during a crucial period of transition. They believe, moreover, that core values corrupted under Milošević were affirmed, at least in part, by Serbian cooperation in ensuring prosecution of war criminals.[6]

Even so, the impact of conditionality on Serbia's political transition has raised complex and consequential questions. On one view, the Tribunal's relentless demands for cooperation, backed by conditionality, at times strengthened ultranationalists in Serbia and distracted reformist leaders from myriad challenges surrounding Serbia's fragile transition.[7] On another, conditionality bolstered the position of reformists in

---

his trial and others at the ICTY disclosed the broad structures of Belgrade's support for Serb forces in Bosnia and Croatia, as well as its more straightforward responsibility for atrocities committed by Serbian forces in Kosovo. *See* HUMAN RIGHTS WATCH, WEIGHING THE EVIDENCE: LESSONS FROM THE MILOŠEVIĆ TRIAL (2006).

[4] *See* Marlise Simons, *Serbia Arrests Its Last Fugitive Accused of War Crimes*, N.Y. TIMES (July 20, 2011). As of September 2017, Serbia had not yet arrested two individuals whom the ICTY charged in December 2014 (along with a third individual who died in June 2017) with contempt of court for threatening witnesses. *See* Dragana Erjavec, *UN Court Ends Case Against Serbian Radical*, BALKAN TRANSITIONAL JUST. (Aug. 19, 2017).

[5] *See* Álvaro de Vasconcelos, *Preface* to WAR CRIMES, CONDITIONALITY, AND EU INTEGRATION IN THE WESTERN BALKANS 5 (Judy Blatt & Jelena Obradović-Wochnik eds., 2009); Mathias Dobbels, *Serbia and the ICTY: How Effective Is EU Conditionality?* 4–5 (C. of Eur., EU Diplomacy Papers 6/2009, 2009).

[6] These and other conceptions of positive ICTY impact in Serbia are explored in Chapter 5.

[7] *E.g.*, interview with Radmila Nakarada, then Associate Professor, Faculty of Political Sciences, in Belgrade, Serb. (Nov. 24, 2006). *See also* NIKOLAS M. RAJKOVIĆ, THE POLITICS OF INTERNATIONAL LAW AND COMPLIANCE: SERBIA, CROATIA AND THE HAGUE TRIBUNAL 79–81 (2012) (arguing that, in late 2003, ill-timed ICTY indictments against four Serbian generals weakened domestic political actors most disposed to cooperate with the Tribunal while strengthening nationalists). *But see* MLADEN OSTOJIĆ, BETWEEN JUSTICE AND STABILITY: THE POLITICS OF WAR CRIMES PROSECUTIONS IN POST-MILOŠEVIĆ SERBIA 12 (2014) (while "the ICTY was indeed used as a catalyst for nationalist mobilization, there is no evidence that it actually generated an increase

post-Milošević governments, widening the political space in which they could advance what they considered a morally imperative project of justice.[8] As will be seen, the reality of Serbia's experience is more complex than either account suggests.

I. DEFIANCE DURING THE MILOŠEVIĆ YEARS

The Milošević government[9] was implacably hostile toward the ICTY from the outset, and maintained its opposition until it collapsed in October 2000. The wartime leader's opposition was foregone: having willfully instigated and sponsored atrocities, Milošević would naturally see The Hague as a threat.

Shortly before the Security Council created the Tribunal, Belgrade threw down the proverbial gauntlet, challenging the legality and legitimacy of the proposed court. In a restrained version of what would become a leitmotif of nationalist narratives, the Federal Republic of Yugoslavia (FRY) alleged the drive to create a tribunal was "politically motivated." Accordingly, the government said it had "doubts about the [proposed tribunal's] impartiality . . . , particularly because of the one-sided approach" of the Council during the Yugoslav conflicts and "the fact [sic] that numerous initiators and advocates of the idea of its establishment have openly stated that this was going to be a tribunal for Serbs."[10] Rejecting the Tribunal's legitimacy, Milošević refused to cooperate with it despite a resolution of the UN Security Council requiring all States to do so.[11]

There were, to be sure, isolated instances in which his government transferred individuals to The Hague, but the circumstances allowed Milošević to maintain a narrative of defiance. In early 1996, Belgrade transferred to the ICTY Dražen Erdemović, a Bosnian Croat who had described his participation in the Srebrenica massacre in an interview with ABC News. At the time of the transfer, Erdemović

---

in public support for nationalist parties in Serbia"). A distinct critique maintains "imposed justice" is unlikely to foster a genuine reckoning with the past. This issue is noted but not explored in depth in CHRISTOPHER K. LAMONT, INTERNATIONAL CRIMINAL JUSTICE AND THE POLITICS OF COMPLIANCE 175–76 (2010). Viktor Peskin warns of a related risk—that an ICT's strategy of shaming a state into compliance "can backfire by hardening domestic opposition to the tribunal" itself. VIKTOR PESKIN, INTERNATIONAL JUSTICE IN RWANDA AND THE BALKANS: VIRTUAL TRIALS AND THE STRUGGLE FOR STATE COOPERATION 62 (2008).

[8] *See* Chapter 10.

[9] Milošević became president of the Presidency of Serbia, then the dominant republic of the SFRY, in late 1989 and was re-elected to this position later that same year. After a new Constitution of Serbia was adopted, Milošević was elected Serbian president in 1990 and was re-elected in 1992. In July 1997, following constitutional changes that transferred many powers from the Serbian to the federal presidency, Milošević was elected president of the FRY, a position he held at the time of his indictment in 1999.

[10] Letter dated May 17, 1993, from the Deputy Prime Minister and Minister for Foreign Affairs of the Federal Republic of Yugoslavia to the Secretary-General, U.N. Doc. A/48/170-S/25801, Annex, pp. 2–3 (May 21, 1993).

[11] The UN Security Council Resolution establishing the ICTY includes a decision that "all States shall cooperate fully with the International Tribunal and its organs in accordance with the present resolution and the Statute of the International Tribunal and that consequently all States shall take any measures necessary under their domestic law to implement the provisions of the present resolution and the Statute, including the obligation of States to comply with requests for assistance or orders issued by a Trial Chamber under Article 29 of the Statute." S.C. Res. 827, ¶ 4 (May 25, 1993).

was sought solely for questioning; only later would he become a suspect. Also in 1996, the government transferred Radoslav Kremenović for questioning by the ICTY Prosecutor (he was remanded back to the FRY). In these circumstances, the Milošević government could claim neither transfer was a precedent for surrendering Serbian indictees.[12]

Despite his general defiance, Milošević faced little pressure to cooperate with the Tribunal.[13] Before the Dayton Peace Agreement (DPA) was concluded, the United States looked to the Serbian leader to help end the conflict then underway in Bosnia. After the DPA was signed in late 1995, the U.S. government relied on Milošević to pressure Bosnian Serbs to abide by the accord, or at least not derail the fragile peace.[14] In any event, in the early post-Dayton period, advocacy efforts to ensure the arrest of Hague fugitives focused on NATO forces deployed in Bosnia, where key Serb suspects were at large, as well as the Croatian government in respect of Croat fugitives.[15]

By the late 1990s, the FRY's increasingly repressive practices in Kosovo brought a fundamental change in Western states' relationship with Milošević. During this period, the Kosovo Liberation Army (KLA) emerged as a collection of small armed resistance groups, whose low-level attacks were met with brutal force by Serbian authorities. With the collapse of diplomatic efforts to end the conflict, in late March 1999 NATO forces launched an eleven-week air campaign aimed at halting Serbian repression, in the course of which some targets in Belgrade were bombed.[16]

In May 1999, with the Kosovo war still underway, the ICTY Prosecutor issued her first indictment of Milošević.[17] The timing would make a lasting impression on many Serbians, reinforcing long-standing nationalist narratives depicting the Tribunal as "an instrument of [Western] power."[18] As a former ICTY prosecutor has noted, "In fact, the opposite was true: . . . there was . . . a fair degree of consternation among some NATO governments," which "saw the indictment as an impediment to ending the war."[19] Yet that hardly mattered to Serbian public opinion. Journalist Filip Švarm

---

[12] See LAMONT, *supra* note 7, at 66–67. Recalling the Erdemović episode, the ICTY's (de facto) first prosecutor, Richard Goldstone, attributed the Serbian government's cooperation to its desire for U.S. financial support: "Fortunately for the Tribunal, Erdemović was not a Serb national and in order to garner financial assistance from the United States, Milošević, to our great surprise, decided to accede to the request and Erdemović was flown to The Hague." Ceremonial Address of Justice Richard J. Goldstone at John Shattuck Inauguration, Nov. 3, 2009, http://www.ceu.hu/article/2009-11-03/transcript-ceremonial-address-justice-richard-j-goldstone-john-shattuck#sthash.oAaiSXE5.dpuf.

[13] See PESKIN, *supra* note 7, at 50–51; LAMONT, *supra* note 7, at 79.

[14] See PESKIN, *supra* note 7, at 50.

[15] See *id.* Although many fugitives were in Bosnia in the early post-Dayton period, several Serbian officers were already under indictment by the ICTY. On November 7, 1995, two weeks before parties agreed to the DPA, the Tribunal confirmed an indictment against three officers in the Yugoslav army, Mile Mrkšić, Miroslav Radić, and Veselin Šljivančanin, in relation to war crimes against Croatians in the city of Vukovar. Prosecutor v. Mrkšić et al., Case No. IT 95-13-1a, Indictment (Int'l Crim. Trib. for the Former Yugoslavia Oct. 26, 1995).

[16] *Preface* to NOEL MALCOLM, KOSOVO: A SHORT HISTORY (1999); THE INDEPENDENT INTERNATIONAL COMMISSION ON KOSOVO, THE KOSOVO REPORT 1–2 (2000).

[17] Prosecutor v. Milošević, Case No. IT-99-37, Indictment (Int'l Crim. Trib. for the Former Yugoslavia May 22, 1999).

[18] Interview with Ljiljana Smajlović, Journalist, in Belgrade, Serb. (Nov. 24, 2006).

[19] Clint Williamson, *Real Justice, in Time: The Initial Indictment of Milošević, in* THE MILOŠEVIĆ TRIAL: AN AUTOPSY 77, 90 (Timothy William Waters ed., 2013).

described a widespread perception this way: "Milošević went to the Hague when he lost the war against NATO."[20]

But if the timing of his indictment provided further grist for anti-Hague narratives, the indictment had wider, salutary effects: journalist Dejan Anastasijević believes it paved the way for the FRY's democratic transition in 2000. In his words, the fact that its "chief of state is indicted for war crimes and therefore internationally isolated did contribute to people being aware there's no future with him."[21]

II. CONFLICTED COOPERATION: THE KOŠTUNICA-ĐINĐIĆ GOVERNMENT (2000–2003)

Serbia's relationship with the Tribunal entered a new phase after Serbians voted Milošević out of office (more precisely, after the wartime leader accepted his electoral defeat on October 5, 2000).[22] With Milošević out of power, Serbian cooperation became a real possibility. But the issue of arrests proved highly contentious for the divided government that succeeded him.

The eighteen-party coalition government, the Democratic Opposition of Serbia (DOS), was led by FRY president Vojislav Koštunica, a nationalist who had long seen the ICTY as an anti-Serb institution and threat to Serbian sovereignty,[23] and Serbian prime minister Zoran Đinđić, a reformist whose administration favored accountability as well as Western integration. DOS's unity in opposing Milošević obscured deep divisions within the coalition. Once in power, the alliance "was paralyzed from the very beginning by deep ideological and political differences over fundamental issues."[24] Although hardly the only point of contention between them, Koštunica and Đinđić divided on the question of cooperation with the ICTY. In Đinđić the Tribunal finally found a partner in the Serbian government. But his room for maneuver was limited by Koštunica's deep antipathy toward the Hague Tribunal.

These divisions went a long way toward demarcating the space in which post-Milošević Serbia would cooperate with the ICTY and, more generally, support accountability for crimes of the Milošević era. As scholars have long recognized, following the collapse of a regime responsible for wholesale violence, the near-term

---

[20] Interview with Filip Švarm, Journalist, in Belgrade, Serb. (Nov. 24, 2006). That the ICTY's first indictment against Milošević included crimes relating solely to Kosovo and not atrocities committed years earlier in Croatia and Bosnia reinforced this perception. For discussion of the reasons the Prosecutor's first indictment focused on atrocities in Kosovo, see DIANE F. ORENTLICHER, OPEN SOCIETY JUSTICE INITIATIVE, SHRINKING THE SPACE FOR DENIAL: THE IMPACT OF THE ICTY IN SERBIA 75–76 (2008).

[21] Interview with Dejan Anastasijević, Journalist, in Belgrade, Serb. (Nov. 20, 2006).

[22] Milošević contested his loss in elections held on September 24, 2000, for two weeks. In the face of massive protests, he accepted his defeat on October 5, 2000. See R. Jeffrey Smith, Anti-Milošević Protests Sweep Across Yugoslavia, WASH. POST (Oct. 3, 2000); R. Jeffrey Smith, Koštunica Takes Reins in Belgrade, WASH. POST (Oct. 8, 2000).

[23] See R. Jeffrey Smith, Koštunica Faces Test over Extradition of Serbs for War Crimes, WASH. POST (Jan. 21, 2001). On the day Milošević fell from power, Koštunica described the ICTY as "a political institution," which "actually . . . is not a court at all." Noting many had asked about surrendering Milošević, Koštunica said, "my answer was clearly no." RTS interview, translated by CNN, Oct. 5, 2000. Soon after, Koštunica told reporters that cooperation with the ICTY "is a fact, but it cannot be one of our priorities." Koštunica: War Crimes Must Wait, BBC NEWS (Oct. 14, 2000).

[24] U.S. INSTITUTE OF PEACE, SPECIAL REP. 128, SERBIA AT THE CROSSROADS AGAIN 7 (2004) [hereinafter SERBIA AT THE CROSSROADS AGAIN].

prospects for retrospective justice depend on the nature of the political transition. Broadly, robust measures are more likely to be undertaken in the years immediately following a "ruptured" transition—one that entails a sharp break with the prior regime—than in the aftermath of a transition entailing significant continuity with the outgoing regime.[25] In the FRY, Koštunica, as well as unreformed security services, represented significant continuity with Milošević-era structures and policies (notwithstanding Koštunica's opposition to Milošević during the 2000 elections).

Despite their differences, for awhile Koštunica and Đinđić shared a common perspective on the foremost issue of cooperation, dispatching Milošević to The Hague. At first both leaders opposed doing so,[26] instead preferring to try the wartime leader in local courts.[27] Đinđić became a proponent of transfer, however, when it became clear Western financial support would turn on sending Milošević to The Hague.[28] Faced with the prospect of losing U.S. direct aid as well as U.S. support for financing from international financial institutions,[29] even Koštunica eventually acquiesced in certain measures to legalize Milošević's surrender, a "lesser evil than what would happen to the country if we did not do it."[30]

For the next decade, Serbian compliance with Tribunal demands would be secured by Western pressure, which bolstered the tenacious efforts of then ICTY Prosecutor Carla del Ponte.[31] Eventually, EU conditionality would provide the most important leverage for securing arrests. But it was Washington that motivated Serbia to arrest Milošević in 2001 (and, indeed, provided crucial impetus for many other arrests). Congress had conditioned financial assistance to the FRY on an executive branch

---

[25] See, e.g., SAMUEL P. HUNTINGTON, THE THIRD WAVE: DEMOCRATIZATION IN THE LATE TWENTIETH CENTURY 215–19 (1991); José Zalaquett, *Confronting Human Rights Violations Committed by Former Governments: Principles Applicable and Political Constraints*, in STATE CRIMES: PUNISHMENT OR PARDON (1989). Recent research suggests the factors that inhibit prosecutions following non-ruptured transitions have a relatively short-term effect, mattering most up to the fourth year of transition. Hun Joon Kim, *Structural Determinants of Human Rights Prosecutions After Democratic Transition*, 49 J. PEACE RES. 305, 313 (2012).

[26] See Steven Erlanger, *New Serbian Leader Vows Fast Improvements*, N.Y. TIMES (Dec. 25, 2000). In the first days of his presidency, Koštunica reportedly did not even favor prosecuting Milošević domestically for electoral fraud. Roger Cohen, *On Milošević: What to Do?*, N.Y. TIMES (Oct. 8, 2000).

[27] Koštunica and Đinđić apparently held different views about appropriate charges. The former reportedly "wanted Milošević to be tried in Belgrade for crimes committed in Serbia," CARLA DEL PONTE IN COLLABORATION WITH CHUCK SUDETIĆ, MADAME PROSECUTOR: CONFRONTATIONS WITH HUMANITY'S WORST CRIMINALS AND THE CULTURE OF IMPUNITY 92 (2008), by implication excluding atrocities committed in Bosnia and Croatia. Đinđić reportedly wanted to press domestic charges relating to corruption and abuse of power first, and perhaps later press war crimes charges against the former Serbian leader. See *Milošević "To Face Justice"*, BBC NEWS (Dec. 24, 2000); Carlotta Gall, *Milošević Facing Arrest by Serbs for a Local Trial*, N.Y. TIMES (Feb. 9, 2001).

[28] See R. Jeffrey Smith, *Serb Leaders Hand Over Milošević for Trial by War Crimes Tribunal*, WASH. POST (June 29, 2001).

[29] See Steven Erlanger, *U.S. Makes Arrest of Milošević a Condition of Aid to Belgrade*, N.Y. TIMES (Mar. 10, 2001).

[30] Carlotta Gall, *Belgrade Begins Process of Sending Milošević to The Hague*, N.Y. TIMES (June 26, 2001). See also R. Jeffrey Smith, *Belgrade Files Court Papers for Milošević Extradition*, WASH. POST (June 26, 2001); R. Jeffrey Smith, *Yugoslavia Moves to Extradite Milošević*, WASH. POST (June 24, 2001).

[31] Del Ponte was not the first Prosecutor to focus on arrests; as described in Chapter 2, this was also a paramount concern of her predecessor. But it was during Del Ponte's eight-year tenure that Belgrade became the principal focus of the Tribunal's arrest efforts.

certification that the government had met certain benchmarks, including cooperation with the ICTY.[32] As the March 31, 2001, certification deadline approached, the U.S. government pressed Belgrade to detain Milošević.[33]

Serbian police tried to arrest Milošević on March 30, 2001, the day before the U.S. certification deadline.[34] After a two-day standoff with police, Milošević surrendered in the early morning of April 1, 2001, reportedly on condition he not be handed over to the Hague Tribunal.[35] Đinđić apparently still hoped the West would agree to let Serbia try Milošević itself. In a radio interview on April 11, 2001, the premier made a powerful case for prosecuting the former leader in his own country: "We have to reconstruct our own past through this legal process, because not only is Milošević a part of our past, but so are we, and because Milošević would not have become what he is without us."[36]

If securing Milošević's arrest was a heavy lift, ensuring his transfer to The Hague was hardly any easier.[37] Once again, significant Western pressure was brought to bear. In the lead-up to a conference of Western donors convened to help rebuild the former Yugoslavia—and confronting a potential U.S. boycott[38]—the Serbian government sought to finalize a legal framework for transferring Milošević.[39] Then, in late June 2001, as the FRY's Constitutional Court blocked a government decree authorizing his transfer, Đinđić repudiated the court's action[40] and arranged for Milošević to be delivered to The Hague on June 28. Although Koštunica denied he knew about the transfer in advance, he reportedly acquiesced in it.[41] Immediately

---

[32] Foreign Operations Export Financing and Related Programs, Fiscal Year 2001, P.L. 106-249, § 594(a), (c), 114 Stat. 1900, 1900A-60 (2000). U.S. failure to certify cooperation with the ICTY would have cost the FRY $100 million in non-humanitarian financial assistance. *See* PESKIN, *supra* note 7, at 68. In principle, it should have also led to a loss of U.S. support for loans to Serbia by international financial institutions, but a 2008 report found that "Serbia's non-cooperation with the ICTY does not seem to have affected its access to international loans, such as those from the IMF and World Bank." STEVEN WOEHREL, CONDITIONS ON U.S. AID TO SERBIA 2, CONG. RES. SERV. (2008).

[33] *See* DEL PONTE WITH SUDETIĆ, *supra* note 27, at 108. The congressional deadline may also have been a factor in Koštunica's decision to establish a Serbian truth commission in late March 2001. The effort never got off the ground, with two members resigning almost immediately. *See* GORDY, *supra* note 2, at 67.

[34] *See* DEL PONTE WITH SUDETIĆ, *supra* note 27, at 110.

[35] *Id.*; *see also* JULIAN BORGER, THE BUTCHER'S TRAIL: HOW THE SEARCH FOR BALKAN WAR CRIMINALS BECAME THE WORLD'S MOST SUCCESSFUL MANHUNT 232–33 (2016).

[36] GORDY, *supra* note 2, at 15.

[37] DEL PONTE WITH SUDETIĆ, *supra* note 27, at 110.

[38] The United States linked its participation in the conference to the FRY taking concrete steps to cooperate with the Hague Tribunal. *See* Carlotta Gall, *Belgrade Begins Process of Sending Milošević to The Hague*, N.Y. TIMES (June 26, 2001); R. Jeffrey Smith, *Yugoslavia Moves to Extradite Milošević*, WASH. POST (June 24, 2001).

[39] *See* Gall, *supra* note 38; R. Jeffrey Smith, *Serb Leaders Hand Over Milošević for Trial by War Crimes Tribunal; Extradition Sparks Crisis in Belgrade*, WASH. POST (June 29, 2001).

[40] Đinđić justified the legality of his action by invoking Article 135(2) of the 1990 Constitution of the Republic of Serbia, which provided: "If acts of the agencies of the Federation or acts of the agencies of another republic, in contravention of the rights and duties it has under the Constitution of the Socialist Federal Republic of Yugoslavia, violate the equality of the Republic of Serbia or in any other way threaten its interests, without providing for compensation, the republic agencies shall issue acts to protect the interest of the Republic of Serbia."

[41] *See* Carlotta Gall, *Serbian Tells of Spiriting Milošević Away*, N.Y. TIMES (July 1, 2001). A former official in the Đinđić government told Viktor Peskin that Koštunica was aware of the arrest and

after Milošević's surrender, Serbia was rewarded with a pledge of $1.28 billion at the donor conference.[42]

The Đinđić government prepared Serbians to support the transfer by publicizing its discovery of mass graves in and around Belgrade of Kosovo Albanian victims, whose remains had been transported by Serbian police to hide evidence of Serbian war crimes.[43] Even so, Đinđić did not think it prudent to justify sending Milošević to The Hague in the language of moral obligation. Instead, Đinđić explained, surrendering Milošević would advance Serbia's economic prosperity and integration in the West: "Our country's place is in the international community."[44] The government's action was taken "not so much for ourselves and for our parents, but for our children. With this decision, we are saving the future of our children."[45]

Đinđić's reliance on pragmatic arguments became a touchstone for debate. Some regret his failure to initiate a national conversation about the crimes for which Milošević was charged, arguing, "Leaders need to lead. They need to grasp the moment."[46] Three years after the transfer, Serbian lawyer Bogdan Ivanišević, then working for Human Rights Watch, faulted Đinđić for "portraying cooperation [with the ICTY] as a means of avoiding economic isolation, rather than as a matter of justice."[47] In his view, this "did more harm than good: most Serbs came to see transfers of indictees to the Tribunal as a business transaction and reacted with revulsion."[48]

In another view, the fact that even Đinđić did not make a moral case for cooperation reflected the cultural politics that prevailed in Serbia and constrained his choices: Đinđić went as far as he could in post-Milošević Serbia, a country by no means eager to confront the moral burden of its immediate past. Indeed, Đinđić's rivals bitterly denounced his action, which Koštunica compared to the "lawless and hasty acts"[49] of the Milošević regime. "Those measures endanger our country,

---

extradition, but "pretended he did not know." PESKIN, *supra* note 7, at 70, quoting then Yugoslav interior minister and later prime minister of Serbia Zoran Živković.

[42] *See* Marlise Simons, *War Crimes Tribunal Expands Milošević Indictment*, N.Y. TIMES (June 30, 2001).

[43] *See* Laura Rozen, *Milošević Goes to The Hague*, SALON (June 28, 2001); Smith, *supra* note 28; BORGER, *supra* note 35, at 237. Julian Borger reports that on the eve of Milošević's transfer, Đinđić surprised Western officials by offering Ratko Mladić for arrest on the same day, provided they arrest Mladić themselves. But neither U.S. nor UK officials were prepared to dispatch troops to Serbia on such short notice, particularly on the basis of an unconfirmed tip about Mladić's location. BORGER, *supra*, at 290.

[44] Smith, *supra* note 28.

[45] Marlise Simons with Carlotta Gall, *Milošević Is Given to U.N. for Trial in War-Crime Case*, N.Y. TIMES (June 29, 2001).

[46] Confidential interview.

[47] Bogdan Ivanišević, *Softly-Softly Approach on War Crimes Doesn't Help Democracy in Serbia*, HUMAN RIGHTS WATCH (June 24, 2004).

[48] *Id.* Ivanišević added: "This, in turn, made cooperation [with the ICTY] more difficult and weakened the government." *Id.* Several scholars have made similar points. *See, e.g.,* PESKIN, *supra* note 7, at 71 ("to many Serbs, this cash-for-suspect transaction only confirmed their belief that international justice is inherently political. That perception was fueled by Đinđić, who justified cooperation not as a moral imperative, but as a way to obtain much needed American dollars."); JELENA SUBOTIĆ, HIJACKED JUSTICE: DEALING WITH THE PAST IN THE BALKANS 47 (2009) (Đinđić's pragmatic justification for the sudden transfer of Milošević "had significant consequences for the process of transitional justice in Serbia, as Serbian citizens came to see it as a business transaction and not an issue of justice").

[49] Simons with Gall, *supra* note 45.

its citizens, and also the damaged peace in our region," he charged.[50] But while Milošević's transfer provoked a crisis within the governing coalition,[51] it did not produce the destabilizing consequences predicted (and implicitly threatened) by Koštunica. In the view of Serbian rights activist Nataša Kandić, "Koštunica wasn't happy, but at that moment Đinđić had the political power to transfer Milošević."[52] Demonstrations against the action were relatively small and scarcely destabilizing.[53] Across a wide political spectrum, many Serbians were relieved to see Milošević removed from their midst.[54]

The public response marked a turning point. A former member of the Đinđić government explained: "Before the Milošević transfer, there may have been reluctance in some parts of the government to deal with this. After the transfer, we realized one can do that and can do much more in the eyes of the public."[55] On this occasion, "coerced cooperation" bolstered Serbian reformists.

The transfer had deep resonance for Serbians who hoped their country would break decisively with the poisonous policies of the past. In the words of Ivan Janković, Đinđić's action "had great symbolic value because it was a clear dissociation of the government from Milošević and everything he stood for."[56] Even if Đinđić did not say as much, his actions expressed a new commitment to moral practice.

Sending Milošević to The Hague did not, however, bridge divisions within the government about Hague cooperation,[57] and Đinđić hoped for a reprieve from pressure for further arrests.[58] Almost a year would pass before Belgrade would take significant steps toward further cooperation. In April 2002, the Yugoslav parliament finally enacted a long-stalled law on cooperation with the ICTY. But the law hardly sanctioned robust cooperation, authorizing the transfer only of Serbian nationals already indicted by the Tribunal.[59] Even so, between April and May 2002, five Serb suspects arrived in The Hague.[60] In May, the U.S. president certified that Serbia had satisfied conditions for U.S. economic assistance.[61]

---

[50] Id.

[51] See R. Jeffrey Smith, Extradition Causes Rift in Belgrade, WASH. POST (June 30, 2001).

[52] Interview with Nataša Kandić, then Executive Director, Humanitarian Law Center, in Belgrade, Serb. (Nov. 27, 2006).

[53] See Serbia Still Coming to Terms with Milošević, DEUTSCHE WELLE (Feb. 11, 2012).

[54] See Ian Fisher, Opinion Is Divided in Serbia over Handover of Milošević, N.Y. TIMES (Jan. 30, 2001).

[55] Interview with Dušan Protić, former Deputy Minister of Justice, in Belgrade, Serb. (Nov. 23, 2006).

[56] Interview with Ivan Janković, Attorney, in Belgrade, Serb. (Nov. 24, 2006).

[57] PESKIN, supra note 7, at 74.

[58] See Carlotta Gall, Serbian Tells of Spiriting Milošević Away, N.Y. TIMES (July 1, 2001).

[59] See Yugoslavia: Cooperation Law Inadequate, HUM. RTS. WATCH (Apr. 12, 2002); PESKIN, supra note 7, at 76. This aspect of the April 2002 law was amended in 2003.

[60] See PESKIN, supra note 7, at 77. Another source reports that six Serbs surrendered to The Hague in this period. WOEHREL, supra note 32, at 2. In his 2002 report to the UN General Assembly and Security Council, the president of the ICTY reported that nine accused came to the Tribunal from the Federal Republic of Yugoslavia, six of whom came voluntarily, from August 1, 2001, to July 31, 2002. Report of the International Tribunal for the Prosecution of Persons Responsible for Serious Violations of International Humanitarian Law Committed in the Territory of the Former Yugoslavia Since 1991, ¶ 227, U.N. Doc. A/57/379-S/2002/985 (Sept. 4, 2002).

[61] See PESKIN, supra note 7, at 77.

For the next three years, further arrests and transfers of ICTY suspects coincided with annual deadlines linking U.S. aid appropriated for Serbia to its satisfaction of criteria that included cooperation with The Hague. A Congressional Research Service (CRS) report aptly described Serbian cooperation from 2001 to 2005:

> Since the coming to power of Serbian democrats in late 2000, Serbian cooper-ation with the ICTY has followed a similar pattern each year: Serbia delivers several indictees to the Tribunal just before or, at most, a few weeks after the certification deadline. The Administration makes the certification as required by the legislation, and urges Serbia to do more. However, Serbian cooperation then slows, with Serbian leaders claiming that political and legal obstacles pre-clude greater efforts. Nevertheless, more indictees are delivered as the next deadline for certification approaches, and so on.[62]

As the CRS study suggests, even when Đinđić was prime minister the ICTY had to fight for every suspect Serbia produced. Its most wanted fugitive, Ratko Mladić, not only lived in Serbia, apparently from 1997[63] until his arrest in 2011,[64] but drew a pension from the Yugoslav Army—approved in 2002 by then president Koštunica—until December 2005.[65]

Several factors beyond the opposition of Koštunica[66] account for Serbia's con-tinued resistance to cooperation long after Milošević fell from power. First, hard-line nationalists who were strongly opposed to war crimes prosecutions constituted a substantial segment of Serbian political leaders and citizens.[67] For years, the ul-tranationalist Serbian Radical Party (SRS), whose founding leader was prosecuted in The Hague, had one of the largest voting blocs in national elections.[68] An article

---

[62] WOEHREL, *supra* note 32, at 2.

[63] *See* BORGER, *supra* note 35, at 283–84. It is not clear whether Mladić remained in Serbia continu-ously from 1997 until 2011. *See id.* at 303–04.

[64] Serbia's failure to arrest Mladić and transfer him to the ICTY was found to constitute a violation of the Convention on the Prevention and Punishment of the Crime of Genocide in a February 2007 judgment of the International Court of Justice. Case Concerning the Application of the Convention on the Prevention and Punishment of the Crime of Genocide (*Bosn. & Herz. v. Serb. and Montenegro*), Judgment, ¶¶ 448, 465, 471(6), 2007 I.C.J. (Feb. 26).

[65] *Serbian PM Koštunica Signed Mladić Retirement in 2002*, AGENCE FRANCE-PRESSE (Feb. 20, 2006). Following Mladić's arrest and transfer to The Hague in 2011, the Serbian government paid his family pension arrears that had accrued since 2005. *Serbia Unfreezes Mladić's Military Pension*, RFE/RL (June 7, 2011).

[66] Koštunica remained president of the FRY until it was succeeded by the state of Serbia and Montenegro in early 2003, having unsuccessfully sought the presidency of Serbia in 2002 during successive elections that failed to produce a winner. One year after he stepped down as president of the FRY, Koštunica became Serbia's prime minister in March 2004, and continued to serve as Serbia's prime minister after Montenegro became independent in June 2006. He resigned from this post in 2008, when the coalition government in which he served collapsed in the fallout from Kosovo's February 2008 declaration of independence from Serbia.

[67] *See* SERBIA AT THE CROSSROADS AGAIN, *supra* note 24.

[68] *See* Sabrina P. Ramet, *The Denial Syndrome and Its Consequences: Serbian Political Culture Since 2000*, 40 COMMUNIST & POST-COMMUNIST STUD. 41, 48 (2007) (parliamentary elections in 2003 revealed that "the most popular political party [was] the neo-fascist Serbian Radical Party"). Even after his trial began at the ICTY, Vojislav Šešelj led the SRS list of candidates for parliamentary elections slated for May 2008. *See Leader Indicted for War Crimes Tops Serb Ultranationalists' List for Parliamentary Elections*, ASSOCIATED PRESS (Mar. 26, 2008). In 2008, Šešelj's former deputy,

published in 2004–2005 began with this telling observation: "Indicted war criminals led at least three of the political parties vying for support in Serbia's parliamentary elections in December 2003, the first held since the downfall of former leader Slobodan Milošević."[69]

At times, developments in The Hague exacerbated constraints induced by Serbian electoral calculations. In late 2006, for example, SRS leader Vojislav Šešelj's hunger strike while in Hague custody "further burnished his nationalist . . . credentials and his electoral prospects" in advance of January 2007 parliamentary elections in Serbia.[70]

Proceedings at another court in The Hague, the International Court of Justice (ICJ), provided further cause for Serbian reluctance to cooperate with the ICTY. In 1993, Bosnia instituted a case against the FRY alleging responsibility for genocide. It would take almost fourteen years for the ICJ to issue its final judgment. As long as the case was pending, Serbian authorities feared ICTY evidence could increase Serbia's exposure in the ICJ case.[71]

A further, formidable obstacle to cooperation came from Serbia's security services, which played a key role in wartime atrocities.[72] Subordinated to Milošević in the 1990s, those services remained unreformed and powerful, and arguably became even more so after Milošević left office. In the assessment of Dejan Anastasijević, "while Milošević was in power, his secret police worked for him. After his demise, they chose not to allow anyone to boss them around."[73] The principal security service, the Security Information Agency (BIA), remained under the effective control of individuals allied with wartime paramilitaries and posed a credible threat to would-be reformists at least until 2008.[74] During this period, the BIA provided crucial support to Hague fugitives.[75]

Tomislav Nikolić, split from the SRS and formed a new party, taking with him many former leaders of Šešelj's party. *See Serb Opposition Leader Resigns*, BBC News (Sept. 7, 2008). For the first time since its founding in 1991, the SRS did not win any seats in Serbia's parliament in 2012. But it returned to parliament in 2016.

[69] Eileen Simpson, *Stop to The Hague: Internal Versus External Factors Suppressing the Advancement of the Rule of Law in Serbia*, 36 Geo. J. Int'l L. 1255, 1255 (2004–2005).

[70] Peskin, *supra* note 7, at 86.

[71] Controversially, the ICJ did not ask Serbia to provide unredacted copies of documents sought by Bosnia. Those documents had been provided by Serbia to the ICTY on the condition that portions Serbia believed would be harmful to its position in the ICJ genocide case would be withheld from the public record. *See* Marlise Simons, *Genocide Court Ruled for Serbia Without Seeing Full War Archive*, N.Y. Times (April 9, 2007). I discuss this episode further in Chapter 6.

[72] Dejan Anastasijević, *What's Wrong with Serbia?*, Eur. Stability Initiative (Mar. 31, 2008).

[73] *Id. See also* Jelena Obradović-Wochnik, *Strategies of Denial: Resistance to ICTY Cooperation in Serbia, in* War Crimes, Conditionality and EU Integration in the Western Balkans 30 (Judy Blatt & Jelena Obradović-Wochnik eds., 2009).

[74] *See* Tanja Nicolić-Đaković, *We Are Still Hostages of Secret Services*, Blic (April 15, 2007) reported by BBC Worldwide Monitoring (Apr. 19, 2007); *Belgrade Daily Slams State Security*, RTV B92 News (Belgrade), (Oct. 10, 2006) (summarizing *Blic* report); International Crisis Group, ICG Balkans Rep. 145, Serbian Reform Stalls Again 14–15 (2003) [hereinafter Serbian Reform Stalls Again]. In 2008, the reformist president Boris Tadić finally replaced Rade Bulatović, whom Koštunica had installed as head of the Security Information Agency, with someone "unburdened by nationalist political allegiances." Borger, *supra* note 35, at 252. Within days, Karadžić was arrested. *Id.* at 300.

[75] *See* Borger, *supra* note 35, at 272 (describing BIA's role in providing Radovan Karadžić false identity documents).

For a time, even Đinđić opted "to live in an uneasy coexistence with the security forces,"[76] which the fledgling government did not believe it could immediately dismantle. Đinđić had other reasons to abide one of the more notorious underworld criminals, Milorad ("Legija") Ulemek, a former special police commander whose infamous Special Operations Unit of Serbia's Secret Police, known as the Red Berets,[77] figured prominently in war crimes committed in Bosnia and later Kosovo.[78] The Serbian premier reportedly believed that, by switching his allegiance from Milošević to Đinđić in 2000, Legija had played a key role in enabling a peaceful transfer of power to take place.[79] In addition, Legija "played the lead role in arresting Milošević in March 2001 . . . on Đinđić's instructions."[80] Besides, with Koštunica commanding the support of the army, Đinđić reportedly relied on the former secret police as a counterpoint to Koštunica's military power base.[81]

By 2003, however, Đinđić moved to crack down on Legija and several organized crime groups, including the Zemun clan with which Legija was associated.[82] By one account, Đinđić saw this as "an important albeit risky way to remove domestic obstacles to political and economic reform."[83] On March 12, 2003, Đinđić's cabinet planned to sign warrants for the arrests of Legija and other leaders of his gang.[84] On that day Đinđić was assassinated. Suspicion immediately centered on Legija and the Zemun clan. On May 23, 2007, a three-and-a-half year trial resulted in the conviction of twelve codefendants, including Legija, for Đinđić's assassination.[85] Serbian prosecutors claimed the defendants wanted to prevent Đinđić from advancing in his campaign against organized crime, ensure no more war criminals were sent to The Hague,[86] and bring hard-line nationalists back to power.[87]

---

[76] Laura Silber, Opinion, *Serbia Loses More than a Leader*, N.Y. TIMES (Mar. 14, 2003).

[77] *See* Misha Glenny, *The Death of Đinđić*, N.Y. REV. BOOKS 32 (July 17, 2003).

[78] Since they were organized by Milošević in 1994, the Red Berets "had acted as paramilitary murderers in Bosnia and Kosovo; as a death squad inside Serbia; as the representatives of organized crime groups inside the Serbian state;" and as trainers of a Macedonian equivalent of the Red Berets. *Id.*

[79] *See id.* at 33; *see also* Daniel Simpson, *Serbs' Premier Is Assassinated; Led in Reforms*, N.Y. TIMES (Mar. 13, 2003).

[80] Michael Dobbs, *Pivotal Alliance Frayed Before Serb's Death*, WASH. POST (Mar. 14, 2003). *See also* Steven Erlanger, *Did Serbia's Leader Do the West's Bidding Too Well?*, N.Y. TIMES (Mar. 16, 2003).

[81] *See* Dobbs, *supra* note 80.

[82] *See* Misha Glenny, *The Death of Đinđić*, N.Y. REV. BOOKS 34 (July 17, 2003). *See also* BORGER, *supra* note 35, at 73 (describing Đinđić's reported decision to assess the criminal responsibility of the Red Berets for wartime conduct).

[83] PESKIN, *supra* note 7, at 79.

[84] *See* Daniel Simpson, *Serbs' Premier Is Assassinated; Led in Reforms*, N.Y. TIMES (Mar. 13, 2003).

[85] *See* Dušan Stojanović, *Milošević Militia Chief, 11 Others Guilty in '03 Killing of Serbian Premier*, ASSOCIATED PRESS (May 23 2007). In December 2008, the Supreme Court of Serbia confirmed the sentences of nine of the twelve who were convicted, including the forty-year sentence given to Legija, reducing the sentences of the other three. *See also Serbian Court Confirms Sentences for Đinđić's Killers*, SETimes (Dec. 30, 2008).

[86] *See* Douglas Hamilton, *Serb to Give Deadly Evidence in Assassination Trial*, REUTERS (Nov. 22, 2006).

[87] *See* Ellie Tzortzi, *Đinđić Verdict Will Leave Unanswered Questions*, REUTERS (May 22, 2007). Echoing the claims of the prosecutors, the Serbian court said the defendants "had conspired to

III. THE AFTERMATH OF THE ĐINĐIĆ ASSASSINATION

In the wake of the assassination, some blamed Western countries and the ICTY, saying they had pressed Đinđić too hard to transfer indicted war criminals to The Hague.[88] Fueling this perspective, just before the assassination a Belgrade paper reported the ICTY was about to bring charges against Legija[89] (although Legija was not, in fact, indicted by the ICTY, he reportedly was concerned about the possibility[90]). Some scholars would later cite the assassination as a prime example of the perils associated with external pressure on fragile democracies to ensure accountability for the wrongs of a prior regime.[91]

The general concern is valid and important. But it is by no means clear pressure on Serbia to cooperate with The Hague cost Đinđić his life. Although Đinđić's assassins said they acted to prevent their colleagues from being sent to The Hague, many believe their principal motivation was "to prevent a crackdown on organized crime" by Đinđić.[92] In a detailed account of the assassination, Eric Gordy describes a "major action against organized crime groups" underway in the lead-up to the assassination; in this setting, Legija proactively sought to discredit the accusations against him by tying them to the "ICTY and the influence of Western countries."[93] After the assassination, "[t]here followed a campaign to displace responsibility for the killing," a key strand of which was to blame the West for Đinđić's assassination. "The implicit blame placed on other countries," Gordy continues,

> carried a barely hidden political message—if the rest of the world would stop expecting things of Serbia, in particular a recognition of responsibility for what its previous regime had done, then the political violence would also stop. The message suggested an implicit threat as to what would happen if, conversely, expectations were to continue.[94]

---

kill Đinđić to halt his pro-Western reforms, bring Milošević's allies back to power and stop further extradition of war crimes suspects to the [ICTY]." *Serbian Court Convicts 12 in PM Assassination*, Associated Press (May 23, 2007).

[88] *See* Erlanger, *supra* note 80; *Serbia Still Coming to Terms with Milošević*, Deutsche Welle (Feb. 12, 2012); Peskin, *supra* note 7, at 81.

[89] Interview with Antonela Riha, Journalist, in Belgrade, Serb. (Nov. 27, 2006).

[90] Interview with Radmila Dragičević-Dičić, Judge, District Court of Belgrade, Organized Crime Division, in Belgrade, Serb. (Nov. 21, 2006); interview with Antonela Riha, Journalist, in Belgrade, Serb. (Nov. 27, 2006). *See also Ulemek Feared Hague*, RTV B92 News (Belgrade) (Mar. 27, 2007).

[91] *See, e.g.*, Jack Snyder & Leslie Vinjamuri, *Trials and Errors: Principle and Pragmatism in Strategies of International Justice*, 28 Int'l Security 5, 23 (2003–2004).

[92] Interview with Ivan Jovanović, then National Legal Advisor, OSCE Mission to Serbia, in Belgrade, Serb. (June 6, 2007). *See also* Morton Abramowitz, Opinion, *Snatching Defeat in the Balkans*, Wash. Post (Jan. 7, 2004) (Đinđić "was killed not because he sent Milošević to The Hague for trial but because he was preparing a crackdown on some of the criminal elements that continue to wield influence in post-Milošević Serbia"); Ivan Đorđević, *The Current Security Situation in Serbia: Challenges Following the Assassination of Prime Minister Đinđić*, 2 Q.J. 39 (2003) (then chief of staff of Serbian Ministry of Internal Affairs attributes assassination to Đinđić government's crackdown on organized crime). Mladen Ostojić bridges these perspectives, writing that the assassins' primary motives "related to [Đinđić's] attempt to tackle organized crime," but "the perceived threat of the Hague tribunal within the armed forces had created a political climate which made this action possible." Ostojić, *supra* note 7, at 78.

[93] Gordy, *supra* note 2, at 70–71.

[94] *Id.* at 81.

When I interviewed him in 2012, the late Srđa Popović, an attorney and activist who represented Đinđić's mother and sister in criminal proceedings against the assassins, rejected the notion Đinđić would still be alive had he not been pressed to surrender suspects to The Hague. In conflict with Koštunica on virtually every fundamental issue,[95] Popović said, Đinđić became a marked man when he lost control of the secret police in November 2001:

> [Đinđić] held the secret police, but just for one year because [the Zemun clan] organized a rebellion in November of 2001 and were able to install their own people as heads of the BIA. And from then on he was an easy target, and [an] obvious target. And he knew it.

In larger perspective, Popović continued, "I don't think [Đinđić] needed to be pressured to do what he did," as he very much "wanted to complete the revolution that was started on October Fifth. It has something to do with ICTY, of course, but with everything else as well. He was talking about lustration. He was talking about the '90s. He was talking about how the whole society was criminalized by Milošević."[96] Still others believe the "real problem" was not that Western governments pressed Đinđić too hard on ICTY cooperation but that government leaders, including Đinđić, did not make adequate efforts sooner to crack down on organized crime, allowing criminal elements to regroup.[97]

---

[95] During my interview with him and in many of his writings, Popović emphasized the existential conflict between Koštunica and Đinđić over the meaning of "October the Fifth," a reference to the collapse of the Milošević regime on that day in 2000. Popović made the point this way:

> [A]fter Milošević fell, [. . .] the state itself was divided between Koštunica and Mr. Đinđić. One was the prime minister, the other was president of the republic. They were as different as you can imagine on *every* point. But the main political argument between them was how to interpret October the Fifth. That was the fight—the interpretation of what happened really. Did we close this chapter of the '90s? Are we clear on Milošević's responsibility? Are we clear about the war crimes? Are we clear about ICTY? And [the two leaders were] diametrically opposed. So The Hague was just one element in this more general, "Are we going into European Union or are we creating ties with Russia?"

Interview with the late Srđa Popović, Attorney, in Belgrade, Serb. (July 9, 2012).
[96] *Id.*
[97] Telephone interview with Bogdan Ivanišević, Attorney (Nov. 3, 2006). Dejan Anastasijević made a similar point: "It was a problem with the revolution in Belgrade. It didn't go far enough." Interview with Dejan Anastasijević, Journalist, in Belgrade, Serb. (Nov. 20, 2006). When I interviewed her in 2006, Jadranka Jelinčić said she was "suspicious of this argument" that Đinđić was "pushed too hard." In 2000, she recalled, the international community was pushing "to make sure Serbia is doing something[;] to develop a policy." Interview with Jadranka Jelinčić, Executive Director, Open Society Fund Serbia, in Belgrade, Serb. (Nov. 24, 2006). Jelinčić added: "Of course there were some moments when more understanding would be helpful, but overall I don't buy the argument that the West pushed too hard. The government has to be responsible." *Id.* Six years later, when we revisited the subject, Jelinčić said that, in light of all the actors who might have wished to remove Đinđić, "we cannot say with certainty" whether a different approach vis-à-vis cooperation with The Hague would have made a difference. But, she said, "I am certain that it would have been better if the international community had been more imaginative in offering prospects for Serbia . . . politically and economically." Interview with Jadranka Jelenčić, Executive Director, Open Society Fund Serbia, in Belgrade, Serb. (July 9, 2012).

There is little dispute about the short-term impact of Đinđić's assassination: public shock triggered a brief but significant period of reform, which included a crackdown on organized crime and renewed cooperation with the ICTY[98] (amidst, it should be noted, concerns about violations of human rights during a state of emergency imposed after the assassination[99]). Summarizing developments in this period, the International Crisis Group wrote:

> In the immediate aftermath of the [Đinđić] shooting, public commitments to cooperate with The Hague Tribunal were made; the army began to be put under civilian control; the highest-profile organised crime gang and parts of the Milošević-era parallel security structures were dismantled; several dozen prominent murders, many dating back to the old dictator's time, were solved; and the new union of Serbia and Montenegro was admitted to the Council of Europe. All this should have happened quickly after Milošević's fall in October 2000, but the reform agenda had been blocked by nationalist forces around former Yugoslav President Vojislav Koštunica until February 2003.[100]

Officials who had previously hesitated to press for cooperation with the ICTY now pledged to support it. As one commentator explained, "Zoran Đinđić's tragic death gave the post-Milošević authorities a kind of a social consensus to face and deal with war crimes."[101] During this period, the ruling coalition used its temporary emergency powers to amend the 2002 Law on Cooperation with the Hague Tribunal, which had previously prevented Serbia from transferring nationals indicted by ICTY after its enactment.[102] In the four months following Đinđić's assassination, four fugitives in Serbia surrendered to the ICTY and a fifth was arrested by authorities of Serbia and Montenegro and transferred to The Hague.[103] The government increased other forms of cooperation as well: for the first time, it "sign[ed] waivers releasing former officers from their obligations to maintain state secrets and permitting [them] to testify," and "turned over unspecified quantities of documents to the ICTY."[104]

The new cooperation reflected a temporary convergence of interests between The Hague and Belgrade. The Tribunal gained custody of individuals who had

---

[98] See Peskin, *supra* note 7, at 81. *But see* Subotić, *supra* note 48, at 76–77, for a more sober assessment of how the assassination affected Serbian politics.

[99] See *Serbia: Emergency Should Not Trump Basic Rights*, Hum. Rts. Watch (Mar. 25, 2003); Amnesty International, Serbia and Montenegro: Alleged Torture During "Operation Sabre" (2003).

[100] Serbian Reform Stalls Again, *supra* note 74, at i. *See also* Borger, *supra* note 35, at 168–69.

[101] Milanka Saponja-Hadžić, *Regional Report: Serbs Finally Back Hague Cooperation*, IWPR (May 29, 2003). Public approval of Slobodan Milošević, whose popularity had surged at the outset of his trial in The Hague, dropped precipitously in the wake of the assassination. *See* Florian Bieber, *The Show and the Trial: The Political Death of Milošević*, in The Milošević Trial: An Autopsy 419, 423 (Timothy William Waters ed., 2013).

[102] See *Report of the International Criminal Tribunal for the Prosecution of Persons Responsible for Serious Violations of International Humanitarian Law Committed in the Territory of the Former Yugoslavia Since 1991*, ¶ 243, U.N. Doc. A/58/297-S/2003/829 (Aug. 20, 2003).

[103] See *id.*, ¶ 232.

[104] Serbian Reform Stalls Again, *supra* note 74, at 4.

"participated in all sorts of paramilitary formations, war crimes, and crimes against humanity. Some turned out to be the actual perpetrators of unbelievably heinous crimes."[105] Belgrade was able to rid itself of two senior Milošević-era security officials, Jovica Stanišić and Franko Simatović, whose continued presence was seen as a threat to the post-Đinđić government.[106]

Public opinion polls showed that, for the first time since the ICTY was established, a majority of the Serbian public favored cooperation with the Tribunal.[107] It was also during this period that the Serbian parliament adopted legislation, which had originated in the Đinđić government, establishing specialized courts to deal with organized crime and war crimes, respectively.[108] The burst of reformist zeal was short-lived, however. Before long, the new government's crackdown on organized crime "gave way to the kind of conflicts and scandals characteristic of the everyday life of a weak government in an unstable state."[109]

By late 2003, moreover, pressure for cooperation with The Hague may have contributed to reformist parties' electoral loss, though any negative fallout was short-lived. During a visit to Belgrade in October 2003, Del Ponte informed then acting prime minister Zoran Živković, a Đinđić ally, of new indictments against four Serb generals. Živković warned that if she went public with the indictments, pro-reformists would pay the price in upcoming presidential and parliamentary elections. Rasim Lajić, the government official formally responsible for ICTY cooperation, warned Del Ponte the right-wing SRS would win the December 2003 parliamentary elections if she went public before the poll.[110] Del Ponte nonetheless unsealed the indictments on October 20, 2003.[111] One month later, the SRS received the largest percentage of votes (47.87) in presidential elections, as well as in parliamentary elections (27.33) in late December 2003.[112] The Radicals' then deputy leader and presidential candidate, Tomislav Nikolić, proclaimed the parliamentary victory a "clear message from the citizens of Serbia that patriotic forces and the anti-Hague lobby have prevailed."[113]

We cannot know if Del Ponte's action changed the outcome of the 2003 elections, but it almost certainly did not help the reformists. Even so, the SRS did not lead the new government: With less than a majority of votes cast for any candidate, the

---

[105] Miloš Vašić, *Patriots by Trade, Criminals by Persuasion; Operation Sabre Illuminates the Overlap of Interests of the ICTY and the Serbian Justice System*, TRANSITIONS ONLINE (Prague) (May 15, 2003).

[106] LAMONT, *supra* note 7, at 71–72; PESKIN, *supra* note 7, at 81. In addition, Đinđić asked Del Ponte to "[t]ake Šešelj," the provocative leader of the SRS, "to the Hague . . . and don't bring him back!" Mirko Klarin, *The Impact of the ICTY Trials on Public Opinion in the Former Yugoslavia*, 7 J. INT'L CRIM. JUST. 89, 91 (2009).

[107] *See* Saponja-Hadžić, *supra* note 101.

[108] *See* SUBOTIĆ, *supra* note 48, at 57. I explore this development in Chapter 10.

[109] GORDY, *supra* note 2, at 85–86.

[110] RAJKOVIĆ, *supra* note 7, at 78.

[111] *Id*. Del Ponte reportedly was pessimistic by then about Živković's commitment to cooperation. PESKIN, *supra* note 7, at 82.

[112] *See* SERBIA AT THE CROSSROADS AGAIN, *supra* note 24, at 8; *see also* IFES, Election Guide, http://www.electionguide.org/elections/id/1908/ (last visited Dec. 9, 2017).

[113] RAJKOVIĆ, *supra* note 7, at 80. While the Radicals' strong performance was understandably worrying, it should be placed in context. Florian Bieber believes the party's success in the 2003 vote can be linked in part to the fact that, with its ultranationalist leader's surrender to The Hague earlier that year, the "more moderate-sounding" Nikolić had ascended to leadership. In addition, Bieber writes, voters endorsed the SRS "mostly due to dissatisfaction with contemporary reforms rather than a desire to resurrect the 1990s." Bieber, *supra* note 101, at 429.

presidential election was annulled. Boris Tadić, who favored cooperation with the ICTY and EU integration, was elected president in a new election held on June 27, 2004.[114] Despite placing first in parliamentary elections, the SRS was unable to form a coalition government. After extended negotiations, Koštunica, whose party won the second-highest number of votes, was able to form a minority government in March 2004.[115] For the next ten months, cooperation with The Hague "amounted to zero," in the words of then U.S. Ambassador-at-Large for War Crimes Issues Pierre Prosper.[116] By January 2005, however, "the message of electoral doom associated with ICTY compliance rapidly and remarkably dissipated."[117]

IV. THE CARROT OF EUROPEAN INTEGRATION

Beginning in late 2004, the Serbian government once again ramped up efforts to secure transfers of indictees to The Hague. By then, as noted, the reformist candidate of the Democratic Party, Boris Tadić, had been elected president. From the outset of his presidency Tadić supported cooperation with the ICTY.[118] But as president of a "highly dysfunctional state run by a minority government based on a shaky coalition,"[119] with Koštunica holding the more powerful position of prime minister and controlling key security sectors,[120] Tadić was unable to ensure full and immediate cooperation with the The Hague. Even so, his election made a palpable difference.

Soon after Tadić became president, Koštunica reconsidered his approach to cooperation. Bridging the positions of coalition partners who pressed for cooperation and hardline nationalists who supported the minority government, Koštunica advanced a new policy of "voluntary surrenders" by Hague fugitives.[121] (In the words of Koštunica's political party, "arrests were not an option."[122]) The period from December 2004 to late Spring 2005 saw what Del Ponte described as "a rapid, almost phantasmagoric, series of voluntary surrenders. All at once, fugitives poured forth from Serbia and the Republika Srpska."[123] In her completion strategy report to the UN Security Council in June 2005, Del Ponte described a "major change" in Serbian cooperation: access to witnesses and documents had been "continuously improving" and Serbia had transferred fourteen fugitives to the Tribunal since December 2004.[124]

---

[114] See SERBIA AT THE CROSSROADS AGAIN, *supra* note 24, at 5.

[115] See JULIE KIM, SERBIA: 2004 PRESIDENTIAL ELECTIONS 2, CONG. RES. SERV. (2004).

[116] RAJKOVIĆ, *supra* note 7, at 81. *See also* PESKIN, *supra* note 7, at 83.

[117] RAJKOVIĆ, *supra* note 7, at 2.

[118] See Boris Tadić, Opinion, *Serbia's Fresh Start*, WASH. POST (July 24, 2004). *See also* SUBOTIĆ, *supra* note 48, at 77.

[119] SERBIA AT THE CROSSROADS AGAIN, *supra* note 24, at 5.

[120] See INTERNATIONAL CRISIS GROUP, EUR. BRIEFING NO. 46, SERBIA'S NEW GOVERNMENT: TURNING FROM EUROPE 8 (2007).

[121] OSTOJIĆ, *supra* note 7, at 89.

[122] LAMONT, *supra* note 7, at 72. As Julian Borger notes, under this policy "very few surrenders were truly voluntary." BORGER, *supra* note 35, at 172. Some suspects who "voluntarily surrendered" were abducted and then dispatched to The Hague. *See id.* at 172–73. The ICTY unit that tracked fugitives considered the surrender of Vojislav Šešelj in February 2003 to be the only truly voluntary surrender during the Koštunica era. *Id.* at 173.

[123] DEL PONTE WITH SUDETIĆ, *supra* note 27, at 316. According to Mladen Ostojić, between October 2004 and September 2005, the policy of "voluntary surrenders" brought sixteen suspects to The Hague. OSTOJIĆ, *supra* note 7, at 90.

[124] U.N. SCOR, 60th Sess., 5199th mtg., at 12, U.N. Doc. S/PV.5199 (June 13, 2005).

Once again, the surge in cooperation could be traced in large part to inducements from the West. In 2005, as in previous years since 2001, the United States conditioned aid to Serbia and Montenegro on transfers of fugitives to The Hague. The prospect of receiving most-favored-nation trade status in the United States, which Serbia thought important to its struggling textile sector, provided further incentive for cooperation.[125] Most important at that time, in January 2005, then European Union (EU) Commissioner on Enlargement Ollie Rehn explicitly linked Serbia's cooperation with the ICTY to its integration into the EU.[126] Nine days later, a high-ranking suspect, Vladimir Lazarević, announced he would voluntarily surrender to The Hague.[127] From that point on, EU conditionality played a more consequential role in securing Serbian cooperation than U.S. pressure.[128]

The uptick in compliance did not, however, signify a watershed in Serbia's moral reckoning with the past. During his presidency, Tadić took a series of significant steps to address wartime atrocities, which are described in Chapter 7. But when it came to selling cooperation to the Serbian public, he, like Đinđić, emphasized the benefits of EU accession rather than Serbia's responsibility to ensure justice for unconscionable crimes. In December 2004, for example, Tadić argued that "without cooperation there is . . . no entry into the EU, no increase in the standard of living. Our poverty rate will rise, we will have no political stability, so long as we are excluded from the international community."[129]

For his part, Koštunica framed his new support for cooperation with the ICTY in terms that divested the policy of moral meaning—or, more precisely, ensured it did not signify remorse for Serbia's role in monstrous crimes. Where Đinđić and Tadić played down the moral case for cooperation, Koštunica called for voluntary surrenders by Serb "patriots," whose brave sacrifice would make it possible for Serbia to advance toward EU membership. The surrender of Lazarević exemplifies this approach. When the retired Serbian general announced he would surrender to the ICTY after meeting with Koštunica, the government released a statement saying the prime minister and other government officials "personally, all appreciate and respect this patriotic, highly moral and honorable decision made by General Lazarević."[130]

---

[125] SUBOTIĆ, *supra* note 48, at 50.

[126] *See* DEL PONTE WITH SUDETIĆ, *supra* note 27, at 316; Dobbels, *supra* note 5, at 10.

[127] RAJKOVIĆ, *supra* note 7, at 83. Lazarević was transferred to The Hague in early February 2005. *ICTY Press Release, Transfer of General Lazarević* (Feb. 3, 2005), http://www.icty.org/en/press/ transfer-general-vladimir-lazarevic.

[128] Although the EU had long called for cooperation with the ICTY, it did not make cooperation a precondition to any specific reward until 2005. Dobbels, *supra* note 5, at 28; *see also id.* at 14. Until then, "[i]t was the US government which had the biggest impact on Serbia's policy of cooperation." *Id.* Dobbels argues that European conditionality began having an effect earlier as a result of an EU summit in Thessaloniki in June 2003. In a declaration adopted at that summit, the European Council committed itself to support integration of Western Balkan states and reiterated the need for cooperation with the ICTY as a condition of further integration. *See id.* at 8–9, 11.

[129] RAJKOVIĆ, *supra* note 7, at 82 (citing B92 NEWS, Dec. 9, 2004).

[130] Nicolas Wood, *Ex-Serbian General Agrees to Surrender to War Crimes Tribunal*, N.Y. TIMES (Jan. 29, 2005). The *Times* article described pressure preceding Lazarević's announcement:

> A refusal by the European Union's high representative for foreign and security policies, Javier Solana, to visit Belgrade last week, and a cut of $10 million in aid by the United States

The statement continued: "The Serbian prime minister said he was convinced that by making this decision General Lazarević acted in accordance with the long tradition of the Serbian Army to have its officers always fight for the interest of his people and of his country."[131] With good reason, the Belgrade-based Humanitarian Law Center protested that, even as the government induced suspects to surrender to the ICTY, it "strengthen[ed] the public's notion of an 'unjust' tribunal."[132] Depicting the indictees as martyrs sacrificing themselves for Serbia, Koštunica inspired portions of the Serbian public to identify and empathize with them.[133] Goran Svilanović, who served as foreign minister in 2000–2004, described the impact of Koštunica's rhetoric this way: "So what has happened [is] we have created a dynamic in which our war criminals have become 'ours'. . . . This is such a political setback, a dramatic setback, for the idea of international war crimes trials."[134]

In other respects, cooperation would now come on Koštunica's terms: Serbian authorities offered financial rewards to ICTY suspects who surrendered "voluntarily" as well as "considerable material compensation for the[ir] families."[135] Koštunica's practice of securing "voluntary surrenders" was part of a broader policy he called "two-way cooperation" between The Hague and Belgrade.[136] Calling for this approach when he was sworn in as prime minister in 2004, Koštunica signaled that other elements of the two-way relationship would include the Tribunal granting provisional release to Serbian indictees, with the Serbian government providing

---

appeared to place additional pressure on the government to act. A European Union delegation is also in Serbia and Montenegro making its last visit before publishing the results of a feasibility study on the country's application for membership.

Id.

[131] *Id.* Two government ministers accompanied Lazarević to the plane that would take him to The Hague. Ramet, *supra* note 68, at 50–51. Years later, the Serbian government would again stoke controversy through its treatment of Lazarević, who was given a hero's welcome when he returned to Belgrade in December 2015 after serving two-thirds of his 14-year sentence. Lazarević reportedly was the first Hague convict to be accompanied home by Serbian cabinet ministers. *See* Marija Ristić, *Serbia Welcomes Freed Yugoslav Army War Criminal*, Balkan Transitional Just. (Dec. 3, 2015). Two years later, the Serbian government again drew international criticism when Lazarević was invited to lecture at the military academy in Belgrade. *See Hague-Convicted General Starts Lecturing at Military Academy*, B92 News (Oct. 26, 2017).

[132] Humanitarian Law Center, Transitional Justice Report: Serbia, Montenegro and Kosovo, 1999–2005, at 9 (2006).

[133] Ostojić, *supra* note 7, at 93.

[134] *Id.* at 93–94.

[135] Humanitarian Law Center, *supra* note 132, at 9. *See also* Ostojić, *supra* note 7, at 92; Rod Nordland, *Pensions for Patriots*, Newsweek (June 25, 2005). In 2004, the Serbian parliament enacted a law providing for payment of salaries to and legal expenses of indictees, along with compensation for their families. The law's implementation was suspended pending a legal challenge, but the government's policy of seeking voluntary surrenders through financial inducements rather than arresting fugitives continued. *See Serbian PM Encouraging Hague Indictees to Surrender with Tycoon Money—Ex-Minister*, HINA Croatian News Agency (Mar. 27, 2005). According to a former Serbian justice minister, much of the financing for the rewards came from "money acquired through the institutionalized racketeering of businessmen and tycoons connected with crime." *Id.*

[136] *See Koštunica Outlines Tough Stance on Hague Cooperation*, news from RTV B92 News (Mar. 2, 2004); *Hague Arrests Not an Option, Say Government*, news from RTV B92 News (Jan. 17, 2005).

guarantees that they would appear in court when their trials began,[137] and the transfer of cases from the ICTY to local courts in Serbia.[138]

In a familiar pattern, the surge in "surrenders" produced tangible rewards; before long, Serbian cooperation would stall again. On the "reward" side of the 2005 cycle, in May 2005, the EU opened Stabilisation and Association Agreement (SAA) talks with Belgrade, a gateway toward EU membership.[139] But Serbia's late 2004–2005 burst of cooperation proved short-lived. With SAA talks underway, Belgrade once again put a brake on cooperation.[140] In the view of Nikolas Rajković, the government's new "hesitancy could be explained to some extent in terms of its own political vulnerability."[141] Among myriad factors behind this perception, the ultranationalist SRS, whose founding leader was awaiting trial in The Hague, was "not only the most popular party but, further still, could form the next government."[142] In addition, the sudden death of Milošević in March 2006 toward the end of his years-long trial in The Hague "only further politicized discussion of the Tribunal within Serbian politics."[143] Even so, in early 2006 Koštunica pledged he would arrest Mladić, now a primary focus of EU efforts; for its part, the EU warned it would suspend SAA talks if Belgrade did not follow through.[144] On May 3, 2006, the EU suspended negotiations in light of Serbia's failure to cooperate with the ICTY.[145]

So far, this account has highlighted the interaction of two variables that account for recurring cycles of Serbian cooperation—Western conditionality on the one hand, and domestic political commitments and constraints on the other. By 2007, an additional factor played a key role in the way EU conditionality was implemented: European unity began to fray. The reasons had less to do with different views among EU Member States about the desirability of arresting fugitives than a dynamic integral to policymaking *within* governments—the need to reconcile a raft of policy objectives. In 2007, a high priority for many European governments was persuading Serbia to accept the inevitable independence of Kosovo at a time when

[137] *See* Eric Jansson, *Serbian Premier Calls for War Crimes Dialogue*, FIN. TIMES (Apr. 8, 2004); *see also* PESKIN, *supra* note 7, at 84.

[138] *See* Cooperation Between Belgrade and Hague Tribunal Should Be Two-Way, Ministry of Foreign Affairs, Serbia and Montenegro, Dec. 10, 2004, http://www.mfa.gov.yu/Policy/Multilaterala/UN/activities_e/icty/111202_e.html. In Chapter 10, I describe how the transfer of cases and dossiers from The Hague to Belgrade actually developed.

[139] *See Serbia Turns a Corner as EU, Hague Give OK*, REUTERS (Sept. 29, 2005).

[140] More specifically: "No further arrests or transfers were made; documents were largely unavailable or inaccessible; witnesses were hard to find." Gareth Evans & James Lyon, Opinion, *No Mladić, No Talks*, INT'L HERALD TRIB. (Mar. 21, 2007). Along with Montenegro and Bosnia-Herzegovina, Serbia was nonetheless admitted into NATO's pre-membership Partnership for Peace in late November 2006, apparently in the hope this would strengthen Serbia's pro-reform sector in the lead-up to parliamentary elections and as the international community prepared to decide on the future status of Kosovo. *See NATO Brought Serbia into Pre-Membership Program to Boost Moderates, Diplomat Says*, ASSOCIATED PRESS (Dec. 3, 2006); Brian Knowlton & Helene Cooper, *Serb's Letter Persuades U.S. to Drop NATO Bar*, INT'L HERALD TRIB. (Dec. 1, 2006).

[141] RAJKOVIĆ, *supra* note 7, at 87.

[142] *Id.* Also, the party of Milošević, whose parliamentary support Koštunica relied upon, declared it would rethink its support for the government if it arrested Mladić. *Id.*

[143] *Id. See also* PESKIN, *supra* note 7, at 85–86.

[144] PESKIN, *supra* note 7, at 86.

[145] *See Please Let Us Join Your Club; Renewed Questions over the Balkans' Future in the European Union*, ECONOMIST (May 6, 2006).

long-protracted negotiations over the territory's status were exhausted without an agreed solution.[146] (In a move vehemently opposed by Serbia, Kosovo declared independence on February 17, 2008.[147])

Added to the policy mix, Europe was confronting worrying signs of robust nationalism in Serbia and wanted to "help the Balkan nation break with its nationalist past."[148] In parliamentary elections held on January 21, 2007, the ultranationalist SRS won the largest number (29.07 percent[149]) of votes cast for any party, and Serbia's parliament selected SRS leader Tomislav Nikolić, who had "presided over rallies feting war criminals,"[150] to be its speaker the following May[151] (though he was forced to resign five days later.)[152] Astute analysts found more cause for encouragement than concern in the election results: in contrast to previous elections, the democratic bloc of parties won an absolute majority, and its liberal wing saw a significant gain in seats.[153] As worrying as the SRS's showing was, moreover, its representation in parliament actually declined by one seat.[154] To others, however, the strong showing of nationalist parties was "a resounding victory for the right wing," in the words of then ICTY Prosecutor Del Ponte.[155]

In this setting, a substantial and growing bloc of European states thought it prudent to ease up on EU insistence that Serbia send Mladić to The Hague as a condition for resuming SAA negotiations.[156] So, too, did EU Enlargement Minister Ollie Rehn, who signaled in March 2007 that SAA talks might be revived if Belgrade showed "a clear commitment" to arrest and transfer ICTY fugitives.[157]

Throughout 2007 and early 2008, what can seem like arcane details of EU procedure—whether, for example, to resume SAA talks, initial an SAA agreement, or conclude one—were the subject of pitched battles among actors who shared a core commitment to justice. For the Tribunal's prosecutor and human rights advocates,

---

[146] To forestall worst-case scenarios threatened by Serbia in the event Kosovo declared independence, reports in December 2007 suggested "Brussels has given a green light for Serbia to become an EU member-candidate through the signing of an SAA" in January 2008, even if Serbia failed to apprehend Mladić. Susanne Simon, *EU Agreement Even Without Surrendering Mladić; Stability More Important than Arrest of War Criminals*, DIE WELT (Dec. 18, 2007). *See also* Ingrid Melander & Mark John, *EU Agrees to Send Mission to Kosovo*, REUTERS, Dec. 13, 2007; Dan Bilefsky, *U.S. and Germany Plan to Recognize Kosovo*, N.Y. TIMES (Jan. 11, 2008); Sandra Lavenex & Frank Schimmelfennig, *Relations with the Wider Europe*, 46 J. COMMON MKT. STUD. 145, 151 (2008).

[147] *See* Dan Bilefsky, *In a Showdown, Kosovo Declares Its Independence; Serbians Express Rage*, N.Y. TIMES (Feb. 18, 2008).

[148] *EU, Serbia Restart Pre-accession Talks After Yearlong Hiatus*, ASSOCIATED PRESS (June 13, 2007). *See also* PESKIN, *supra* note 7, at 86.

[149] IFES, Election Guide, http://www.electionguide.org/elections/id/1908/ (last visited Dec. 9, 2017).

[150] Dan Bilefsky, *Nationalist Wins Serbian Presidency, Clouding Ties to the West*, N.Y. TIMES (May 20, 2012).

[151] PESKIN, *supra* note 7, at 88.

[152] *See Serbian Ultra-Nationalist Resigns as Assembly Speaker*, DEUTSCHE PRESSE-AGENTUR (May 13, 2007).

[153] *See* Eric Gordy, *Serbia's Elections: Less of the Same*, OPEN DEMOCRACY (Jan. 23, 2007).

[154] *Id.*

[155] DEL PONTE WITH SUDETIĆ, *supra* note 27, at 345.

[156] *See* Lavenex & Schimmelfennig, *supra* note 146, at 151; Dobbels, *supra* note 5, at 14–15.

[157] Anna McTaggart et al., *In Depth: EU Split on Fast-Track Serbian Membership*, BALKAN INSIGHT (Mar. 16, 2007).

the matter was clear: the EU must not waver in demanding Mladić's arrest before resuming negotiations (or, once they lost that battle, before concluding an SAA agreement). Meeting with the EU's foreign policy chief, Javier Solana, in late January 2007, Del Ponte argued EU conditionality had played a crucial part in securing custody of former fugitives.[158] "Now," she said, "is the crucial moment to get Mladić." Noting "Spain, Italy, Slovenia, Austria, Hungary and others want to resume the [SAA] talks because of Kosovo," Del Ponte argued: "This will have the worst possible effect."[159] As 2007 progressed, few EU states supported her position, eventually leaving only The Netherlands and Belgium in Del Ponte's camp.[160]

Through a new push for arrests in mid-2007, Belgrade provided other European states and EU officials sufficient grounds for resuming SAA talks. Revived cooperation with The Hague followed the formation of a new government in May, with Koštunica serving as prime minister alongside President Tadić.[161] At the end of May, less than a week before Del Ponte was to visit Serbia, authorities in Belgrade and Republika Srpska launched a successful operation to arrest Zdravko Tolimir, then the third-most wanted ICTY fugitive,[162] who would later be convicted of genocide and sentenced to life in prison.[163]

Del Ponte proclaimed her June 2007 visit to Serbia (her first at the invitation of the Serbian government) "the best" she had in her eight years as prosecutor, in part because she thought the government would arrest Mladić "within the next three months."[164] Instead, Serbia produced a different fugitive in an apparent bid to cooperate no more than necessary to revive SAA talks.[165] The European Commission

---

[158] Del Ponte told Solana: "Ninety percent of our accused are in custody thanks to the European Union." DEL PONTE WITH SUDETIĆ, *supra* note 27, at 347. Although widely-cited, this estimate is exaggerated. Some thirty-five suspects from Serbia and Republika Srpska were transferred to The Hague before EU conditionality became the most influential incentive for Serbian transfers, the overwhelming majority prompted by U.S. conditionality. Email from Nina Bang-Jensen, Former Executive Director, Center for International Justice, to Diane Orentlicher (Aug. 21, 2017).

[159] DEL PONTE WITH SUDETIĆ, *supra* note 27, at 347.

[160] *See* Stephen Castle, *Negotiations Put Europeans Closer to Pact with Serbia*, N.Y. TIMES (Apr. 28, 2008). Later, The Netherlands was the sole EU Member insisting on Mladić's surrender as an absolute requirement. *See* Dan Bilefsky & Doreen Carvajal, *Fewer Protect Serb Wanted in War Crimes; European Union Bid Tied to Mladić Case*, N.Y. TIMES (Oct. 22, 2010).

[161] By one account, President Tadić agreed Koštunica could remain on as prime minister if he, in turn, would agree to cooperate with the ICTY. Nicholas Wood, *New Round of EU Talks with Serbia Confirmed; In a Turnaround, Belgrade Shifts Its Focus to the West*, INT'L HERALD TRIB. (June 8, 2007).

[162] Immediately after Tolimir's arrest, EU enlargement commissioner Olli Rehn indicated SAA negotiations between the EU and Belgrade might resume soon. Sara Goodman, *Is Tolimir Arrest Evidence of New Cooperation?*, IWPR (June 1, 2007). On June 7, 2007, the EU confirmed it would resume SAA negotiations. *See* Wood, *supra* note 161.

[163] Prosecutor v. Tolimir, Case No. IT-05-88/2-T, Trial Judgment, ¶¶ 1173, 1176, 1242 (Int'l Crim. Trib. for the Former Yugoslavia Dec. 12, 2012). While overturning some counts for which Tolimir had been found guilty at trial, the ICTY Appeals Chamber affirmed his genocide convictions and sentence. Prosecutor v. Tolimir, Case No. IT-05-88/2-A, Appeal Judgment ¶ 649 (Int'l Crim. Trib. for the Former Yugoslavia Apr. 8, 2015).

[164] *See* Wood, *supra* note 161. Later, however, Del Ponte wrote her meeting with Koštunica during that visit "was not a pleasant encounter," and that she "was not at all sure" she could trust Koštunica's assurance he had the political will to arrest Mladić. DEL PONTE WITH SUDETIĆ, *supra* note 27, at 360–61.

[165] Within weeks of Del Ponte's visit, Serbian authorities played a major part in securing the arrest of Vlastimir Đorđević, who was found in Montenegro. Acting on intelligence provided by the

announced SAA negotiations would resume on June 13[166] and initialed an SAA agreement in November,[167] but said it would postpone final signature until Serbia achieved "full cooperation" with the ICTY.[168] In the months that followed, Del Ponte, advocacy groups, and others intensified efforts to forestall a final SAA agreement until Serbia dispatched Mladić to The Hague, fearing Europe was about to squander what leverage remained to secure his arrest.[169]

Ultimately, a still-divided EU reached a series of compromises that augmented the electoral prospects of pro-European candidates and parties. Following an inconclusive presidential election in January 2008, in which the SRS candidate received more votes than the moderate incumbent, Boris Tadić,[170] a significant number of EU states sought to bolster Tadić's prospects by signing the SAA as he headed into a runoff. But they were blocked by The Netherlands, which continued to insist on the transfer of Mladić.[171]

Unusually, by that time there were also divisions within civil society about how to approach the issue. Some organizations (not only within Serbia but also outside) continued to oppose SAA progress until Mladić was arrested, while others advocated immediate signing of the SAA. In a letter to EU Member States and officials dated January 18, 2008, nineteen Serbian organizations argued that "any postponement in signing the [SAA] would only play into the hands of [Serbia's] conservative and nationalistic forces which are leading the country towards self-isolation and away from

---

ICTY, Serbian intelligence services reportedly helped track down Đorđević, whom Serbian media had previously reported to be hiding in Russia. Serbian and Montenegrin authorities disputed how long the fugitive had lived in Montenegro. *See* Douglas Hamilton, *Charges Fly after Serb Fugitive's Surprise Arrest,* Reuters (June 18, 2007). After this arrest, only four ICTY suspects remained at large. *See* Peskin, *supra* note 7, at 90. In addition to its mid-2007 arrests, Serbia made a show of trying to arrest Mladić. In October 2007, for example, the government offered a reward of €1,000,000 (approximately $1.4 million) for information leading to Mladić's arrest. *See Serbia: $1.4 Million Reward Offered for Fugitive General,* N.Y. Times (Oct. 13, 2007). Serbian authorities also periodically staged raids on the homes of individuals thought to be harboring Mladić and arrested alleged members of his support network. *See* Peskin, *supra* note 7, at 87. In retrospect, however, it seems likely these actions were designed to send signals to the fugitive so he could go deeper underground.

[166] Nicholas Wood, *After Key Arrest by Serbia, European Union Is to Reopen Talks,* N.Y. Times (June 8, 2007); Lavenex & Schimmelfennig, *supra* note 146, at 153.

[167] In the following months, there was speculation the EU might even offer to sign the agreement with Serbia in late January 2008, potentially putting Serbia on a fast track toward membership. *See EU Leaders Clash over Kosovo, Serbia,* Deutsche Press-Agentur (Dec. 14, 2007).

[168] Rajković, *supra* note 7, at 90. As noted below, to the extent this condition meant arresting Mladić, it was later relaxed.

[169] *See, e.g., Call for Tougher Approach to Serbia,* Press Ass'n (June 13, 2007) (reporting remarks of former High Representative for Bosnia Lord Paddy Ashdown); *Serbia Not Fully Cooperating with UN War Crimes Court: Prosecutor,* Agence France-Presse (Oct. 15, 2007); Eric A. Witte & Kurt Bassuener, *Holding the Reins of Balkan Justice,* 13 Eur. Voice (Sept. 13, 2007); *EU/Serbia: Don't Compromise on Mladić: EU Should Insist on Full Cooperation with Yugoslav Tribunal,* Hum. Rts. Watch (Nov. 6, 2007). *See also* James Lyon, Opinion, *Conceding to Serbia Is a Risky, Short-Term Strategy,* Fin. Times (Oct. 2, 2007) (arguing "a hard international line," including on Serbia's duty to hand over war criminals, "is the only political cover Serbia's 'democrats' have and . . . whenever the west lowers its standards, the 'democrats' inevitably suffer and nationalists profit").

[170] In the first ballot on January 20, 2008, SRS candidate Tomislav Nikolić received 40.76 percent of the votes against the incumbent President Tadić's 36.08 percent. *See* IFES, Election Guide, http://www.electionguide.org/elections/id/2061/ (last visited Dec. 9, 2017).

[171] Gjeraqina Tuhina, *EU Offers New Deal to Serbia,* Balkan Insight (Jan. 31, 2008).

the rule of law and accountability."[172] While emphasizing "Serbia still has an obligation to fully and unconditionally cooperate with the ICTY," the signatories argued that, as "all other possibilities to influence positive developments in Serbia have been exhausted," signing the SAA would provide desperately-needed incentive for Serbia to reignite its stalled democratic transition.[173]

In a compromise, EU states agreed to offer Serbia an unprecedented political agreement, "providing a framework for cooperation on free trade, visa liberalization and educational exchanges," which would be signed February 7.[174] By offering benefits that would appeal to Serbian citizens but were not in the SAA, the offer sought to signal in advance of elections that Serbia had a future in Europe without shortchanging the matter of Mladić's arrest. The gambit worked: by a slim margin, Tadić won the runoff on a platform of strengthening Serbia's ties with Europe.[175] Prime Minister Koštunica denounced the EU package as a ploy to induce Serbian acquiescence in Kosovo's independence.[176] Deeply divided, the Serbian government collapsed in March and scheduled parliamentary elections for May 11, 2008.[177]

A similar standoff among EU Members played out as Serbia headed toward the May vote. In late March, The Netherlands and Belgium drew a line in the sand, saying they opposed steps to make Serbia an EU candidate until it delivered Karadžić and Mladić to The Hague.[178] A month later, however, the two countries agreed to another compromise. Serbia could sign the SAA now, but would not "see the rewards of the SAA deal, such as funds, until it is deemed to be fully cooperating with the Hague Tribunal."[179] On April 29, 2008, Serbia signed the deal.[180]

---

[172] Letter to EU Member States, President of the EU Commission, EU High Representative for Foreign Policy and Security, and EU Commissioner for Enlargement, from 19 Serbian civil society organizations, Jan. 18, 2008 (on file with author).

[173] *Id.* Two of the organizations that signed onto this letter, Women in Black and Civic Initiatives, had previously signed a letter urging the EU to hold firm in demanding full cooperation with the ICTY as a precondition to concluding an SAA with Serbia. *See* Letter from the Humanitarian Law Center, Youth Initiative for Human Rights, Women in Black, and Civic Initiatives to EU Member State leaders, Apr. 2, 2007 (on file with author).

[174] *EU: Serbia Offer Still on the Table*, BALKAN INSIGHT (Mar. 10, 2008); *see also Ball Now in Serbia's Court on EU Ties: Denmark*, AGENCE FRANCE-PRESSE (Jan. 30, 2008).

[175] *See* Dan Bilefsky, *Pro-West Incumbent Wins Serbia's Presidential Runoff*, N.Y. TIMES (Feb. 4, 2008).

[176] *See* Dan Bilefsky, *Rift over Closer Ties to Europe Ignites Serbian Political Crisis*, N.Y. TIMES (Feb. 6, 2008). According to the *New York Times*, Koštunica "appeared to have hardened his stance partly because the European Union [had just] approved plans to send a police and judicial mission to take over administration of Kosovo from the United Nations." *Id.*

[177] *See Election Time: The Government Quits, Paving the Way for an Early Election*, ECONOMIST (Mar. 2008).

[178] *Belgium, Netherlands Against EU Warming to Serbia; Want War Crimes Suspects in Court First*, ASSOCIATED PRESS (Mar. 28, 2008).

[179] *EU Signs Pre-membership Deal with Serbia*, BALKAN INSIGHT (Apr. 29, 2008). An article in the *New York Times* indicated that, under the compromise agreement, the SAA would not be signed until June, and would not take effect until Serbia fully cooperated with the ICTY. Stephen Castle, *Negotiations Put Europeans Closer to Pact with Serbia*, N.Y. TIMES (Apr. 28, 2008). But the agreement was signed the following day. While press accounts are somewhat muddled, a source within the OTP provided this clarification in a confidential communication in early May 2008: "On 29 April, the Council issued two separate decisions. In the first, it stated that the SAA Interim Agreement would only enter into force if the Council finds that there is full cooperation with the ICTY. . . . In another binding decision, the Council decided that the SAA will only be ratified by national parliaments once the Council decides that there is full cooperation with the ICTY."

[180] *See Tadić Travels to Luxembourg for SAA Signing*, RTV B92 NEWS (Apr. 29, 2008).

Koštunica condemned the signing, saying it amounted to recognition of Kosovo's independence.[181] Others denounced it for rather different reasons, calling it a "blow to the Bosnian victims and their families" and a costly surrender of principle, sacrificing Europe's most important inducement for Serbia to arrest Mladić.[182] Once again, however, Europe's calculation paid off: Tadić's commitment to EU accession, coupled with Europe's inducements in the lead-up to the May vote,[183] are widely thought to have propelled his party to first place.[184]

As for cooperation with the ICTY, those who argued Europe relinquished powerful leverage to secure Mladić's near-term arrest could claim history proved them right: it would take several more years for Serbia to arrest him. Yet the election of a pro-European president and government led to other high-profile arrests in short order: Serbia arrested one of four remaining fugitives, Stojan Župljanin, as post-election negotiations over the formation of a new government ensued.[185] Soon after the new government was formed, the ICTY received long-awaited news: on July 21, 2008, Serbian authorities announced they had arrested wartime Bosnian Serb leader Radovan Karadžić, who had been living under an assumed identity in suburban Belgrade.[186] EU leaders saw the arrest as validation for their strategy, noting their pragmatic approach had given Tadić the crucial edge in elections and asserting, "[i]f not for the current government in place, we wouldn't have Karadžić in The Hague."[187]

---

[181] Simon Jennings, *EU-Serbia Agreement Sparks Controversy*, IWPR (May 9, 2008).

[182] *Id.*

[183] In addition to the April 29, 2008, SAA signing, two other developments may have contributed to the outcome of the May 11, 2008 vote: First, shortly before the elections seventeen European countries eased their visa fees for Serbian citizens. *See* Oana Lungescu, *Serbs to Have Easier Travel in EU*, BBC News (May 6, 2008). Second, the Italian auto manufacturer Fiat signed a memorandum of understanding to buy a plant in Serbia that, when implemented, would represent a major investment. *See* Colleen Barry, *Fiat Signs Agreement to Buy Zastava Car Plant in Serbia*, Associated Press (Apr. 30, 2008); *Serbian Election Watchdog Expects High Turnout Following SAA, Fiat Deal*, BBC (May 6, 2008). For economic reasons, implementation of the Fiat deal was delayed until late 2009. *The Balkans and the European Union: Lightening Gloom?*, Economist (Jan. 2010).

[184] *See* Jasna Dragović-Soso, *Apologising for Srebrenica: The Declaration of the Serbian Parliament, the European Union and the Politics of Compromise*, 28 East Eur. Pol. 173, 169 (2012). Although pre-election polls had placed the SRS ahead of other parties, it received only 29 percent of the vote, with the party of President Tadić winning approximately 39 percent. *See Nationalist Premier of Serbia Teams Up with Radical Party*, Reuters (May 14, 2008); Dan Bilefsky, *Tilt to West Is Seen in Elections in Serbia*, N.Y. Times (May 12, 2008). When a new government was formed, a member of Tadić's party succeeded Koštunica as prime minister. Dan Bilefsky, *Serbs Set Up Government That Favors the West*, N.Y. Times (July 8, 2008). The new government resulted from "an unlikely alliance" between Tadić's pro-West party and the Socialist Party, previously led by Milošević. Dan Bilefsky, *Serbs Choose New Premier for Coalition*, N.Y. Times (June 28, 2008).

[185] *See* Ivana Sekularac & Dina Kyriakidou, *Serbia Arrests Top Bosnian Serb War Crimes Fugitive*, Reuters (June 11, 2008).

[186] *See* Dan Bilefsky & Marlise Simons, *Bosnian Serb Under Arrest in War Crimes*, N.Y. Times (July 22, 2008). Karadžić's Belgrade lawyer claims he was actually arrested several days before July 21 and held incommunicado until his arrest was announced. *See Deadline for Appeal of Bosnian's Extradition Passes*, Associated Press (July 26, 2008).

[187] Stephen Castle & Steven Erlanger, *Quiet Pressure Behind EU Success*, N.Y. Times (Europe) (July 22, 2008) (quoting Cristina Gallach, spokeswoman for then-EU foreign policy chief Javier Solana). *See also* Dan Bilefsky, *Karadžić Arrest Is Big Step for a Land Tired of Being Europe's Pariah*, N.Y. Times (July 23, 2008) (some experts say pivotal moment leading to Karadžić's arrest came on eve of parliamentary elections in late April 2008, when the EU allowed Serbia to sign SAA agreement, even though it had not yet fulfilled conditions for full benefits).

Karadžić's impunity had lasted so long, Serbians who had tirelessly sought his arrest were "in shock" when it finally happened.[188] What had long seemed inconceivable soon became fact: Karadžić was transferred to The Netherlands on July 30, 2008,[189] and made an initial appearance before the ICTY the next day.[190] His arrest, a long-time Serbia observer wrote, was "[m]ore than just the closing of a chapter of bloody history[;] it is a signal about the future. The newly formed government in Belgrade is demonstrating that it is serious about bringing Serbia into the European fold."[191]

Recalling Karadžić's arrest years later, Serbians interviewed for this study rued the sensational way his capture was covered by the local media. Instead of in-depth stories about the atrocities for which he was charged, which might have advanced a Serbian reckoning with the past, gossipy media reports focused on Karadžić's life under cover as "David Dabić," a faith healer with flowing locks.[192] Yet the arrest of Karadžić also signified progress in Serbian responsibility for ensuring justice. Notably, upon his arrest Karadžić was brought before Serbia's War Crimes Chamber, by then five years old.[193] In accordance with Serbian law, the chamber ruled Karadžić could be transferred to the ICTY. That a Serbian court cleared the legal path for Karadžić's transfer to the ICTY stood in striking contrast to the circumstances of Milošević's transfer to The Hague seven years earlier, in defiance of the country's constitutional court and in the face of then president Koštunica's strident opposition.[194] This time, the transfer of a notorious Serb fugitive took place *through* Serbian judicial process.

It would take another three years for Serbia to meet what had become the ultimate test of cooperation with The Hague—arresting Ratko Mladić. On the afternoon of May 26, 2011, then president Tadić called an "urgent news conference" in which he confirmed Mladić had been arrested "on the soil of the Republic of Serbia" that morning. Tadić said: "Today we closed one chapter of our recent history that will help us one step closer to reconciliation in the region." Not incidentally, he suggested, the arrest would ease Serbia's entry into the European Union: "I believe that the doors for Serbia to join the EU are open."[195]

---

[188] Bilefsky & Simons, *supra* note 186 (quoting Nataša Kandić).

[189] *See* Peter Finn, *Karadžić Extradited to The Hague to Face War Crimes Charges*, WASH. POST (July 30, 2008).

[190] *See* Marlise Simons, *Karadžić Calmly Hears Tribunal's Charges of Genocide and War Crimes*, N.Y. TIMES (Aug. 1, 2008).

[191] Laura Silber, Opinion, *Serbia's Arresting Development*, L.A. TIMES (July 23, 2008).

[192] *See* Dragana Erjavec, *Biserko: Serbia Still "At War', Using Other Means*, JUSTICE REP. (Nov. 4, 2009). International press coverage also featured lengthy stories about Karadžić's life under cover. *See, e.g.*, Nicholas Kulish & Graham Bowley, *The Double Life of an Infamous Serbian Fugitive*, N.Y. TIMES (July 23, 2008).

[193] *See* Bilefsky & Simons, *supra* note 186. The ICTY's role in catalyzing the creation of this chamber is explored in Chapter 10.

[194] *See* Simons with Gall, *supra* note 45.

[195] *Ratko Mladić Arrest—Thursday 26 May 2011*, GUARDIAN: NEWS BLOG (May 26, 2011). *Time Magazine* reported:

> Aptly, Mladić's capture occurred on the eve of the release of a report on Serbia's coopera-tion with the ICTY, which will now be rewritten, and on the day E.U. Foreign-policy chief Catherine Ashton was in Belgrade. After news of Mladić's arrest broke, Ashton herself indicated that Brussels would meet the challenge laid down by Serbia's president. "People will be thinking about Serbia and its future in the European Union," she said. "We will approach that with renewed energy because of today."

Leo Cendrowicz, *After Mladić's Arrest, the E.U. Whispers Sweet Nothings to Serbia*, TIME (May 28, 2011).

Notably, the arrest resulted from close and intense collaboration between the Tadić government and the Office of the Prosecutor (OTP) of the Hague Tribunal. Reflecting on the process culminating in Mladić's capture, OTP Chief of Operations Bob Reid told me: "We worked really, really closely, we had a really good working relationship" with Serbian authorities, functioning as a virtually unified team.[196] Against Serbia's previous policy of defiance, its collaboration with the OTP was remarkable.

Yet the new collaboration did not signify a broad social movement to confront the crimes with which Mladić was charged. Much as media reporting on Karadžić's arrest focused on sensational aspects of his life as a fugitive, press coverage of Mladić's arrest focused on such trivia as "whether he asked for strawberries" as he awaited transfer to the ICTY.[197] As Jadranka Jelinčić observed, "nobody spoke about his deeds, his crimes, *why* he was wanted by the ICTY."[198] Then, once Mladić was transferred to The Hague, "the story was over."[199] To Jelinčić, this signified that, "all in all, once Serbia accepted that all those charged should be transferred . . . , Serbia was happy to fulfill the quota to solve the problem. But [when it comes to exploring] other questions, the public is not so much interested."[200] Nor did then president Tadić use the occasion of Mladić's arrest to raise these questions. While repeatedly invoking Serbia's "moral responsibility," he did not elaborate on its nature or the crimes for which Mladić was charged.[201] (As elaborated in Chapter 7, however, Tadić used other occasions to express remorse for Serb atrocities.)

Less than two months after Mladić's arrest, Serbia arrested the last ICTY fugitive, Goran Hadžić, and transferred him to The Hague.[202] His arrest came three months before EU leaders would decide whether to open membership talks with Serbia.[203] Announcing Hadžić's arrest, Tadić said: "With this, Serbia has now concluded its most difficult chapter in the cooperation with The Hague tribunal."[204] Serbia had, in his words, fulfilled its "legal duties" as well as its "moral duty."[205] In March 2012, Serbia gained EU candidacy status.[206]

---

[196] Interview with Bob Reid, Chief of Operations, Office of the Prosecutor, ICTY, in The Hague, Neth. (May 28, 2015). As a U.S. government official during the final year and a half of Serbia's push to apprehend Mladić, I closely observed the collaboration Reid described.

[197] Interview with Jadranka Jelinčić, Executive Director, Open Society Foundation Serbia, in Belgrade, Serb. (July 9, 2012).

[198] *Id.*

[199] *Id.*

[200] *Id.*

[201] Marlene Spoerri & Mladen Jokšić, *The Ethics of a Justice Imposed: Ratko Mladić's Arrest and the Costs of Conditionality*, CARNEGIE COUNCIL ETHICS INT'L AFF. (June 2, 2011). ICTY Prosecutor Serge Brammertz called on Serbia's leaders to "help the public understand why Ratko Mladić has been arrested and why justice demands that he stand trial." Serge Brammertz, Prosecutor of the International Criminal Tribunal for the Former Yugoslavia, Address at the UN Security Council (June 7, 2011).

[202] *See* Marlise Simons, *Serbia Arrests Its Last Fugitive Accused of War Crimes*, N.Y. TIMES (July 20, 2011).

[203] *See id.*

[204] *Id.*

[205] *Id.* The ICTY ultimately dismissed the case against Hadžić in light of his terminal illness. Hadžić died in July 2016. *Goran Hadžić, 58, Ex-chief of Rebel Serbs*, N.Y. TIMES (July 14, 2016).

[206] *See European Neighbourhood Policy and Enlargement Negotiations: Serbia*, EC, http://ec.europa. eu/enlargement/countries/detailed-country-information/serbia/index_en.htm (last visited Sept. 18, 2017).

Soon afterward, amidst widespread concerns about economic stagnation, unemployment (estimated at 24–25 percent), corruption, and "authoritarianism" during his tenure,[207] Tadić was voted out of office. His rival in two previous elections, Tomislav Nikolić, was elected president (by then, Nikolić had split from the SRS and now espoused a pro-European stance).[208] While substantial issues of cooperation with the ICTY did not, in fact, end with Hadžić's arrest,[209] Serbia's relationship with the Tribunal in the post-Tadić years, as well as its approach to broader questions of accountability, are more productively addressed in later chapters.[210]

V. CONCLUDING OBSERVATIONS

That all of the ICTY's indictments eventually were answered is widely seen as a landmark achievement, and understandably so: the Tribunal's sister court, the International Criminal Tribunal for Rwanda, formally closed at the end of 2015 with eight suspects still at large,[211] while nine suspects facing charges before the International Criminal

---

[207] Dan Bilefsky, *Nationalist Wins Serbian Presidency, Clouding Ties to the West*, N.Y. TIMES (May 20, 2012). *See also* Dan Bilefsky, *Next Premier of Serbia Is from Party of Milošević*, N.Y. TIMES (July 26, 2012). In protest against Tadić's record, some Serbian citizens cast "white ballots" during elections on May 6, 2012. Although opposed to Nikolić, they could not bring themselves to vote for Tadić either. *See* Charles Recknagel, *As Serbia Votes, a Sense of Déjà Vu*, RFE/RL (May 5, 2012).

[208] *See Protest Days; Angry Demonstrations Reflect Some Deep-Seated Grievances*, ECONOMIST (Apr. 23, 2011).

[209] Although the arrest of Hadžić ended demands for the arrest and transfer of accused war criminals, the ICTY continued to request information from Serbia in connection with ongoing cases. Soon after former SRS leaders assumed leadership positions, the new Serbian government assured ICTY Prosecutor Brammertz it would continue to cooperate with the Hague Tribunal. Marija Ristić, *ICTY Chief Prosecutor Meets Serbia's New Government*, BALKAN TRANSITIONAL JUST. (Oct. 9, 2012). Following the November 2012 acquittal of the ICTY's top Croatian suspect, which provoked bitter denunciations from Serbia, however, Belgrade reduced cooperation with the ICTY to a "technical level." *See* Enis Zebić et al., *Croatian Joy, Serbian Anger at Gotovina Acquittal*, IWPR (Nov. 19, 2012). The Serbian government continued to cooperate with the OTP by providing evidence. As of late May 2015, an ICTY official told me, "if we need anything, we get it immediately. . . . So on the technical level, nothing really changed. . . . If we needed documentation, yeah, it was business as usual." Interview with Bob Reid, Chief of Operations, Office of the Prosecutor, ICTY, in The Hague, Neth. (May 28, 2015). But Serbia's minister of education canceled an ICTY outreach project in Serbian high schools. Interview with Georgia Tortora, Chief of Communications, MICT, in The Hague, Neth. (May 28, 2015); interview with Almir Alić, Liaison Officer, Registry, ICTY, in Sarajevo, Bosn. & Herz. (Sept. 12, 2014). As previously noted, moreover, Serbia has continued to defy an ICTY request for the arrest and transfer of three (later two, as a result of the death of one) individuals to stand trial on contempt charges for allegedly threatening witnesses in the trial of Vojislav Šešelj, as well as "judicial orders . . . to provide updates to the Tribunal on its efforts to execute the arrest warrants." *Report of Serge Brammertz, Prosecutor of the International Tribunal for the Former Yugoslavia, Provided to the Security Council under Paragraph 6 of Security Council Resolution 1534 (2004)*, ¶ 15, U.N. Doc. S/2016/976, Annex II (Nov. 17, 2016). *See also* Marija Ristić, *Serbian Court Refuses to Extradite Wanted Radicals*, BALKAN TRANSITIONAL JUST. (May 18, 2016).

[210] Chapter 7 explores the degree to which Serbian authorities and society have forthrightly acknowledged and condemned the country's role in 1990s atrocities, while Chapter 10 explores the development and record of Serbia's war crimes prosecutor and chamber.

[211] *See* Laura Heaton, *Last Days for UN Court Trying Suspects in Rwanda Genocide*, N.Y. TIMES (Dec. 14, 2015). Of the eight remaining fugitives, three were expected to be tried by the MICT if apprehended, while the ICTR Prosecutor recommended that the others be referred for trial in

Court were at large as of December 2017.[212] Against Belgrade's resistance to cooperation with the Hague Tribunal, Western policies of conditionality were, overall, a remarkable success. Even so, the protracted delay in arresting Karadžić and Mladić profoundly diminished Bosnian survivors' satisfaction with Hague justice and may have exacted a more enduring toll on Bosnia's recovery from calamitous conflict.[213]

The overall impact of conditionality on Serbia's political transition is more challenging to assess. At certain times, Western conditionality seemed to bolster nationalists, at least in the immediate term. Yet it also enlarged the space in which reformists could advance their agendas. Western diplomats in Belgrade, including one who was hardly a fan of U.S. conditionality requirements, have said moderates in the post-Milošević government "used conditionality to win internal arguments."[214]

Moreover the arrests of several high-profile fugitives, secured through conditionality, removed spoilers from Serbia's political landscape. In the view of Filip Švarm, if Serbia's leading war criminals had not been prosecuted in The Hague, "we would have had a mafia oligarchy as our leaders."[215]

Even so, some believe Western conditionality diminished Serbians' willingness to reckon with wartime atrocities, a process the ICTY's champions in Serbia hoped it would help advance.[216] By "diverting the dynamics of national discussion away from past wrongs to a national fixation on the fruits of ICTY compliance," the argument runs, conditionality made it "harder for Serbia to come to terms with its role in past wrongs."[217] Yet it is hardly clear Serbia would have undertaken a robust reckoning had it not been pressed to surrender suspects. Throughout the post-Milošević era in Serbia, "there . . . existed . . . a strong undercurrent of general public reluctance towards any kind of open discussion of the 1990s wars and war crimes."[218] As elaborated later, some Serbians believe that, without the issue of cooperation pushing wartime atrocities into the headlines, citizens would not have addressed wartime depredations even to the extent they did during the first decade of the twenty-first century.[219]

A related question is whether policies of conditionality could have been implemented more effectively. As we have seen, on several occasions the EU deftly managed its dual objectives of securing arrests of Hague fugitives and advancing Serbia's democratic transition by bolstering moderate political leaders. A key question is whether it could have done so more consistently. In the view of Jadranka Jelinčić, there is little doubt: "It would have been better if the international

---

Rwanda. *See* United Nations Mechanism for International Criminal Tribunals, *Searching for the Fugitives*, http://www.unmict.org/en/cases/searching-fugitives (last visited Dec. 9, 2017).

[212] *See* ICC website, https://www.icc-cpi.int/Pages/cases.aspx?k=at%20large (last visited Dec. 9, 2017).

[213] *See* Chapter 2.

[214] Email from Nina Bang-Jensen, Former Executive Director, Coalition for International Justice, to Diane Orentlicher (Aug. 21, 2017).

[215] Interview with Filip Švarm, Journalist, in Belgrade, Serb. (Nov. 24, 2006). *See* Chapter 5.

[216] *See* Chapter 5.

[217] Spoerri & Jokšić, *supra* note 201. *See also* LAMONT, *supra* note 7, at 175–76 (the experience of both Croatia and Serbia suggests "consequentialist approaches to human rights regime enforcement may undermine human rights norm internalization as compliance is no longer perceived as a legal obligation but rather a subject of inter-state negotiation").

[218] Obradović-Wochnik, *supra* note 73, at 32.

[219] I explore this question in Chapter 7.

community had been more imaginative in offering prospects for Serbia . . . politically and economically."[220]

A distinct question is whether Hague officials could have done more to link their insistence on arrests with core values underpinning the Tribunal's work. In the view of former FRY foreign minister Goran Svilanović, the answer is clear. Svilanović faults then-Prosecutor Carla del Ponte for relentlessly insisting on surrenders without conveying a fundamental message: that "this should never happen again."[221] To be sure, Svilanović added, the government he served "missed the opportunity" to convey a moral message behind cooperation with The Hague itself—"absolutely."[222] Whether Serbians would have seen cooperation in a different light had Del Ponte emphasized the values underlying Hague prosecutions is unknowable.[223] But Svilanović is surely right that an ICT's officials should consistently voice a moral message, particularly when the very meaning of its work is deeply contested.

---

[220] Interview with Jadranka Jelenčić, Executive Director, Open Society Fund Serbia, in Belgrade, Serb. (July 9, 2012). As noted in several later chapters, improved economic prospects may make it more likely a society will confront a difficult past. At the same time, the very rigidity of Western conditionality—and the timing of its adoption, when Western countries' support for the ICTY was high—may have been necessary to its success. Nina Bang-Jensen makes the case this way:

> [H]ad the U.S. or other member states of the UN waited until more nuanced instruments (careful diplomacy, cajoling with more targeted packages of carrots and sticks, non-legislated or more flexible conditionality) were developed, the moment to produce defendants . . . might have been lost. Hitting while the political support [for the Tribunal] was arguably at its peak and could have been quickly lost was important.

Email from Nina Bang-Jensen, Former Executive Director, Coalition for International Justice, to Diane Orentlicher (Aug. 21, 2017).

[221] Interview with Goran Svilanović, Former Minister of Foreign Affairs, FRY, in Belgrade, Serb. (Nov. 20, 2006).

[222] Id.

[223] As previously noted, Del Ponte's successor, Serge Brammertz, pressed Serbian authorities to convey a moral message when announcing arrests.

PART TWO

Measuring ICTY Success

Local Perspectives

4

Some Kind of Justice

Bosnian Expectations of the ICTY

My mind is very overburdened with sad things. . . . We just trust in God and justice. I am glad there is justice. . . . .

—Sadik Trako[1]

Justice will never be reached—just a little satisfaction.

—Fatima Fazlić[2]

[S]urvivors in Bosnia want atrocity trials.

—Lara J. Nettelfield[3]

Bosnia is filled with survivors of harrowing crimes, and with the graves of loved ones they lost.[4] No measure of redress can restore lives shattered by ethnic cleansing, but many survivors "desperately need justice."[5] Asta Zinbo, who worked with survivors searching for missing relatives, made the point this way: "They weren't just hit by a

---

[1] Interview with Sadik Trako, President, Association of Victims and Missing Persons in Lašva Valley, in Vitez, Bosn. & Herz. (Dec. 6, 2006).

[2] Interview with Fatima Fazlić, President, Izvor, in Prijedor, Bosn. & Herz. (July 23, 2009).

[3] Lara J. Nettelfield, Courting Democracy in Bosnia and Herzegovina: The Hague Tribunal's Impact in a Postwar State 278 (2010).

[4] In the words of Nihad Ključanin, "the map of our land is covered with graves." Ed Vulliamy, *Bosnia's Survivors Gather and Grieve as the Soil Endlessly Gives Up Its Dead*, Guardian (Aug. 8, 2015). *See also* Selma Jatić, *22 Years After the War: Exhumations, Postmortem Identifications and Collective Burials Remain a Reality in Bosnia*, RTV Slon (Apr. 21, 2017). As of late July 2017, more than 6,500 victims of the Srebrenica massacre were buried in the cemetery in Potočari. *See* Humanitarian Law Center, *Newsletter No. 16*, 16 Through Accession Towards Just. 2 (2017).

[5] Interview with Mirsad Tokača, President, Research and Documentation Center (Sarajevo), in Sarajevo, Bosn. & Herz. (Dec. 6, 2006).

bus. Someone did terrible things many times over. . . . People don't expect perfect justice but they want some kind of justice."[6] If victims did not expect perfect justice, many had "great, great expectations of international justice" when the Tribunal was launched.[7] In this chapter I explore the kind of justice they expected the ICTY to provide—the benchmarks, if you will, by which they would assess its successes and failures—and their evolving expectations of justice over time.

Several preliminary points merit brief mention. While I interviewed individuals from each major ethnic group in Bosnia, the experiences of Bosniaks loom especially large in this chapter. The principal reason follows from this chapter's focus, the benchmarks of Tribunal "success" in the eyes of Bosnians who support its work. From the beginning of the Tribunal's life, Bosniaks, who suffered the vast majority of atrocities committed in the 1990s conflict,[8] have been significantly more likely than other Bosnians to embrace the ICTY.[9]

Second, particularly in light of grievous crimes committed in Bosnia *based on victims' ethnicity*, exploring victims' perspectives through an ethnic lens raises nettlesome questions. My natural inclination mirrors that of many Bosnians whom I interviewed, who made it clear that, precisely because of the lethal effects of ethnic mobilization in the 1990s, they were loath to identify themselves as anything other than Bosnian or Yugoslav (to be clear: I did not ask anyone their ethnicity but some of my sources raised this point). To do otherwise, they believed, would affirm the pernicious premise of ethnic cleansing.

Yet it is impossible to provide a meaningful account of Bosnian expectations of Hague justice without recognizing the role of ethnicity in shaping them. Bosnia's ethnic divisions refract across myriad social and political spheres. Among them, most civil society organizations advocating on behalf of wartime victims comprise members of a single ethnic group.[10] More to the present point, ethnic cleavages are deeply relevant to Bosnians' experience of the ICTY: as has often been noted, there is a striking correlation between Bosnians' views of the Tribunal and the ethnic group to which they belong.

---

[6] Interview with Asta Zinbo, then Director, Civil Society Initiatives Program, International Commission on Missing Persons, in Sarajevo, Bosn. & Herz. (Dec. 6, 2006).

[7] Interview with Fadil Budnjo, President, Association of Families of Killed and Missing from Foča and Kalinovik, in Ilidža, Bosn. & Herz. (July 24, 2009). See generally Chapter 2.

[8] Of the civilians whose death or disappearance during the Bosnian war has been confirmed by the Research and Documentation Center in Sarajevo, 83.33 percent were Bosniak, 10.27 percent were Serb, 5.45 percent were Croat, and almost 1 percent had another ethnicity. Research and Documentation Center (Sarajevo), *Ljudski Gubici u Bosni i Hercegovni 91–95 (Human Losses in Bosnia and Herzegovina 1991–95)*, graph 36, www.idc.org.ba/.

[9] See Stuart Ford, *A Social Psychology Model of the Perceived Legitimacy of International Criminal Courts: Implications for the Success of Transitional Justice Mechanisms*, 45 VAND. J. TRANSNAT'L L. 405, 416–17 (2012); Mirko Klarin, *The Impact of the ICTY Trials on Public Opinion in the Former Yugoslavia*, 7 J. INT'L CRIM. JUST. 89, 90 (2009); Isabelle Delpla, *In the Midst of Injustice: The ICTY from the Perspective of Some Victim Associations, in* THE NEW BOSNIAN MOSAIC: IDENTITIES, MEMORIES AND MORAL CLAIMS IN A POST-WAR SOCIETY 213 (Xavier Bougarel et al. eds., 2007); Donna E. Arzt, *Views on the Ground: The Local Perception of International Criminal Tribunals in the Former Yugoslavia and Sierra Leone*, ANNALS AM. ACAD. POL. & SOC. SCI. 223, 232 (2006).

[10] A number of grassroots efforts have sought to transcend these divisions, addressing the wartime past in terms, as one person put it, of "the act that happened" rather than the ethnic group whose members committed the crime. Interview with Emir Hodžić, Jer Me Se Tiče, in Sarajevo, Bosn. & Herz. (Sept. 13, 2014).

None of this is to suggest Bosnian citizens share uniform perspectives with other members of their ethnic group. Many have mobilized to counter dominant narratives of their in-group and to reconstitute bonds of civic community across ethnic lines. Ethnic Serbs were among the most ardent advocates for Serb acknowledgment of Serb atrocities whom I interviewed for this study, while many Bosniaks condemned Bosniak leaders' failure adequately to acknowledge and condemn war crimes committed by Bosniak soldiers. Štefica Galić, whose experience is highlighted in this chapter, has courageously addressed wartime atrocities by other Bosnian Croats. In larger perspective, each survivor's conception of justice is shaped by his or her unique humanity and experience.[11] In the course of interviews I found, for example, that highly educated urban elites were more likely than rural victims to describe Tribunal "success" in terms of abstract principles and to situate its achievements in a global context.[12]

Third, while this chapter explores Bosnian expectations of the ICTY, its focus should not be taken to imply Bosnian survivors of ghastly crimes believe the *only* appropriate response is criminal punishment. Many endured every conceivable permutation of tragic loss, and have a raft of pressing needs. Although many place a high value on prosecutions, this is hardly their only priority; for many, it is not even their first.[13]

In myriad ways Bosnians' broader experience of loss has colored their expectations and experience of Hague justice. Crimes that shattered their lives are woven into a broader canvas of trauma and deeply felt injustices—the haunting remembrance that it took years before the international community ended their suffering, the division of their country under terms many Bosniaks experience as the ratification of ethnic cleansing, and the daily injustice of exile from homes in which generations of their families lived. These are hardly the kind of harms criminal trials can redress. Even so, in part because the ICTY was the principal institution on offer to address survivors' needs in the aftermath of savage war, many Bosnians developed exorbitant expectations of what it would deliver.

---

[11] A study based on qualitative interviews of 171 Bosnians found that victims who had survived internment, lost close relatives, been internally displaced, been injured in a landmine explosion, and/or been subjected to sexual violence tended to have the highest expectations of the ICTY at the outset, resulting in greater disappointment later. Janine Natalya Clark, *The Limits of Retributive Justice: Findings of an Empirical Study in Bosnia and Hercegovina*, 7 J. INT'L CRIM. JUST. 463, 467 (2009) [hereinafter Clark, *Limits of Retributive Justice*].

[12] While the elites to whom I refer often spoke of others as "direct victims," most of my sources in Sarajevo endured three-and-a-half years of perilous siege themselves. A survey conducted by two other scholars captures the extent of victimization by residents of Sarajevo, where many of the elites whom I interviewed live. More than 70 percent of Sarajevo respondents "reported themselves to be victims of war crimes and crimes against humanity." Approximately 90 percent "reported the victimization of a family member or close friend." Sanja Kutnjak Ivković & John Hagan, *The Politics of Punishment and the Siege of Sarajevo: Toward a Conflict Theory of Perceived International (In)justice*, 40 L. & SOC'Y REV. 369, 383 (2006).

[13] Based on her work helping Bosnians identify the remains of loved ones who disappeared during the war, Asta Zinbo described "truth" as the "number one" priority for those survivors. In her words, "they want to know what happened and who did it." Zinbo characterized "justice" as their "number two" priority, adding: "Both are very important." Interview with Asta Zinbo, then Director, Civil Society Initiatives Program, International Commission on Missing Persons, in Sarajevo, Bosn. & Herz. (Dec. 6, 2006).

I. "JUSTICE IS IMPORTANT FOR ITS OWN SAKE"

The purpose of a trial is to render justice, and nothing else . . . Hence, to the question most commonly asked about the Eichmann trial: What good does it do?, there is but one possible answer: It will do justice.

—HANNAH ARENDT[14]

Today, it is commonplace to ask in relation to international tribunals much the same question that, in Arendt's words, was "most commonly asked about the Eichmann trial" more than a half a century ago—What good do they do?[15] But for many who survived ghastly crimes, the question answers itself.

Mirsad Duratović was seventeen when Bosnian Serbs detained him in the notorious Omarska camp, and lost some sixty relatives during the Serb takeover of Prijedor. Thus he was perplexed when I asked why he supported the ICTY despite his profound disappointment in its performance. "What I have gone through," he replied, "I think whoever was in my shoes would actually like to see some justice being done." If I ever endured what he had, Duratović said, "then it would be clear to you . . . why you want [justice]."[16] Srebrenica survivor Kada Hotić implicitly made the same point when she explained the ICTY's importance: "If the court were not established at all, it would be very difficult to reach any sentence [for wartime atrocities]. That's a little piece of justice."[17] Sadik Trako, who headed the Association of Victims and Missing Persons in Lašva Valley in Central Bosnia when I interviewed him, said all he thought necessary when I asked why he supported the ICTY: "For me, the Hague Tribunal is an extremely important institution because it is that court which is going to punish the perpetrators."[18]

Over the course of scores of interviews in Bosnia, I heard richly varied views of what prosecutions in The Hague would achieve. But for many, the moral satisfaction derived from punishment was elemental. Law professor Jasna Bakšić Muftić captured the irreducible importance of punishment for thousands of victims: "After all kinds of war crimes and genocide, the people need some sort of satisfaction . . . that someone guilty be punished."[19] Explaining why many victims support the ICTY despite their

---

[14] HANNAH ARENDT, EICHMANN IN JERUSALEM: A REPORT ON THE BANALITY OF EVIL 253–54 (Penguin Books 1994) (1963).

[15] *See, e.g.,* Ralph Zacklin, *The Failings of Ad Hoc International Tribunals,* 2 J. INT'L CRIM. J. 541 (2004); Helena Cobban, *Think Again: International Courts,* FOREIGN POL'Y (May 8, 2006).

[16] Interview with Mirsad Duratović, in Prijedor, Bosn. & Herz. (Dec. 8, 2006.) Among those whom Duratović lost were his father and fifteen-year-old brother.

[17] Interview with Kada Hotić, Vice President, Association of Mothers of Srebrenica and Žepa Enclaves, in Sarajevo, Bosn. & Herz. (July 24, 2009).

[18] Interview with Sadik Trako, President, Association of Victims and Missing Persons in Lašva Valley, in Vitez, Bosn. & Herz. (Dec. 6, 2006).

[19] Interview with Jasna Bakšić Muftić, Professor, Faculty of Law, University of Sarajevo, in Sarajevo, Bosn. & Herz. (Nov. 30, 2006). Bakšić Muftić's observation so aptly captured a widely-shared perspective in Bosnia, I incorporated it in the title of my earlier study of the ICTY's impact there. DIANE F. ORENTLICHER, OPEN SOCIETY JUSTICE INITIATIVE & INTERNATIONAL CENTER FOR TRANSITIONAL JUSTICE, THAT SOMEONE GUILTY BE PUNISHED: THE IMPACT OF THE ICTY IN BOSNIA (2010).

frustrations with its work, Mirsad Tokača made much the same point: "Simply, they desperately need justice. It's some kind of satisfaction, moral satisfaction."[20]

While profoundly important to those who survived ethnic cleansing, it is not just victims who expressed support for the ICTY in terms of "justice for its own sake."[21] During the war, Štefica Galić, a Bosnian Croat, courageously rescued Bosniak neighbors from ethnic cleansing carried out by ethnic Croats in 1993. When I asked Galić how she reacted when the ICTY was created, she replied: "I thought finally justice will be served" in the sense that those responsible for monstrous crimes would "be put behind bars for good, ... something that they really deserved for [the] crimes they committed."[22] Like virtually all of my Bosnian interlocutors, Galić is disappointed in some aspects of the Tribunal's performance. Even so, she said, "thanks to that court, I believe in justice as such."[23]

These perspectives evoke what scholars call a "just deserts" or retributivist theory of criminal punishment. While there are myriad permutations, retributivist theories commonly hold "that when an individual harms society by violating its rules in some normatively unallowable way, ... the perpetrator deserves to be punished in proportion to the past harm he or she committed."[24] In contrast to consequentialist theories, which justify punishment in terms of their presumed social benefits, classic retributivist theories see punishment as "an end in itself [that] needs no further justification."[25]

The value of "justice for its own sake" was not lost on those who launched the ICTY, and has loomed large in the Tribunal's sentencing judgments. In the resolution creating the Tribunal, the UN Security Council cited its determination not only to deter further atrocities and restore peace—distinctly consequentialist goals—but also "to take effective measures to bring to justice the persons who are responsible for them."[26] The ICTY's first president evoked this goal with elegant simplicity, noting one of the Tribunal's principal aims was "to do justice."[27] In line with the Council's

---

[20] Interview with Mirsad Tokača, President, Research and Documentation Center (Sarajevo), in Sarajevo, Bosn. & Herz. (Dec. 6, 2006).

[21] *E.g.,* interview with Zdravko Grebo, Director, Center for Interdisciplinary Postgraduate Studies, University of Sarajevo, in Sarajevo, Bosn. & Herz. (Dec. 4, 2006). The precise wording of this section's title ("justice is important for its own sake") comes from my interview with Professor Grebo.

[22] Interview with Štefica Galić, Editor, Tačno.net, in Mostar, Bosn. & Herz. (Sept. 10, 2014). Although Galić was not a victim of ethnic cleansing during the conflict, she later became the target of sustained attacks by Bosnian Croats who resented her public recognition of war crimes committed by Croat perpetrators. *See* Boris Pavelić, *Dangerous Life of Štefica Galić, Ljubuški's Oskar Schindler,* BALKAN TRANSITIONAL JUST. (Aug. 9, 2012).

[23] *Id.* I describe Galić's criticisms of the ICTY's performance in Chapter 6.

[24] Kevin M. Carlsmith et al., *Why Do We Punish? Deterrence and Just Deserts as Motives for Punishment,* 83 J. PERSONALITY & SOC. PSYCHOL. 284, 284 (2002). *See also* Mirko Bagaric & John Morss, *International Sentencing Law: In Search of a Justification and Coherent Framework,* 6 INT'L CRIM. L. REV. 191, 241 (2006).

[25] Carlsmith et al., *supra* note 24, at 284. *See also* Diane Marie Amann, *Group Mentality, Expressivism, and Genocide,* 2 INT'L CRIM. L. REV. 93, 116 (2002). Even so, as I explain later, some versions of retributivism emphasize social functions advanced by punishment.

[26] S.C. Res. 827, preamble (May 25, 1993).

[27] ICTY President, *Report of the International Tribunal for the Prosecution of Persons Responsible for Serious Violations of International Humanitarian Law Committed in the Territory of the Former Yugoslavia since 1991,* ¶ 11, U.N. Doc. A/49/342-S/1994/1007 (Aug. 29, 1994) [hereinafter *First Annual Report*]. The ICTY's website folds this objective into others, stating: "By

justifications for creating the ICTY, its judges have frequently cited retribution as one of the principal considerations (along with deterrence) guiding their determination of sentences.[28]

Many Bosnians are convinced their only hope for retributive justice was through the ICTY. Hatidža Mehmedović, who lost her husband, two teenage sons, brothers, parents, and scores of other relatives in the Srebrenica genocide, described her disappointments in the ICTY at some length when I interviewed her in July 2009.[29] Yet she concluded our meeting this way:

> My opinion is that it is good that the Hague Tribunal was established and that the Hague Tribunal exists simply because of the point that if the court was not established, no instance would be able to issue . . . verdicts in the case of these crimes.[30]

In a similar vein, former judge Vehid Šehić told me: "I only know for a fact that in case the Hague Tribunal was never established war criminals would have never been tried or prosecuted."[31]

Others, emphasizing conditions that prevailed when the Tribunal was created, believe the "only possibility"[32] for justice during and in the immediate aftermath of the 1990s conflict was through "a neutral, impartial institution"[33] like the ICTY. As I elaborate in Chapter 9, the ICTY eventually, if belatedly, catalyzed domestic war crimes prosecutions in Bosnia, and key actors should have prepared domestic institutions to prosecute wartime atrocities sooner. For Mervan Miraščija, however, it is hard to imagine war crimes prosecutions taking place in Bosnia at all were it not for the Hague Tribunal: "If there were no ICTY," he said, "I don't know how the whole process would start. We definitely didn't have any possibility to process war crimes" in local courts.[34]

---

bringing perpetrators [of atrocities] to trial, the ICTY aims to deter future crimes and *render justice to thousands of victims and their families*, thus contributing to lasting peace in the former Yugoslavia." ICTY website, http://www.icty.org/en/about (last visited Feb. 3, 2017) (emphasis added).

[28] The ICTY Appeals Chamber summarized the practice of the Tribunal itself and of the ICTR in a 2009 judgment, recalling: "It is well established that, at the Tribunal and at the ICTR, retribution and deterrence are the main objectives of sentencing." Prosecutor v. Krajišnik, Case No. IT-00-39-A, Appeal Judgment, ¶ 775 (Int'l Crim. Trib. for the Former Yugoslavia Mar. 17, 2009). *See also* Prosecutor v. Stakić, Case No. IT-97-24-T, Trial Judgment, ¶ 900 (Int'l Crim. Trib. for the Former Yugoslavia July 31, 2003); Prosecutor v. Aleksovski, Case No. IT-95-14/1-A, Appeal Judgment, ¶ 185 (Int'l Crim. Trib. for the Former Yugoslavia Mar. 24, 2000).

[29] I describe her criticisms in Chapter 6.

[30] Interview with Hatidža Mehmedović, President, Association of Srebrenica Mothers, in Potočari, Bosn. & Herz. (July 21, 2009).

[31] Interview with Vehid Šehić, President, Citizens Forum of Tuzla, in Tuzla, Bosn. & Herz. (July 15, 2009).

[32] Interview with Zdravko Grebo, Director, Center for Interdisciplinary Postgraduate Studies, University of Sarajevo, in Sarajevo, Bosn. & Herz. (Dec. 4, 2006).

[33] Interview with Sinan Alić, then Director, Foundation Truth, Justice, Reconciliation, in Tuzla, Bosn. & Herz. (Dec. 5, 2006).

[34] Interview with Mervan Miraščija, Law Program Coordinator, Open Society Fund BiH, in Sarajevo, Bosn. & Herz. (Nov. 29, 2006).

II. "WE ARE HERE TO SAY IT'S NOT GOOD TO DO THAT"

Now a noted writer, Nidžara Ahmetašević was a teenager living with her family in Sarajevo when Serb snipers launched "the first big shelling"[35] of Bosnia's capital on May 2, 1992. Ahmetašević describes what happened later that month:

> Then, on May 28, I was wounded. It was the night [Ratko] Mladić had said; "burn it all!" . . . I was outside, sitting with my friends. It was destiny. I went in the house with my family. All the others stayed outside. A rocket hit the balcony. I was behind the glass doors. I still have two pieces of shrapnel covered with blood in my home. Because there was shooting we could not get to the hospital. My father was also injured. I was given first aid. Only next day did I get to hospital.
>
> I was 17. It was strange. They asked how old I was and when I told them they said they would not cut my leg off because I was too young. They cleaned the wound in my leg everyday but the flesh was burned. It was horrible and so painful. I remember once I had ten people around me, holding me down. In the first week in hospital I lost 22 kilos and more in the next few months. I could not walk.[36]

When I asked Ahmetašević to explain why she supported the ICTY, she emphasized its potential to affirm core precepts of morality betrayed by ethnic cleansing. At the time we spoke, the two Bosnians many hold most responsible for wartime atrocities, Ratko Mladić and Radovan Karadžić, were still at large. Capturing and prosecuting these two men was of paramount importance, Ahmetašević said, because of the moral meaning their eventual punishment would ascribe to their acts: "The whole world will say, 'these people committed that and that and we are here to say, it's not good to do that. You cannot do that and go around unpunished.'"[37]

Tarik Jusić evoked a similar theme. We spoke a week after the ICTY Appeals Chamber imposed a life sentence on Stanislav Galić based on his command responsibility for the siege of Sarajevo from September 1992 to August 1994.[38] Jusić told me the life sentence (the most severe penalty the ICTY can impose) was "very important" because "it re-establishes the basic preconditions for society as such. It cannot be that someone bombs you for four years and it's fine. . . . It's a re-establishing of basic, underlying values of civilization and society."[39]

Others made a similar point while emphasizing fundamental principles of universal law. For example, the first time I interviewed law professor Jasna Bakšić Muftić, she extolled ICTY judgments' role in "confirm[ing] minimum" standards set

---

[35] *Return to Europe: Portrait of Nidžara Ahmetašević*, EUR. STABILITY INITIATIVE WEBSITE, www. esiweb.org (last visited Dec. 11, 2017).

[36] *Id.*

[37] Interview with Nidžara Ahmetašević, then Editor, BIRN in BiH, in Sarajevo, Bosn. & Herz. (July 13, 2009). The title of this section ("we are here to say it's not good to do that") comes from this interview.

[38] Prosecutor v. Galić, Case No. IT-98-29-A, Appeal Judgment (Int'l Crim. Trib. for the Former Yugoslavia Nov. 30, 2006).

[39] Interview with Tarik Jusić, then Program Director, Mediacentar Sarajevo, in Sarajevo, Bosn. & Herz. (Dec. 6, 2006).

forth in treaties like the 1949 Geneva Conventions on armed conflict and the 1948 Genocide Convention.[40] In an interview eight years later, she emphasized the "very important message" of the ICTY's work, whose value extends beyond "the region" to the "whole European, maybe global, context." That message, she said, was that encouraging ethnic hatred can lead to explosive violence, in which people "justify killing people who do not belong with you."[41]

The observations of Ahmetašević, Jusić, and Bakšić Muftić evoke what many scholars call the *expressive* function of international criminal tribunals—that is, their "messaging effect."[42] In David Luban's words, international trials are "expressive acts broadcasting the news that mass atrocities are, in fact, heinous crimes."[43] By punishing individuals who breached the basic code of humanity, Robert Sloane argues, the international community seeks "authoritatively to disavow that conduct, to indicate symbolically its refusal to acquiesce in the crimes, to vindicate international human rights norms and the laws of war."[44] ICTY judges have embraced this function, justifying sentences in terms of their role in "duly expressing the outrage of the international community at [the] crimes" for which they are imposed.[45]

While expressivist theories justify international prosecutions in terms of normative messaging aimed at an abstract and diffuse audience,[46] at least in some

---

[40] Interview with Jasna Bakšić Muftić, Professor, Faculty of Law, University of Sarajevo, in Sarajevo, Bosn. & Herz. (Nov. 30, 2006).

[41] Interview with Jasna Bakšić Muftić, Professor, Faculty of Law, University of Sarajevo, in Sarajevo, Bosn. & Herz. (Sept. 17, 2014).

[42] MARK A. DRUMBL, ATROCITY, PUNISHMENT AND INTERNATIONAL LAW 17 (2007). *See also* Robert Sloan, *The Expressive Capacity of International Punishment* (Colum. Public L. & Legal Theory, Working Paper 06100, 2006).

[43] David Luban, *Fairness to Rightness: Jurisdiction, Legality, and the Legitimacy of International Criminal Law, in* THE PHILOSOPHY OF INTERNATIONAL LAW 569, 576 (Samantha Besson & John Tasioulis eds., 2010).

[44] Sloane, *supra* note 42, at 39. *See also* DRUMBL, *supra* note 42, at 174.

[45] Prosecutor v. Krajišnik, Case No. IT-00-39-A, Appeal Judgment, ¶ 775 (Int'l Crim. Trib. for the Former Yugoslavia Mar. 17, 2009); Prosecutor v. Aleksovski, Case No. IT-95-14/1-A, Appeal Judgment, ¶ 185 (Int'l Crim. Trib. for the Former Yugoslavia Mar. 24, 2000); Prosecutor v. Stakić, Case No. IT-97-24-T, Trial Judgment, ¶ 900 (Int'l Crim. Trib. for the Former Yugoslavia July 31, 2003). While victims stress the need for punishment that is adequate in light of the gravity of the offenses for which a defendant was convicted, the ICTY has also recognized the notion of retribution as incorporating a "principle of restraint" in sentencing. *See, e.g.*, Prosecutor v. Krajišnik, Case No. IT-00-39-A, Appeal Judgment, ¶ 804 (Int'l Crim. Trib. for the Former Yugoslavia Mar. 17, 2009); Prosecutor v. Kordić et al., Case No. IT-95-14/2-A, Appeal Judgment, ¶ 1075 (Int'l Crim. Trib. for the Former Yugoslavia Dec. 17, 2004); Prosecutor v. Aleksovski, Case No. IT-95-14/1-A, Appeal Judgment, ¶ 185 (Int'l Crim. Trib. for the Former Yugoslavia Mar. 24, 2000).

[46] For example, one scholar explains the expressive function of ICTs this way:

> International criminal tribunals can contribute most effectively to world public order as self-consciously expressive penal institutions: publicly condemning acts deplored by international law, acting as an engine of jurisprudential development at the local level, and encouraging the legal and normative internalization of international human rights and humanitarian law.

Sloane, *supra* note 42, at 44. While the goals enunciated by Sloane may seem removed from consequentialist concerns, ICTs' role in norm projection is thought to promote behavior in accordance with the norms they help entrench. *See* DRUMBL, *supra* note 42, at 174; Margaret M. deGuzman, *Choosing to Prosecute: Expressive Selection at the International Criminal Court*, 33 MICH. J. INT'L L. 265, 313 (2012). Writing about the impact of domestic human rights trials, Kathryn Sikkink described their significance this way: "Human rights prosecutions . . . are not

versions,[47] many Bosnians whom I interviewed embrace the ICTY's expressive function for deeply personal reasons. As victims of monstrous crimes the world failed to prevent, many crave a clarion judgment that what happened to them was grievously wrong. The harms they endured transcend tangible measures of human loss: the moral universe was shattered. Many survivors experienced ethnic cleansing in much the same way Primo Levi described Holocaust survivors' experience of "concentration camps, in their most offensive and unforeseen aspect," as "a world turned upside down."[48]

Speaking from her own experience as an Auschwitz survivor, Eva Benda evoked the message many Bosnians internalized when they became targets of ethnic cleansing: "Once you have to defend yourself it is too late. When you are left to defend yourself, *it is as if you are already guilty*."[49] Conversely, as Ahmetašević suggested, when an international court convicts the architects and foot soldiers of mass atrocities, it is as if "the whole world" has said, "it's not good to do that."[50]

III. ESTABLISHING THE TRUTH AND DISPELLING DENIAL

We still had the hope that establishing this court will help to reveal the truth so that justice will be reached.

—SEAD GOLIĆ[51]

A. Dispelling Serb Denial

As Bosnian Serbs laid merciless siege to predominantly Muslim towns, their wartime leaders routinely inverted reality, attributing their attacks to their victims.[52] The perverse cruelty of their lies crystalized in a haunting image: arriving in Srebrenica in July 1995 to oversee the slaughter of some 8,000 Muslims in a matter of days, Bosnian Serb military leader Ratko Mladić gave chocolate to eight-year-old Izudin Alić, whose Muslim family had sought safety in Srebrenica. Patting Alić on the head, Mladić offered his personal assurance everyone in Srebrenica would be treated well, in full accordance with the Geneva Conventions.[53] Later, many Bosnian Serbs would deny there was a massacre in Srebrenica, minimize the numbers who were killed,

---

only instances of punishment or enforcement but also high-profile symbolic events that communicate and dramatize norms *and socialize actors to accept those norms*." KATHRYN SIKKINK, THE JUSTICE CASCADE: HOW HUMAN RIGHTS PROSECUTIONS ARE CHANGING WORLD POLITICS 173 (2011) (emphasis added).

[47] In other versions of expressivism, the principal audience for the moral message of punishment is the wrongdoer who is punished. *See* Pablo de Greiff, *Deliberative Democracy and Punishment*, 5 BUFF. CRIM. L. REV. 373, 397–98 (2002).

[48] MIRNA CICIONI, PRIMO LEVI: BRIDGES OF KNOWLEDGE 61 (1995).

[49] Ms. Benda's remarks were recalled at her funeral in January 2017. Rabbi Daniel G. Zemel, Eulogy for Eva Benda, Temple Micha, Washington, DC (Jan. 5, 2017).

[50] Interview with Nidžara Ahmetašević, then Editor, BIRN in BiH, in Sarajevo, Bosn. & Herz. (July 13, 2009).

[51] Interview with Sead Golić, Secretary, Association of Forcibly Taken Away and Missing from Brčko, in Brčko, Bosn. & Herz. (July 22, 2009).

[52] *See* Mark Danner, *Bosnia: The Turning Point*, N.Y. REV. BOOKS (Feb. 5, 1998).

[53] *See A Child's Meeting with Ratko Mladić, Hours Before the Massacre of Thousands*, ASSOCIATED PRESS (June 2, 2011).

imply Bosnian victims bore equal responsibility for wartime atrocities,[54] or justify the killings as a "gesture of revenge" for war crimes committed by Bosniaks against Serbs.[55]

In this setting, many Bosniaks told me one of the most important contributions the ICTY would make was establishing "the truth" of what happened during the 1990s conflict. Some suggested an authoritative rendering of facts was a form of justice in itself. Ahmetašević's reference to the Tribunal's factual findings ("these people committed that and that") evokes many victims' need not only for an authoritative affirmation that they were *wronged*, but also for validation of the basic facts of the crimes they survived.[56] Exploring the healing potential of ICTY trials, Lepa Mladjenović noted:

> For trauma victims, one of the most important functions of therapy is the validation of their experiences. By prosecuting war crimes and crimes against humanity, the ICTY reveals how, by whom, and under what circumstances these crimes were carried out. The experiences of the victims of the wars in the former Yugoslavia are therefore validated in an international forum.[57]

In the view of Muharem Murselović, who survived internment in Omarska, the ICTY's authoritative rendering of facts was a form of justice in itself. In his words, "the realistic reflection [in ICTY verdicts] of what happened in Prijedor," Murselović's hometown, was a "major achievement."[58]

But most Bosniaks who placed store in the ICTY's role in establishing the truth emphasized its expected social impact: they considered it "an important test of the Hague Tribunal to prevent denial."[59] Kada Hotić, whose husband and brother were among those exterminated in Srebrenica,[60] recalled that "when the Hague Tribunal was established it gave us a big hope, not only to convict criminals . . . but

---

[54] *E.g.*, interview with Neđeljko Mitrović, President, Republika Srpska Association of Families of Missing Persons, in Banja Luka, Bosn. & Herz. (July 23, 2009) (asserting it takes at least "two sides to fight"); interview with Đoren Kalajdžić, Executive Secretary, Association of Republika Srpska Veterans, in Foča, Bosn. & Herz. (July 20, 2009).

[55] Interview with Đoren Kalajdžić, Executive Secretary, Association of Republika Srpska Veterans, in Foča, Bosn. & Herz. (July 20, 2009). The phenomenon of denialism in Bosnia is the focus of Chapter 8.

[56] U.S. Prosecutor Telford Taylor made the same point with characteristic eloquence in one of the postwar prosecutions of Nazis in Nuremberg. Evoking the singular role of the proceedings, Taylor elaborated that, for victims, "it is far more important that these incredible events be established by clear and public proof, so that no one can ever doubt that they were fact and not fable." Telford Taylor, *Opening Argument in Medical Trial, in* I Trials of War Criminals Before the Nurenberg Military Tribunals Under Control Council Law No. 10 27 (1948).

[57] Lepa Mladenović, *The ICTY: The Validation of the Experiences of Survivors, in* International War Crimes Trials: Making a Difference? 60 (Steven R. Ratner & James L. Bischoff eds., 2004).

[58] Interview with the late Muharem Murselović, then Member, Republika Srpska National Assembly, President, RS Parliamentarians Club for the Party for BiH, in Banja Luka, Bosn. & Herz. (July 15, 2009).

[59] Interview with Zdravko Grebo, Director, Center for Interdisciplinary Postgraduate Studies, University of Sarajevo, in Sarajevo, Bosn. & Herz. (Dec. 4, 2006).

[60] *See* Udo Ludwig & Ansgar Mertin, *"A Toast to the Dead"; Srebrenica Widows Sue UN, Dutch Government*, Spiegel Online Int'l (July 4, 2006).

we expected to have the truth in this country revealed and proved, because we have a big problem here regarding acknowledgement of the truth."[61] Omarska survivor Nusreta Sivac believed ICTY verdicts "would influence the conscience of people around here, the minds of people, their way of thinking."[62] While recognizing that discourses of denial were still prevalent when we spoke in 2009, Emsuda Mujagić told me it mattered enormously that the ICTY had already produced "the evidence and proof that will someday make [Bosnian Serbs] understand they lied to themselves."[63]

A common critique of international justice holds that local processes are better suited than ICTs to influence local perspectives.[64] While this may generally be true, many Bosnians insist that, in light of their country's ethnic fractures, *only* an international court could dispel denial through judicial fact-finding. Emir Hodžić made the point this way: The "Hague Tribunal itself is very important because it's the only . . . independent body that we can cite, that we can quote, that we can use in regards to war crimes to say 'this, this, this, this happened, it has been proven.'" The ICTY's authority derives, in Hodžić's view, from the very fact that "it is an international court, . . . the only independent court that we can talk about tomorrow and today" to affirm who "committed war crimes as a fact, established fact."[65]

Many survivors of Serb atrocities hoped the ICTY would not only establish ethnic Serbs' responsibility for atrocities, but also Serbian "aggression."[66] Even before the ICTY was established, the Bosnian government turned to the International Court of Justice (ICJ) in March 1993, seeking its help in ending violence by the Federal Republic of Yugoslavia. Although the case was instituted before the Srebrenica genocide, its survivors placed considerable hope in the ICJ case. In particular, they hoped it would provide "legal acknowledgment that the Serbian state shared blame for their fate."[67]

For many survivors of Serb atrocities, dispelling Serb denial is a matter of justice. But for many Bosnian Serbs, it is a moral imperative. Among the most passionate

---

[61] Interview with Kada Hotić, Vice President, Association of Mothers of Srebrenica and Žepa Enclaves, in Sarajevo, Bosn. & Herz. (July 24, 2009). Victims of grave crimes often seek social validation they were unjustly harmed. *See* Bar-Tal et al., *A Sense of Self-Perceived Collective Victimhood in Intractable Conflicts*, 91 INT'L REV. RED CROSS 229, 232 (2009). *See also id.* at 234.

[62] Interview with Nusreta Sivac, Former Judge, in Prijedor, Bosn. & Herz. (Sept. 16, 2014).

[63] Interview with Emsuda Mujagić, President, Srcem do Mira, in Kozarac, Bosn. & Herz. (July 23, 2009).

[64] José Alvarez has made a more nuanced argument—that in the wake of mass atrocities, "international processes for criminal accountability need to encourage and adapt to local processes directed toward the same end." José E. Alvarez, *Crimes of States/Crimes of Hate: Lessons from Rwanda*, 24 YALE J. INT'L L. 365, 370 (1999).

[65] Interview with Emir Hodžić, Jer Me Se Tiče, in Sarajevo, Bosn. & Herz. (Sept. 13, 2014).

[66] In the words of Aleksandra Letić, "From the early beginning," Bosniaks "were counting very much on the ICTY" to say "yes, the major victims of the war in B-H were the Bosniaks, and really stating that, yes, the crimes committed in Bosnia were the result of an aggression." Interview with Aleksandra Letić, Secretary-General, Helsinki Committee for Human Rights in Republika Srpska, in Sarajevo, Bosn. & Herz. (Sept. 8, 2014). See also Chapter 2.

[67] LARA J. NETTELFIELD & SARAH E. WAGNER, SREBRENICA IN THE AFTERMATH OF GENOCIDE 113 (2014).

advocates for acknowledgment whom I have met are Bosnian Serbs, such as Goran Zorić, who have courageously confronted Serb denial. In alliance with non-Serb activists, Zorić has participated in grassroots initiatives that seek to "challenge the ways we look at . . . dealing with the past,"[68] transcending wartime narratives that divide Bosnians. Explaining how he came to devote himself to this work, Zorić told me: "I was so full of frustration I *had* to start to speak about genocide, because that's the only thing that can make amends."[69] Zorić does not consider himself an expert on the ICTY and doubts it has contributed "in any way to social changes" in Bosnia. Nevertheless, he and his colleagues "use it" in their advocacy. More specifically, Zorić said, "we use facts from the court verdicts as relevant facts."[70]

Like Zorić, Aleksandar Trifunović passionately believes "Serbs must understand what really happened" during the war."[71] In his view, it is morally necessary to "analyze this period" and "say, 'yes, this is bad.'" Beyond Serbs' moral burden of reckoning, Trifunović believes acknowledgment "is absolutely normal, if you want to live normally in your country." Most of all, he fears that, unless Serbs "start a conversation" about the past and acknowledge "what happened, . . . we can repeat this. This is my big fear, that we can repeat all this stuff."[72]

B. Fostering Acknowledgment by Each Ethnic Group

If many Bosnian Serbs have failed to acknowledge the full extent and nature of Serb atrocities, much less condemn them unequivocally, many Bosniaks have been reluctant to express robust condemnation of war crimes committed by the Bosnian Army against Serbs and Croats, concerned "this could be seen as equalizing guilt."[73] Bosnian Croats, too, have evinced scant readiness to address Croats' wartime depredations.[74] In this setting, some of my interlocutors assessed Tribunal success in part by the degree to which leaders and members of *each* ethnic group acknowledge and condemn atrocities committed by members of their in-group.[75]

Several Bosnian sources noted a tension between this type of acknowledgment and a principle the ICTY has been at pains to emphasize—that criminal guilt is

---

[68] International Center for Transitional Justice, *Young Activists in Bosnia Discuss Transitional Justice and Media at the Site of a Former Camp* (Aug. 6, 2015) (quoting Goran Zorić).

[69] Interview with Goran Zorić, Executive Director, KVART, in Sarajevo, Bosn. & Herz. (Sept. 17, 2014).

[70] *Id.*

[71] Interview with Aleksandar Trifunović, Editor, BUKA, in Banja Luka, Bosn. & Herz. (Sept. 15, 2014).

[72] *Id.*

[73] Interview with Dobrila Govedarica, Executive Director, Open Society Fund BiH, in Sarajevo, Bosn. & Herz. (Nov. 29, 2006).

[74] Interview with Štefica Galić, Editor, Tačno.net, in Mostar, Bosn. & Herz. (Sept. 10, 2014). *See also* Janine Natalya Clark, International Trials and Reconciliation: Assessing the Impact of the International Criminal Tribunal for the Former Yugoslavia 103 (2014).

[75] This point is distinct from the aspirations described in the previous section, which emphasized: (1) many victims' hope that those responsible for the crimes they suffered will acknowledge the facts and wrongfulness of their conduct, and (2) some Bosnian Serbs' belief that their ethnic group and leaders must acknowledge and condemn atrocities committed by Serbs.

individual.[76] To suggest Serbs (or Croats or Bosniaks) should acknowledge and condemn Serb (or Croat or Bosniak) atrocities could, they feared, reinforce the ethnicization of Bosnian discourses about war crimes. In line with the Tribunal's own messaging, many Bosnians believe "individualizing guilt is important."[77] Even so, many who made this point also stressed the importance they attach to acknowledgment by leaders and members of each ethnic group that members of their in-group committed war crimes, a notion that implies collective responsibility.[78] For example, while insisting "someone who belongs to an ethnic group should not be stigmatized" because of the guilt of individuals who share her ethnicity, Dobrila Govedarica said:

> It was not just individuals who were responsible by directly perpetrating crimes. There were witnesses who were silent. They weren't accomplices but they were silent. Some who opposed crimes committed by members of their ethnic group were punished, but how come they're *still* silent? . . . It was impossible not to see that your neighbor was tortured just because he belonged to an ethnic group. So you shouldn't stigmatize an entire group, but maybe there should be an acceptance of political responsibility. These individuals didn't come from nowhere. There had to be either an overall political/societal climate that supported such acts or there had not been awareness that it was wrong.[79]

IV. RECONCILIATION

The word *reconciliation* is not used in the Security Council resolution establishing the ICTY,[80] and some of its judges have balked at the suggestion their work is justified, even in part, as contributing to reconciliation.[81] Even so, many scholars have assumed the Security Council's determination that the ICTY would contribute to

---

[76] Scholars and others have long debated the circumstances in which collective responsibility is morally justified. Key threads of that debate are summarized in Nenad Dimitrijević, *Moral Responsibility for Collective Crime*, Eurozine (July 5, 2006).

[77] Interview with Dobrila Govedarica, Executive Director, Open Society Fund BiH, in Sarajevo, Bosn. & Herz. (Nov. 29, 2006).

[78] I believe Sabina Čehajić-Clancy captures the notion expressed by many Bosnians who made this point in interviews when she uses the phrase "collective responsibility" to connote "the whole community and its members accepting responsibility for crimes" already committed in their name. Sabina Čehajić-Clancy, *Dealing with the Past (II): The Issue of Collective Responsibility*, Puls Demokratije (2007).

[79] Interview with Dobrila Govedarica, Executive Director, Open Society Fund BiH, in Sarajevo, Bosn. & Herz. (Nov. 29, 2006).

[80] In contrast, the Security Council resolution establishing a tribunal for Rwanda explicitly invokes the notion of *reconciliation*, expressing the conviction "that in the particular circumstances of Rwanda, the prosecution of persons responsible for serious violations of international humanitarian law would . . . contribute to the process of national reconciliation and to the restoration and maintenance of peace." S.C. Res. 955, preamble (Nov. 8, 1994).

[81] For example, ICTY judge Fausto Pocar insisted that, whatever goals the Security Council might have had in mind when it established the ICTY, the Tribunal cannot pursue "political" goals such as fostering reconciliation. Instead, its task is to "deal with cases as any other court would do," ensuring that principles of due process are applied. Interview with Fausto Pocar, Judge and then President, ICTY, in The Hague, Neth. (Mar. 5, 2007). *See also* Denis Džidić, *Hague Tribunal President: "We Offered Truth, Not Reconciliation,"* Balkan Insight (June 21, 2017).

peace includes the notion of reconciliation,[82] and ICTY judgments[83] and other official statements have at times endorsed this view.[84]

As elaborated in early ICTY reports and elsewhere, the theory behind such claims has several strands. One holds that, by prosecuting individuals one by one, the Tribunal avoids the taint of collective responsibility, which would heighten the risk of future conflicts. Then ICTY president Antonio Cassese made the point this way in his first report to the UN General Assembly and Security Council in 1994:

> Far from being a vehicle for revenge, [the ICTY] is a tool for promoting reconciliation and restoring true peace. If responsibility for the appalling crimes perpetrated in the former Yugoslavia is not attributed to individuals, then whole ethnic and religious groups will be held accountable for these crimes and branded as criminal. In other words, "collective responsibility"—a primitive and archaic concept—will gain the upper hand; eventually whole groups will be held guilty of massacres, torture, rape, ethnic cleansing, the wanton destruction of cities and villages. The history of the region clearly shows that clinging to feelings of "collective responsibility" easily degenerates into resentment, hatred and frustration and inevitably leads to further violence and new crimes.[85]

A second strand draws on familiar justifications for punishment in domestic settings: by satisfying victims' need for retributive justice, punishment prevents vigilante violence. Judge Cassese made the case this way in a 1997 lecture: "[W]hen there is no justice in response to the extermination of a people, the result is that victims are led to take the law into their own hands."[86] In a similar spirit, upon completion of the Dayton peace negotiations, Cassese and then ICTY Prosecutor Richard Goldstone

---

[82] *See, e.g.*, Bagaric & Morss, *supra* note 24, at 242; Laurel E. Fletcher & Harvey M. Weinstein, *Violence and Social Repair: Rethinking the Contribution of Justice to Reconciliation*, 24 HUM. RTS. Q. 573, 578–79 & 579 n.17 (2002). Others, while recognizing that the Security Council did not explicitly link the ICTY's work to reconciliation, have nonetheless assessed its impact on reconciliation. *See, e.g.*, James Meernik & José Raul Guerrero, *Can International Criminal Justice Advance Ethnic Reconciliation? The ICTY and Ethnic Relations in Bosnia-Herzegovina*, 14 SOUTHEAST EUR. & BLACK SEA STUD. 383 (2014); Janine Natalya Clark, *Judging the ICTY: Has It Achieved Its Objectives?*, 9 SOUTHEAST EUR. & BLACK SEA STUD. 123 (2009) [hereinafter *Judging the ICTY*]. While noting the UN Security Council did not mention reconciliation when it established the ICTY, Clark notes "it has subsequently been heavily accentuated" by Tribunal officials. Clark, *supra*, at 132.

[83] *See, e.g.*, Prosecutor v. Erdemović, Case No. IT-96-22-T, Sentencing Judgment, ¶ 58 (Int'l Crim. Trib. for the Former Yugoslavia Nov. 29, 1996); Prosecutor v. Furundžija, Case No. IT-95-17/1-T, Trial Judgment, ¶ 288 (Int'l Crim. Trib. for the Former Yugoslavia Dec. 10, 1998).

[84] Indeed, in remarks delivered in Sarajevo in 2001, then ICTY president Claude Jorda conflated the Security Council's explicit assertion that the Tribunal would help restore and maintain peace with reconciliation. After citing the first claim, set forth in Security Council resolution 827, Jorda continued: "Stated otherwise, [the ICTY's] mission is to promote reconciliation through the prosecution, trial and punishment of those who perpetrated war crimes, crimes against humanity and genocide." Claude Jorda, *The ICTY and the Truth and Reconciliation Commission in Bosnia and Herzegovina*, remarks delivered in Sarajevo (May 12, 2001), set forth in ICTY Press Release, JL/ P.I.S./591-e, May 17, 2001.

[85] *First Annual Report, supra* note 27, ¶¶ 16–17.

[86] Antonio Cassese, *Reflections on International Criminal Justice*, 61 MODERN L. REV. 1, 1 (1998). *See also id.* at 6; Sanja Kutnjak Ivković, *Justice by the International Criminal Tribunal for the Former Yugoslavia*, 37 STAN. J. INT'L L. 255, 262 (2001) [hereinafter *Justice by the ICTY*] (quoting Cassese, in 1995 interview, stating "Justice is an indispensable ingredient of the process of national

averred: "Justice is an indispensable ingredient of the process of national reconciliation. . . . It breaks the cycle of violence, hatred and extra-judicial retribution."[87]

By 2004, Judge Cassese voiced doubts about his earlier expectations, writing: "The much-hoped-for beneficial impact of ICTY trials on persons and groups living in the former Yugoslavia is meager and tardy. In some cases, . . . proceedings are even having an adverse effect on and are ultimately rekindling nationalism and ethnic animosity."[88] But if, as several of my Bosnian interlocutors suggested, ICTY officials retreated from earlier claims along these lines,[89] advancing reconciliation still figured in the Tribunal's account of its goals at the end of its life. As of December 2017 the ICTY website made the following, comparatively modest claim: "Simply by removing some of the most senior and notorious criminals and holding them accountable the Tribunal has been able to lift the taint of violence, contribute to ending impunity and *help pave the way for reconciliation*."[90]

In the course of interviews over eight years, many Bosnians brought up the ICTY's potential role in fostering reconciliation. Those who did so expressed widely divergent views, however, about whether it is appropriate to expect a criminal court to contribute to reconciliation,[91] what reconciliation means in this context, and *how* criminal trials might foster reconciliation.

As previously noted, many Bosnians hoped the ICTY's work would dispel denial about wartime atrocities and stimulate acknowledgment and remorse. For some, acknowledgment of the "trial truth" established in The Hague is a precondition to reconciliation; for others, such as Edin Ramulić, it is a proxy for reconciliation—a key measure of how far Bosnia has come in the arduous process of social repair. Ramulić, who survived internment in Trnopolje but whose father and brother were killed in Keraterm, said that for him, *reconciliation* means "above all" that the Serbs who were responsible for these abominations "admit[] what was committed."[92]

---

reconciliation" and (in her partial paraphrase) "a critical factor in quelling the cycles of violence and 'extra-judicial retribution' among people who have lived under a reign of terror").

[87] Press Release, ICTY, Joint Statement by the President and the Prosecutor, ICTY Doc. CC/PIO/027-E (Nov. 24, 1995). *See also* Kutnjak Ivković, *Justice by the ICTY, supra* note 86, at 263 (quoting similar views by Goldstone in a 1995 publication).

[88] Antonio Cassese, *The ICTY: A Living and Vital Reality*, 2 J. INT'L CRIM. JUST. 585, 595 (2004).

[89] *E.g.*, interview with Gojko Berić, Journalist & Columnist, Oslobođenje, in Sarajevo, Bosn. & Herz. (July 17, 2009); interview with Emir Suljagić, Author, in Sarajevo, Bosn. & Herz. (Sept. 11, 2014).

[90] ICTY website, http://www.icty.org/en/about (last visited Dec. 11, 2017) (emphasis added). In a similarly modest manner, when asked during a visit to Serbia if the ICTY was contributing to reconciliation, Judge Theodor Meron responded that the Tribunal had contributed to the rule of law in the territory of the former Yugoslavia and that this indirectly influenced reconciliation. *Meron: Judges Work in Accordance with Best Practices of Law*, TANJUG SERBIAN NEWS AGENCY (July 16, 2013). The ICTY Prosecutor has made stronger claims. *See, e.g.*, Serge Brammertz, Prosecutor of the International Tribunal for the Former Yugoslavia, *Report provided to the Security Council under Paragraph 6 of Security Council Resolution 1534*, ¶ 40 (2004), U.N. Doc. S/2014/827, Annex II (Nov. 19, 2014) ("The effective prosecution of war crimes committed during the conflicts in the former Yugoslavia is fundamental to building and sustaining the rule of law, as well as to truth-seeking and reconciliation").

[91] In a variation on this theme, Nerma Jelačić said "it was always wrong to expect the Tribunal to have a direct impact on reconciliation." She nonetheless implied its work would contribute to reconciliation, along with "many [other] things that have to happen." Interview with Nerma Jelačić, then Director, BIRN in BiH, in Sarajevo, Bosn. & Herz. (Dec. 1, 2006).

[92] Interview with Edin Ramulić, Project Coordinator, Izvor, in Prijedor, Bosn. & Herz. (Dec. 8, 2009).

The late civil society leader Srđan Dizdarević made an impassioned case for justice as "the key pillar of reconciliation" when I interviewed him in 2006. Whatever the reasons for the 1990s conflict, Dizdarević said, it created "hatred" and "disturbed the traditional, existing relationships" among Bosnia's ethnic groups. In this setting, he said, "justice will bring a part of the solution." Dizdarević did not believe prosecutions alone could "rebuild trust"; other mechanisms were also needed. But, he insisted, "justice is the starting point, the basic point."[93] In a similar vein, Senad Pećanin was convinced "there is no way to think about reconciliation without justice. Justice is the minimum requirement for any attempts of reconciliation, building ethnic trust between people."[94]

Jasna Bakšić Muftić also said "justice is . . . necessary to create good inter-ethnic relations and stability in the region,"[95] and explained why in terms of historical experience. After World War II, ethnic violence committed during the war "was minimized and put under the carpet." Without a serious process of reckoning, "a double history" developed. Official textbooks omitted discussion of wartime atrocities, which then became part of a "secret history" within families. Those who lost loved ones at the hands of ethnic slaughter endured a "double trauma—that it happened, and that you couldn't talk about what happened." Long repressed, the secret history "completely opened up in the last conflict. All the people know what happened in the Second World War and there was sort of a revenge in the 1990s war."[96]

Some, such as Tarik Jusić, invoked the principle of individual responsibility often emphasized by ICTY leaders to explain why the Tribunal's work would contribute to reconciliation. For Jusić, "It's really essential that the guilt is individual. They [i.e., members of an ethnic group] didn't all commit these crimes."[97]

When I interviewed her in 2006, Sevima Sali-Terzić suggested the international community placed more importance on reconciliation than on the fundamental goal of bringing war criminals to justice. Even so, she considered justice a precondition to reconciliation. Noting *reconciliation* has myriad meanings, Sali-Terzić said the "best meaning" is "we have to know what happened and we have to reconcile with that."[98] She explained:

People here have different understandings of the same facts and all are blaming others. And the real thing is to know what your people did and to reconcile with that. And then you can live with each other. A lot of Serbs do not accept [that Serbs committed genocide in] Srebrenica. Unless you accept that, you cannot reconcile with the past in order to live with your neighbors. For example, people

---

[93] Interview with the late Srđan Dizdarević, then President, Helsinki Committee for Human Rights in Bosnia and Herzegovina, in Sarajevo, Bosn. & Herz. (Dec. 1, 2006).

[94] Interview with Senad Pećanin, then Editor, Dani, in Sarajevo, Bosn. & Herz. (Dec. 6, 2006). Similarly, Mirsad Tokača insisted "there is no social reconstruction without justice." Interview with Mirsad Tokača, Director, Research and Documentation Center (Sarajevo), in Sarajevo, Bosn. & Herz. (Dec. 6, 2006).

[95] Interview with Jasna Bakšić Muftić, Professor, Faculty of Law, University of Sarajevo, in Sarajevo, Bosn. & Herz. (Nov. 30, 2006).

[96] *Id.*

[97] *Id.*

[98] Interview with Sevima Sali-Terzić, Senior Legal Adviser, Constitutional Court of BiH, in Sarajevo, Bosn. & Herz. (Nov. 30, 2006).

here [i.e., Bosniaks] do not accept that Serbs were killed in Srebrenica. . . . The point is that I understand that somebody allegedly in my name killed people and I say 'I don't like this, and they should be punished.' Only then can there be reconciliation.

Sali-Terzić added: "If you just push it under the carpet it will grow and be a real problem."[99]

V. BEARING WITNESS

According to the ICTY's website, more than 4,650 witnesses had testified before the Tribunal as of mid-2015.[100] The majority were "people who survived crimes, who witnessed them, or whose family members were victims of crimes."[101] Although only a fraction of Bosnian survivors have been witnesses in The Hague, many who testified derived deep satisfaction from the experience.[102] For these witnesses, Jasna Bakšić Muftić noted, ICTY trials have provided a "chance to tell their personal history and to have it officially recognized."[103]

For Nusreta Sivac, testifying fulfilled a vow she made to herself before the Tribunal was even created. Sivac, who testified in several ICTY trials, was one of thirty-seven women repeatedly raped while detained in Omarska in the early months of the war.[104] In the darkest days of her captivity, Sivac told me, "I promised myself that I was going to talk about my imprisonment and detention as much as I can" once freed, "mainly because of those who are not here with us anymore." For Sivac, "this was a strong motivation" to testify in The Hague.[105]

VI. PREVENTING FUTURE CRIMES

In the future, others would be thinking twice before committing such crimes.
—Emsuda Mujagić[106]

---

[99] *Id.* Yet as noted in Chapter 9, Sali-Terzić despairs about whether, however necessary, justice came too late for Bosnia.

[100] ICTY website, http://www.icty.org/en/about/registry/witnesses/statistics (last visited Feb. 6, 2017). This figure is lower than those provided in other ICTY-related sources. For example, a study citing the ICTY's Victim and Witness Section as its source reported that, as of June 2009, 5,494 witnesses had been assisted by that unit. Gabriela Mischkowski & Gorana Mlinarević, Medica Mondiale, "... And That It Does Not Happen to Anyone Anywhere in the World": The Trouble with Rape Trials—Views of Witnesses, Prosecutors and Judges on Prosecuting Sexualised Violence During the War in the Former Yugoslavia 50 (2009).

[101] ICTY website, http://www.icty.org/en/about/registry/witnesses (last visited Feb. 6, 2016).

[102] *See, e.g.,* the account of the late Muharem Murselović in Chapter 6.

[103] Interview with Jasna Bakšić Muftić, Professor, Faculty of Law, University of Sarajevo, in Sarajevo, Bosn. & Herz. (Nov. 30, 2006).

[104] *See* Aida Čerkez, *Bosnian Woman Helped Make Rape a War Crime,* Associated Press (Mar. 8, 2013).

[105] Interview with Nusreta Sivac, Former Judge, in Prijedor, Bosn. & Herz. (Sept. 16, 2014).

[106] Interview with Emsuda Mujagić, President, Srcem do Mira, in Kozarac, Bosn. & Herz. (July 23, 2009). Mujagić was describing the effect she thought the trials of Radovan Karadžić and Ratko Mladić, neither of which had yet taken place, would have.

Many Bosnians interviewed for this study expressed the hope that, through its work, the Tribunal would prevent future crimes. While this expectation was often conveyed in terms redolent of expressivism, the views explored in this section were explicitly framed in terms of prevention.

When I first interviewed Mirsad Tokača, he described the value of Hague prosecutions this way: "Simply, it's a message for people that crime will never be accepted. . . . There is a strong message to society that there is not anybody who committed a crime who can stay untouched, unpunished."[107] In a similar vein, Tarik Jusić told me the "message" of the ICTY "is that you can't go around and kill people just because you want to. There are basic civilizational norms you have to obey even in war." And, Jusić continued, "If you don't, you'll have to pay the consequences."[108] Dino Đipa told me "the most useful" impact of the ICTY was that it helped make "people . . . aware that war crimes are wrong" and, in consequence, "in the event of a future war, everyone would be so careful about not committing war crimes because of the work of the ICTY."[109] For Tokača, Jusić, and Đipa, then, the Tribunal's expressive function was important in part because of its supposed deterrent effect.

Branko Todorović, who led the Helsinki Committee for Human Rights in Republika Srpska when I interviewed him in 2009, was painfully aware mass atrocities were committed in Bosnia even after the ICTY was created. Even so, he believed "some very bad crimes would have been committed" in the region but for the Tribunal.[110] Yet he had greater confidence in the deterrent potential of the ICTY's global message: "The best thing the Tribunal in The Hague has done is not related to Bosnia and Herzegovina only or to Kosovo or Rwanda," Todorović said. "It has to do with the world as such and the message is clear: 'Think before you commit a crime. You could certainly be held responsible for what you did.'"[111]

ICTY judges, too, have expressed the hope the Tribunal's work would prevent future crimes. In a 2007 interview, for example, then ICTY judge Wolfgang Schomburg told me he was "convinced that in the future" potential perpetrators would be deterred from committing atrocities as a result of the work of contemporary international tribunals. Asserting that leaders who instigate campaigns of atrocity include "highly intelligent people," he predicted: "When confronted with . . . whether to commit crimes, they will see a real risk of being convicted, being brought to prison."[112]

The hope these individuals voiced may seem to align with one of the purposes for which the Tribunal ostensibly was created. The resolution creating the ICTY expressed the Security Council's belief that the measure would help "put an end" to the "widespread and flagrant violations of international humanitarian law" then underway in Bosnia and contribute to ensuring the crimes "are halted."[113] Reflecting

---

[107] Interview with Mirsad Tokača, President, Research and Documentation Center (Sarajevo), in Sarajevo, Bosn. & Herz. (Dec. 6, 2006).

[108] Interview with Tarik Jusić, then Program Director, Mediacentar Sarajevo, in Sarajevo, Bosn. & Herz. (Dec. 6, 2006).

[109] Interview with Dino Đipa, Research Director, PRISM Research, in Sarajevo, Bosn. & Herz. (July 13, 2009).

[110] Interview with Branko Todorović, then President, Helsinki Committee for Human Rights in Republika Srpska, in Sarajevo, Bosn. & Herz. (July 14, 2009).

[111] *Id.*

[112] Interview with Wolfgang Schomburg, then Judge, ICTY, in The Hague, Neth. (Mar. 5, 2007).

[113] S.C. Res. 827, preamble (May 25, 1993).

this justification, then ICTY president Antonio Cassese noted in 1994, "[o]ne of the main aims" of the Security Council when it established the Tribunal "was to establish a judicial process capable of dissuading the parties to the conflict from perpetrating further crimes."[114] "In short," Cassese wrote, "the Tribunal is intended to act as a powerful deterrent to all parties against continued participation in inhuman acts."[115]

Yet, setting aside the question whether members of the Security Council actually believed creating the ICTY would help end ethnic cleansing,[116] the Bosnians quoted here knew nothing of the sort had happened. Murderous conflict continued in Bosnia for more than two-and-a-half years after the Council launched the Tribunal, culminating in the Srebrenica genocide.[117] Indeed, Nura Begović, a leader of the organization Women of Srebrenica, told me she holds the ICTY responsible for Srebrenica, noting the Tribunal was established two years "before this tragedy occurred." In her view, ICTY prosecutors should have pressed charges sooner, but "they didn't do it."[118] Thus, Bosnians who cited the Tribunal's potential to prevent atrocities seemed to suggest that, now fully operational, the ICTY could send a message to the future that those who may contemplate horrific crimes risk prosecution.[119]

In recent years, several social scientists have developed empirical support for the deterrent impact of human rights prosecutions.[120] While recognizing that, under some conditions, international trials might contribute to prevention of future atrocities, I do not explore the ICTY's impact in this sphere further for two related reasons. First, despite anecdotal evidence suggesting the Tribunal deterred some individuals from committing crimes, it failed to prevent crimes of surpassing scope and cruelty, notably including the Srebrenica massacre. Second, for that reason no one interviewed for this study counts the prevention of atrocities in Bosnia as an ICTY "success."

---

[114] *First Annual Report, supra* note 27, ¶ 13.

[115] *Id.*

[116] The Security Council used its extraordinary powers under Chapter VII of the UN Charter to create the Tribunal. Under the law of the Charter, the Council can take measures under Chapter VII to maintain or restore international peace and security. *See* UN Charter, art. 39. Legally, then, the Council had to link creation of the ICTY to restoring peace, and S.C. resolution 827 implied that preventing further atrocities was integral to that goal.

[117] As well, atrocities later prosecuted in The Hague occurred in Kosovo in 1998–1999.

[118] Interview with Nura Begović, Member of the Presidency, Women of Srebrenica, in Tuzla, Bosn. & Herz. (July 21, 2009). Begović lost sixteen relatives, including her brother, during the Srebrenica massacre. *See* Aida Alić, *Peace of Mind Still Eludes Srebrenica Families*, Just. Rep. (July 9, 2009).

[119] As noted in Chapter 2, however, one of my interlocutors recalled that when the Tribunal was created, many Bosnians' "expectation was . . . that the aggressor states . . . will stop or at least reduce their aggression-related activities simply for the fact that they are now aware of such a UN-organized international tribunal." Interview with Smail Čekić, Professor of History and then Director, Institute for Research of Crimes against Humanity and International Law, University of Sarajevo, in Sarajevo, Bosn. & Herz. (July 16, 2009).

[120] *See, e.g.*, Sikkink, *supra* note 46, at 183–85; Kathryn Sikkink & Hun Joon Kim, *The Justice Cascade: The Origins and Effectiveness of Prosecutions of Human Rights Violations*, 9 Ann. Rev. L. Soc. Sci. 269 (2013). For a more cautious assessment of consequentialist claims, see Leslie Vinjamuri, *Deterrence, Democracy, and the Pursuit of International Justice*, 24 Ethics & Int'l Aff. 191 (2010).

VII. REMOVING WAR CRIMINALS

Although my interlocutors in Bosnia did not identify incapacitation and/or removal of dangerous individuals as a goal they hoped the ICTY would achieve, many implied as much. As I elaborate in Chapter 6, a common and powerful criticism of the ICTY among victims is that, as a result of overly lenient sentences, perpetrators returned to their communities soon after they were convicted of atrocious crimes. In a similar vein, some fault the Tribunal for failing ever to indict many perpetrators, leaving them in positions of influence in local communities.[121] As previously noted, moreover, NATO forces' initial failure to arrest ICTY suspects allowed wartime leaders to regroup and consolidate power during a crucial period of transition,[122] to the lasting regret of many Bosnians. Conversely, NATO arrests beginning in July 1997 contributed, along with other factors, to a significant number of Bosniaks' willingness to return to homes from which they had been forced to flee by ethnic cleansing.[123]

VIII. CATALYZING JUSTICE AT HOME

As noted earlier, many Bosnians believed the ICTY was the only institution that could provide the kind of justice they needed. So, too, did the UN Security Council; its decision to create an international tribunal represented a judgment that local courts in the former Yugoslavia were unable or unwilling to mount credible prosecutions.[124] Thus no one interviewed for this study suggested his or her early support for the Hague Tribunal was based, even in small part, on its capacity to catalyze domestic war crimes prosecutions. As elaborated in Chapter 9, however, the Tribunal eventually did just that. In partnership with the Office of the High Representative as well as Bosnian lawyers, the ICTY played a key role in planning for a specialized war crimes chamber, launched in 2005, in the new Court of Bosnia and Herzegovina, and a Special Department for War Crimes in the office of the state prosecutor. Once this happened, the ICTY's role in launching local war crimes prosecutions was widely seen as one of its "major achievements."[125]

IX. CONCLUDING OBSERVATIONS

As this chapter has elucidated, Bosniak victims in particular hoped the ICTY would meet a raft of pressing needs. In part because the Tribunal was, for many years, the principal institutional response to the crimes they endured, it became a major focus

---

[121] *See* Chapter 6. Another study found that Bosnians "who had particularly suffered" were especially likely to fault the Tribunal for failing to effect the removal of those they blame for their suffering. These individuals had expected the ICTY "to severely punish all war criminals with harsh prison sentences and to have a significant impact at the level of their communities; they had expected to be able to go about their daily lives without encountering people whom they claim are guilty of war crimes." Clark, *Limits of Retributive Justice, supra* note 11, at 467.

[122] *See* Chapter 2.

[123] *See id.*

[124] *See* Chapter 9.

[125] Interview with Gojko Berić, Journalist & Columnist, Oslobođenje, in Sarajevo, Bosn. & Herz. (July 17, 2009).

of soaring expectations. ICTY officials have at times compounded this propensity, raising unrealistic expectations of the Tribunal's social impact.

To the extent victims' expectations were consequentialist, they would be largely disappointed. In particular, as Chapter 8 elucidates, denialism was not only pervasive decades after the ICTY began its work, but was on the rise as its official life drew to an end. The gap between daily encounters with denialism and early expectations is vast, highlighting the crucial importance of establishing and communicating realistic expectations of what international criminal courts can achieve—and what they cannot. Despite Bosnians' disappointments, the Hague Tribunal provided something harder to measure but undeniably precious to many survivors of wartime atrocities: justice.

5

Dealing with the Past

Serbian Perspectives on ICTY Success

As we have seen, Serbian authorities were unremittingly hostile to the ICTY during the Milošević years,[1] and used "tremendous anti-Hague propaganda"[2] to discredit the Tribunal in the eyes of the Serbian public. Since the end of the wartime regime, Serbia's leaders have rarely voiced robust support for the Tribunal's core mission. Even leaders who favored accountability, like Zoran Đinđić and Boris Tadić, were reluctant publicly to justify cooperation with the Hague Tribunal on principled rather than pragmatic grounds, in no small part because they did not want to alienate key sectors of the Serbian public.[3] In contrast to their reticence, nationalist

---

[1] *See* Chapter 3.

[2] Interview with the late Vojin Dimitrijević, then Director, Belgrade Centre for Human Rights, in Belgrade, Serb. (Nov. 28, 2006).

[3] There have, to be sure, been exceptions to the discursive patterns described in Chapter 3. Čedomir Jovanović, leader of the Liberal Democratic Party, has long called for Serbia to "face our historical heritage." Ana Marija Vojković, *Interview: Čedomir Jovanović*, Javno (Apr. 16, 2007). In striking contrast to many other Serbian politicians, Jovanović has publicly recognized that Serbs committed genocide in Srebrenica, *see Čedomir Jovanović in Potočari, Srebrenica Hurts*, Radio Sarajevo (July 11, 2016), and linked the Serbian government's long-running failure to arrest Ratko Mladić to its refusal "to recognize that they are responsible for a genocide." Sylvie Matton, *Pièces à Conviction*, France 3 (Oct. 9, 2007). In 2007, then foreign minister Vuk Jeremić said the Serbian government was committed to transferring both Mladić and Radovan Karadžić to The Hague not only because doing so is "our international obligation, but also our moral duty toward neighbors." *Serb Suspects Must Face U.N. War Crimes Court, Council of Europe Says*, Associated Press (May 24, 2007). But as Bogdan Ivanišević noted, few political leaders confronted Serbian society with "unequivocally clear condemnations" of Serb conduct during the 1990s wars, much

elites aggressively propagated discourses reviling the Tribunal long after Milošević was voted out of power, and with palpable effect: a majority of Serbian citizens have consistently expressed negative views of the ICTY.[4]

Yet Serbian hostility toward the ICTY has never been monolithic. A dedicated corps of citizens has championed the Tribunal, embracing its mission.[5] Several Serbian nongovernmental organizations (NGOs), including the Humanitarian Law Center, Helsinki Committee for Human Rights, Belgrade Centre for Human Rights, and Youth Initiative for Human Rights, advocated for Serbian cooperation with the ICTY and, in various ways, provided tangible support for its work. During the long years in which there was scant prospect of accountability through domestic institutions, the ICTY was a key focus of their advocacy efforts, often at considerable risk to their leaders.[6]

Like Bosnians who embraced the Hague Tribunal, its most staunch supporters in Serbia had "huge expectations from the ICTY."[7] Civil society leader Marijana Toma summarized early expectations this way: "We attributed all these *amazing* powers to the court, like 'it will . . . establish the whole truth about [the] conflict. . . . It will punish everyone. It will contribute to reconciliation. It will *be* reconciliation.'"[8]

This chapter identifies the principal reasons these Serbians supported the ICTY.[9] More specifically, it explores what NGO leaders and other citizens who supported the Hague Tribunal expected it to achieve and, by implication, how they would measure its success. With respect to certain goals, such as dispelling impunity, this chapter also reflects sources' views about how well the Tribunal had already met their expectations by the time I interviewed them. I explore Serbian assessments of two other benchmarks of Tribunal success identified in this chapter, advancing acknowledgment and catalyzing domestic war crimes prosecutions, in later chapters.[10]

I. ENSURING PROSECUTION OF ATROCIOUS CRIMES; DISPELLING IMPUNITY

Some Serbians framed their support for the ICTY in terms redolent of retributivism, saying a key function of the Tribunal is to ensure punishment of individuals

---

less framed cooperation with the ICTY in terms of Serbia's moral debt. Telephone interview with Bogdan Ivanišević, Attorney (Nov. 3, 2006).

[4] *See* Marko Milanović, *The Impact of the ICTY on the Former Yugoslavia: An Anticipatory Postmortem*, 110 Am. J. Int'l L. 233, 240-41 (2016).

[5] Public opinion surveys conducted between 2001 and 2011 suggest these citizens constituted roughly 15 percent of the population in that period. At various points, larger percentages of Serbians said they supported cooperation with the ICTY for pragmatic reasons, such as avoiding new sanctions and ensuring EU membership. But the roughly 15 percent of Serbians to whom I refer here said their country should cooperate with the ICTY "to achieve justice."

[6] While this chapter explores the reasons these citizens supported the ICTY, many have pressed for accountability on multiple fronts. For example, Nataša Kandić, for many years the most prominent Serbian proponent of cooperation with the ICTY, has also led efforts to establish a regional truth commission.

[7] Interview with Maja Mičić, then Executive Director, Youth Initiative for Human Rights, in Belgrade, Serb. (June 11, 2014).

[8] Interview with Marijana Toma, then Deputy Director, Humanitarian Law Center, in Belgrade, Serb. (June 10, 2014).

[9] For obvious reasons, this chapter reflects the views of Serbians interviewed for this study in particular.

[10] *See* Chapters 7 (acknowledgment) and 10 (domestic prosecutions).

responsible for atrocious crimes.[11] In the words of Bogdan Ivanišević, the Tribunal's work "is important for its own sake, because of justice."[12] Some emphasized its importance for victims of Serb war crimes in particular. For example journalist Filip Švarm noted that, despite many victims' disappointment in ICTY sentences, "when you talk to victims there is a sense that justice has been done."[13] Virtually every Serbian source whom I interviewed who supports the ICTY believes, as well, that "if The Hague didn't exist, there would be no trials" for wartime atrocities.[14] Švarm made the point this way: "It's simple. If not for the Hague Tribunal, no one would ever actually bring to trial anyone who committed these crimes."[15] With no prospect of local justice during the Milošević era, Bruno Vekarić said, "The Hague Tribunal was the necessity of the moment."[16]

These Serbians' expectations accord with the views of ICTY judges interviewed for this study, which were noted in Chapter 4. When asked to articulate his understanding of the Tribunal's objectives, for example, Judge Fausto Pocar, then president of the Tribunal, replied: "I would take it that the ICTY was entrusted with prosecuting and holding trials for the main perpetrators . . . and that's the only task."[17] Although the Security Council may have contemplated additional objectives, such as fostering "peace, stability and reconciliation," he continued, the Tribunal itself cannot act as though it has a "political mandate."[18] Judge (later ICTY and MICT president) Theodor Meron expressed a similar sentiment. In his view, "the primary goal of an international tribunal is to do justice and punish atrocities."[19]

Some Serbian sources emphasized the Tribunal's role in establishing that atrocious crimes have consequences.[20] Civil society activist Andrej Nosov said that, by prosecuting Slobodan Milošević, the ICTY helped the Serbian public understand that "there is no one who can order killings and stay unpunished."[21] In a similar vein, Filip Švarm said: "The Hague Tribunal demonstrated that not everything can be legalized."[22] Bogdan Ivanišević believes the ICTY helped dispel the corrosive effects of impunity in Serbia, and evoked the specter of lawless license he believes would have prevailed had it not been established. Convinced there would have been no prosecutions of war criminals in Serbia with the ICTY, Ivanišević said its work was

---

[11] For a brief discussion of retributivism, see Chapter 4. Subject to caveats noted earlier, Serbian citizens were not victims of atrocities that are the focus of this study, although many "felt themselves as victims" of NATO bombings in 1999. Interview with Antonela Riha, Journalist, in Belgrade, Serb. (Nov. 27, 2006). Accordingly, Serbian sources did not explain their support for the ICTY in terms of a personal need for justice.

[12] Telephone interview with Bogdan Ivanišević, Attorney (Nov. 3, 2006).

[13] Interview with Filip Švarm, Journalist, in Belgrade, Serb. (Nov. 24, 2006). It may be important to note the date of my interview. As elucidated in Chapter 6, victims have grown increasingly frustrated with the ICTY in the years since I interviewed Švarm.

[14] Interview with Svetlana Logar, then Deputy General Director, Strategic Marketing Research, in Belgrade, Serb. (Nov. 21, 2006).

[15] Interview with Filip Švarm, Journalist, in Belgrade, Serb. (Nov. 24, 2006).

[16] Interview with Bruno Vekarić, Deputy War Crimes Prosecutor, in Belgrade, Serb. (Nov. 21, 2006).

[17] Interview with Fausto Pocar, Judge and then President, ICTY, in The Hague, Neth. (Mar. 5, 2007).

[18] Id.

[19] Interview with Theodor Meron, Judge, ICTY, in The Hague, Neth. (Mar. 6, 2007).

[20] Some of these sources evoked expressivist as well as deterrence rationales for punishment. The former is explained in Chapter 4.

[21] Interview with Andrej Nosov, then Executive Director, Youth Initiative for Human Rights, in Belgrade, Serb. (Nov. 23, 2006).

[22] Interview with Filip Švarm, Journalist, in Belgrade, Serb. (Nov. 24, 2006).

important in part "because the message otherwise will be one can do whatever he wants to do because he's in power and that's it. That kind of message would be disastrous. The ICTY prevented that from happening."[23]

Journalist Dejan Anastasijević, too, evoked the toxic effects of impunity: "When a crime occurs and it's unpunished, a hole is opened in the fabric of society, like a hole in your stocking. If it's left unattended, it tends to spread all over. . . . Because if it's OK to kill or rape a human being because the victim is a member of a community which we tend to see as our enemy, where do we draw the line?"[24] Anastasijević recalled a case in which a drug dealer had defended himself by claiming he was trafficking heroine to "get even" with North Atlantic Treaty Organization countries that bombed Serbia in the 1999 Kosovo war. Paraphrasing the dealer's claim ("They gave us bombs, we gave drugs to their children"), Anastasijević observed: "Once a crime is justified for patriotic reasons, you can put that label on anything. Not processing war crimes right away creates an atmosphere of impunity that tends to spread to the whole society."[25]

Like more straightforward retributivist claims noted earlier, the perspective articulated by Nosov, Švarm, Ivanišević, and Anastasijević aligns with the views of ICTY judges interviewed for this study. In the words of Judge Meron, "Ending impunity for the terrible crimes [committed in the former Yugoslavia] was always a primary goal." He added: "That goal is largely being achieved."[26] In the view of then judge Wolfgang Schomburg, "By the very existence of the Tribunal, the culture of impunity has found an end."[27] Judge Schomburg elaborated: The ICTY is "fulfilling for the first time in history in the area of our responsibility the promise enshrined in . . . the International Covenant on Civil and Political Rights . . . that 'All persons shall be equal before the courts and tribunals.' There are no longer untouchables!"[28]

II. REMOVING WAR CRIMINALS

In domestic legal systems, a widely-cited justification for imprisonment of convicted felons is incapacitation: as long as they are behind bars, individuals who committed heinous crimes cannot do so again, at least against individuals beyond prison walls.[29] Serbian supporters of the ICTY cited a similar, yet somewhat distinct, justification for the Tribunal's work: by "physically removing some of the worst criminals" from Serbia,[30] the ICTY provided the country a viable chance to chart a new path going forward.[31]

---

[23] Telephone interview with Bogdan Ivanišević, Attorney (Nov. 3, 2006).

[24] Interview with Dejan Anastasijević, Journalist, in Belgrade, Serb. (Nov. 20, 2006).

[25] Id.

[26] Interview with Theodor Meron, Judge, ICTY, in The Hague, Neth. (Mar. 6, 2007).

[27] Interview with Wolfgang Schomburg, then Judge, ICTY, The Hague, Neth. (Mar. 5, 2007).

[28] Id.

[29] See, e.g., Kent Greenawalt, Punishment, in CRIMINAL LAW: CASES AND MATERIALS 39 (Joshua Dressler & Stephen P. Garvey eds., 7th ed. 2007).

[30] Interview with Dejan Anastasijević, Journalist, in Belgrade, Serb. (Nov. 20, 2006).

[31] Removing spoilers from positions of responsibility has been a "significant practical contribution of transitional justice processes" in other post-conflict settings. Rachel Kerr, Transitional Justice in Post-Conflict Contexts: Opportunities and Challenges, in JUSTICE MOSAICS: HOW CONTEXT SHAPES TRANSITIONAL JUSTICE IN FRACTURED SOCIETIES 116, 122 (Roger Dutie & Paul Seils eds., 2017).

Describing this as an important contribution of the Tribunal "that is usually neglected by experts," Dejan Anastasijević observed: "It was good not to have them around, at all levels."[32] In fact, Anastasijević believes, the 1999 indictment of then president Slobodan Milošević helped bring about Serbia's transition to a democratically-elected government the following year.[33] Filip Švarm suggested that if Serbia's leading war criminals had not been prosecuted in The Hague, "we would have had a mafia oligarchy as our leaders."[34]

An official who served in the first post-Milošević government in Serbia, Dušan Protić, told me the "removal of Milošević was something that had to be done in order to make the next step in our democratization process."[35] Why not remove Milošević from public life by prosecuting him in Serbia, then? For awhile, both leaders of the coalition government that succeeded Milošević supported doing so.[36] But in Protić's view, Milošević "would have been an unbearable burden [if he were tried] in Serbian jurisdiction." Characterizing the apparently-evolved view of the Serbian government led by Prime Minister Zoran Đinđić, Protić continued: "The government probably felt, . . . they can handle him [in The Hague]; we cannot."[37] In much the same vein, Goran Svilanović, who handled negotiations with the ICTY on behalf of the FRY government, believes that "if Milošević had not been extradited, he would never be prosecuted here."[38]

Not everyone agrees. Professor Radmila Nakarada believes that "if Milošević had remained, he would have likely been prosecuted here. There was a widespread feeling that what he did was very painful for his citizens—that was in the air."[39] Others, however, emphasized the risks to which Protić alluded. Noting "some say [Milošević] should have been tried in Belgrade," Antonela Riha said: "If that happened, there would be thousands outside [the courthouse]. That would be a mess. He'd be even more of a hero if he were tried here."[40] Describing former Serbian prime minister Zoran Đinđić's decision to transfer Milošević to The Hague as "maybe the most important decision" he made, Riha added: Milošević "may be in a cave, but you never know when he'll come out."[41]

---

[32] Interview with Dejan Anastasijević, Journalist, in Belgrade, Serb. (Nov. 20, 2006).

[33] *Id.* Anastasijević explained: the fact that Serbia's "chief of state is indicted for war crimes and therefore internationally isolated did contribute to people being aware there's no future with him." *Id.*

[34] Interview with Filip Švarm, Journalist, in Belgrade, Serb. (Nov. 24, 2006).

[35] Interview with Dušan Protić, Former Deputy Minister of Justice, Serbia, in Belgrade, Serb. (Nov. 23, 2006).

[36] *See* Chapter 3.

[37] Interview with Dušan Protić, Former Deputy Minister of Justice, Serbia, in Belgrade, Serb. (Nov. 23, 2006).

[38] Interview with Goran Svilanović, Former Minister of Foreign Affairs, FRY, in Belgrade, Serb. (Nov. 20, 2006).

[39] Interview with Radmila Nakarada, then Associate Professor, Faculty of Political Sciences, University of Belgrade, in Belgrade, Serb. (Nov. 24, 2006). It is by no means clear, however, that Milošević would have faced war crimes charges in Serbia. Instead, when he was arrested in 2001, it was on corruption-related charges. *See* Steven Erlanger & Carlotta Gall, *The Milošević Surrender: The Overview; Milošević Arrest Came with Pledge for a Fair Trial*, N.Y. TIMES (Apr. 2, 2001).

[40] Interview with Antonela Riha, Journalist, in Belgrade, Serb. (Nov. 27, 2006).

[41] *Id.*

The perspective shared by Anastasijević, Švarm, Protić, Svilanović, and Riha is noteworthy not only because, as Anastasijević suggested, it is "usually neglected by experts": it provides a counterpoint to the claim that international prosecutions can imperil efforts to contain the power of spoilers during a fragile transition.[42] This is not to suggest international prosecutions invariably have the effect Serbian sources praised. But Serbia is an important case study of a situation in which international prosecutions *removed* spoilers during a particularly fragile period of political transition.[43]

Even in Serbia, however, prosecutions in The Hague carried political risks. Ana Miljanić suggested the ICTY's then ongoing prosecution of one high-profile Serbian defendant, Serbian Radical Party leader Vojislav Šešelj, might have boosted his stature. "Being prosecuted in The Hague means you're special," Miljanić noted, and "this helped mystify [Šešelj]."[44] Saying the "Šešelj case so belonged in Belgrade," Miljanić nonetheless noted Serbia's own war crimes prosecutor "didn't want him prosecuted here."[45]

III. DEALING WITH THE PAST

For me, the acknowledgment is the key for everything.

—MARIJANA TOMA[46]

Many Serbian sources who support the ICTY placed special emphasis on its expected role in advancing a national process of "dealing with the past."[47] In their view, both Serbian society and the Serbian government must acknowledge atrocities that were committed in the name of ethnic Serbs and condemn them unequivocally. Doing so would entail a rupture with widespread *denial*, a concept I use in this book, along with *denialism*, to capture a spectrum of related phenomena, including: literal denial of fundamental facts; distortion of such facts, including by minimizing the scale of crimes conceded to have occurred; silence; and interpretive denial. While the first

---

[42] *See* Jack Snyder & Leslie Vinjamuri, *Trials and Errors: Principle and Pragmatism in Strategies of International Justice*, 28 INT'L SECURITY 5 (2003–2004).

[43] There have been a number of instances in which leaders of fragile post-conflict states wanted an international court to prosecute their predecessor on the ground domestic prosecutions would be destabilizing. In 2006, Liberian president Ellen Johnson Sirleaf asked that her predecessor, Charles Taylor, be prosecuted outside the region for this reason. Taylor had been indicted by the Special Court for Sierra Leone (SCSL), which was based in Freetown, Sierra Leone. Although the SCSL held all of its other trials in Freetown, it conducted Taylor's trial in The Hague to honor Sirleaf's request. Marlise Simons, *Former Liberian President in The Hague for Trial*, N.Y. TIMES (June 21, 2006).

[44] Interview with Ana Miljanić, Center for Cultural Decontamination, in Belgrade, Serb. (Nov. 22, 2006). Ten years after I interviewed Miljanić, Šešelj's marathon trial ended in acquittal at the trial level. The trial verdict was widely thought to have bolstered the popularity of Šešelj's political party in the short term. I discuss this case in Chapter 6.

[45] Interview with Ana Miljanić, Center for Cultural Decontamination, in Belgrade, Serb. (Nov. 22, 2006). Indeed, Serbia's long-time war crimes prosecutor, Vladimir Vučkević, told me he believed it would be destabilizing to try Šešelj in Belgrade. Interview with Vladimir Vučković, then War Crimes Prosecutor, in Belgrade, Serb. (Nov. 21, 2006).

[46] Interview with Marijana Toma, then Deputy Director, Humanitarian Law Center, in Belgrade, Serb. (June 10, 2014).

[47] Interview with Maja Mičić, then Executive Director, Youth Initiative for Human Rights, in Belgrade, Serb. (June 11, 2014).

three phenomena are self-explanatory, I use the phrase *interpretive denial* to connote circumstances in which someone does not deny certain facts occurred, but denies their appropriate meaning or implications, including their moral implications.[48]

In the context of pervasive Serbian denialism, the acknowledgment Serbian advocates said they hoped the ICTY would catalyze has several layers, beginning with citizens' actual knowledge of the occurrence and nature of wartime atrocities and *public recognition* of those facts without distortion.[49] Nataša Kandić, the longtime (now former) director of the Humanitarian Law Center, justified the ICTY's work this way: "[O]ne of the tasks for the [ICTY] is to put an end to the practice of . . . passing over in silence or denying atrocities, or persistently broadcasting . . . distorted and biased versions of the past."[50] Ana Miljanić said a key measure of ICTY success would be that "people remember over time things that were brought into public knowledge by the ICTY's work."[51]

Miljanić's notion of bringing facts "into public knowledge" evokes Thomas Nagel's conception of acknowledgment. Seeking to explain the difference between knowledge and acknowledgment, Nagel described the latter as "what happens and can only happen to knowledge . . . when it is made part of the public cognitive scene."[52] Kandić's and Miljanić's conceptions of acknowledgment also call to mind Stanley Cohen's notion of "coming to terms with the past":

> For the collective, as for the individual, "coming to terms with the past" is to know (*and admit to knowing*) exactly what happened.[53]

Beyond spurring citizens publicly to recognize the fundamental facts of wartime atrocities, these Serbians hoped the ICTY would stimulate acknowledgment in

---

[48] My usage departs somewhat from Stanley Cohen's definition of *interpretive denial*. In Cohen's usage, interpretive denial does not entail denying the "raw facts" of what happened, but instead entails giving those facts "a different meaning from what seems apparent to others." STANLEY COHEN, STATES OF DENIAL: KNOWING ABOUT ATROCITIES AND SUFFERING 7 (2001). An example of this type of denial is calling what others recognize as "ethnic cleansing" a "population transfer." *Id.* Cohen used the phrase *implicatory denial* to connote denying or minimizing "the psychological, political or moral implications that conventionally follow" from knowing certain facts. *Id.* at 8. I use the phrase *interpretive denial* to capture both categories. For a similar approach, see Nenad Dimitrijević, *Serbia After the Criminal Past: What Went Wrong and What Should Be Done*, 2 INT'L J. TRANSITIONAL JUST. 5, 5–6 (2008) (illustrating "interpretive denial" with the example of admitting that Serbs killed thousands of Muslims in Srebrenica while arguing the acts were legitimate acts of self-defense).

[49] As I explain in Chapter 7, many Serbian citizens know what happened during the war but are unwilling to say so outside their most intimate circles of family and friends, if at all.

[50] Nataša Kandić, *The ICTY Trials and Transitional Justice in Former Yugoslavia*, 38 CORNELL INT'L L.J. 789, 789 (2005).

[51] Interview with Ana Miljanić, Center for Cultural Decontamination, in Belgrade, Serb. (Nov. 22, 2006). Some, however, faulted the ICTY for overreaching with respect to the *nature* of the facts its prosecutor sought to establish. In particular, Dejan Anastasijević said, the prosecutor sought to establish the "historical truth" through the vehicle of the Milošević trial, and "that was a mortal mistake." In his view, "No court in the world should aim to discover the historical truth," but should instead establish only those facts that bear on the defendant's criminal responsibility. Interview with Dejan Anastasijević, Journalist, in Belgrade, Serb. (Nov. 20, 2006).

[52] Nagel offered this distinction at a seminal meeting in 1988. *See* LAWRENCE WESCHLER, A MIRACLE, A UNIVERSE: SETTLING ACCOUNTS WITH TORTURERS 4 (1991).

[53] COHEN, *supra* note 48, at 222 (emphasis added).

another sense: citizens would attach appropriate moral meaning to the basic facts of Serb depredations and Serbia's role in sponsoring them, thereby dispelling a pernicious form of *interpretive denial*, and condemn Serb atrocities without equivocation. Thus, Miljanić suggested, a vital role of the ICTY is "to promote the ethical message, however difficult."[54] This conception corresponds to two scholars' definition of *acknowledgment* as "a conscious and public acceptance that the in-group's actions have violated some important moral precepts . . . In other words, acknowledgment refers to a psychological readiness to publicly *accept the meaning* of the in-group's immoral behavior."[55] It also evokes the German notion of *Vergangenheitsbewältigung*—coming to terms with the past—which is well known to some of my Serbian interlocutors. As Susanne Karstedt explains, the German concept "includes the moral dimension of dealing with the past, as well as the process of the general public's reorientation and reevaluation of the past."[56]

Some evoked the notion of *collective responsibility*, in the sense of "realization of in-group responsibility for some negative behavior."[57] Describing the ICTY as a mechanism for reconciliation, Marijana Toma explained: "For me, reconciliation is about reconciling with your past, reconciling with the accountability for the crimes that were committed either in your name or somebody from your community committed them, so it's about reconciling with the fact that your state committed genocide. It is about acknowledgment more than anything else."[58]

Toma and others suggested Serbians owe a moral debt of acknowledgment to victims of Serb atrocities. Saying "acknowledgment is the key for everything," Toma continued: "The knowledge exists between the victim and the perpetrator. But unless it is acknowledged, then the victim is not recognized. Its suffering is not recognized, and somehow the full truth is not there."[59]

Several emphasized acknowledgment as a foundation for the future. Goran Svilanović hoped the ICTY's work would inspire Serbian citizens "to discuss the crimes"[60] and make a moral and political commitment that "this should never happen again."[61] Andrej Nosov, who founded an organization "as an answer to denial

---

[54] Interview with Ana Miljanić, Center for Cultural Decontamination, in Belgrade, Serb. (Nov. 22, 2006).

[55] Sabina Čehajić & Rupert Brown, *Silencing the Past: Effects of Intergroup Contact on Acknowledgment of In-Group Responsibility*, 1 SOC. PSYCHOL. & PERSONALITY SCI. 190, 191 (2010).

[56] Susanne Karstedt, *Coming to Terms with the Past in Germany After 1945 and 1989: Public Judgments on Procedures and Justice*, 20 L. & POL'Y 15, 16 (1998).

[57] Čehajić & Brown, *supra* note 55, at 191.

[58] Interview with Marijana Toma, then Deputy Director, Humanitarian Law Center, in Belgrade, Serb. (June 10, 2014).

[59] *Id.* In similar terms, Pablo de Greiff has often argued that a key function of transitional justice measures is to recognize the moral value of victims. The acknowledgment provided through the work of truth commissions, he writes, "is important precisely because it constitutes a form of recognizing the significance and value of persons— . . . as individuals . . . and as victims." Pablo de Greiff, *DDR and Reparations: Establishing Links Between Peace and Justice Instruments, in* BUILDING A FUTURE ON PEACE AND JUSTICE 321, 346 (Kai Ambos et al. eds., 2009). *See also* Chapter 1.

[60] Interview with Goran Svilanović, Former Minister of Foreign Affairs, FRY, in Belgrade, Serb. (Nov. 20, 2006).

[61] *Id.* Svilanović's focus on the future evoked a theme Martha Minow has eloquently captured:

> Living after genocide, mass atrocity, totalitarian terror . . . makes remembering and forgetting not just about dealing with the past. The treatment of the past through

of crimes" that focuses on youth, told me he "strongly believes the only way to build a future" for Serbia "is to take responsibility for the past."[62] While making the case for a truth commission rather than cooperation with the ICTY, Nenad Dimitrijević has also evoked the moral consequences of Serbian citizens' failure to come to terms with the wartime past: "The wall of silence built around the recent past only fosters a situation in which there are too many people who are either incapable or unwilling to distinguish between right and wrong."[63]

Some suggested a social reckoning would mark the growing maturity of Serbia's fragile democracy. At a time when Serbia still resisted demands that it arrest remaining ICTY fugitives, the Humanitarian Law Center linked cooperation with the Hague Tribunal to the "building of Serbia's democratic future based on respect for the Law and human rights."[64] It maintained, moreover, that "Serbia's political system . . . can invigorate its democratic culture only in so far as it has created room for memory of 'that past,'" and that cooperation was key to this process.[65] Ivan Janković characterized the ICTY's role in educating Serbians about their former leaders' responsibility for atrocious crimes as "extremely important." He, too, explained why in terms of Serbia's capacity to function as a mature democracy: "If they're not informed, the public will not be aware of crimes, [which is necessary] in order to make correct choices" as citizens.[66]

As elaborated in Chapter 7, Serbian supporters of the ICTY (and other Serbian proponents of accountability) believe, as well, that it is not enough that citizens address the past. In their view, the Serbian government must formally acknowledge, condemn, and apologize for Serb atrocities and Serbian state institutions' role in sponsoring them.

IV. RECONCILIATION

You need justice for reconciliation.

—Andrej Nosov[67]

Some of my Serbian interlocutors linked the ICTY's work to reconciliation and stability, even if (as one source suggested in 2006), its work "can have negative effects on stabilization" in the near-term.[68] As has often been recognized, *reconciliation* has

---

remembering and forgetting crucially shapes the present and future for individuals and entire societies.

Martha Minow, Between Vengeance and Forgiveness: Facing History After Genocide and Mass Violence 119 (1998).

[62] Interview with Andrej Nosov, then Executive Director, Youth Initiative for Human Rights, in Belgrade, Serb. (Nov. 23, 2006).

[63] Dimitrijević, *supra* note 48, at 14.

[64] Humanitarian Law Center, *Political Elites in Serbia Show No Responsibility for Legacy of the Past* (Dec. 11, 2006).

[65] Humanitarian Law Center, Transitional Justice Report: Serbia, Montenegro and Kosovo, 1999–2005, at 6 (2006).

[66] Interview with Ivan Janković, Attorney, in Belgrade, Serb. (Nov. 24, 2006).

[67] Interview with Andrej Nosov, then Executive Director, Youth Initiative for Human Rights, in Belgrade, Serb. (Nov. 23, 2006).

[68] Interview with Filip Ejdus, then Research Fellow, Center for Civil-Military Relationships, in Belgrade, Serb. (Nov. 23, 2006).

multiple meanings and "is rarely defined clearly."[69] I have already noted one of the meanings Marijana Toma attached to *reconciliation*, which she equated with a societal process of addressing the past and acknowledging wrongdoing. Later in the same interview, Toma articulated a somewhat different notion: By establishing the "facts . . . about the crimes" committed during the 1990s conflict, the ICTY could help forge a common version of historical truth among former Yugoslav communities. Noting there are now multiple versions of the truth, Toma said:

> What we are seeing now, there are . . . sort of conflicts *of* memory. We have wars of memory, like . . . Serbian version of the past or this Croatian version of the past, in conflict with each other. And you have . . . wars *for* memory. And that is what we are waging here.[70]

Forging a common and accurate understanding, some suggested, is necessary to avoid future manipulation of the past. Recalling how Milošević and other nationalist leaders weaponized the past to foment ethnic violence in the 1990s, Filip Ejdus said: "If you don't have justice, you can always manipulate the past. . . . A lot of space is left for manipulation, [as happened] after the Second World War. You have different historiographies." But "once you have a sentence by a legal authority, you have firm ground [for discussion]."[71]

Ejdus' view is grounded, as he suggested, in Yugoslavia's postwar history. Although Yugoslavia's major ethnic groups committed mass atrocities against each other during World War II, the country's leader, Josip Broz Tito, "largely dispens[ed] with war crimes trials like those the Allies convened at Nuremberg."[72] Against this background, nationalist leaders in the former Yugoslavia were able to tap a deep reservoir of latent interethnic fear to provoke violence during the 1990s.

While some suggested the ICTY's work was important in part because it would advance reconciliation, this view was hardly universal among Serbian sources who supported the Tribunal. Whatever *reconciliation* means, Jadranka Jelinčić said, it has no place in the Hague Tribunal's mission. In her words, "it is not the work of any judicial tribunal."[73]

---

[69] Oskar N.T. Thoms et al., *The Effects of Transitional Justice Mechanisms* 26 (Ctr. Int'l Stud., Working Paper 2008).

[70] Interview with Marijana Toma, then Deputy Director, Humanitarian Law Center, in Belgrade, Serb. (June 10, 2014). Toma made this point when I asked her to clarify why she thought establishing facts would contribute to reconciliation.

[71] Interview with Filip Ejdus, then Research Fellow, Center for Civil-Military Relationships, in Belgrade, Serb. (Nov. 23, 2006).

[72] ARYEH NEIER, WAR CRIMES: BRUTALITY, GENOCIDE, TERROR, AND THE STRUGGLE FOR JUSTICE 5 (1998). The few trials carried out in postwar Yugoslavia were controversial; Tito's goal in prosecuting two prominent postwar defendants, Aryeh Neier writes, was to silence opponents of the Communist government. *Id.* at 115–16.

[73] Interview with Jadranka Jelinčić, Executive Director, Open Society Foundation Serbia, in Belgrade, Serb. (July 9, 2012).

V. STRENGTHENING THE RULE OF LAW BY CATALYZING DOMESTIC WAR CRIMES PROSECUTIONS

As noted, many Serbians who championed cooperation with the ICTY believed accountability had to come through the Hague Tribunal because, at the time of its creation and for a long time after, there was no other viable option. Credible prosecutions by the Serbian government were unimaginable.[74] In consequence, Serbians who supported the Tribunal did not initially conceive of it as a vehicle for catalyzing domestic prosecutions.

By the time of my first research visit in 2006, however, the Tribunal had done just that. As I explore in depth in Chapter 10, the ICTY spurred Serbia to create a domestic war crimes chamber and Office of the War Crimes Prosecutor, and in myriad ways worked to strengthen these institutions. Virtually all of my Serbian interlocutors, including those who have otherwise been at best ambivalent about the Tribunal, considered this contribution invaluable. Yet as I elaborate in Chapter 10, this legacy has always been fragile; in the final years of the ICTY's formal life, Serbia's war crimes institutions suffered the increasingly corrosive effects of political pressure.

---

[74] *E.g.*, interview with Dejan Anastasijević, Journalist, in Belgrade, Serb. (Nov. 20, 2006). Although Serbia, Bosnia, and Croatia had all undertaken war crimes prosecutions by the time we spoke, Anastasijević said none of these countries could handle high-profile war crimes cases "for a long time to come," and added: "That's quite clear." *Id.*

PART THREE

The Quality of Victims' Justice

6

The Quality of Justice

Bosnian Assessments

As far as the Hague Tribunal, I'm not happy with its work. But the great thing was to have it established. It was excellent that it was established.

—Džafer Deronjić[1]

I hate the Tribunal but I need the Tribunal.

—Saša Madacki[2]

The literature on ICTs presents a damning indictment of international justice (along with robust defenses, to be sure). With respect to the ICTY, victims are said to be frustrated with the imposition of "trifling, even laughable" sentences,[3] intolerably long proceedings,[4] plush conditions of detention for individuals who brought Bosnia

---

[1] Interview with Džafer Deronjić, Association of the Families of Missing, Forcibly Detained and Murdered Bosniaks of Bosnia and Herzegovina, in Brčko, Bosn. & Herz. (July 22, 2009).

[2] Interview with Saša Madacki, Director, Human Rights Centre, University of Sarajevo, in Sarajevo, Bosn. & Herz. (July 17, 2009).

[3] ERIC STOVER, THE WITNESSES: WAR CRIMES AND THE PROMISE OF JUSTICE IN THE HAGUE 142 (2005); *see also* Mirko Klarin, *The Impact of the ICTY Trials on Public Opinion in the Former Yugoslavia*, 7 J. INT'L CRIM. JUST. 89, 90 (2009); Kelly Askin, *International Criminal Tribunals and Victim-Witnesses, in* INTERNATIONAL WAR CRIMES TRIALS: MAKING A DIFFERENCE? 49, 57 (Steven R. Ratner & James L. Bischoff eds., 2004) [hereinafter Askin, *Victim-Witnesses*]; Janine Natalya Clark, *The Limits of Retributive Justice: Findings of an Empirical Study in Bosnia and Hercegovina*, 7 J. INT'L CRIM. J. 463, 471 (2009); Janine Natalya Clark, *Judging the ICTY: Has It Achieved Its Objectives?*, 9 SOUTHEAST EUR. & BLACK SEA STUD. 123, 130 (2009).

[4] *See, e.g.,* Janine Natalya Clark, *The Impact Question: The ICTY and the Restoration and Maintenance of Peace, in* THE LEGACY OF THE INTERNATIONAL CRIMINAL TRIBUNAL FOR THE FORMER YUGOSLAVIA 55, 62 (Bert Swart et al. eds., 2011) [hereinafter Clark, *The Impact Question*]; Klarin, *supra* note 3, at 90.

to ruinous violence,[5] the limited number of perpetrators tried in The Hague,[6] controversial acquittals,[7] judges' failure to rein in disruptive defendants,[8] the ICTY's limited engagement with local populations,[9] the persistence of widespread denial of facts adjudicated in The Hague,[10] and on and on.[11]

My interviews with Bosnians generated a similar catalogue of discontent, which this chapter explores in some depth. For the most part, however, I heard nuanced assessments of the ICTY from individuals whose point of departure was to support its work. With rare exception,[12] no one in this category assessed the Tribunal in terms implying it should not have been created (though other reports suggest the possible exception in my interviews is hardly alone).[13] For many, the Tribunal has rendered a measure of justice that, however flawed, is infinitely preferable to no justice at all. In their eyes, the Tribunal's creation was amply justified because it rendered "a little piece of justice."[14] Particularly at a time of robust debate about the goals we can responsibly assign to ICTs, this tells us something deeply important: while the Hague Tribunal could not imaginably achieve some goals ascribed to its work, it could and did provide victims meaningful redress.

---

[5] See JULIAN BORGER, THE BUTCHER'S TRAIL: HOW THE SEARCH FOR BALKAN WAR CRIMINALS BECAME THE WORLD'S MOST SUCCESSFUL MANHUNT 317 (2016); Askin, *Victim-Witnesses, supra* note 3, at 58; GABRIELA MISCHKOWSKI & GORANA MLINAREVIĆ, MEDICA MONDIALE, " . . . AND THAT IT DOESN'T HAPPEN TO ANYONE ANYWHERE IN THE WORLD": THE TROUBLE WITH RAPE TRIALS—VIEWS OF WITNESSES, PROSECUTORS AND JUDGES ON PROSECUTING SEXUALISED VIOLENCE DURING THE WAR IN THE FORMER YUGOSLAVIA 53 (2009).

[6] See, e.g., Isabelle Delpla, *In the Midst of Injustice: The ICTY from the Perspective of Some Victim Associations, in* THE NEW BOSNIAN MOSAIC: IDENTITIES, MEMORIES AND MORAL CLAIMS IN A POST-WAR SOCIETY 214 (Xavier Bougarel et al. eds., 2007); Clark, *The Impact Question, supra* note 4, at 68; Klarin, *supra* note 3, at 90.

[7] See *Hague Tribunal Prepares for Shutdown in 2017*, BALKAN TRANSITIONAL JUST. (Jan. 4, 2017).

[8] See generally PATRICIA M. WALD, OPEN SOCIETY JUSTICE INITIATIVE, TYRANTS ON TRIAL: KEEPING ORDER IN THE COURTROOM (2009).

[9] See, e.g., Refik Hodžić, *Accepting a Difficult Truth: ICTY Is Not Our Court*, BALKAN TRANSITIONAL JUST. (Mar. 6, 2013); KRISTEN CIBELLI & TAMY GUBEREK, JUSTICE UNKNOWN, JUSTICE UNSATISFIED? (2000).

[10] See, e.g., Delpla, *supra* note 6, at 216; Dejan Guzina & Branka Marijan, *Local Uses of International Criminal Justice in Bosnia-Herzegovina: Transcending Divisions or Building Parallel Worlds?*, 7 STUD. SOC. JUST. 245, 251 (2013).

[11] Jelena Subotić summarizes key disappointments this way: "ICTY legal proceedings have been staggeringly difficult for the local population to understand and internalize . . . For many victims, ICTY sentences have been shockingly low, plea bargains overused, and the percentage of acquittals too high." JELENA SUBOTIĆ, HIJACKED JUSTICE: DEALING WITH THE PAST IN THE BALKANS 132 (2009).

[12] I refer here to my 2014 interview with Sevima Sali-Terzić, which I describe below. Sali-Terzić did not literally say the Tribunal should not have been created, but her critique is consistent with this view.

[13] See, e.g., *Bosnia 1992: The Omarska Camp*, AL JAZEERA (May 10, 2017) (quoting Omarska survivor Rezak Hukanović saying: "The very establishment of the tribunal in The Hague was just a naïve story for the gullible that justice would finally be done. Now we all know it hasn't.").

[14] Interview with Kada Hotić, Vice President, Mothers of Srebrenica and Žepa Enclaves, in Sarajevo, Bosn. & Herz. (July 24, 2009). Based on her own fieldwork in Bosnia, Janine Natalya Clark similarly found that, "In general, Bosnian Muslims are extremely glad that the ICTY exists." Yet, in line with the findings presented here, Clark also found "deep-felt dissatisfaction with the quantity and quality of the 'justice' it delivers." JANINE NATALYA CLARK, INTERNATIONAL TRIALS AND RECONCILIATION: ASSESSING THE IMPACT OF THE INTERNATIONAL CRIMINAL TRIBUNAL FOR THE FORMER YUGOSLAVIA 59 (2014).

That victims of ethnic cleansing would nonetheless be disappointed in myriad aspects of Hague justice was inevitable. As many survivors readily acknowledge, after enduring crimes of surpassing cruelty, no measure of justice *could* meet their needs.[15] As well, "since the ICTY was long the most visible institution of transitional justice in Bosnia," many Bosnians trained frustrations on The Hague they might otherwise direct toward local institutions.[16] Believing "the judicial paradigm would do everything" in terms of "dealing with the past," Edin Hodžić reflected, many Bosnians experienced the "full circle of high expectations in the beginning and big disappointment" later.[17]

But if victims were bound to be disappointed in the ICTY, much of their frustration derives from aspects of its performance that, by common accord, are problematic. At the same time, some aspects of its work have been gratifying for many survivors. This chapter explores both dimensions of the Tribunal's record.

I. BROAD PATTERNS IN BOSNIAN ASSESSMENTS OF THE ICTY

A. Overall Decline in Positive Assessments

As noted in Chapter 2, when the ICTY was created, many Bosnians had "great, great expectations of international justice."[18] Years later, most believed the ICTY had only "partially" fulfilled their early expectations.[19] In 2006, Dobrila Govedarica aptly summarized views I heard often during interviews at that time: most Bosnians recognized "some positive developments" as a result of the ICTY's work, "but all of us would have expected to see much more."[20]

---

[15] Kada Hotić made the point this way: "We know very well what the court can do for us . . . [It] cannot bring our loved ones back." Interview with Kada Hotić, Vice President, Association of Mothers of Srebrenica and Žepa Enclaves, in Sarajevo, Bosn. & Herz. (Sept. 18, 2014).

[16] SUBOTIĆ, *supra* note 11, at 135.

[17] Interview with Edin Hodžić, Director, Public Law Program, Center for Social Research Analitika, in Sarajevo, Bosn. & Herz. (Sept. 11, 2014).

[18] Interview with Fadil Budnjo, President, Association of Families of Killed and Missing from Foča and Kalinovik, in Ilidža, Bosn. & Herz. (July 24, 2009).

[19] *E.g.*, interview with Nusreta Sivac, Former Judge, in Prijedor, Bosn. & Herz. (Sept. 16, 2014); interview with Sead Golić, Secretary, Association of the Families of Missing, Forcibly Detained and Murdered Bosniaks of Bosnia and Herzegovina, in Brčko, Bosn. & Herz. (July 22, 2009); and interview with Mirsad Tokača, President, Research and Documentation Center (Sarajevo), in Sarajevo, Bosn. & Herz. (Dec. 6, 2006).

[20] Interview with Dobrila Govedarica, Executive Director, Open Society Fund BiH, in Sarajevo, Bosn. & Herz. (Nov. 29, 2006). While virtually everyone I interviewed in 2006–09 expressed a version of this appraisal, sources expressed a wide range of views about the *degree* to which the ICTY had met their expectations. At one end of the spectrum was Vehid Šehić, who told me the Tribunal had "absolutely" achieved what he hoped it would within the limits of its judicial role. Šehić noted, however, that "very few" of the ICTY's verdicts "fulfilled justice 100 percent simply because of the point that a court is limited by the procedures and facts it can use to reach a final decision." Interview with Vehid Šehić, President, Citizens Forum of Tuzla, in Tuzla, Bosn. & Herz. (July 15, 2009). At the other end of the spectrum was Fadil Budnjo, who said that, sixteen years after the ICTY was established, "very little is left of what we could have expected." Like others who spoke of disappointed hopes, however, Budnjo added: "All in all, we still believe it was positive to have it established." Interview with Fadil Budnjo, President, Association of Families of Killed and Missing from Foča and Kalinovik, in Ilidža, Bosn. & Herz. (July 24, 2009).

In subsequent interviews, Bosnians were increasingly critical of the Tribunal's performance.[21] The views of two exemplify this trend. When I interviewed Mirsad Tokača in 2006, he told me he was "80 percent satisfied" with what the ICTY had achieved.[22] Eight years later, Tokača said, "With time passing, I am less and less satisfied." While reserving final judgment until the final outcomes of proceedings against Radovan Karadžić and Ratko Mladić, Tokača said that, on a scale of "one to five," the ICTY was "a good two"[23]—presumably signifying a decrease from 80 percent "satisfaction" in 2006 to 40 percent in 2014.

Sevima Sali-Terzić did not quantify her appraisal of the ICTY. But her frustrations with its work intensified between 2006 and 2014. Though already disappointed in many aspects of its performance in 2006, she could readily identify positive achievements that year.[24] By 2014, Sali-Terzić was hard-pressed to cite any achievements by the Hague Tribunal; the best she could muster was that its "treatment of sexual violence" was "okay." Whatever its achievements, Sali-Terzić said, the "negatives outweigh the positives."[25]

Section II explores aspects of the ICTY's performance, both positive and negative, that shaped Bosnians' assessments, with the following exceptions: First, I do not revisit here aspects of the Tribunal's record addressed in previous chapters, such as the impact of arrests on displaced Bosnians' willingness to return to their prewar homes. Second, I address in later chapters two key aspects of the ICTY's impact—the degree to which it has fostered knowledge and acknowledgment of wartime atrocities, and its impact on domestic war crimes institutions.

B. Ethnic Divisions in Overall Assessments of the Tribunal

As a foundation for this inquiry, it is necessary to note that Bosnians' views about the ICTY bear a strong correlation to their ethnicity, as myriad studies have shown.[26] In surveys administered between 2002 and 2012, Bosniak respondents have usually

---

[21] Other researchers have charted increasingly negative assessments by Bosnians. *See, e.g.,* SANJA KUTNJAK IVKOVIĆ & JOHN HAGAN, RECLAIMING JUSTICE: THE INTERNATIONAL TRIBUNAL FOR THE FORMER YUGOSLAVIA AND LOCAL COURTS 50 (2011) (surveys conducted in former Yugoslav states between 1997 and 2005 showed "substantially more negative attitudes toward the ICTY" after 2003 than before); Refik Hodžić, *Living the Legacy of Mass Atrocities,* 8 J. INT'L CRIM. JUST. 113, 118–21 (2010) [hereinafter Hodžić, *Living the Legacy*] (describing change over time in Prijedor victims' perceptions of justice).

[22] Interview with Mirsad Tokača, President, Research and Documentation Center (Sarajevo), in Sarajevo, Bosn. & Herz. (Dec. 6, 2006).

[23] Interview with Mirsad Tokača, President, Research and Documentation Center (Sarajevo), in Sarajevo, Bosn. & Herz. (Sept. 11, 2014).

[24] Among them, even though Karadžić and Mladić were then still at large, they did not "live freely, they [had] to hide." Without the ICTY, moreover, "there would never have been a war crimes chamber here." Interview with Sevima Sali-Terzić, Senior Legal Counsel, Constitutional Court of BiH, in Sarajevo, Bosn. & Herz. (Nov. 30, 2006).

[25] Interview with Sevima Sali-Terzić, Senior Legal Counsel, Constitutional Court of BiH, in Sarajevo, Bosn. & Herz. (Sept. 9, 2014).

[26] As Marko Milanović writes, "it is almost meaningless to draw conclusions from average responses [to a survey on war crimes issues] on the level of Bosnia as a whole, because of persistent divisions in post-conflict Bosnian society." Marko Milanović, *The Impact of the ICTY on the Former Yugoslavia: An Anticipatory Postmortem,* 110 AM. J. INT'L L. 233, 238 (2016).

registered the most positive views of the Tribunal, Serbs the most negative, with Croat views fluctuating.[27]

In 2002, the International Institute for Democracy and Electoral Assistance administered a survey of all states and entities of the former Yugoslavia. Only 3.6 percent of respondents in the predominantly Serb entity of Republika Srpska (RS) said they trusted the ICTY,[28] while 50.5 percent of those surveyed in the predominantly Bosniak-Croat Federation said they trusted the Tribunal.[29] When responses are broken down by ethnicity, the divisions are even more stark: only 1.8 percent of RS respondents who identified themselves as Serb said they trusted the ICTY, while 42.2 percent of RS respondents who identified themselves as "other" said they trusted the Tribunal. Within the Federation, 70.2 percent of respondents who identified as Muslim said they trusted the Tribunal, compared to 14.4 percent of Croat respondents.[30]

Surveys undertaken by PRISM Research between April 2001 and May 2004 asked a different question—"To what degree do you support the work of the Tribunal?" Over the period these surveys were administered, the percentage of Serbs who said they support the ICTY's work ranged from 17.60 to 32.90, the percentage of Bosniaks ranged from 89.10 to 92.50, while the percentage of Croats fluctuated the most—from 47.80 to 68.70.[31]

A June 2005 survey commissioned by the United Nations Development Programme (UNDP) produced a somewhat different picture but nonetheless registered striking correlations between respondents' ethnicity and their assessments of the ICTY. As with other surveys, the percentage of respondents who reported a positive view was significantly higher in the Federation than in RS. Unusually, however, a higher percentage of Croat respondents (31.9 percent) said they thought the ICTY "has done a good job and justified its existence" than Bosniak respondents

---

[27] In a 2006 interview, Dubravka Piotrovski summarized Bosnian views of the ICTY this way: "It seems that Bosniaks are more or less satisfied, Croats somewhat, and Serbs not at all." Interview with Dubravka Piotrovski, then Program Coordinator, American Bar Association Central European and Euroasian Law Initiative, in Sarajevo, Bosn. & Herz. (Nov. 29, 2006). As indicated below, surveys conducted four and six years later suggested Croat views of the ICTY had become nearly as negative as those of Serbs.

[28] Int'l Inst. Democracy & Electoral Assistance, *South East Europe Public Agenda Survey, January-February 2002, Republika Srpska*, 24, http://archive.idea.int/balkans/results/Srpska/Srspka_rtf.rtf. (This online source no longer contains the detailed information cited in the text).

[29] *Id.* at 26.

[30] *Id.*

[31] These data were provided by Dino Đipa, who undertook the surveys for the United Nations Development Programme. Curiously, there did not appear to be an inverse relationship between surges in, say, Serbs' support and that of other groups. The highest percentage of Serb respondents supporting the ICTY's work, 32.90 percent, was registered in the September 2003 survey; that same month saw the highest percentage of Bosniak respondents reporting that they support the Tribunal's work (93.60 percent) and the second largest percentage of Croat respondents reporting that they support its work (67.20 percent) during the period for which Đipa provided survey results. These results seem broadly consistent with those undertaken by Strategic Marketing Research, a Belgrade-based company, in 2007. In response to its survey question about whether they support the ICTY, 28 percent of RS residents said yes, while 76 percent of Federation residents responded affirmatively. The results were quoted in *Najviše Građana RS za Izručenje* ("Most RS Citizens Favor Surrender [of Radovan Karadžić and Ratko Mladić]"), *B92* News, (Belgrade) (July 23, 2007).

(24 percent).[32] Only 18.8 percent of Serb respondents said they thought the Tribunal "has done a good job and justified its existence."[33] A different pattern emerged when respondents were asked whether the ICTY has "not done a good job, but is necessary." Here, 46.4 percent of Bosniak respondents, 22.2 percent of Croat respondents, and 29.8 percent of Serb respondents responded affirmatively.[34]

Notably, stark divisions largely disappeared when respondents were asked what, in principle, should happen to those who "caused unjustifiable harm to others during the war." Across each major ethnic group, roughly two-thirds of respondents said these individuals "should be held accountable, without exception."[35]

Another survey, conducted in late 2008, asked whether the ICTY was helping reconciliation or keeping past conflicts alive. Once again, responses "differed distinctively across ethnic lines."[36] Sixty-one percent of Federation respondents said they believed the Tribunal was helping reconciliation and strengthening peace, while only 9 percent of RS respondents chose this response. Seventy-one percent of RS respondents said the Tribunal did not serve the best interests of the region, and was instead keeping past conflicts alive.[37]

In 2010, the UNDP commissioned a survey assessing Bosnian views relating to transitional justice. Since its focus was on domestic needs and approaches, it touched only lightly on the ICTY, asking whether respondents agreed with the statement, "The documentation of international courts (the ICTY and the International Court of Justice) represents the best basis for discussions about what happened during the war in BiH." More than 80 percent of Bosniak respondents agreed (either "fully" or "mainly"), compared to 25.3 percent of Serb respondents and 55.9 percent of Croat respondents.[38]

The Belgrade Centre for Human Rights commissioned two surveys in Bosnia, one in 2010 and the other in 2012. As with other surveys, respondents' overall view of the ICTY reflected a strong correlation with their ethnicity. In contrast to most of the surveys described above, however, Croat respondents no longer expressed somewhat more positive views of the ICTY than Serb respondents. In aggregate, Croat responses were almost indistinguishable from the low appraisal of Serb respondents. In response to the question, "What is your attitude toward the ICTY in general?," 59 percent of respondents from the Federation reported a positive assessment in

---

[32] These results are presented in Stefan Priesner et al., *Transitional Justice in Bosnia and Herzegovina: Findings of a Public Survey*, 2 LOCAL-GLOBAL JUSTICE: IDENTITY, SECURITY, COMMUNITY 119, 124 (2006). The authors speculate that the reason for relatively low opinions of the ICTY's performance might include "the slowness of the court's proceedings, lightness of sentencing, allegations of political bias, and the fact that indicted war criminals Radovan Karadžić, Ratko Mladić and Ante Gotovina were still at large at the time the polls were conducted." *Id.* Of these factors, "lightness of sentencing" and the fugitive status of Karadžić and Mladić would be most pertinent to Bosniaks' relatively low satisfaction in the ICTY's performance, while the fact that Gotovina was still at large would more likely translate into Serb dissatisfaction (and, perhaps, satisfaction on the part of Croats).

[33] *Id.*

[34] *Id.*

[35] Specifically, 64.9 percent of Bosniak respondents, 67.2 percent of Croat respondents, and 63.8 percent of Serb respondents chose this answer. *Id.*

[36] GALLUP BALKAN MONITOR, INSIGHTS AND PERCEPTIONS: VOICES OF THE BALKANS 48 (2008).

[37] *Id.*

[38] ZORAN PAJIĆ & DRAGAN M. POPOVIĆ, FACING THE PAST AND ACCESS TO JUSTICE FROM A PUBLIC PERSPECTIVE 50 (2011).

2012, yet only 15 percent of those living in the predominantly Croat area of the Federation reported a positive view. That same year, 15 percent of RS residents said they held a positive view of the Tribunal.[39]

In part because these surveys asked somewhat different questions, it is difficult to draw robust conclusions about changes over time in respondents' views about the ICTY. Still, several preliminary observations are warranted. Most obviously, across time and methodology, all of the Bosnia surveys showed significant ethnic cleavages in responses to general questions about the ICTY. Mirko Klarin, who covered the Tribunal longer and more closely than any other journalist, explains the divisions this way: a favorable view of the ICTY among Bosnians, as other former Yugoslav citizens, "is inversely proportional to the number of accused that come from [the survey respondents'] ethnic communities."[40]

As a generalization, Klarin's point is amply warranted: two-thirds of those indicted by the Tribunal were ethnic Serbs, and ethnic Serbs have generally registered the most negative views of the ICTY; 5.5 percent were Bosniak, and Bosniaks have generally been most supportive of the ICTY; while 21.1 percent were ethnic Croats, who, as a broad generalization, have been more ambivalent than Serbs or Bosniaks. Yet perceptions of the ICTY are more complex than Klarin's point reflects. For one thing, perceptions *within* Bosnia's ethnic groups are hardly monolithic. Notably, for example, several studies show that Serbs who live in predominantly non-Serb communities are, in general, more likely to have a favorable view of the ICTY than Serbs living in RS.[41]

Beyond differences among Bosnian Serbs (and, similarly, among Bosniaks and Croats), ethnic groups' average responses to survey questions have shifted over time. In line with Klarin's generalization, before 2010 Croat responses to questions probing general assessments of the ICTY tended to fall somewhere between Bosniaks' comparatively positive responses and Serbs' comparatively negative responses. But in a departure from this pattern, a higher percentage of Croat respondents (31.9 percent) in the 2005 UNDP survey said they thought the ICTY had done a good job than Bosniak respondents (24 percent). By the time this survey was done, the ICTY had indicted thirty-four ethnic Croats (of whom twenty-nine were Bosnian Croats), and only nine Bosniaks. (Because the ICTY issued its last indictment at the end of 2004, the ethnic breakdown of suspects had not changed since then.)

Even if it were consistently true that Bosniaks had the most favorable view of the ICTY, Serbs the lowest, and Croats in-between, this would not mean each ethnic group has maintained essentially the same opinion of the Tribunal over time. As noted earlier, overall assessments became increasingly critical during the final years of the ICTY's work. In Chapter 8, I argue that basic circumstances of Bosnians' lives—in particular, declining economic and social prospects, rising nationalism and political dysfunction—have influenced their assessments of the Hague Tribunal. In this chapter, I make a fundamentally different point: Bosnian assessments of the ICTY have to a considerable extent turned on its performance.

---

[39] Ipsos Strategic Marketing, Public Opinion Survey in Bosn. & Herz. 9–10 (2012).
[40] Klarin, *supra* note 3, at 92.
[41] I discuss these studies in Chapter 8.

II. THE QUALITY OF JUSTICE

Among those who invested hope in the ICTY, Bosnians have not experienced Hague justice as indivisible, something the Tribunal either provided or did not. Instead, they have found much to fault in its performance while deriving deep gratification from specific judgments as well as the moral message of its overall work. This section explores aspects of the ICTY's performance that loomed large in the assessments of Bosnians interviewed for this study, whose experience of international justice offers valuable lessons for other ICTs.

A. Sentencing Practices

1. SENTENCE LENGTHS

We who survived these tortures believe that all of those convicted have gotten insignificant or small punishments.

—DŽAFER DERONJIĆ[42]

The sentences are not strong enough to adequately reflect the crime committed.

—NUSRETA SIVAC[43]

Perhaps no factor weighs more heavily in victims' assessments of the Hague Tribunal than whether, in line with retributivist as well as expressivist theories of punishment, sentences bear a just relationship to the gravity of a defendant's crimes.[44] Srebrenica survivor Zumra Šehomerović evoked the importance of this when she said: "We would all expect *appropriate* sentences to be issued so that the victims can carry on living more easily."[45] Understandably, victims see the length of sentences imposed by The Hague "as a reflection of the gravity of crimes committed against them and thus as a mean[s] of acknowledging their trauma and suffering."[46] In their eyes, short sentences are "an implicit denial or . . . a failure to acknowledge the depth and gravity of their suffering."[47] By this measure, the Hague Tribunal has, overall, profoundly disappointed and even angered many victims, although not invariably so.

Before I elaborate, it should be noted that the average length of ICTY sentences has gradually increased over time, in part because the Tribunal's early cases involved

---

[42] Interview with Džafer Deronjić, Association of the Families of Missing, Forcibly Detained and Murdered Bosniaks of Bosnia and Herzegovina, in Brčko, Bosn. & Herz. (July 22, 2009).

[43] Interview with Nusreta Sivac, Former Judge, in Prijedor, Bosn. & Herz. (Sept. 16, 2014).

[44] As noted in Chapter 4, retributivism holds that, when a fundamental norm is breached, "the perpetrator deserves to be punished *in proportion to* the past harm he or she committed." Kevin M. Carlsmith et al., *Why Do We Punish? Deterrence and Just Deserts as Motives for Punishment*, 83 J. PERSONALITY & SOC. PSYCHOL. 284, 284 (2002) (emphasis added).

[45] Interview with the late Zumra Šehomerović, Member, Association of Mothers of Srebrenica and Žepa Enclaves, in Sarajevo, Bosn. & Herz. (Sept. 18, 2014).

[46] Refik Hodžić, *Living the Legacy of Mass Atrocities: Victims' Perspectives on War Crimes Trials*, 8 J. INT'L CRIM. JUST. 113, 134 (2010),

[47] *Id.* A study conducted in Croatia also found that sentences loom large in citizens' assessments of whether a trial outcome is just. *See* Roman David, *International Criminal Tribunals and the Perception of Justice: The Effect of the ICTY in Croatia*, 8 INT'L J. TRANSITIONAL JUST. 476, 492 (2014).

low-ranking perpetrators while later cases focused on senior suspects.[48] As former ICTY judge Patricia Wald has noted, early in the Tribunal's life, when comparatively low-level perpetrators dominated its docket, judges were inclined to "leave space for even more severe punishment" for the higher-level perpetrators they anticipated sentencing in later trials.[49] Some of the views quoted below were likely shaped by relatively early sentences in particular. Even so, victims have decried more recent sentences. For example, when an ICTY trial chamber sentenced Radovan Karadžić, widely seen as a mastermind of ethnic cleansing, to forty years in prison in March 2016, victims were disappointed he did not receive a life sentence, the highest sentence the ICTY can impose. A Srebrenica survivor expressed her disappointment in terms redolent of retributivism: "I am disappointed because with this sentence Europe again underestimated his crimes and all sufferings that my people and my family went through. It should be a life sentence, but even that I don't find fair enough."[50]

Victims from municipalities that saw extreme brutality, such as Foča and Prijedor, describe ICTY sentencing practices with a mixture of incredulity and anger. Their reactions highlight an often profound gap between enthusiastic global reactions to jurisprudence set forth in Hague judgments on the one hand, and victims' experiences on the other hand.

Crimes of sexual violence committed in Foča were condemned in a pathbreaking judgment in the *Kunarac* case.[51] Yet Fadil Budnjo, leader of an association of survivors from Foča, was appalled by the sentences imposed in that case, which he characterized as "basically nothing."[52] The defendants received sentences of twelve, twenty, and twenty-eight years in prison;[53] two other defendants convicted of crimes in Foča received fifteen-year sentences.[54]

---

[48] See Barbora Holá et al., *International Sentencing Facts and Figures: Sentencing Practice at the ICTY and ICTR*, 9 J. Int'l Crim. Just. 411, 420 (2011) [hereinafter Holá et al., *Sentencing Facts and Figures*]. In general, high-ranking defendants have received the longest sentences at the Tribunal. *Id.* at 431. Holá et al. found that low-ranking suspects on average received the next longest sentences, while mid-ranking defendants received the lowest. *Id.* They believe this "puzzling" finding is explained by factors that have been more important determinants of sentence length than rank, such as the cruelty and apparent enthusiasm of hands-on perpetrators. *Id.* at 431–32.

[49] Patricia Wald, Comments at Conference on the Occasion of IntLawGrrls! 10th Birthday, University of Georgia School of Law, Athens, GA (Mar. 3, 2017). For a critique of this approach, see Jens David Ohlin, *Proportional Sentences at the ICTY, in* The Legacy of the International Criminal Tribunal for the Former Yugoslavia 322 (Bert Swart et al. eds., 2011).

[50] Garret Tankosić-Kelly, *War Crimes Tribunal Still Invaluable Despite Šešelj Ruling*, Irish Times (Apr. 6, 2016) (quoting survivor identified as "AH").

[51] Prosecutor v. Kunarac et al., Case Nos. IT-96-23-T & IT-96-23/1-T, Trial Judgment, ¶¶ 883, 886 (Int'l Crim. Trib. for the Former Yugoslavia Feb. 22, 2001). The *Kunarac* trial judgment was the first in history to find that crimes of sexual violence constitute the crime against humanity of enslavement. *See* Kelly D. Askin, *Prosecuting Wartime Rape and Other Gender-Related Crimes Under International Law: Extraordinary Advances, Enduring Obstacles*, 21 Berkeley J. Int'l L. 288, 333 (2003) [hereinafter Askin, *Prosecuting Wartime Rape*].

[52] Interview with Fadil Budnjo, President, Association of Families of Killed and Missing from Foča and Kalinovik, in Ilidža, Bosn. & Herz. (July 24, 2009).

[53] Prosecutor v. Kunarac et al., Case Nos. IT-96-23-T & IT-96-23/1-T, Trial Judgment, ¶¶ 871, 877, 882 (Int'l Crim. Trib. for the Former Yugoslavia Feb. 22, 2001). These sentences were upheld by the Appeals Chamber. Prosecutor v. Kunarac et al., Case Nos. IT-96-23 & IT-96-23/1-A, Appeal Judgment, 125-27 (Int'l Crim. Trib. for the Former Yugoslavia June 12, 2002).

[54] The Appeals Chamber raised the sentence of Milorad Krnojelac, initially sentenced to seven and one-half years, to fifteen years' imprisonment. Prosecutor v. Krnojelac, Case No. IT-97-25-A,

As the ICTY's website recalls, atrocities in Prijedor, where nondescript warehouses became nightmarish camps, had a formative impact on the Tribunal:

> On 6 August 1992, British journalists from *ITN* and the *Guardian* unveiled to the world the existence of camps for non-Serb civilians in the area of Prijedor in north-western Bosnia and Herzegovina. Shocking images of emaciated inmates circled the planet in just a few days and shook the conscience of humanity. Barely two months later, a process was set in motion which would change the face of international criminal justice forever.[55]

Like crimes in Foča, those in Prijedor gave rise to pathbreaking jurisprudence.[56] But while gratified by the Tribunal's attention to their experience, survivors in Prijedor expressed profound frustration with sentences imposed on some defendants. When we spoke in 2006, Trnopolje camp survivor Edin Ramulić summarized the views of local victims: "In Prijedor, generally speaking people aren't satisfied with Hague sentencing policy."[57] Small wonder. Individuals found criminally responsibility for atrocities in camps in Prijedor received sentences as short as three,[58] five,[59] six,[60] seven,[61] and eight[62] years' imprisonment. (The ICTY has at times imposed longer sentences for these crimes, including twenty-five years in prison for Zoran Žigić,[63] twenty years for Mlađo Radić,[64] and fifteen years for Duško Sikirica.[65]) Ramulić reiterated this concern in 2014, citing as one of three troubling aspects of the ICTY's

---

Appeal Judgment, ¶ 246 (Int'l Crim. Trib. for the Former Yugoslavia Sept. 17, 2003). The Appeals Chamber sustained the Trial Chamber's sentence of fifteen years' imprisonment for Dragan Zelenović. Prosecutor v. Zelenović, Case No. IT-96-23/2-A, Appeal Judgment, 13 (Int'l Crim. Trib. for the Former Yugoslavia Oct. 31, 2007).

[55] ICTY, *Crimes before the ICTY: Prijedor*, http://www.icty.org/en/in-focus/documentaries/crimes-icty-prijedor (last visited Dec. 5, 2017).

[56] For example, the Tribunal's first trial, against Omarska camp guard Duško Tadić, generated novel jurisprudence concerning the laws of war. *See* Alexander Zahar, *Civilizing Civil War: Writing Morality as Law at the ICTY, in* THE LEGACY OF THE INTERNATIONAL CRIMINAL TRIBUNAL FOR THE FORMER YUGOSLAVIA 507, 475–76 (Bert Swart et al. eds., 2011).

[57] Interview with Edin Ramulić, Project Coordinator, Izvor, in Prijedor, Bosn. & Herz. (Dec. 8, 2006).

[58] Prosecutor v. Sikirica et al., Case No. IT-95-8-S, Sentencing Judgment, ¶ 243 (Int'l Crim. Trib. for the Former Yugoslavia Nov. 13, 2001) (sentencing Dragan Kolundžija).

[59] *Id.* ¶ 239 (sentencing Damir Došen); Prosecutor v. Kvočka et al., Case No. IT-98-30/1, Appeal Judgment, 243 (Int'l Crim. Trib. for the Former Yugoslavia Feb. 28, 2005) (affirming trial chamber's sentence of five years' imprisonment for Dragoljub Prcać).

[60] Prosecutor v. Kvočka et al., Case No. IT-98-30/1-T, Trial Judgment, ¶ 760 (Int'l Crim. Trib. for the Former Yugoslavia Nov. 2, 2001) (sentencing Molojica Kos to six years' imprisonment).

[61] Prosecutor v. Kvočka et al., Case No. IT-98-30/1, Appeal Judgment, 242 (Int'l Crim. Trib. for the Former Yugoslavia Feb. 28, 2005) (affirming trial chamber's sentence of seven years' imprisonment for Miroslav Kvočka).

[62] Prosecutor v. Banović, Case No. IT-02-65/1-S, Sentencing Judgment, ¶ 96 (Int'l Crim. Trib. for the Former Yugoslavia Oct. 28, 2003).

[63] Prosecutor v. Kvočka et al., Case No. IT-98-30/1, Appeal Judgment, 243 (Int'l Crim. Trib. for the Former Yugoslavia Feb. 28, 2005) (affirming trial chamber's sentence of twenty-five years' imprisonment for Zoran Žigić).

[64] *Id.* (affirming trial chamber's sentence of twenty years' imprisonment for Mlađo Radić).

[65] Prosecutor v. Sikirica et al., Case No. IT-95-8-S, Sentencing Judgment, ¶ 235 (Int'l Crim. Trib. for the Former Yugoslavia Nov. 13, 2001).

overall record "whether those who have been prosecuted have been adequately sentenced."[66]

The late Muharem Murselović, an Omarska survivor who testified in several ICTY trials, described the overall attitude of Muslims from Prijedor this way: "We had a very positive attitude towards those trials in The Hague, always very welcome. But we have always been disappointed with the sentences."[67] Recalling "Bosnians had big hopes, major expectations from the fact that the Hague Tribunal was established," Emsuda Mujagić told me that "in a certain way, the victims feel to be even more offended and damaged very often by those sentences issued by the court in the Hague in relation to what they have originally expected."[68]

Already offended by sentences imposed upon conviction, survivors have been further aggrieved by the Tribunal's "consistent practice" of granting early release after defendants have served two-thirds of their sentences.[69] Noting most of the Prijedor defendants who received short sentences were released soon after they were convicted (beyond the effect of the ICTY's early release practice, all received credit for time served before they were sentenced), Ramulić asked, "What message do you think that sends here to the local Serb community?"[70]

If painfully short sentences subvert the moral message of the Tribunal's work, they have sometimes had a retraumatizing effect as well: with perpetrators back in their communities a few years after their arrests, some victims have frequently encountered men who visited grievous harm on them as they go about their daily lives. Consider the experience of Nusreta Sivac, who was repeatedly raped in Omarska while detained there in 1992.[71] In 2002, Sivac returned to Prijedor to reclaim her apartment, which had been given to a former Serb colleague.[72] One of her neighbors was

---

[66] Interview with Edin Ramulić, Project Coordinator, Izvor, in Prijedor, Bosn. & Herz. (Sept. 16, 2014).

[67] Interview with the late Muharem Murselović, then Member of Republika Srpska National Assembly, President of the RS Parlamentarians Club for the Party for BiH, in Banja Luka, Bosn. & Herz. (July 15, 2009).

[68] Interview with Emsuda Mujagić, President, Srcem do Mira, in Kozarac, Bosn. & Herz. (July 23, 2009).

[69] Prosecutor v. Tadić, Case No. IT-95-9, Decision of the President on the Application for Pardon or Commutation of Sentence of Miroslav Tadić, ¶ 4 (June 24, 2004). See also Barbora Holá & Joris van Wijk, Life After Conviction at International Criminal Tribunals, 12 J. INT'L CRIM. JUST. 109, 124 (2014); Jonathan H. Choi, Early Release in International Criminal Law, 123 YALE L.J. 1784, 1788, 1792–94 (2014). The president of the Tribunal may grant early release to a convicted person when he or she becomes eligible under the law of the state where that person is serving his or her sentence. Updated Statute of the International Criminal Tribunal for the Former Yugoslavia, art. 28, Sept. 2009. The state where a defendant is serving his or her sentence must notify the Tribunal of his or her eligibility for pardon or commutation of sentence under its own law. Rules of Procedure and Evidence, Int'l Crim. Trib. for the Former Yugoslavia, U.N. Doc. IT/32/Rev. 49, Rule 123 (May 22, 2013). Typically, states that have agreed to receive defendants for purposes of serving sentences imposed by the ICTY allow early release when a convict has served two-thirds of his or her sentence. It falls to the Tribunal president to determine, in light of factors set forth in the ICTY's rules of procedure and after consulting with officials specified therein, whether to grant pardon or commutation.

[70] Interview with Edin Ramulić, Project Coordinator, Izvor, in Prijedor, Bosn. & Herz. (Dec. 8, 2006).

[71] See United Nations Office of the High Commissioner for Human Rights, The Story of Nusreta Sivac (June 23, 2009).

[72] See Felix Blake, Nusreta Survived the Rape Camp, But Her Torture Is Unending, INDEPENDENT (Nov. 23, 2002).

Miroslav Kvočka, against whom Sivac had testified in The Hague. Sentenced to serve seven years, Kvočka was granted early release in March 2005. Until Kvočka sold his apartment in 2008, Sivac encountered him almost daily. Alluding to Sivac's experience, Fatima Fazlić said: "And that is only one example, and there are hundreds of those."[73]

For many survivors, the harms associated with short sentences are amplified by the enduring legacy of ethnic cleansing. As Sivac noted, defendants granted early release "are coming back to carry on living in their home towns, where we are still looking for the people who were murdered and executed during wartime and whose remains have not yet been found."[74]

Several sources readily acknowledged no sentence would seem adequate for the crimes they survived.[75] Using her own experience to illustrate the point, Nidžara Ahmetašević, who was wounded by Serb snipers early in the years-long siege of Sarajevo, described her reaction when Stanislav Galić was condemned to a life sentence for his role in the siege:[76] "I'm from Sarajevo, and I'm *really* disappointed with the life sentence for Galić. You're always unsatisfied."[77] (As noted below, however, many who lived through the siege were deeply gratified by Galić's sentence.)

Hatidža Mehmedović, who lost her husband, brothers, teenage sons, parents, and scores of extended family members in the Srebrenica genocide, evinced a similar self-awareness when she described survivors' views of ICTY sentences: "[W]e are . . . not happy with the sentences, with the verdicts, because what would be the verdict that would be convenient for a crime committed here in Srebrenica of which you have seen the consequences?"[78] So, too, did Sead Golić, who told me his brother was shot at close range and buried in a mass grave in Brčko: "No matter how strict or serious or high [a sentence] would be, no verdict would replace my brother or some other victim."[79]

Even so, it would be unfair to discount victims' dissatisfaction on the ground no sentence could satisfy them. ICTY sentencing patterns have been widely criticized[80] by international legal experts as well as victims.[81] During interviews, moreover,

---

[73] Interview with Fatima Fazlić, President, Izvor, in Prijedor, Bosn. & Herz. (July 23, 2009).

[74] Interview with Nusreta Sivac, Former Judge, in Prijedor, Bosn. & Herz. (Sept. 16, 2014).

[75] *See also* MISCHKOWSKI & MLINAREVIĆ, *supra* note 5, at 53 (citing similar sentiments among victims of sexual violence in the former Yugoslavia who have testified in war crimes trials).

[76] Prosecutor v. Galić, Case No. IT-98-29-A, Appeal Judgment (Int'l Crim. Trib. for the Former Yugoslavia Nov. 30, 2006). The trial chamber had sentenced Galić to twenty years in prison. Prosecutor v. Galić, Case No. IT-98-29-T, Trial Judgment (Int'l Crim. Trib. for the Former Yugoslavia Dec. 5, 2003).

[77] Interview with Nidžara Ahmetašević, then Editor, BIRN in BiH, in Sarajevo, Bosn. & Herz. (July 13, 2009).

[78] Interview with Hatidža Mehmedović, President, Association of Srebrenica Mothers, in Potočari, Bosn. & Herz. (July 21, 2009). In a similar vein, Zumra Šehomerović told me victims are "not happy with any of the verdicts passed" by the ICTY "because no sentence can bring life back." Interview with the late Zumra Šehomerović, Member, Association of Mothers of Srebrenica and Žepa Enclaves, in Sarajevo, Bosn. & Herz. (Sept. 18, 2014).

[79] Interview with Sead Golić, Association of the Families of Missing, Forcibly Detained and Murdered Bosniaks of Bosnia and Herzegovina, in Brčko, Bosn. & Herz. (July 22, 2009).

[80] *See* Barbora Holá, *Sentencing of International Crimes at the ICTY and ICTR: Consistency of Sentencing Case Law*, 4 AMSTERDAM L.F. 3, 4 (2012) [hereinafter Holá, *Sentencing of International Crimes*].

[81] *See, e.g.*, MARK A. DRUMBL, ATROCITY, PUNISHMENT, AND INTERNATIONAL LAW 59 (2007).

individuals who condemned short sentences readily acknowledged their satisfaction when the Tribunal imposed sentences they thought commensurate with defendants' crimes. For example, while highly critical of short sentences imposed on some Prijedor defendants, Edin Ramulić was gratified when another, Milomir Stakić, received a longer sentence. At trial, Stakić received a sentence of life in prison,[82] and this "was very important for us symbolically," Ramulić recalled. Although Stakić's sentence was reduced to forty years on appeal,[83] Ramulić had feared it would be reduced to half that amount and was both relieved and philosophical about the reduced sentence.[84]

Some of my interviews took place the week the ICTY Appeals Chamber raised the sentence of Stanislav Galić, whom a trial chamber had sentenced to twenty years' imprisonment for his role in the siege of Sarajevo, to life in prison. Following the trial verdict in December 2003, Sarajevans who participated in a survey "overwhelmingly indicated that they regarded [the then recently imposed 20-year sentence] as too lenient."[85] The final sentence, delivered in November 2006, was a milestone; no previous ICTY defendant had received a life sentence after exhausting the appeals process. Many Sarajevans were deeply gratified, and spontaneously expressed this during conversations and more formal interviews that week.[86]

I heard similar reactions to sentences rendered during my July 2009 research visit. On July 20, 2009, an ICTY Trial Chamber sentenced Milan Lukić to life in prison and his cousin, Sredoje Lukić, to thirty years' imprisonment for their roles in sadistic crimes in Višegrad.[87] While many victims were disappointed the Prosecutor did not include rape charges in the indictment, some found the defendants' sentences to be appropriately severe.[88]

For some (perhaps many), the satisfaction that comes with verdicts of guilt at least partially offsets their disappointment in sentences. Sadik Trako recalled that he and others in Lašva Valley "were really pleased" when an ICTY Trial Chamber sentenced Tihomir Blaškić to forty-five years in prison but "were very sad" when the Appeals Chamber reduced his sentence to nine years.[89] While he "could not accept" the court's reasons for reducing the sentence, Trako said he was "still very glad that the

---

[82] Prosecutor v. Stakić, Case No. IT-97-24-T, Trial Judgment, Disposition, 253 (Int'l Crim. Trib. for the Former Yugoslavia July 31, 2003).

[83] Prosecutor v. Stakić, Case No. IT-97-24-A, Appeal Judgment, Disposition, 142 (Int'l Crim. Trib. for the Former Yugoslavia Mar. 22, 2006).

[84] Interview with Edin Ramulić, Project Coordinator, Izvor, in Prijedor, Bosn. & Herz. (Dec. 8, 2006).

[85] Sanja Kutnjak Ivković & John Hagan, *The Politics of Punishment and the Siege of Sarajevo: Toward a Conflict Theory of Perceived International (In)justice*, 40 L. & Soc'y Rev. 369, 397 (2006).

[86] E.g., interview with Mervan Miraščija, Law Program Coordinator, Open Society Fund BiH, in Sarajevo, Bosn. & Herz. (Nov. 2006).

[87] Prosecutor v. Lukić et al., Case No. IT-98-32/1-T, Trial Judgment, Disposition, 333-34 (Int'l Crim. Trib. for the Former Yugoslavia July 20, 2009). On appeal, Milan Lukić's life sentence was sustained while Sredoje Lukić's sentence was reduced to twenty-seven years' imprisonment. Prosecutor v. Lukić et al., Case No. IT-98-32/1-A, Appeal Judgment, Disposition, 221 (Int'l Crim. Trib. for the Former Yugoslavia Dec. 4, 2012).

[88] E.g., interview with Sead Golić, Association of the Families of Missing, Forcibly Detained and Murdered Bosniaks of Bosnia and Herzegovina, in Brčko, Bosn. & Herz. (July 22, 2009).

[89] Prosecutor v. Blaškić, Case No. IT-95-14-A, Appeal Judgment, Disposition, 258 (Int'l Crim. Trib. for the Former Yugoslavia July 29, 2004).

court pronounced [Blaškić] guilty."[90] Speaking more generally, Jasna Bakšić Muftić told me: "Though sometimes I am disappointed in [defendants'] punishment, I am glad to see their punishment, which is more important [than the sentence they receive]. This brings some sense of justice. In public, on TV, all of us can hear who did what. The whole story has been heard."[91]

Just as many Bosniaks fault the ICTY for imposing lenient sentences on individuals who committed atrocities against Muslims, many Serbs have condemned sentences the ICTY imposed on Bosniaks as "so small compared to [the penalty imposed on] Serbs."[92] Particularly troubling for many was the two-year sentence imposed by a trial chamber on a prominent Bosniak defendant, Naser Orić,[93] who was later acquitted by the ICTY.[94]

I heard analogous complaints from Bosnian Croats. When we spoke in 2006, Fabijan Barać, president of the Association for Tracking of Killed and Missing Croats of Central Bosnia and Herzegovina, told me Croats in Central Bosnia "are generally very mad with the Hague Tribunal." The reason: short sentences then recently imposed on Bosniak defendants for crimes against Croats compared to harsher sentences imposed on Bosnian Croat defendants for crimes against Bosniaks.[95] Srećko Mišković described the sentences imposed against two Bosniak defendants for crimes against Bosnian Croats as "shameful."[96]

As these interviews suggest, many Bosnians have been especially critical of short sentences when the defendant was convicted of committing crimes against members of their own ethnic group. But some sentences have been criticized across ethnic lines as derisorily short. While highly critical of the ICTY for imposing inappropriately short sentences on Serb defendants, Senad Pećanin found the trial chamber's

---

[90] Interview with Sadik Trako, President, Association of Victims and Missing Persons in Lašva Valley, in Vitez, Bosn. & Herz. (Dec. 6, 2006).

[91] Interview with Jasna Bakšić Muftić, Professor, Faculty of Law, University of Sarajevo, in Sarajevo, Bosn. & Herz. (Nov. 30, 2006).

[92] Interview with Ljubiša Simović, President, Association of Displaced and Refugees in Republika Srpska, in Foča, Bosn. & Herz. (July 20, 2009).

[93] Prosecutor v. Orić, Case No. IT-03-68-T, Trial Judgment, Disposition, 269 (Int'l Crim. Trib. for the Former Yugoslavia June 30, 2006).

[94] Prosecutor v. Orić, Case No. IT-03-68-A, Appeal Judgment (Int'l Crim. Trib. for the Former Yugoslavia July 3, 2008). As explored in Chapter 10, Serbian prosecutors subsequently indicted Orić, who was later tried before, and acquitted by, Bosnia's state court.

[95] Interview with Fabijan Barać, President, Association for Tracking of Killed and Missing Croats of Central Bosnia and Herzegovina, in Lašva Valley, Bosn. & Herz. (Dec. 7, 2006). Barać appeared to have in mind the prison sentences imposed on Enver Hadžihasanović (five years) and Amir Kubura (two-and-a-half years) for crimes committed principally against Bosnian Croats but also against Bosnian Serbs in Central Bosnia. See Prosecutor v. Hadžihasanović et al., Case No. IT-01-47-T, Trial Judgment, Disposition, 625, 627 (Int'l Crim. Trib. for the Former Yugoslavia Mar. 15, 2006). On appeal (after I interviewed Barać), Kubura's sentence was reduced to two years' imprisonment, and Hadžihasanović's was reduced to three-and-half years in prison. Prosecutor v. Hadžihasanović et al., Case No. IT-01-47-A, Appeal Judgment, Disposition, 133-34 (Int'l Crim. Trib. for the Former Yugoslavia Apr. 22, 2008). Barać contrasted the two-and-a-half year original sentence imposed on Kubura with the twenty-five-year sentence imposed on Bosnian Croat commander Dario Kordić for crimes committed against Muslims in Central Bosnia.

[96] Interview with Srećko Mišković, Administrative Secretary, War Veterans of Travnik, in Lašva Valley, Bosn. & Herz. (Dec. 7, 2006). Mišković apparently was referring to the sentences imposed on Enver Hadžihasanović and Amir Kubura earlier that year. See supra note 95.

two-year sentence for Naser Orić to be so short as to defy rational meaning. "It's really funny, two years," Pećanin said, adding:

> He should be either [found] innocent or seriously punished. For most people, that's nothing, that's no solution at all—a guy who was indicted for terrible crimes and then you have two years. What does it mean? . . . That decision in my view discredited the authority of the Tribunal.[97]

Branko Todorović, a Bosnian Serb who worked tirelessly to educate others about the work of the ICTY, was at a loss to explain Orić's sentence: "There is no one here in Republika Srpska who is able to explain to a person here that the verdict in the Naser Orić case was justified." Todorović added: "[T]he type of verdict he got was almost icing on the cake for those who were claiming the worst things" about the ICTY.[98]

2. Apparent Inconsistency in Sentencing

Beyond concerns about sentence lengths, Bosnians interviewed for this study were highly critical of apparent inconsistencies in ICTY sentences. Dobrila Govedarica made the point this way: "You can't say this person will get 45 years, the other 25 years [for essentially similar crimes]. . . . They applied really different sentences depending on trial chamber judges." Govedarica added: This is "about the law," and "the law shouldn't be a matter of free judgment of judges. Not absolutely free."[99] Mirsad Tokača made much the same point, noting that, on the one hand, Momčilo Krajišnik, a Bosnian Serb leader, was sentenced to twenty years in prison while "some small fish" from "Krajina" was sentenced to forty years.[100]

As noted in my previous study of the ICTY's impact in Bosnia,[101] legal experts who have studied the Tribunal's sentencing patterns have voiced similar concerns, describing sentencing practices of the ICTY and its sister tribunal for Rwanda as "erratic"[102] and finding "troubling disparities" among ICTY sentences.[103] In subsequent

---

[97] Interview with Senad Pećanin, then Editor, Dani, in Sarajevo, Bosn. & Herz. (Dec. 6, 2006). I interviewed Pećanin before Orić's conviction was reversed on appeal.

[98] Interview with Branko Todorović, then President, Helsinki Committee for Human Rights in Republika Srpska, in Bijeljina, Bosn. & Herz. (Dec. 5, 2006). As with Pećanin, I interviewed Todorović before Orić's conviction was reversed.

[99] Interview with Dobrila Govedarica, Executive Director, Open Society Fund BiH, in Sarajevo, Bosn. & Herz. (Nov. 29, 2006).

[100] Interview with Mirsad Tokača, President, Research and Documentation Center (Sarajevo), in Sarajevo, Bosn. & Herz. (Dec. 6, 2006). Tokača apparently was referring to Milomir Stakić, whom the Appeals Chamber sentenced to forty years in prison for crimes committed in Prijedor, which is located in the northwest area of Bosnian known as Bosanska Krajina. *See Prosecutor v. Stakić*, Case No. IT-97-24-A, Appeal Judgment, Disposition, 142 (Int'l Crim. Trib. for the Former Yugoslavia Mar. 22, 2006).

[101] Diane F. Orentlicher, Open Society Justice Initiative & International Center for Transitional Justice, That Someone Guilty Be Punished: The Impact of the ICTY in Bosnia 56 (2010).

[102] Drumbl, *supra* note 81, at 59.

[103] Jennifer J. Clark, *Zero to Life: Sentencing Appeals at the International Criminal Tribunals for the Former Yugoslavia and Rwanda*, 96 Geo. L.J. 1685, 1691 (2009) [hereinafter Clark, *Zero to Life*]. *See also* Robert Sloane, *The Expressive Capacity of International Punishment* 36 (Colum. Public L. & Legal Theory, Working Paper 06100, 2006); Judith Armatta, *The Need for Sentencing Standards*, Coalition Int'l Just. (Feb. 28, 2003).

publications, however, several scholars have concluded, based on in-depth analyses of ICTY sentences, that there may be greater consistency than previously believed. Broadly, they found that many apparent inconsistencies can be explained by relevant distinctions among defendants, such as differences in the charges for which they were convicted, the extent to which they cooperated with the Prosecutor, the defendant's rank, and the nature of his or her participation in the crimes for which he or she was convicted.[104] Even so, these scholars have "detected some instances of disparity across cases," along with "a considerable amount of confusion in the ICTY . . . case law regarding the objectives of punishment."[105]

Perhaps more important than the disparities cited in these studies, the ICTY has not communicated a coherent framework for sentencing.[106] Instead, its judges eschewed proposals by the Prosecutor and others that they adopt "basic sentencing principles" aimed at ensuring sentencing consistency,[107] in large part on the ground this would compromise their duty to individualize penalties.[108] Yet as recent studies indicate, a coherent sentencing policy can leave ample space for individualizing sanctions. What such a policy would have offered is a framework that *made sense* of different sentence lengths—a particularly important form of transparency for a tribunal often accused by local leaders of operating in a biased fashion.

3. PLEA AGREEMENTS/CONFESSIONS

We, the families of the victims, are not satisfied. We are not pleased with bargaining between the court and the perpetrators. It doesn't give us any satisfaction.

—SEAD GOLIĆ[109]

[C]riticisms of ICTY sentences have been particularly sharp in respect of sentences imposed in cases of plea agreements.

—MARK B. HARMON AND FERGAL GAYNOR[110]

---

[104] *See, e.g.*, Holá et al., *Sentencing Facts and Figures, supra* note 48, at 411.

[105] Holá, *Sentencing of International Crimes, supra* note 80, at 22–23.

[106] *See* Ohlin, *supra* note 49, at 325.; Mirko Bagaric & John Morss, *International Sentencing Law: In Search of a Justification and Coherent Framework*, 7 INT'L CRIM. L. REV. 191, 207–08 (2006).

[107] Prosecutor v. Delalić et al., Case No. IT-96-21-A, Appeal Judgment, ¶ 715 (Int'l Crim. Trib. for the Former Yugoslavia Feb. 20, 2001); *see also* Clark, *Zero to Life, supra* note 103, at 1697–98.

[108] *See* Prosecutor v. Delalić et al., Case No. IT-96-21-A, Appeal Judgment, ¶ 717 (Int'l Crim. Trib. for the Former Yugoslavia Feb. 20, 2001) (noting that trial chambers exercise considerable discretion in sentencing, the Appeals Chamber explained: "This is largely because of the overriding obligation to individualise a penalty to fit the individual circumstances of the accused and the gravity of the crime"); Prosecutor v. Blaškić, Case No. IT-95-14-A, Appeal Judgment, ¶ 680 (Int'l Crim. Trib. for the Former Yugoslavia July 29, 2004) ("The Appeals Chamber has emphasised in previous judgements that sentencing is a discretionary decision and that it is inappropriate to set down a definitive list of sentencing guidelines.[] The sentence must always be decided according to the facts of each particular case and the individual guilt of the perpetrator.").

[109] Interview with Sead Golić, Association of the Families of Missing, Forcibly Detained and Murdered Bosniaks of Bosnia and Herzegovina, in Brčko, Bosn. & Herz. (July 22, 2009).

[110] Mark B. Harmon & Fergal Gaynor, *Ordinary Sentences for Extraordinary Crimes*, 5 J. INT'L CRIM. JUST. 683, 707 n.101 (2007).

Twenty ICTY defendants entered guilty pleas between May 1996 and December 2007,[111] usually following negotiations with prosecutors who hoped to convince the suspects to plead guilty in exchange for a steep reduction in sentence.[112] From the prosecutors' perspective, plea agreements offered distinct advantages: most obviously, they usually averted lengthy and costly trials.[113] (Tellingly, most guilty pleas were entered in 2002 and 2003, a period in which the ICTY faced intensive pressure to wrap up its work expeditiously.[114]) In addition, some defendants who pleaded guilty provided "vital new evidence, as in the case of . . . two Bosnian Serb officers who pleaded guilty to playing a role in the Srebrenica massacre and provided the first high-level account of how and by whom it was planned."[115]

That someone responsible for savage crimes could "bargain" for a reduced sentence is anathema to many victims, however.[116] As Srebrenica survivor Hajra Čatić put it: "In the case of some sentences, [the ICTY was] like bargaining as people do in marketplaces—'admit some, we will forgive the rest.'"[117] Professor Zdravko Grebo expressed similar disdain, saying whatever utility plea agreements may have in ordinary criminal cases, they are "questionable, both from a legal and moral point of view," in war crimes cases. "Can you bargain about war crimes?," he asked.[118]

If these general perspectives informed Bosnian reactions, two high-profile guilty pleas, those of Dražen Erdemović and Biljana Plavšić, made a particularly strong impression. As explained below, both cases epitomized the distance between ICTY judges' conceptions of justice on the one hand, and that of victims on the other hand.

a. Dražen Erdemović

At his initial appearance before the ICTY on May 31, 1996, Erdemović, a Bosnian Croat who served with Bosnian Serb forces during the 1990s war, became the first

---

[111] More precisely, prosecutors agreed to withdraw certain charges and/or recommend reduced sentences in exchange for defendants' guilty pleas, a process commonly known as plea bargaining.

[112] The first two ICTY defendants who entered guilty pleas did so without such negotiations. *See* Nancy Amoury Combs, *Procuring Guilty Pleas for International Crimes: The Limited Influence of Sentence Discounts*, 59 Vanderbilt L. Rev. 69, 87–88 (2006) [hereinafter Combs, *Procuring Guilty Pleas*].

[113] Occasionally, however, defendants entered guilty pleas well into their trials. *See id.* at 89–90 (2006) (discussing the *Sikirica* case, involving three defendants); Janine Natalya Clark, *Plea Bargaining at the ICTY: Guilty Pleas and Reconciliation*, 20 Eur. J. Int'l L. 415, 418 n.11 (2009) [hereinafter Clark, *Plea Bargaining*] (guilty plea was entered by Stevan Todorović more than two years after his first appearance before the ICTY).

[114] Combs, *Procuring Guilty Pleas*, *supra* note 112, at 92. The pressures to which I allude are described in Chapter 9.

[115] Marlise Simons, *Plea Deals Being Used to Clear Balkan War Tribunal's Docket*, N.Y. Times (Nov. 18, 2003). *See also* Combs, *Procuring Guilty Pleas*, *supra* note 112, at 92.

[116] A survey administered in Sarajevo in December 2003 found that only 6 percent of respondents approved of the Tribunal's use of plea bargaining. Kutnjak Ivković & Hagan, *supra* note 85, at 396. The ICTY does not use the phrase "plea bargaining," referring instead to "plea agreements." *See* Marlise Simons, *In a Startling Plea, a Serbian Policeman Confesses to Atrocities*, N.Y. Times (July 27, 2003).

[117] Interview with Hajra Čatić, President, Women of Srebrenica, in Tuzla, Bosn. & Herz. (July 21, 2009).

[118] Interview with Zdravko Grebo, Director, Center for Interdisciplinary Postgraduate Studies, University of Sarajevo, in Sarajevo, Bosn. & Herz. (July 13, 2009).

suspect to enter a guilty plea before the Tribunal.[119] By his own account, Erdemović personally killed 70 of the estimated 7,000-8,000 victims of the Srebrenica massacre at the Branjevo farm near Pilica on July 16, 1995.

From the perspective of the ICTY Prosecutor and judges, Erdemović earned leniency despite his participation in what is routinely called the worst massacre in Europe since World War II. Not only did Erdemović surrender and plead guilty, but he willingly cooperated with the prosecution in other cases.[120] In addition, Erdemović expressed what judges considered "sincere and genuine remorse"[121] for his actions.

Erdemović's initial sentence of ten years' imprisonment was later reduced to five,[122] this time based on a charge-reduction agreement with the Prosecutor.[123] While recognizing the Tribunal's role expressing the outrage of the international community at crimes such as those of Erdemović,[124] Trial Chamber II noted countervailing considerations. Among them, the defendant's cooperation advanced the Tribunal's institutional interests by, for example, encouraging other perpetrators to "come forward."[125] The chamber also accepted Erdemović's claim he committed the crimes under threat of death;[126] accordingly, it recognized "duress" as a factor in mitigation.[127] In addition, the chamber claimed, the Tribunal "has a duty . . . to contribute to . . . reconciliation and establishing the truth behind the evils perpetrated in the former Yugoslavia."[128] In its view:

> Discovering the truth is a cornerstone of the rule of law and a fundamental step on the way to reconciliation: for it is the truth that cleanses the ethnic and religious hatreds and begins the healing process. The International Tribunal must demonstrate that those who have the honesty to confess are treated fairly as part

---

[119] During this appearance Erdemović pleaded guilty to the count of murder as a crime against humanity without any promise of leniency. *See* Combs, *Procuring Guilty Pleas, supra* note 112, at 88. He later entered a plea of guilty to a war crimes charge pursuant to a plea agreement. *See infra* note 123.

[120] Six weeks after he first pleaded guilty, Erdemović testified in proceedings against Ratko Mladić and Radovan Karadžić and later provided valuable testimony in cases against other senior suspects. *See* Monika Nalepa, Why Do They Return? Evaluating the Impact of ICTY Justice on Reconciliation 17–18 n.20 (Jan. 26, 2007) (unpublished manuscript) (on file with author).

[121] Prosecutor v. Erdemović, Case No. IT-96-22-T, Sentencing Judgment, ¶ 55 (Int'l Crim. Trib. for the Former Yugoslavia Nov. 29, 1996); *see also id.* ¶¶ 95–97. As an ICTY prosecutor noted, however, Erdemović's expression of remorse was "rather unmemorable." Alan Tieger, *Remorse and Mitigation in the International Criminal Tribunal for the Former Yugoslavia*, 16 LEIDEN J. INT'L L. 777, 780 (2003).

[122] Erdemović received a ten-year sentence upon his first guilty plea. After ruling his initial plea had not been fully informed, the Appeals Chamber remanded Erdemović's case to a different trial chamber. Prosecutor v. Erdemović, Case No. IT-96-22-A, Appeal Judgment (Int'l Crim. Trib. for the Former Yugoslavia Oct. 7, 1997). That chamber imposed a five-year sentence in March 1998.

[123] Erdemović pleaded guilty to a war crimes charge; the ICTY Prosecutor withdrew the crime against humanity charge. Prosecutor v. Erdemović, Case No. IT-96-22-T*bis*, Sentencing Judgment, ¶ 8 (Int'l Crim. Trib. for the Former Yugoslavia Mar. 5, 1998).

[124] *Id.* ¶ 21.

[125] *Id.*

[126] *Id.* ¶ 14.

[127] *Id.* ¶ 17.

[128] *Id.* ¶ 21.

of a process underpinned by principles of justice, fair trial and protection of the fundamental rights of the individual.[129]

The Chamber's lofty sentiments could not have been more distant from the outrage many survivors felt when they learned a mass murderer had received a five-year sentence. Kada Hotić, a leader of the Association of Mothers of Srebrenica and Žepa Enclaves, decried the sentence as "ridiculous," and explained why in terms redolent of retributive justice: "I believe that each crime has its price, regardless of [a defendant's] further cooperation."[130] Other Srebrenica survivors became agitated when we discussed Erdemović's sentence. Saying they derived no comfort from his cooperation in other cases, they demanded, "Why didn't he turn down the orders to kill? If I'm ordered to kill you I would rather ask them to kill me. He should have turned down the order from those who ordered him to kill."[131]

Zdravko Grebo shared their indignation, characterizing Erdemović's sentence as "unacceptable."[132] Mirsad Tokača denounced the sentence as "ridiculous," "unacceptable," and so short "it's like a blanket forgiving of a crime." "Without appropriate reason," he said, the ICTY reduced Erdemović's sentence to "a level that's absurd."[133] This reaction was not universal, however. Nidžara Ahmetašević believes Erdemović's plea "*was* groundbreaking." Not only was Erdemović the first Srebrenica perpetrator to come forward and confess, she noted, "he is still coming to the ICTY as a witness" against other defendants.[134]

b. Biljana Plavšić

If *Erdemović* shaped many Bosnians' initial view of guilty pleas in The Hague, no case made a stronger impression than that of Biljana Plavšić. Her case highlights the degree to which scholars, human rights advocates, diplomats, and judicial officers ascribed redemptive power to international justice, and exposed a huge chasm between our collective hopes on the one hand and victims' experiences on the other.

On October 2, 2002, Plavšić, who served as a member of the Bosnian Serbs' presidency during the war, pleaded guilty to the crime against humanity of persecution.[135] At the time she entered her plea, Plavšić issued a statement saying that, by "accepting responsibility and expressing her remorse fully and unconditionally," she

---

[129] *Id.*

[130] Interview with Kada Hotić, Vice President, Association of Mothers of Srebrenica and Žepa Enclaves, in Sarajevo, Bosn. & Herz. (July 24, 2009).

[131] Interview with Hatidža Mehmedović, Mejra Đogaz, & Hanifa Đogaz, Association of Srebrenica Mothers, in Potočari, Bosn. & Herz. (July 21, 2009). At a hearing preceding his first sentencing, Erdemović said that in one instance, when he was able to resist an order to execute Muslim men without being killed himself, he refused the order. *See* Prosecutor v. Erdemović, Case No. IT-96-22-T, Sentencing Judgment, ¶ 81 (Int'l Crim. Trib. for the Former Yugoslavia Nov. 29, 1996).

[132] Interview with Zdravko Grebo, Director, Center for Interdisciplinary Postgraduate Studies, University of Sarajevo, in Sarajevo, Bosn. & Herz. (July 13, 2009).

[133] Interview with Mirsad Tokača, Director, Research and Documentation Center (Sarajevo), in Sarajevo, Bosn. & Herz. (Dec. 6, 2006).

[134] Interview with Nidžara Ahmetašević, then Editor, BIRN in BiH, in Sarajevo, Bosn. & Herz. (July 13, 2009).

[135] Plavšić surrendered to the ICTY after learning there was a sealed indictment against her. *See* Carla del Ponte with Chuck Sudetić, Madam Prosecutor: Confrontations with Humanity's Worst Criminals and the Culture of Impunity 161 (2008).

hoped "to offer some consolation to the innocent victims" of the Bosnian war.[136] Although seven ICTY defendants had by then entered guilty pleas, this was the first time someone of her rank had confessed and expressed remorse.[137] Sounding themes more commonly voiced by international and transitional justice advocates than participants in mass atrocities, Plavšić said:

> To achieve any reconciliation or lasting peace in BH, serious violations of humanitarian law during the war must be acknowledged by those who bear responsibility—regardless of their ethnic group. This acknowledgement is an essential first step.[138]

Some hoped Plavšić's "admittedly noble example of . . . public remorse"[139] would have a catalytic effect on "the process of reconciliation" in Bosnia.[140] The Humanitarian Law Center, a leading nongovernmental organization (NGO) in Serbia, welcomed her confession, saying it "opens the way to the reconciliation of individuals and ethnic groups, and to restoring the dignity of the victims."[141]

If, as some have suggested, international criminal trials are didactic exercises in judicial theater,[142] Plavšić's December 2002 sentencing hearing was staged as a lesson in the restorative potential of global justice. A pantheon of luminary witnesses, including former U.S. secretary of state Madeleine K. Albright, the late Nobel laureate Elie Wiesel, and then president of the International Center for Transitional Justice Alex Boraine, hailed her confession as a gesture of acknowledgement that could advance reconciliation.[143] So, too, did Bosnian NGO leader Mirsad Tokača, who testified that Plavšić's admission of guilt was "an extremely courageous, brave and important gesture."[144] In its sentencing brief, the prosecution wrote: "Mrs. Plavšić's

---

[136] Prosecutor v. Plavšić, Case No. IT-00-39 & 40/1-S, Sentencing Judgment, ¶ 71 (Int'l Crim. Trib. for the Former Yugoslavia Feb. 27, 2003) (quoting Plavšić Written Statement).

[137] See Marlise Simons, Ex-Bosnia Leader Enters Guilty Plea to The Hague, N.Y. TIMES (Oct. 3, 2002).

[138] Prosecutor v. Plavšić, Case No. IT-00-39 & 40/1-S, Sentencing Judgment, ¶ 74 (Int'l Crim. Trib. for the Former Yugoslavia Feb. 27, 2003) (quoting Plavšić Written Statement).

[139] Michael Bohlander, Last Exit Bosnia—Transferring War Crimes Prosecution from the International Tribunal to Domestic Courts, 14 CRIM. L.F. 59, 59 (2003).

[140] Simons, supra note 137.

[141] Humanitarian Law Center, Acknowledgment, Taking of Responsibility, Remorse—The Way to Reconciliation (Oct. 3, 2002).

[142] See LAWRENCE DOUGLAS, THE MEMORY OF JUDGMENT: MAKING LAW AND HISTORY IN THE TRIALS OF THE HOLOCAUST 2–3 (2001); DRUMBL, supra note 81, at 175.

[143] See Marlise Simons, Crossing Paths: Albright Testifies in War Crimes Case, N.Y. TIMES (Dec. 18, 2002). Weisel testified that, "whereas others similarly accused deny the truth about their crimes and thereby assist those who want to falsify history, Mrs. Plavšić, who once moved in the highest circles of power, has made an example by freely and wholly admitting her role in the crime." Prosecutor v. Plavšić, Case No. IT-00-39 & 40/1-S, Sentencing Judgment, ¶ 69 (Int'l Crim. Trib. for the Former Yugoslavia Feb. 27, 2003) (summarizing testimony of Elie Wiesel). Wiesel urged, however, that the value of Plavšić's confession be weighed against the "pain and suffering of all the victims" and that she receive a stern sentence. Wiesel Urges Stern Hague Term, N.Y. TIMES (Dec. 17, 2002). In advance of his testimony, Wiesel said he would not testify in support of mitigation but instead "to say that it is important for a person of [Plavšić's] importance to have the courage to admit her guilt." Stephanie van den Berg, Nobel Laureate Wiesel to Testify Against Ex-Bosnian Serb Leader, AGENCE FRANCE-PRESSE (Dec. 13, 2002).

[144] Prosecutor v. Plavšić, Case No. IT-00-39 & 40/1-S, Sentencing Judgment, ¶ 78 (Int'l Crim. Trib. for the Former Yugoslavia Feb. 27, 2003) (quoting testimony of Mirsad Tokača).

plea of guilty and acceptance of responsibility represents an unprecedented contribution to the establishment of truth and a significant effort toward the advancement of reconciliation."[145]

In Bosnia, reactions to the confession "ranged from pleasant surprise to suspicion that the tribunal somehow compromised its values by making a deal" with Plavšić.[146] While some believed her confession could be a watershed, others doubted her sincerity. Srebrenica survivor Munira Subašić thought Plavšić had confessed "so she can get a lighter sentence"[147] (a suspicion later confirmed by Plavšić). Another survivor, Sabra Kolenović, noted Plavšić stopped short of actually apologizing,[148] while Emir Suljagić, who spent much of the war in Srebrenica, did not detect even a "note of apology" in Plavšić's words.[149] Suljagić later recalled: "Another thing that really hurt was the long line of international officials willing to testify in her defense."[150]

Two months after the sentencing hearing, the ICTY sentenced Plavšić to eleven years' imprisonment for crimes against humanity,[151] of which she would actually serve only two-thirds.[152] Without explaining precisely how it determined her sentence, the Trial Chamber gave substantial weight to the views of witnesses who testified about the impact Plavšić's guilty plea "could have for the reconciliation process."[153]

Far from celebrating the potential impact of Plavšić's confession on reconciliation, many Bosnians were stunned and incensed by her sentence. Mujesira Memišević, whose husband, children, and other relatives were slaughtered, decried the "outrageously low" penalty, saying: "I am speechless. I cannot talk at all. I am shivering, I am completely shaken."[154] The late Muharem Murselović was flabbergasted: "Eleven years for all those lives, for all the sufferings is only a drop in the ocean and we, the former camp inmates, cannot be satisfied with that."[155] Several years later, Nerma

---

[145] *Id.* ¶ 67 (quoting Prosecution Sentencing Brief); *see also id.* ¶ 67.

[146] *Southeastern Europe Praise for Bosnian Serb Leader's Admission of Guilt*, RFE/RL NewsLine (Oct. 3, 2002).

[147] Abigail Levene, *"Iron Lady" in Dock for Ethnic Cleansing*, Reuters (Dec. 18, 2002).

[148] *Id.*

[149] Simons, *supra* note 143. Carla del Ponte, who was the ICTY Prosecutor during the Plavšić proceedings, would later write that she was horrified when she heard the defendant's confession (notwithstanding the above-quoted sentencing brief). Del Ponte described the courtroom scene this way:

> [Plavšić] got up during her sentencing hearing and read out a statement full of generalistic mea culpas but lacking compelling detail. I listened to her admissions in horror, knowing she was saying nothing.

Del Ponte with Sudetić, *supra* note 135, at 161.

[150] Interview with Emir Suljagić, Author, in Sarajevo, Bosn. & Herz. (July 14, 2009). In a similar vein but more generally, Omarska survivor Mirsad Duratović told me he found "very offensive" the way defendants who plead guilty to unspeakable atrocities "get praised by the [ICTY] for being very cooperative." Interview with Mirsad Duratović in Prijedor, Bosn. & Herz. (Dec. 8, 2006).

[151] Prosecutor v. Plavšić, Case No. IT-00-39 & 40/1-S, Sentencing Judgment, ¶¶ 132, 134 (Int'l Crim. Trib. for the Former Yugoslavia Feb. 27, 2003). The Trial Chamber had previously accepted a plea agreement between Plavšić and the Prosecutor pursuant to which charges of genocide were dropped. *See id.* ¶ 5.

[152] *See* Ian Traynor, *Leading Bosnian Serb War Criminal Released from Swedish Prison*, Guardian (Oct. 27, 2009).

[153] Prosecutor v. Plavšić, Case No. IT-00-39 & 40/1-S, Sentencing Judgment, ¶ 75 (Int'l Crim. Trib. for the Former Yugoslavia Feb. 27, 2003) (describing testimony of Alex Boraine).

[154] Daria Sito-Sučić, *Muslim Victims Outraged, Say Plavšić Sentence Low*, Reuters (Feb. 27, 2003).

[155] *Id.*

Jelačić reflected: "There was no impact of Biljana Plavšić's confession [on victims]. It got lost in the injustice they saw with the sentence given."[156]

Although critical of Plavšić's sentence, some Bosnians were heartened by her "guilty plea and call to other leaders to follow her example."[157] Dobrila Govedarica praised Plavšić's confession when we spoke four years later, saying: "Plavšić verbally made herself guilty. That was one of the most important things that happened in the ICTY. A high official really confessed and found herself guilty."[158] Still, Govedarica made clear, she hoped Bosnian Serbs would build on Plavšić's example.[159] Others who initially welcomed Plavšić's confession had already revised their views. Edina Residović explained why she did this way: "We somehow were expecting the others [i.e., other Bosnian Serbs] to realize what was going on but we were wrong. Serbs proclaimed her as a traitor and victims thought it was her way to get out with a short term of imprisonment."[160]

By the time of my July 2009 research visit, it was infinitely more difficult (though not impossible) for Bosnians to find value in Plavšić's plea.[161] Earlier that year Plavšić disavowed her confession, saying in an interview that she had pleaded guilty to crimes against humanity to avoid facing a lengthy trial on other charges, including genocide. Against her earlier gesture of remorse, Plavšić now insisted: "I have done nothing wrong."[162] (Not long after, Plavšić was warmly welcomed by nationalist leader Milorad Dodik when she returned to Belgrade.[163])

---

[156] Interview with Nerma Jelačić, then Director, BIRN in BiH, in Sarajevo, Bosn. & Herz. (Dec. 1, 2006). Reflecting on the same sentence, Sevima Sali-Terzić said: "It doesn't really look like an institution that can bring justice." Interview with Sevima Sali-Terzić, Senior Legal Counsel, Constitutional Court of BiH, in Sarajevo, Bosn. & Herz. (Nov. 30, 2006).

[157] Sito-Sučić, *supra* note 154 (quoting Omarska survivor Nusreta Sivac).

[158] Interview with Dobrila Govedarica, Executive Director, Open Society Fund BiH, in Sarajevo, Bosn. & Herz. (Nov. 29, 2006). Jasna Bakšić Muftić made a similar point, describing Plavšić as "the first one who really said everything[;] she really accepted responsibility." Interview with Jasna Bakšić Muftić, Professor, Faculty of Law, University of Sarajevo, in Sarajevo, Bosn. & Herz. (Nov. 30, 2006).

[159] Srđan Dizdarević said he did not believe the situation in Bosnia was "mature enough" to benefit from Plavšić's confession, which he nonetheless considered "an enormous qualitative step forward." Interview with the late Srđan Dizdarević, then President, Helsinki Committee in BiH, in Sarajevo, Bosn. & Herz. (Dec. 1, 2006). Dizdarević noted many devalued Plavšić's confession because they thought the sentence inadequate. *Id.*

[160] Interview with Edina Rešidović, Attorney; then-Member of ICTY Defence Attorney Chamber, in Sarajevo, Bosn. & Herz. (Nov. 30, 2006).

[161] Ivan Lovrenović still considered Plavšić's guilty plea "one of those strong moments that would have never happened if the Hague Tribunal were not established." Interview with Ivan Lovrenović, then Editor-in-Chief, Dani, in Sarajevo, Bosn. & Herz. (July 17, 2009).

[162] Margaretha Nordgren, *Mötet med Biljana Plavšić* ("Meeting with Biljana Plavšić"), Vi (Stockholm) (Jan. 25, 2009). Plavšić explained that her defense lawyer had advised her to plead guilty to some charges to reduce the length of the trial. *See also* Simon Jennings, *Plavšić Reportedly Withdraws Guilty Plea*, IWPR (Jan. 30, 2009). Plavšić suggested as early as March 2005 that her confession was not genuine. She told an independent TV station in Republika Srpska that she admitted guilt because she was unable to bring in appropriate witnesses to testify on her behalf, and added: "When I got to see how all that goes in the Hague Tribunal, I told myself I should do something for myself. At least I could spare myself the trouble of sitting there and listening to false witnesses." *Zatvorski Dani B. Plavšić* ("B. Plavšić's Prison Days"), website B92 News, (Belgrade) (Mar. 12, 2005).

[163] *See* Iva Martinović, *Outcry at Plavšić's Belgrade Welcome*, IWPR (Nov. 4, 2009).

Noting Plavšić "negated everything" in her interview, Mirsad Tokača regretted his testimony at her sentencing hearing. "Now we see it was also my mistake," Tokača reflected. "I believed she would confess sincerely and others would follow." But the reality had instead been "absolutely disappointing."[164] Tokača believes the ICTY also made a "big mistake," though of a different order: It did not require Plavšić to testify in other cases as a precondition to accepting her plea agreement.[165] Former ICTY Prosecutor Carla del Ponte blames herself, saying she made a "fundamental error" by "not obliging [Plavšić] to agree on paper to testify against the other accused. I accepted verbal assurances and was deceived."[166] The ICTY apparently learned a lesson; defendants who pleaded guilty after Plavšić generally agreed to testify in other proceedings or at least provide "complete" information.[167]

c. Other Confessions

In the summer and fall of 2003, the ICTY saw a cascade of detailed confessions by Bosnian Serb perpetrators, including several relatively senior commanders involved in the Srebrenica massacre.[168] Some provided crucial information not previously available as evidence.[169] Despite his concerns about Plavšić's guilty plea, Emir Suljagić hoped these confessions would finally breach Bosnian Serb denial: "If

---

[164] Interview with Mirsad Tokača, Director, Research and Documentation Center (Sarajevo), in Sarajevo, Bosn. & Herz. (July 24, 2009).

[165] Id.

[166] DEL PONTE WITH SUDETIĆ, *supra* note 135, at 161.

[167] The following suspects pleaded guilty after Biljana Plavšić entered a guilty plea and agreed to cooperate with the Prosecutor: Momir Nikolić (*see* Prosecutor v. Nikolić, Case No. IT-02-60/1-S, Sentencing Judgment, ¶¶ 153, 155 (Int'l Crim. Trib. for the Former Yugoslavia Dec. 2, 2003)); Dragan Obrenović (*see* Prosecutor v. Obrenović, Case No. IT-02-60/2-S, Sentencing Judgment, ¶ 128 (Int'l Crim. Trib. for the Former Yugoslavia Dec. 10, 2003)); Darko Mrđa (*see* Prosecutor v. Mrđa, Case No. IT-02-59-S, Sentencing Judgment, ¶ 74 (Int'l Crim. Trib. for the Former Yugoslavia March 31, 2004)); Miroslav Deronjić (*see* Prosecutor v. Deronjić, Case No. IT-02-61-S, Sentencing Judgment, ¶¶ 241–255 (Int'l Crim. Trib. for the Former Yugoslavia Mar. 30, 2004)); Miodrag Jokić (*see* Prosecutor v. Jokić, Case No. IT-01-42/1-S, Sentencing Judgment, ¶ 95 (Int'l Crim. Trib. for the Former, 2004); Dragan Nikolić (*see* Prosecutor v. Nikolić, Case No. IT-94-2-S, Sentencing Judgment, ¶ 260 (Int'l Crim. Trib. for the Former Yugoslavia Dec. 18, 2003)); Ranko Češić (*see* Prosecutor v. Češić, Case No. IT-95-10/1-S, Sentencing Judgment, ¶¶ 61–62 (Int'l Crim. Trib. for the Former Yugoslavia Mar. 11, 2004)); Milan Babić (*see* Prosecutor v. Babić, Case No. IT-03-72-S, Sentencing Judgment, ¶ 73-5 (Int'l Crim. Trib. for the Former Yugoslavia June 29, 2004)); and Ivica Rajić (*see* Prosecutor v. Rajić, Case No. IT-95-12-S, Sentencing Judgment, ¶ 154 (Int'l Crim. Trib. for the Former Yugoslavia May 8, 2006)); Predrag Banović (*see* Prosecutor v. Banović, Case No. IT-02-65/1-S, Sentencing Judgment, ¶ 60 (Int'l Crim. Trib. for the Former Yugoslavia Oct. 28, 2003)); and Dragan Zelenović (*see* Prosecutor v. Zelenović, Case No. IT-96-23/2-S, Sentencing Judgment, ¶ 52 (Int'l Crim. Trib. for the Former Yugoslavia Apr. 4, 2007)). In the case of Miroslav Bralo, the Tribunal assessed the defendant's cooperation as merely "moderate," and weighed it accordingly. Prosecutor v. Bralo, Case No. IT-95-17-S, Sentencing Judgment ¶ 81 (Int'l Crim. Trib. for the Former Yugoslavia Dec. 7, 2005).

[168] *See* Judith Armatta, *Srebrenica Guilty Pleas Have Many Repercussions*, COALITION INT'L JUST. (May 21, 2003); Marlise Simons, *In a Startling Plea, a Serbian Policeman Confesses to Atrocities*, N.Y. TIMES (July 27, 2003); Arthur Max, *Yugoslav Tribunal Is Court Making History*, ASSOCIATED PRESS (Aug. 3, 2003); Marlise Simons, *Serb at Hague Pleads Guilty to Brutalities*, N.Y. TIMES (Sept. 5, 2003); Marlise Simons, *Officers Say Bosnian Massacre Was Deliberate*, N.Y. TIMES (Oct. 12, 2003).

[169] *See* Simons, *supra* note 115.

you punched that wall, I thought the rest would fall like dominoes. . . . I was really hopeful: 'This is it, it's happened now.' "[170]

What Suljagić hoped would happen is that the commanders' detailed confessions would "open up a space in the media that was not there before for others to admit to wrongdoing; that [the confessions] would make it easier for Serbs who were not complicit in crimes to talk to their non-Serb neighbors." But, he continued, "it was not that simple[;] obviously I was way too naïve."[171] Still, the confessions were gratifying. Soon after one of the Srebrenica defendants pleaded guilty, Suljagić told a reporter: "I was crying in court. When [the defendant] said, 'I plead guilty,' I ran upstairs and locked myself in the toilet and cried my eyes out. It was a genuine relief to hear someone like him saying, 'Yes, we killed seven thousand or eight thousand people.' "[172]

While the wave of guilty pleas yielded valuable evidence, the Prosecutor's failure to demand crucial information from one of the suspects pained survivors.[173] Darko Mrđa, who pleaded guilty in the summer of 2003, bore major responsibility for a notorious massacre, the execution in Korićanske Stijene of some 200 non-Serbs transferred from Prijedor in August 1992. Survivors were astonished to learn Mrđa did not reveal in court "where the bodies are."[174] For victims, Mirsad Duratović told me, "that was the most important thing."[175] A couple of years after I interviewed

---

[170] Interview with Emir Suljagić, Author, in Sarajevo, Bosn. & Herz. (July 14, 2009).

[171] *Id.* Suljagić recalled that in the period that followed these confessions, the Serbian government geared up to counter evidence of its involvement in the Srebrenica massacre as the International Court of Justice moved toward resolution of a case the Bosnian government instituted a decade earlier alleging that the FRY had violated the Genocide Convention. *Id.*

[172] Tim Judah, *The Fog of Justice*, 51 N.Y. REV. BOOKS (Jan. 15, 2004).

[173] Interview with Mirsad Duratović in Prijedor, Bosn. & Herz. (Dec. 8, 2006). The ICTY website includes this paragraph in its summary of the Mrđa sentencing judgment:

> As to the mitigating circumstances, the Chamber took into consideration Mrđa's cooperation with the Prosecution. The Chamber also held that Mrđa's guilty plea had helped to establish the truth surrounding the crimes committed at Korićanske Stijene and could contribute to promoting reconciliation between the peoples of Bosnia and Herzegovina. It was noted incidentally that his plea made it possible to obviate the expense of a lengthy trial and the need for a large number of victims and witnesses to come and testify at the Tribunal. Therefore, his guilty plea was considered to be a mitigating factor. In addition, the Chamber found the accused's expression of remorse to be sincere and took this into account in mitigation. The Chamber found that Mrđa's personal circumstances should be considered in mitigation, but that little weight should be attached to them.

ICTY, CASE INFORMATION SHEET: DARKO MRĐA, http://www.icty.org/x/cases/mrda/cis/en/cis_mrdja_en.pdf (last visited Dec. 5, 2017).

[174] Interview with Mirsad Duratović in Prijedor, Bosn. & Herz. (Dec. 8, 2006). Sadik Trako made much the same point about the ICTY's failure to ensure that another defendant who pleaded guilty, Miroslav Bralo, provided accurate information about the location of victims' corpses. According to Trako, although Bralo had provided information about the location, authorities did not discover bodies there. Noting that local residents were still searching for relatives' bodies, Trako said: "They're angry because the Tribunal didn't get the correct information [from Bralo]. I see it as if he's playing with The Hague." Interview with Sadik Trako, President, Association of Victims and Missing Persons in Lašva Valley, in Vitez, Bosn. & Herz. (Dec. 6, 2006).

[175] Interview with Mirsad Duratović in Prijedor, Bosn. & Herz. (Dec. 8, 2006). *See also* Hodžić, *Living the Legacy, supra* note 21, at 128 (one reason Prijedor victims have reacted negatively to guilty pleas of certain Prijedor defendants is because they "left unanswered questions as to the whereabouts of missing persons").

Duratović, the war crimes chamber of the Court of Bosnia and Herzegovina applied the lesson of the ICTY's misstep: it identified the remains of victims of the Korićanske Stijene massacre through the testimony of defendants who pleaded guilty.[176] Noting that defendants' testimony before the Bosnian court had led to the discovery of mass graves, Nidžara Ahmetašević said, "that's how you will find out about the destiny of some of your relatives."[177]

In contrast to the Mrđa episode, at times proceedings in The Hague have answered survivors' urgent need to learn the fate of their loved ones. Former ICTY prosecutor Dan Saxon recalls such a moment:

> [I]n September 2003, Dragan Nikolić, the warden of the notorious Sušica prison camp in the Republika Srpska, confessed to his responsibility for atrocities committed against detainees. At his sentencing hearing . . . , an extraordinary event occurred when a Prosecution witness, the mother of two Bosnian Muslim men who disappeared from the Sušica prison camp during the war, asked Mr. Nikolić if he could provide her with any information about the fate of her lost sons. Mr. Nikolić explained to the witness that 11 years earlier, . . . Bosnian Serb forces murdered her two children. It will be difficult to find another example of courtroom testimony that so powerfully and quickly advanced the process of truth-seeking and (hopefully) reconciliation in the former Yugoslavia.[178]

The ICTY website, which has featured this moment, indicates Nikolić provided information that might lead to the identification of the graves of the witness's sons.[179] But as a former staff member of the International Commission on Missing Persons observed, the ICTY did not always ask, "where did you put the bodies?"[180]

Even so, some Bosnians believe, in the words of Ivan Lovrenović, that the "tens of confessions saying in an unambiguous way that war crimes have been committed" was an important achievement. In Lovrenović's view (as of 2009), such confessions helped counter attempts by many to equalize crimes committed during the 1990s war, which have "dehumanize[ed] victims' suffering." Through the detailed confirmation of specific atrocities that comes with guilty pleas, Lovrenović said, the ICTY is "taking our attention back to the concrete problem which is most important here, which is the misery that victims have been through."[181]

Some victims suggested expressions of remorse that appear genuine can be reparative. For example, Sadik Trako told me victims in Lašva Valley were gratified when they were contacted by Tihomir Blaškić, a Bosnian Croat commander who

---

[176] See Exhumation at Korićanske Stijene Begins, Justice Rep. (July 21, 2009); Bosnian Authorities Recover Remains of War Crime Victims, Deutsche Presse-Agentur (Aug. 5, 2009).

[177] Interview with Nidžara Ahmetašević, then Editor, BIRN in BiH, in Sarajevo, Bosn. & Herz. (July 13, 2009).

[178] Dan Saxon, Exporting Justice: Perceptions of the ICTY Among the Serbian, Croatian, and Muslim Communities in the Former Yugoslavia, 4 J. Hum. Rts. 559, 560 (2005) (citations omitted).

[179] See ICTY, Achievements: Establishing the Facts, http://www.icty.org/sid/324 (last visited Aug. 7, 2017).

[180] Interview with Asta Zinbo, then Director, Civil Society Initiatives Program, International Commission on Missing Persons, in Sarajevo, Bosn. & Herz. (Dec. 6, 2006).

[181] Interview with Ivan Lovrenović, then Editor-in-Chief, Dani, in Sarajevo, Bosn. & Herz. (July 17, 2009). As explored in Chapter 8, virulent forms of denialism have intensified in the period since I interviewed Lovrenović.

had been convicted of war crimes against Bosniaks in the region, upon his release from prison. Blaškić wanted to meet with the organization Trako led "to apologize to the families of victims." Although Trako thought it too early for such a meeting and told Blaškić as much, he was "still glad Blaškić apologized."[182] Blaškić did not benefit from a plea agreement, and victims are more likely to perceive an apology as insincere when accompanied by a reduced sentence.[183] But victims often *do* discern meaningful differences among defendants who express remorse based on their apparent sincerity. And as one commentator has noted, "guilty pleas that seem to be motivated by sincere remorse and a genuine acknowledgement of wrongdoing are much more likely to encourage dialogue and forgiveness than guilty pleas that appear motivated solely by sentencing concessions."[184]

Yet defendants' expressions of remorse—whether in the context of plea agreements or otherwise—can contribute to victims' sense of justice only if they are known, and this does not happen automatically. According to Fatima Fazlić, when the ICTY sentences defendants who have pleaded guilty, the local media report the sentences but not the details set forth in confessions, "because they still see [confessions] as a betrayal of Serb interests."[185]

Until December 2008, the ICTY made scant effort to publicize confessions.[186] Mirsad Duratović, who was highly critical of plea agreements, suggested his view could change if he knew the details of defendants' cooperation. In his words, "It would mean a lot, by all means, yes, if we knew that the defendant's cooperation [with the Prosecutor] led to mass graves or the conviction of others who were even more responsible."[187]

---

[182] Interview with Sadik Trako, President, Association of Victims and Missing Persons in Lašva Valley, in Vitez, Bosn. & Herz. (Dec. 6, 2006). Another person told me he does "not think that justice will be served" until the man who was most responsible for his brother's death "comes before the people and apologizes" after he serves the twenty-one-year sentence he received upon pleading guilty in Bosnia's war crimes chamber. Interview with Sabahudin Garibović, Association of Former Camp Detainees, in Kozarac, Bosn. & Herz. (July 23, 2009).

[183] In her own research interviews in 2008, Janine Natalya Clark found that Bosnian victims overwhelmingly thought ICTY defendants who expressed regret for their crimes were "being disingenuous and [were] simply seeking . . . a reduced sentence." Clark, *Plea Bargaining, supra* note 113, at 432.

[184] Nancy Amoury Combs, *Copping a Plea to Genocide: The Plea Bargaining of International Crimes*, 151 U. PA. L. REV. 1, 150 (2002). *See also* Clark, *Plea Bargaining, supra* note 113, at 432–33. Conversely, a study of Prijedor victims found that one of the most important factors accounting for negative views of guilty pleas "is the perceived lack of sincerity and narrow scope of the acknowledgment of responsibility by defendants." Hodžić, *Living the Legacy, supra* note 21, at 129.

[185] Interview with Fatima Fazlić, President, Izvor, in Prijedor, Bosn. & Herz. (July 23, 2009). Refik Hodžić notes, however, that "ICTY pleas have generated a great deal of discussion and debate among victims in Prijedor," Hodžić, *Living the Legacy, supra* note 21, at 129, but does not state whether details of these pleas were well known in Prijedor.

[186] That month the ICTY launched a new website, which included a substantial section on guilty pleas and confessions, with transcripts and video extracts from proceedings. *See* ICTY, http://www.icty.org/sid/203 (last visited Dec. 5, 2017). An ICTY source told me this page was the twelfth-most viewed of the entire site during 2009.

[187] Interview with Mirsad Duratović in Prijedor, Bosn. & Herz. (Dec. 8, 2006).

B. Length and Complexity of ICTY Proceedings

It's only that these trials took too long, way too long. And I also think these whole proceedings are too complicated.

—MUHAREM MURSELOVIĆ[188]

These trials of war criminals are taking way too long.

—KADA HOTIĆ[189]

Along with sentencing practices, the length and complexity of proceedings ranks high among Bosnian criticisms of Hague justice,[190] and understandably so: in some instances years elapsed between the time the Tribunal gained custody of a suspect and the beginning of his trial;[191] then, the trial typically lasted well over a year.[192] More than a dozen trials lasted over two years;[193] some of them made a deep impression on many Bosnians. Following a trial verdict, additional years often elapsed before final judgment was rendered.[194]

The sheer length of proceedings has exacted a heavy toll, comprising three broad categories. The first, explored in the following subsection, entails tangible effects on prosecutions, notably including the death of suspects before their trials are completed,[195] and the loss of valuable evidence as crucial witnesses pass

---

[188] Interview with the late Muharem Murselović, then Member of Republika Srpska National Assembly, President of the RS Parlamentarians Club for the Party for BiH, in Banja Luka, Bosn. & Herz. (July 15, 2009).

[189] Interview with Kada Hotić, Vice-President, Association of Mothers of Srebrenica and Žepa Enclaves, in Sarajevo, Bosn. & Herz. (Sept. 18, 2014).

[190] This criticism is long-standing. *See* Sonja Kutnjak Ivković, *Justice by the International Criminal Tribunal for the Former Yugoslavia*, 37 STAN. J. INT'L L. 255, 329 (2001). Although my focus here is on the views of Bosnians, the Tribunal's cumbersome procedures have been widely criticized by scholars and practitioners of international justice. As Alex Whiting succinctly notes, "A central and enduring critique" of the ICTY "is that the trials are too slow, too long, and inefficient." Alex Whiting, *The ICTY as a Laboratory of International Criminal Procedure, in* THE LEGACY OF THE INTERNATIONAL CRIMINAL TRIBUNAL FOR THE FORMER YUGOSLAVIA 83, 95 (Bert Swart et al. eds., 2011) [hereinafter Whiting, *Laboratory*]. *See also* Alex Whiting, *In International Criminal Prosecutions, Justice Delayed Can Be Justice Delivered*, 50 HARV. INT'L L.J. 323, 323–24 (2009).

[191] Based on calculations by one of my research assistants, Alanna Kennedy, in 2017, the average time between a suspect's arrest or surrender and the beginning of his trial or guilty plea was more than two years. These figures do not, of course, capture the unique toll exacted by the extended impunity of Ratko Mladić and Radovan Karadžić, as described in Chapter 2.

[192] Based on calculations by my research assistants Mona Adabi, Sonja Balić, and Chase Dunn, the average length of trials completed by August, 24, 2017, was approximately one year and nine months. This calculation was based solely on cases in which there was a full trial, and thus excluded trials that ended before closing arguments because a defendant pleaded guilty.

[193] Based on a review undertaken in 2017 by my former research assistant Alanna Kennedy, 15 trials lasted more than two years.

[194] Of the cases analyzed by Alanna Kennedy in 2017 (see previous footnotes), an average of just over two-and-a-half years elapsed between the date a trial judgment was issued and, if there was an appeal, the date an appeal judgment was issued.

[195] Although the best-known instance is the death of Slobodan Milošević, whose case is discussed below, he was not the only ICTY defendant to die before judgment. The last fugitive transferred to The Hague, Goran Hadžić, became terminally ill before his trial was completed. First indicted in May 2004, Hadžić was not arrested until July 2011. *See* Julian Borger, *Serbia Arrests Goran Hadžić, the Last Yugoslav War Fugitive*, GUARDIAN (July 20, 2011). Hadžić's trial began in October 2012; in October 2014, the case was adjourned due to the defendant's illness. The case

away.[196] Although subjective, a second harm is by no means speculative: the extended life of the ICTY—longer than that of any other ICT—has profoundly diminished many victims' experience of justice, as the second subsection makes clear. The third type of harm, explored in Chapter 2, comprises lost opportunities for the ICTY to have a positive social impact. By its nature speculative,[197] this loss is nonetheless keenly felt and lamented by Bosnians who invested soaring hopes in the Hague Tribunal.

1. The Trial without End: Slobodan Milošević

If they made a huge mistake it was the Milošević case.

—Dobrila Govedarica[198]

In the case of Milošević's trial, we all have been deprived of justice.

—Edin Ramulić[199]

A lot of victims felt cheated when he died.

—Damir Arnaut[200]

To many Bosnians and others, the marathon trial of former Yugoslav president Slobodan Milošević is emblematic of a pervasive problem in The Hague—trials whose length extends beyond tolerable limits[201]—and a cautionary tale. After more than four years, the trial was within weeks of ending[202] when the defendant died in his detention cell in March 2006,[203] abruptly terminating what was to have been the Tribunal's capstone case.

Gojko Berić reflected the views of many Bosnians I interviewed when he said, "the pace of the proceedings . . . went before any expectations. This was really too much."[204] The "whole thing turned into a bureaucratic labyrinth," Ivan Lovrenović

---

against Hadžić was dismissed ten days after his death in July 2016. *See* ICTY, Case Information Sheet: Goran Hadžić, http://www.icty.org/x/cases/hadzic/cis/en/cis_hadzic_en.pdf (last visited Dec. 5, 2017).

[196] See Whiting, *Laboratory, supra* note 190, at 99.

[197] A classic counterfactual, this category of loss assumes earlier trials of prominent suspects would have had significant implications for postwar Bosnia's social and political development.

[198] Interview with Dobrila Govedarica, Executive Director, Open Society Fund BiH, in Sarajevo, Bosn. & Herz. (Nov. 30, 2006).

[199] Interview with Edin Ramulić, Project Coordinator, Izvor, in Prijedor, Bosn. & Herz. (Sept. 16, 2014).

[200] Interview with Damir Arnaut, then Advisor for Legal and Constitutional Affairs, Cabinet of Haris Silajdžić, in Sarajevo, Bosn. & Herz. (July 16, 2009).

[201] As legal commentators have noted, "[t]he most ardent criticism of [the Milošević] trial was that it was simply allowed to go on for too long." Gideon Boas & Timothy L.H. McCormack, *Learning the Lessons of the Milošević Trial*, 9 Y.B. Int'l Humanitarian L. 65, 68–69 (2006).

[202] At the time of Milošević's death, the prosecution had completed presenting its case and forty hours remained for the defendant to present his case. Del Ponte with Sudetić, *supra* note 135, at 332.

[203] *See* Molly Moore & Daniel Williams, *Milošević Found Dead in Prison; Genocide Trial Is Left Without a Final Judgment*, Wash. Post (Mar. 12, 2006); Marlise Simons, *Milošević's Trial Ends but Inquiries Continue*, N.Y. Times (Mar. 15, 2006).

[204] Interview with Gojko Berić, Journalist & Columnist, Oslobođenje, in Sarajevo, Bosn. & Herz. (July 17, 2009). Although a lawyer herself, Sevima Sali-Terzić had a hard time "understand[ing]

said, and, in the end, "we had no appropriate verdict."[205] Like many Bosnians, Tarik Jusić linked Milošević's death to the length of ICTY trials, which he described as the "weakest" dimension of the Tribunal's work.[206]

The need to accommodate the defendant's precarious health situation was a major factor behind the trial's length.[207] Even so, many blame Milošević's death without judgment on the Tribunal's "extreme inefficiency."[208] Some, including Berić, place primary blame on the Prosecutor for "prolonging this process for so long." In his view, then Prosecutor Carla del Ponte tried to prove too much, and in the end lost the chance to prove anything: she "wrote an indictment that is a novel. . . . It's too extensive, unnecessarily."[209]

Before I continue, it should be noted that, while the indictment was indeed comprehensive,[210] its sweep was in no small part a reflection of prosecutors' effort to address victims' hopes the Tribunal would do more than prosecute individuals one by one, and instead render an authoritative history of the 1990s conflicts.[211] Had Milošević lived to see judgment and been convicted as charged, it is fair to assume criticism of the indictment's breadth would have been significantly muted.

Like Berić, legal experts recognize that the lengthy indictment made for a "long and arduous trial,"[212] but cite other factors as well. Former ICTY judge Patricia Wald

---

why the *Milošević* trial lasted so long." Interview with Sevima Sali-Terzić, Senior Legal Counsel, Constitutional Court of BiH, in Sarajevo, Bosn. & Herz. (Nov. 30, 2006).

[205] Interview with Ivan Lovrenović, then Editor-in-Chief, Dani, in Sarajevo, Bosn. & Herz. (July 17, 2009). Lovrenović said "everybody's opinion" is that one of the major failures of the ICTY is its "extreme inefficiency, its slow pace." *Id.*

[206] Jusić said the ICTY "allowed that [Milošević] was not sentenced," and described Milošević's death without judgment as the "most negative" aspect of its record. Interview with Tarik Jusić, then Program Director, Mediacentar Sarajevo, in Sarajevo, Bosn. & Herz. (Dec. 6, 2006).

[207] *See* WALD, *supra* note 8, at 13; HUMAN RIGHTS WATCH, WEIGHING THE EVIDENCE: LESSONS FROM THE SLOBODAN MILOŠEVIĆ TRIAL 60–61 (Dec. 2006) [hereinafter HRW, WEIGHING THE EVIDENCE]; Nancy Amoury Combs, *Regulation of Defence Counsel: An Evolution Towards Restriction and Legitimacy, in* THE LEGACY OF THE INTERNATIONAL CRIMINAL TRIBUNAL FOR THE FORMER YUGOSLAVIA 306–08 (Bert Swart et al. eds., 2011) [hereinafter Combs, *Regulation of Defence Counsel*].

[208] Interview with Ivan Lovrenović, then Editor-in-Chief, Dani, in Sarajevo, Bosn. & Herz. (July 17, 2009).

[209] Interview with Gojko Berić, Journalist & Columnist, Oslobođenje, in Sarajevo, Bosn. & Herz. (July 17, 2009). Like Berić, Mirsad Tokača faults the Prosecutor for framing an indictment that was "too wide" and lacked focus. Interview with Mirsad Tokača, President, Research and Documentation Center (Sarajevo), in Sarajevo, Bosn. & Herz. (Dec. 6, 2006).

[210] As Timothy Waters has noted, "what made this trial extraordinary" was the way it wove together the many crimes charged in the Tribunal's overall work: "What had been isolated, disparate acts, told and tested in separate trials, was now joined in a single case, under a single theory that implied a claim about the wars as a whole. The case that was brought against Milošević placed him at the very center of a web of criminality." Timothy William Waters, *Preface to* THE MILOŠEVIĆ TRIAL: AN AUTOPSY, at xv, xvii (Timothy William Waters ed., 2013). Fatefully, the Prosecutor chose to join three distinct indictments in a single case, and successfully appealed the trial chamber's ruling against her on this point. Had the Appeals Chamber sustained the Trial Chamber's ruling, Milošević likely would have lived to see judgment on at least one set of charges.

[211] *See* Whiting, *Laboratory, supra* note 190, at 101; David Wippman, *The Costs of International Justice*, 100 AM. J. INT'L L. 861, 875–76 (2006).

[212] WALD, *supra* note 8, at 14. The quoted language is Judge Wald's characterization of views expressed by Gideon Boas, who, in his former capacity as senior legal officer, was responsible for managing the *Milošević* trial for the ICTY Chambers.

has noted, for example, "There is a strong argument . . . that it is less the length or scope of the indictment that makes for needlessly long trials than the management of time by the prosecutor, the defense, and the court. If the court sets reasonable time allotments and sticks to them, the trial will stay on a timely course."[213]

Analysts have generated a raft of practical suggestions for how ICTY and other ICT trials can be made more efficient without detracting from the historic nature of alleged crimes,[214] and the Tribunal itself progressively worked to streamline proceedings, albeit with mixed success.[215] Former ICTY prosecutor Alex Whiting recalls that, particularly as the completion strategy gained steam around 2005, judges imposed stricter deadlines on the parties. In the same period, "judges would ask the prosecution to submit its list of witnesses and exhibits and then issue an order to the prosecution to cut their anticipated time by a third. It was always one-third."[216] Whiting prosecuted Dragomir Milošević under such an order, which "certainly shortened the trial (and made it no less effective)."[217] More generally, in Whiting's assessment, this approach "was effective in shortening some of the later trials," though not those of senior suspects.[218]

For many former Yugoslav citizens, the trial without judgment cannot be redeemed. In the eyes of Serbians who had long championed the ICTY, Milošević's death without judgment deprived Serbia of a crucial foundation for a necessary process of national reckoning. For Bosniak victims, his death was a grave breach in the edifice of justice. Noting Milošević's trial went on "for too long, way too long, so that he was not in a position to even live long enough to be faced with a verdict," Srebrenica survivor Hatidža Mehmedović said: "This was a huge price for not only victims of . . . crimes committed in Srebrenica but for all of Bosnia as such."[219] One reason relates to a hope many Bosniaks directed toward the Tribunal—that it would unequivocally proclaim the rump Yugoslavia (then comprising Serbia and Montenegro) to be the "aggressor" in the 1990s war.[220] The Milošević prosecution offered a prime opportunity to prove, in Mehmedović's words, "that Serbia and

---

[213] *Id.* at 18.

[214] *See, e.g.*, HRW, WEIGHING THE EVIDENCE, *supra* note 207, at 53.

[215] For an overview of ICTY efforts to expedite proceedings and their limited success, see Whiting, *Laboratory, supra* note 190, at 95–105. As many commentators have noted, a key reason for lengthy proceedings before ICTs is the complexity of typical cases, which arise from mass atrocities, usually committed in countries other than the one where the Tribunal conducts cases. *See, e.g., id.* at 96; Wippman, *supra* note 211, at 875; Stuart Ford, *Complexity and Efficiency at International Criminal Courts*, 29 EMORY INT'L L. REV. 1, 15, 35 (2014). But this is hardly the sole reason for lengthy trials. Whiting identifies several contributing factors that could, in principle, be addressed more effectively. For example, in light of the high stakes of international trials, prosecutors are prone to produce redundant evidence to minimize the risk of acquittal. Whiting, *Laboratory, supra* note 190, at 96. In addition, pretrial judges at the ICTY, who were usually unfamiliar with the facts of cases, have "had little basis on which to seek a narrowing of the issues for trial, encourage agreement, or focus the proceedings" even though ICTY rules would allow them to do so. *Id.* at 100.

[216] Email from Alex Whiting, Professor of Practice, Harvard Law School, to Diane Orentlicher (Sept. 3, 2017).

[217] *Id.*

[218] *Id.*

[219] Interview with Hatidža Mehmedović, Association of Srebrenica Mothers, in Potočari, Bosn. & Herz. (July 21, 2009).

[220] *See* Chapter 2.

Montenegro made an aggression."[221] Saying "this case should have been completed," Kada Hotić evoked what was lost in similar terms. "Truth be told," she said, it was not the goal of any victim "to have defendants suffer, but simply to have them serve their sentences so this whole story becomes a part of the truth of everything that happened."[222]

Sevima Sali-Terzić sees Milošević's death before judgment as "one of the biggest flaws" in the ICTY's record, and laments the loss of what should have been a historic ruling: "The creator of the whole evil, you might say, is dead and now you don't have the court sentence that would say, well, 'he was the one.'"[223] Jasna Bakšić Muftić, who was "personally very sad that Milošević died" before his trial ended, made a similar point. Since the ICTY "didn't have the possibility . . . to go to the end of the process" for "one of the main actors" in the tragedy that befell Bosnia, the absence of a final judgment left "room for speculation and future manipulation." This, Bakšić Muftić said, "is the big damage."[224]

Nusreta Sivac noted another consequence of delayed justice: "Witnesses are literally dying."[225] So, too, are many victims, including several whom I interviewed for this book who did not live to see judgment rendered in two trials they had long awaited—those of Radovan Karadžić and Ratko Mladić.[226]

2. The Heavy Weight of Lengthening Time

The whole process . . . , for sure has to be shorter.

—Jasna Bakšić Muftić[227]

Everything is too, too, too long.

—Mirsad Tokača[228]

Concerns about the length of specific cases shade into a related yet distinct frustration: a pervasive sense that the ICTY has taken far too long to complete its work. Saša

---

[221] Interview with Hatidža Mehmedović, Association of Srebrenica Mothers, in Potočari, Bosn. & Herz. (July 21, 2009).

[222] Interview with Kada Hotić, Vice President, Mothers of Srebrenica and Žepa Enclaves, in Sarajevo, Bosn. & Herz. (July 24, 2009).

[223] Interview with Sevima Sali-Terzić, Senior Legal Counsel, Constitutional Court of BiH, in Sarajevo, Bosn. & Herz. (Sept. 9, 2014).

[224] Interview with Jasna Bakšić Muftić, Professor, Faculty of Law, University of Sarajevo, in Sarajevo, Bosn. & Herz. (Sept. 17, 2014).

[225] Interview with Nusreta Sivac, Former Judge, in Prijedor, Bosn. & Herz. (Sept. 16, 2014).

[226] As noted in Chapter 2, although first indicted in July 1995, Karadžić was not arrested until July 2008. His trial began on October 26, 2009, and ended almost five years later. On March 24, 2016, Karadžić was convicted of genocide, crimes against humanity, and war crimes and sentenced to forty years in prison. *See* ICTY, Case Information Sheet: Radovan Karadžić, http://www.icty.org/x/cases/karadzic/cis/en/cis_karadzic_en.pdf (last visited Dec. 5, 2017). Ratko Mladić eluded capture even longer than Karadžić. Arrested in 2011, Mladić was convicted of genocide and other crimes on November 22, 2009, and sentenced to life in prison. *See* ICTY, Case Information Sheet: Ratko Mladić, http://www.icty.org/x/cases/mladic/cis/en/cis_mladic_en.pdf (last visited Dec. 5, 2017).

[227] Interview with Jasna Bakšić Muftić, Professor, Faculty of Law, University of Sarajevo, in Sarajevo, Bosn. & Herz. (Sept. 17, 2014).

[228] Interview with Mirsad Tokača, President, Research and Documentation Center (Sarajevo), in Sarajevo, Bosn. & Herz. (Sept. 11, 2014).

Madacki made the point this way when we spoke in 2009: "Ordinary people will ask you how Nuremberg took one year and this [process] is taking 20 years."[229] Indeed, many Bosnians "feel cheated," in Emir Hodžić's words, precisely because they expected the ICTY to resemble Nuremberg, "where you go 'boom, boom, boom, you're guilty, you had a trial,' and, you know, done deal."[230]

Even Bosnians who champion its work have long seen the Tribunal as a heavy bureaucratic machine, wholly impervious to their country's urgent need for justice. Branko Todorović evoked this when he contrasted the toxic chokehold of many wartime Bosnian Serb leaders[231] with the lumbering bureaucracy he observed in The Hague:

> I want to tell you that in my opinion they made a first mistake: the majority of people working there are most probably the highest ranking in the judicial profession, but at the same time they are a high-ranking supreme bureaucracy, too. They have bylaws of the court, documents of the court, "we have certain international standards and of course we are backed up with the United Nations and we'll do our job the best we know based on justice, law." And to them it must have seemed pretty perfect. At the same time, here there were people who were running the country in high political circles who were the people who committed the crimes.[232]

But if these concerns are long-standing, a palpably deeper despair had taken hold by the time of my last research trip. Mirsad Tokača verbalized what many conveyed, saying he was "tired, sincerely speaking, of such extensive, slow" proceedings in The Hague. "For me," he added, "it's time wasting."[233] For many Bosnians, there is a painful paradox, which Emir Suljagić expressed this way: as years multiplied without the ICTY finishing its work, Suljagić lost interest in its cases. And yet, he said, he "still want[s] to see and [would] dedicate [his] life to see[ing] these guys in prison."[234]

A crucial point to be made here is that Bosnians did not experience long-awaited trials, such as that of Radovan Karadžić, the same way they would have years earlier.[235] When Karadžić was convicted of genocide and other charges in March

---

[229] Interview with Saša Madacki, Director, Human Rights Centre, University of Sarajevo, in Sarajevo, Bosn. & Herz. (July 17, 2009).

[230] Interview with Emir Hodžić, Jer Me Se Tiče, in Sarajevo, Bosn. & Herz. (Sept. 13, 2014).

[231] *See* Chapter 2.

[232] Interview with Branko Todorović, then President, Helsinki Committee for Human Rights in Republika Srpska, in Sarajevo, Bosn. & Herz. (July 14, 2009).

[233] Interview with Mirsad Tokača, President, Research and Documentation Center (Sarajevo), in Sarajevo, Bosn. & Herz. (Sept. 11, 2014).

[234] Interview with Emir Suljagić, Author, in Sarajevo, Bosn. & Herz. (Sept. 11, 2014).

[235] Whether the passage of time inevitably would have such an effect is hardly obvious; elsewhere, victims have felt a great sense of empowerment and vindication in finally bringing former leaders to justice after decades of impunity. This appears to be the case in Guatemala, where former dictator José Efraín Ríos Montt was brought to trial in 2013 on charges relating to massacres of indigenous Ixil Mayans that took place in 1982 and 1983. On May 10, 2013, Ríos Montt was convicted of genocide and crimes against humanity and sentenced to eighty years' imprisonment. Although his conviction was overturned by Guatemala's constitutional court, a retrial began in January 2015. Perhaps because Ixil survivors did not have reason to expect justice, Ríos Montt's trial some three decades after his alleged crimes did not seem to exact the kind

2016, Srebrenica survivor Kada Hotić lamented: "It's unbelievable to me that people like that were unpunished for so long," adding: "Many victims did not live to see the day when the organiser of all that violence gets punished."[236] For Bida Smajlović, whose husband and two brothers-in-law were killed in Srebrenica, "This came too late."[237]

Even so, when the ICTY rendered its final trial verdict in late November 2017, convicting Ratko Mladić of genocide and other crimes and sentencing him to life in prison, many survivors savored the moment. In the lead-up to judgment, many feared that, like Milošević before him, Mladić would die before judgment after a years-long trial (indeed, his defence lawyers sought to postpone judgment in light of their client's deteriorating health[238]). While Bosnians experienced a mix of emotions when the verdict was rendered, it brought more than relief for many. Survivors watching proceedings from Bosnia "exulted as the verdict was broadcast live," weeping along with those who found their way to The Hague.[239]

C. The Collateral Damage of Self-Representation

Across the years of its work, key benchmarks for assessing the ICTY's "success" have evolved, some looming especially large in its early years and receding in importance later, as others became more salient.[240] But in the eyes of Tribunal judges, one standard has consistently been of "paramount importance"[241]—the ICTY's adherence to the highest standards of fair and impartial process. Devotion to fair procedures is, to be sure, fundamental to any court's legitimacy. But it is especially vital for an ICT. By their nature and design, ICTs are detached from political communities and

---

of toll ICTY delays have taken on Bosnian survivors. I am grateful to Naomi Roht Arriaza for this point.

[236] Julian Borger, *"Is the Tribunal Not Ashamed?" Karadžić Sentence Angers Victims*, GUARDIAN (Mar. 24, 2016).

[237] *Id.*

[238] *See* Marlise Simons, *Judge Rejects Bid to Delay Verdict for Ratko Mladić in Bosnian Genocide*, N.Y. TIMES (Nov. 12, 2017). Thus, the *Guardian* reported, when the trial chamber announced its verdict, "the most common response" among Bosnian Muslims "was relief that the trial was finally over and that Mladić—unlike . . . Milošević—had lived long enough to hear the guilty verdict." Julian Borger, *Bosnians Divided Over Ratko Mladić Guilty Verdict for War Crimes*, GUARDIAN (Nov. 22, 2017).

[239] Dimitar Dilkoff, *Ratko Mladić Will Be Convicted in 1990s Slaughter of Bosnian Muslims* (Nov. 22, 2017).

[240] For example, during the Tribunal's early years, many observers as well as ICTY officials focused overwhelmingly on the Tribunal's ability to gain custody of its suspects—which is to say, to actually conduct trials. Early legal scholarship about the ICTY focused overwhelmingly on its contributions to the development of international humanitarian law. On the evolution of benchmarks for measuring ICTs' success, see Diane Orentlicher, *Review Essay: From Viability to Impact: Evolving Metrics for Assessing the International Criminal Tribunal for the Former Yugoslavia*, 7 INT'L J. TRANSITIONAL JUST. 536 (2013).

[241] The Tribunal's website includes this statement:

> While its judgments demonstrate that all parties in the conflicts [in the former Yugoslavia] committed crimes, the Tribunal regards its fairness and impartiality to be of paramount importance. . . . The Judges ensure a fair and open trial. . . .

ICTY website, http://www.icty.org/en/about (last visited Dec. 5, 2017).

institutions of self-government, which in myriad ways anchor the legitimacy of national courts.[242] In this setting, as Yuval Shany has observed:

> Due process fulfills a critical role in establishing and maintaining the institutional legitimacy of international criminal tribunals. By invoking internationally accepted standards of judicial practice, these courts project an image of fairness and procedural justice that alleviates some of the unique legitimacy deficits associated with having trials conducted by foreign judges who lack the usual connections with and accountability toward the people and polities over which they preside.[243]

Beyond these general considerations, ICTY judges, mindful of Serb narratives casting the Tribunal as anti-Serb and, more broadly, of the Tribunal's historic role in the development of international criminal justice, have been at pains to ensure Hague trials are models of fair process.

The value of their commitment has not been lost on Bosnians. Recalling early reports suggesting the UN Security Council created the ICTY "to have its own conscience clear so it can wash its hands of what was going on in Bosnia," Dženana Karup Druško praised the institution that emerged in The Hague: "Something happened in terms of the people who came to the ICTY, and how seriously they regarded it, and how they committed themselves to justice."[244] Nusreta Sivac, who was a judge before the war and has testified in several ICTY trials, said she would not offer any suggestions for how they could be expedited. Despite the much-criticized length of Hague proceedings, Sivac said, she understands the reasons "perhaps better than others." ICTY judges have "procedures they have to follow, [which] meet extremely high standards that give rights to both the defendant and the victims."[245]

In several crucial respects, however, the Tribunal's exemplary commitment to fair process—in particular, its exquisite regard for defendants' rights—has compromised its credibility in the eyes of countless victims. Fadil Budnjo lamented: "Sometimes I see the Hague Tribunal on television and my hair goes up seeing how much they care about human rights for killers," who showed no regard for the rights of others when "they had power in their hands, killing people, chopping bodies."[246]

These concerns have been raised most acutely by trials in which high-profile defendants, notably including Slobodan Milošević and Vojislav Šešelj, chose to represent themselves.[247] Milošević notoriously exploited that right, with corrosive effect

---

[242] See Diane F. Orentlicher, *Whose Justice? Reconciling Universal Jurisdiction with Democratic Principles*, 92 Geo. L.J. 1057, 1093–1100 (2004).

[243] Yuval Shany, *The Legitimacy Paradox of Self-Representation*, in The Milošević Trial: An Autopsy 174, 175 (Timothy William Waters ed., 2013).

[244] Interview with Dženana Karup Druško, Director, Transitional Justice, Accountability and Remembrance, in Sarajevo, Bosn. & Herz. (Sept. 8, 2014). Karup Druško told me she did not know of this account of the ICTY's creation until years after it was launched.

[245] Interview with Nusreta Sivac, Former Judge, in Prijedor, Bosn. & Herz. (Sept. 16, 2014).

[246] Interview with Fadil Budnjo, President, Association of Families of Killed and Missing from Foča and Kalinovik, in Ilidža, Bosn. & Herz. (July 24, 2009).

[247] Article 21(4)(d) of the ICTY's Statute provides that the accused "shall be entitled . . . to defend himself in person or through legal assistance of his own choosing." This right is not absolute, however. The Tribunal's interpretation of this right in several controversial cases has been widely criticized by legal scholars and practitioners. *See, e.g.*, Stefan Trechsel, *Rights in Criminal*

on Bosnian perceptions of the Hague Tribunal. Frequently "disrespectful of the Tribunal and obstreperous,"[248] Milošević transformed "the ICTY courtroom [into] a stage for his performance."[249] For victims of merciless violence, it was excruciating to see Milošević treat judges "without respect."[250] Srebrenica survivor Kada Hotić decried the ease with which "a defendant simply makes a circus of this court whenever they are willing."[251] As well, Milošević's skill "in delaying proceedings through defiance, complaints and filibustering" contributed significantly to the length of his trial,[252] the consequences of which have already been noted.

Yet judges were reluctant to use the authority they possessed to rein Milošević in, no matter how far his forays into Serbian nationalism strayed beyond the bounds of legal relevancy. While myriad factors account for this,[253] it is almost surely the case that, acutely aware of Serbian accusations the Tribunal is anti-Serb, judges bent over backward to demonstrate their fairness.[254]

If Milošević challenged the Tribunal's dignity, the courtroom antics of Serbian firebrand Vojislav Šešelj, who flagrantly abused his right to defend himself, surpassed all others.[255] As he prepared to fly to The Hague in February 2003, Šešelj vowed to destroy "that anti-Serbian political institution."[256] In the view of many, he succeeded beyond measure.[257] That Šešelj repeatedly raised "irrelevant or specious

---

Proceedings Under the ECHR and the ICTY Statute—A Precarious Comparison, in THE LEGACY OF THE INTERNATIONAL CRIMINAL TRIBUNAL FOR THE FORMER YUGOSLAVIA 149, 174–88 (Bert Swart et al. eds., 2011); Göran Sluiter, *Compromising the Authority of International Justice*, 5 J. INT'L CRIM. JUST. 529 (2007); Michael P. Scharf, *Self-Representation Versus Assignment of Defence Counsel Before International Criminal Tribunals*, 4 J. INT'L CRIM. JUST. 31 (2006).

[248] Mirjan Damaška, *Assignment of Counsel and Perceptions of Fairness*, 3 J. INT'L CRIM. JUST. 3, 4 (2005) [hereinafter Damaška, *Assignment of Counsel*]. *See also* Combs, *Regulation of Defence Counsel, supra* note 207, at 306.

[249] Interview with Nidžara Ahmetašević, Journalist, in Sarajevo, Bosn. & Herz. (Sept. 12, 2014). *See also* Ian Fisher & Marlise Simons, *Defiant, Milošević Begins His Defense by Assailing NATO; Calls U.N. Charges "Lies"*, N.Y. TIMES (Feb. 15, 2002).

[250] Interview with Kada Hotić, Vice President, Association of Mothers of Srebrenica and Žepa Enclaves, in Sarajevo, Bosn. & Herz. (July 24, 2009).

[251] *Id.*

[252] Damaška, *Assignment of Counsel, supra* note 248, at 4. *See also* Combs, *Regulation of Defence Counsel, supra* note 207, at 306.

[253] Among them, judges believed "allowance had to be made for [Milošević's] insufficient grasp of legal relevancy." Damaška, *Assignment of Counsel, supra* note 248, at 4. ICTY judges have at times faced unenviable dilemmas. For example in late 2006, Vojislav Šešelj went on a hunger strike to protest the Trial Chamber's amply justified decision to impose counsel in his case. By any reasonable standard, Šešelj had forfeited the right to represent himself. But the Appeals Chamber faced a Hobson's choice: severely weakened by his hunger strike, Šešelj was on the precipice of death and seemed determined to reject sustenance if the Trial Chamber's decision was upheld. *See Serbian Politician Ends His Hunger Strike*, N.Y. TIMES (Dec. 9, 2006). Yet reversing the Trial Chamber's ruling—the path the Appeals Chamber took—would be seen as capitulation to a defendant bent on destroying the Tribunal. For a summary of this episode, see Combs, *Regulation of Defence Counsel, supra* note 207, at 309–11.

[254] *See* Combs, *Regulation of Defence Counsel, supra* note 207, at 308.

[255] As one commentator put it, Šešelj's trial "managed to outdo the spectacle and failure of the Milošević trial in almost every respect." Eugene Cerruti, *Self-Representation in the International Arena: Removing a False Right of Spectacle*, 40 GEO. J. INT'L L. 919, 979 (2009). *See also* Alexander Zahar, *Legal Aid, Self-Representation, and the Crisis at the Hague Tribunal*, 19 CRIM. L.F. 241, 242 (2008) ("Milošević's case was not half as fraught as Vojislav Šešelj's").

[256] Zorana Suvaković, *Vojislav Šešelj's Ghost of Future Past*, AL-JAZEERA ONLINE (Nov. 18, 2014).

[257] *Id. See also* Zahar, *supra* note 255, at 261.

matters"[258] and flouted the court's rules[259] were the least of the challenges he presented during a trial lasting over five years. As the *New York Times* reported, Šešelj "quickly became notorious for his loutish outbursts, . . . disrupting the proceedings with exceptional demands and long speeches."[260] In the course of his trial, Šešelj harassed and threatened witnesses and disclosed confidential information about three protected witnesses. (Šešelj was later convicted of contempt for doing so.) Šešelj's chronically disruptive behavior, in the words of the *Times*, "caused profound embarrassment for the tribunal"[261]—an assessment shared by every Bosnian and Serbian who addressed his case in interviews for this book.[262]

Weeks into Šešelj's marathon trial, Sevima Sali-Terzić wondered "why [he] has all the power to mock the court and the judges just sit there in all their dignity. He offends the victims again. The procedure is terrible. I'm a lawyer and I just don't understand."[263] Eight years later, her assessment was even harsher, and understandably so. Saying Šešelj and other defendants were "making fools of these judges" and "abusing" the trial process, Sali-Terzić continued: "The Hague Tribunal became a great protector of all little process details rather than protecting . . . the rights of victims" and the moral principles that apply even in war. "I just see it as a machinery to make money and make good careers."[264] Jasna Bakšić Muftić had a generally more positive assessment of the Tribunal but singled out its handling of Šešelj and several other defendants as examples of when "the whole procedure" went "very bad." She added: "They allowed them to be a theater player, you know, . . . piece of the public theater."[265]

While my focus here is on perceptions of Bosnians, they have not been exceptionally critical of how ICTY judges managed these trials. As Alex Whiting has written, the "perception that Milošević and Šešelj succeeded in hijacking their trials and using the proceedings to their own ends is at the heart of many critiques of the ICTY and international criminal proceedings generally."[266]

In the lead-up to his trial in 2009, Radovan Karadžić—who, like Milošević and Šešelj, chose to be his own defense counsel—threatened to tie the ICTY up

---

[258] Prosecutor v. Šešelj, Case No. IT-03-67-PT, Decision on Assignment of Counsel, ¶ 34 (Int'l Crim. Trib. for the Former Yugoslavia Aug. 21, 2006).

[259] *See id.* ¶ 41.

[260] Marlise Simons, *Vojislav Šešelj, Serbian Nationalist, Is Acquitted of War Crimes by Hague Tribunal,* N.Y. TIMES (Mar. 31, 2016). As Eugene Cerruti observed, moreover, "[t]he vulgarity alone of his extensive written submissions to the [ICTY] became extraordinary." Cerruti, *supra* note 255, at 980.

[261] Simons, *supra* note 260.

[262] After noting other concerns about the ICTY's performance, for example, Nidžara Ahmetašević said: "Not to mention Šešelj! It's just embarrassing! It's just embarrassing!" Interview with Nidžara Ahmetašević, Journalist, in Sarajevo, Bosn. & Herz. (Sept. 12, 2014).

[263] Interview with Sevima Sali-Terzić, Senior Legal Counsel, Constitutional Court of BiH, in Sarajevo, Bosn. & Herz. (Nov. 30, 2006).

[264] Interview with Sevima Sali-Terzić, Senior Legal Counsel, Constitutional Court of BiH, in Sarajevo, Bosn. & Herz. (Sept. 9, 2014). At the time of this interview, Šešelj's trial had concluded but judgment would not be rendered for another year-and-a-half.

[265] Interview with Jasna Bakšić Muftić, Professor, Faculty of Law, University of Sarajevo, in Sarajevo, Bosn. & Herz. (Sept. 17, 2014).

[266] Whiting, *Laboratory, supra* note 190, at 102.

in a blizzard of motions.[267] Nidžara Ahmetašević noted at the time that Bosnians were "really disappointed because the court is letting him do that. People are losing confidence in the ICTY because of that."[268] Yet despite some criticisms of Karadžić's conduct at trial, the Tribunal took greater control of the proceedings in his case,[269] "keeping Karadžić on a tighter leash than previous self-representing accused."[270]

The confluence of several factors accounts for the contrast between Karadžić's conduct and that of Šešelj (beyond those attributable to their distinct personalities). To its credit, the ICTY applied lessons painfully learned from its experience in the *Milošević* case and, more broadly, from its overall experience regulating defense counsel in the later trial of Karadžić.[271] Without detracting from the Tribunal's course corrections, another factor may have been more important: different judges presided over the trials of Karadžić and Šešelj, respectively. The judge assigned to preside in the trial of the ICTY's most challenging defendant, Šešelj, was assuredly the one least capable of doing so competently.[272] In a trial plagued by embarrassments, Judge Jean-Claude Antonetti's indulgence of Šešelj was all too consistent.[273]

D. The Unindicted

Bosnia is full of crimes that no one has been prosecuted for.
—MATIAS HELLMAN[274]

For Trnopolje camp survivor Edin Ramulić, there is one paramount measure of Tribunal success. Speaking on behalf of himself and other members of the organization Izvor, Ramulić said: "What is really important to us was actually those statistics—to bring as many perpetrators as possible before the face of justice."[275] Each time I have spoken to Ramulić, he has called attention to the fact that ICTY judgments in cases from Prijedor mention in passing men, such as Radovan Vokić,

---

[267] Saying he planned to challenge everything other than whether it was "sunny outside or raining," Karadžić told ICTY judges his trial would be "far greater than any before it." Rachel Irwin, *Karadžić to Dispute Everything but the Weather*, IWPR (Apr. 3, 2009).

[268] Interview with Nidžara Ahmetašević, then Editor, BIRN in BiH, in Sarajevo, Bosn. & Herz. (July 13, 2009).

[269] Combs, *Regulation of Defence Counsel*, *supra* note 207, at 311–12.

[270] *Id.* at 315. Even so, Ahmetašević remained frustrated by Karadžić's courtroom conduct, faulting ICTY judges for allowing him to do "whatever he wants in that courtroom again. And it's enough of that. I mean, it's really enough of that." Interview with Nidžara Ahmetašević, Journalist, in Sarajevo, Bosn. & Herz. (Sept. 12, 2014).

[271] *See* Combs, *Regulation of Defence Counsel*, *supra* note 207, at 311–12.

[272] Judge Jean-Claude Antonetti was assigned as pretrial judge in Šešelj's case in February 2007 and presided over the trial as well. *See* Zahar, *supra* note 255, at 244.

[273] Eric Gordy has fairly described the Šešelj trial as "principally notable for the grotesque theatrics that have accompanied it, in which an insane man plays a swearier and more bloated Jeanne D'Arc and an incompetent man plays a judge." Eric Gordy, *This Week's Predictions: Ko Te Karadžić Nek Ti Piše Pjesme*, EAST ETHNIA (Mar. 21, 2016), https://eastethnia.wordpress.com/2016/03/21/this-weeks-predictions-ko-te-karadzic-nek-ti-pise-pjesme/.

[274] Interview with Matias Hellman, then ICTY Liaison Officer, in Sarajevo, Bosn. & Herz. (Nov. 29, 2006).

[275] Interview with Edin Ramulić, Project Coordinator, Izvor, in Prijedor, Bosn. & Herz. (Sept. 16, 2014).

who played crucial roles in ethnic cleansing yet were never indicted.[276] Recognizing that neither the ICTY nor Bosnian courts would "take care of" all those responsible for wartime atrocities, Ramulić affirmed what he thought they *should* do—"take care that the least number of war crimes perpetrators stays unprosecuted."[277]

Like Ramulić, Emir Suljagić believes the ICTY's failure to indict thousands of individuals responsible for wartime atrocities is a fundamental failure. When we spoke in 2014, Suljagić said the ICTY had failed to "end impunity," one of the goals it assigned to itself. When asked to explain what he meant, Suljagić said: "It means there are still thousands of people who are still up their shoulders in blood . . . roaming free around . . . Bosnia" and neighboring countries.[278]

E. Removing Dangerous Individuals

If many Bosnians lament the ICTY's failure to prosecute a larger number of suspects or to sentence them more harshly,[279] some are grateful for Tribunal's role in removing dangerous men from positions of power. When I interviewed him in 2009, journalist Gojko Berić seemed to tremble at the thought of what the region would be like were it not for the ICTY:

If there was no Hague, Milošević would probably still be in power. If nothing else, he would at least be the head of his political party. Many ICTY convicts would still

---

[276] For example the first time I interviewed Ramulić he brought up the trial verdict in the case of Milomir Stakić, the most senior person from Prijedor to face trial before the ICTY. The judgment describes how Radovan Vokić arranged for the transfer on two buses of some 120 Muslim men from Keraterm, a detention camp to which they had been taken from their homes in Prijedor, to the Omarska camp. One trial witness had compiled a list of "about 60 people he knew personally who were taken away on those buses and killed." Prosecutor v. Stakić, Case No. IT-97-24-T, Trial Judgment, ¶ 211 (Int'l Crim. Trib. for the Former Yugoslavia July 31, 2003). The corpses of some victims, who had been killed by gunshot, were found in mass graves. *Id.* ¶ 212. One was Ramulić's brother. Interview with Edin Ramulić, Project Coordinator, Izvor, in Prijedor, Bosn. & Herz. (Dec. 8, 2006). Despite this finding, the ICTY never indicted Vokić, whom Ramulić routinely encountered until the boutique Vokić owned burned down. Interview with Edin Ramulić, Project Coordinator, Izvor, in Prijedor, Bosn. & Herz. (July 23, 2009).

As in previous interviews, in 2014 Ramulić decried the fact that the ICTY indicted only three members of the Crisis Staff of Prijedor even though, as he put it: "It has been well established that the Crisis Headquarters was responsible for everything that was going on here during the wartime; it is indisputably established that [it] was issuing orders for everything that happened during the wartime." Interview with Edin Ramulić, Project Coordinator, Izvor, in Prijedor, Bosn. & Herz. (Sept. 16, 2014). Indeed, the *Stakić* Trial Judgment identified five Prijedor Crisis Staff members who were never indicted by the ICTY. *See* Prosecutor v. Stakić, Case No. IT-97-24-T, Trial Judgment, ¶ 89 (Int'l Crim. Trib. for the Former Yugoslavia July 31, 2003). In consequence, those men, who in Ramulić's words were among those "deciding who would live and who would die" in Prijedor, were "freely walking around town." More troubling in his view, some of them held positions of influence in Prijedor's municipal government or in publicly-owned companies. Interview with Edin Ramulić, Project Coordinator, Izvor, in Prijedor, Bosn. & Herz. (Sept. 16, 2014).

[277] Interview with Edin Ramulić, Project Coordinator, Izvor, in Prijedor, Bosn. & Herz. (Sept. 16, 2014).

[278] Interview with Emir Suljagić, Author, in Sarajevo, Bosn. & Herz. (Sept. 11, 2014).

[279] Even in towns, such as Prijedor and Kozarac, where survivors routinely encounter perpetrators who served short sentences or were never prosecuted, the Tribunal's work had a palpable and positive impact for a time. As discussed in Chapter 2, the arrests of key figures in Prijedor beginning in July 1997 encouraged many refugees to return there. For a variety of reasons, not all of which relate to the ICTY, this impact dissipated however. Among the factors that do not relate

be active in politics and at this moment, summertime, these individuals would probably be having their vacations in some summer resort.[280]

Senad Pećanin, too, imagined a parallel universe without the ICTY:

Probably Radovan Karadžić would be a Member of Parliament. Ratko Mladić could be Chief of Staff of the Army. Hundreds of war criminals could be highly ranked in all parts of state institutions. Without the ICTY, there would be no chance to have prosecutions of these most responsible people. If we put a hundred minuses, this one thing is heavier than all handicaps.[281]

F. Symbolically Resonant Judgments

In terms redolent of expressivism, some Bosnians interviewed for this study yearned for an authoritative condemnation, expressed on behalf of the international community, of the grievous harms they endured.[282] While I heard a range of views about the degree to which the Tribunal satisfied this hope, there is no doubt some of its judgments provided profound moral satisfaction to many.

1. CALLING A MASSACRE BY ITS PROPER NAME

Srebrenica was sentenced to death, disappearance. These people in Srebrenica, their destiny was to be disappeared from the face of the earth. [The Bosnian Serbs] killed all they could[;] fortunately they failed to kill us all.
—ZUMRA ŠEHOMEROVIĆ[283]

The ICTY's determination, first reached in the case of Radislav Krstić, that "Bosnian Serb forces committed genocide" in Srebrenica is singularly important in this regard.[284] In 2004, the ICTY Appeals Chamber affirmed in clarion terms the Trial Chamber's 2001 determination that the Srebrenica massacre met the stringent definition of genocide:

The Appeals Chamber states unequivocally that the law condemns, in appropriate terms, the deep and lasting injury inflicted, and calls the massacre

---

to the ICTY, many refugees had put down roots elsewhere and were no longer tempted to return to their prewar homes, if they ever were. Thus, at a certain point, most refugees who might have wished to return had already done so.

[280] Interview with Gojko Berić, Journalist & Columnist, Oslobođenje, in Sarajevo, Bosn. & Herz. (July 17, 2009).

[281] Interview with Senad Pećanin, then Editor, Dani, in Sarajevo, Bosn. & Herz. (Dec. 6, 2006).

[282] As explained in Chapter 4, expressivist theories hold that the distinctive importance of punishment lies in its "symbolic significance." Joel Feinberg, *The Expressive Function of Punishment*, in DOING AND DESERVING: ESSAYS IN THE THEORY OF RESPONSIBILITY 95, 98 (1970). More particularly, punishment expresses "attitudes of resentment and indignation, and . . . judgments of disapproval and reprobation" on behalf of either the punishing authority or "those 'in whose name' the punishment is inflicted." *Id.*

[283] Interview with the late Zumra Šehomerović, Association of Mothers of Srebrenica and Žepa Enclaves, in Sarajevo, Bosn. & Herz. (Sept. 18, 2014).

[284] Prosecutor v. Krstić, Case No. IT-98-33-A, Appeal Judgment, ¶ 37 (Int'l Crim. Trib. for the Former Yugoslavia Apr. 19, 2004). At trial, Krstić was found guilty of genocide and sentenced to

at Srebrenica by its proper name: genocide. Those responsible will bear this stigma, and it will serve as a warning to those who may in future contemplate the commission of such a heinous act.²⁸⁵

Describing the impact of this ruling two-and-a-half years later, Nerma Jelačić said: "It's still important—this is a huge judgment to this day. [*Krstić* is] probably the only one that gave victims a sense of the most complete thing to justice."²⁸⁶ In a similar vein, civil society leader Dobrila Govedarica said "clarifying that Srebrenica was a genocide" was the Tribunal's "most important achievement and without the ICTY it wouldn't be possible." She described the judgment's significance this way: "For history and for the future, you can never question that . . . and that's definitely important for victims."²⁸⁷ Mirsad Tokača, too, called *Krstić* "one of the most important" accomplishments of the ICTY, adding: "Only based on this decision, the ICTY is successful." In his view, the Tribunal's genocide ruling was important not only "theoretically [and] in terms of judicial practice," but also "for Bosnian society. Finally there is no dilemma. . . . After this decision, there is no negation and refusing of the fact that genocide happened."²⁸⁸ (As will be seen in Chapter 8, however, there is pervasive negation of "the fact that genocide happened" in Republika Srpska.)

Jasna Bakšić Muftić described what the ruling meant to women who lost their sons in Srebrenica. Rural and largely uneducated, many of these women became deeply "engaged as mothers" in trying to find justice. In Bakšić Muftić's view, their daily protesting would have deepened their suffering if their goals remained unfulfilled: "You're always waiting for, waiting for, waiting for; this is the way to madness." But once the ICTY ruled that thousands of Muslim men were victims of genocide, "their family members were recognized, named. They got a sense of life; [they were able] to start life again."²⁸⁹

During interviews, Srebrenica survivors expressed profound appreciation for the ICTY's genocide rulings, even as they protested myriad other aspects of its performance. For example, after describing her concerns about Hague justice, Hatidža Mehmedović added: "Despite [these concerns,] we have to be honest and say the Hague was the one who sentenced and reached the verdict of *Krstić* for the . . . crime of genocide committed here in Srebrenica. This is what matters to us, this is what is

---

forty-six years' imprisonment. Prosecutor v. Krstić, Case No. IT-98-33-T, Trial Judgment (Int'l Crim. Trib. for the Former Yugoslavia Aug. 2, 2001). The Appeals Chamber ruled Krstić was guilty of aiding and abetting genocide rather than committing genocide, and reduced his sentence to thirty-five years in prison. Prosecutor v. Krstić, Case No. IT-98-33-A, Appeal Judgment (Int'l Crim. Trib. for the Former Yugoslavia Apr. 19, 2004).

²⁸⁵ Prosecutor v. Krstić, Case No. IT-98-33-A, Appeal Judgment, ¶ 37 (Int'l Crim. Trib. for the Former Yugoslavia Apr. 19, 2004).

²⁸⁶ Interview with Nerma Jelačić, then Director, BIRN in BiH, in Sarajevo, Bosn. & Herz. (Dec. 1, 2006).

²⁸⁷ Interview with Dobrila Govedarica, Executive Director, Open Society Fund BiH, in Sarajevo, Bosn. & Herz. (Nov. 30, 2006).

²⁸⁸ Interview with Mirsad Tokača, President, Research and Documentation Center (Sarajevo), in Sarajevo, Bosn. & Herz. (Dec. 6, 2006).

²⁸⁹ Interview with Jasna Bakšić Muftić, Professor, Faculty of Law, University of Sarajevo, in Sarajevo, Bosn. & Herz. (Nov. 30, 2006). Bakšić Muftić placed this judgment in a wider context, saying it confirmed that "at the end of the 20th Century in Europe" it is possible for genocide to occur. "After that, we could believe there could be a genocide anywhere. It's always a potential danger." *Id.*

the most important to us, to the families, to the victims, that justice is reached."[290] While highly critical of the ICTY's failure to indict UN peacekeepers for failing to protect Srebrenica, Hajra Čatić added: "We can't say they did nothing good; Krstić was convicted of genocide."[291]

Along with thousands of other Bosniaks, Emir Suljagić and his family sought refuge in Srebrenica before it became the most dangerous place on earth. Even so, he derived scant satisfaction when he first learned a trial chamber had found Krstić guilty of genocide. When we spoke in 2009, Suljagić recalled that, upon hearing the news, he told a journalist, "I really don't care what you do to this guy." But his views changed when he read the Appeals Chamber's 2004 judgment. "That was the moment I realized, my god, we are in that select group of nations whose existence has been brought into question, literally, physically, and that's when the importance of this judgment—that's when I realized it."[292] When I interviewed Suljagić five years later, he rued the fact that the *Krstić* judgment had had no discernible impact in dispelling Serb denial. Despite this, he said, the judgment still held the same personal meaning he had described in 2009.[293]

2. ABSENCE OF GENOCIDE CONVICTIONS OUTSIDE THE CONTEXT OF SREBRENICA

However gratifying he found *Krstić* and later Srebrenica-related genocide convictions, Suljagić has a "problem with this whole Srebrenica thing": "This whole thing started as genocide in Bosnia [in 1992] and it ended with genocide in Srebrenica [in July 1995] and it's so unfair to those tens of thousands of people" who died elsewhere in Bosnia that the ICTY has not ruled them victims of genocide.[294]

Like Suljagić, Mirsad Tokača, who developed the most meticulous database about wartime casualties, is disappointed the ICTY did not rule that genocide occurred outside the context of Srebrenica.[295] Tokača believes Srebrenica was the "final point" in a genocide that began and "happened" between April and September 1992,[296] and

[290] Interview with Hatidža Mehmedović, Association of Srebrenica Mothers, in Potočari, Bosn. & Herz. (July 21, 2009).

[291] Interview with Hajra Čatić, President, Women of Srebrenica, in Tuzla, Bosn. & Herz. (July 21, 2009). While the ICTY rendered its first, and therefore historic, ruling on genocide in the *Krstić* case, later cases have found other defendants guilty of genocide-related charges. In January 2015, the Appeals Chamber upheld the conviction of three Bosnian Serb officers of genocide-related charges, two of whom were convicted of genocide itself—the first time the Appeals Chamber had done so (as noted, Krstić was convicted of aiding and abetting genocide). Prosecutor v. Popović et al., Case No. IT-05-88-A, Appeal Judgment (Int'l Crim. Trib. for the Former Yugoslavia Jan. 30, 2015). Later that year, the Appeals Chamber sustained General Zdravko Tolimir's conviction for genocide as well as conspiracy to commit genocide, affirming his life sentence. Prosecutor v. Tolimir, Case No. IT-05-88/2-A, Appeal Judgment (Int'l Crim. Trib. for the Former Yugoslavia Apr. 8, 2015). As already noted, ICTY trial chambers subsequently rendered genocide convictions in the cases of Radovan Karadžić (in March 2016) and Ratko Mladić (in November 2017) in relation to Srebrenica.

[292] Interview with Emir Suljagić, Author, in Sarajevo, Bosn. & Herz. (July 14, 2009).

[293] Interview with Emir Suljagić, Author, in Sarajevo, Bosn. & Herz. (Sept. 11, 2014).

[294] Interview with Emir Suljagić, Author, in Sarajevo, Bosn. & Herz. (July 14, 2009).

[295] Interview with Mirsad Tokača, Director, Research and Documentation Center (Sarajevo), in Sarajevo, Bosn. & Herz. (July 24, 2009).

[296] Interview with Mirsad Tokača, Director, Research and Documentation Center (Sarajevo), in Sarajevo, Bosn. & Herz. (Sept. 11, 2014).

is convinced his data prove this. Tokača showed me charts based on his documentation, which show two spikes in wartime killings during the Bosnian conflict—one during the early months of the war in 1992, the other in July 1995—towering like skyscrapers over a jagged series of smaller spikes.[297]

Survivors in Prijedor voiced the same criticism, and for them the point was deeply personal. Recalling "there were approximately 3,300 registered civilian victims of war here in Prijedor," Mirsad Duratović said just under 1,000 of them were killed in concentration camps. Since the ICTY's convictions for murders in Prijedor involved concentration camps, he suggested, the Tribunal distorted the meaning of the systematic killing of non-Serbs outside the camps.[298] Sudbin Musić was equally aggrieved, saying the concentration camps that were the focus of the ICTY's Prijedor prosecutions "were the last thing that happened in this chain of crime." Before the camps were established, "there was planned, systematic killing in six villages" in Prijedor, including his own.[299]

At the time of these interviews, judgment had not yet been rendered in either the Karadžić or Mladić trials, both of which provided an opportunity to find a defendant guilty of genocide in Bosnia outside (as well as in) Srebrenica. Duratović told me that if neither suspect was convicted of genocide outside Srebrenica, "we will certainly lose every hope and trust not only in the ICTY, but in justice as such. We will consider it another crime against the victims, who already were murdered."[300] Indeed, he said, "we [would] consider the ICTY a co-collaborator in the crime."[301]

The criticism lodged by Suljagić, Tokača, Duratović, Musić, and others evokes a perennially vexing irony. Raphael Lemkin, who coined the word *genocide* and tirelessly campaigned for a convention outlawing it, hoped the crime would be imbued with a uniquely powerful stigma. Regrettably, the success of Lemkin's vision has, in the experience of many victims, downgraded the stigma associated with other international crimes, however grave.

For many Bosnians, the Tribunal's failure to convict certain high-level defendants of genocide is inexplicable. A notable case in point is that of Momčilo Krajišnik, a senior member of the Bosnian Serb leadership during the war. On September 27, 2006, ICTY Trial Chamber I found Krajišnik responsible for "the killing, through murder or extermination, of approximately 3,000 Bosnian Muslims and Bosnian Croats" in thirty Bosnian municipalities during the period of the indictment.[302] It also found that "the perpetrators of the killings chose their victims on the basis of their Muslim and Croat identity."[303] Yet the chamber was not convinced the prosecution

---

[297] *Id. See also* Emir Suljagić with Mirsad Tokača, *Genocide Is Not a Matter of Numbers*, BOSNIAN INSTITUTE (Jan. 19, 2006).

[298] Interview with Mirsad Duratović, Chairman, Prijedor '92, in Prijedor, Bosn. & Herz. (Sept. 16, 2014).

[299] Interview with Sudbin Musić, Secretary, Prijedor '92, in Prijedor, Bosn. & Herz. (Sept. 16, 2014).

[300] Interview with Mirsad Duratović, Chairman, Prijedor '92, in Prijedor, Bosn. & Herz. (Sept. 16, 2014).

[301] *Id.* Duratović made the same point in an interview with Julian Borger, saying: "If the judges fail to convict Karadžić for genocide in 1992 in Prijedor, it will be a slap in the face of the victims. Everything else will be a reward for Karadžić and Republika Srpska." Borger, *supra* note 236.

[302] Prosecutor v. Krajišnik, Case IT-00-39-T, Trial Judgment, ¶¶ 1143, 717, 792 (Int'l Crim. Trib. for the Former Yugoslavia Sept. 27, 2006).

[303] *Id.* ¶ 793.

had proven beyond a reasonable doubt that "any of these acts were committed with the intent to destroy, in part, the Bosnian-Muslim or Bosnian-Croat ethnic group, as such,"[304] an element of the crime of genocide.

Several months after the verdict was rendered Nerma Jelačić told me it was "a huge thing" for victims that Krajišnik "wasn't found guilty of genocide."[305] Reflecting on the verdict several years later, historian Smail Čekić said, "I am completely disappointed. . . . For all of us investigators and victims of genocide, this is like a shock, like a major hit. . . . [They] proved the existence of the *actus reus* of the crime of genocide but they failed in proving the intention of the crime."[306] Srebrenica survivor Kada Hotić found it "ridiculous, silly" that Krajišnik was acquitted of genocide-related charges "when there was so much evidence" against him.[307]

Others were not so much shocked as disappointed. When asked to describe public reactions to Krajišnik's acquittal on genocide-related charges, Nidžara Ahmetašević said: "People didn't even expect that Krajišnik would be convicted of genocide. People don't . . . trust that people will finally recognize that we survived genocide. . . . In a way, people expected that decision because they just lost confidence in international justice."[308]

In the days leading up to the trial verdict in the case of Radovan Karadžić, Bosnian and Croat victims associations said they would be "totally disappointed if there is no punishment for genocide in all eight municipalities in BiH" for which genocide charges were leveled.[309] Not surprisingly, some expressed disappointment when the verdict, convicting Karadžić of genocide in relation to Srebrenica but nowhere else, was released.[310] But victims apparently were even more disturbed by the forty-year sentence Karadžić received.[311] In carefully-chosen words, civil society lawyer Mervan Miraščija acknowledged that, on a personal level, his reaction was similar: "As a man I'm disappointed with judgment or to be more precise with a measured punishment. I emphasize as a man, not as a lawyer, and I expected life in prison for Karadžić."[312]

---

[304] *Id.* ¶ 867.

[305] Interview with Nerma Jelačić, then Director, BIRN in BiH, in Sarajevo, Bosn. & Herz. (Dec. 1, 2006).

[306] Interview with Smail Čekić, Professor of History, University of Sarajevo, and Director of Sarajevo University Institute for Research of Crimes against Humanity and International Law, in Sarajevo, Bosn. & Herz. (July 16, 2009).

[307] Interview with Kada Hotić, Vice President, Association of Mothers of Srebrenica and Žepa Enclaves, in Sarajevo, Bosn. & Herz. (July 24, 2009).

[308] Interview with Nidžara Ahmetašević, then Editor, BIRN in BiH, in Sarajevo, Bosn. & Herz. (July 13, 2009).

[309] Email from Mirvan Miraščija, Law Program Coordinator, Open Society Fund BiH, to Diane Orentlicher (Mar. 24, 2016). In addition to genocide charges stemming from the 1995 massacre in Srebrenica, the Prosecutor brought genocide-related charges against Karadžić in relation to atrocities in seven other municipalities in 1992.

[310] *See* Denis Džidić, *Karadžić Verdict: Mixed Reactions Reflect Divided Bosnia*, BALKAN TRANSITIONAL JUST. (Mar. 24, 2016); Ed Vulliamy, *I Saw Karadžić's Camps. I Cannot Celebrate While Many of His Victims Are Denied Justice*, GUARDIAN (Mar. 26, 2016).

[311] *The Guardian* quoted Srebrenica survivor Kada Hotić reacting this way: "Is the tribunal not ashamed? Do the Bosnian Muslims and Bosnian Croats not have a right to justice? He got 40 years. That's not enough." Julian Borger, *Radovan Karadžić Sentenced to 40 Years for Srebrenica Genocide*, GUARDIAN (Mar. 24, 2016). *See also* Borger, *supra* note 236; Marlise Simons, *Radovan Karadžić, a Bosnian Serb, Is Convicted of Genocide*, N.Y. TIMES (Mar. 24, 2016).

[312] Email from Mirvan Miraščija, Law Program Coordinator, Open Society Fund BiH, to Diane Orentlicher (Mar. 24, 2016).

Some, however, voiced satisfaction, noting Karadžić had been convicted of the most grave crimes imaginable.[313] Bakir Izetbegović, the Bosniak member of Bosnia's three-person presidency, hailed the trial judgment as "the most important verdict since Nuremberg."[314]

Not surprisingly, some survivors expressed disappointment in the November 2017 trial verdict of Ratko Mladić, who, like Karadžić, had been charged with genocide in relation to other municipalities but was convicted of this charge only in relation to Srebrenica.[315] Yet as already noted, Mladić's conviction and, perhaps just as important, his sentence of life in prison were deeply gratifying to many.

3. Gender Jurisprudence

Women became visible, personalized, recognized as one kind of victim.
—Jasna Bakšić Muftić[316]

When wartime atrocities occur on a large scale they invariably include crimes of sexual violence. While there should be no doubt these constitute war crimes, genocide, and/or crimes against humanity when other elements of those crimes are established, sexual violence remained largely in the shadows in postwar prosecutions.[317] The work of the ICTY and its sister tribunal for Rwanda changed that, building a rich jurisprudence recognizing that crimes of sexual violence are among those meriting the strongest condemnation.

Reflecting on the ICTY's achievements more than a dozen years after it was launched, Jasna Bakšić Muftić said that, through its judgments, the ICTY had "created a new kind of awareness that women had been used as a means" of warfare. "They became visible, personalized, recognized as one kind of victim."[318] In her view, the recognition provided by ICTY judgments enabled rape survivors "to become more active" in asserting their rights. Bakira Hasečić, a rape survivor who has been called "the Bosnian Wiesenthal,"[319] exemplifies this. The organization Hasečić leads, the Association of Women Victims of War, "rallies rape victims across Bosnia and Herzegovina and has provided key testimonies in rape and sexual abuse trials linked to the conflict."[320]

---

[313] *See Bosnia Leaders Trade Barbs over Karadžić Sentence*, Balkan Insight (Mar. 25, 2016) (citing view of Vlado Adamović).

[314] *Id.*

[315] *See, e.g.,* Sanya Burgess, *The Butcher of Bosnia: Ratko Mladić Given Life Sentence in Dramatic Court Hearing*, National (Nov. 22, 2017).

[316] Interview with Jasna Bakšić Muftić, Professor, Faculty of Law, University of Sarajevo, in Sarajevo, Bosn. & Herz. (Nov. 30, 2006).

[317] Although "countless women and girls were . . . singled out for rape, sexual slavery and other forms of sexual violence and persecution" during World War II and substantial evidence of these offenses was presented during the Nuremberg trial of major Nazi war criminals, these crimes were largely buried in the Nuremberg judgment. Askin, *Prosecuting Wartime Rape, supra* note 51, at 300. Crimes of sexual violence received greater attention in postwar prosecutions in Asia. *See id.* at 302–03.

[318] Interview with Jasna Bakšić Muftić, Professor, Faculty of Law, University of Sarajevo, in Sarajevo, Bosn. & Herz. (Nov. 30, 2006).

[319] Interview with Nidžara Ahmetašević, then Editor, BIRN in BiH, in Sarajevo, Bosn. & Herz. (July 13, 2009).

[320] Nidžara Ahmetašević, Nerma Jelačić & Selma Boračić, *Investigation: Višegrad Rape Victims Say Their Cries Go Unheard*, Balkan Insight (Nov. 29, 2008).

Yet Hasečić's own case points up the limits of Hague justice for crimes of sexual violence. On July 20, 2009, an ICTY trial chamber convicted the man who raped her, Milan Lukić, and his cousin Sredoje Lukić for their roles in sadistic atrocities committed in Višegrad during the war. Milan Lukić was sentenced to life in prison; his cousin received a sentence of thirty years[321] (later reduced to twenty-seven).[322] But while the mass rapes associated with the two have received international attention for over a decade, rape-related charges were left out of their indictment.[323]

A month before the *Lukić* case went to trial, the prosecution sought leave to amend the indictment, but the Trial Chamber denied its motion on the ground it "had not acted with the required diligence in submitting the motion in a timely manner so as to provide adequate notice to the Accused."[324] While the judgment is replete with testimony of women describing multiple rapes by the defendants, the chamber held it could not make "any determination of guilt in relation to these non-indicted crimes."[325]

The prosecution's failure diligently to pursue rape charges was hardly unprecedented. In many instances where sex crime charges were warranted, they were absent from indictments, often with a view to expediting trials and completing the Tribunal's work. Even as the ICTY and other international courts have highlighted crimes of sexual violence in some of their cases, others "continue[d] to be plagued by prosecutorial omissions and errors as well as by a tendency on the part of the judges to require that the prosecution meet higher evidentiary standards in these cases than in other types of cases."[326] Thus here, as in other aspects of its work, the ICTY's contributions have at once been incalculable and fallen short of many survivors' expectations.

In 2014, I asked Bakšić Muftić if she still believed the ICTY's gender jurisprudence had had a transformative impact on rape survivors. Without hesitation she said she considered this to be one of the Tribunal's "really very important" achievements. Even so, Bakšić Muftić noted the "other side of the story": political leaders did not "pay real attention, the kind women deserve," to survivors' social and economic needs.[327] Indeed, 60 percent of Bosnian women who had testified about sexual violence and who were interviewed for another study "lived under very poor economic

---

[321] Prosecutor v. Lukić et al., Case No. IT-98-32/1-T, Trial Judgment, ¶¶ 1101, 1106 (Int'l Crim. Trib. for the Former Yugoslavia July 20, 2009).

[322] Prosecutor v. Lukić et al., Case No. IT-98-32/1-A, Appeal Judgment, ¶ 672 (Int'l Crim. Trib. for the Former Yugoslavia Dec. 4, 2012).

[323] For an account of factors behind this omission, see Michelle Jarvis & Kate Vigneswaran, *Challenges to Successful Outcomes in Sexual Violence Cases*, in PROSECUTING CONFLICT-RELATED SEXUAL VIOLENCE AT THE ICTY 33, 51–53 (Serge Brammertz & Michelle Jarvis eds., 2016).

[324] Prosecutor v. Lukić et al., Case No. IT-98-32/1-T, Trial Judgment, ¶ 36 (Int'l Crim. Trib. for the Former Yugoslavia July 20, 2009).

[325] *Id.* ¶ 37. The testimony about multiple rapes had been allowed with a view to rebutting an alibi defense.

[326] Susana SáCouto & Katherine Cleary, *The Importance of Effective Investigation of Sexual Violence and Gender-Based Crimes at the International Criminal Court*, 17 AM. U. J. GENDER, SOC. POL'Y & L. 337, 348 (2009). Michelle Jarvis and Kate Vigneswaran provide an overview of the challenges surrounding prosecution of sexual violence at the ICTY in Jarvis & Vigneswaran, *supra* note 323.

[327] Interview with Jasna Bakšić Muftić, Professor, Faculty of Law, University of Sarajevo, in Sarajevo, Bosn. & Herz. (Sept. 17, 2014).

conditions with hardly enough money to sustain their families."[328] More than half were unemployed.[329]

G. Beyond Individual Judgments

Beyond the satisfaction many Bosnians have derived from landmark judgments, some value the broader significance of the Tribunal's work. Dženana Karup Druško made the point this way: "And for us, the survivors, whether of the siege of Sarajevo or other parts of Bosnia, the judgments have given us a sense that there is justice."[330] After providing a nuanced assessment of its by-then extensive record and impact in 2014, Bakšić Muftić offered a "final . . . impression: It is very good that ICTY was founded." Noting the Tribunal may not have satisfied everyone's expectations, she continued: "But they *helped*, and they give the certain message—not always the good message and the clear message—but they sent the message that there is no untouchable people."[331]

Although Mirsad Duratović said he was disappointed in "all the rulings passed by the court," he believes "there was a good point in the work of the Hague Tribunal," which is "that the court was established, that the war crimes were recognized as such."[332] Duratović seemed proud, as well, that the ICTY's first trial involved a "case from Omarska," where he was detained at the age of seventeen, and that "the crime of rape was finally classified as a general war crime as a result of the witnesses of the systematic rapes" committed in Omarska.[333]

While many victims have been outraged by acquittals in The Hague, some told me they experienced a measure of justice even when the ICTY failed to convict defendants they held responsible for atrocious crimes. For example Josip Drežnjak said that, even though the ICTY had not found a particular defendant guilty, he derived satisfaction from the fact that the Tribunal found beyond a reasonable doubt that crimes under international law had been committed.[334] Fatima Fazlić, who lost her husband during the war, said she would derive satisfaction "[just] in the fact that some of the suspects have been arrested even if the court decides there is not sufficient evidence and he is released. . . . Even that is satisfaction."[335]

---

[328] MISCHKOWSKI & MLINAREVIĆ, *supra* note 5, at 51.

[329] *Id. See also* AMNESTY INTERNATIONAL, "WE NEED SUPPORT, NOT PITY": LAST CHANCE FOR JUSTICE FOR BOSNIA'S WARTIME RAPE SURVIVORS 37–38 (2017).

[330] Interview with Dženana Karup Druško, Director, Transitional Justice, Accountability and Remembrance, in Sarajevo, Bosn. & Herz. (Sept. 8, 2014).

[331] Interview with Jasna Bakšić Muftić, Professor, Faculty of Law, University of Sarajevo, in Sarajevo, Bosn. & Herz. (Sept. 17, 2014).

[332] Interview with Mirsad Duratović, Chairman, Prijedor '92, in Prijedor, Bosn. & Herz. (Sept. 16, 2014).

[333] *Id.*

[334] Interview with Josip Drežnjak, President, Association of Missing Croat Persons from Grabovica, in Mostar, Bosn. & Herz. (July 18, 2009).

[335] Interview with Fatima Fazlić, President, Izvor, in Prijedor, Bosn. & Herz. (July 23, 2009). In a similar vein, Marin Brkić, who was seeking justice in an entity court for the wartime murder of family members, told me if those responsible spent even one day in prison, "that would mean so much to me[;] I would then say . . . that justice has been served." Interview with Marin Brkić, Association of Missing, Forcibly Taken Away and Fallen Croats of Brčko District, in Brčko, Bosn. & Herz. (July 22, 2009).

H. Bearing Witness

Duratović is frustrated he was not asked to testify in The Hague, as he believes he could have provided better evidence than some witnesses in Prijedor cases.[336] While his reason is specific, Duratović's disappointment is not uncommon: many survivors interpret their exclusion from the Prosecutor's witness list as a judgment of their worth.[337] Yet despite his own experience, Duratović counts as a signal achievement the fact "that many victims finally got the chance to speak loudly before the world thanks to the ICTY."[338]

As studies have documented, testifying in war crimes trials can be frustrating and stressful;[339] for victims, describing devastating experiences can be retraumatizing. Particularly during the ICTY's early years, the experiences of some witnesses were far from ideal.[340] Witnesses who were the subject of protective measures—their names were not publicly disclosed in judgments; their identity was obscured in court, for example—enjoyed little protection when they returned home, if home was still in Bosnia.[341] While most witnesses have not faced problems as a result of their testimony, some were harassed or threatened.[342]

---

[336] Duratović explained that before he was detained in Omarska, he was used as a human shield by Bosnian Serbs as they went "from one house to another, . . . taking civilians out, shooting them all," before moving on to the next house. "So I was an eye-witness to all these murders," whereas others who testified in The Hague were not in a position to witness those executions. Yet "they didn't find me interesting to witness before the Hague Tribunal." Interview with Mirsad Duratović, Chairman, Prijedor '92, in Prijedor, Bosn. & Herz. (Sept. 16, 2014).

[337] See Hodžić, *Living the Legacy, supra* note 21, at 124–25. The resulting feeling of "inadequacy," Hodžić writes, affects survivors' overall perceptions of war crimes trials. *Id.*

[338] Interview with Mirsad Duratović, Chairman, Prijedor '92, in Prijedor, Bosn. & Herz. (Sept. 16, 2014).

[339] See STOVER, *supra* note 3, at 127–30; MISCHKOWSKI & MLINAREVIĆ, *supra* note 5, at 56–57; Hodžić, *Living the Legacy, supra* note 21, at 124–25. See also Eduardo Reyes, *Yugoslavia Tribunal: Legacy of War,* LAW SOC'Y GAZETTE (July 20, 2015) (ICTY source notes that for many witnesses, stress "starts when they hear they have been admitted to the witness list and called for the purpose of trial").

[340] Several former witnesses volunteered during interviews that they found the Tribunal's treatment of witnesses to be highly professional (my interviews do not, however, provide a basis for assessing how representative their experience was). Describing his testimony in an ICTY case, Mirko Zelenika told me: "I came back very happy, very satisfied for the fact that the ICTY has a very supportive, very well organized service for witness support." Interview with Mirko Zelenika, Acting President, Association of Croat Detainees of BiH, in Mostar, Bosn. & Herz. (Sept. 10, 2014). Nusreta Sivac, too, extolled the ICTY's professionalism, as well as the "very human approach" of its personnel, including their "sensitivity for victims" as well as defendants. Interview with Nusreta Sivac, Former Judge, in Prijedor, Bosn. & Herz. (Sept. 16, 2014). Both Zelenika and Sivac found their experiences as ICTY witnesses more satisfying than their experiences with Bosnia's war crimes chamber.

[341] Eric Stover interviewed eighty-seven witnesses in ICTY proceedings for his 2005 book. The majority of the protected witnesses he interviewed "said the measures taken in The Hague to guard their anonymity as witnesses failed, leaving them open for recriminations on their returning home from the tribunal." STOVER, *supra* note 3, at 98. Someone I interviewed said she knew of a witness who, by virtue of the ICTY's travel arrangements, flew home on the same plane as relatives of the defendant against whom she had just testified as a "protected witness." Interview with Jasminka Džumhur, then National Legal Officer, Office of the High Commissioner for Human Rights, in Sarajevo, Bosn. & Herz. (June 11, 2007).

[342] See U.N. HIGH COMMISSIONER FOR REFUGEES, UPDATE ON CONDITIONS FOR RETURN TO BOSNIA AND HERZEGOVINA 2 (2005); STOVER, *supra* note 3, at 100–01.

Despite these concerns, many witnesses derived deep satisfaction from testifying in The Hague.[343] Their chief reason is moral, not instrumental, and sifts down to a deeply felt need to bear witness for those who did not survive ethnic cleansing. In his 2005 study of ICTY witnesses, Eric Stover wrote that many, having "survived unspeakable crimes while others had perished," believed it "their 'moral duty' to ensure that the truth about the death of family members, neighbors, and colleagues was duly recorded and acknowledged."[344] I heard the same sentiment in interviews with former witnesses, such as the late Muharem Murselović. Murselović was detained in Omarska for the crime of being Muslim and was a willing witness in several ICTY cases. He explained his motivation when I interviewed him in 2009: "I am obliged to witness, to testify on behalf of hundreds of my friends who have been murdered in Prijedor whose guilt was the same as mine. I survived that hell and I never regretted for the fact that I witnessed."[345]

Džafer Deronjić, who testified against Goran Jelisić, made much the same point. Jelisić has the shameful distinction of standing out even among ICTY defendants for his monstrous depravity. Arriving in Brčko during the war, Jelisić introduced himself as the "Serb Adolf" and announced he had come to kill Muslims. In May 1992, hundreds of Muslim and Croat victims were taken to the Luka camp, formerly a warehouse facility, where many were systematically killed. Jelisić routinely entered the camp's main hangar, selected detainees for interrogation, beat them mercilessly, and then shot and killed some.[346]

Deronjić narrowly escaped being killed in Luka but was tormented by his perfect recall. Explaining why he was asked to testify in the *Jelisić* case, Deronjić said: "I remember everything. I remember each time somebody lost a piece of his body" in Luka. For the past eight years, Deronjić told me, "I do not sleep at all," and testifying against Jelisić did nothing to calm his nightmares. Yet when I asked if he had wanted to testify, Deronjić did not hesitate: "Absolutely yes. It is in the interest of us all who survived the tortures to tell the truth, to tell the world what it was like. . . . "[347]

Nusreta Sivac, who survived repeated rape while detained in Omarska, testified in several ICTY cases and, at the time I interviewed her, at least one trial before Bosnia's state court. Sivac knew "it was going to be difficult" to testify "because each time you do it, you refresh your memory and then you are living through all that again and again," which is "so difficult."[348] When I asked why she was nonetheless willing to testify so often, Sivac answered:

> Even when I was in the concentration camp, I promised myself I was going to talk about it. If I happen to survive my detention, my imprisonment, I promised

---

[343] Seventy-seven percent of the witnesses Eric Stover interviewed reported that, on balance, testifying in The Hague was a positive experience. STOVER, *supra* note 3, at 134. He cautioned, however, that some might revise their assessments following the Appeals Chamber's reversal of guilty verdicts imposed by the chamber before which they testified. *Id.*

[344] *Id.* at 126.

[345] Interview with the late Muharem Murselović, Member of Republika Srpska National Assembly, President of the RS Parlamentarians Club for the Party for BiH, in Banja Luka, Bosn. & Herz. (July 15, 2009).

[346] Prosecutor v. Jelisić, Case No. IT-95-10-T, Trial Judgment (Int'l Crim. Trib. for the Former Yugoslavia Dec. 14, 1999).

[347] Interview with Džafer Deronjić, Association of the Families of Missing, Forcibly Detained and Murdered Bosniaks of Bosnia and Herzegovina, in Brčko, Bosn. & Herz. (July 22, 2009).

[348] Interview with Nusreta Sivac, Former Judge, in Prijedor, Bosn. & Herz. (Sept. 16, 2014).

myself that I was going to talk about it as much as I can, once freed, mainly because of those who are not here with us anymore. This was a strong motive, for those who are not alive to talk about all atrocities, all the misery that we all have been through.[349]

I. "This Is a Political Court"

Created by a quintessential political body, the ICTY faced a singular challenge establishing confidence in its independence. Even so, it was widely seen as fair and impartial at least among Bosniaks for much of its working life. Yet a series of decisions, beginning with a procedural ruling in the *Milošević* case, eroded even Bosniaks' confidence while providing grist for longtime critics.[350]

1. NONDISCLOSURE OF EVIDENCE IN THE *MILOŠEVIĆ* CASE

Among the most legally consequential documents sought by then Prosecutor Carla del Ponte in the *Milošević* case were wartime records of the Supreme Defense Council of the FRY, which "the prosecution team knew would be crucial to establishing beyond a reasonable doubt the links between Milošević and the rest of the political leadership in Belgrade with the war crimes committed in Croatia, Bosnia and Herzegovina, and Kosovo."[351] Although legally bound to comply with ICTY requests for evidence, Serbian authorities repeatedly said they would provide these documents only if they were kept under protective order. The reason, Serbian officials made clear, was they feared the records would be the proverbial nail in the coffin of their defense to the genocide case Bosnia had brought against the FRY in the International Court of Justice (ICJ).[352]

Del Ponte later explained how and why she resolved the dilemma Serbian resistance presented: "The Serbs were ready to provide records in a way that would help us sink Milošević with the millstone of genocide tied around his neck. If we did not seize this break in the political cloud cover, the Office of the Prosecutor might not acquire these documents for months or years."[353] Yet the Tribunal's rules allowed this evidence to be kept secret only to protect legitimate "national security interests,"[354] not to shield a state from accountability before another court. In a decision for which she has been strongly criticized,[355] the Prosecutor agreed to support in general terms Serbia's application for protective measures on the understanding the application

---

[349] *Id.* Sivac's early efforts to document crimes of sexual violence are noted in Chapter 2. In a separate interview, Emsuda Mujagić told me Sivac remained willing to bear witness because she knew what her testimony "means to justice, which has a higher importance." Interview with Emsuda Mujagić, President, Srcem do Mira, in Kozarac, Bosn. & Herz. (July 23, 2009).

[350] The title of this section ("This is a political court") is taken from an interview with Kada Hotić, Vice President, Association of Mothers of Srebrenica and Žepa Enclaves, in Sarajevo, Bosn. & Herz. (Sept. 18, 2014).

[351] DEL PONTE WITH SUDETIĆ, *supra* note 135, at 99.

[352] *See id.* at 199, 202.

[353] *Id.* at 200.

[354] Rules of Procedure and Evidence, Int'l Crim. Trib. for the Former Yugoslavia, U.N. Doc. IT/32/Rev.49, Rule 54 *bis* (May 22, 2013).

[355] *See, e.g.*, Ruth Wedgwood, *The Strange Case of Florence Hartmann*, THE AMERICAN INTEREST. COM (2009).

would be "reasonable" and "take into consideration the interest of transparency of the court proceedings."[356]

The Trial Chamber agreed not to disclose the crucial evidence on a broad reading of Serbia's "vital national interest," a standard not contemplated in the ICTY's rules of procedure. When the Appeals Chamber eventually ruled on the matter, it found the Trial Chamber had erred in applying this standard. Nevertheless, and even though Serbia "made no secret" of the fact that it sought the protective order to avert a genocide ruling by the ICJ,[357] the Appeals Chamber ruled in two confidential decisions that, since Serbia had relied on the Trial Chamber's ruling when it provided the documents—which it was legally required to provide in any case—it was entitled to the protection afforded by the Trial Chamber.[358] The Trial Chamber would be able to see the unredacted documents for purposes of assessing Milošević's guilt, and so the principal effect of the ruling would be to shield Serbia from liability in the ICJ case against it. Fatefully, however, the ICTY never passed judgment in the Milošević case, as the defendant's death brought his trial to an end.

As for the case before the ICJ, on February 26, 2007, the Court ruled that genocide was committed in Srebrenica;[359] Serbia bore responsibility for failing to prevent that genocide,[360] but Bosnia had not proved the genocidal conduct of Bosnian Serb forces could be legally attributed to Serbia.[361] Crucially, the ICJ had refused Bosnia's request that it seek the unredacted Supreme Defense Council documents from Serbia; nor did it ask the ICTY to consider modifying its protective measures so the ICJ could obtain access to the Tribunal's unredacted documents. The ICJ nonetheless "observe[d] that the Applicant has extensive documentation and other evidence available to it, especially from the readily accessible ICTY records"[362]—which of course did not include the very documents at issue.

Unknowable, of course, is whether the secret evidence would have produced a different outcome. What is clear is that Serbia thought it would, and for that reason mounted an aggressive effort to ensure it remained hidden.[363]

The episode tarnished both Hague courts in the eyes of many Bosnians. Emir Suljagić wondered, "How could [ICTY] judges accept that hiding of evidence of participation in genocide is a legitimate national interest? . . . What's worse, the ICJ never asked [for the redacted documents]! . . . Good god!"[364] Zdravko Grebo characterized the ICTY's decision to "intentionally hide some documents" and thereby "influence"

---

[356] DEL PONTE WITH SUDETIĆ, supra note 135, at 200.

[357] Marlise Simons, Genocide Court Ruled for Serbia Without Seeing Full War Archive, N.Y. TIMES (Apr. 9, 2007).

[358] See Yuval Shany, Two Sides of the Same Coin? Judging Milošević and Serbia Before the ICTY and ICJ, in THE MILOŠEVIĆ TRIAL: AN AUTOPSY 441, 451 (Timothy William Waters ed., 2013).

[359] Application of the Convention on the Prevention and Punishment of the Crime of Genocide (Bosn. & Herz. v. Serb. & Montenegro), 2007 I.C.J. 43, Judgment, ¶ 297 (Feb. 26, 2007).

[360] Id. ¶ 438.

[361] Id. ¶ 415.

[362] Id. ¶ 206.

[363] One of the dissenting judges in the ICJ case thought it "reasonable" to expect "that those documents would have shed light on . . . central questions" pertaining to the FRY's legal responsibility for genocide. Id., Dissenting Opinion of Vice President Al-Khasawneh, ¶ 35.

[364] Interview with Emir Suljagić, Author, in Sarajevo, Bosn. & Herz. (July 14, 2009).

the outcome in the ICJ case as "scandalous."[365] Srebrenica survivor Kada Hotić lamented: "If the court can clearly express that they are protecting Serbian national interests, this means that this is a political court, this is not a court of justice."[366] Saša Madacki expressed concern in gentler terms: "Sometimes we are not able to understand the decisions of the Tribunal," particularly those relating to the Supreme Defense Council. "This is something that's not understandable."[367]

For Bosniaks, the suppression of seemingly crucial evidence imperiled an aspiration many cherished—that the ICTY would establish authoritatively Serbia's pivotal role in the Bosnian war. The late Muharem Murselović explained how many reacted: "What especially upsets people here in Bosnia and Herzegovina and hurts them," he told me, "is that some information proving the direct involvement of Serbia has been hidden in agreement with the Government of Serbia[;] the Hague Tribunal protected the state of Serbia by hiding documentation of the involvement of Serbia in the conflict in Bosnia. So this creates a certain mistrust, a suspicion of its good intentions."[368]

This reaction was later compounded by the ICTY's action against a former employee, Florence Hartmann. Hartmann, who served as spokesperson for then Prosecutor Carla del Ponte from 2000 to 2006, later wrote about the Appeals Chamber's key rulings authorizing protective measures for the Supreme Defense Council documents.[369] A Special Chamber of the ICTY found Hartmann guilty of "knowingly and wilfully interfering with the Tribunal's administration of justice"[370] for having disclosed the "contents and purported effect"[371] of the rulings in breach of the chamber's orders that they remain confidential.[372] Hartmann was fined €7,000,[373] a penalty subsequently converted to seven days in jail.[374]

Some of my interlocutors found Hartmann's own conduct troubling, either because they thought she should have gone public sooner or because they thought her publication was conduct unbecoming senior court staff. But victims' associations were offended by her prosecution. Several Bosniak victims sought unsuccessfully to be heard at her trial so they could advise the Special Panel its punitive action could "destabilize relations in the region, inflame victims' frustrations, [and] endanger

---

[365] Interview with Zdravko Grebo, Director, Center for Interdisciplinary Postgraduate Studies, University of Sarajevo, in Sarajevo, Bosn. & Herz. (July 13, 2009).

[366] Interview with Kada Hotić, Vice President, Association of Mothers of Srebrenica and Žepa Enclaves, in Sarajevo, Bosn. & Herz. (Sept. 18, 2014).

[367] Interview with Saša Madacki, Director, Human Rights Centre, University of Sarajevo, in Sarajevo, Bosn. & Herz. (July 17, 2009).

[368] Interview with the late Muharem Murselović, then Member of Republika Srpska National Assembly, President of the RS Parlamentarians Club for the Party for BiH, in Banja Luka, Bosn. & Herz. (July 15, 2009).

[369] See Edward Cody, From War Crimes to Contempt Case; U.N. Yugoslav Tribunal's Prosecution of Ex-spokeswoman Draws Criticism, Wash. Post (June 21, 2009); International Court Fines Journalist for Secrecy Violation; No Jail Time in Contempt Finding, Wash. Post (Sept. 15, 2009).

[370] In the Case against Hartmann, Case No. IT-02-54-R77.5, Judgment on Allegations of Contempt ¶ 89 (Int'l Crim. Trib. for the Former Yugoslavia Sept. 14, 2009).

[371] Id. ¶ 47.

[372] Id. ¶ 62.

[373] Id. ¶ 90.

[374] Ed Vulliamy, French Journalist Florence Hartmann Jailed by War Crimes Tribunal, Guardian (Mar. 26, 2016).

the founding principles of the work of the [ICTY]."[375] As a result of its action, they wrote, "Trust in the [Tribunal] and international justice might be lost."[376] (At the Tribunal itself, many believe that, because Hartmann violated the court's protective orders, it had a duty to prosecute the violation, as it has in other contempt proceedings.) Following Hartmann's conviction, many Serbs—both Serbian and Bosnian—who had supported the ICTY denounced its action, saying they "now have serious worries about what is happening there."[377] Already controversial, the Tribunal's pursuit of Hartmann was crystalized in an indelible image when its officers arrested the former spokeswoman as she spoke with victims' groups while they awaited the trial verdict in the *Karadžić* case.[378]

2. CONTROVERSIAL ACQUITTALS

> *Unfortunately we're now seeing a reversal. Now, . . . the judgments resemble . . . politically-aligned rulings rather than rulings related to justice.*
> —DŽENANA KARUP DRUŠKO[379]

As we have seen, the ICTY's early trials were of relatively low-level perpetrators, while men widely considered most responsible for ethnic cleansing eluded arrest for years.[380] Thus many Bosnians hoped the Tribunal's later years would redeem the protracted delay in bringing senior suspects, particularly Radovan Karadžić and Ratko Mladić, before the bar of justice. As well, the long-awaited trials of several Serbian officials nurtured hopes the Tribunal would definitively link Serbian state institutions to atrocities carried out by Bosnian Serbs—a cherished hope of many Bosniak victims in particular. Some hoped as well that the trial of three senior Croatian military officials, Ante Gotovina, Mladen Markač, and Ivan Čermak, would illuminate and condemn "the responsibility of the Croatian army in the crimes committed against Serb civilians in Croatia and Bosnia."[381] In short, many hoped that, in its final years, the Tribunal would write a definitive history of the Yugoslav wars, clarifying the roles of Serbia and Croatia while holding the masterminds of ethnic cleansing to account.

Far from what they envisioned, the ICTY's later years were marked by unprecedented controversy, triggered by controversial acquittals of several high-profile suspects. Virtually any acquittal would, of course, disappoint many victims. But these were notable above all because they seemed indefensible even in the eyes of the Tribunal's staunchest supporters.

[375] Simon Jennings, *Victims' Request to Speak in Hartmann Trial Dismissed*, IWPR (May 8, 2009).
[376] *Id.*
[377] Merima Husejnović, *Hague Tribunal's Prestige Fades as Closure Looms*, BALKAN INSIGHT (Sept. 17, 2009).
[378] Marlise Simons, *Tribunal Releases Journalist Held 5 Days in a Prison for War Criminals*, N.Y. TIMES (Mar. 30, 2016).
[379] Interview with Dženana Karup Druško, Director, Transitional Justice, Accountability and Remembrance, in Sarajevo, Bosn. & Herz. (Sept. 8, 2014).
[380] See Chapter 2. *See also* Tim Judah, *Why Are Balkan War-Crimes Convictions Getting Overturned?*, BLOOMBERG (June 6, 2013).
[381] Caterina Bonora, *Dženana Karup Druško: The Painful Importance of the ICTY*, OSSERVATORIO BALCANI E CAUCASO (Dec. 4, 2013).

a. Gotovina and Haradinaj Acquittals

The cascade of controversial judgments began with the November 16, 2012, judgment of the ICTY Appeals Chamber overturning the conviction of Croatian generals Ante Gotovina and Mladen Markač. Some background will be helpful in explaining why this was the ICTY's "most controversial judgment" up to that point:[382] In April 2011, a unanimous trial chamber convicted Gotovina and Markač of crimes against humanity committed against Serbs during Operation Storm,[383] the Croatian offensive launched in August 1995 to rout Serb rebels from the Krajina region of Croatia.[384] Gotovina was sentenced to twenty-four years and Markač to eighteen years in prison.

The trial verdict was—or at least seemed at the time—to be a landmark in the Tribunal's work. Its conviction of senior Croatian military officials for crimes against ethnic Serbs offered a compelling rebuttal to long-standing Serb claims that the Tribunal was organized to convict Serbs, and brought a sense of vindication in Serbia.[385] Some hoped the conviction would counter widespread denial in Croatia that Croats committed war crimes during Operation Storm.[386] In part because of its historic nature, the case had long been the stuff of high drama, entailing an epic struggle to secure custody of Gotovina[387] and induce Croatia to turn over artillery logs deemed crucial to his prosecution.[388] The trial verdict had powerful regional reverberations: if Serbs found vindication in Gotovina's conviction, Croatian citizens were shocked. Croatia's leaders condemned the Trial Chamber's finding that an operation they considered purely defensive entailed a "joint criminal enterprise" whose purpose was to permanently remove Serbs from Krajina.[389]

An "unfortunate"[390] aspect of the judgment made it vulnerable on appeal: faced with the question of whether the Croatian army indiscriminately (and thus unlawfully) fired hundreds of artillery projectiles into four towns in Krajina, the separatist Serb region of Croatia, the Trial Chamber developed and applied a presumption: artillery projectiles that fell more than 200 meters away from a legitimate military target would, absent contrary evidence, be presumed to have been fired indiscriminately

---

[382] Bogdan Ivanišević, *Hague Failed to Justify Gotovina Acquittal*, Balkan Transitional Just. (Nov. 19, 2012).

[383] Prosecutor v. Gotovina et al., Case No. IT-06-90-T, Trial Judgment (Int'l Crim. Trib. for the Former Yugoslavia April 15, 2011). A third defendant, Ivan Čermak, was acquitted.

[384] This region had been controlled by Serb forces since 1991. See Mark A. Summers, *The Surprising Acquittals in the* Gotovina *and* Perišić *Cases*, 13 Rich. J. Global L. & Bus. 649, 663–64 (2015).

[385] See Enis Zebić & Branka Mihajlović, *Gotovina Conviction Riles Croats, Mollifies Serbs*, IWPR (Apr. 22, 2011).

[386] See Bonora, *supra* note 381; Janine Natalya Clark, *Courting Controversy: The ICTY's Acquittal of Croatian Generals Gotovina and Markač*, 11 J. Int'l Crim. Just. 399, 401 (2013) [hereinafter Clark, *Courting Controversy*].

[387] See Borger, *supra* note 5, at 120–26.

[388] See Prosecutor v. Gotovina et al., Case No. IT-06-90-T, Decision on Prosecution's Application for an Order Pursuant to Rule 54*bis* Directing the Government of the Republic of Croatia to Produce Documents or Information, ¶¶ 1–11 (Int'l Crim. Trib. for the Former Yugoslavia July 26, 2010).

[389] See Enis Zebić & Branka Mihajlović, *Gotovina Conviction Riles Croats, Mollifies Serbs*, IWPR (Apr. 22, 2011); Radmila Nakarada, *Case Note: Acquittal of Gotovina and Markač: A Blow to the Serbian and Croatian Reconciliation Process*, 29 Merkourios 102, 103 (2013).

[390] Marko Milanović, *The Gotovina Omnishambles*, EJIL: Talk! (Nov. 18, 2012).

and thus unlawfully.[391] Using this presumption, the Trial Chamber concluded that four towns in Krajina had been subjected to unlawful artillery fire.[392]

In a "surprise" ruling[393] aptly described as "a disaster at almost every level,"[394] a starkly divided Appeals Chamber reversed the generals' convictions and released them from prison. All five appellate judges agreed the Trial Chamber failed to provide a reasoned foundation for the 200-meter standard.[395] But they sharply disagreed about the consequences of its error. The majority considered the standard to have been the lower chamber's "cornerstone and organising principle" for determining the lawfulness of artillery fire.[396] In its view, if the standard was invalid, the trial judgment could not be redeemed.[397] In the view of dissenting judges, the majority failed to show why conclusions in the trial verdict that were "not at all linked to the 200 Metre Standard" were invalid.[398] Undertaking a de novo review rather than simply correcting what it considered a legal error,[399] the majority "swept aside" not only the trial verdict's conclusions based on the 200-meter standard, "but also all the other evidence of Gotovina's guilt" in the trial judgment.[400]

---

[391] See Prosecutor v. Gotovina et al., Case No. IT-06-90-T, Trial Judgment, ¶¶ 1903–1906; 1919–1921; 1932–1933, 1940–1941. (Int'l Crim. Trib. for the Former Yugoslavia Apr. 15, 2011).

[392] Id. ¶¶ 1913, 1925, 1937, 1945. The Trial Chamber's legal analysis was more complex than this account may imply, but it suffices for present purposes. Western (especially U.S.) military experts were deeply concerned, believing the 200-meter test departed from long-standing jurisprudence concerning the mens rea element of a disproportionate military attack, effectively imposing a strict liability standard. See EMORY INT'L HUMANITARIAN CLINIC, OPERATIONAL LAW EXPERTS ROUNDTABLE ON THE GOTOVINA JUDGMENT: MILITARY OPERATIONS, BATTLEFIELD REALITY AND THE JUDGMENT'S IMPACT ON EFFECTIVE IMPLEMENTATION AND ENFORCEMENT OF INTERNATIONAL HUMANITARIAN LAW (2012); see also Rachel Irwin, Do Overturned Convictions Undermine Hague Tribunal?, IWPR (Mar. 20, 2013) (quoting legal scholar Jens David Ohlin characterizing the trial chamber's 200-meter test as a "mistake").

[393] Serbia Launches Fightback over Hague Verdicts, BALKAN TRANSITIONAL JUST. (Nov. 23, 2012); Summers, supra note 384, at 650. See also Rhodri C. Williams, Breaking News—Gotovina and Markač Convictions Overturned (updated), TERRANULLIUS (Nov. 16, 2012) (describing the appellate ruling as a "shock reversal"); Marlise Simons, Hague Court Overturns Convictions of 2 Croatian Generals over a 1995 Offensive, N.Y. TIMES (Nov. 17, 2012) (describing the judgment as "the most dramatic reversal in the 19-year-history" of the ICTY).

[394] Milanović, supra note 390.

[395] Prosecutor v. Gotovina et al., Case No. IT-06-90-A, Appeal Judgment, ¶¶ 61, 64 (Int'l Crim. Trib. for the Former Yugoslavia Nov. 16, 2012).

[396] Id. ¶ 64.

[397] See id. ¶¶ 2–3 (Dissenting Opinion of Judge Carmel Agius).

[398] Id. ¶ 18 (Dissenting Opinion of Judge Fausto Pocar); ¶ 4 (Dissenting Opinion of Judge Carmel Agius) ("the Majority erroneously regards the 200 Metre Standard as the critical piece underpinning all of the Trial Chamber's findings regarding the unlawfulness of the attacks on the Four Towns").

[399] This aspect of the majority's approach has been harshly criticized not only by dissenting judges, but also legal commentators. See, e.g., Summers, supra note 384, at 670–73; Nakarada, supra note 389, at 104.

[400] Summers, supra note 384, at 667. Other aspects of the majority's analysis have been vigorously criticized as well. See, e.g., Bogdan Ivanišević, Hague Failed to Justify Gotovina Acquittal, BALKAN TRANSITIONAL JUST. (Nov. 19, 2012); Clark, Courting Controversy, supra note 386. A favorable commentary was published by Gary Solis, one of the former military advisors who, as explained below, urged the Appeals Chamber to reject the 200-meter standard. Gary D. Solis, The Gotovina Acquittal: A Sound Appellate Course Correction, 215 MILITARY L. REV. 78 (2013).

Marko Milanović bluntly captured the judgment's repercussions for the Tribunal, saying its "credibility is now not just in tatters—it is nil."[401] Sense News Agency reported:

The difference between the conviction and 24-year sentence [by the Trial Chamber] and an acquittal, rendered without a single new fact, testimony or evidence being presented, is a serious blot on the practice of the ICTY; either the Trial Chamber or the Appeals Chamber made a severe error."[402]

Bosnian journalist and transitional justice advocate Dženana Karup Druško described the judgment's impact this way: "The contribution of the ICTY is priceless, but . . . it took a turn when it comes to the *Gotovina* judgment." As a result, she continued, "the ICTY is being seen as an institution constructing a new approach to the interpretation of international law and how it is applied."[403]

Had it not been followed by other stunning acquittals, the *Gotovina* Appeal Judgment might be remembered principally for its effect on Serb victims of Gotovina's alleged crimes[404] and wider Serb concerns about the ICTY's "ethnic balance": with the acquittal, the ICTY would close its doors without convicting Croatian Croats for crimes against Serbs (though it has convicted Bosnian Croats of wartime atrocities).[405] In light of subsequent acquittals described below, however, the judgment assumed another layer of meaning: many believe the majority opinion was motivated by judges' desire to avoid a legal precedent against which Western military forces might more readily be judged guilty of war crimes.[406]

---

[401] Milanović, *supra* note 290.

[402] *The Way to Avoid Being Condemned to Conflict Based on a Verdict*, SENSE NEWS AGENCY (Nov. 26, 2012). The scathing tone of the two dissents compounded this perception. *See, e.g.*, Prosecutor v. Gotovina et al., Case No. IT-06-90-A, Appeal Judgment, ¶ 2 (Int'l Crim. Trib. for the Former Yugoslavia Nov. 16, 2012) (Dissenting Opinion of Judge Fausto Pocar) ("Given the sheer volume of errors and misconstructions in the Majority's reasoning and the fact that the Appeal Judgement misrepresents the Trial Chamber's analysis, I will not discuss everything in detail"); *id.* ¶ 26 (characterizing contentions of the Majority in a passage of its opinion as "simply grotesque").

[403] Interview with Dženana Karup Druško, Transitional Justice, Accountability and Remembrance, in Sarajevo, Bosn. & Herz. (Sept. 8, 2014).

[404] Several years after Gotovina's acquittal in The Hague, Bosnian Serb authorities pressed charges against Gotovina, accusing him of war crimes against Serbs in the Bosnian region of Livno. *See Bosnian Serbs Accuse Croatia's Gotovina of War Crimes*, AGENCE FRANCE-PRESSE (Apr. 12, 2017).

[405] Another Croatian wartime commander indicted by the ICTY, Janko Bobetko, died on April 29, 2003, before he was arrested. *See* ICTY, CASE INFORMATION SHEET: JANKO BOBETKO, http://www.icty.org/x/cases/bobetko/cis/en/cis_bobetko_en.pdf (last visited Dec. 6, 2017). The cases of two other Croatians indicted for crimes against Serbs, Mirko Norac and Rahim Ademi, were transferred to Croatia for trial there. The Zagreb District Court sentenced Norac to seven years' imprisonment; Ademi was acquitted. *See* ICTY, CASE INFORMATION SHEET: ADEMI & NORAC, http://www.icty.org/x/cases/ademi/cis/en/cis_ademi_norac.pdf (last visited Dec. 6, 2017).

[406] Several facts fueled this narrative. First, a group of retired military advisors from the United States and other Western countries prepared an amicus brief urging the Appeals Chamber to reject the 200-meter standard. Application and Proposed Amicus Curiae Brief Concerning the 15 April 2011 Trial Chamber Judgment and Requesting that the Appeals Chamber Reconsider the Findings of Unlawful Artillery Attacks During Operation Storm, submitted in Prosecutor v. Gotovina et al., Case No. IT-06-90-A (Int'l Crim. Trib. for the Former Yugoslavia Jan. 12, 2012). Second, the trial verdict convicting Gotovina and Markač of participating in a "joint criminal

Less than two weeks after the *Gotovina* reversal, an ICTY trial chamber acquitted Ramush Haradinaj and two other Kosovo Albanians of crimes committed against Serb civilians in Kosovo.[407] Widely anticipated, their acquittals did not have the dramatic impact of the *Gotovina* judgment. Nevertheless, the verdict reinforced a pervasive Serb belief that the ICTY was biased against Serbs,[408] and contributed to a growing perception the Tribunal was racking up acquittals at a point in its life when many expected landmark convictions.

b. "Specific Direction"

I no longer believe in the ICTY because this is political judgment.

                                —SABAHETA FEJZIĆ[409]

As already noted, some Bosniaks hoped the ICTY would render an authoritative judgment that Serbia committed aggression against Bosnia. Technically, it cannot do so: the Tribunal does not have jurisdiction over the international crime of aggression. Yet its judgments can establish fundamental facts of Serbian support for Bosnian Serbs who carried out the murderous program of ethnic cleansing and genocide, and a number of judgments have done so.[410]

The trial of former Yugoslav army chief of staff Momčilo Perišić offered a singular opportunity to establish the role of Serbian state institutions in atrocities carried out by Bosnian Serbs, and was widely anticipated for that reason.[411] As Bogdan Ivanišević noted, the indictment against Perišić was the ICTY's first "to specifically target the nature and the degree of the Belgrade government's military involvement in the wars in Bosnia and Croatia."[412] The prosecution claimed Perišić established and ran two sections of the Yugoslav Army's General Staff, one of which provided myriad forms of support, including salaries, for the Bosnian Serb army. In September 2011,

---

enterprise" to expel Serbs from Krajina had "raised fresh questions about the role Croatia says American advisers played in the campaign." Marlise Simons, *U.N. Court Convicts Two Croatian Generals of War Crimes and Frees a Third*, N.Y. TIMES (Apr. 16, 2011). Finally, American judge Theodor Meron was among those voting for acquittal.

[407] Prosecutor v. Haradinaj et al., Case No. IT-04-84*bis*-T, Trial Judgment (Int'l Crim. Trib. for the Former Yugoslavia Nov. 29, 2012).

[408] Interview with Ivan Jovanović, Attorney, in Belgrade, Serb. (June 9, 2014) (noting the acquittal contributed to the overall "result that . . . there is a high number of convictions of Serbs, whereas . . . very few convictions of crimes against Serbs" by the ICTY).

[409] *Bosnia Ethnically Split over Perišić's Acquittal*, BALKAN TRANSITIONAL JUST. (Mar. 1, 2013) (quoting Sabaheta Fejzić reacting to the acquittal of Momčilo Perišić).

[410] The crimes over which the ICTY has jurisdiction include a broad range of war crimes committed in international armed conflict on the one hand, and a more limited number of war crimes committed in a non-international conflict. To determine which category applied in its first trial, the ICTY examined Belgrade's role in the Bosnian conflict. It held that Bosnian Serb armed forces acted under the "overall control" of the Federal Republic of Yugoslavia at relevant times. Prosecutor v. Tadić, Case No. IT-94-1-A, Appeal Judgment, ¶ 162 (Int'l Crim. Trib. for the Former Yugoslavia July 15, 1999).

[411] *See* Rachel Irwin, *Perišić First Belgrade Official Convicted for Bosnia Crimes*, IWPR (Sept. 12, 2011). Upon Perišić's acquittal by the Appeals Chamber, discussed below, Serbian government officials made the reverse claim, saying his acquittal "proved there was no aggression by the Yugoslav army against Bosnia and Croatia." Ognjen Zorić, *Serbian Relief at Perišić Ruling*, IWPR (Mar. 4, 2013) (quoting then Serbian prime minister Ivica Dačić).

[412] Ana Uzelac, *Momčilo Perišić Trial May Have Great Implications*, BOSNIA REP. (2005).

with one judge dissenting, Trial Chamber I convicted Perišić of knowingly aiding and abetting murderous attacks in Sarajevo and Srebrenica and sentenced him to twenty-seven years in prison.[413] This marked the first time the ICTY had convicted a Serbian official for crimes committed in Bosnia.[414]

But in another stunning reversal, on February 28, 2013, the Appeals Chamber acquitted Perišić, with one judge dissenting.[415] Srebrenica survivor Fadila Memišević decried the "scandalous" verdict, saying that, through its acquittal of "Perišić, the tribunal has started to lose credibility. It's a harsh blow to all those victims who were expecting justice."[416] Hatidža Mehmedović denounced what she called a "reward for crimes and punishment for victims."[417] Fazila Efendić, also a Srebrenica survivor, was incredulous: "I have waited 20 years for justice. Where is that justice now?"[418]

For many others, the Appeals Chamber decision "further darken[ed the] shadow" recent acquittals had cast over the ICTY, breathing "new life into the longstanding argument of nationalists" that the Tribunal is a political court.[419] Mirsad Tokača gave voice to a concern rapidly gaining ground in Bosnia:

> Instead of being a completely neutral judicial institution that only judges the facts and evidence and does not deal with anything else, the last few decisions have shown that the Hague tribunal has become highly politicized. These acquittals are only fueling claims that this is a political court that delivers political judgements.
>
> That is not good. It's not good for international justice, it's not good for the whole region, and I think that everything that the Hague tribunal has been building for years has been put in jeopardy by these acquittals.[420]

Other longtime Bosnian supporters of the Tribunal found it difficult to believe recent acquittals resulted from the neutral application of legal precedent. Instead, many

---

[413] Prosecutor v. Perišić, Case No. IT-04-81-T, Trial Judgment (Int'l Crim. Trib. for the Former Yugoslavia Sept. 6, 2011). Perišić was also convicted of aiding and abetting crimes committed in Zagreb, Croatia, and of superior responsibility for failing to punish certain war crimes and crimes against humanity in Zagreb.

[414] ICTY, Press Release, *Tribunal Convicts Momčilo Perišić for Crimes in Bosnia and Herzegovina and Croatia* (Sept. 6, 2011); J. David Goodman, *Serbian Official Convicted of War Crimes*, N.Y. Times (Sept. 6, 2011); *Serbian General Perišić Jailed for 27 Years at Hague*, BBC News (Sept. 11, 2011). Even so, some Bosnians victims expressed disappointment in the Trial Chamber's failure to impose a life sentence and its acquittal of Perišić on certain charges. *See* Rachel Irwin, *Perišić First Belgrade Official Convicted for Bosnia Crimes*, IWPR (Sept. 12, 2011).

[415] Prosecutor v. Perišić, Case No. IT-04-81-A, Appeal Judgment (Int'l Crim. Trib. for the Former Yugoslavia Feb. 28, 2013).

[416] Ognjen Zorić & Dženana Karabegović, *Serbian Relief at Perišić Ruling*, IWPR (Mar. 4, 2013). Memišević is identified in this article as the "head of the Society for Threatened Peoples in Bosnia."

[417] *Id.* Mehmedović is president of the Association of Srebrenica Mothers.

[418] *Id.*

[419] Christophe Solioz & Srđa Pavlović, *Requiem for a Court*, Open Democracy (Mar. 5, 2013). A *Sense* commentary averred that the judgment "only strengthened the public's deep-rooted skepticism and contempt towards the Tribunal, providing fresh fodder for scornful comments at the Tribunal's expense." *Specific Direction of Appeals Chamber's Latest Judgments*, Sense News Agency (Mar. 6, 2013).

[420] Solioz & Pavlović, *supra* note 419.

could not "ignore what appear to be obvious political motives" behind the spate of acquittals.[421]

If, as some suggested, the Tribunal was rendering politically-motivated judgments, what did they suppose judges' motives to be? In one view, "the powers behind the bench" thought the time had come to distribute among the former belligerents equal measures of relief from accountability—in short, to "forgive, forget, and close the court files on the wars in the former Yugoslavia."[422] Jasna Bakšić Muftić offered a variation on this theme: "By the end of the whole process, sometimes I do believe that they calculate, you know, in the political way . . . to make the ethnic justice"—that is, to achieve "a certain balance" in the ethnic representation of those acquitted.[423] A related view holds that the Tribunal "wanted to show that it was not 'entirely anti Serb.' "[424]

Another view placed Perišić's acquittal in the same column as Gotovina's: the ICTY Appeals Chamber was increasingly mindful of how its precedents might affect military officials who command Western armies.[425] In the *Gotovina* case, this meant rejecting the 200-meter test, which even well-trained armies might find challenging to satisfy despite best efforts to comply with international humanitarian law. In *Perišić*, it meant tightening the test for accessorial liability. Briefly, the *Perišić* majority held that, at least when a suspect is "remote" from the crimes he allegedly assisted, he cannot be convicted of aiding and abetting those crimes even when his assistance was extensive, and (by implication) even when the murderous conduct of those he assisted was well known and continuous, absent proof his assistance was "specifically directed" to the crimes themselves rather than, say, toward the perpetrators' general prosecution of war aims.[426]

---

[421] Hodžić, *supra* note 9.

[422] Solioz & Pavlović, *supra* note 419.

[423] Interview with Jasna Bakšić Muftić, Professor, Faculty of Law, University of Sarajevo, in Sarajevo, Bosn. & Herz. (Sept. 17, 2014). Professor Bakšić Muftić thought this dynamic was at play in the Tribunal's acquittals of Gotovina-Markač and Stanišić-Simatović, the latter of which is noted below.

A commentary published after Perišić's acquittal noted another "common explanation":

> Perišić was acquitted because he was "America's man" and the CIA "takes care of its minions". It was therefore no wonder that he was acquitted by the Appeals Chamber presided [over] by an "American judge" [i.e., Theodor Meron]. In Serbia, Perišić was suspected of delivering confidential military documents to an American diplomat but the case was dropped when Perišić surrendered to the Tribunal.

Specific Direction of Appeals Chamber's Latest Judgments, SENSE NEWS AGENCY (Mar. 6, 2013).

[424] *Specific Direction of Appeals Chamber's Latest Judgments*, *supra* note 423.

[425] *See The Yugoslav Tribunal Shuts Down, a Kosovo Tribunal Starts Up*, ECONOMIST (Jan. 14, 2017).

[426] *See* Prosecutor v. Perišić, Case No. IT-04-81-A, Appeal Judgment, ¶¶ 25–40 (Int'l Crim. Trib. for the Former Yugoslavia Feb. 28, 2013). The majority elaborated:

> [I]n most cases, the provision of general assistance which could be used for both lawful and unlawful activities will not be sufficient, alone, to prove that this aid was specifically directed to crimes of principal perpetrators. In such circumstances, in order to enter a conviction for aiding and abetting, evidence establishing a direct link between the aid provided by an accused individual and the relevant crimes committed by principal perpetrators is necessary.

Id. ¶ 44. In the jargon of criminal law, the "specific direction" requirement was part of the actus reus—the conduct requirement, as distinct from the mens rea, or mental element—of liability

In a decision later reversed, an ICTY trial chamber rendered another stunning acquittal on May 30, 2013, following the three-year trial of Jovica Stanišić and Franko ("Frenki") Simatović. As reported in advance of the verdict, a conviction of the two "could provide the crucial link legally tying many war crimes in Bosnia and Croatia to the Serbian state."[427] During the 1990s conflicts, Stanišić served as chief of the Serbian Interior Ministry's State Security Service and Simatović as commander of that service's Special Operations Unit. In these capacities, the two "had the largest hand in creating, training, arming, financing and directing" some of the most notorious paramilitary groups responsible for ethnic cleansing in Bosnia and Croatia.[428] While confirming their roles in damning detail, the Trial Chamber acquitted the two in a 2-1 judgment, which the *New York Times* described as "one of the most surprising verdicts" of the ICTY's by then "checkered prosecution of Balkan war crimes."[429] The acquittal turned in part on application of the "specific direction" test set forth in the Appeals Chamber's judgment in *Perišić*, which the majority believed it was bound to follow. Applied in the *Stanišić/Simatović* case, the result was a verdict that reads as a road map for how to organize, train, and finance brutal paramilitaries and get away with it.

Now, commentators outside as well as in former Yugoslav states speculated that judges restrictively applied the "specific direction" test to avoid a legal precedent that could imperil military officials from their own countries who assist armed forces elsewhere.[430] Eric Gordy wrote: "[N]o conspiracy is needed to explain that judges represent the states that nominated them to the tribunal. . . . To an outside observer it looks as though the [ICTY] was on its way to establishing groundbreaking precedent, saw what this implied, and jumped backward."[431]

---

for aiding and abetting a crime. Some commentators defended this approach as a reasonable interpretation of previous jurisprudence, or at least as desirable on policy grounds. *See* Bogdan Ivanišević, *Falling Out of Love with the Hague Tribunal*, BALKAN TRANSITIONAL JUST. (June 11, 2013); Kevin Jon Heller, *Why the ICTY's "Specifically Directed" Requirement Is Justified*, OPINIO JURIS (June 2, 2013). Other legal experts condemned the *Perišić* appeals judgment as a marked departure from precedent. In their assessment, while some ICTY cases had made reference to "specific direction," the concept had not played a significant part in prior jurisprudence. *See, e.g.*, James G. Stewart, *Guest Post: The ICTY Loses Its Way on Complicity—Part 1*, OPINIO JURIS (Apr. 3, 2013); Kenneth Roth, *A Tribunal's Legal Stumble*, N.Y. TIMES (July 9, 2013). Instead, the Tribunal had generally found the actus reus element of accessorial responsibility satisfied when a defendant provided practical assistance, encouragement, or moral support that had a substantial or significant effect on the direct perpetrator's commission of the relevant crime. *See, e.g.*, Prosecutor v. Orić, Case No. IT-03-68-T, Trial Judgment, ¶ 284 (Int'l Crim. Trib. for the Former Yugoslavia June 30, 2006); Prosecutor v. Blagojević et al., Case No. IT-02-60-T, Trial Judgment, ¶ 726 (Int'l Crim. Trib. for the Former Yugoslavia Jan. 17, 2005); Prosecutor v. Furundžija, Case No. IT-95-17/1-T, Trial Judgment, ¶ 249 (Int'l Crim. Trib. for the Former Yugoslavia Dec. 10, 1998).

[427] Marlise Simons, *Verdicts Expected Soon for 2 Milošević Agents*, N.Y. TIMES (May 26, 2013).

[428] Eric Gordy, Opinion, *What Happened to the Hague Tribunal?*, N.Y. TIMES (June 2, 2013).

[429] Marlise Simons, *U.N. Court Acquits 2 Serbs of War Crimes*, N.Y. TIMES (May 31, 2013).

[430] For example, speculating about motives behind the *Perišić* appeals judgment, Kenneth Roth told journalist David Rohde: "My guess is that the tribunal was trying to narrow the concept of aiding and abetting to avoid far right fears in the United States that U.S. military aid would lead to criminal liability if the recipients unexpectedly committed war crimes." David Rohde, *How International Justice Is Being Gutted*, ATLANTIC (July 14, 2013).

[431] Gordy, *supra* note 428. Not everyone thought such concerns improper; Kevin Jon Heller defended the "specific direction" test precisely because it offered protection to states, like the United Kingdom and United States, that might assist rebel forces combatting brutal dictators

Whether one sees merit or malice in the majority's approach, what was widely (though not universally) seen as a departure from the ICTY's previous caselaw, coming on the heels of the Tribunal's unexpected acquittal of Gotovina and Markač, "jettisoned" the court's legacy—or so it seemed at the time.[432] Prijedor native Refik Hodžić warned that its late-life acquittals "will have a serious and irreparable effect."[433]

At that moment, it was hard to imagine confidence in the ICTY sinking any lower. But two weeks after the *Stanišić/Simatović* verdict, a "bombshell"[434] further tarnished its credibility. Danish media published a "private" letter from ICTY judge Frederick Harhoff to "56 contacts" sharing concerns about Appeals Chamber decisions starting with *Gotovina*. Criticizing recent judgments that "suddenly back-tracked" on previous ICTY jurisprudence, Harhoff implied American and Israeli pressure was behind the judicial retrenchment:

> You would think that the military establishment in leading states (such as USA and Israel) felt that the courts in practice were getting too close to the military commanders' responsibilities. . . . In other words: The court was heading too far in the direction of commanding officers being held responsible for every crime their subordinates committed.[435]

Raising the question of "*how* this military logic pressures the international justice system," Harhoff speculated that then ICTY president Theodor Meron, a naturalized American who once served in the Israeli Foreign Ministry, played a key role:

> Have any American or Israeli officials ever exerted pressure on the American presiding judge (the presiding judge for the court that is) to ensure a change of direction? We probably will never know. But reports of the same American presiding judge's tenacious pressure on his colleagues in the Gotovina-Perišić case makes you think he was determined to achieve an acquittal . . .[436]

Harhoff's speculation about American-Israeli influence was just that. But in the eyes of many Bosnians, it was the proverbial smoking gun, proving the Tribunal

---

elsewhere. Even though their assistance had salutary aims, Heller argued, the rebels would inevitably commit war crimes. Heller, *supra* note 426.

[432] Gordy, *supra* note 428.

[433] Tim Judah, *Why Are Balkan War-Crimes Convictions Getting Overturned?*, BLOOMBERG (June 6, 2013).

[434] *"Bombshell" at the Tribunal*, SENSE NEWS AGENCY (June 12, 2013). *See also* Marlise Simons, *Judge at War Crimes Tribunal Faults Acquittals of Serb and Croat Commanders*, N.Y. TIMES (June 15, 2013).

[435] E-mail from Frederik Harhoff, Ad Litem Judge, ICTY, to 56 Contacts (June 6, 2013), http://a.bimg.dk/node-files/511/6/6511917-letter-english.pdf.

[436] *Id.* Further to this same theme, after referring to the "specific direction" requirement (in terms of "demanding a *direct intention* to commit crime"), Harhoff wrote:

> Most of the cases will lead to commanding officers walking free from here on. So the American (and Israeli) military leaders can breathe a sigh of relief. . . . I am sitting here with a very uncomfortable feeling that the court has changed the direction [because] of pressure from "the military establishments" in certain dominant countries.

Id.

was a political court, as Serb nationalists had long charged. Although Dženana Karup Druško said she still considered the ICTY "invaluable, just priceless," she lamented: "Unfortunately, now we're seeing a reversal" of its judicial legacy, characterized by "politically-aligned rulings." Already "suspicious" such a trend was emerging, Karup Druško believes Harhoff "confirmed" it.[437]

Although widespread, this view was not universal among those I interviewed in 2014. For example Štefica Galić told me the principal inference she drew from Gotovina's acquittal was that the "indictments were pretty weak."[438] Another Bosnian implicitly endorsed the view that ICTY judges are responsive to broader political developments but found nothing sinister in this: "I always understood that courts, yeah, come from the political side . . . , so courts are not divine products. I mean, they exist in certain political circumstances." She continued: "I'm just saying that [courts like the ICTY] are humanly constructed in political and social circumstances, and . . . those circumstances were different at the time [the ICTY] was created to the circumstances of the world today."[439]

More recent judgments offered grounds for renewed confidence in the Tribunal, moving its jurisprudence on aiding and abetting closer to its previous approach.[440] In its judgment in the Šainović case, a four-judge majority of the five-person Appeals Chamber "unequivocally reject[ed]" the specific direction test elucidated in the Perišić Appeal Judgment.[441] In two subsequent judgments, the Appeals Chamber followed its approach in Šainović rather than Perišić.[442] One of those judgments reversed the acquittal of Jovica Stanišić and Franko Simatović, in part because the Trial Chamber had improperly applied the specific direction test,[443] and ordered a new trial. As the retrial began before the MICT (the residual mechanism for the ICTY and ICTR) on June 13, 2017, the New York Times foreshadowed its potential place in the Tribunal's legacy: "The fate of Mr. Stanišić and Mr. Simatović will be crucial in legally determining the role of the Serbian state in the wars in Bosnia and Croatia that killed more than 130,000 people."[444]

---

[437] Interview with Dženana Karup Druško, Transitional Justice, Accountability and Remembrance, in Sarajevo, Bosn. & Herz. (Sept. 8, 2014). An organization with which Karup Druško is affiliated, Journalists of Bosnia and Herzegovina, joined with several other organizations in writing to the United Nations to ask the Secretary-General to investigate "the role of Meron, based on the allegations that Harhoff expressed in his letter." Bonora, supra note 381.

[438] Interview with Štefica Galić, Editor, Tačno.net, in Mostar, Bosn. & Herz. (Sept. 10, 2014).

[439] Confidential interview, in Sarajevo, Bosn. & Herz. (Sept. 2014).

[440] See Leila Nadya Sadat, Can the ICTY Šainović and Perišić Cases Be Reconciled?, 108 Am. J. Int'l L. 475, 483 (2014).

[441] Prosecutor v. Šainović et al., Case No. IT-05-87-A, Appeal Judgment, ¶ 1650 (Int'l Crim. Trib. for the Former Yugoslavia Jan. 23, 2014). In its view, that approach was "in direct and material conflict with the prevailing jurisprudence on the actus reus of aiding and abetting liability and with customary international law in this regard." Id. See also id. ¶ 1663. Notably, one of the dissenters in Perišić, Judge Fausto Pocar, wrote the majority opinion in Šainović.

[442] The first was Prosecutor v. Popović et al., Cases No. IT-05-88-A, Appeal Judgment, ¶ 1758 (Int'l Crim. Trib. for the Former Yugoslavia Jan. 30, 2015).

[443] Prosecutor v. Stanišić et al., Case No. IT-03-69-A, Appeal Judgment, ¶¶ 106, 108 (Int'l Crim. Trib. for the Former Yugoslavia Dec. 9, 2015). Three of the five judges on this appeals panel supported the majority ruling on "specific direction."

[444] Marlise Simons, Retrial Begins for 2 Serbs at U.N. War Crimes Tribunal, N.Y. Times (June 13, 2017).

c. Trial Chamber's Acquittal of Vojislav Šešelj

This is the lowest point of the Hague Tribunal.

—SENAD PEĆANIN[445]

As we have seen, gross mismanagement of the Šešelj trial was widely considered a "profound embarrassment" for the Tribunal.[446] Thus, while many hoped the verdict would redeem the case, few expected a satisfactory conclusion.[447] Even so, the March 31, 2016, acquittal of Šešelj on all counts by a 2-1 decision was stunning,[448] and not just because of the fact of his acquittal. Much of the Trial Chamber's reasoning appeared "so far-fetched," in the words of the *Economist*, "that it defies belief."[449]

Despite statements by the defendant along the lines "not a single [Croat] should leave Vukovar [Croatia] alive," the majority deemed the ideology of "Greater Serbia" espoused by Šešelj to be "in principle a political plan, not a criminal one."[450] The defendant was merely "lifting his troops' morale" when he ordered Serb forces to "spare no one" in Vukovar.[451] The majority interpreted Šešelj's call to "cleanse Bosnia of Muslims" as merely "galvanizing the Serb forces."[452] Buses organized to deport non-Serbs from Vukovar were a "humanitarian gesture by Serb paramilitaries."[453] As Marko Milanović noted, the majority's conclusions in a "comprehensively bad judgment" were "at odds with literally dozens of previous [ICTY] judgments."[454]

Bosnians denounced the "absolutely shocking decision," which Senad Pećanin called "the lowest point of the Hague Tribunal."[455] Bosnian Croats and Muslims saw the acquittal as "a humiliation of the victims and the continuation of their suffering, but now in The Hague."[456] And yet, Mervan Miraščija noted, denunciations of Hague verdicts by victims associations and other civil society actors have generally been short-lived. In his view, one reason is Bosnians had grown accustomed to disappointing verdicts from the Hague Tribunal. "In addition," Miraščija said, "I think it's been so much time since the war ended. People are facing everyday problems and

---

[445] *Croatia Shocked as UN Court Acquits Serb Nationalist Šešelj*, TRIB. NEWS SERVS. (Mar. 31, 2016) (quoting Senad Pećanin).

[446] Marlise Simons, *Tribunal Acquits Serbian Nationalist of War Crimes*, N.Y. TIMES (Apr. 1, 2016).

[447] *See, e.g.*, Gordy, *supra* note 273.

[448] *See* Jelena Subotić, *How Šešelj's Verdict Got History Terribly Wrong*, BALKAN TRANSITIONAL JUST. (Apr. 1, 2016); *Croatia Shocked as UN Court Acquits Serb Nationalist Šešelj, supra* note 445; *Vojislav Šešelj's Acquittal Is a Victory for Advocates of Ethnic Cleansing*, ECONOMIST (Mar. 31, 2016); Neil Buckley, *Karadžić and Šešelj Decisions Risk Reputation of ICTY*, FIN. TIMES (Apr. 1, 2016); Tena Prelec, *Will the ICTY's Acquittal of Vojislav Šešelj Heighten Tensions in the Balkans?*, EUR. WESTERN BALKANS (May 19, 2016).

[449] *Vojislav Šešelj's Acquittal Is a Victory for Advocates of Ethnic Cleansing, supra* note 448.

[450] *See* Prelec, *supra* note 448.

[451] Subotić, *supra* note 448.

[452] *See id.*

[453] Garret Tankosić-Kelly, *War Crimes Tribunal Still Invaluable Despite Šešelj Ruling*," IRISH TIMES (Apr. 6, 2016).

[454] Marko Milanović, *The Sorry Acquittal of Vojislav Šešelj*, EJIL TALK! (Apr. 4, 2016).

[455] *Croatia Shocked as UN Court Acquits Serb Nationalist Šešelj, supra note 445* (quoting Senad Pećanin). *See also* Gordana Knezević, *The Long Shadow of the Šešelj Verdict*, RFE/RL (Apr. 7, 2016) (describing Tuzla war veterans' bitter denunciation of the Šešelj verdict).

[456] Email from Mervan Miraščija, Law Program Coordinator, Open Society Fund BiH, to Diane Orentlicher (Apr. 4, 2016).

injustices, and they're tired of waiting [for] international and national courts to end the war crimes trials."[457]

Even so—perhaps in part *because* of mounting frustrations—many Bosnians, like Mirsada Malagić, derived profound satisfaction from the Tribunal's final trial verdict. Malagić, who lost her husband, two sons, and other relatives during the war, was a witness in the trial of Ratko Mladić. The day he was convicted and sentenced to life in prison, Malagić responded this way when asked if the Tribunal had made any difference in the lives of survivors: "It is good that the Hague Tribunal exists. . . . [T]he killing of so many people has been proven. They were sentenced. Just enough for us to get some peace in our souls. Just that much."[458]

III. CONCLUDING OBSERVATIONS

In light of myriad and substantial disappointments in the ICTY's performance, it is notable that many Bosnians continued to affirm the importance of its existence long after their early expectations were upended. In a typical exchange during my last set of research interviews, I asked Mirsad Duratović, by then gravely dissatisfied with the ICTY's performance, if he still believed—as he had when we spoke in 2006—that it was good the Tribunal was created. Without hesitating, he replied: "It's far from being not good. It is of course very good that the Tribunal was formed."[459] Emir Suljagić railed against the Tribunal's "failures" when we spoke in 2014, but when I asked if he now believed it should not have been established, Suljagić did not hesitate: "Ah, it should have been established, that's not an issue." If it did not solve a raft of problems many once thought it would, the ICTY "provided a modicum of justice."[460] Many still believed, in the words of Prijedor native Refik Hodžić, that the Tribunal remained "the best thing that happened to the people of the former Yugoslavia since 1991."[461]

---

[457] *Id.*

[458] *News Hour*, BBC WORLD SERVICE (Nov. 22, 2017), http://www.bbc.co.uk/programmes/w172vr1h1kzbc88 (last visited Dec. 6, 2017).

[459] Interview with Mirsad Duratović, Chairman, Prijedor '92, in Prijedor, Bosn. & Herz. (Sept. 16, 2014).

[460] Interview with Emir Suljagić, Author, in Sarajevo, Bosn. & Herz. (Sept. 11, 2014).

[461] Hodžić, *supra* note 9.

PART FOUR

Impact on Acknowledgment

7

Denial and Acknowledgment in Serbia

For the collective, as for the individual, "coming to terms with the past" is to know (and admit to knowing) exactly what happened.

—Stanley Cohen[1]

I would say that ICTY contributed greatly to the establishment of truth, however not enough, primarily because its facts were never accepted and acknowledged here in the region.

—Marijana Toma[2]

In his masterful meditation on "the question of German guilt," Karl Jaspers condemned the idea that a "whole people" could bear criminal guilt,[3] and insisted as well that moral guilt can only ever be personal.[4] In his words, "The categorical judgment of a people is always unjust," resulting "in the debasement of the human being as an individual."[5] Jaspers nonetheless implored his fellow Germans to explore questions of "German guilt"—to "analyze, judge and cleanse" themselves—in the dialogue of fellow citizens, not solely in the silence of private conscience.[6]

The questions Jaspers probed were rooted in the singular experience of postwar Germany. But his call for communal reckoning with the malevolence of a prior regime has reverberated across decades and regions. In much the same spirit as Jaspers' appeal for collective engagement with Germany's immediate past, a committed corps of citizens has pressed Serbian society to "address the past."

---

[1] Stanley Cohen, States of Denial: Knowing About Atrocities and Suffering 222 (2001).
[2] Interview with Marijana Toma, then Deputy Director, Humanitarian Law Center, in Belgrade, Serb. (June 10, 2014).
[3] Karl Jaspers, The Question of German Guilt 34 (E.B. Ashton trans., 2000) (1947).
[4] *Id.* at 34–35.
[5] *Id.* at 35.
[6] *Id.* at 43.

As elaborated in Chapter 5, for these Serbians, addressing the past has myriad dimensions, whose core elements sift down to ensuring: (1) Serbian citizens know about and accept as true the full extent of Serb perpetrators' and Serbian state institutions' responsibility for wartime atrocities; (2) Serbia's society and government publicly acknowledge and condemn without equivocation crimes committed by Serbs as well as Serbia's role in those crimes, the latter in recognition of what Jaspers would have called *political guilt*;[7] and (3) Serbia undertake appropriate gestures of penance and redress.

A commitment to these goals does not inexorably translate into support for the ICTY.[8] But in interviews with Serbians who support the Tribunal, many emphasized they hoped its work would educate Serbians about the full extent of atrocities committed by Serbs and underwritten by Serbia, which had been occluded by discourses of denial. Serbian activist Nataša Kandić has made the point this way:

> If attempts at rewriting history, such as the denial in Germany of the Holocaust, are to be prevented, the courts must do everything possible to bring out the truth. In this context, one of the tasks for the [ICTY] is to put an end to the practice of the successor states of the former Yugoslavia of passing over in silence or denying atrocities, or persistently broadcasting their distorted and biased versions of the past . . .[9]

Taking these Serbians' aspirations as its point of departure, this chapter assesses the degree to which their hopes have been met. As a baseline for assessment, the first section notes key facts relating to ethnic Serbs' and Serbia's responsibility for wartime atrocities. The chapter next explores Serbian citizens' evolving beliefs about those atrocities, drawing on periodic public opinion surveys. The chapter separately explores the degree to which Serbian officials and state institutions have acknowledged and expressed remorse for atrocities committed by Serbs and for Serbia's role underwriting their conduct.

---

[7] In Jaspers' lexicon of guilt, political guilt involves "the deeds of statesmen and of the citizenry of a state," and "results in my having to bear the consequences of the deeds of the state whose power governs me and under whose order I live." JASPERS, *supra* note 3, at 25. Although political guilt is collective, Jaspers recognized the interconnectedness of (individual) moral guilt and (collective) political guilt. *See id.* at 27. In his words, moral failings "cause the conditions out of which both crime and political guilt arise. The commission of countless little acts of negligence, of convenient adaptation, of cheap vindication, and the imperceptible promotion of wrong; the participation in the creation of a public atmosphere that spreads confusion and thus makes evil possible—all that has consequences that partly condition the political guilt involved in the situation and the events." *Id.* at 28.

The notion that Serbian citizens should acknowledge and condemn crimes committed by ethnic Serbs corresponds to two scholars' definition of acknowledgment as "a conscious and public acceptance that the in-group's actions have violated some important moral precepts . . . In other words, acknowledgment refers to a psychological readiness to publicly *accept the meaning* of the in-group's immoral behavior." Sabina Čehajić & Rupert Brown, *Silencing the Past: Effects of Intergroup Contact on Acknowledgment of In-Group Responsibility*, 1 SOC. PSYCHOL. & PERSONALITY SCI. 190, 191 (2010) [hereinafter Čehajić & Brown, *Silencing the Past*].

[8] Conversely, as one of my interlocutors insisted, anti-ICTY views should not be equated with "total denial." Interview with Radmila Nakarada, then Associate Professor, Faculty of Political Sciences, University of Belgrade, in Belgrade, Serb. (Nov. 24, 2006).

[9] Nataša Kandić, *The ICTY Trials and Transitional Justice in Former Yugoslavia*, 38 CORNELL INT'L L.J. 789, 789 (2005).

As will be seen, the ICTY has not had the transformative impact on citizens' beliefs or official acknowledgment many of its Serbian supporters hoped it would have. At least for a time, however, its work likely contributed to incremental progress in Serbian citizens' awareness of and readiness to acknowledge Serb atrocities. Indirectly, it may also have played a part in a series of official apologies for Serb atrocities.

Together, insights derived from interviews in Serbia, social science research, and experience in other countries provide a compelling account of why judgments rendered in The Hague have failed to persuade most Serbians to acknowledge the full extent of Serb atrocities and condemn them without equivocation. Beyond explaining the Serbian experience to date, this account illuminates conditions in which any international criminal tribunal (ICT) can reasonably be expected to shape a society's beliefs.

I. SERBIAN CITIZENS' AWARENESS AND ACKNOWLEDGMENT OF CRIMES COMMITTED BY SERBS AND THE ROLE OF SERBIAN INSTITUTIONS

A. What Might We Expect Serbian Citizens to Know and Acknowledge?

As a foundation for evaluating Serbian citizens' awareness and acceptance of information concerning Serb atrocities, it is necessary to recall fundamental facts they should, in the view of Serbians pressing for acknowledgment, be expected to know, acknowledge, and condemn. Three broad categories loomed large in my interviews with Serbians. First is the scale and nature of atrocities committed by ethnic Serbs against members of other groups during the conflicts of the 1990s. Second, and closely related to the first, is the scale of wartime atrocities perpetrated by Serbs *relative to those committed by members of other groups*. Third is the role of Serbian state institutions in sponsoring war crimes committed by ethnic Serbs.[10] To focus this inquiry, the following summary of relevant facts is limited to patterns in Bosnia, which experienced the highest levels of wartime atrocities.

Data developed by the Research and Documentation Center of Sarajevo (RDC), which has undertaken the most meticulous accounting of wartime deaths in Bosnia, provide a basic sense of the first two categories. Although the Center does not try to establish who was the victim of a war crime, which entails a legal assessment, it documents civilians who died or disappeared during the 1990s conflict—a rough proxy for victims of wartime atrocities.[11] The overwhelming number of civilians who died or disappeared during the conflict (approximately 83 percent) were Bosniak.[12]

---

[10] These points are developed in Chapter 4. I use the phrase *war crimes* here as a shorthand for international crimes, including genocide and crimes against humanity as well as violations of international humanitarian law.

[11] The picture is rough because, under the laws of war, not all civilian killings are war crimes and some killings of combatants are.

[12] Daria Sito-Sučić & Matt Robinson, *After Years of Toil, Book Names Bosnian War Dead*, REUTERS (Feb. 15, 2013). The database includes 96,895 wartime casualties (wartime killings and disappearances), of which approximately two-thirds (64,003) were Bosniak and roughly one-quarter (24,826) were Serb. This figure does not reflect the total number who might have

These figures hardly represent the whole picture of war crimes committed during the conflict. For example, they do not measure instances of sexual violence, which was committed on a vast scale.[13] They nonetheless provide a basis for assessing the degree to which Serbian citizens' perceptions of relative victimization in Bosnia correspond to well-established facts.[14]

The RDC did not compile data on those *responsible* for wartime casualties.[15] While hardly a precise or uncontested measure, the ICTY's charging distribution is generally in line with patterns one would expect to find based on the RDC's data on civilian casualties and the nature of ethnic conflict in Bosnia—in particular, which ethnic groups were engaged in conflict with each other. Two-thirds of those indicted by the Tribunal were ethnic Serbs, 21.1 percent were ethnic Croats, 5.5 percent were Bosniaks, 5 percent were Kosovo Albanians, 1.2 percent were ethnic Macedonians, and 1.2 percent were ethnic Montenegrins.[16]

As previously noted, Serbian citizens who supported the ICTY were also "trying to establish accountability and responsibility [for wartime atrocities] on the level of Serbian authorities," and hoped the Tribunal would help ensure this.[17] Nataša Kandić, for decades Serbia's most prominent champion of the Hague Tribunal, explained why she thought it essential to prosecute Serbian officials: "Without Serbian state security leaders, . . . it was impossible to create the war strategy" that produced so many atrocities.[18]

It is difficult to provide an overview of key facts concerning Serbia's role that is both concise and uncontroversial.[19] In terms of general context, those facts include a sharp turn in the late 1980s toward Serb nationalism within the SFRY leadership, in which Slobodan Milošević played a pivotal part, which ignited developments culminating in ruinous wars of secession. Milošević's recourse to nationalist rhetoric

---

been killed, but instead a more conservative number of those whose death or disappearance was verified in accordance with the Center's methodology. Roughly 80 percent (20,000) of the 24,826 Serbs killed in Bosnia were soldiers and another 661 were police. *See* Patrick Ball et al., The Bosnian Book of Dead: Assessment of the Database 4 (2007).

[13] At least 20,000 women were raped or sexually abused in seventy-three municipalities in Bosnia during the conflict there. *See* Denis Džidić, *"20,000 Women Sexually Assaulted" During Bosnian War*, Balkan Insight (Sept. 29, 2015). This figure may well substantially underestimate the number of victims of sexual violence. *See* Amnesty International, "We Need Support, Not Pity": Last Chance for Justice for Bosnia's Wartime Rape Survivors 16 n.10 (2017).

[14] A substantial majority of ICTY prosecutions involved atrocities in Bosnia, reflecting the fact that civilian casualties there far surpassed those in Croatia and Kosovo.

[15] *See* Ball et al., *supra* note 12, at 32.

[16] These figures are based on research by Alanna Kennedy, then a student at the Washington College of Law.

[17] Interview with Maja Mičić, then Executive Director, Youth Initiative for Human Rights, in Belgrade, Serb. (June 11, 2014).

[18] Interview with Nataša Kandić, Former Executive Director, Humanitarian Law Center, in Belgrade, Serb. (June 8, 2014). *See also* Natasha Kandić, *The Shame of Serbia*, N.Y. Times (June 6, 2011) (expressing concern about Serbian efforts to dissociate the state from the Srebrenica genocide). As noted below, despite her long-standing support, Kandić became highly critical of the Tribunal in light of a series of controversial judgments rendered in its final years.

[19] As Timothy William Waters aptly notes, "There is little about the history of Yugoslavia, its dissolution, or the violence that followed that is uncontested, and the prospects of saying something both meaningful and uncontroversial are vanishingly small." Timothy William Waters, *The Context, Contested: Histories of Yugoslavia and Its Violent Dissolution*, in The Milošević Trial: An Autopsy 3, 3 (Timothy William Waters ed., 2013).

was accompanied by a steady recentralization of authority in the SFRY, which in turn "had destabilizing consequences" for the country.[20] During this period, Milošević came to dominate the Yugoslav National Army (JNA), which became "an instrument of specifically Serb interests."[21] As the SFRY disintegrated, the JNA (and, later, its successor, the Army of Yugoslavia, or VJ) provided substantial and direct support to Serb militias in Croatia and Bosnia, whose atrocities have been the subject of numerous ICTY prosecutions. Paramilitary units responsible for infamous atrocities in Bosnia were directly incorporated in Serbian security services.[22]

Much of the discussion that follows assesses the degree to which the ICTY's work has influenced Serbian acknowledgment of facts falling into the first two categories noted earlier, relating to (1) the scale and nature of atrocities committed by ethnic Serbs, and (2) the scale of Serb atrocities relative to those committed by members of other ethnic groups. With respect to the third category, involving the nature of Serbian state institutions' support for Serb atrocities, the ICTY's own performance has disappointed the expectations of Serbians who have pressed for acknowledgment. At the time I conducted final research interviews in Serbia and wrote this book, the ICTY had not imposed a final judgment convicting *Serbian* officials for the roles they played in relation to atrocities in Bosnia.[23] While its verdicts in several cases nonetheless include richly detailed accounts of Serbian support for murderous paramilitaries in Bosnia, former Yugoslav citizens often perceive ICTY judgments in reductionist terms: if a Serbian official is acquitted based on insufficient evidence of his own guilt, the Tribunal in effect absolved Serbia of responsibility.[24]

---

[20] *Id.* at 15–16.

[21] *Id.* at 16.

[22] *Id.* at 17–23.

[23] In December 2015, the ICTY Appeals Chamber reversed a Trial Chamber's acquittal of two Serbian officials who provided extensive support for Bosnian Serb forces, and ordered a retrial. Prosecutor v. Stanišić et al., Case No. IT-03-69-A, Appeal Judgment (Int'l Crim. Trib. for the Former Yugoslavia Dec. 9, 2015). The two suspects' retrial before the ICTY's residual body, the Mechanism for International Criminal Tribunals (MICT), began on June 13, 2017. *See* Marlise Simons, *Retrial Begins for 2 Serbs at U.N. War Crimes Tribunal*, N.Y. Times (June 13, 2017). Thus, at the time this book was written, it remained possible the MICT would convict at least these former officials for their roles in sponsoring atrocities in Bosnia.

The ICTY has entered final judgments convicting several JNA officers of war crimes committed in Croatia. *See, e.g.*, Prosecutor v. Mrkšić et al., Case No. IT-95-13/1-T, Trial Judgment (Int'l Crim. Trib. for the Former Yugoslavia Sept. 27, 2007); Prosecutor v. Mrkšić et. al., Case No. IT-95-13/1-A, Appeal Judgment (Int'l Crim. Trib. for the Former Yugoslavia May 5, 2009); Prosecutor v. Jokić, Case No. IT-01-42/1-S, Sentencing Judgment (Int'l Crim. Trib. for the Former Yugoslavia Mar. 18, 2004); Prosecutor v. Jokić, Case No. IT-01-42/1-A, Judgment on Sentencing Appeal (Int'l Crim. Trib. for the Former Yugoslavia Aug. 30, 2005); Prosecutor v. Strugar, Case No. IT-01-42-T, Trial Judgment (Int'l Crim. Trib. for the Former Yugoslavia Jan. 31, 2005); Prosecutor v. Strugar, Case No. IT-01-42-A, Appeal Judgment (Int'l Crim. Trib. for the Former Yugoslavia July 17, 2008).

[24] Characterizing local reactions to the acquittal of senior Serbian official Momčilo Perišić, for example, Marijana Toma said the judgment "means that Serbia didn't have anything to do with war in Bosnia" even though the verdict established extensive facts relating to Serbian support for Serb paramilitaries in Bosnia. Interview with Marijana Toma, then Deputy Director, Humanitarian Law Center, in Belgrade, Serb. (June 10, 2014).

In the wake of the ICTY's then recent acquittal of top Serbian security officials, Nataša Kandić rued what she believed was the aging Tribunal's new aim—"to remove state responsibility" from its judicial legacy.[25] For Maja Mičić, the Tribunal's failure to convict any Serbian defendants for atrocities in Bosnia raised the troubling prospect that Serbian society would "end up blaming everything on the Bosnian Serbs, . . . completely leaving Serbia as a state and state institutions out of the equation" for atrocities in Bosnia.[26]

B. Awareness of War Crimes as Reflected in Surveys

Public opinion surveys provide a notoriously imperfect way to gauge beliefs,[27] particularly when it comes to highly fraught subjects—as responsibility for wartime depredations surely is for much of the Serbian public.[28] Serbians' expressions of knowledge and belief about wartime atrocities, in public opinion surveys as in other contexts, often obscure the complex, contradictory, and ambivalent views many hold privately or communicate only within their most intimate circles,[29] as well as the diversity of views aggregated in each survey result.[30]

Noting a distinction between what Serbians believe about Serb atrocities and what they tell pollsters, Bogdan Ivanišević cautioned: "Many, many, many see themselves as having a mission when they are polled. The mission is, 'Don't acknowledge. Don't contribute anything that may be used eventually as an argument against the Serbs. . . . Don't add to the percentage that in another day, somebody will show and say, See, a great majority of Serbs do accept that [a specific incident] was a crime.'"[31]

Surveys administered periodically from 2001 through 2011 nonetheless provide important information. With relevant caveats about methodology,[32] they at least tell

---

[25] Interview with Nataša Kandić, Former Executive Director, Humanitarian Law Center, in Belgrade, Serb. (June 8, 2014). The acquittals faulted by Kandić are described in Chapter 6.

[26] Interview with Maja Mičić, then Executive Director, Youth Initiative for Human Rights, in Belgrade, Serb. (June 11, 2014).

[27] *See, e.g.*, Denis Chong & James N. Druckman, *Framing Theory*, 10 Ann. Rev. Pol. Sci. 103, 104 (2007) (even minor changes in the phrasing of a question in a public opinion survey can produce a large change in the surveyed population's responses).

[28] *See* Eric Gordy, Guilt, Responsibility and Denial: The Past at Stake in Post-Milošević Serbia 22 (2013); Diane Orentlicher, Review Essay: *From Viability to Impact: Evolving Metrics for Assessing the International Criminal Tribunal for the Former Yugoslavia*, 7 Int'l J. Transitional Just. 536 (2013). *See also* Jelena Obradović-Wochnik, *Knowledge, Acknowledgement and Denial in Serbia's Responses to the Srebrenica Massacre*, 17 J. Contemp. Eur. Stud. 61, 69 (2009) [hereinafter Obradović-Wochnik, *Srebrenica*] (war crimes "occupy contentious places in the psyche of private individuals in Serbia").

[29] *See* Jelena Obradović-Wochnik, Ethnic Conflict and War Crimes in the Balkans; The Narratives of Denial in Post-Conflict Serbia (2013) [hereinafter Obradović-Wochnik, Narratives of Denial].

[30] *See* Jelena Obradović-Wochnik, *The "Silent Dilemma" of Transitional Justice: Silencing and Coming to Terms with the Past in Serbia*, 7 Int'l J. Transitional Just. 328, 338 (2013) [hereinafter Obradović-Wochnik, *Silent Dilemma*].

[31] Interview with Bogdan Ivanišević, Attorney, in Belgrade, Serb. (July 9, 2012).

[32] Beyond those already noted, Ivan Jovanović, who worked for the OSCE Mission to Serbia when it sponsored or co-sponsored surveys undertaken in 2006, 2009, and 2011, cautioned that the methodology might not have been the same for all years the surveys were administered. Interview with

us what Serbian respondents were willing to *say* they knew and believed about wartime atrocities when asked by a professional survey organization at a time of political transition. Surveys addressing a wide range of war-crimes-related issues were administered from 2004 to 2011 by the Belgrade-based Strategic Marketing Research and, following its acquisition by Ipsos in 2008, Ipsos Strategic Marketing (hereafter collectively referred to as "Strategic Marketing") on behalf of a somewhat varying group of client organizations.[33] In addition, a survey administered by Strategic Marketing in 2001 on behalf of B92, a radio, television, and Internet broadcaster, included several questions on this subject.[34]

Among myriad issues relating to war crimes, these surveys tracked awareness of and beliefs about several well-documented episodes. Responses relating to two of them exemplify gaps between the "trial truth" established in The Hague and Serbian citizens' stated beliefs. One is the July 1995 massacre of an estimated 8,000 individuals in Srebrenica, Bosnia, which the ICTY has ruled a genocide.[35] The other is the siege of Sarajevo by Serb forces, which started in April 1992 and lasted over

---

Ivan Jovanović, then National Legal Advisor, OSCE Mission to Serbia, in Belgrade, Serb. (July 12, 2012).

[33] Surveys published in August 2004 and April 2005 were commissioned by the Belgrade Centre for Human Rights (BCHR). A survey published in December 2006 was commissioned by the Organization for Security and Co-operation in Europe (OSCE) Mission to Serbia and BCHR. The April 2009 survey was commissioned by the OSCE Mission to Serbia, and the final survey, published in October 2011, was commissioned by the OSCE Mission to Serbia and BCHR. The BCHR also commissioned a survey probing attitudes toward the ICTY in 2003. I do not discuss the 2003 survey because it did not ask questions about specific war crimes. In addition to surveys undertaken by Strategic Marketing, a number of scholars have undertaken attitudinal surveys in Serbia and other former Yugoslav countries that touch on war crimes issues. *See, e.g.,* SANJA KUTNJAK IVKOVIĆ & JOHN HAGAN, RECLAIMING JUSTICE: THE INTERNATIONAL TRIBUNAL FOR THE FORMER YUGOSLAVIA AND LOCAL COURTS (2011); JANINE NATALYA CLARK, INTERNATIONAL TRIALS AND RECONCILIATION: ASSESSING THE IMPACT OF THE INTERNATIONAL CRIMINAL TRIBUNAL FOR THE FORMER YUGOSLAVIA (2014) [hereinafter CLARK, INTERNATIONAL TRIALS AND RECONCILIATION].

[34] Perception of Truth in Serbia (abridged), SMMRI on behalf of B92 (2001) [hereinafter 2001 Survey].

[35] As of December 2017, the ICTY had rendered final convictions of five Bosnian Serbs on genocide-related charges in connection with Srebrenica, and two other genocide convictions of Bosnian Serbs at the trial level. Its first trial verdict finding that genocide was committed in Srebrenica was rendered in 2001. Prosecutor v. Krstić, Case No. IT-98-33-T, Trial Judgment, ¶¶ 599 (Int'l Crim. Trib. for the Former Yugoslavia Aug. 2, 2001). On April 19, 2004, the ICTY Appeals Chamber sustained the trial chamber's conclusion that the Srebrenica massacre met the legal definition of genocide. Prosecutor v. Krstić, Case No. IT-98-33-A, Appeal Judgment, ¶ 37 (Int'l Crim. Trib. for the Former Yugoslavia Apr. 19, 2004). In January 2015, the Appeals Chamber upheld the convictions of two Bosnian Serb officers on the charge (among others) of genocide itself—the first time it had done so (Krstić was convicted on appeal of aiding and abetting genocide). Prosecutor v. Popović et al., Case No. IT-05-88-A, Appeal Judgment, ¶¶ 472, 486, 494 (Int'l Crim. Trib. for the Former Yugoslavia Jan. 30, 2015). Later that year, the Appeals Chamber also sustained the conviction of Zdravko Tolimir on the charge (among others) of genocide in relation to Srebrenica. Prosecutor v. Tolimir, Case No. IT-05-88/2-A, Appeal Judgment, ¶ 648 (Int'l Crim. Trib. for the Former Yugoslavia Apr. 8, 2015). In March 2016, an ICTY trial chamber convicted Radovan Karadžić of genocide and other charges in connection with Srebrenica. Prosecutor v. Karadžić, Case No. IT-95-5/18-T, Trial Judgment, ¶ 6022, 6071 (Int'l Crim. Trib. for the Former Yugoslavia Mar. 24, 2016). Ratko Mladić was convicted of genocide in relation to Srebrenica in November 2017. Prosecutor v. Mladić, Case No. IT-09-92-T, Trial Judgment, ¶ 5188, 5191 (Int'l Crim. Trib. for the Former Yugoslavia Nov. 22, 2017).

three years, during which many citizens of Sarajevo were killed by Serb snipers.[36] Each survey asked whether respondents had heard of these and several other events, and if so, whether they believed the reported events actually happened. In addition, the surveys asked questions concerning the legal and moral meaning respondents ascribed to these crimes: respondents who said they believed what they had heard about an event were asked whether they thought what happened was "inevitable in the course of war or a war crime for which the perpetrators should answer."[37] With respect to Srebrenica, the last two surveys (in 2009 and 2011) also asked, "Do you think that murders of Bosniaks in Srebrenica are genocide?"[38]

The survey results confound the aspirations of those who hoped the ICTY's work would dispel Serbian denial.[39] Consider, for example, responses to a question concerning sniper deaths in Sarajevo, which show a sharp decline in reported awareness between the first survey year (92 percent in 2001)[40] and the next time the question was polled (68 percent in 2004), followed by a less steep overall decline between 2004 and 2011 (64 percent), the final year this survey was administered (Figure 7.1):[41]

---

[36] The surveys asked two sets of questions relating to the Sarajevo siege. One asked whether respondents had heard/believed that "Sarajevo was under siege for over 1,000 days"; the other asked whether they had heard/believed that "many civilians were killed by snipers in Sarajevo." The following discussion focuses on responses to the second set of questions.

Several individuals were prosecuted before the ICTY for crimes committed during the siege of Sarajevo. A landmark conviction was rendered in December 2003 in a case against Stanislav Galić, who was sentenced by the Trial Chamber to twenty years' imprisonment for his role in the siege. Prosecutor v. Galić, Case No. IT-98-29-T, Trial Judgment, ¶ 769 (Int'l Crim. Trib. for the Former Yugoslavia Dec. 5, 2003). The Appeals Chamber raised Galić's sentence to life in prison. Prosecutor v. Galić, Case No. IT-98-29-A, Appeal Judgment, 185 (Int'l Crim. Trib. for the Former Yugoslavia Nov. 30, 2006). A second major conviction relating to the Sarajevo siege was rendered in December 2007. Prosecutor v. Milošević, Case No. IT-98-29/1-T, Trial Judgment (Int'l Crim. Trib. for the Former Yugoslavia Dec. 12, 2007). Both Radovan Karadžić and Ratko Mladić were convicted of charges relating to the Sarajevo siege as well as other crimes. Prosecutor v. Karadžić, Case No. IT-95-5/18-T, Trial Judgment, ¶ 6048 (Int'l Crim. Trib. for the Former Yugoslavia Mar. 24, 2016); Prosecutor v. Mladić, Case No. IT-09-92-T, Trial Judgment, ¶ 5190 (Int'l Crim. Trib. for the Former Yugoslavia Nov. 22, 2017). Another suspect, Momčilo Perišić, was initially convicted for his role in the Sarajevo siege and other crimes, see Prosecutor v. Perišić, Case No. IT-04-81-T, Trial Judgment, ¶¶ 1815–1817 (Int'l Crim. Trib. for the Former Yugoslavia Sept. 6, 2011), but was acquitted of all charges on appeal. Prosecutor v. Perišić, Case No. IT-04-81-A, Appeal Judgment (Int'l Crim. Trib. for the Former Yugoslavia Feb. 28, 2013).

[37] See, e.g., ORGANIZATION FOR SECURITY AND CO-OPERATION IN EUROPE, MISSION TO SERBIA, BELGRADE CENTRE FOR HUM. RTS. & IPSOS PUB. AFFAIRS., ATTITUDES TOWARDS WAR CRIMES ISSUES, ICTY AND THE NATIONAL JUDICIARY 85 (Oct. 2011) [hereinafter 2011 Survey].

[38] See id. at 86 (providing percentages for both 2009 and 2011 surveys).

[39] Here, I use the word *denial* to capture the cluster of phenomena described as such in Chapter 5, including outright denial or distortion of facts, silence about those facts, and failure to acknowledge the moral significance of those facts, by, for example, claiming Serb atrocities were acts of self-defense.

[40] 2001 Survey, *supra* note 34, at 35. This was the highest percentage of respondents who said they had heard of reports for any event in which Serbs committed crimes against other ethnic groups. The event about which the largest percentage of 2001 survey respondents (93 percent) said they had heard was framed as "The Croats killed a lot of civilians" during the Storm and Flash operations. *Id.* at 34. The primary victims of these 1995 military operations were ethnic Serbs. Curiously, in 2001 a larger percentage of respondents (92 percent) said they were familiar with the "event" that "a lot of civilians were killed in Sarajevo by sniper shots" than the percentage (70 percent) who said they were familiar with the "event" that "Sarajevo was under siege for more than 1,000 days." *Id.* at 35.

[41] 2011 Survey, *supra* note 37, at 83 (providing percentages for all six survey years).

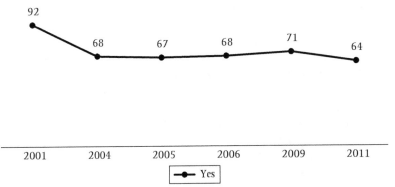

Have you heard that many civilians were killed by snipers in Sarajevo? (percentage)

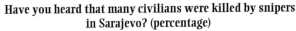

Figure 7.1 Stated Awareness of Sniper Killings in Sarajevo.

The decline in reported awareness between 2001 and 2004 is particularly striking in light of previously-noted expectations about the ICTY's impact. In December 2003, a trial chamber of the ICTY for the first time convicted a defendant of crimes in relation to the Sarajevo siege.[42] Yet the next time Strategic Marketing asked Serbian respondents about the siege, far fewer said they had heard about the sniper killings than the previous time Serbians were polled on this question (68 percent of respondents in 2004 compared to 92 percent of respondents in 2001).

Two figures starkly depict the degree to which Serbians' reported beliefs diverge from factual findings in ICTY judgments—the total percentage of respondents who said they *believed* that (1) "Many civilians were killed in Sarajevo by snipers"; and (2) "A large number of Muslim/Bosniak civilians were killed in Srebrenica" (Figure 7.2):[43]

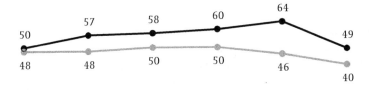

Total surveyed who said they believe Srebrenica massacre and Sarajevo sniper killings really happened (percentage)

Figure 7.2 Total Survey Population Who Said They Believed Srebrenica Massacre and Sarajevo Killings Happened.

---

[42] Prosecutor v. Galić, Case No. IT-98-29-T, Trial Judgment (Int'l Crim. Trib. for the Former Yugoslavia Dec. 5, 2003).

[43] Data reflected in Figure 7.2 are set forth in the 2011 Survey, *supra* note 37, at 84.

Yet a closer look at survey responses reveals a more complex picture than one of consistent denialism over time. I noted earlier that, despite the ICTY's December 2003 judgment convicting a Bosnian Serb commander in relation to the Sarajevo siege, the percentage of respondents who said they had heard about siege-related killings in 2004 was lower than the percentage in 2001. But among those who said they had heard about siege-related killings, there was a steep *rise* in the percentage who said they *believed* what they had heard between 2001 (55 percent)[44] and 2004 (84 percent)[45] (Figure 7.3). The percentage of "believers" among those who said they had heard of the sniper killings continued to rise in the next three surveys before declining in the final survey. Even with the last shift, among respondents who said they had heard of the sniper killings, the percentage who said they believed what they had heard was higher in 2011 (77 percent) than in 2001 (55 percent)—a significant overall increase (Figure 7.3):[46]

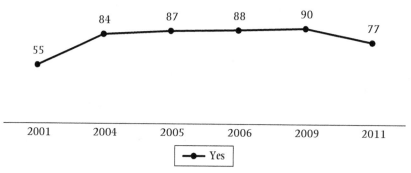

Among those who have heard of Sarajevo sniper killings: Do you believe it really happened? (percentage)

| 2001 | 2004 | 2005 | 2006 | 2009 | 2011 |

◆ Yes

Figure 7.3 Among Respondents Who Said They Heard of Sarajevo Sniper Killings, Percentage Who Said They Believed the Killings Happened.

For this particular question, then, the overall picture of relative continuity in the percentage of total respondents who said they believed large numbers of civilians had been killed by snipers (from 50 percent in 2001 to 49 percent in 2011) masks a significant overall increase (from 55 percent in 2001 to 77 percent in 2011) in respondents who, having said they heard about the killings, also said they *believed* the killings occurred (see Figure 7.4):

---

[44] 2001 Survey, *supra* note 34, at 35.

[45] BELGRADE CENTRE FOR HUMAN RIGHTS & STRATEGIC MARKETING RESEARCH, PUBLIC PINION IN SERBIA: ATTITUDES TOWARDS THE ICTY (Aug. 2004) [hereinafter 2004 Survey] (not paginated).

[46] Data in Figure 7.3 are derived from information set forth in the 2011 Survey, *supra* note 37, at 84.

In Sarajevo, many civilians were killed by snipers (percentage responding "yes")
2001–2011

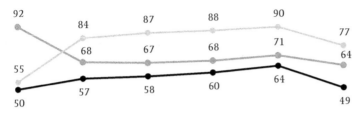
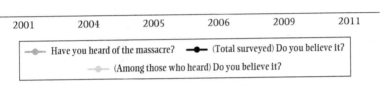

Figure 7.4 Responses to Three Questions about Sarajevo Sniper Killings.

The overall rise in the percentage of respondents who said they believed what they had heard (the light grey line in Figure 7.4) did not, however, mean respondents were increasingly likely to condemn the sniper killings. Vacillating percentages said they considered the casualties a "war crime for which the perpetrators should answer" rather than an inevitable byproduct of war, from a high of 50 percent in 2001 to a low of 30 percent in 2011 (Figure 7.5).[47] As Jadranka Jelinčić observed when I interviewed her in 2006, Serbians' awareness of Serb atrocities did not "necessarily make [them] regret" the crimes.[48]

Sarajevo sniper attacks are war crimes for which the
perpetrators should answer (percentage)

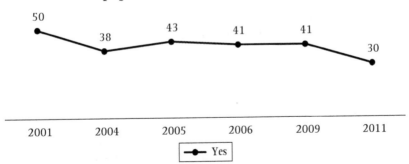

Figure 7.5 Stated Beliefs about Blameworthiness of Sniper Killings.

---

[47] These percentages are provided in the 2011 Survey, *supra* note 37, at 85. They reflect the percentage of total survey respondents who said they had heard of and believed what they had heard about the Sarajevo sniper killings and also considered those killings a "war crime for which the perpetrators should answer."

[48] Interview with Jadranka Jelinčić, Executive Director, Open Society Fund Serbia, in Belgrade, Serb. (Nov. 24, 2006).

Responses to questions about Srebrenica also paint a complex picture. In 2001, 77 percent of those surveyed said they had heard "A large number of Moslem/Bosniak civilians were killed in Srebrenica."[49] The 2001 survey was administered before the ICTY rendered its first genocide conviction for the Srebrenica massacre in the *Krstić* case.[50] Over the next few survey years, the percentage who said they had heard about Srebrenica fluctuated between a high of 78 percent in 2004 (the first time Serbians were surveyed about the massacre after the *Krstić* trial judgment) to a low of 71 percent in 2006. By 2011, 72 percent of respondents said they had heard large numbers of Muslim/Bosniak civilians were killed in Srebrenica,[51] the highest percentage for any crime committed by Serbs included in the 2011 survey (Figure 7.6).

While it is surprising that only 72 percent of respondents in the 2011 survey said they had heard about the massacre, which received substantial attention globally, this figure compares favorably to responses among residents of the majority-Serb entity Republika Srpska in Bosnia. In a 2012 survey of Bosnian respondents, only 59 percent of those living in Republika Srpska said they had heard about the slaughter in Srebrenica—which is *in* that entity.[52]

Have you heard of the Srebrenica massacre? (percentage)

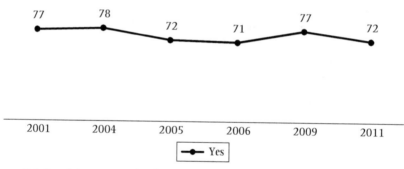

Figure 7.6 Stated Awareness of Srebrenica Massacre.

Between 2001 and 2006, a rising percentage of Serbian respondents who said they had heard about the Srebrenica massacre said they *believed* what they had heard (from 62 percent in 2001[53] to 70 percent in 2006), before the percentage dropped to 60 percent in 2009, and finally to 56 percent in 2011, the final survey year (Figure 7.7):[54]

---

[49] 2011 Survey, *supra* note 37, at 83 (providing percentages for six survey years).

[50] As noted previously, the trial judgment in *Krstić* was issued in August 2001; the 2001 Survey is dated May 2001.

[51] 2011 Survey, *supra* note 37, at 83. In the same survey, 85 percent of respondents said they had heard of Kosovo Liberation Army (KLA) crimes during the 1999 war between the KLA and Serbian forces, while 84 percent said they had heard of Croatian war crimes against Serbs during 1995 military operations. *Id.* at 81.

[52] *See* Chapter 8.

[53] 2001 Survey, *supra* note 34, at 35.

[54] These percentages are derived from data provided in the 2011 Survey, *supra* note 37, at 83–84.

Among those who said they heard of the Srebrenica massacre: Do you believe it really happened? (percentage)

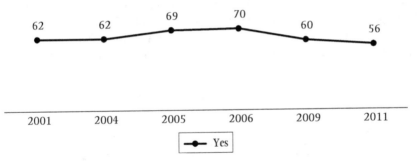

Figure 7.7 Among Respondents Who Said They Heard of Srebrenica Massacre, Percentage Who Said They Believed the Massacre Happened.

Despite a growing tendency from 2001 until 2006 for respondents who said they had heard about Srebrenica to say they believed what they had heard, when the higher percentage of acknowledged believers is applied to the diminishing percentage who said they had *heard* of the massacre, the total population percentage who said they believed the massacre occurred rose only modestly during this period, from 48 percent in 2001 to 50 percent in 2006 (Figure 7.8). Again, then, what may appear to be an astonishing picture of enduring denialism (see in particular the black line in Figure 7.8) masks a more complex pattern of shifting perspectives.

Have you heard/do you believe that a large number of Muslim/Bosniak civilians were killed in Srebrenica? (percentage responding "yes")

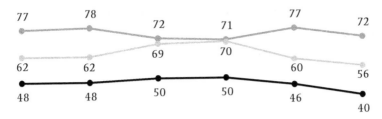

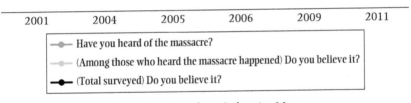

Figure 7.8 Responses to Three Questions about Srebrenica Massacre.

Were respondents prepared to condemn the massacre? Survey responses reflect complex views and trends. On the one hand, in 2011 a smaller percentage (33 percent) of total survey respondents said the Srebrenica killings were "a war crime for which the perpetrators should answer" than in 2001 (48 percent). Notably, too, a smaller percentage (37 percent) characterized the killings as a war crime in 2004, after the ICTY rendered its first genocide conviction, than in 2001 (48 percent) (Figure 7.9):[55]

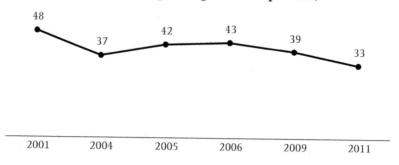

Figure 7.9 Stated Beliefs about Blameworthiness of Srebrenica Massacre.

Yet the surveys do not reflect consistently diminishing moral acknowledgment. After declining between 2001 and 2004, the percentage characterizing Srebrenica as a war crime rose the next two survey years before declining again. (Figure 7.9.) Among those who said they believed what they had heard, moreover, between 84 to 86 percent characterized the massacre as a war crime between 2005 and 2011. Not surprisingly, however, fewer respondents characterized Srebrenica as a genocide in the years (2009 and 2011) the survey included a relevant question (Figure 7.10):[56]

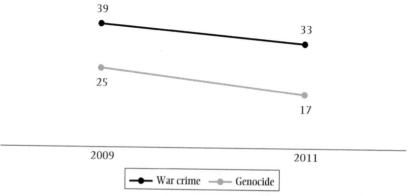

Figure 7.10 Characterization of Srebrenica as War Crime and Genocide.

---

[55] The percentages in Figure 7.9 are provided in the 2011 Survey, *supra* note 37, at 85.
[56] The percentages in Figure 7.10 are derived from data set forth in *id.* at 85–86, as clarified by Ivan Jovanović. The percentages for those who said they believed the massacre occurred are derived from data set forth in *id.* at 83–85 and from page 184 of statistical tables for the 2011 survey.

C. Resistance to Reports of Serb Atrocities

Another pattern merits emphasis: survey responses reflect significantly greater read-iness by Serbian citizens, a majority (roughly 83 percent) of whom are ethnic Serbs,[57] to believe reports of war crimes committed by others against Serbs than reports of Serb crimes committed against members of other groups.[58] (Generally, members of each ethnic group in the region are more likely to say they believe reports of crimes committed against members of their group than reports of crimes committed *by* members of their group, but since this chapter explores Serbian acknowledgment of Serb atrocities and Serbia's role in those crimes, I focus here on the stated beliefs of Serbians.) For example, in contrast to the 40 percent of total respondents in the 2011 survey who said they believed large numbers of Bosniak civilians had been killed in Srebrenica, 80 percent said they believed reports that "Croats killed many civilians in the Storm and Flash operations,"[59] whose principal victims were ethnic Serbs. Similarly, 82 percent of total respondents in the 2011 survey said they believed the Kosovo Liberation Army, the Serbian government's adversary in the 1999 Kosovo war, committed crimes during that conflict.[60] In a further disappointment to Serbians who have pressed their society to condemn atrocities committed by Serbs, Serbian respondents have been much more likely to characterize crimes committed by individuals belonging to other ethnic groups as war crimes that deserve to be punished than crimes committed by ethnic Serbs.[61]

Finally, Serbian respondents have repeatedly and by large majorities said they believed Serbs constituted the largest victim group other than Slovenians and committed the fewest war crimes. Even so, survey results show movement over time, with decreasing percentages saying Serbs suffered the largest number of wartime casualties (from 84 percent in 2004 to 69 percent in 2011) (Figure 7.11). The surveys do not, however, reflect meaningful changes in respondents' willingness to acknowl-edge that Serbs committed the most wartime atrocities (Figure 7.11).[62]

In sum, the trends captured in Strategic Marketing surveys are more complex than a pattern of continuously diminishing knowledge of, belief in, and condemnation of Serb atrocities. Overall, however, they undeniably disappoint the early expecta-tions of some Serbians that the ICTY's judgments would spur Serbian society to

---

[57] Index Mundi, Serbia Demographics Profile 2014, http://www.indexmundi.com/serbia/demographics_profile.html (last visited December 2, 2017).

[58] The authors of the 2004 survey report summarized the pattern this way: "A significantly larger percentage of [Serbian] citizens are familiar with events and believe them to be true if the victims were Serbs and the culprits belonged to a different ethnic group." 2004 Survey, *supra* note 45, at PowerPoint Slide 26.

[59] 2011 Survey, *supra* note 37, at 84. Although comparatively high, the 80 percent response to this question in 2011 is lower than the 90 percent of respondents in 2001 who said they believed Croats had killed many Serbs in these military operations. *See id.* (comparing responses in six surveys undertaken between 2001 and 2011).

[60] *Id.* at 81.

[61] *See id.*

[62] Figure 7.11 reflects responses by the total respondent population. While only 7 percent of this population said Serbs committed the most war crimes, an even lower percentage of respondents *who identified as ethnic Serb*—5 percent—said they thought Serbs committed the most war crimes in 2011. ORGANIZATION FOR SECURITY AND CO-OPERATION IN EUROPE, MISSION TO SERBIA, BELGRADE CENTRE FOR HUM. RTS., & IPSOS STRATEGIC MARKETING, REPORT: STATISTICAL TABLES, ATTITUDES TOWARDS WAR CRIMES, THE ICTY AND THE NATIONAL JUDICIARY 159 (Oct. 2011).

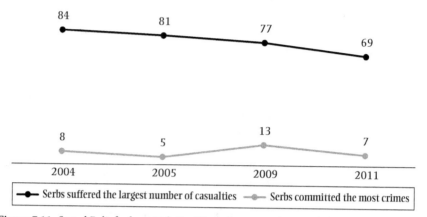

Figure 7.11 Stated Beliefs about Relative Victimization and Responsibility.

acknowledge the enormity of Serb atrocities, both in absolute and relative terms, and condemn them without equivocation. In the sections that follow, I explore why many Serbians either have not accepted fundamental facts concerning Serb atrocities or are unwilling to acknowledge what they privately suspect or believe, as well as factors that account for shifting patterns in this sphere.

II. ACCOUNTING FOR PERSISTENTLY HIGH LEVELS OF DENIAL

A. Serbian Perspectives

Serbians interviewed for this study, including individuals who played key roles designing and implementing Strategic Marketing surveys, provided rich insights into the dynamics behind trends highlighted in the previous section. As later sections elucidate, studies across several social science disciplines provide striking support for their core insights.

1. KNOWING/NOT KNOWING

As previously noted, survey results reflecting high levels of denial may be attributable in part to some respondents' calculated desire to advance a "mission."[63] If Belgrade attorney Ivan Janković is correct, a substantial portion of respondents acted on that impulse. When I interviewed him in 2006, Janković insisted that, when it comes to Serb crimes of surpassing savagery and scope, most Serbians could not help but know what happened yet "often deny their knowledge."[64]

---

[63] Here I refer to Bogdan Ivanišević's observation that many respondents "see themselves as having a mission when they're polled. The mission is, 'Don't acknowledge . . . anything that may be used . . . as an argument against the Serbs.'"

[64] Interview with Ivan Janković, Attorney, in Belgrade, Serb. (Nov. 24, 2006). *See also* Nenad Dimitrijević, *Serbia After the Criminal Past: What Went Wrong and What Should Be Done*, 2 INT'L J. TRANSITIONAL JUST. 5, 5 (2008) (many Serbians' denial that mass killings took place in

For some survey respondents, what appears on the surface as literal denial may reflect a more complex state of simultaneously knowing and not knowing a disquieting truth.[65] The late Vojin Dimitrijević, whose Belgrade Centre for Human Rights sponsored or co-sponsored many of the Strategic Marketing surveys, evoked this phenomenon when he said: "The question is whether you really don't know or you refuse to know."[66] For Dimitrijević, many Serbians' stated lack of awareness of or belief in well-documented atrocities is a form of self-deception—in Stanley Cohen's formulation, "a way to keep secret from ourselves the truth we cannot face"[67] (and in Sissela Bok's words, "a person's failure to acknowledge" even to herself "what is too obvious to miss"[68]). In another variation on this theme, Jadranka Jelinčić said she believes "the majority [of Serbian citizens] know . . . what happened in their hearts." But if "the underlying knowledge is there," most "don't want to recognize" what they know.[69] Similar dynamics can operate on a social level. In the words of Antonela Riha, "No one wants to deal with his own shame. This is also true of countries."[70]

For many Serbians, there is no greater shame than accepting the legal judgment that ethnic Serbs committed genocide in Srebrenica. Srđan Bogosavljević made the point this way: "Everybody committed war crime" [sic] during the 1990s conflicts, but "genocide is not [something] everybody committed. So we want to be normal, to be among the normal people which committed just war crime but not organized genocide."[71] In similar terms, Jelinčić said "genocide is a turning point for any society," and noted the association the crime evokes for Serbians: "If you say [Serbs committed] genocide, you are equal to" the Nazis. After all, "that's how genocide entered our consciousness."[72]

Did this mean the ICTY's determination that Serbs committed genocide in Srebrenica was *antithetical* to Serbian acknowledgment that a terrible crime was committed? Branko Rakić, a law professor who helped defend Milošević in The Hague, suggested it was. Rakić believes most Serbians now accept "there was a horrible crime in Srebrenica." But, he told me, "very few of them would qualify it as

---

Srebrenica "was not necessarily due to a lack of knowledge of the facts" but instead "reflected the lack of readiness to publicly acknowledge facts that were privately known").

[65] Cohen, *supra* note 1, ch. II.

[66] Interview with the late Vojin Dimitrijević, then Director, Belgrade Centre for Human Rights, in Belgrade, Serb. (Nov. 28, 2006).

[67] Cohen, *supra* note 1, at 39.

[68] Sissela Bok, Secrets: On the Ethics of Concealment and Revelation 60 (1982), *quoted in* Cohen, *supra* note 1, at 39.

[69] Interview with Jadranka Jelinčić, Executive Director, Open Society Fund Serbia, in Belgrade, Serb. (July 9, 2012).

[70] Interview with Antonela Riha, Journalist, in Belgrade, Serb. (Nov. 27, 2006).

[71] Interview with Srđan Bogosavljević, Director, Ipsos Strategic Marketing, in Belgrade, Serb. (July 10, 2012).

[72] Interview with Jadranka Jelinčić, Executive Director, Open Society Fund Serbia, in Belgrade, Serb. (July 9, 2012). Ivan Jovanović made a similar point, saying many Serbians resist the ICTY's genocide rulings "because of what genocide means in the memory of Serbs . . . and because of the wishful thinking to regard our nation only as the victims of the genocide committed in World War II, and not as the perpetrators of some other genocide (a feeling/attitude otherwise common for all the nations). . . . Now you have to join the same line of perpetrators" as the Nazis. Interview with Ivan Jovanović, then National Legal Advisor, OSCE Mission to Serbia, in Belgrade, Serb. (July 12, 2012); email from Ivan Jovanović, Attorney, to Diane Orentlicher (May 31, 2017).

a genocide." In his view, the fact that the ICTY did so had "a bad effect," which he described this way:

> If you want the population to accept and to face the fact that a crime was committed within them . . . Then, if you . . . —this may sound bad from my side—but if you exaggerate, if you give the accusations, it produces a counter effect. . . . I am partial, I am biased, I would like my people to be less criminal than they perhaps [are], and that is natural.[73]

Like Rakić, Ivan Jovanović (a longtime ICTY supporter) believes the Tribunal's genocide rulings made Serbians less inclined to acknowledge the moral magnitude of Srebrenica (indeed, as depicted in Figure 7.9, fewer respondents characterized Srebrenica as a war crime worthy of punishment *after* the ICTY rendered its first genocide conviction in August 2001 than before). In Jovanović's words, the Tribunal's determination that Bosnian Serbs committed genocide in Srebrenica made the truth "harder for Serbs to swallow, that's absolutely true." But, Jovanović insisted, this did not mean it would have been preferable for the ICTY to reach a different conclusion. "Because had [ICTY judges] defined [the massacre] differently, maybe they would have done an injustice to the victims."[74]

2. Time, Memory, and Context

If a human disposition to resist painful truths partially explains some survey responses, Bogosavljević believes similar dynamics contributed to *diminishing* knowledge over time, in his view through their operation on memory. When I first interviewed Bogosavljević in November 2006, the surveys his organization conducted already showed a decline since 2001 in affirmative responses to the question whether respondents had heard of several well-known instances of Serb atrocities, the most notable drop occurring between the first (2001) and second (2004) surveys. Reflecting on this trend, Bogosavljević said: "These things happened thirteen, fourteen years ago. Over time, people are forgetting."[75]

Strategic Marketing's survey data provide grounds to believe respondents were indeed forgetting fundamental facts about the 1990s conflicts as they receded in time. When I first interviewed Bogosavljević, Serb respondents were registering somewhat lower levels of affirmative responses not only to questions asking whether they had heard about crimes committed *by* Serbs, but also to a question asking if they had heard about crimes *against* Serbs committed by Croats eleven years earlier,[76]

---

[73] Interview with Branko Rakić, Professor, Faculty of Law, University of Belgrade, in Belgrade, Serb. (July 11, 2012).

[74] Interview with Ivan Jovanović, then National Legal Advisor, OSCE Mission to Serbia, in Belgrade, Serb. (July 12, 2012).

[75] Interview with Srđan Bogosavljević, Director, Strategic Marketing Research, in Belgrade, Serb. (Nov. 21, 2006).

[76] *See* Belgrade Centre for Human Rights, OSCE Mission to Serbia & Strategic Marketing Research, Public Opinion in Serbia: Views on Domestic War Crimes, Judicial Authorities and the Hague Tribunal 24 (Dec. 2006) [hereinafter 2006 Survey]. Between the first (2001) and second (2004) surveys, there was already a decline in the percentage of respondents who said they had heard that "Croats killed many civilians during the Storm and Flash operations," whose principal victims were Serbs. In 2001, 93 percent of respondents said

suggesting respondents were not simply deleting from their memory banks events that challenged their collective self-esteem. Vojin Dimitrijević told me this finding was unexpected; he and his colleagues had "assumed people would remember crimes against Serbs."[77]

But if it makes sense that wartime memories would fade over time, many Serbs vividly "remember" the 1389 Battle of Kosovo as though it happened yesterday.[78] How, then, could some survey respondents' memories of notorious events in their own lifetimes ebb so quickly?

Bogosavljević believes the psychology of selective memory is at play. Reflecting on respondents' awareness of Serb atrocities, he said: "People like to forget" this part of their history.[79] When I interviewed him again in 2012, Bogosavljević made the point more emphatically, insisting: "People don't *like* to, don't *like* to, don't *like* to remember, because you know when something is blaming you for something, you don't like. . . ."[80] For Bogosavljević, to say many Serbians do not want to remember unsettling facts is not to deny they are actually forgetting them. In his words: "And that's real. People are forgetting and they're not able to tell you [what happened]. We checked from time to time, and 'there [are] no crimes committed by Serbs.' We can speak about Srebrenica, and that's it."[81]

Svetlana Logar, who oversaw the surveys for Strategic Marketing, also said "people are forgetting," which she believes the 2011 survey demonstrated.[82] Later in the same interview, however, she noted two other factors that contributed to declining levels of self-reported knowledge, one of which suggests the survey trends may partially reflect changing demographics. The first was growing public fatigue with the topic of war crimes. When I interviewed Logar in 2012, Serbia had recently arrested the last ICTY fugitive and, with this, the topic of "the past" had fallen off the proverbial radar for most Serbians. In Logar's words, "No one cares" about the subject anymore. "People are forgetting everything," she continued. "What [happened] in Sarajevo—let's forget about it."[83]

Before I introduce the second factor cited by Logar, it may be useful to foreshadow here a point I develop in Chapter 11: the apparent disposition of many

---

they had heard about this, compared to 85 percent in 2004. By 2006, the first year I interviewed Bogosavljević, the percentage had dropped to 78 percent (though it would rise to 88 percent in 2009). *See* 2011 Survey, *supra* note 37, at 83.

[77] Interview with the late Vojin Dimitrijević, then Director, Belgrade Centre for Human Rights, in Belgrade, Serb. (Nov. 28, 2006). As previously noted, the organization Dimitrijević led commissioned or co-sponsored many of the surveys discussed here.

[78] This battle holds powerful resonance for Serbian nationalists. *See* WARREN ZIMMERMANN, ORIGINS OF A CATASTROPHE: YUGOSLAVIA AND ITS DESTROYERS—AMERICA'S LAST AMBASSADOR TELLS WHAT HAPPENED AND WHY 11–12 (1996).

[79] Interview with Srđan Bogosavljević, Director, Strategic Marketing Research, in Belgrade, Serb. (Nov. 21, 2006).

[80] Interview with Srđan Bogosavljević, Director, Ipsos Strategic Marketing, in Belgrade, Serb. (July 10, 2012). The ellipses in the quoted statement do not reflect an edit. Bogosavljević trailed off before completing this sentence, presumably assuming he had already made himself clear.

[81] *Id.* With respect to Srebrenica, Bogosavljević said, the mass executions there were so well documented no one denied it happened. *Id.*

[82] In Logar's words: "What's very important is that you can see in our survey forgetting, the people forget." Interview with Svetlana Logar, then Research Director, Ipsos Strategic Marketing, in Belgrade, Serb. (July 10, 2012).

[83] *Id.* As elaborated later in this chapter, sources made the same point during my final research visit two years later.

Serbians to "forget" rather than confront the recent past is strikingly reminiscent of many postwar Germans' orientation toward the Nazi past (to note this is not to suggest a general equivalency in the two countries' experiences). For many years, Juergan Baumann wrote, "most German citizens made all possible efforts to forget what happened in twelve ill-fated years. They made their gaps in memory systematic."[84] It was not just postwar Germans who were keen to "behave[e] as though the past was indeed dead and buried"; the sentiment was common in postwar Europe.[85] Broadly, then, comparative experience bolsters Bogosavljević's and Logar's intuition.[86]

The second factor identified by Logar involves changing demographics, layered onto a broader social exhaustion with the subject of war crimes. Noting that each year approximately 75,000 young adults enter the pool of survey respondents, Logar said: "So new and new generations [are participating in our surveys, and] they are bored with this boring topic, again, this war past."[87] As well, Bogosavljević noted, "more people are dying": in each of the previous ten years, he estimated, roughly 35,000 Serbians had passed away.[88] Accordingly, survey responses that seem to signify declining levels of awareness of Serb atrocities may be partly attributable to continuously changing pools of survey respondents.[89]

Alongside these factors, Ivan Jovanović believes the political-economic landscape of post-Milošević Serbia influenced the psychological dynamics of denial/ acknowledgment. He believes Serbians' new optimism after ousting their wartime leader partially accounts for the comparatively high percentage of respondents in 2001 who said they had heard of specific Serb atrocities.[90] At that time, which "was immediately after we got rid of Milošević, everyone except for those close to the previous regime . . . were very enthusiastic. They suddenly felt a big relief after a decade of frustrations and defeats. So everything looked bright." In this setting, Jovanović recalled, "people had a feeling of encouragement, acceptance by [the] international

---

[84] JUERGAN BAUMANN, DER AUFSTAND DES SCHLECTEN GEWISSENS (1965), *quoted and translated in* Christoph Burchard, *The Nuremberg Trial and Its Impact on Germany*, 4 J. INT'L CRIM. JUST. 800, 812 (2006).

[85] TONY JUDT, POSTWAR: A HISTORY OF EUROPE SINCE 1945, at 62 (2005). *See also id.* at 52.

[86] This is not to suggest all societies emerging from an experience of mass atrocities follow this pattern. For further discussion of this point, see Chapter 11.

[87] Interview with Svetlana Logar, then Research Director, Ipsos Strategic Marketing, in Belgrade, Serb. (July 10, 2012).

[88] Interview with Srđan Bogosavljević, Director, Ipsos Strategic Marketing, in Belgrade, Serb. (July 10, 2012).

[89] The obvious implication of Bogosavljević's and Logar's comments was that younger respondents were less likely to know about wartime atrocities than older respondents. Consistent with this inference, the 2009 survey offered the following commentary to its compilation of survey responses to questions about "awareness of events": "In average, younger generations are less aware than the older." ORGANIZATION FOR SECURITY AND CO-OPERATION IN EUROPE, MISSION TO SERBIA, VIEWS ON WAR CRIMES, THE ICTY, AND THE NATIONAL WAR CRIMES JUDICIARY 90 (Apr. 2009). Ivan Jovanović, who helped design later surveys on behalf of the OSCE Mission to Serbia, believes changing demographics affected the results only by a few percentage points. Email from Ivan Jovanović, Attorney, to Diane Orentlicher (May 31, 2017) (on file with author).

[90] As noted, 92 percent of those surveyed said they had heard that large numbers of civilians were killed by snipers in Sarajevo; this percentage dropped to 68 percent in 2004. In addition, 70 percent of respondents in 2001 said they had heard Sarajevo was under siege for more than 1,000 days; in 2004, only 51 percent said they had heard this. *See* 2011 Survey, *supra* note 37, at 83.

community." He believes this made it "easier for them to swallow these bitter pieces from the past." At that time, too, it was relatively easy for Serbians to convince themselves they "had nothing to do with that [and] attribute everything to the former regime."[91] Also relevant, Jovanović believes, the Đinđić administration had "started revealing some facts" implicating the previous regime in war crimes in Kosovo,[92] which further primed Serbian society to believe what they were hearing from independent sources, including the ICTY, about Serb war crimes.[93]

When, however, Serbians realized "that there's a price to pay," meaning Serbia would have to "surrender the accused to the ICTY and if you fail to do so there will be some consequences to bear, then it . . . causes a spiral of new frustrations and a sense of injustice."[94] (Here, Jovanović was referring to Western policies of conditionality, the focus of Chapter 3.) Jovanović believes Serbians would naturally resist "look[ing] at the unpleasant facts about [their] own nation and [their] own past" in any event. Even so, he believes their "resistance is less strong and determined if [they] do not have to pay a price for that."[95]

It is, of course, impossible to test Jovanović's theory about the impact of Western conditionality (which does not in any case account for the moderate *rise* in survey respondents' stated awareness of and belief in Serb crimes after 2004, or the slight rise between 2001 and 2004 in the percentage of respondents who said they had heard about Srebrenica).[96] Yet his basic intuition—that a society may be comparatively willing to confront a difficult past if it has "some prospect of a better future"[97]—seems plausible, and worthy of attention in future comparative research studies.

---

[91] Interview with Ivan Jovanović, then National Legal Advisor, OSCE Mission to Serbia, in Belgrade, Serb. (July 12, 2012). This dynamic calls to mind German citizens' contemporaneous reaction to the Nuremberg prosecution of major Nazi war criminals. As discussed in Chapter 11, many German citizens embraced Nuremberg while the trial was underway, in significant part because they saw the landmark trial as exonerating most Germans. Before long, however, German opinion turned against Nuremberg.

[92] As noted in Chapter 3, the Đinđić government disclosed the discovery of mass graves of Kosovo Albanians, whose bodies had been reburied in Serbia as part of a Serbian cover-up.

[93] In 2001, 57 percent of survey respondents said they had heard "Albanians were expelled and killed [in] Kosovo even before the bombing." This is significantly higher than the percentage (49 percent) who said in 2004 that they had heard about this. See 2011 Survey, *supra* note 37, at 83.

[94] Interview with Ivan Jovanović, then National Legal Advisor, OSCE Mission to Serbia, in Belgrade, Serb. (July 12, 2012).

[95] *Id.*

[96] *See* Figure 7.6, *supra*. In addition to previously-noted survey responses to questions about Srebrenica and the Sarajevo siege, responses to a question asking if respondents had heard about Serb killings of Croat civilians in Vukovar, Croatia, showed steadily rising levels of self-reported awareness between 2005 (47 percent) and 2011 (62 percent, which approached the highest percentage for any survey year, 64 percent in 2001). *See* 2011 Survey, *supra* note 37, at 83.

[97] JUDT, *supra* note 85, at 106. In the passage from which the quoted text is drawn, Judt did not draw a direct a link between a society's economic prospects and its willingness to confront the past, but the implications of his point are suggestive. Describing the views of Americans who opposed taking a harshly punitive approach to postwar Germany, Judt wrote: "It was all very well forcibly bringing Germans to a consciousness of their own defeat, but unless they were given some prospect of a better future the outcome might be the same as [after World War I]: a resentful, humiliated nation vulnerable to demagogy. . . . " As Judt elaborated, in the immediate postwar years Germany's prospects for recovery seemed gloomier than they would later prove to be. *See id.* at 89. For much of this period, most Germans were in no mood to address the Nazi past. *See* Chapter 11.

To the extent Jovanović linked Serbians' frustrations to their economic prospects,[98] recent research suggests countries with relatively strong economies are more likely than others to confront a prior regime's depredations by undertaking prosecutions.[99] Notably, as well, Germany's economic stability is believed to be one of many "key factors" behind its "retrospective embracing of 'Nuremberg[.]'"[100]

The significance of economic prospects for citizens' readiness to confront painful truths emerged as a recurring theme in interviews.[101] During my 2012 research visit to Serbia, not long after Strategic Marketing's final war crimes survey showed decreasing levels of stated knowledge since the previous (2009) survey, several interlocutors linked this decline and related discursive trends to Serbia's dire political and economic situation. Radmila Nakarada described prevailing conditions this way: "The problems here are ever growing and becoming bitterly dramatic."[102] Referring to the economic depression that had spread across Europe at that time, she said: "I think this whole sort of widespread depression or lack of cheerfulness . . . makes the local problems even greater, because you can't see anything across the fence that sort of gives you more hope."[103]

---

[98] Jovanović's point may also encompass Serbians' frustration with the perpetuation of Serbia's pariah status, implied by Western conditionality, which they might have experienced as a form of shame. A number of social science studies have explored the impact of shame (as well as guilt) on individuals' readiness to undertake reparative measures. Several studies suggest people are more likely to take a constructive approach, which in this context would include acknowledgment, if they believe a shame-producing failure is reparable. *See, e.g.,* Colin Wayne Leach & Atilla Cidam, *When Is Shame Linked to Constructive Approach Orientation?: A Meta-analysis,* 109 J. PERSONALITY & SOC. PSYCHOL. 983, 997 (2015). Research also suggests that people who have been offered opportunities for self-affirmation are more likely to acknowledge harm inflicted by members of their in-group. *See, e.g.,* Sabina Čehajić-Clancy, *Dealing with Ingroup Committed Atrocities: Moral Responsibility and Group-Based Guilt, in* THE SOCIAL PSYCHOLOGY OF INTRACTABLE CONFLICTS 103, 109 (Eran E. Halperin & Keren Sharvit eds., 2015). Seemingly inconsistent results among studies make it premature, however, to apply their findings to the context explored here.

[99] Hun Joon Kim, *Structural Determinants of Human Rights Prosecutions After Democratic Transition,* 49 J. PEACE RES. 305, 315 (2012).

[100] Donald Bloxham, *The Nuremberg Trials and the Occupation of Germany,* 27 CARDOZO L. REV. 1599, 1600 (2005–2006). *See also* THOMAS U. BERGER, WAR, GUILT, AND WORLD POLITICS AFTER WORLD WAR II, at 80 (2012) (practical obstacles to penitence diminished in the face of "increased German prosperity" by the second half of the 1960s).

[101] Although our analysis differs in other respects, Izabela Steflja makes a similar point:

It is understandable that people might not have the incentive to change their opinions of Milošević, Karadžić, and Mladić, and their interpretation of the past if nothing has changed for the better in their lives. . . . A real transformation, including important changes in people's daily lives and their standard of living, is perhaps required to motivate moral transformation.

Izabela Steflja, *Identity Crisis in Post-Conflict Societies: The ICTY's Role in Defensive Nationalism Among the Serbs,* 22 GLOBAL CHANGE, PEACE & SECURITY 231, 246 (2010).

[102] Interview with Radmila Nakarada, Professor of Peace Studies, Faculty of Political Sciences, University of Belgrade, in Belgrade, Serb. (July 9, 2012). Professor Nakarada made this point in the course of explaining why she thought the then-recent conviction (later overturned) of Croat General Ante Gotovina for crimes against Serbs had not had a major impact on Serbians' assessment of the ICTY. As noted below, others linked dire economic conditions more directly to Serbians' general disinclination to confront wartime depredations.

[103] *Id.*

At a time when "people are thinking how to feed their children tomorrow," Svetlana Logar noted, they have scant capacity to contemplate questions of historical truth.[104] In the view of Marijana Toma, Serbians' growing weariness with the topic of war crimes shaded into a wider social fatigue. In her words, a "majority of people [are] tired of talking about war crimes . . . , and I see that fatigue in, you know, we are tired of living bad."[105] In a similar vein, Maja Mičić, then director of the Youth Initiative for Human Rights, reflected: "It's even more difficult to put human rights on the agenda when you have a poor society that is focused only on their day-to-day essential survival."[106]

If citizens are comparatively likely to confront a painful past when their economic prospects are promising, is it possible that Western policies of conditionality (described in Chapter 3) had an unintended impact on Serbian acknowledgment? Any reflections on this question must be tentative, not least because we are still far from understanding the relationship between a country's economic conditions and its readiness to confront the past. With this caveat, several observations may be offered.

First, to the extent there was any trade-off between addressing survivors' need for justice and Serbians' disposition to confront the past, it is important to keep sight of the fact that the Tribunal's mandate embraces only the first.[107] This is appropriate: for reasons elaborated later in this chapter, we should have modest expectations about *any* ICT's capacity to transform social beliefs, particularly in the immediate aftermath of mass atrocities. Economic prospects are but one of many factors that, in combination, determine a society's readiness to confront a difficult past. Even if we knew how to ensure a prosperous economy, doing so would hardly ensure a robust reckoning with the past. In contrast to the speculative and attenuated connection between economic prospects and acknowledgment, it is clear the ICTY *was* capable of addressing victims' need for justice, however imperfectly,[108] and that Western conditionality was necessary to achieve that aim.[109]

Jovanović's observation might, nonetheless, reinforce a point made in Chapter 3: even if policies of conditionality are necessary to ensure fugitives are arrested, they can (at least in some circumstances) be implemented with a view to advancing other objectives. As we have seen, at crucial times the European Union deftly managed its policy of conditionality to offer Serbian society a sense of hope without abandoning its determination to ensure full cooperation with the ICTY.[110]

---

[104] Interview with Svetlana Logar, then Research Director, Ipsos Strategic Marketing, in Belgrade, Serb. (July 10, 2012).

[105] Interview with Marijana Toma, then Deputy Director, Humanitarian Law Center, in Belgrade, Serb. (June 10, 2014).

[106] Interview with Maja Mičić, then Executive Director, Belgrade, Youth Initiative for Human Rights, in Belgrade, Serb. (June 11, 2014).

[107] The Security Council resolution establishing the Tribunal makes no mention of advancing acknowledgment; it does, however, express the Council's determination "to take effective measures to bring to justice the persons who are responsible" for "widespread and flagrant violations of international humanitarian law occurring within the territory of the former Yugoslavia, and especially in the Republic of Bosnia and Herzegovina, including . . . mass killings, massive, organized and systematic detention and rape of women, and . . . 'ethnic cleansing.'" S.C. Res. 827, preamble (May 24, 1993).

[108] *See* Chapter 6.

[109] I develop the foundation for this claim in Chapter 3.

[110] *See id.*

Yet Western conditionality might have been implemented in a manner even more conducive to Serbia's political and social transformation. Speaking in a somewhat different context, Jadranka Jelinčić offered a reflection equally relevant here: "I am certain that it would have been better if the international community had been more imaginative in offering prospects for Serbia . . . politically and economically," even as it insisted on Serbian cooperation with the Hague Tribunal.[111]

3. Sources of Information about Wartime Conduct: Official and Elite Discourses

The ways in which most people remember the past is powerfully conditioned by the narratives generated by the state, which are, in turn, driven primarily by practical considerations. . . .

—Thomas U. Berger[112]

As several Serbian interlocutors intimated, the way information is processed is not solely a private matter. An account of reality that involves some form of denial (e.g., "many Muslims were killed in Srebrenica, but not as many as the ICTY has found—and anyway, it wasn't a genocide") can, in Stanley Cohen's words, be "learnt by ordinary cultural transmission, . . . drawn from a well-established, collectively available pool."[113] People may, in fact, adopt a particular account in part *because* of its "public acceptability."[114]

In line with Cohen's insight, several individuals interviewed for this study explained the disparity between facts established in The Hague and many Serbians' stated beliefs by emphasizing Serbians' sources of information. Crucially important were official narratives widely disseminated during the 1990s conflicts. Initially portraying Serbs as targets of an ominous and imminent threat[115] and then as victims of ethnically-motivated atrocities, the Milošević regime "presented both its actions and their consequences as politically legitimate and morally right. . . ."[116] At times, official narratives literally inverted reality, attributing Serb attacks to their victims.[117] State-controlled media dutifully disseminated the official narrative, which had a powerful shaping influence on many Serbians' beliefs.[118] Svetlana Logar described

---

[111] Interview with Jadranka Jelinčić, Executive Director, Open Society Fund Serbia, in Belgrade, Serb. (July 9, 2012). Jelinčić offered this perspective while addressing the question whether Western pressure to arrest Hague fugitives heightened the risks faced by the late Serbian prime minister Zoran Đinđić.

[112] Berger, *supra* note 100, at 2.

[113] Cohen, *supra* note 1, at 59.

[114] *Id. See also* Obradović-Wochnik, *Srebrenica, supra* note 28, at 68 ("Public and political discourses delineate the limits of what is acceptable").

[115] *See* Vojin Dimitrijević, *Serbia: Towards European Integration with the Burden of the Past?, in* The Violent Dissolution of Yugoslavia: Causes, Dynamics and Effects 211, 211 (Miroslav Hadžić ed., 2004).

[116] Kutnjak Ivković & Hagan, *supra* note 33, at 101.

[117] *See* Sabrina P. Ramet, *The Denial Syndrome and Its Consequences: Serbian Political Culture Since 2000,* 40 Communist & Post-Communist Stud. 41, 47 (2007); Payam Akhavan, *Justice in the Hague, Peace in the Former Yugoslavia? A Commentary on the United Nations War Crimes Tribunal,* 20 Hum. Rts. Q. 737, 763–64 (1998).

[118] In Eric Gordy's words, "As long as the Milošević regime controlled most media in Serbia, denial and claims of victimization were the most generally available perspectives on guilt." Gordy,

media coverage during the 1990s this way: "The only source [of information] was our official TV, in which, as you know, you only saw suffering from one side, the Serbs."[119]

While Logar's characterization is somewhat overstated,[120] independent journalists who provided more balanced accounts during the 1990s faced formidable obstacles and pressure.[121] Media reporting on Srebrenica provides a window into those challenges. Reflecting twenty years later on how Serbian journalists covered the massacre, Dejan Radulović said: "Keeping silent about it or minimizing it—that was the official policy. Media control was overpowering and any attempt to write anything about it roused the [pro-government] 'journalists on watch duty' who didn't spare the insults."[122] Another journalist, Dušan Veličković, recalled that "potential sources of information [about the Srebrenica massacre] were buried under war propaganda and misinformation of different forms."[123] Meanwhile, journalists working for state-controlled media dutifully reported Bosnian Serb military commander Ratko Mladić's perverse claim that Srebrenica's civilians were safe, and that "Muslim soldiers [who] fled to the hills" and were captured were "being treated in compliance with the Geneva Convention."[124]

With the collapse of the Milošević government it became easier to find balanced accounts in the local media.[125] Between 2001 and 2004, even the state media broadcast

---

supra note 28, at 46. *See also* Kutnjak Ivković & Hagan, *supra* note 33, at 101 (as a result of wartime narratives, the prevailing view was either one of complete denial that Serbs committed atrocities or justification of Serb behavior in terms of heroic self-defense). In the lexicon of denial introduced in Chapter 5, justification narratives are classic forms of interpretive denial.

[119] Interview with Svetlana Logar, then Research Director, Ipsos Strategic Marketing, in Belgrade, Serb. (July 10, 2012).

[120] Logar likely was not speaking literally when she described Serbian state television as Serbians' "only" source of news. But her basic point is widely accepted. In its 2001 survey, administered soon after Milošević was arrested and thus closest in time to his regime, Strategic Marketing asked respondents what their sources of information were "during the wars." 2001 Survey, *supra* note 34, at 53. By far the most often-cited source (selected by 80 percent of respondents) was state media. *Id.* at 54. Yet the largest percentage of respondents (43 percent) to another question—"to what extent do you trust the sources of information?"—said they "did not trust" state media. *Id.* at 55.

[121] *See* Obradović-Wochnik, *Silent Dilemma, supra* note 30, at 331.

[122] Antonela Riha, *Reporting Srebrenica: Hear No Evil, Speak No Evil*, Transitions Online (July 13, 2015). Radulović was a correspondent for Radio Free Europe.

[123] *Id.*

[124] *Id.*

[125] Interview with Ivan Jovanović, then National Legal Advisor, OSCE Mission to Serbia, in Belgrade, Serb. (July 12, 2012); *Remarks of Igor Bandović, in* International War Crimes Trials: Making a Difference? 90, 92 (Steven R. Ratner & James L. Bischoff eds., 2004). Nevertheless, a large majority of Serbians continued to rely on state-owned media as their principal source of news, *see, e.g.*, 2011 Survey, *supra* note 37, at 123–24 (reporting results for both 2009 and 2011), and the mainstream media continued to reflect dominant discourses of nationalist figures. *See* Obradović-Wochnik, *Srebrenica, supra* note 28, at 63 & 67.

More recently, the Serbian media—like media in a number of other former Yugoslav countries—have faced growing pressure to conform to state-sanctioned views. *See* Freedom House Report, Freedom of the Press 2015, at 6–7, 22–23 (2015); Igor Jovanović, *Balkan Media in 'Worrying' State, Conference Hears*, Balkan Insight (Sept. 3, 2015). Reflecting on these pressures in 2014, Bogdan Ivanišević observed: "What I can say for sure is that there's a lot of either . . . censorship or self-censorship." Interview with Bogdan Ivanišević, Attorney, in Belgrade, Serb. (June 9, 2014).

documentaries about Srebrenica and other war crimes;[126] so, too, did the independent B92 station.[127] In the view of Jadranka Jelinčić and others, these documentaries "influenced a part of public opinion," contributing to "public discussion about whether genocide happened."[128] As already noted, moreover, in 2001 the Đinđić government and other sources disclosed information about recently-discovered mass graves of victims of Serbian war crimes, which sensitized the public to the criminality of the Milošević regime.[129] But for those whose views were already entrenched, Logar said, it was difficult to displace the "basic picture [that] was already in peoples' minds."[130]

Had the first post-Milošević government made a sharp break with the past, a wider space for confronting Serbian responsibility might have opened up.[131] As noted earlier, however, that government comprised a deeply divided coalition, with a strongly nationalist FRY president and reformist Serbian prime minister; the political strength of nationalists meant the reformist wing operated in a constrained and contested space.[132] Electoral calculations were a key reason then Prime Minister Đinđić appealed to Serbians' self-interest rather than precepts of morality to marshal support for arresting fugitives.[133] Several years on, the persistence of nationalists'

---

[126] Interview with Žarko Marković, then Legal Officer, Belgrade Centre for Human Rights, in Belgrade, Serb. (June 11, 2014). According to Marković, although journalists continued to make documentaries about Serb atrocities, they were no longer routinely broadcast on state-owned television and other state media after Vojislav Koštunica became prime minister of Serbia in March 2004. Koštunica took control of state media for the next few years, Marković said, "and war crimes issues pretty much disappeared" from this source of information. *Id.*

[127] Interview with Jadranka Jelinčić, Executive Director, Open Society Fund Serbia, in Belgrade, Serb. (Nov. 24, 2006).

[128] *Id.*

[129] Interview with Žarko Marković, then Legal Officer, Belgrade Centre for Human Rights, in Belgrade, Serb. (June 11, 2014). The Đinđić government's release of information about these graves is noted in Chapter 3.

[130] Interview with Svetlana Logar, then Research Director, Ipsos Strategic Marketing, in Belgrade, Serb. (July 10, 2012).

[131] In a forthcoming publication, Marko Milanović plausibly posits that a key predictor of whether a country or substate unit will acknowledge abuses committed by a prior regime is whether the elites of the successor state or group "are the same or substantially similar to those that led the group" or state during the period in which atrocities took place, "and whether they adhere to or espouse the same or substantially similar ideology." Marko Milanović, Draft, *Courting Failure: When Are International Criminal Courts Likely to Be Believed by Local Audiences?*, in The Oxford Handbook of International Criminal Law (Kevin Jon Heller et al. eds., forthcoming 2017). It is not clear, however, whether the persistence of denialism is caused above all by leadership continuity, popular opinion (reflected in the election of leaders who share the perspectives of a prior regime), a combination of both, or more complex factors. As suggested below, even leaders who do not represent continuity with a prior regime's ideology may be constrained by the voting power of citizens who embrace that ideology.

[132] *See* Chapter 3; *see also* Jasna Dragović-Soso, *Apologising for Srebrenica: The Declaration of the Serbian Parliament, the European Union and the Politics of Compromise*, 28 East Eur. Pol. 163, 165 (2012) (a key reason "there was little political will to investigate the wars of the 1990s" after the collapse of the Milošević regime was that "deals struck" between new authorities and elements of the "old regime—which had ensured the peaceful transition of power but which was now hampering any substantive transformation of the state, the judiciary and the security services— meant that attempts to investigate the recent past were inevitably going to be slow and precarious").

[133] A similar dynamic was at play in postwar Germany. West Germany's two major parties realized "they would have to fish for their votes from a people whose overwhelming majority some ten years earlier would have voted for Hitler in a free and secret election." Fritz Stern, *Foreward* to Norbert Frei, Adenauer's Germany and the Nazi Past: The Politics of Amnesty and Integration, at vii, viii (Joel Gold trans., 2002).

political clout meant "even the most progressive politicians, such as President Boris Tadić, . . . failed to offer a strong and credible counter-discourse" to nationalist narratives even as they took steps to advance accountability.[134]

Noting that Serbians' perceptions of "the past" are shaped more "by political elites, the media, [and] the intellectual elites" than by "facts," Bogdan Ivanišević observed that, in the former Yugoslavia, there have "simply never been these kind of political elites or intellectual elites that could decisively affect the already existing unwillingness of the majority of people to confront the past in a fair manner."[135] In the same vein, scholars Sanja Kutnjak Ivković and John Hagan believe Serbian leaders' general failure to offer a robust alternative to Milošević-era narratives explains why respondents in surveys administered between 2001 and 2006 "were more likely to report hearing about atrocities involving Serbs as victims, more likely to believe that these events really happened, and more likely to label them as war crimes."[136]

Meanwhile, years after Milošević lost power, nationalists continued to dominate Serbia's discursive landscape to a degree often disproportionate to their political support.[137] In a 2009 publication, Jelena Subotić wrote: "It is difficult to overestimate the saturation in the public discourse" in Serbia of the idea that Serbs are "a victimized nation."[138] In consequence, she concluded, "there has simply been no discursive space open for" a new message urging Serbians to examine their past.[139]

While these factors help explain the persistence of high levels of denialism, it would be a mistake to suggest differences between the discourses of reformist and nationalist leaders were inconsequential. As previously noted, Strategic Marketing surveys show significant fluctuations in Serbian beliefs about wartime atrocities between 2004 and 2011. Serbians who helped design these surveys believe the fluctuations are attributable, at least in part, to the contrasting discourses of the reformist president, Boris Tadić, and nationalist prime minister, Vojislav Koštunica. Ivan Jovanović notes that Koštunica's ascension to the position of prime minister in 2004 produced a rise in denialist discourses, which he believes had a depressing effect on citizens' knowledge of/belief in wartime atrocities. Despite "the unfriendly political environment during . . . Koštunica's term," however, other sources countered denialist influences to some extent. "NGOs, the media and some public figures kept talking about wartime atrocities" during this period.[140] Among the more significant public figures in this respect, Jovanović believes that "Tadić and his party gave some boost to facing the past when he replaced Koštunica" as president in 2004.[141]

---

[134] Obradović-Wochnik, *Srebrenica, supra* note 28, at 63.

[135] Interview with Bogdan Ivanišević, Attorney, in Belgrade, Serb. (July 9, 2012).

[136] KUTNJAK IVKOVIĆ & HAGAN, *supra* note 33, at 102.

[137] *See* Obradović-Wochnik, *Srebrenica,* supra note 28, at 63. Obradović-Wochnik suggests Serbian leaders' relative silence on the subject of wartime atrocities "allowed for the public sphere to be monopolized by a large number of revisionist pundits, religious leaders and far-right groups that periodically engage in war crimes denial." Obradović-Wochnik, *Silent Dilemma, supra* note 30, at 336.

[138] JELENA SUBOTIĆ, HIJACKED JUSTICE: DEALING WITH THE PAST IN THE BALKANS 69 (2009).

[139] *Id.*

[140] Email from Ivan Jovanović, Attorney, to Diane Orentlicher (May 31, 2017).

[141] *Id.* Jovanović believes these and other factors produced fluctuations in survey results in 2005, 2006, 2009, and 2011. Among other factors that may have contributed to declining knowledge/acknowledgment at relevant times, Jovanović cited disappointment in the ICTY, frustration with the international community's support for Kosovo's independence from Serbia, pressure on Serbia to arrest Radovan Karadžić and Ratko Mladić, and general "war crimes fatigue." *Id.*

4. Vilifying the Hague Tribunal

If nationalist discourses shaped and then helped sustain many Serbians' beliefs, they also undermined an alternative source of information about wartime atrocities: the ICTY. As a source of information, the Tribunal does not communicate directly with many Serbians (exceptions include public statements made by senior ICTY officials during periodic visits to Belgrade[142] and Tribunal personnel's engagement with victims' associations and other supportive members of civil society). For most Serbians, then, the Tribunal's work is mediated, and the most influential intermediaries have been political and intellectual elites whose views are widely disseminated in the Serbian media.

The official narrative of the wartime government played a crucial role in shaping many Serbians' initial views about the ICTY. From the time it was established, Milošević and other leaders wove the Tribunal into a wider narrative of Serb victimization. Their motivations were obvious and self-serving; as Mirko Klarin has noted, "it was not in the best interests" of the Milošević regime, key leaders of whom were deeply implicated in war crimes, "for the public in [Serbia] to have a positive image of the ICTY's mission and work."[143] Instead, the regime's leaders "did all they could to convince their subjects that the Tribunal was biased and hostile" toward Serbia.[144]

This pattern continued long after Milošević left office. While a large majority of Serbians holds an extremely low opinion of the ICTY,[145] few have direct knowledge of its work. Most Serbians rarely if ever follow ICTY trials[146] and only a handful has read any of the Tribunal's judgments.[147] When it comes to the ICTY, Svetlana Logar

---

[142] Even when successive ICTY Prosecutors came to Belgrade, Svetlana Logar noted, "it is not themselves who are talking" to the Serbian public. They "have some small . . . press conference, saying a few words, but it is the interpretation . . . which goes on the media." A news story reporting on ICTY Prosecutor Serge Brammertz's latest visit might, for example, say something along the lines: "Brammertz is here again to press us, to press Serbia for this or that." Interview with Svetlana Logar, then Research Director, Ipsos Strategic Marketing, in Belgrade, Serb. (July 10, 2012).

[143] Mirko Klarin, *The Impact of the ICTY Trials on Public Opinion in the Former Yugoslavia*, 7 J. Int'l Crim. Just. 89, 90 (2009).

[144] *Id.*

[145] During both of the last two years in which Strategic Marketing conducted surveys on war crimes issues (2009 and 2011), only 14 percent of respondents said they had positive views of the ICTY while 15 percent said they had no opinion. The remaining 71 percent had either "mainly negative" or "extremely negative" views. *See* 2011 Survey, *supra* note 37, at 65 (reporting results for both 2009 and 2011 surveys). *See also* Kutnjak Ivković & Hagan, *supra* note 33, ch. 3; Donna E. Arzt, *Views on the Ground: The Local Perception of the International Criminal Tribunals in the Former Yugoslavia and Sierra Leone*, 603 Annals Am. Acad. Pol. & Soc. Sci. 226, 232–33 (2006); Bandović, *supra* note 125, at 91–93.

[146] *See* 2011 Survey, *supra* note 37, at 60. This has fluctuated, however. Many Serbians followed at least portions of the Milošević trial. *See* Klaus Bachmann, *Framing the Trial of the Century; Influences of, and on, International Media, in* The Milošević Trial: An Autopsy 260, 261 (Timothy William Waters ed., 2011) ("No other trial" before the ICTY "drew so many citizens of the former Yugoslavia to their TV screens"); *see also* Michael P. Scharf, Opinion, *Making a Spectacle of Himself; Milošević Wants a Stage, Not the Right to Provide His Own Defense*, Wash. Post (Aug. 29, 2004).

[147] *See* 2011 Survey, *supra* note 37, at 55 (90 percent of respondents said they had never read a Tribunal judgment). This is not surprising; ICTY judgments typically run hundreds of pages. The trial judgment in the Karadžić case ran more than 2,500 pages, while Mladić's trial verdict was 2,473 pages long. Prosecutor v. Karadžić, Case No. IT-95-5/18-T, Trial Judgment (Int'l Crim. Trib. for the Former Yugoslavia Mar. 24, 2016); Prosecutor v. Mladić, Case No. IT-09-92-T, Trial

said, "We just have interpretations, not facts."[148] Although "people don't have faith in our politicians," she added, "they're receptive to their message that the ICTY is anti-Serb."[149]

Ivan Jovanović, who helped design some of the surveys on war crimes issues discussed earlier, has a somewhat different view. While he acknowledges politicians are partly responsible for public hostility toward the Hague Tribunal, Jovanović believes the most influential opinion leaders in post-Milošević Serbia are intellectual elites who serve as "talking heads" in media coverage of the Tribunal.[150] The difference between his and Logar's views may be inconsequential, however; those whom Jovanović identifies as highly influential share the anti-Hague perspectives of nationalist politicians.[151]

Serbian lawyers who have represented defendants in The Hague are, Jovanović believes, among the most influential "talking heads" when it comes to the ICTY. In a 2012 interview, Jovanović said there was "more accurate reporting . . . about ICTY" than in earlier years; at that time, the print media were likely to call an ICTY spokesperson for comment when they covered a Tribunal-related development. "But," he continued,

> then they give a slot to a defense attorney [or someone with similar views] saying something different, and then the public is supposed to choose between the two truths. And of course, if you have two truths on the market, which one are you going to prefer? The one [that] is closer to your own conviction, the one which says, "you guys are good, and those guys are bad."[152]

Among the "truths" put forth by Serbian defense lawyers are critiques calling into question key aspects of the ICTY's genocide rulings, as well as legal arguments impugning the Tribunal itself. In the first category, Branko Rakić, the law professor who helped Slobodan Milošević prepare his defense before the ICTY, reprised several strands of this discourse when I interviewed him in 2012. In Rakić's words, "genocide includes the intention to eliminate a group or a substantial part of it, and even if it is 8,000 people from Srebrenica [who were killed, an] even bigger number was

---

Judgment (Nov. 22, 2017). The trial judgment in *Prosecutor v. Prlić et al.* was over 2,600 pages. *Prosecutor v. Prlić et al.*, Case No. IT-04-74-T, Trial Judgment (Int'l Crim. Trib. for the Former Yugoslavia May 29, 2013). More generally, as I discuss later in this chapter, people commonly count on trusted sources to mediate their assessment of complex information.

[148] Interview with Svetlana Logar, then Research Director, Strategic Marketing Research, in Belgrade, Serb. (Nov. 21, 2006).

[149] *Id.*

[150] For that reason, Jovanović ensured that the 2009 and 2011 survey question asking which sources most influenced respondents' views about war crimes proceedings included among possible responses "local analysts (political analysts, writers, intellectuals)" as well as "local lawyers," some of whom have been frequent commentators on news programs about ICTY cases. Interview with Ivan Jovanović, then National Legal Advisor, OSCE Mission to Serbia, in Belgrade, Serb. (July 12, 2012).

[151] The survey results from 2009 and 2011 appear to bear out Jovanović's thesis. More respondents cited local analysts as having a strong influence on their views than any other source, with local lawyers ranking second-highest, media reports third, representatives of state institutions fourth, and local politicians sixth. *See* 2011 Survey, *supra* note 37, at 114.

[152] Interview with Ivan Jovanović, then National Legal Advisor, OSCE Mission to Serbia, in Belgrade, Serb. (July 12, 2012).

sent . . . to Tuzla by the Serbian military authority there."[153] This, he insisted, "does not correspond to the notion of any intention to eliminate them."[154]

Alert to this argument's inherent appeal to a Serbian audience, Rakić continued: "Many people believe that the figures [of those killed] are a little bit inflated." When I asked how many people he believes were killed in Srebrenica, Rakić replied: "I can't tell exactly . . . I cannot estimate. It could be, I wouldn't be surprised if it were [1,000]," far less than the widely-used estimates of 7,000–8,000.[155] In Jovanović's view, these and other arguments by Serbian lawyers, which have received extensive publicity in Serbia,[156] reinforced many Serbians' natural inclination to reject the ICTY's genocide rulings.

It is worth pausing to consider whether (as several Serbians suggested), public challenges to Hague rulings merit condemnation. After all, citizens in open societies routinely criticize judicial rulings, and respected international legal experts have questioned specific ICTY judgments.[157] Serbian journalist Ljiljana Smajlović passionately pressed this point when I asked her about a then-recent Strategic Marketing survey showing declining levels of knowledge about Srebrenica. Noting that internationally-respected scholars had raised questions about the ICTY's genocide determination in relation to Srebrenica, Smajlović fairly exploded:

> And I very much resent being told that if I am not willing to accept that this legal definition fits the Srebrenica crime, that this means that I'm a denier. I am not a denier. . . . And in this region, with internationals . . . as soon as someone says, "Well, I have some doubts about whether this is genocide," you're in denial . . . ; that's not true! And it's frankly somewhat offensive to intimate that anytime one objects to anything, that's, you know, that's somehow ethically . . . wrong, and I should say "Whatever the ICTY said is the truth and I will swear by it and I will never question it." . . . If you're a Serb and you say, "Look, this doesn't exactly seem like what I've been taught to believe genocide is," or "This doesn't exactly chime in with the Holocaust," then you're somehow suspect, you know, you are morally suspicious. And so that, that annoys me.[158]

I raised this perspective with several Serbians who support the ICTY. Their common response was a version of "context is everything." In the Serbian context, they said, challenges to the ICTY's genocide rulings were integral to discourses of denial. Focusing on arguments, such as those of Rakić, that subtract several thousand from the internationally-accepted estimate of victims killed in Srebrenica, Jovanović said

[153] Interview with Branko Rakić, Professor, Faculty of Law, University of Belgrade, in Belgrade, Serb. (July 11, 2012).

[154] *Id.*

[155] *Id.* These arguments track with what Eric Gordy describes as a nationalist strategy "to partly acknowledge the commission of crimes in Srebrenica while raising doubt and fear on the question of whether they constituted genocide." GORDY, *supra* note 28, at 135. The claim that far fewer Bosniaks were killed in Srebrenica than the ICTY and others have found is a classic instance of *minimization*, a form of denial. *See* Chapter 5.

[156] *See* GORDY, *supra* note 28, at 141.

[157] As noted later in this chapter, even the ICTY's most staunch champions in Serbia found themselves sharply criticizing a series of Hague judgments, beginning with the Appeals Chamber's November 2012 acquittal of Ante Gotovina.

[158] Interview with Ljiljana Smajlović, Journalist, in Belgrade, Serb. (July 10, 2012).

these claims "are getting into relativization" and amount "to denying Srebrenica."[159] In his view, such arguments obscure the most salient point: "What you have to remember is that Serbs killed as many Bosnian men as they were able to kill on that particular place in those few days."[160] Marijana Toma, then deputy director of the Humanitarian Law Center, acknowledged that even some of her "friends who are lawyers … are actually questioning" the ICTY's ruling that genocide can be committed on the scale of a single municipality (Srebrenica). But, Toma added, their questions come from an entirely different perspective than that of "our politicians," most of whom "are actually questioning it from the position of somebody who wants to justify the Serbian policy during the wars."[161]

Buttressing their critiques of specific judgments, Serbia's legal pundits have continued to espouse Milošević-era narratives discrediting the Tribunal's institutional legitimacy.[162] Jovanović described the impact this way:

It suffices that you have a few individuals who are seen as [possessing the] most authority on a field and then everyone relies on them and their interpretation. And here you had some law professors and also defense attorneys who were working at the Tribunal, who …, once they [return to Serbia], they're more often denigrating the Tribunal than describing how it works—which was often mistaken, deliberately.[163]

As Jovanović implied, these attorneys may not believe all of the views they espouse.[164] But this hardly matters in terms of their impact. Their anti-Hague claims generate a reservoir of arguments upon which credulous citizens can draw to rationalize rejecting ICTY judgments.

Whatever the sources of Serbians' views, opinion polls registered highly negative views of the Hague Tribunal long after Milošević lost power. A majority of Serbian respondents in a survey described as "recent" in 2009 identified the ICTY as the institution posing "the greatest danger to national security."[165] In the words of Serbian

---

[159] Interview with Ivan Jovanović, then National Legal Advisor, OSCE Mission to Serbia, in Belgrade, Serb. (July 12, 2012).

[160] Id.

[161] Interview with Marijana Toma, then Deputy Director, Humanitarian Law Center, in Belgrade, Serb. (June 10, 2014).

[162] One of their principal arguments is that any such tribunal should have been created by treaty. E.g., interview with Branko Rakić, Professor, Faculty of Law, University of Belgrade, in Belgrade, Serb. (July 11, 2012). This aspect of local lawyers' discourses is reminiscent of robust critiques of the International Military Tribunal (IMT) developed by German lawyers during the 1950s. The emergence of their critique (many components of which were eminently reasonable) coincided with the onset in German society of a "general suppression process"—a keen desire to forget the Nazi past. Christoph Burchard, *The Nuremberg Trial and Its Impact on Germany*, 4 J. Int'l Crim. Just. 800, 811–12 (2006). For further discussion of the German experience, see Chapter 11.

[163] Interview with Ivan Jovanović, then National Legal Advisor, OSCE Mission to Serbia, in Belgrade, Serb. (July 12, 2012).

[164] In Jovanović's assessment, these lawyers are often "telling the public what they think the public would like to hear." Id.

[165] Klarin, *supra* note 143, at 89. Only 5 percent of Serbian Serbs who participated in a 2002 survey said they considered the ICTY trustworthy. See Stuart Ford, *A Social Psychology Model of the Perceived Legitimacy of International Criminal Courts: Implications for the Success of Transitional Justice Mechanisms*, 45 Vand. J. Transnat'l L. 405, 416 (2012). In a separate poll five years later, 7 percent of Serbians said they considered the ICTY unbiased. See id.

political scientist Nenad Dimitrijević, the "reigning attitude toward the ICTY" in Serbia "is one of open animosity."[166]

In remains to be noted that some aspects of the ICTY's record were seized upon by Serbians already disposed to reject evidence of Serb atrocities to support nationalist claims of Tribunal bias. Two merit brief mention here. First, as noted earlier, two-thirds of those indicted by the Tribunal were ethnic Serbs. Among those charged by the Hague Prosecutor whose cases reached final judgment as of late September 2017, moreover, Serb suspects were convicted (some through plea agreements) at somewhat higher rates than were suspects of Bosniak and Croat ethnicity.[167]

Second, the ICTY trial many Serbians hoped would illuminate the criminality of the Milošević regime—that of Slobodan Milošević himself—frustrated their expectations, and not just because the defendant died before judgment. As noted in Chapter 6, Milošević "transform[ed] the courtroom into his political platform."[168] Of particular relevance to the point developed here, Milošević, who chose to represent himself, mounted a defense calculated to reinforce Serbian antipathy toward the Hague Tribunal.

The Prosecutor's initial indictment against Milošević, issued while Serbians were experiencing NATO attacks during the FRY-Kosovo conflict,[169] related solely to crimes committed in Kosovo. In this setting, many Serbians believed the ICTY was acting as "an instrument of power," not an impartial court of justice.[170] Fueling Serbian suspicions in his opening statement, the bellicose defendant charged that the case against him was " 'an ocean of lies' concocted by Western powers to justify NATO's attack on Serbian forces during the 1999 Kosovo war." [171] Throughout his trial Milošević sought to undermine a central claim of Tribunal officials—that the ICTY determined the guilt or innocence of individuals one by one, not the

---

[166] Dimitrijević, *supra* note 64, at 17.

[167] Excluding cases in which initial ICTY charges were dismissed, cases in which the Prosecutor had issued an indictment were transferred to domestic courts for trial, ICTY proceedings were terminated in light of defendants' death, or final judgments had not yet been rendered by the ICTY, an analysis undertaken by Sonja Balić, one of my research assistants at the Washington College of Law, found that 90 percent of Serb defendants were found guilty of at least some charges, compared to 75 percent of Bosniak suspects, 73 percent of Croat suspects, and 33 percent of Kosovo Albanian suspects.

[168] Ian Fisher & Marlise Simons, *Defiant, Milošević Begins His Defense by Assailing NATO*, N.Y. TIMES (Feb. 15, 2002).

[169] Although Milošević was later indicted for crimes committed in Bosnia and Croatia in the early to mid-1990s, the ICTY did not issue its first indictment against him until May 1999, when his country was at war with NATO. *See* Chapter 3. To Serbians, the correlation is straightforward. As journalist Filip Švarm put it, "Milošević went to the Hague when he lost the war against NATO." Interview with Filip Švarm, Journalist, in Belgrade, Serb. (Nov. 24, 2006). More generally, since "people here felt themselves as victims" during the NATO bombardment, it was difficult for "ordinary people" to accept that Milošević could be "guilty of war crimes" against Kosovo Albanians, whom they considered "enemies of Serbia." Interview with Antonela Riha, Journalist, in Belgrade, Serb. (Nov. 27, 2006). I address the ICTY Prosecutor's reasons for indicting Milošević during the Kosovo war, and initially only for war crimes committed in Kosovo, in DIANE F. ORENTLICHER, OPEN SOCIETY JUSTICE INITIATIVE, SHRINKING THE SPACE FOR DENIAL: THE IMPACT OF THE ICTY IN SERBIA 75–76 (2008).

[170] Interview with Ljiljana Smajlović, Journalist, in Belgrade, Serb. (Nov. 24, 2006).

[171] *Milošević on Trial*, ECONOMIST (Feb. 13, 2002).

responsibility of an ethnic group.[172] In Milošević's counter narrative, the Tribunal was prosecuting Serbia's former leader as a proxy for persecuting Serbs.[173] In myriad ways, then, Milošević used his trial to perpetuate the anti-Hague narrative he had honed as wartime president.

5. OTHER SOURCES OF INFORMATION ABOUT WAR CRIMES

Individuals interviewed for this study cited several other factors that, in their view, contributed to many Serbians' poor grasp of or belief in reports of Serb atrocities. Refik Hodžić, who served as Acting Head of the Media Outreach and Web offices of the ICTY when I interviewed him in November 2006,[174] said that, because "there were no crimes committed in Serbia" itself, "the people have no day-to-day connection" to wartime atrocities.[175]

Many Serbians do, however, routinely encounter ethnic Serbs whom they see as victims of wartime atrocities. Srđan Bogosavljević noted that hundreds of thousands of Serbs fled to Serbia during the 1990s conflicts; many married local Serbians and were integrated in their spouses' social networks.[176] Bogosavljević continued:

> And they have their own stories about their own truth about what had happened. So not only that we have these nationalist journalists and a lot of nationalistically-oriented publications which were showing that Serbs are the only right, everybody else was against Serbs, and that we are good, and all are bad, but there are people which are witnessing that they suffered and they never killed anybody, they just escaped.[177]

In Bogosavljević's experience, when someone tries to balance these accounts by raising the "broader picture, what came from Serbia," citizens who interact with Serbs displaced during the wars reply, "Yes, but you know, this and this guy, how he suffered. His son was killed, his house was burned, and so on." This, in Bogosavljević's view, helped perpetuate a widespread perception of "Serbs as a victim, not as somebody who caused" harm.[178]

---

[172] *See* Chapter 2. *See also* Brammertz: *ICTY Did Not Try Nation but War Criminals*, HINA CROATIAN NEWS AGENCY (Dec. 2, 2017).

[173] *See* NEVENKA TROMP, PROSECUTING SLOBODAN MILOŠEVIĆ: THE UNFINISHED TRIAL 30 (2016).

[174] Hodžić later served as Spokesperson for the ICTY Registry and Chambers, and since March 2011 has served as director of communications for the International Center for Transitional Justice.

[175] Interview with Refik Hodžić, then Acting Head of the Media Outreach and Web offices, ICTY, in The Hague, Neth. (Nov. 17, 2006). This is a slight overstatement. As noted earlier, some war crimes were committed in Serbia during the 1990s. ICTY charges against Vojislav Šešelj included an accusation relating to forced deportation of the non-Serb population from parts of Vojvodina, Serbia. Prosecutor v. Šešelj, Case No. IT-03-67-T, Third Amended Indictment, ¶ 6 (Int'l Crim. Trib. for the Former Yugoslavia Dec. 7, 2007).

[176] Interview with Srđan Bogosavljević, Director, Ipsos Strategic Marketing, in Belgrade, Serb. (July 10, 2012). Another source states that, as of 2015, Serbia still hosted "around 220,000 displaced persons from Kosovo, and 44,000 from elsewhere in former Yugoslavia, who could not or did not want to move back to their pre-war places of residence." Davide Denti, *Serbia, the Unexpected Friend of Syrian Refugees*, BOULEVARD EXTÉRIEUR (Sept. 3, 2015).

[177] Interview with Srđan Bogosavljević, Director, Ipsos Strategic Marketing, in Belgrade, Serb. (July 10, 2012).

[178] *Id.*

Yet displaced Serbs also brought intimations of atrocities committed *by* Serbs. Indeed, by June 2016 some 3,000 individuals suspected of committing war crimes in Bosnia, Croatia, and Kosovo were estimated to be living in Serbia.[179] Still, Bogosavljević noted, "our killers are hidden, they're not going around and speaking about how many [Serb] people killed" others.[180] Instead, their accounts are likely to be shared, if at all, only obliquely and privately. Describing her own interviews with Serbians who made veiled references to rumored Serb atrocities, Jelena Obradović-Wochnik observes: "[T]here is something at the very core of such stories that is not openly discussed, or even articulated. That 'something' was the implicit knowledge that not only had someone died a terrible, brutal and often undignified death, but that, if the rumours were true, they died at the hands of Serbs."[181]

Implicit knowledge of Serb atrocities is hardly likely to dispel public manifestations of denial. Instead, as Obradović-Wochnik notes, the very "*presence* of informal knowledge and rumour [might reinforce] the silence, because what most respondents came to know through informal channels is that the reality of what was happening was much worse than what was being presented."[182] The rumors "could be true, or they could be false, and the possibility of their truth often rendered them unspeakable."[183]

B. Social Science Perspectives

By their nature, theories offered by Serbians to explain high levels of denialism cannot be proven correct. But research across several social science disciplines provides striking support for many of them. As will be seen, myriad studies offer compelling accounts of dynamics likely to limit any ICT's capacity to transform beliefs about a dark chapter in a society's immediate past.

A note of caution is in order first: many of the studies on which I draw took place in laboratory settings, where participants' exposure to information was limited and controlled. The studies typically transpired over a brief period, sometimes as short as an hour.[184] These circumstances are crucial to a study's results, which often "fail to replicate if we change the context."[185] And as I have emphasized throughout this

---

[179] *FHP: U Srbiji Živi 3,000 Osumnjičenih za Ratne Zločine*, Vesti (June 17, 2016).

[180] Interview with Srđan Bogosavljević, Director, Ipsos Strategic Marketing, in Belgrade, Serb. (July 10, 2012).

[181] Obradović-Wochnik, Narratives of Denial, *supra* note 29, at 104. In another publication, Obradović-Wochnik argues that Serbs who privately circulated these accounts were, by doing so, "actively resist[ing] the silencing of the Milošević era." Obradović-Wochnik, *Silent Dilemma*, *supra* note 30, at 342. She also suggests, however, that many of her sources said they did not speak of these crimes because they were unspeakable—that is, "too horrible." *Id.*

[182] Obradović-Wochnik, Narratives of Denial, *supra* note 29, at 105.

[183] *Id.*

[184] *See, e.g.*, Charles S. Taber & Milton Lodge, *Motivated Skepticism and the Evaluation of Political Beliefs*, 50 Am. J. Pol. Sci. 755, 757 (2006) (describing research study conditions in terms of "a single session lasting less than one hour"). Recognizing this, some social psychologists have undertaken longitudinal studies. *See* Rupert Brown & Sabina Čehajić, *Dealing with the Past and Facing the Future: Mediators of the Effects of Collective Guilt and Shame in Bosnia and Herzegovina*, 38 Eur. J. Soc. Psychol. 669 (2008).

[185] Lisa Feldman Barrett, Opinion, *Psychology Is Not in Crisis*, N.Y. Times (Sept. 1, 2015). Many social science studies have proved difficult to replicate even in controlled laboratory settings. A study conducted by 270 researchers tried to replicate the results of 100 psychology experiments whose results were published in prestigious journals. They were able to do so only thirty-nine

book, context matters enormously when it comes to how a society reckons with (or fails to face) a disturbing chapter in its past.

1. IMPACT OF OFFICIAL NARRATIVES: HEURISTICS AND FRAMING

If widespread denial of wartime atrocities raises profound questions of communal conscience, it also reflects the most prosaic patterns of human cognition. Even in societies that have not experienced dramatic upheavals or national traumas, beliefs are often poorly informed or, put differently, are based on factual errors. Social scientists across several disciplines have tried to explain why.[186]

In an influential account published in 1974, Amos Tversky and Daniel Kahneman attributed many mistaken beliefs to people's reliance on *heuristics*—cognitive shortcuts we use to assess the probability that something is factually true.[187] Adapting their approach to the context explored here, we might imagine Serbian citizens subconsciously[188] asking themselves, "What is the probability that reports I have heard of Serb atrocities are true?" As people process such questions, Tversky and Kahneman theorized, they rely on judgmental heuristics to guide their assessments. While often useful, these rules of thumb can produce profoundly mistaken beliefs.

A key judgmental heuristic is that of *availability*, which connotes "the ease with which instances or occurrences [of a phenomenon] can be brought to mind."[189] The notion of availability is central to contemporary versions of *framing theory*,[190] which offer a plausible account of how elite Serbian narratives shaped many citizens' beliefs about wartime atrocities. Framing theorists believe that the way we assess a claim turns in part on the availability in our memory of potentially relevant considerations.[191] When confronted with facts or possibilities that require evaluation (e.g., "Serbs killed thousands of Muslims in Srebrenica"), several rather different perspectives may be *available* to guide a person's assessment. Framing theory suggests that the perspective that is most readily *accessible* is likely to

---

times. OPEN SCIENCE COLLABORATION, *Estimating the Reproducibility of Psychological Science,* 349 SCI. 943 (2015).

[186] For relatively recent examples, *see* Brendan Nyhan & Jason Reifler, *When Corrections Fail: The Persistence of Political Misperceptions,* 32 POL. BEHAV. 303 (2010); Taber & Lodge, *supra* note 184; James N. Druckman, *The Implications of Framing Effects for Citizen Competence,* 23 POL. BEHAV. 225 (2001).

[187] Amos Tversky & Daniel Kahneman, *Judgment Under Uncertainty: Heuristics and Biases,* 185 SCI. 1124 (1974). In a more recent publication, Kahneman defined a heuristic as "roughly, a rule of thumb," which is often used "to make a difficult judgment." DANIEL KAHNEMAN, THINKING, FAST AND SLOW 7 (2011).

[188] The processes that form our views about reality are not wholly conscious, but instead transpire to a great extent "in the silence in our mind." KAHNEMAN, *supra* note 187, at 4.

[189] Tversky & Kahneman, *supra* note 187, at 1127. The concept has been refined since Tversky and Kahneman's early writing. *See* KAHNEMAN, *supra* note 187, at 129. *See also* CASS R. SUNSTEIN & REID HASTIE, WISER: GETTING BEYOND GROUPTHINK TO MAKE GROUPS SMARTER 44 (2015) ("When people use the availability heuristic, they answer a question of probability by asking whether examples come readily to mind").

[190] Although Tversky and Kahneman did pioneering work on framing, the following account of framing theory draws primarily on more recent work of other scholars.

[191] James Druckman explains the concept this way: "A consideration must be stored in memory to be *available* for retrieval and use in constructing an attitude." James N. Druckman, What's It All About?: Framing in Political Science 9 (2009) [hereinafter Druckman, *Framing in Political Science*]. *See also* Chong & Druckman, *supra* note 27, at 111.

prevail.[192] Accessibility typically increases "through regular or recent exposure to a communication . . . emphasizing the consideration,"[193] and is also thought to be a function of *salience*, which is likely to be high when a consideration triggers strong emotions.[194]

Shrewd politicians have long grasped the power of framing, honing their communications to emphasize the perspective they hope their audience will adopt. If they succeed, they will have produced a *framing effect*—that is, they will have shaped their audience's beliefs.[195] Notably, strong frames "can be built around exaggerations and outright lies playing on [people's] fears and prejudices."[196] As we have seen, Milošević was a master of the technique: throughout the 1990s he invoked the specter of Serb victimization[197] at the hands of Croats, Bosniaks, and Kosovo Albanians to mobilize Serbs and justify their wartime conduct.[198] In line with this frame, Milošević cast global efforts to halt and punish Serb atrocities as proof of the international community's anti-Serb bias.

This not to suggest Serbians uniformly adopted official narratives as their own. In the lead-up to war, throughout the 1990s conflicts, and after they ended, a robust corps of Serbian activists challenged their government's narrative and policies.[199] My point here is that framing theory maps neatly onto Serbian sources' ascription of a powerful belief-shaping influence to official and dominant elite discourses.[200] In

---

[192] In Druckman's words, "*Accessibility* refers to the likelihood that an available consideration exceeds an activation threshold to be used in an evaluation." Druckman, *Framing in Political Science, supra* note 191, at 9. (emphasis in original).

[193] Chong & Druckman, *supra* note 27, at 110. *See also* Druckman, Framing in Political Science, *supra* note 191, at 10.

[194] *See* Cass R. Sunstein, *What's Available? Social Influences and Behavioral Economics Empirical Legal Realism: A New Social Scientific Assessment of Law and Human Behavior*, 97 Nw. U. L. Rev. 1295, 1297–98 (2003). *See also* Tversky & Kahneman, *supra* note 187, at 1127. Reflecting on his and Tversky's earlier work, Kahneman wrote in 2011 that "an important advance" in the intervening years "is that emotion now looms much larger in our understanding of intuitive judgments and choices than it did in the past." Kahneman, *supra* note 187, at 12.

[195] *See* Druckman, *supra* note 186, at 230 (by emphasizing a perspective, a speaker can "lead individuals to focus on [that perspective] when constructing their opinions," a type of framing effect). *See also* Chong & Druckman, *supra* note 27, at 109.

[196] Chong & Druckman, *supra* note 27, at 111.

[197] In doing so, Milošević used a classic technique. As Daniel Bar-Tal et al. have noted, "Politicians often use collective victimization as a source of political power, and reminders of past and present victimization are a potent theme for recruitment and mobilization." Daniel Bar-Tal et al., *A Sense of Self-Perceived Collective Victimhood in Intractable Conflicts*, 91 Int'l Rev. Red Cross 229, 247 (2009).

[198] While this book emphasizes developments beginning with the ascendance of Slobodan Milošević as a nationalist leader, nationalist Serbian narratives predate the Milošević era. *See* Ramet, *supra* note 117, at 44–46.

[199] *See* Emily Shaw, The Role of Social Identity in Resistance to International Criminal Law: The Case of Serbia and the ICTY 12–13 (Berkeley Program in Soviet and Post-Soviet Studies Working Paper Series, 2003). Serbia saw mass protests against the Milošević regime after the conflicts in Bosnia and Croatia ended. *See also* Florian Bieber, *Popular Mobilization in the 1990s: Nationalism, Democracy and the Slow Decline of the Milošević Regime, in* New Perspectives on Yugoslavia: Key Issues and Controversies ch. 9 (Dejan Djokić & James Ker-Lindsay eds., 2011).

[200] Framing theory can also account for the views of Serbians who rejected official narratives. In some iterations, framing theory holds that the way individuals assess information is influenced by their "frame in thought." *See, e.g.,* Chong & Druckman, *supra* note 27, at 105–06. Individuals' deeply-held values can define their dominant frame in thought. *See id.* Thus two

their account, described earlier, those discourses shaped the views of a great part of Serbian society, not all Serbians' beliefs.

Framing theory also accommodates Bogosavljević's belief that many Serbians' views were influenced by daily encounters with Serbs from other parts of the former Yugoslavia. Scholars recognize that, however powerful, dominant public discourses are by no means the only shaping influence on peoples' beliefs. Instead, "citizens regularly adopt frames they learn in discussions with other citizens."[201] In a similar vein, some scholarship on judgmental heuristics places special emphasis on "the social and cultural dimensions of judgment under uncertainty,"[202] recognizing the independent influence of citizens' conversations on the formation of political views.[203]

2. Motivated Reasoning and Social Identity

The role of motivation in shaping beliefs is central to other streams of social psychology, which offer striking support for Serbian perspectives explored earlier. Particularly relevant here is scholarship on *motivated reasoning*,[204] whose core insight is that unconscious preferences bias the way we reason, with the result that people "are more likely to arrive at those conclusions that they want to arrive at."[205] As Charles Taber and Milton Lodge have written, "It is not that [people] openly lie to themselves" when they process new information and evidence.[206] Instead, people often "unconsciously process information" in ways that advance "goals or interests extrinsic to the decisionmaking task at hand,"[207] even when they consciously strive to be objective. More specifically, they employ a permissive standard when evaluating information they wish to believe, and a more rigorous standard to assess evidence of unwelcome facts.[208]

Social identity theory adds another layer to this account, which is highly pertinent here. As conceived by Henri Tajfal, social identity is "that *part* of an individual's self-concept which derives from his knowledge of his membership of a social group (or groups) together with the value and emotional significance attached to that membership."[209] Linking social identity to motivated reasoning, much as individuals are motivated to maintain a positive self-image, many are disposed to maintain a positive

---

people with fundamentally different values can evaluate the same information in profoundly different ways.

[201] *Id.* at 109.

[202] Sunstein, *supra* note 194, at 1299.

[203] *See, e.g.,* James N. Druckman & Kjersten R. Nelson, *Framing and Deliberation: How Citizens' Conversations Limit Elite Influence,* 47 Am. J. Pol. Sci. 729 (2003).

[204] Following Ziva Kunda's definition, I use the word *motivation* to connote wishes, desires, or preferences that influence reasoning processes such as "forming impressions, determining one's beliefs and attitudes, evaluating evidence, and making decisions." Ziva Kunda, *The Case for Motivated Reasoning,* 108 Psychol. Bull. 480, 480 (1990).

[205] *Id.* at 495.

[206] Taber & Lodge, *supra* note 184, at 757.

[207] Dan M. Kahan, *The Supreme Court 2010 Term—Foreward: Neutral Principles, Motivated Cognition, and Some Problems for Constitutional Law,* 125 Harv. L. Rev. 1, 7 (2011). *See also id.* at 19.

[208] Erica Dawson et al., *Motivated Reasoning and Performance on the Wason Selection Task,* 28 Personality & Soc. Psychol. Bull. 1379, 1379–380 (2002).

[209] Henri Tajfal, Human Groups and Social Categories: Studies in Social Psychology 255 (1981) (emphasis in original).

view of their social group(s).[210] Accordingly, they are generally disposed to believe information that conforms to a positive view of themselves *and the groups to which they belong.*[211] Conversely, people are more likely to reject than accept propositions "that impugn the character" of groups to which they belong and on whom they depend for psychic support, from family members to ethnic communities.[212] These dynamics readily account for both outright rejection by some Serbians of evidence implicating Serbs in mass atrocities, as well as the refusal of many to characterize as blameworthy conduct they say they believe occurred.[213]

Although he has not been exposed to literature on motivated reasoning or social identity, Ivan Jovanović illustrated their central insights when he explained Serbians' resistance to the "trial truth" established in The Hague this way:

- You need more evidence to be persuaded that somebody of your own creed did something bad than evidence that all what you hear [about Serb atrocities] is a lie.[214]
- And of course, if you have two truths on the market, which one are you going to prefer? The one . . . which says, "you guys are good, and those guys are bad."[215]

Srđan Bogosavljević enunciated a theory of "motivated forgetting" when he suggested many Serbians "are forgetting" what they once knew about Serb atrocities because they "don't *like* to remember" unsettling facts about their in-group.[216]

Social scientists have identified a manifestation of motivated reasoning common in situations of inter-group conflict, which tracks with previously-noted responses to Strategic Marketing survey questions about relative victimization.[217] In these settings,

---

[210] *See* Sabina Čehajić-Clancy et al., *Affirmation, Acknowledgment of In-Group Responsibility, Group-Based Guilt, and Support for Reparative Measures*, 101 J. PERSONALITY & SOC. PSYCHOL. 256, 256 (2011); Čehajić-Clancy, *supra* note 98, at 103.

[211] *See* Dawson et al., *supra* note 208, at 1379–87.

[212] Kahan, *supra* note 207, at 20. Not surprisingly, this effect has been especially pronounced among "people who identified strongly with [their] in-group," who have "required more evidence to judge their group's actions as harmful and felt less collective guilt than people who identified less strongly." Masi Noor et al., *When Suffering Begets Suffering: The Psychology of Competitive Victimhood Between Adversarial Groups in Violent Conflicts*, 16 PERSONALITY & SOC. PSYCHOL. REV. 351, 366 (2012). *See also* Anca M. Miron et al., *Motivated Shifting of Justice Standards*, 36 PERSONALITY & SOC. PSYCHOL. BULL. 768 (2010).

Social identity theory suggests, as well, that the wartime context of the 1990s might have elevated the salience of many Serbians' self-identification *as Serbs*. When a social group with which one identifies comes under threat, group identification may be heightened, with significant implications for how group members process information. *See* Shaw, *supra* note 199, at 10–11. Alternatively, some members of the group may maintain a positive self-image by *dissociating* from a social group whose conduct conflicts with their personal values. *See id.*

[213] The latter is reflected in previously-discussed responses to Strategic Marketing survey questions asking respondents who said they believed certain events had occurred whether they considered the underlying conduct to be a war crime meriting punishment or, instead, an inevitable by-product of war.

[214] Interview with Ivan Jovanović, then National Legal Advisor, OSCE Mission to Serbia, in Belgrade, Serb. (July 12, 2012).

[215] *Id.*

[216] Interview with Srđan Bogosavljević, Director, Ipsos Strategic Marketing, in Belgrade, Serb. (July 10, 2012).

[217] *See supra* Figure 7.11.

people's general motivation to preserve a positive social identity has often produced "a belief that [one's own group] has suffered more than the out-group" even though the in-group committed grave crimes against the latter.[218] A perception of "collective victimhood"[219] typically entails the belief that another group is "responsible for unjust and immoral acts"[220] while the conduct of one's own group is justified and fundamentally moral. Accordingly, belief in the collective victimhood of one's in-group can "become[] an institutionalized way of escaping guilt, shame or responsibility."[221]

3. DISSONANCE

Social psychology in the dissonance tradition offers complementary insights about the dynamics underlying denialism. Dissonance theory generally holds that individuals who possess inconsistent beliefs, or whose beliefs are inconsistent with their behavior, experience psychological discomfort that they are motivated to alleviate, particularly when the dissonance is acute.[222] Of particular relevance here, dissonance can arise when one's personal values conflict with the conduct, beliefs, or values of groups with which one identifies.[223]

If one believes members of her family or ethnic group committed atrocities, she can live uneasily with the resulting dissonance[224]—as many Serbians surely do. Jadranka Jelinčić evoked this state when she explained widespread resistance among Serbians to information about wartime atrocities: if you believe someone "you love could have done" grievous harm, you have a "very difficult psychological dialogue" with yourself.[225]

While some live uneasily with dissonance, others may instead engage in dissonance-reduction strategies, such as attitudinal change. This could entail rejecting official narratives casting Serbs primarily as victims. Alternatively, it could entail much the opposite, manifesting as denial: to minimize dissonance with their deepest values or devotion to family, Serbians might discredit evidence that Serbs committed mass atrocities. Among dissonance-reduction techniques other than attitudinal change, Serbians might resort to "repression or deverbalization."[226]

---

[218] Čehajić & Brown, *Silencing the Past*, supra note 7, at 192. *See also* Čehajić-Clancy, *supra* note 98, at 105.

[219] *See* Daniel Bar-Tal et al., *supra* note 197, at 229; Noor et al., *supra* note 212.

[220] Bar-Tal et al., *supra* note 197, at 244.

[221] *Id.* at 246. *See also* Noor et al., *supra* note 212, at 359.

[222] The seminal work on cognitive dissonance is LEON FESTINGER, A THEORY OF COGNITIVE DISSONANCE (1957).

[223] *See, e.g.*, Demis E. Glasford et al., *Intragroup Dissonance: Responses to Ingroup Violation of Personal Values*, 44 J. EXPERIMENTAL SOC. PSYCHOL. 1057 (2008); David C. Matz & Wendy Wood, *Cognitive Dissonance in Groups: The Consequences of Disagreement*, 88 J. PERSONALITY & SOC. PSYCHOL. 22, 22–37 (2005). Conversely, Festinger posited that individuals whose cherished views are challenged by inconsistent information may reduce the accompanying dissonance through their social interaction with others who share their commitment to those beliefs. *See* FESTINGER, *supra* note 222, ch. 8.

[224] As Festinger recognized, people have varying tolerances for dissonance. FESTINGER, *supra* note 222, at 266.

[225] Interview with Jadranka Jelinčić, Executive Director, Open Society Fund Serbia, in Belgrade, Serb. (July 9, 2012). As for those who actually saw battle, Jelinčić said: "The generation that participated in all this is not ready to face with itself." *Id.*

[226] Patrick Gosling et al., *Denial of Responsibility: A New Mode of Dissonance Reduction*, 90 J. PERSONALITY & SOC. PSYCHOL. 722, 723 (2006). *See* Ford, *supra* note 165, at 427, for discussion of other dissonance-reduction techniques.

In a different interview than the one just quoted, Jelinčić evoked dissonance-related dynamics to explain Serbia's "culture of denial": "When you have a brother or a husband" who participated in a war, "you don't think of him as someone who could take a knife to a child."[227] Jelinčić continued: "For very personal reasons you can't change the framework in which you think."[228]

The state of mind Jelinčić evoked is not solely a function of citizens' identification with individuals who committed atrocities. For many Serbians, confronting the past would require a discomforting reckoning with their *own* wartime choices. Bogdan Ivanišević explained Serbian resistance to the ICTY's factual findings this way: "Most of the people don't want to confront [the subject of Serb atrocities] because . . . they invested so heavily in the '90s, rooting for their own side and ignoring all the bad things that their own side was doing against the other side somehow. So there's a natural tendency among a great number of people not to reexamine oneself—'Who [did] I support? What did I do during the war?'—because that's a difficult thing for anyone to do."[229]

In a similar vein, Serbian psychologist Žarko Korać evoked the dynamics of dissonance to explain why many Serbians deny or ignore Serb responsibility for two notorious massacres during the siege of Sarajevo. The first occurred on February 5, 1994, when a shell detonated in Sarajevo's outdoor Markale market, killing sixty-eight and wounding over a hundred and forty.[230] Eighteen months later, five mortar shells landed in Markale, this time killing at least forty-three and wounding eighty-eight.[231] Both times, Serbs claimed government forces deliberately attacked their own citizens.[232] Even after the ICTY found Serb forces responsible for both massacres, Serbs "still routinely denied, or ignored" them.[233] In the view of Professor Korać, the massacres are rarely even mentioned in Serbia because, like Srebrenica, they implicate "above all, . . . the responsibility of the Serbian side for these crimes." "As a psychologist," he told a journalist, "I would call it a grand negation of reality, signifying an unwillingness to confront one's own responsibility."[234]

Dissonance theory suggests a possible effect of coerced compliance with the ICTY, as described in Chapter 3, on Serbian beliefs about wartime atrocities. As previously noted, Serbian advocates for cooperation hoped Serbian arrests and transfers of Hague suspects would signify social condemnation of those crimes. Yet research suggests that, when people are *compelled* to take action inconsistent with their beliefs, they are unlikely to adjust their views to align with their conduct precisely because they understand the latter to have been externally compelled.[235] If a similar dynamic

---

[227] Interview with Jadranka Jelinčić, Executive Director, Open Society Fund Serbia, in Belgrade, Serb. (Nov. 24, 2006).

[228] *Id.*

[229] Interview with Bogdan Ivanišević, Attorney, in Belgrade, Serb. (July 9, 2012).

[230] Prosecutor v. Mladić, Case No. IT-09-92-T, Trial Judgment, ¶ 2097 (Nov. 22, 2017).

[231] *Id.* ¶ 2150 (Nov. 22, 2017).

[232] *See Serbs Resist Guilt for Markale Massacres*, Just. Rep. (Feb. 3, 2012).

[233] *Id.*

[234] *Id.*

[235] An example from a laboratory setting is captured in the notion, "I did this because the experimenter asked me to, so I am not responsible." Gosling et al., *supra* note 226, at 723 (illustrating the findings of an earlier study by Daniel R. Stalder and Robert S. Baron). *See also* Festinger, *supra* note 222, at 85.

was at play in Serbia,[236] successive leaders reinforced it by justifying their arrests of Hague fugitives on pragmatic rather than moral grounds.

Yet it is also plausible that, at least in some contexts, coerced cooperation can catalyze normative change. Lara Nettelfield suggests something like this could happen in Bosnia: recalling that Bosnian leaders who opposed the ICTY were nonetheless compelled to support it "in order to receive specific benefits," she argues that, in line with experience elsewhere, "such adaptation can be the first step in the process of internalization of norms."[237]

4. Belief Perseverance/Confirmation Biases

Generally, people prefer information consistent with their beliefs, views and prior behaviors, and avoid information that's inconsistent.

—James Shepperd[238]

If there was a conscious theory behind the expectations of Serbians who thought the ICTY would catalyze a national reckoning, it went something like this: in the face of new facts about Serb atrocities, established in the crucible of trial before an independent, impartial tribunal, Serbian citizens would reexamine their beliefs, acknowledge the full extent of Serb atrocities and Serbia's role in sponsoring them, and condemn both. Instead, as Svetlana Logar observed, it proved difficult to displace the "basic picture [that] was already in peoples' minds."[239]

Scholars across several disciplines have explored the phenomenon Logar evoked, *belief perseverance*. A large body of research shows that once people form a belief, they are prone to bring a *confirmation bias* to bear in assessing new evidence and arguments about the subject.[240] That is, they "tend to interpret [new] evidence so as to maintain their initial beliefs,"[241] bringing comparatively exacting standards to bear in assessing information that challenges established views.[242]

Confirmation biases operate in the most mundane spheres of human cognition. But they are magnified when individuals have a distinct motivation, conscious or not, to maintain established beliefs.[243] As we have seen, as *motivated reasoners*,

---

[236] This is a substantial caveat; the studies to which I refer involved individual participants in a research study, not a large segment of a society whose leaders pursued policies inconsistent with these citizens' beliefs.

[237] Lara J. Nettelfield, Courting Democracy in Bosnia and Herzegovina: The Hague Tribunal's Impact in a Postwar State 274 (2010).

[238] James Shepperd, Professor of Psychology, University of Florida, *quoted in* Kevin Quealy, *Media Bias of Different Sort: Readers Skip Some Stories*, N.Y. Times (Feb. 21, 2017).

[239] Interview with Svetlana Logar, then Research Director, Ipsos Strategic Marketing, in Belgrade, Serb. (July 10, 2012).

[240] *See* Dawson et al., *supra* note 208, at 1380.

[241] Charles G. Lord et al., *Biased Assimilation and Attitude Polarization: The Effects of Prior Theories on Subsequently Considered Evidence*, 37 J. Personality & Soc. Psychol. 2098, 2099 (1979). *See also* Taber & Lodge, *supra* note 184, at 756 (people "are typically unable to control their preconceptions," and this tends to produce "belief perseverance" in the face of new information even as we strive to reach accurate conclusions").

[242] *See* Dawson et al., *supra* note 208, at 1379–80.

[243] On the interaction between motivated reasoning and confirmation biases, see David P. Redlawsk et al., *The Affective Tipping Point: Do Motivated Reasoners Ever "Get It"?*, 31 Pol. Psychol. 563 (2010).

people bring different standards to bear in evaluating information they wish to be true than evidence they would rather find false.[244] Research has shown, as well, "that important and extreme attitudes are more resistant to change than unimportant and nonpolarized attitudes."[245]

Studies by political scientists Charles Taber and Milton Lodge illuminate cognitive processes underlying this phenomenon. Individuals who are strongly attached to a position are more likely to seek out information that supports their belief than information that calls it into question,[246] and "will spend more time and cognitive resources denigrating and counterarguing" evidence and arguments that contravene their existing position.[247] This research might explain the influential role of legal commentators in Serbia, as described by Ivan Jovanović: nationalist lawyers who denigrate the ICTY generate a reservoir of arguments upon which Serbian citizens can draw to confirm an established belief that Hague prosecutions reflect an anti-Serb bias.[248]

While cognitive processes theorized by Taber and Lodge typically operate subconsciously,[249] denigration and counterarguing can be readily observed in the reactions of some Serbians to evidence of Serb atrocities. A striking instance occurred in June 2005, when the ICTY prosecution introduced a video in the trial of Slobodan Milošević. The video showed members of the Scorpions, a Serb paramilitary unit operating under the command of the Serbian Ministry of Interior, executing six Bosnian Muslims. The victims, who were cruelly taunted and forced to dig their own graves before they were slain, had been taken from Srebrenica during the 1995 genocide to the nearby town of Trnovo, where they were killed. The day after the video was shown in The Hague, it was broadcast repeatedly on Serbian television.[250] The impact was immediate and profound. Atrocities depicted in the video were denounced "across the political spectrum";[251] even then prime minister Koštunica, who had consistently treated indicted Serb war criminals as patriots, condemned the Scorpions' crimes unequivocally.[252] While this episode had a lasting impact on many Serbians, others apparently used the cognitive techniques of denigration and counterarguing to maintain established beliefs in Serb innocence.

---

[244] Dawson et al., *supra* note 208, at 1379–80.

[245] Andrew J. Elliot & Patricia G. Devine, *On the Motivational Nature of Cognitive Dissonance: Dissonance as Psychological Discomfort*, 67 J. PERSONALITY & SOC. PSYCHOL. 382, 387 (1994).

[246] Taber & Lodge, *supra* note 184, at 764.

[247] *Id.* at 757. Experiments conducted by Taber and Lodge appeared to support their expectation that this would happen. *See id.* at 763. *See also* Redlawsk et al., *supra* note 243, at 567 (when confronted with information at odds with their beliefs about a candidate, people may bolster their existing evaluation by mentally arguing against the new information).

[248] At the same time, the arguments they espouse help sustain the *availability* and *accessibility* of anti-Hague perspectives, producing a framing effect within a significant portion of their target audience.

[249] *See* Taber & Lodge, *supra* note 184, at 757 ("people are largely unaware of the power of their [prior beliefs]. It is not that they openly lie to themselves").

[250] In addition, print media coverage of the Srebrenica massacre skyrocketed. One study showed that at least 676 stories about the genocide were published in the Serbian print media in June 2005, the month the Scorpions video was broadcast, compared to 816 stories on Srebrenica in the previous two years. *See* SUBOTIĆ, *supra* note 138, at 63 n.107.

[251] Tim Judah, *Serbia Struggles to Face the Truth About Srebrenica*, BALKAN WITNESS (June 17, 2005).

[252] Beti Bilandžić, *Serbs Are Stunned by Video of Srebrenica*, REUTERS (June 3, 2005).

One-third of respondents in a public opinion survey taken shortly after the video was broadcast said they thought it had been fabricated,[253] a classic instance of denigration. In a bid to expand the ranks of doubters, nationalist discourses of trivialization, denial of responsibility, and justification[254] shifted into high gear. The ultranationalist Serbian Radical Party (SRS) produced a film titled *Istina* ("the truth") depicting mistreatment of Serbs by other ethnic groups. Introducing *Istina* at a public screening about five weeks after the Scorpions videotape was broadcast in The Hague, Tomislav Nikolić, then deputy leader of the SRS (and later president of Serbia), acknowledged Serbs committed crimes. But, he suggested, Serbs were being unfairly singled out for blame, pivoting from a discourse of factual denial to one of equivalency and trivialization.[255]

It is not simply the case that strongly-held views are particularly resistant to change; several studies suggest exposure to new information and arguments challenging such views may actually cement them,[256] at least under certain circumstances and for some people.[257] In research settings, this "backfire effect"[258] has been especially pronounced among participants who already possess a deep commitment to a position.[259]

5. A Tipping Point: When Does New Information Change Minds?

The social science literature explored so far has significant implications for an issue much debated among international legal scholars: What goals should we ascribe to

---

[253] Beth Kampschror, *Serbs Divided over Grim Video*, Christian Sci. Monitor (June 15, 2005). Among those who said they saw the video, the percentage who said they thought it was authentic was higher (45 percent). *See* Subotić, *supra* note 138, at 64. A somewhat higher percentage (53.5) of respondents in a separate survey, administered in August 2005, said they believed the videotape was authentic. Kutnjak Ivković & Hagan, *supra* note 33, at 108.

[254] While I am describing discourses rather than psychological techniques, each of the strategies mentioned here (trivialization, denial of responsibility, and justification) has been recognized as a technique for dissonance reduction. *See* Gosling et al., *supra* note 226, at 722–24.

[255] *See* Gordy, *supra* note 28, at 134–35. In the period that followed, nationalists continued to espouse an equivalency discourse, arguing that some 3,000 Serbians were killed in the villages surrounding Srebrenica in the three years before Muslims were slaughtered. Weaving this claim into a discursive tapestry of Serb victimization, a nationalist group circulated a petition that argued: "Putting the suffering of one group on a pedestal necessarily derogates from the right of the other group—in this case Serbian non-combatants in the devastated villages surrounding the enclave of Srebrenica." *Id.* at 136. Denouncing the "media campaign that is being conducted against the Serbian people and the state," then SRS general secretary (later Serbian prime minister and president) Aleksandar Vučić said members of the Scorpions neither were from Serbia nor had any connections to Serbian institutions, despite clear evidence linking them to Serbia's interior ministry. *Id.* at 138–39.

[256] *See* Nyhan & Reifler, *supra* note 186, at 303; Lord et al., *supra* note 241. *See also* Emily Thorson, Opinion, *Let Trump's Falsehoods Lie*, N.Y. Times (Jan. 10, 2016); Cass R. Sunstein, Opinion, *Breaking Up the Echo*, N.Y. Times (Sept. 18, 2012); Michael Cooper, *Political Memo: Fact-Checkers Howl, But Campaigns Seem Attached to Dishonest Adds*, N.Y. Times (Sept. 1, 2012).

[257] *See* Lord et al., *supra* note 241, at 2104 ("inconclusive or mixed data will lead to increased polarization rather than to uncertainty and moderation" of existing views).

[258] Nyhan & Reifler, *supra* note 186, at 307.

[259] Taber & Lodge, *supra* note 184, at 765 (also finding a pronounced backfire effect among "sophisticated participants"). Studies conducted by Nyhan and Reifler have found that the backfire effect triggered by corrective information is most likely to occur among participants who possess views that align with a political ideology (e.g., "conservatives"). Nyhan & Reifler, *supra* note 186, at 319–20.

ICTs?[260] The clearest implication is that it is misguided to expect an ICT to transform social beliefs simply by making new information publicly available.[261] This body of research does not, however, suggest the ICTY's work *could not* influence the views of *any* Serbian citizens. As intimated but not emphasized earlier, several studies have found exposure to new information actually *did* change some participants' minds, even as it failed to change or even hardened the views of others.[262]

Reasoning that "[a]t some point even the most strongly held [view] should flag in the face of repeated [contradictory] information,"[263] researchers have recently explored the limits of cognitive biases underlying belief perseverance. An early effort found that, when study participants were introduced to relatively small amounts of information inconsistent with their views about a preferred fictional political candidate, the information produced a backfire effect: evaluations of the candidate became *more* positive. When, however, subjects were exposed to relatively large amounts of such information, their views were likely to change.[264] In short, "motivated reasoning does not continue ad infinitum."[265]

In a similar vein, Ivan Jovanović, who suggested Serbians' resistance to evidence emanating from The Hague may have intensified in light of frustrations associated with Western conditionality, went on to say he did not believe this resistance was insurmountable. Instead, he said, in this setting, "you need more evidence to be persuaded that somebody of your own creed did something bad than evidence that . . . what you hear [about Serb atrocities] is a lie."[266]

III. IS THERE LESS DENIAL AND GREATER ACKNOWLEDGMENT THAN THERE WOULD HAVE BEEN WITHOUT THE ICTY?

If the ICTY's work could have influenced some Serbians' views about wartime atrocities, it remains to be considered whether and to what extent it did so. As a classic counterfactual (we cannot know what Serbian views about wartime atrocities would have been without the ICTY), this cannot be answered definitively. Even so, Serbians interviewed for this study, including individuals who are hardly Tribunal enthusiasts, are convinced its work led to greater acceptance by many Serbians of fundamental facts concerning Serb atrocities, at least for a while and perhaps with more lasting effect.[267]

---

[260] *See, e.g.,* Mirjan Damaška, *What Is the Point of International Criminal Justice?*, 3 CHI.-KENT L. REV. 329 (2008); Stuart Ford, *A Hierarchy of the Goals of International Criminal Courts*, 27 MINN. J. INT'L L. (forthcoming 2017).

[261] Indeed, Serbians who once thought ICTY judgments would dispel denial now recognize this was an impossible hope. As noted in Chapter 5, for example, Marijana Toma reflected that those who actively supported the ICTY "made the mistake; we had too many expectations from the court." In particular, "we attributed all these *amazing* powers to the court, like 'it will . . . establish the whole truth about [the] conflict.' " Interview with Marijana Toma, then Deputy Director, Humanitarian Law Center, in Belgrade, Serb. (June 10, 2014).

[262] *See, e.g.,* Nyhan & Reifler, supra note 186, at 316–17.

[263] Redlawsk et al., *supra* note 243, at 564.

[264] *Id.* at 579–83.

[265] *Id.* at 589. As the study's authors acknowledge, it may be harder to change the attitudes of committed ideologues (though their own study did not test this). *Id.* at 590.

[266] Interview with Ivan Jovanović, then National Legal Advisor, OSCE Mission to Serbia, in Belgrade, Serb. (July 12, 2012).

[267] For Serbians who have long supported the ICTY, the perception that its work helped reduce levels of denial might in part be attributable to belief perseverance. Thus it is notable that even critics of the ICTY expressed this view.

To be sure, any such impact was far from transformative. As we have seen, Tribunal judgments did not and surely could not have a profound impact on beliefs in post-Milošević Serbia, where nationalists still have an outsize influence on social beliefs. Even in the constrained political space already described, however, meaningful shifts in public leadership and discourses alternately expanded and diminished citizens' readiness to accept evidence of Serb atrocities.

A. Growing Acceptance of Facts concerning Serb Atrocities

During each of my research visits to Serbia, perspectives expressed in myriad interviews coalesced around an overarching theme. In 2006 and 2007, it was this: despite significant minimization and outright denial of Serb atrocities, there had been palpable progress in Serbian acknowledgment. Recalling earlier narratives of denial relating to Srebrenica, for example, Bogdan Ivanišević said: "Now, people who [voice those positions] are from the margins[;] there is incomparably less distortion of the past."[268] Jadranka Jelinčić made much the same point, noting: "It's now very difficult to deny that certain things happened and that cultural elites were responsible."[269]

To what extent can the progress they described be attributed to the ICTY? Serbians interviewed in 2006 and 2007 were convinced the Tribunal played a key role. In the view of Ivan Janković, evidence adduced in The Hague had significantly "shrunk the public space" in which political leaders could credibly deny the truth about notorious crimes.[270] Janković's observation so well captured a recurring theme in my 2006–2007 interviews, it inspired the title of a previous publication on the ICTY's impact in Serbia.[271]

Alongside palpable changes in elite discourses,[272] Strategic Marketing surveys depicted growing public awareness of Serb atrocities (or at any rate, growing willingness to admit awareness), while also highlighting limits to these changes. Despite persistently high levels of reported disbelief in reports of Serb atrocities as described earlier, surveys charted *rising* levels of stated belief in reports of emblematic Serb crimes during the first five or six years of post-Milošević Serbia. Applying the percentage of respondents who believed what they heard to those who said they had heard of certain crimes, the resulting portion of total respondents who said they believed large numbers of civilians in Sarajevo were killed by snipers rose from 50 percent in 2001 to 60 percent in 2006 (see Figure 7.4).[273] The corresponding percentage for Srebrenica showed more modest growth, rising from 48 percent in 2001 to 50 percent in 2006 (see Figure 7.8).[274]

---

[268] Telephone Interview with Bogdan Ivanišević, Attorney (Nov. 3, 2006).

[269] Interview with Jadranka Jelinčić, Executive Director, Open Society Fund Serbia, in Belgrade, Serb. (Nov. 24, 2006).

[270] Interview with Ivan Janković, Attorney, in Belgrade, Serb. (Nov. 24, 2006).

[271] ORENTLICHER, *supra* note 169.

[272] As noted earlier, elite discourses were hardly uniform during this period. The point here is that, even with competing narratives in play, on the whole extreme forms of denial were relegated to the margins of public discourse during the early post-Milošević years.

[273] *See* 2011 Survey, *supra* note 37, at 84 (showing data for all survey years). The percentage rose to 64 percent in 2009, before dropping to 49 percent in 2011. *Id.*

[274] *Id.* The percentage dropped to 46 in 2009 and to 40 in 2011. *Id.*

Žarko Marković, who worked with one of the organizations that commissioned these surveys, believes facts established in The Hague played a key role in reducing levels of denial during this period. Marković recalled that, during the Tribunal's early years, "there was a lot of space for denial before all these facts were established" in ICTY trials.[275] And Serbian denialists occupied much of that space: "On TV shows, you could hear people denying" basic facts about wartime atrocities "in a very loud way." But this changed once trials got underway and compelling witness testimony was broadcast in the media. Then, Marković recalls, "it became obvious something happened" and people "stopped denying."[276]

Although hardly a fan of the ICTY, journalist Ljiljana Smajlović, too, credited the Tribunal with educating the Serbian public about war crimes and Serbia's role in supporting them when I interviewed her in late 2006: "There's no question that the ICTY has educated the public; we've found out more about war crimes and the . . . inner workings of the government than we would ever have found out—and about the criminal aspects of the regime."[277] Smajlović said she believed the "findings of the Tribunal are more accepted now" (i.e., in late 2006) than previously. As a result of "what we've found out in The Hague," she said, the public now "accepts that Serbs committed enormous crimes," including the Srebrenica massacre.[278]

There were, of course, other sources of information about Serb atrocities; indeed, it is safe to assume facts established in The Hague would have influenced few citizens' beliefs without the efforts of local intermediaries. Jadranka Jelinčić recalled that documentaries about Serb atrocities, broadcast on both state and independent media, "contributed to public discussion about whether genocide happened." These sources, many of which relied on evidence used in The Hague, "helped us come over the phase of denial."[279] Marković recalled that, for many Serbians, the information revealed in documentaries broadcast in this period "was completely new and shocking."[280]

Even in 2006, however, Serbian citizens were more prepared to acknowledge Serbs committed atrocities than to condemn them or accept political responsibility for their country's wartime policies. For example, while 60 percent of total respondents in Strategic Marketing's 2006 survey said they believed many civilians were killed by snipers in Sarajevo (see Figure 7.4),[281] only 41 percent characterized the killings

---

[275] Interview with Žarko Marković, then Legal Officer, Belgrade Centre for Human Rights, in Belgrade, Serb. (June 11, 2014). As noted in Chapter 2, during its early years the ICTY struggled to gain custody of suspects whom it could prosecute.

[276] Interview with Žarko Marković, then Legal Officer, Belgrade Centre for Human Rights, in Belgrade, Serb. (June 11, 2014). Jelena Obradović-Wochnik similarly believes ICTY cooperation and trials "ensured that war crimes can no longer be categorically denied nor ignored, as was the case during the Milošević era." Even so, she writes, political figures were reluctant to expose war crimes after the Đinđić assassination, "fearing retaliation from the as-yet unreformed security sector." Obradović-Wochnik, Srebrenica, supra note 28, at 65.

[277] Interview with Ljiljana Smajlović, Journalist, in Belgrade, Serb. (Nov. 24, 2006).

[278] Id.

[279] Interview with Jadranka Jelinčić, Executive Director, Open Society Fund Serbia, in Belgrade, Serb. (Nov. 24, 2006).

[280] Interview with Žarko Marković, then Legal Officer, Belgrade Centre for Human Rights, in Belgrade, Serb. (June 11, 2014). Marković said that, until early 2004, some of these documentaries were broadcast "in prime time on national television." Id.

[281] This figure derives from applying the percentage of those who said they believed what they had heard about this years-long episode to the percentage who said they had heard about it. See 2011 Survey, supra note 37, at 84.

as war crimes that deserved to be punished rather than an inevitability in war (see Figure 7.5).[282] As for Srebrenica, 50 percent of total respondents in the 2006 survey said they believed the massacre had occurred (see Figure 7.8); only 43 percent condemned it as a war crime (see Figure 7.9).[283] Smajlović described the limits to Serbians' then growing acknowledgment of Serb atrocities this way: "You can only say this person committed this crime. People can accept that, but not that they're responsible for failing to go on the streets"[284]—that is, that they bear political responsibility for failing to protest crimes committed or sponsored by their leaders.

B. Regression . . . ?

By 2012, Serbians interviewed for this study were more circumspect about the Tribunal's impact on beliefs and acknowledgment than during 2006–2007 interviews. Ivan Janković, who previously credited the ICTY with shrinking "the public space" for credibly denying Serb atrocities, responded this way when I asked if he still believed it had had this effect:

> Denial is most often a conscious, chosen strategy aimed at self-protection. In that sense the ICTY probably did not reduce the quantity of denial, but it provided the firm points from which to attack denial and make it more relative, to bring it into question, to show it as questionable.[285]

Bogdan Ivanišević, who in late 2006 described "incomparably less distortion of the past" in elite discourses, now perceived "an almost universal tendency among Serbs in the former Yugoslavia *not* to call [the Srebrenica massacre] genocide."[286] To be sure, it was never commonplace for Serbian elites to call the massacre a genocide; what had changed was an uptick in discourses *challenging* the ICTY's genocide rulings. Now, Ivanišević said, it was "considered legitimate both to say [Srebrenica] was a horrible crime but no genocide and to say it was a horrible crime but not nearly as bad as the ICTY would have us believe."[287] Still, Ivanišević emphasized, there had not been a complete reversal of previous gains; even the "fiercest nationalists" still acknowledged "a lot of people in Srebrenica were killed."[288] Srđan Bogosavljević similarly noted that, while many Serbians resisted labeling Srebrenica a genocide, "nobody denies" anymore that "people [were] killed by somebody in [an] organized way."[289] Indeed, he said, "everybody of the political elites" agreed that large numbers of Bosniaks were killed in Srebrenica, because "they have seen real evidence."[290]

Consistent with Bogosavljević's account, citizens still registered relatively high levels of reported awareness of Srebrenica in the last (2011) Strategic Marketing

---

[282] *Id.* at 85.

[283] *Id.* at 84–84.

[284] Interview with Ljiljana Smajlović, Journalist, in Belgrade, Serb. (Nov. 24, 2006).

[285] Interview with Ivan Janković, Attorney, in Belgrade, Serb. (July 11, 2012).

[286] Interview with Bogdan Ivanišević, Attorney, in Belgrade, Serb. (July 9, 2012).

[287] *Id.*

[288] *Id.*

[289] Interview with Srđan Bogosavljević, Director, Ipsos Strategic Marketing, in Belgrade, Serb. (July 10, 2012).

[290] *Id.*

survey on war crimes issues. As noted earlier, 72 percent of respondents said they had heard about the massacre—the same percentage as in 2005, and a slightly higher percentage than in 2006 (71 percent) (see Figure 7.6).[291] Commenting on the 2011 survey results, Ivan Jovanović observed: "Srebrenica still ranks first, because it's the topic that's been most spoken about. So when you keep something at the head of public discourse and discussion, over time people start incorporating it."[292] That said, only 56 percent of respondents who said they had heard about Srebrenica in 2011 said they believed what they had heard—a notable decline from the 70 percent of respondents who said they believed what they had heard about Srebrenica in 2006 (see Figure 7.7). There was also a decline between 2009 and 2011 in affirmative responses to the question "Do you think that murders of Bosniaks in Srebrenica are genocide?"[293] Among respondents who said they believed large numbers of Bosniaks were killed in Srebrenica, 25 percent said they thought the massacre was a genocide in 2009, compared to 17 percent in 2011 (see Figure 7.10).

What, then, accounts for the discursive shifts Ivanišević and others perceived, as well as the decline in survey respondents' stated belief in reports about Srebrenica and willingness to characterize the massacre as genocide? Focusing on the former, Ivanišević ascribed a "big impact" in Serbia to the negationist rhetoric of Republika Srpska president Milorad Dodik, who has aggressively denied Serbs committed genocide in Srebrenica.[294] Ivanišević added: "And there haven't been voices who would state that it's unacceptable to speak in these terms in the absence of serious credible information that puts a different light on what the ICTY established."[295]

Instead, he said, even Serbia's most liberal leader since Zoran Đinđić, former president Boris Tadić, had "made nationalism more respectable" by virtue of a general rightward shift during his presidency.[296] Explaining, Ivanišević said Tadić's shift centered on the contested status of Kosovo at a time when Europe was pressing Serbia to accept its independence. Even so, Ivanišević believes, coming from "the highest authority," then president Tadić's increasingly nationalist positions "just made it so much easier for all sorts of completely insane arguments to be heard and accepted."[297] In short, a "general shift to a more nationalist direction compared to the beginning of the last decade" opened up a wider space for discourses of denial.

The political shifts Ivanišević cited had nothing to do with the ICTY. But in Ivanišević's assessment, they diminished Serbians' readiness to credit evidence of Serb atrocities. In his words, "All of the political leaders and intellectual elites in Serbia have moved since [the] mid-2000's in a direction that makes the acceptance of the facts established by the ICTY more difficult than in the previous period."[298]

---

[291] Data for all of these survey years are provided in the 2011 Survey, *supra* note 37, at 83.

[292] Interview with Ivan Jovanović, then National Legal Advisor, OSCE Mission to Serbia, in Belgrade, Serb. (July 12, 2012). This perception accords with previously-discussed research on heuristics and framing, which emphasizes the importance of *availability* in shaping the way people assess the probability that a proposition is true.

[293] As previously noted, this question was included for the first time in the 2009 survey.

[294] *See* Chapter 8.

[295] Interview with Bogdan Ivanišević, Attorney, in Belgrade, Serb. (July 9, 2012).

[296] *Id.*

[297] *Id.*

[298] *Id.*

Several sources attributed declining levels of reported knowledge in part to another development: with the arrest of the last ICTY fugitive in July 2011, the issue of cooperation no longer drove the subject of war crimes onto the daily headlines and into public consciousness. This perspective offers an intriguing counterpoint to concerns addressed in Chapter 3. As noted there, many Serbians who supported cooperation with the ICTY regretted the way local leaders justified arrests of Hague fugitives on pragmatic rather than principled grounds, squandering the opportunity to mold public opinion on questions of accountability. In retrospect, however, some believed cooperation-related debates had elevated public awareness of war crimes in a fashion conducive to acknowledgment (even if, as suggested earlier, they also thought the public had grown weary of the subject). As long as the ICTY was in the news, Svetlana Logar said, it "had a lot of impact" in Serbia: "It was due to the existence of ICTY [the topic of Serb atrocities] was discussed" at all.[299] Bogdan Ivanišević reflected that, because "there are no [longer] requirements from the ICTY, . . . there is no trigger" for provoking public discussion about trials in The Hague.[300]

Another contextual factor is crucial: my 2012 interviews took place just weeks after former SRS deputy Tomislav Nikolić became Serbia's president. As recounted in Chapter 3, in previous elections the specter of Nikolić becoming president or premier had been so worrying, Western countries used the tools at their disposal to try to avert this outcome. Although Nikolić separated from the SRS in October 2008 and campaigned for the presidency on a pro-European platform in 2012, many doubted the depth of his transformation. (Others, however, saw the transformation of Nikolić and other former SRS leaders in a different light. In the view of Jadranka Jelinčić, the shift showed that "extreme nationalism is not in fashion anymore."[301])

Almost immediately after he was sworn in, Nikolić confirmed the apprehensions of human rights advocates. In a televised interview, he declared, "There was no genocide in Srebrenica." Instead, Nikolić said, "grave war crimes were committed by some Serbs, who should be found, prosecuted and punished."[302] Although Marijana Toma had grown concerned the subject of war crimes was "becoming passé," she believes the way Nikolić brought Srebrenica back into public consciousness was "actually worse."[303]

For those who hoped Serbia would advance toward a robust reckoning with the past, Nikolić's comments signified a reversal of hard-won gains. Outside Serbia, they drew swift condemnation. The Bosniak member of Bosnia's presidency, Bakir

[299] Interview with Svetlana Logar, then Research Director, Ipsos Strategic Marketing, in Belgrade, Serb. (July 10, 2012).

[300] Interview with Bogdan Ivanišević, Attorney, in Belgrade, Serb. (July 9, 2012).

[301] Interview with Jadranka Jelinčić, Executive Director, Open Society Fund Serbia, in Belgrade, Serb. (July 9, 2012). Parliamentary elections in August 2016 reinforced this trend. Eighty-seven percent of representatives elected to parliament belonged to pro-Europe parties. Ivan Vejvoda, *Serbia Votes to Continue Its EU Integration Path*, GERMAN MARSHALL FUND WEBSITE (Apr. 25, 2016).

[302] *Srebrenica "Not Genocide"—Serbia's President Nikolić*, BBC NEWS (June 1, 2012); *Serbia's New President Denies Srebrenica Massacre Was Genocide*, SOFIA NEWS AGENCY (June 1, 2012); Olivera Nikolić, *War Crimes, Not Genocide in Srebrenica: Serbian President*, AGENCE FRANCE-PRESSE (June 1, 2012).

[303] Interview with Marijana Toma, then Deputy Director, Humanitarian Law Center, in Belgrade, Serb. (June 10, 2014).

Izetbegović, decried his remarks as "an insult to the victims" of the genocide[304] and a "source of new misunderstandings and tension" in the region.[305] The office of the EU foreign policy chief condemned them as well, saying "the EU strongly rejects any intention to rewrite history."[306] In his next report to the UN Security Council, ICTY Prosecutor Serge Brammertz said: "Such rhetoric is a backwards step, aggravates the victims' suffering, and jeopardizes the fragile process of reconciliation in the former Yugoslavia."[307]

As explained later, Nikolić would soon temper his remarks. By the time of my 2014 research visit, however, Serbians who supported the ICTY were even more concerned about its enduring impact on acknowledgment. Strategic Marketing was no longer updating its earlier surveys on war crimes issues,[308] but some suggested that, if surveys had been administered recently, they would show declining awareness of wartime atrocities.

Contextual changes loomed large in their accounts of what they assumed such surveys would show. As in 2012 interviews, Serbians interviewed in 2014 noted the topic of war crimes had largely vanished from Serbia's discursive landscape, in part because the issue of cooperation no longer drove it there. In the words of Maja Mičić, the Tribunal was "not a topic" anymore; "ICTY trials and proceedings are done story when we come to Serbia."[309] In a similar vein, Žarko Marković noted that, in recent years, the ICTY "was already out of the top five topics" in the Serbian public's consciousness. The Tribunal was "everywhere for 20 years," and people "simply became a bit tired" of it. Drawing a link, Marković characterized the contemporary period as one "of total ignorance" about the past. "There's no denial anymore; there's almost complete silence."[310]

Also coloring many of my interviews in 2014, another former SRS leader, Aleksandar Vučić, had assumed the position of prime minister following elections in March 2014.[311] Like Nikolić, Vučić had split from the Radicals in 2008 and helped found the Serbian Progressive Party (SNS). But his reputation was forged during his years as a protégé of the ultranationalist firebrand Vojislav Šešelj. Days after the

---

[304] *Serbia's New President Revives Balkan Tensions*, ASSOCIATED PRESS (June 4, 2012).

[305] Olivera Nikolić, *War Crimes, Not Genocide in Srebrenica: Serbian President*, AGENCE FRANCE-PRESSE (June 1, 2012).

[306] *Serbia's New President Revives Balkan Tensions*, FOX NEWS (June 4, 2012).

[307] Serge Brammertz, Prosecutor, Int'l Crim. Trib. for the Former Yugoslavia, Address to the United Nations Security Council (June 7, 2012).

[308] Clients who had commissioned previous surveys were no longer able to secure funding. Interviews with Žarko Marković, then Legal Officer, Belgrade Centre for Human Rights, in Belgrade, Serb. (June 11, 2014); Ivan Jovanović, Attorney, in Belgrade, Serb. (June 9, 2014).

[309] Interview with Maja Mičić, then Director, Youth Initiative for Human Rights, in Belgrade, Serb. (June 11, 2014). *See also* Slobodan Georgijev, *Delicacies and Denial at The Hague*, BALKAN TRANSITIONAL JUST. (Jan 25, 2013) ("The Serbian media lost any substantial interest in covering trials at the . . . ICTY after Slobodan Milošević died and the last of the top suspects were arrested and transferred to The Hague. When Ratko Mladić was [arrested], it was said that we were finished with the Tribunal.").

[310] Interview with Žarko Marković, then Legal Officer, Belgrade Centre for Human Rights, in Belgrade, Serb. (June 11, 2014).

[311] After serving as prime minister for three years, Vučić won a presidential election in early April 2017 by a landslide. *Serbian PM Elected President as EU Warns over Increased Powers*, GUARDIAN (Apr. 3, 2017).

Srebrenica massacre, Vučić defended the infamous crime, saying: "You kill one Serb and we will kill 100 Muslims."[312] Twelve years later, as a member of Serbia's parliament, Vučić declared his home "would always be a safe house for general Ratko Mladić."[313] By 2014, Vučić had adopted "European" perspectives, and since then has undertaken several gestures of acknowledgment, described later in this chapter (while at the same time raising concerns about what is often described as an increasingly authoritarian style[314]). At the time of my 2014 interviews, his ultranationalist history was foremost in the minds of many I interviewed. Maja Mičić said: "In this moment we're dealing definitely with the changing of the government" from a disappointing, but fundamentally democratic, one to a government led by "people who have war crimes in their background."[315]

While these developments alone might have diminished the ICTY's impact on Serbian acknowledgment (as well as sources' perceptions of changing social beliefs), another factor loomed large in accounts of the Tribunal's declining influence—its own performance. Since my last research visit, Tribunal chambers had rendered a series of controversial judgments, starting with the acquittal of Croatian general Ante Gotovina in November 2012, riling not only longtime ICTY detractors but also its most staunch defenders in Serbia.[316] Now, Serbians who had long pressed their country to "deal with the past" faced a new challenge—how to criticize recent ICTY rulings, as many were doing, while urging other Serbians to accept Tribunal judgments convicting Serbs of wartime atrocities.

Like many Serbian advocates of accountability, Mičić was unnerved: "We felt that ICTY, which we supported and [with which we] cooperated, gave us slap in the face." This was "difficult," she said, "because everyone was turning to us, . . . the promoters and advocators of ICTY as something that would bring some kind of justice, being one step toward reconciliation, and asking the question, 'So what now? What do you say now?'"[317] In a similar vein, Ivan Jovanović said that, while Serbians who long supported the ICTY still did, their assessments were increasingly "sliding into a general description of [its] record as being permeated with a lot of stains, which in their view are irreparable."[318] In short, the Tribunal's late-life performance made

---

[312] Katarina Subašić, *Serbia's Hard-Line Premier Turned Friend of West*, Dawn (Apr. 22, 2016).

[313] *Id. See also Radicals: Parliament Is Mladić Safe House*, RTV B92 News (Oct. 5, 2007).

[314] *See, e.g.*, Editorial, *A Serbian Election Erodes Democracy*, N.Y. Times (Apr. 9, 2017); Jasmin Mujanović, *Vučić's Brand of "Stability" Will Be Short-Lived*, Balkan Insight (Apr. 19, 2017).

[315] Interview with Maja Mičić, then Director, Youth Initiative for Human Rights, in Belgrade, Serb. (June 11, 2014).

[316] These rulings are discussed in Chapter 6.

[317] Interview with Maja Mičić, then Director, Youth Initiative for Human Rights, in Belgrade, Serb. (June 11, 2014).

[318] Interview with Ivan Jovanović, Attorney, in Belgrade, Serb. (June 9, 2014). Jovanović referred in particular to the acquittals of Ante Gotovina and Momčilo Perišić by the ICTY Appeals Chamber, and the then-recent acquittal at the trial level of Jovica Stanišić and Franko Simatović, all of which are discussed in Chapter 6. (The last acquittal was reversed in 2015, and a retrial of the two suspects began in June 2017.) At the time of the quoted interview, Vojislav Šešelj had not yet been acquitted. In an email following his acquittal, Jovanović characterized the trial judgment as "a bomb, a dirty bomb!" and "really unbelievable!" As the presiding judge read out his verdict in the Šešelj case, Jovanović "was realizing it was [an] 'I can't believe my ears' moment in the history of international justice." Email from Ivan Jovanović, Attorney, to Diane Orentlicher (Apr. 6, 2016).

it infinitely more challenging for domestic interlocutors to counter Serbian denial based on facts adjudicated in The Hague.[319]

Despite these developments, Jovanović believes Serbia has not seen a complete reversal of earlier gains in the sphere of acknowledgment. While critical of the Tribunal's then-recent performance when I interviewed him in 2014, Jovanović said:

> At least the Tribunal brought up, [dug] out some facts and brought it up to day-light. And without the work of the Tribunal, people in Serbia would hardly know anything about Srebrenica. There still is denial of Srebrenica, there is more relativ-ization than denial about Srebrenica, but still people are aware, and they do accept that some terrible crimes were committed by Serbs in Srebrenica. Without the work of the Tribunal, it would have been impossible. There is also this . . . general acceptance that Serbs committed crimes, which, again, without the work of the Tribunal would have not been possible.[320]

Žarko Marković made much the same point. After describing recent ICTY blunders (emphasizing in particular the Tribunal's disastrous handling of the Šešelj trial[321]), Marković said the ICTY had "changed the political discourse here . . . , and not only here but in Croatia and Bosnia. At least people are willing to accept that some crimes were committed by their own ethnic group."[322]

IV. OFFICIAL ACKNOWLEDGMENT

Previous portions of this chapter have addressed official and other elite discourses to highlight their influential role in shaping citizens' beliefs. Beyond their explan-atory significance, official statements can be consequential in their own right. In particular, official apologies for moral transgressions have a distinctive restorative potential.[323] At least when accompanied by acceptance of responsibility and remorse,

---

[319] The impact Mičić, Jovanović, and others described transcends what they experienced as a loss of credibility in an already challenging context. As previously noted, the social impact of an ICT depends in no small part on the degree to which its work mobilizes civil society actors. *See* Chapter 1. Even if the Tribunal's longtime Serbian partners maintained their overall support, their shaken confidence deflated their enthusiasm.

[320] Interview with Ivan Jovanović, Attorney, in Belgrade, Serb. (June 9, 2014).

[321] *See* Chapter 6.

[322] Interview with Žarko Marković, then Legal Officer, Belgrade Centre for Human Rights, in Belgrade, Serb. (June 11, 2014). Nevertheless, Serbians previously convicted of war crimes have attended high-profile events hosted by political parties, a pattern the HLC called "glorifica-tion of war criminals." Filip Rudić, *Serbia Failing to Prosecute War Crimes, HLC Says*, BALKAN TRANSITIONAL JUST. (May 18, 2017). Controversially, in 2017 a former Serbian general whom the ICTY convicted of crimes against humanity and who was released from prison in 2015 was invited to lecture cadets at a military academy in Belgrade. *See* Matthew Brunwasser, *Serbia's Brand of Reconciliation: Embracing Old War Criminals*, N.Y. TIMES (Nov. 23, 2017).

[323] That potential is reflected in international law's recognition that an official apology, "including acknowledgement of the facts and acceptance of responsibility," is a key component of the repa-ration owed for breaching core precepts of human rights and humanitarian law. Basic Principles and Guidelines on the Right to a Remedy and Reparation for Victims of Gross Violations of International Human Rights Law and Serious Violations of International Humanitarian Law and Serious Violations of International Humanitarian Law, G.A. Res. 60/147, Guiding Principle 22(e). (Mar. 21, 2006). *See also* Human Rights Committee, General Comment No. 31, The Nature

an apology offered on behalf of Serbia would answer a moral imperative to amend past wrongs,[324] and a deeply felt need of many survivors: as previous chapters have explored, many experience enduring Serb denial as a tormenting wrong.

The ICTY's influence on official gestures of acknowledgment described below is attenuated. Those gestures were more clearly responsive to Western pressure and domestic advocacy than to judgments in The Hague (though Serbian authorities would not have been pressed to condemn the Srebrenica massacre as a genocide if the ICTY and ICJ had not ruled the tragedy a genocide). Yet beyond whatever indirect influence the ICTY may have had, Serbian apologies add an important dimension to our inquiry, placing in perspective previously-noted concerns about whether questions of cooperation with the ICTY diverted attention from the moral weight of Serb atrocities. Although, as we have seen, Serbian leaders were reluctant to justify *cooperation with the ICTY* on moral grounds,[325] this did not prevent senior officials from addressing Serbia's political responsibility, however tentatively.

A. Early Post-Milošević Years

The first post-Milošević government did not take significant steps in the direction of apologizing for Serbia's role in wartime atrocities.[326] To be sure, reformist members of the coalition government initiated a highly consequential process of accountability by creating dedicated war crimes institutions in Serbia's judiciary.[327] Yet their leader, Zoran Đinđić, demurred when urged to apologize for Belgrade's role in the murderous actions of Serb forces. In October 2002, then U.S. senator Joseph Biden stated that a condition for full renewal of U.S. aid was that the coalition government apologize publicly for Serbia's wartime actions. Đinđić emphatically rejected the premise of Biden's position:

> I do not think that I have anything to do with those war crimes. Neither my Government nor I. The situation with the governments of Croatia, Bosnia and some others is quite opposite. They are the governments of continuity, while our Government made discontinuity and it is the only one in this region without representatives of former regime. That is why I think that Biden's request is without grounds.[328]

---

of the General Legal Obligation Imposed on States Parties to the Covenant, U.N. Doc. CCPR/C/ 21/Rev.1/Add.13, ¶ 16 (Mar. 29, 2004).

[324] *See* Elazar Barkan & Alexander Karn, *Group Apology as an Ethical Imperative, in* TAKING WRONGS SERIOUSLY: APOLOGIES AND RECONCILIATION 5 (Elazar Barkan & Alexander Karn eds., 2006).

[325] *See* Chapter 3.

[326] Even before Milošević lost power, however, then president of Montenegro Milo Đukanović apologized (in June 2000) for the republic's involvement in war operations in the Croatian town of Vukovar. *See* Michel-André Horelt, *Serbia-Croatia, Bosnia and Herzegovina: Different Apology Packages, Different Successes, in* APOLOGY AND RECONCILIATION IN INTERNATIONAL RELATIONS: THE IMPORTANCE OF BEING SORRY 168 (Christopher Daase et al. eds., 2016).

[327] *See* Chapter 10. While my focus here is on official statements and symbolic gestures such as visits to gravesites, it is possible to conceive of official narratives about past atrocities in a more comprehensive way, encompassing retrospective prosecutions as well as other measures. *See, e.g.,* BERGER, *supra* note 100, at 12 (official narratives comprise government policies across five domains, including rhetoric, education, commemoration, compensation, and punishment).

[328] *Koštunica and Đinđić Have to Apologise for "Genocide,"* BLIC (Oct. 5, 2002).

By all accounts, Đinđić was deeply devoted to Serbia's "discontinuity" with the Milošević regime. Yet his response was striking in its departure from the practice of leaders elsewhere who have drawn a stark line between the government they led and a prior regime.[329] In myriad countries across the globe, leaders of new, or newly-restored, democracies have sought to demonstrate their fidelity to human rights by *accepting* political responsibility for the depredations of their predecessor, implicitly recognizing a morally consequential form of continuity.[330]

Đinđić's coalition partner, Vojislav Koštunica, made a gesture toward addressing the past, but it hardly amounted to acknowledgment of political responsibility for Serbian-sponsored atrocities, much less an apology for them. On March 30, 2001, Koštunica promulgated a presidential decision to establish a Truth and Reconciliation Commission.[331] In some countries, the final report of such a body has served as a foundation for the government's formal apology for the depredations of its predecessor. For this reason, Koštunica's move enjoyed cautious support from several prominent civil society leaders, both within and outside Serbia. But the initiative quickly collapsed. The commission began with an ambiguous mandate, which emphasized causes of the 1990s conflicts rather than war crimes,[332] and disbanded without issuing a report.[333]

B. Apologies by Subsequent Serbian Governments

Successive Serbian leaders have expressed remorse to neighbors of Serbia, typically in terms that elide institutional responsibility for wartime atrocities and situate Serb atrocities within a broader canvas of interethnic violence. For many victims, these qualifications have subverted the apologies' restorative potential.[334] Serbian

---

[329] Under international law, moreover, a successor government generally must discharge international legal obligations arising from the actions of its predecessor, such as a duty to provide reparations, if they have not yet been fulfilled. *See* Diane F. Orentlicher, *Settling Accounts: The Duty to Prosecute Human Rights Violations of a Prior Regime*, 100 YALE L.J. 2537, 2595 (1991).

[330] For example, after reading the report of a Chilean commission established to investigate torture during the reign of military dictator Augusto Pinochet, then president Patricio Aylwin begged for victims' forgiveness on behalf of the Chilean state. *See* PRISCILLA B. HAYNER, UNSPEAKABLE TRUTHS: TRANSITIONAL JUSTICE AND THE CHALLENGE OF TRUTH COMMISSIONS 48 (2d ed. 2011).

    Although Đinđić offered no apologies, Goran Svilanović, who served as foreign minister in the coalition government that succeeded Milošević, expressed his personal regret for the "suffering to which citizens of . . . Croatia, both Croats and Serbs, as well as citizens of FR Yugoslavia, were exposed [in] recent years" when he visited Croatia in December 2001. Svilanović framed his remarks as the expression of "an emotion," suggesting he spoke in a personal rather than official capacity. Horelt, *supra* note 326, at 168–69.

[331] *Decision on the Establishment of the Truth and Reconciliation Commission*, OFFICIAL GAZETTE OF THE FEDERAL REPUBLIC OF YUGOSLAVIA, No. 15/2001 (Mar. 30, 2001) [hereinafter Decision on TRC].

[332] The commission's principal mandate was to "organize research work on the uncovering of evidence on the social, inter-ethnic and political conflicts which led to the war and to shed light on the causal links among those events." Jelena Pejić, *The Yugoslav Truth and Reconciliation Commission: A Shaky Start*, FORDHAM INT'L L.J. 1, 9 (2001) (quoting Decision on TRC). *See also id.* at 10–13.

[333] Two members resigned over disagreements about the body's mandate and composition. *See Truth Commission: Serbia and Montenegro*, U.S. INST. OF PEACE (Feb. 1, 2002); Dimitrijević, *supra* note 64, at 18.

[334] In his classic work on apologies, Nicholas Tavuchis wrote that an authentic apology—one capable of transforming social relations sundered by wrongful conduct—"clearly announces that 'I have

advocates for accountability have often expressed a different reaction: set against the enduring influence of wartime narratives, any movement in the direction of remorse represented welcome progress, a new resting place from which to reach for the next milestone in an ongoing process of regional repair.

In a precursor to the first apology by a Serbian president, in 2003 Svetozar Marović, then president of Serbia and Montenegro (SaM) apologized to then president of Croatia Stjepan Mesić when the latter visited Belgrade. During Mesić's visit, Marović surprised his guest by saying: "As President of our Union, in the name of that past that we cannot forget I want to apologize for all the evils that any citizen of Serbia and Montenegro inflicted upon or committed against any citizen of Croatia."[335] Mesić accepted the apology and added his own: "In my name, I also apologize to all those who have suffered pain or damage at any time from the citizens of Croatia who misused the law or abused their position."[336]

While stopping short of acknowledging state institutions bore responsibility for atrocities (referring instead to evils inflicted by "any citizen"), Marović conveyed SaM's political responsibility by explicitly offering the apology in his capacity *as* "President of our Union."[337] Even so, his apology did not symbolize Serbian penance: Marović is a Montenegrin politician, and has always identified as such. Accordingly, Serbians did not see his remarks as those of a Serbian leader;[338] indeed, a press account reports that "some" in SaM "said it was not for Marović—himself a Montenegrin—to do something no Serbian president had done."[339]

During a visit to Sarajevo two months after his exchange with Mesić, Marović expressed an apology to Bosnians (also unexpectedly[340]), saying: "I want to use this opportunity to apologize for every evil or misfortune which anyone in Bosnia-Herzegovina suffered from anyone from Serbia and Montenegro."[341] Marović's gesture was hardly robust, referring obliquely to harm inflicted by "anyone" from SaM, not to Belgrade's central role in underwriting atrocities.[342] Missing from his words were "admission of fault and responsibility for . . . violation" of a moral rule, a core element of apologies thought capable of repairing grievous harms.[343] Indeed, Marović

---

no excuses for what I did or did not do'. . . . " Nicholas Tavuchis, Mea Culpa: A Sociology of Apology and Reconciliation 19 (1991).

[335] Horelt, *supra* note 326, at 170 (quoting Svetozar Marović).

[336] *Id.*

[337] *See* Ruti Teitel, *The Transitional Apology*, *in* Taking Wrongs Seriously: Apologies and Reconciliation (Elazar Barkan & Alexander Karn eds., 2006) [hereinafter *Transitional Apology*] for an excellent account of the significance of a *presidential* apology on behalf of the state as a measure of transitional justice.

[338] Comment by Ivan Jovanović on draft chapter (provided May 31, 2017). Jovanović believes Marović's ethnicity "is most likely a main reason why it was him to be the first to decide to apologize, or, in other words, why it was easier for him (both politically and, I presume, psychologically) to make such a move." *Id.*

[339] *Balkans: When Is It Time to Apolgize?*, RFE/RL (Dec. 5, 2003). This account does not specify the ethnicity of individuals who expressed this view.

[340] *See* Anes Alić, *Marović Apologizes to Bosnians*, Transitions Online (Nov. 17, 2003) (Marović "surprised everyone . . . during his first official visit to Sarajevo when he made an apology to the citizens of Bosnia for the suffering caused by the 1992–1995 war").

[341] *Calling for Forgiveness, Serbia Leader Apologizes to Bosnia for War*, N.Y. Times (Nov. 14, 2003).

[342] Marović's phrasing, which placed responsibility for Serb atrocities on individuals rather than state policy, was likely crafted with a view to the then-pending genocide case against SaM before the International Court of Justice. *See* Horelt, *supra* note 326, at 176.

[343] Tavuchis, *supra* note 334, at 3.

later clarified that "his apology did not translate into a confession that the Belgrade authorities were involved in the war in Bosnia."[344] Even so, his gesture elicited positive responses from a number of Bosniak leaders and Federation citizens.[345]

The presidency of Boris Tadić, who began his first term as president of Serbia (then still part of SaM) in July 2004, saw a series of official apologies to Serbia's neighbors. Like those of Marović, Tadić's expressions of regret stopped short of recognizing Serbia's political responsibility for underwriting Serb atrocities, but they included symbolic gestures that enlarged their restorative message. On December 6, 2004, Tadić visited Sarajevo—a symbolically resonant gesture—and apologized "to all against whom a crime was committed by the Serb people." He immediately added: "But it was not committed by the Serb people, since the criminals are individuals and it is impossible to accuse a people."[346]

Tadić's caveat was a clever if somewhat misplaced appropriation of the ICTY's own messaging. From the outset of its work, the Tribunal's top leadership insisted the ICTY would establish criminal responsibility one person at a time, not the collective guilt of a people or nation.[347] Coming from Tadić, however, the point elided the difference between a criminal court and head of state, whose office invests him with singular authority to address his country's *political* responsibility for mass atrocities.[348] Tadić added that Serbs were victims as well as perpetrators: "It is impossible to blame one nation for this because the same crimes had been committed against the Serbs." Accordingly, he said, "we all need to apologise to one another, and if I need to be the first to do so here I am."[349]

Seven months later, Tadić attended the tenth anniversary commemoration of the Srebrenica slaughter in Potočari, Bosnia, paying respect to victims buried there.[350] In an interview two years later, Tadić elaborated on the meaning of his participation, noting he had "assumed a part of the responsibility for what had been done to Bosniaks on behalf of Serbian people."[351] While condemning ethnic killings carried out "supposedly in the name of the Serbian nation and state," Tadić added: "At the

[344] Anes Alić, *Marović Apologizes to Bosnians*, TRANSITIONS ONLINE (Nov. 17, 2003).

[345] *Id*. Transitions Online conducted a "random telephone poll survey of 15 people," and reported that "citizens from the Federation mostly applauded Marović's apology, while citizens from Republika Srpska expressed varying attitudes." *Id*.

[346] This translation is adapted from that provided by Denisa Kostovicova, *Airing Crimes, Marginalizing Victims: Political Expectations and Transitional Justice in Kosovo*, in THE MILOŠEVIĆ TRIAL: AN AUTOPSY 249, 251 n.3 (Timothy William Waters ed., 2013). For a somewhat different translation, see *Serb Leader Apologises in Bosnia*, BBC NEWS (Dec. 6, 2004). Ivan Jovanović believes Tadić's reference to "Serb people" likely refers to ethnic Serb citizens of Serbia. Comment on draft chapter by Ivan Jovanović (provided May 31, 2017).

[347] *See* Chapter 2.

[348] For offenses of "the many against the many," an effective apology must be undertaken by someone in a representational capacity. *See* TAVUCHIS, *supra* note 334, at 98. And as Ruti Teitel notes, a country's president possesses symbolic power to apologize "on behalf of the political body" he leads. *Transitional Apology*, *supra* note 337, at 104. *See also* More than Words: Apologies as a Form of Reparation 13 (International Center for Transitional Justice 2015).

[349] *Serb Leader Apologises in Bosnia*, BBC NEWS (Dec. 6, 2004).

[350] *See Srebrenica Divides Serbs*, SUNDAY'S ZAMAN (July 13, 2005). Obradović-Wochnik attributes this gesture to the impact of the previously-mentioned Scorpions video. Obradović-Wochnik, *Srebrenica*, *supra* note 28, at 64.

[351] *Tadić Apologizes to Croatian Citizens*, B92 NEWS (June 24, 2007). Another source translates the last phrase as "on behalf of the Serb people." Horelt, *supra* note 326, at 171–72.

same time, I cannot overlook the fact that the same happened to my people as well."[352]
In 2015, Tadić once again expanded on the political significance and moral meaning
of his 2005 gesture. Affirming he had apologized "in the name of Serbia and its citizens"[353] when he attended the Potočari ceremony, Tadić said his gesture had to be a
"unilateral act of apology as a precondition to reconciliation . . . without any requests
for reciprocity."[354] He elaborated:

> You would not apologize in order to get something back, because then it
> becomes business, bookkeeping, but because you are morally obliged to do so.
> The act of apology is your act and it does not entail a condition, "I will do so
> if you do it for me, so we meet in the middle"—that is nonsense. That is infra-
> structure in moral relations. The unilateral act is exceptionally important, his-
> torically and civilly.[355]

During an interview on Croatian television in June 2007, Tadić apologized for Serb
crimes committed in Croatia,[356] saying: "I extend my apologies to all the citizens of
Croatia who suffered because of what the members of my nation have done, for which
I take responsibility."[357] The apology required no small measure of courage: then
SRS secretary-general Aleksandar Vučić denounced Tadić as "a disgrace for Serbia,"
characterizing his remarks as "an apology to Croatia for killing and exiling Serbs."[358]
An official of the Socialist Party of Serbia called the apology a "major disappoint-
ment," saying Tadić had "owned up to something that did not actually happen."[359]

Čedomir Jovanović, the Serbian politician who has gone farthest in condemning
Serb atrocities, welcomed Tadić's remarks while "stressing on the other hand that
words were not enough."[360] Nataša Kandić hailed the apology as "the most serious
expression of regret ever heard in the region."[361] Especially important, in her view,

---

[352] *Tadić Apologizes to Croatian Citizens, supra* note 351.

[353] *Tadić: Ćosić Vio Protiv Mog Odlaska u Srebrenicu*, Radio Slobodna Evropa (July 10, 2015)
(translation by Sonja Balić).

[354] Tadić made these remarks as a member of a panel organized on the twentieth anniversary of
the Srebrenica massacre, which was reported in *Srebrenica, Twenty Years Later*, Vreme (July
16, 2015).

[355] *Id.* Even as former president, however, Tadić declined to characterize the Srebrenica massacre
as a genocide, explaining that representatives of the state must protect its interests (presumably
against the legal responsibility Serbia could incur if it acknowledged responsibility for genocide),
and recalling that the International Court of Justice had not found Serbia legally responsible for
genocide, only for failing to prevent it. *Tadić: Why the Serbian Authorities Will Not Say Genocide*,
Al Jazeera (June 20, 2015).

[356] *See* Lidija Popović, *Tadić Apology to Croats Divides Serbia*, Balkan Insight (June 26, 2007);
Tadić: It Was My Duty to Apologize, RTV B92 News (June 25, 2007); *Serbian President Apologizes
to Croatia for War Crimes*, Deutsche Presse-Agentur (June 24, 2007).

[357] *Tadić Apologizes to Croatian Citizens*, B92 News (June 24, 2007).

[358] *Id.*

[359] *Id. See also* Lidija Popović, *Tadić Apology to Croats Divides Serbia*, Balkan Insight (June
26, 2007). Tadić's apologies were often overwhelmed in Serbia's public space by the strident
discourses of ultranationalists. In the view of Jelena Obradović-Wochnik, this was partly because
Tadić "failed to offer a strong and credible counter-discourse" to the discourse of ultranationalist
parties. Obradović-Wochnik, *Srebrenica, supra* note 28, at 63.

[360] This quotation comes from Horelt, *supra* note 326, at 172, but did not appear in the online
version of the source cited by Horelt.

[361] The quoted language is an apparent paraphrase of Kandić's comments. *See Tadić Apologizes to
Croatian Citizens*, B92 News (June 24, 2007).

was the fact that Tadić had assumed responsibility as Serbian president for crimes committed by Serb forces. In her words: "Assuming responsibility gives the gravest tone to his apology."[362]

C. The Parliamentary Declaration on Srebrenica

The measure of official acknowledgment best known outside Serbia is a parliamentary declaration, adopted in March 2010, condemning the Srebrenica massacre.[363] While the idea originated within Serbian civil society,[364] Tadić was "the main force"[365] behind the declaration. The acrimonious debate surrounding its passage and its heavily negotiated text highlighted the polarized nature of public discourse surrounding Srebrenica even fifteen years after the slaughter.

In light of strident opposition by nationalist parties, Serbia's parliament did not explicitly describe the massacre as a genocide, as proponents of the text had hoped it would.[366] In a compromise, the legislature adopted a resolution implying as much, alluding to the ICJ's determination (which, in turn, was heavily influenced by ICTY case law) that what happened in Srebrenica met the legal definition of genocide: "The parliament of Serbia strongly condemns the crime committed against the Bosnian Muslim population of Srebrenica in July 1995, as determined by the International Court of Justice ruling."[367] Members of parliament also expressed "their condolences and an apology to the families of the victims because not everything possible was done to prevent the tragedy."[368]

Contemporaneous reporting suggests Bosnian survivors (at least those quoted in the media) focused more on what the resolution failed to acknowledge than the condemnation it expressed. Dismissing the gesture as a "political game," Srebrenica survivor Sabra Kolenović said: "This resolution means nothing to us and we will not accept it. We will hail a resolution . . . that mentions the term genocide."[369] In contrast, while Serbian activists were acutely aware of the declaration's limits, many saw its adoption as progress in what inevitably would be a long journey toward unequivocal acknowledgment.[370] Nataša Kandić described the move as "a good step,"

---

[362] *Id.* In another gesture of atonement, in November 2010, Tadić and then newly-elected president of Croatia Ivo Josipović visited Vukovar, Croatia, together, paying homage to Serb and Croat victims killed in Ovčara and Paulin Dvor. *See* Davide Denti, *Sorry for Srebrenica? Public Apologies and Genocide in the Western Balkans, in* Disputed Memory: Emotions and Memory in Central, Eastern and South-Eastern Europe (Tea Sindbœk Andersen et al. eds., 2016).

[363] *Serbia Adopts Resolution Condemning Srebrenica Massacre*, Balkan Transitional Just. (Mar. 31, 2010) The declaration was adopted with a majority of only two votes. Dragović-Soso, *supra* note 132, at 172.

[364] Dragović-Soso, *supra* note 132, at 167.

[365] *Id.* at 163. *See also Tadić: Zašto Vlasti u Srbiji Neće da Kažu Genocid*, Al Jazeera (June 20, 2015).

[366] *See* Dragović-Soso, *supra* note 132, for an account of the political debate and compromises surrounding this resolution.

[367] *Serbia Adopts Resolution Condemning Srebrenica Massacre*, Balkan Transitional Just. (Mar. 31, 2010). The Liberal Democratic Party condemned the resolution for not explicitly calling the massacre a genocide, while other politicians criticized it for singling out Srebrenica. *See id.*

[368] *Serbia Apologises for Srebrenica Massacre*, Mail & Guardian (Mar. 31, 2010).

[369] *Id. See also* Tim Judah, Opinion, *Serbia's Honest Apology*, N.Y. Times (Apr. 2, 2010).

[370] *See* Dragović-Soso, *supra* note 132, at 163. Indeed, Serbia's parliament went farther than its Bosnian counterpart. As noted in Chapter 8, soon after the former passed the Srebrenica resolution, Serb MPs blocked a Bosnian resolution on Srebrenica.

adding: "It's the first step."[371] Ivan Jovanović similarly saw the declaration as "a good political step: a sign of state recognition of a mass crime, which, in the future, may be used (and is used) as a reference and a bridgehead to keep the discourse about Srebrenica alive and, step by step, make the fact about the massacre and its magnitude internalized by the Serbs (at least in Serbia) even if it's not called genocide." While he believes it is "important" to characterize Srebrenica as a genocide, Jovanović reckons that, for now, this is "secondary" and that, in the long run, Serbians will accept that designation.[372]

The process culminating in the declaration merits brief note in light of concerns, described in Chapter 3, that Western policies of conditionality failed to emphasize a moral message behind demands for Serbian arrests of Hague fugitives. Perhaps as a corrective, external actors have increasingly pressed Serbia to acknowledge and condemn Serb atrocities,[373] and Western pressure may have played a key role in the declaration's adoption. Two previous efforts to secure a parliamentary resolution had foundered in the face of nationalist opposition.[374] The third produced a resolution, even if less robust than its proponents had sought, reportedly in part because of EU pressure for "symbolic reparation" for Srebrenica.[375]

D. Acknowledgment by "Reformed" Nationalists

Serbia saw further gestures of acknowledgment even in the post-2012 political landscape, in which "reformed" nationalists have held top leadership positions. Like previous official gestures, their limitations were glaring in the eyes of survivors. At least some Serbians, however, placed greater emphasis on the fact that men who had long been in the vanguard of Serbian denialism now expressed regret for Serb atrocities. Although none said so explicitly, they seemed to understand these leaders' apologies as elements of an "extended process[]" potentially "culminating in reconciliation.[376]

As previously noted, upon becoming president in 2012, former SRS leader Tomislav Nikolić stoked controversy by proclaiming, "There was no genocide in Srebrenica." Several months later, under pressure from regional and Western governments, Nikolić took his own turn apologizing for Srebrenica during an interview on Bosnian

---

[371] Christiane Amanpour, Transcript, *A View of Serbia's Future Through the Lens of Its Past*, CNN (Apr. 15, 2010).

[372] Comment by Ivan Jovanović on draft chapter (provided May 31, 2017). In line with Kandić's and Jovanović's assessments, Tim Judah believes that, in view of Serbia's deeply divided polity, simply proposing the Srebrenica resolution was "an achievement" and its adoption a "political landmark." Tim Judah, Opinion, *Serbia's Honest Apology*, N.Y. TIMES (Apr. 1, 2010). Writing in the immediate aftermath of the resolution's passage, Judah characterized negative appraisals as "shockingly churlish and cynical." *Id.*

[373] *See, e.g.,* Maja Živanović, *Council of Europe Calls for Serbia to Acknowledge Genocide*, BALKAN TRANSITIONAL JUST. (May 16, 2017).

[374] *See* Dragović-Soso, *supra* note 132, at 167–69.

[375] *Id.* at 169. In the view of Jasna Dragović-Soso, the Srebrenica declaration was "of dubious moral integrity and devoid of genuine remorse." *Id.* at 173. The principal takeaway from this episode, she argues, is that "external actors have a limited capacity to influence domestic processes of confronting a traumatic recent past." *Id.* Others, such as Ivan Jovanović, do not believe that, in this particular instance, Western pressure was counterproductive. Comment by Ivan Jovanović on draft chapter (provided May 31, 2017).

[376] Michael R. Marrus, *Official Apologies and the Quest for Historical Justice*, 3 CONTROVERSIES IN GLOBAL POL. & SOCIETIES 1, 7 (2006).

television taped in April 2012. English-language press accounts provide somewhat inconsistent accounts of his apology, a telling reflection of its ambiguity.[377] Most reported that Nikolić apologized for Srebrenica without using the word *genocide*,[378] angering victims' associations in Bosnia.[379] But at least one Serbian journalist reported Nikolić used the word,[380] and several Serbians interviewed for this study recalled that he "said it was genocide."[381]

A translation of Nikolić's comments by Sonja Balić makes clear why there is confusion. Her translation suggests Nikolić started to use the word *genocide* but then treated it as a verbal slip:

> I kneel because of it. Here, I kneel. And I seek forgiveness for Serbia for a crime that resulted in genocide, in Srebrenica [he finishes the word "genocide" abruptly and looks down and says "in Srebrenica" as though that was what he wanted to say instead of "genocide"]. I apologize for the crimes that were committed in the name of our country by any [Serb] individual.[382]

Later, the interviewer asked Nikolić whether he agreed the Srebrenica massacre was a genocide in light of all the evidence, and whether he thought it had the characteristics of genocide. Nikolić replied: "All that happened in the wars in the former Yugoslavia has characteristics of genocide."[383]

As with earlier apologies, Srebrenica survivors (again, it should be emphasized, at least those quoted in the media) found more to fault than welcome in Nikolić's remarks. One source reported:

> [Srebrenica survivor] Munira Subašić . . . said she was "not convinced" of Nikolić's sincerity. It was not about someone kneeling and asking for forgiveness, she said. What the relatives of the victims of the war crimes needed, she said, was sincerity and true remorse. And they wanted to "hear the Serbian president and Serbia say the word 'genocide,'" she said, adding that stealing a handbag would also classify as "crime".[384]

---

[377] Scholars believe that, to be effective tools of reconciliation, official apologies must be unambiguous. *See* Johanna Kirchhoff & Sabina Čehajić-Clancy, *Intergroup Apologies: Does It Matter What They Say?*, 20 PEACE & CONFLICT: J. PEACE PSYCHOL. 430, 432 (2014).

[378] Typical of these reports is a *Telegraph* article quoting Nikolić saying: "I am down on my knees because of it. Here, I am down on my knees. And I am asking for a pardon for Serbia for the crime that was committed in Srebrenica. I apologise for the crimes committed by any individual on behalf of our state and our people." Damien McElroy, *Serbian President in Historic Srebrenica Massacre Apology*, TELEGRAPH (Apr. 25, 2013).

[379] *See, e.g., Bosnians Are Not Enthusiastic About Apology*, DEUTSCHE WELLE (Apr. 26, 2013); *Serbian President Apologises for Srebrenica "Crime"*, BBC NEWS (Apr. 25, 2013).

[380] Marija Ristić, *Serbian President Apologises for War Crimes*, BALKAN TRANSITIONAL JUST. (Apr. 25, 2013).

[381] Interview with Marijana Toma, then Deputy Director, Humanitarian Law Center, in Belgrade, Serb. (June 10, 2014).

[382] Translated by Sonja Balić, then a student at Washington College of Law, American University. The bracketed account is that of Ms. Balić.

[383] This, too, is based on Sonja Balić's translation. One press account that mentioned the interviewer's question reported that Nikolić said in response, "That charge remained to be proven." Damien McElroy, *Serbian President in Historic Srebrenica Massacre Apology*, TELEGRAPH (Apr. 25, 2013).

[384] *Bosnians Are Not Enthusiastic About Apology*, DEUTSCHE WELLE (Apr. 26, 2013).

Within Serbian civil society, Nikolić's comments evoked wide-ranging assessments. Bogdan Ivanišević recalled the "apology" as bordering on sarcasm (in the spirit of, "What do you expect—Do you expect an apology from me? . . . OK, if that's what . . . I'm supposed to do, OK, I'm apologizing.").[385] Journalist Marija Ristić had a different reaction; in her view, the statement was "important" despite manifest shortcomings in light of Nikolić's ultranationalist past: "At least he said it on Bosnian TV to Bosnian people. Bearing in mind who was Nikolić, that is important. I don't know if it was sincere, but it's a step forward from the beginning of his presidency, when he said Vukovar [Croatia] is Serbian."[386] Nataša Kandić also saw Nikolić's remarks as a milestone, noting: "Nobody has ever said anything like it in Serbia. We know [the symbolism of kneeling and asking for forgiveness] from Willy Brandt and that's what makes his apology so important."[387] (Unlike Willy Brandt, however, Nikolić did not actually drop to his knees.) In Kandić's view, considering "his own past," Nikolić's apologizing at all was more important than whether he used the word *genocide*.[388]

Bridging these views and Ivanišević's perception, Marijana Toma recalled Nikolić's remarks this way:

> Actually he said that [Srebrenica] was genocide, but he said also that there are so many genocides, he would apologize for Srebrenica and for all the other genocides. What he basically meant was that, you know, "yes, it may be genocide, but then everything else is genocide." . . . On the other hand, I think his apology was more significant than [that of former President] Tadić . . . because of his background. I think that it is far more important to hear somebody who belonged to that nationalist politics . . . saying that he apologized, irrespective of who, what, does he really think.[389]

Three years after Nikolić's remarks, Serb leaders in Serbia and Bosnia came under mounting pressure to address Srebrenica as the twentieth anniversary of the massacre approached. In the lead-up to the anniversary, the British government introduced a draft UN Security Council resolution stressing "acceptance of the tragic events at Srebrenica as genocide is a prerequisite for reconciliation" and condemning

---

[385] Interview with Bogdan Ivanišević, Attorney, in Belgrade, Serb. (June 9, 2014).

[386] Interview with Marija Ristić, Journalist, in Belgrade, Serb. (June 13, 2014).

[387] *Bosnians Are Not Enthusiastic About Apology*, Deutsche Welle (Apr. 26, 2013). Kandić was, of course, referring to the iconic moment in 1970 when German chancellor Willy Brandt dropped to his knees at the Memorial of the Warsaw Uprising, "which is considered the most famous gesture of state penance in international politics." Stefan Engert, *German-Israel: A Prototypical Political Apology and Reconciliation Process, in* Apology and Reconciliation in International Relations: The Importance of Being Sorry 29, 30 (Christopher Daase et al. eds., 2016).

[388] *Bosnians Are Not Enthusiastic About Apology*, Deutsche Welle (Apr. 26, 2013).

[389] Interview with Marijana Toma, then Deputy Director, Humanitarian Law Center, in Belgrade, Serb. (June 10, 2014). While hailing the significance of an apology by a leader who personified Serbia's nationalist past, Toma added:

> I would not have a problem with his apology being insincere, right, if it was followed by some concrete steps, like slowly, slowly . . . slowly ignoring the Republika Srpska, which Serbian government is slowly doing that. . . . But also what I would want to see . . . would be some kind of concrete measures when it comes to reparations.

genocide denial.[390] Serbia's foreign minister denounced the text as "unbalanced, unnecessary and detrimental," while Nikolić implored Russian leader Vladimir Putin to veto the draft resolution.[391] During negotiations, Nikolić reportedly "repeated his denial of the Srebrenica genocide and stated he had no intention of attending" the upcoming anniversary commemoration of the massacre.[392] Although the proposed text acknowledged responsibility by all sides for committing atrocities in the 1990s conflict and did not name Serbs as those responsible for genocide, Russia vetoed the draft on the asserted ground it "singled out one party."[393] A grateful Nikolić hailed Russia as a true friend for preventing attempts to "smear the entire Serbian nation as genocidal."[394]

While then prime minister (later president) Vučić, too, opposed the draft resolution,[395] he attended the twentieth anniversary commemoration ceremony in Potočari, reportedly "after much . . . pressure from the West,"[396] but also, in one view, out of a conviction that it is not in Serbia's interest "to stand behind anyone's crimes."[397] (The following year, however, Serbia's interior minister banned rallies in Belgrade on July 11, leading to charges against a civil society activist who organized a demonstration to commemorate the victims of Srebrenica.[398])

Bogdan Ivanišević acknowledged Vučić's expressions of remorse might have been prompted more by Western pressure than the stirrings of conscience. But until this is shown to be the case, Ivanišević said, "I cannot disregard" what Vučić has said and done.[399] Ivanišević continued:

I have to take into consideration that . . . good things he said are different than what he said in the past. And, you know, words have a . . . performative effect—I mean they matter. If people who are in the position—he's been in a position in the

---

[390] *UN Council Headed for Showdown over Srebrenica*, AGENCE FRANCE-PRESSE (July 7, 2015). *See also Serbia Slams "Destabilising" UN Srebrenica Resolution*, BALKAN TRANSITIONAL JUST. (June 23, 2015).

[391] Edith M. Lederer, *Serbia Asking Russia to Veto Srebrenica Massacre Resolution*, ASSOCIATED PRESS (July 7, 2015).

[392] Hajrudin Somun, Opinion, *Who Is to Blame for the Srebrenica Incident?*, TODAY'S ZAMAN (Aug. 4, 2015).

[393] Karen DeYoung, *Russia Vetoes U.N. Resolution*, WASH. POST (July 9, 2015).

[394] *Id.*

[395] *Serbia Slams "Destabilising" UN Srebrenica Resolution*, BALKAN TRANSITIONAL JUST. (June 23, 2015); Marija Ristić & Saša Dragojlo, *Serbia's Genocide Denial Ensures an Annual Fiasco*, BALKAN TRANSITIONAL JUST. (July 7, 2016).

[396] Marko Milanović, *The Shameful Twenty Years of Srebrenica*, EJIL TALK! (July 13, 2015).

[397] Snežana Čongradin, *Srđan Bogosavljević: Vučić Changing Attitude of the Citizens of Srebrenica*, DANAS (June 29, 2015). Vučić had by then already addressed wartime atrocities in terms markedly different from his earlier stance. In September 2013, then deputy prime minister Vučić said: "We must continue to establish facts and prosecute crimes, we must name all the victims, maintain the memory and respect for all the victims, we must draw a line under all that happened, inform our citizens about all that information and educate [future] generations so that such crimes never happen again." Boris Pavelić, *Serbia and Croatia "Will Never Fight Again"*, BALKAN TRANSITIONAL JUST. (Sept. 2, 2013).

[398] Ivana Nikolić, *Serbian Activist Faces Court for Commemorating Srebrenica*, BALKAN TRANSITIONAL JUST. (Jan. 29, 2016).

[399] Although Ivanišević did not make this point, many celebrated apologies were the product of political negotiations.

government now for quite a few years—keep repeating these things, . . . at some point they must have some impact on the millions who are listening.[400]

As noted, survivors have often regarded Serbian apologies skeptically. Thus it is notable that Vučić's participation in the twentieth anniversary commemoration was welcomed by the Association of Mothers of Srebrenica and Žepa Enclaves. Regrettably, however, its reparative message was overshadowed by an angry mob, who pelted the Serbian leader with debris.[401] Denouncing their action, Munira Subašić, president of the Srebrenica mothers' association, declared: "This was not an attack on Vučić, but on all of us, on our dignity. . . . I am deeply disappointed."[402]

* * *

To varying degrees, apologies by Serbian leaders have fallen well short of a "consummate apology"[403] (most official apologies have). Bosnian survivors have seen many as insincere and incomplete, and none has stimulated or reflected a "genuine societal reckoning with war crimes and questions of responsibility."[404] Flawed apologies, prompted in part by Western pressure, raised anew a perennial question about the "role that external factors can play in instigating and facilitating . . . deep and durable social change."[405] It is surely right, as Jasna Dragović-Soso argues, that "external actors have a limited capacity to influence domestic processes of confronting a traumatic recent past."[406] Yet it is equally true that outside pressure can, depending on the

---

[400] Interview with Bogdan Ivanišević, Attorney, in Belgrade, Serb. (June 9, 2014). Ivanišević's point about the performative effect of Vučić's apology evokes a widely-recognized function of official apologies. *See, e.g.,* Tavuchis, *supra* note 334, at 22; Barkan & Karn, *supra* note 324, at 5.

[401] Marko Milanović, *The Shameful Twenty Years of Srebrenica,* EJIL Talk! (July 13, 2015).

[402] *Mothers of Srebrenica: This Was Not an Attack on Vučić, But on Our Dignity,* Sarajevo Times (July 12, 2015). The next year, no Serbian leader attended the twenty-first anniversary ceremony in Potočari, in part because survivors feared that a reprise of the attack against Vučić would detract from the victims themselves. *Thousands Gather at Ceremony for Victims of Srebrenica Massacre,* World Post (July 11, 2016). In addition, Srebrenica's mayor said those who would not accept that genocide was committed in Srebrenica were not welcome. Talha Ozturk, *Bosnia-Serbia Tensions Rise Ahead of Srebrenica Event,* Anadolu Agency (July 6, 2016). In response, then prime minister Vučić said, "If you have a problem with us placing a flower and laying wreaths, we will not come." Marija Ristić & Saša Dragojlo, *Serbia's Genocide Denial Ensures an Annual Fiasco,* Balkan Transitional Just. (July 7, 2016). Vučić visited the memorial center in November 2015, laying flowers as a gesture of respect for Srebrenica's victims, and announced Serbia was donating approximately $5.4 million to support economic development in Srebrenica. Dan Bilefsky, *Serbia Gives Bosnia Town $5.4 Million in Good Will,* N.Y. Times (Nov. 12, 2015). During this visit, Vučić noted Serbia had condemned "the serious and heinous crimes in Srebrenica" and that, since becoming prime minister, he had "never said it either was or wasn't" a genocide, as he did "not want to hurt any Bosniak by telling them" the massacre was "not it." *Izetbegović "Disappointed" with Vučić,* BETA (Nov. 5, 2015).

[403] Tavuchis, *supra* note 334, at 14. Michael Marrus writes that students of political apologies seem to be "remarkably in agreement" on the elements of effective apologies. In his account, those elements are (1) "acknowledgment of a wrong committed, including the harm it caused"; (2) "acceptance of responsibility for having caused the wrong"; (3) "expression of regret or remorse both for the harm and for having committed the wrong"; and (4) "a commitment . . . to reparation and, when appropriate, to non-repetition of the wrong." Marrus, *supra* note 376, at 8. Others, however, have noted wide-ranging scholarly views about the elements of an effective apology.

[404] Dragović-Soso, *supra* note 132, at 173.

[405] *Id.*

[406] *Id.* As well, because apologies for grievous wrongs pay "homage to a moral order rendered problematic by the very act that calls it forth," they transcend the concern of the perpetrators and the community they represent. Tavuchis, *supra* note 334, at 14.

circumstances, bolster domestic advocacy efforts in this sphere. Notably, advances in Germany's widely-extolled process of acknowledgment were not solely the product of domestic political factors; at times, progress was catalyzed by external pressure.

These considerations hardly assure that Western pressure will, in the long run, help Serbia develop a more robust process of reckoning and redress. Whether it does will be determined by myriad, now unknowable, developments. Some Serbian advocates are convinced, however, that external pressure is indispensable to progress in this sphere. Far from worrying such pressure might backfire, Maja Mičić voiced concern when I interviewed her in 2014 about the waning engagement of the EU and other external "allies" of Serbian human rights organizations. At a time when Serbian advocacy organizations faced formidable challenges, their longtime allies were, in effect, signaling: "You've had enough time [to address wartime atrocities]. That story's over, you need to turn to something else."[407]

V. A FOUNDATION FOR FUTURE ACKNOWLEDGMENT?

Sometimes the public is not ready to digest the truth.

—MARTIN LUTHER KING JR.[408]

Two broad conclusions emerge from this chapter's account. First, at least in the absence of a political transition entailing a sharp break with a prior regime and other auspicious conditions, the work of an ICT is unlikely to have a profound impact on beliefs about recent atrocities committed, inspired, or abetted by a society's government. And yet: ICTs are most likely to become involved in situations that have *not* seen such a transition. Officials and supporters of ICTs raise false hopes when they claim a tribunal's work will dispel denial or otherwise transform social conditions; instead, social conditions profoundly affect the way its work is understood. To be sure, the "trial truth" of an ICT might provide a factual foundation for a robust reckoning in the future.[409] But it falls to domestic governments and citizens to lead that effort, bolstered by outside actors when helpful and possible.[410]

---

[407] Interview with Maja Mičić, then Director, Youth Initiative for Human Rights, in Belgrade, Serb. (June 11, 2014). Marijana Toma, too, was concerned that the subject of war crimes was "becoming passé, because the international community does not insist on it anymore." Interview with Marijana Toma, then Deputy Director, Humanitarian Law Center, in Belgrade, Serb. (June 10, 2014).

[408] Martin Luther King, Jr., quoted in David J. Garrow, Opinion, *When Martin Luther King Came Out Against Vietnam*, N.Y. TIMES (Apr. 4, 2017).

[409] Ivan Jovanović evoked this possibility when he answered my question about whether it was useful for the ICTY to disclose evidence of Serb atrocities if Serb communities rejected that information:

> It's different when you're not getting information at all and when you're getting information but you're ignoring it because you don't like it. . . . Because credibility could be built over time by change of generations or change in intermediaries, which would here be crucial. . . . So once you had someone who collected the facts and who compiled the facts in the form of a judicial truth, then you're shrinking the space for denial. You're creating a record, a historical and juridical record for future generations.

Interview with Ivan Jovanović, then National Legal Advisor, OSCE Mission to Serbia, in Belgrade, Serb. (July 12, 2012).

[410] While many civil society advocates for accountability are understandably disheartened, others—not only in Serbia but in the region—have redoubled efforts to build on the Tribunal's legacy. As

Second, ICTs might nonetheless help reduce *levels* of denial within a society even without a decisive political transition, at least in some circumstances. In the context of a muddled transition such as Serbia's, even if a distant court's rulings do not alter the beliefs of many citizens, they might persuade *some* that an ethnic group or state to which they belong bears responsibility for inexcusable wrongs. The ICTY apparently had such an impact in Serbia during relatively auspicious periods in its political transition, persuading some Serbians to believe Serbs committed atrocities worthy of condemnation. The degree to which an ICT actually has this effect will turn on myriad contextual factors, as the Serbia case study exemplifies.[411]

Serbians who hoped the Tribunal would have a more substantial impact in the early post-Milošević era now focus on the future. Even if their society is not ready to "face the past," I heard repeatedly, the Tribunal's work has laid a firm foundation for future acknowledgment. Sonja Stojanović made the point this way during my first research visit: the Hague Tribunal "managed to compile information and archives that will prevent future mythologies. For any researcher in the future, ICTY evidence will be crucial for all sides."[412] But, she said, "unfortunately" Serbian society (which Stojanović described as "very frustrated") was "not yet ready to handle" this information.[413]

This theme became even more pronounced in later interviews. By 2012, Bogdan Ivanišević had concluded "it's too early" for Serbian society to face the past. When and if that time comes, however, Ivanišević believes the ICTY will have "laid the foundation for that by helping numerous facts to come to the surface" and ensuring they were "credibly established."[414] Maja Mičić predicted that, in the future, "we will be looking back to . . . many things that were gathered and that were made public through the work of the ICTY."[415] Now, however, it had become abundantly clear "it will take much more time than we expected" for Serbian society to accept key facts authenticated in The Hague.[416]

---

the ICTY prepared to end its work in late 2017, the Sense News Agency, which provided the most consistent reporting on the Tribunal over its lifetime, transformed itself into the Sense Transitional Justice Center. Based in Pula, Croatia, the new center aims "to make visible and permanently available the facts established by the ICTY about the events in the former Yugoslavia" and, in doing so, provide a "focal point for regional transitional justice initiatives." Letter from Mirko Klarin, Director, Sense Transitional Justice Center, to Diane Orentlicher (Sept. 11, 2017).

[411] As previously discussed, Serbian sources believe rising levels of acknowledgment during certain periods in the post-Milošević era are attributable in part to the stewardship and discourses of reformist leaders, as well as widely-viewed documentaries chronicling Serb atrocities.

[412] Interview with Sonja Stojanović, Executive Director, Center for Civil-Military Relations, in Belgrade, Serb. (Nov. 23, 2006).

[413] *Id.*

[414] The issue now, Ivanisević said, "is how to translate that [established knowledge] from something that is the property of a limited number of persons in the region to something that everyone in the region, or most people of the region, would own." Interview with Bogdan Ivanišević, Attorney, in Belgrade, Serb. (July 9, 2012).

[415] Interview with Maja Mičić, then Director, Youth Initiative for Human Rights, in Belgrade, Serb. (June 11, 2014). *See also* Ivan Jovanović, *From History to Courtroom and Back: What Can Historiography Obtain from Judgments for Crimes in the Wars in the Former Yugoslavia, in* FORUM FOR TRANSITIONAL JUSTICE 156 (2017) ("the ICTY leaves us a legacy, a huge reservoir of facts and findings").

[416] *Id.* Germany's relationship to Nuremberg, which I explore briefly in Chapter 11, provides grounds to believe an ICT *can* make a much-delayed contribution to the kind of reckoning Mičić and other Serbians hoped the ICTY would inspire.

8

Living in Compulsory Denial (Bosnia)

The official history of our region is being written in The Hague. There are so many different histories being offered here. . . . Now, through the Hague process, . . . we can get the complete picture.

—Jasna Bakšić Muftić[1]

We have a big problem here regarding acknowledgment of the truth. Because you see it is well known to all that several alleged truths exist—Muslims' truth, Serbs' truth and Croats' truth.

—Kada Hotić[2]

Those who committed the war crimes against us are still winning. They are killing our truth.

—Bakira Hasečić[3]

Expressing U.S. support for a Security Council resolution formally creating the ICTY, Ambassador Madeleine Albright vowed: "The only victor that will prevail in this endeavor is the truth. . . . And it is only the truth that can cleanse the ethnic and religious hatreds and begin the healing process."[4] Though she could not have known it then, Albright ascribed to the Tribunal a mission many Bosnians would avidly

---

[1] Interview with Jasna Bakšić Muftić, Professor, Faculty of Law, University of Sarajevo, in Sarajevo, Bosn. & Herz. (Nov. 30, 2006).
[2] Interview with Kada Hotić, Vice President, Association of Mothers of Srebrenica and Žepa Enclaves, in Sarajevo, Bosn. & Herz. (July 24, 2009).
[3] Julian Borger, The Butcher's Trail: How the Search for Balkan War Criminals Became the World's Most Successful Manhunt 330 (2016) (quoting Bakira Hasečić, Survivor).
[4] Provisional Verbatim Record, U.N. SCOR, 3,217th mtg., at 12, U.N. Doc. S/PV.3217 (May 25, 1993). *See also* Provisional Verbatim Record, U.N. SCOR, 3175th mtg., at 11, U.N. Doc. S/PV.3175 (Feb. 22, 1993) (session in which Ambassador Albright first made this point).

4

embrace. They hoped and believed that, by rendering a definitive factual record, the ICTY would dispel denial[5] about wartime depredations, foster acknowledgment and remorse, forge a shared understanding of the 1990s conflict among Bosnia's ethnic groups, and advance reconciliation.[6]

Using their expectations as benchmarks for assessment, this chapter explores several interlocking questions: To what extent have Bosnian citizens accepted key factual conclusions set forth in judgments, as well as the ICTY's implicit allocation, through charging patterns, of relative responsibility for wartime atrocities? Have Bosnians developed a *common* understanding of basic facts concerning wartime atrocities? To what extent have government officials and institutions acknowledged and condemned war crimes, including those committed by members of officials' own ethnic group? What role, if any, did the Tribunal play in advancing or hindering acknowledgment?

Moving from description to explanation, this chapter explores factors that account for persistently high levels of denial in Bosnia. To avoid repeating analysis developed in Chapter 7, it does not provide an in-depth account of social science research that supports and deepens the perspectives of Bosnians interviewed for this study. Instead, it builds on the foundation developed in Chapter 7, introducing additional social science perspectives principally to the extent they have not been previously addressed. In light of Bosnia's ethnic diversity and divisions, those perspectives center on questions of *mutual* acknowledgment by leaders and members of each major ethnic group of harms committed by members of their in-group against others. In particular, this chapter draws upon social science research on *competitive victimhood* to deepen the insights of Bosnians, explored in this chapter, about dynamics underlying contesting narratives about wartime atrocities.

Portions of this assessment dealing with Serb discourses will come as no surprise in light of the analysis set forth in Chapter 7. As in Serbia, Bosnia saw meaningful progress in Serb acknowledgment for several years in the early 2000s, but has seen rising levels of denialism since then. Yet despite these parallels, Serb denialism has had a distinct trajectory and nature in Bosnia. Notably, it has been even more pronounced in Bosnia than Serbia, although Bosnian Serbs have every reason to know the brutal facts of ethnic cleansing. These and other differences are instructive, highlighting the independent influence of contextual factors on the phenomenon of denial.

I. BOSNIAN CITIZENS' ACCEPTANCE OF FUNDAMENTAL FACTS OF WARTIME ATROCITIES

A. What Should Bosnians Know, Say They Know, and Condemn?

Although widely recognized, it bears repeating that historical truth is always provisional, unsettled, and constructed in no small part by subjective interpretation.[7]

---

[5] The phrase "living in compulsory denial" used in the title of this chapter comes from Nidžara Ahmetašević, *Bosnia's Unending War*, NEW YORKER (Nov. 4, 2015) (quoting sociologist Eric Gordy saying that activists in Prijedor "are conscious that the community has no future living in compulsory denial").

[6] I develop these points in Chapter 4.

[7] *See, e.g.*, RUTI G. TEITEL, TRANSITIONAL JUSTICE 69–70 (2000). While generally true, this is especially so in Bosnia. As Svjetlana Nedimović reflected, in a country of "open wounds," as she described Bosnia, the past is profoundly "unsettled." Interview with Svjetlana Nedimović, Activist, in Sarajevo, Bosn. & Herz. (Sept. 18, 2014).

In deeply divided societies, "the past" is fertile ground for clashing narratives, each shaped as much by (instrumentalized) mythology as objective facts.[8] But if the past does not lend itself to a fixed meaning, many Bosnians hoped the Hague Tribunal would, through the crucible of legal procedure, place the hard facts of ethnic cleansing beyond the realm of plausible denial. More extravagantly, they hoped the Tribunal would generate consensus about the *meaning* of those facts, above all their moral meaning.

Bosnians interviewed for this study identified several broad categories of "truth" they hoped ICTY judgments would persuade Bosnians to accept. Many victims of Serb atrocities hoped the Tribunal would definitively establish broad patterns of wartime atrocities, including the *relative extent* of atrocities committed by members of each ethnic group and, conversely, of each group's victimization ("in effect" because broad historical conclusions of this type transcend the Tribunal's remit), as well as the nature of those crimes. On a related note, many Bosniaks hoped the Tribunal's judgments would make clear that, while members of each ethnic group committed war crimes, Serbs initiated armed violence and crafted a strategy of systematic persecution to achieve their war aims.

As explained in Chapter 4, many Bosniaks in particular (though by no means exclusively) hoped the ICTY's factual findings would stimulate acknowledgment of and remorse for wartime atrocities, particularly on the part of ethnic Serbs. As in Serbia, the Srebrenica massacre is widely seen as a litmus test of Serb acknowledgment. Judged to meet the stringent definition of genocide in several ICTY cases,[9] the July 1995 slaughter "has become a symbol of collective suffering" for many Bosniaks.[10] Thus, emphasizing the necessity of "messages of reconciliation" through "public acknowledgment of the crimes," Dženana Karup Druško told me the "well known" case of Srebrenica was an obvious place to start.[11] Many also hoped Bosniaks would condemn war crimes committed by their in-group against others.

---

[8] Michael Ignatieff explored some of these themes in *Articles of Faith*, 5 INDEX ON CENSORSHIP 110 (1996).

[9] The ICTY convicted five Bosnian Serbs of genocide-related charges in connection with Srebrenica after appeals were exhausted, and two others—Radovan Karadžić and Ratko Mladić—at the trial level (the Tribunal's residual mechanism has jurisdiction over appeals from the latter two). The ICTY's first Srebrenica conviction at the trial level—in which it also for the first time ruled the Srebrenica massacre a genocide—was rendered in 2001. Prosecutor v. Krstić, Case No. IT-98-33-T, Trial Judgment, ¶¶ 599, 653 (Int'l Crim. Trib. for the Former Yugoslavia Aug. 2, 2001). On April 19, 2004, the ICTY Appeals Chamber sustained the trial chamber's conclusion that the Srebrenica massacre met the legal definition of genocide. Prosecutor v. Krstić, Case No. IT-98-33-A, Appeal Judgment, ¶¶ 21, 23 (Int'l Crim. Trib. for the Former Yugoslavia Apr. 19, 2004). In January 2015, the Appeals Chamber upheld the convictions of three Bosnian Serb officers on genocide-related charges, two of whom were convicted of genocide itself—the first time the Appeals Chamber had rendered such a verdict (Krstić was convicted on appeal of aiding and abetting genocide). Prosecutor v. Popović et. al, Case No. IT-05-88-A, Appeal Judgment (Int'l Crim. Trib. for the Former Yugoslavia Jan. 30, 2015). Later that year, the Appeals Chamber convicted General Zdravko Tolimir of genocide and other charges, affirming his life sentence. Prosecutor v. Tolimir, Case No. IT-05-88/2-A, Appeal Judgment, (Int'l Crim. Trib. for the Former Yugoslavia Apr. 8, 2015).

[10] Maja Zuvela, *Thousands Gather at Ceremony for Victims of Srebrenica Massacre*, REUTERS (July 11, 2016).

[11] Interview with Dženana Karup Druško, Transitional Justice, Accountability and Remembrance, in Sarajevo, Bosn. & Herz. (Sept. 8, 2014).

As elaborated in Chapter 2, the Bosnian Serb leadership strongly opposed the Tribunal's creation. Once the Tribunal became a reality, however, many Bosnian Serbs hoped it would recognize war crimes committed against their in-group, such as those noted below, in equal measure to those committed by Serbs against others.[12] Other Bosnian Serbs, whose perspectives loom large in this account, have supported the Tribunal for reasons similar to those of Serbians who have pressed their leaders and society to "address the past":[13] They believe Bosnian Serbs are morally bound to acknowledge and condemn atrocities committed in their name.

As previously noted, for the most part Bosnian Croats neither enthusiastically embraced nor strongly rejected the ICTY when it was created.[14] Once it became a reality, the hope of many was that the Tribunal's judgments would essentially validate the "purity" of their wartime aims.[15]

Other Croat citizens have condemned war crimes committed by Bosnian (as well as Croatian) Croats, and hoped ICTY judgments would help advance a wider reckoning by their in-group. Broadly, the Tribunal's prosecution of Bosnian Croats involved crimes by members of the *Hrvatsko Vijeće Obrane* (HVO)—the wartime Bosnian Croat militia—during a military campaign that began in late 1992 and lasted until 1994.[16] The campaign's aim was to establish exclusive Croat control over territory in Bosnia the HVO called "Herceg-Bosna." Acting in concert with Croatia's wartime president, Franjo Tuđman, the HVO hoped eventually to attach Herceg-Bosna to Croatia.[17] To achieve its aims, the HVO "ethnically cleansed" non-Croats. For example, almost all Bosniaks in the Lašva Valley region were either killed or forced to flee. In the hamlet of Ahmići, Croats massacred over a hundred Bosniaks, burning some alive in their homes. Among the victims were thirty-two women and eleven children.[18]

While Bosniaks experienced the highest level of wartime atrocities among Bosnia's ethnic communities, Bosniak forces also committed war crimes, some of which

---

[12] See DIANE F. ORENTLICHER, OPEN SOCIETY JUSTICE INITIATIVE & INTERNATIONAL CENTER FOR TRANSITIONAL JUSTICE, THAT SOMEONE GUILTY BE PUNISHED: THE IMPACT OF THE ICTY IN BOSNIA 50 (2010) (recounting interviews with Bosnian Serbs who described their desire for justice).

[13] The views of Serbians who pressed for accountability are addressed in Chapters 5 and 7.

[14] See Chapter 2.

[15] The word "purity" was used by a Bosnian source who distilled Croat commentary about ICTY cases.

[16] Croatian Croats were prosecuted before the ICTY for war crimes committed in the context of Croatia's campaign to recover Croatian territory seized by Croatian Serb rebels, culminating in Operations Storm and Flash in 1995.

[17] See Prosecutor v. Prlić et al., Case No. IT-04-74-T, Trial Judgment, ¶¶ 414, 423, 428 (Int'l Crim. Trib. for the Former Yugoslavia May 29, 2013) [hereinafter Prlić Trial Judgment]; Denis Džidić, *Hague Jails Bosnian Croat Leaders for 111 Years*, BALKAN TRANSITIONAL JUST. (May 29, 2013); CARLA DEL PONTE WITH CHUCK SUDETIĆ, MADAME PROSECUTOR: CONFRONTATIONS WITH HUMANITY'S WORST CRIMINALS AND THE CULTURE OF IMPUNITY 242 (2009). Under pressure from the United States, Tuđman eventually abandoned this goal and persuaded Bosnian Croats to unite with Bosniaks against Serb combatants. See BORGER, *supra* note 3, at 107. Before the HVO campaign to establish Herceg-Bosna, Bosniak and Croat forces had cooperated in combatting Serb forces. See Prlić Trial Judgment, *supra*, ¶ 440.

[18] See Prosecutor v. Kordić et al., Case No. IT-95-14/2, Trial Judgment, ¶ 625 (Int'l Crim. Trib. for the Former Yugoslavia Feb. 26, 2001); see also DEL PONTE WITH SUDETIĆ, *supra* note 17, at 247–48.

were prosecuted in The Hague. For example, Bosniaks as well as Croats in Konjic retaliated against Serbs when their town was shelled by Serb forces in May 1992. Serb prisoners of war, as well as some local Serbs, were taken to the Čelebići prison camp, where they were sadistically tortured, killing some.[19] In June 1993, the Bosniak-led Bosnian Army, as well as foreign Muslim forces known as "Mujahedin" who fought with that army, attacked HVO forces in Travnik, killing and wounding many Croat and Serb civilians as well as captured HVO forces.[20]

B. Awareness of War Crimes as Reflected in Surveys

In contrast to Serbia, where Strategic Marketing and its clients administered periodic surveys for roughly a decade, no single organization has periodically explored Bosnian views of war crimes issues.[21] The Belgrade Centre for Human Rights (BCHR) did, however, commission surveys in Bosnia in 2010 and 2012, administered by Ipsos Strategic Marketing, that probed beliefs about this subject. As with surveys administered in Serbia, it is safe to assume that, on a subject as fraught as this, many Bosnian respondents felt social pressure to align their answers with dominant group discourses.[22] Even so, the BCHR surveys are a telling barometer of Bosnian citizens' acknowledgment, illuminating at the very least what respondents were willing to *say* they believe about wartime atrocities in response to survey questions.

The BCHR surveys did not ask respondents to identify themselves by ethnicity; instead, they requested information about residence. In light of Bosnia's high degree of de facto ethnic segregation,[23] however, the residence of respondents serves as a

---

[19] *See* Prosecutor v. Delalić et al., Case No. IT-96-21-T, Trial Judgment (Int'l Crim. Trib. for the Former Yugoslavia Nov. 16, 1998). Four suspects were prosecuted in this case, of whom three were convicted.

[20] *See* Prosecutor v. Delić, Case No. IT-04-83-T, Trial Judgment (Int'l Trib. for the Former Yugoslavia Sept. 15, 2008); Prosecutor v. Hadžihasanović et al., Case No. IT-01-47-T, Trial Judgment (Int'l Crim. Trib. for the Former Yugoslavia Mar. 15, 2006).

[21] As summarized in Chapter 6, a number of surveys conducted between 2002 and 2012 asked at least one or more questions about the ICTY and/or war crimes.

[22] Indeed, all of the methodological caveats noted in respect of Serbia surveys noted in Chapter 7 apply to the Bosnia surveys discussed here. Survey responses discussed in this section are drawn from *Javno Mnenje u BiH i Stavovi Prema Međunarodnom Krivičnom Tribunalu za Bivšu Jugoslaviju u Hagu ICTY 2010—Detaljne Tabele*, http://www.bgcentar.org.rs/bgcentar/wp-content/uploads/2013/10/Javno-mnenje-u-BiH-i-stavovi-prema-Me%C4%91unarodnom-krivi%C4%8Dnom-tribunalu-za-biv%C5%A1u-Jugoslaviju-u-Hagu-ICTY-2010-detaljne-tabele.pdf [hereinafter 2010 BCHR Survey] and *Javno Mnenje u BiH i Stavovi Prema Međunarodnom Krivičnom Tribunalu za Bivšu Jugoslaviju u Hagu ICTY 2012—Detaljne Tabele*, http://www.bgcentar.org.rs/bgcentar/wp-content/uploads/2013/10/Javno-mnenje-u-BiH-i-stavovi-prema-Me%C4%91unarodnom-krivi%C4%8Dnom-tribunalu-za-biv%C5%A1u-Jugoslaviju-u-Hagu-ICTY-2012-detaljne-tabele.pdf [hereinafter 2012 BCHR Survey].

[23] According to the 2013 Bosnian census, 92 percent of Bosnian Serbs live in Republika Srpska, 82 percent of whose population is Serb. Approximately 93 percent of Federation residents are either Bosniak or Croat. Within the Federation, there is significant de facto segregation as well. For example, ethnic Croats constitute approximately 69 percent of residents in the contiguous cantons of Herzegovina Neretva, West Herzegovina, and Canton 10, and 77 percent of the geographically separate Posavski canton, while almost 82 percent of residents in the remaining six Federation cantons (Una-Sana, Tuzla, Zenica-Doboj, Bosnian-Podrinje, Central Bosnia, and Sarajevo) are Bosniak. These percentages are derived from population statistics in the Census of Population, Households and Dwellings in Bosnia and Herzegovina, 2013, Final Results at 54–55,

rough proxy for their ethnicity.[24] Accordingly, the following discussion uses BCHR regional response data to approximate responses by members of each major ethnic group.[25]

As will be seen, survey results depict sobering levels of persisting denialism. It should be emphasized, however, that persistence is not the same as consistency over time. Later, I explore significant changes in Bosnian discourses of acknowledgment and denial over roughly two decades. As already intimated and developed in greater detail later, Bosnia saw meaningful progress in this sphere in the early years of the twenty-first century.

1. OVERVIEW OF SURVEY RESULTS: ETHNIC CLEAVAGES

The BCHR surveys captured stark differences in the responses of citizens in predominantly Serb, Croat, and Bosniak regions, respectively, to questions about relative victimization and responsibility for war crimes.[26] In 2010, 75 percent of respondents in the Federation said the largest number of victims were Bosniak, while only 3 percent of respondents in Republika Srpska chose this answer. While these figures suggest a striking Federation/RS divide, responses *within* the Federation also break sharply along ethnic lines: almost 89 percent of those living in majority Bosniak regions identified Bosniaks as the largest victim group, while only 12 percent of respondents in majority Croat regions chose this response. (Figure 8.1.)

In the same survey, 32 percent of respondents in majority Serb areas said Serbs were the greatest victims of wartime atrocities, while 42 percent said all groups suffered equally. Among respondents in majority Croat areas, 39 percent identified

---

http://www.popis2013.ba/popis2013/doc/Popis2013prvoIzdanje.pdf [hereinafter 2013 Bosnia Census].

[24] Residence is only a rough proxy for ethnicity for two reasons. First, the regions surveyed by BCHR are not ethnically homogeneous (see previous footnote). Second, even when BCHR survey results are broken down by regions smaller than entities, they do not uniformly group together regions in which one ethnic group predominates. For example, BCHR presents findings for the Herzegovina region, in which Croats constitute 67 percent of the population, but folds two other Croat-majority cantons (Posavski and Canton 10), in both of which Croats are 77 percent of the population, into regions in which Croats are a minority.

[25] In the charts provided in this section I use the phrase "majority Serb region" to encompass two regions BCHR identifies as "Northern Republika Srpska and Brčko" and "Eastern Republika Srpska," despite the fact that Brčko is not predominantly Serb. While 82 percent of Republika Srpska's citizens are ethnic Serbs, only 35 percent of Brčko's residents are Serbs. See 2013 Bosnia Census, *supra* note 23, at 54. Serbs constitute roughly 79 percent of the combined survey regions of Northern RS, Brčko, and Eastern RS. BCHR survey results broken down by entity residence (Federation and Republika Srpska) also fold Brčko into Republika Srpska.

The charts in this section use the phrase "majority Croat region" to refer to the Herzegovina region, and the phrase "majority Bosniak region" to refer to regions in the Federation other than Herzegovina. The areas comprised in the "majority Bosniak region" are Sarajevo (almost 84 percent of whose residents are Bosniak, according to the 2013 Bosnia Census, *supra* note 23, at 55), Northern Federation (which is not defined in the BCHR survey), and Cazin, a municipality in Una Sana Canton almost 96 percent of whose residents are Bosniak. See 2013 Bosnia Census, *supra* note 23, at 57. I assumed (and a BCHR source confirmed) that BCHR survey references to "Northern Federation" include those portions of the Federation other than four areas—Sarajevo, Cazin, Herzegovina Neretva, and West Herzegovina—for which survey results are provided separately. Based on data in the 2013 Bosnian Census, more than 74 percent of the residents of "Northern Federation" as thus defined are Bosniak.

[26] The percentages used in this and the next paragraph come from the 2010 BCHR Survey, *supra* note 22, at 135–36.

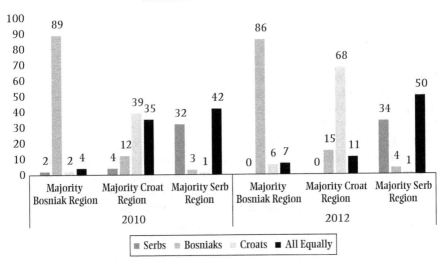

Which side incurred the most victims?

Figure 8.1 Stated Beliefs about Relative Victimization.

Croats as the largest group of wartime victims, while 35 percent said all suffered equally. (Figure 8.1.) Thus, with the exception of respondents living in majority Bosniak regions, whose aggregate responses are warranted by well-established facts, significant numbers of Croats and Serbs either inflated their own group's relative victimization or equalized victimization levels across ethnic groups.

Also in the 2010 survey, respondents in majority Bosniak regions overwhelmingly (89 percent) identified Serbs as having committed the most war crimes, while 67 percent of respondents in predominantly Croat areas chose this response. Notably in light of well-established facts about the extent of crimes committed by Serbs, only 1 percent of respondents in majority Serb areas said Serbs committed the most war crimes. Roughly 44 percent of respondents in those areas said all groups were equally responsible, 24 percent identified Bosniaks as most responsible, and 24 percent said they did not know.[27] (Figure 8.2.) Again, responses in the 2010 survey by individuals in predominantly Bosniak regions correspond most closely to well-established facts.

Although the 2012 survey results also show striking cleavages along ethnic lines, they reflect several shifts since 2010. For example, respondents living in majority Bosniak areas were somewhat less likely (86 percent) to say Bosniaks constituted the largest group of victims than in 2010 (89 percent). Respondents in majority Croat areas were, in contrast, much more likely (68 percent) than in 2010 (39 percent) to say Croats constituted the largest number of wartime victims.[28] Among respondents in

[27] *Id.* at 137-38.

[28] Here, it may be relevant to note that the survey was conducted early in 2012, before the ICTY Appeals Chamber acquitted Croatian general Ante Gotovina of crimes against Serbs. It is unfortunate the BCHR did not administer another survey following Gotovina's acquittal; the resulting data might shed greater light on whether or how ICTY judgments affect assessments of war crimes by members of one's in-group.

majority Serb areas, in 2012 roughly 50 percent said all sides were equally victimized, a significant increase from 2010, when 42 percent chose this response. (Figure 8.1.) This change cannot be attributed principally to a shift since 2010 in Serb assessments of Serb victimization levels, which was relatively small.[29] Instead, compared to 2010, residents of majority Serb areas were significantly more likely in 2012 to *equalize victimization* than to say they did not know who was most victimized.[30]

Correspondingly, the 2012 survey reflects shifts since 2010 in responses to the question "Who committed the most war crimes?"[31] Fewer respondents in majority Serb areas (16 percent) chose Bosniaks as the group most responsible for crimes in 2012 than in 2010 (24 percent). Yet this did not translate into a comparable shift in the percentage who identified Serbs as the primary perpetrators: 4 percent of respondents in majority Serb areas chose this answer in 2012, compared to 1 percent in 2010. (Figure 8.2.) The most striking shift in responses to this question by persons in majority Serb areas is a sizable increase in the percentage who chose the option "all equally." In 2010, 44 percent of residents in majority Serb areas chose this response, while in 2012, 66 percent did. As will be seen later, the notion that all sides were equally responsible for war crimes is a dominant theme in Bosnian Serb discourses. What the surveys seem to show is that Serb citizens' commitment to this narrative hardened between 2010 and 2012. (Figure 8.2.)

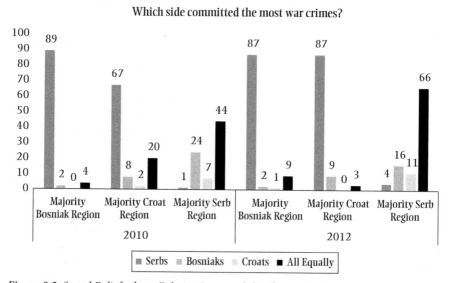

Figure 8.2 Stated Beliefs about Relative Responsibility for War Crimes.

[29] Roughly 32 percent of respondents in predominantly Serb regions identified Serbs as the largest victim group in 2010, compared to 34 percent in 2012. (Figure 8.1.)

[30] In 2010, roughly 21 percent of respondents from predominantly Serb areas said they did not know who was most victimized. In 2012, only 11 percent chose this response. The data for 2012 survey responses concerning relative victimization come from 2012 BCHR survey, *supra* note 22, at 138–39.

[31] Data for 2012 survey responses to this question come from *id.* at 140–41.

Turning to emblematic crimes, survey responses to questions about Srebrenica show a marked cleavage between the stated beliefs of respondents in the (predominantly Bosniak and Croat) Federation on the one hand, and those in (the predominantly Serb) Republika Srpska on the other. In 2010, more than 96 percent of respondents in the Federation said they had heard "over seven thousand Bosniak civilians and war prisoners were executed in Srebrenica" in 1995, while only 54 percent of RS respondents said they had heard this.[32] (Figure 8.3.)

Among those who said they had heard about the massacre, almost 100 percent of respondents from the Federation said they believed it happened in 2010, meaning 96 percent of total Federation respondents said they believed more than seven thousand Bosniaks were executed in Srebrenica. In contrast, only 53 percent of RS respondents who said they had heard of the massacre said they believed it happened, with the result that only 29 percent of total RS respondents said they believed thousands had been executed in Srebrenica.[33] (Figure 8.3.)

Of those who said they believed what they had heard, approximately 100 percent of Federation respondents and 88 percent of Republika Srpska respondents characterized Srebrenica as a "war crime for which the perpetrators should answer" rather than "an inevitable consequence of war."[34] Applying these percentages to the percentages who said they believed what they had heard about Srebrenica, the ethnic divide appears more stark: while 96 percent of total Federation respondents characterized Srebrenica as a war crime, a little more than 25 percent of total RS respondents did.[35] (Figure 8.4.)

Survey responses in 2012 likewise reflect striking cleavages in responses to Srebrenica-related questions, but also show some movement on this question. In 2012, a higher percentage (59 percent)[36] of RS respondents said they had heard about the Srebrenica massacre than in 2010 (54 percent). While this may seem to signify modest progress, among those who said they had heard of the massacre, RS respondents were less likely (35 percent)[37] to say they believed what they had heard than in 2010 (53 percent). Applying the percentage who said they believed what they had heard about Srebrenica to the percentage who said they had heard about the massacre, only 21 percent of total RS respondents said they believed more than 7,000 Bosniaks were massacred in Srebrenica (compared to 97 percent of Federation respondents).[38] (Figure 8.3.)

Notably, however, in both regions respondents who said they believed what they had heard about Srebrenica were highly likely to characterize the massacre as a war crime for which people should answer rather than an inevitable act during war: 99 percent of Federation respondents and 97 percent of RS respondents who said they believed more than 7,000 Bosniaks were killed in Srebrenica chose this answer in 2012.[39] When the percentage of those who characterized the massacre as

---

[32] 2010 BCHR survey, *supra* note 22, at 37–39.

[33] *Id.* at 48, 50.

[34] *Id.* at 60–61.

[35] *Id.*

[36] 2012 BCHR Survey, *supra* note 22, at 38.

[37] *Id.* at 48.

[38] *Id.* at 52.

[39] *Id.* at 61–62.

a war crime is applied to the percentage who said they believed it happened, how-ever, the ethnic divide once again is striking: in 2012, 96 percent of total Federation respondents characterized Srebrenica as a war crime, compared to only 20 percent of RS respondents.[40] (Figure 8.4.)

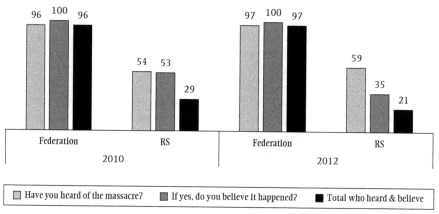

Have you heard that over 7,000 Bosniak civilians and war prisoners were executed in Srebrenica? (Percentage responding "yes")

Figure 8.3 Stated Beliefs about Srebrenica Massacre.

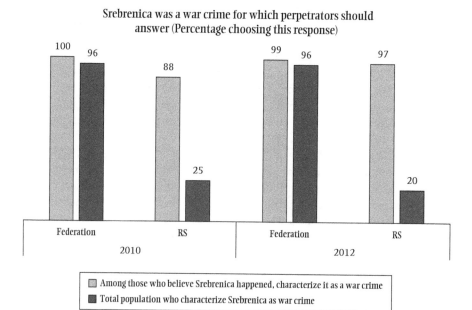

Srebrenica was a war crime for which perpetrators should answer (Percentage choosing this response)

Figure 8.4 Stated Beliefs about Blameworthiness of Srebrenica Massacre.

---

[40] *Id.*

The Srebrenica-related responses are particularly striking. If beliefs were based above all on readily available information, we would expect Bosnian Serbs to know more than Serbians about Srebrenica. Indeed, during interviews in Serbia I sometimes heard observations to the effect that Serb denialism is less pronounced in Bosnia than in Serbia precisely because Bosnians lived through (and, in many instances, committed) atrocities in Bosnia, and thus could hardly deny what happened. Contrary to this expectation, however, surveys administered in Bosnia and Serbia, respectively, suggest denialism is more pronounced among Bosnian Serbs than citizens of Serbia. Notably, in 2012 a smaller proportion of respondents in Republika Srpska (59 percent) said they had even *heard* about the Srebrenica massacre than the proportion of *Serbian* respondents (72 percent) who answered the same question in a 2011 survey administered by Strategic Marketing/Ipsos.[41]

More striking still are differences between responses to the question whether survey participants believed what they had heard about Srebrenica: for the 2012 Bosnia survey, only 35 percent of (majority-Serb) RS respondents who said they had heard about Srebrenica said they believed the massacre happened, compared to 56 percent of respondents in the 2011 *Serbia* survey. It may well be the case, as several Serbian interlocutors suggested, that Bosnians are more likely than Serbians to know/believe members of their own ethnic group committed atrocities precisely because it was impossible not to know. But as the survey results remind us, this is not the same as *acknowledging* what they know, even in an anonymous survey.

Although the BCHR surveys reflect deep, and apparently deepening, Serb denialism in respect of war crimes committed by Serbs, they also reflect a surprisingly low level of acknowledged Serb awareness of war crimes committed *against* Serbs. In 2012, only 33 percent of respondents in Republika Srpska said they had heard of rapes committed against Serb women in Čelebići—an even lower percentage than the portion of Federation respondents (38 percent) who said they had heard of these crimes against Serbs.[42] (Figure 8.5.) This is notable not least because these crimes would lend support to a key theme in Serb discourses—that all sides were equally responsible for war crimes. Addressing this surprising, Marko Milanović writes: "This indicates a general desire within the Bosnian Serb population toward the suppression of collective memories—or the expression of those memories—regarding the conflict as a whole."[43]

Responses to a separate question about war crimes committed by foreign Muslims who fought with the Bosniak armed forces also reflect a disparity between Federation and RS responses, though the cleavage breaks in a somewhat unexpected way: in response to the question asking whether respondents had heard that "in 1993, Mudjahedins committed crimes against Serb and Croat civilians in Travnik and its vicinity," respondents in the Federation were more likely (52 percent) to answer yes than respondents in Republika Srpska (38 percent).[44] (Figure 8.6.)

---

[41] *See* Figure 7.6, Chapter 7.

[42] *See* 2012 BCHR Survey, *supra* note 22, at 38. Among respondents who said they had heard of these rapes, respondents in the Federation were slightly more likely to say they believed what they had heard (95 percent) than respondents in RS (91 percent). *Id.* at 46-47.

[43] Marko Milanović, *The Impact of the ICTY on the Former Yugoslavia: An Anticipatory Postmortem*, 110 Am. J. Int'l L. 233, 250 (2016).

[44] 2012 BCHR Survey, *supra* note 22, at 38. Among those who said they had heard of this, an overwhelming majority in both the Federation (97 percent) and RS (92 percent) said they believed

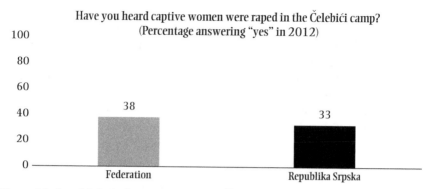

Figure 8.5 Stated Beliefs about War Crimes in Čelebići.

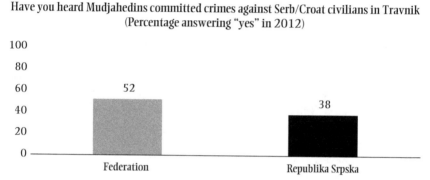

Figure 8.6 Stated Beliefs about War Crimes in Travnik.

C. Encounters with Denial and Acknowledgment

During interviews in several municipalities, Bosnians expressed views about what happened in the 1990s that broadly conform to the BCHR survey results, while presenting a more nuanced picture of citizens' stated beliefs. In addition to expressions of their own views, several sources described prevailing discourses about wartime atrocities that illuminate key features of the BCHR survey results.

1. SERB CITIZENS

In 2009 (the year before the first BCHR survey discussed above), I visited the RS town of Foča, whose prewar Muslim population, roughly 51 percent of the town, was almost entirely routed by ethnic cleansing.[45] In the landmark case of *Kunarac*, the ICTY convicted three Serbs from Foča for their roles in killing, raping, and sexually enslaving non-Serb residents, among whom Muslim women were a "specific target

---

what they had heard. *Id.* at 46-47. Among those who believed this happened, roughly 99 percent of respondents in both regions said they believed what happened was a war crime rather than an inevitable consequence of war. *Id.* at 61–62.

[45] *See* Prosecutor v. Plavšić, Case No. IT-00-39 & 40/1-S, Sentencing Judgment, ¶ 32 (Int'l Crim. Trib. for the Former Yugoslavia Feb. 27, 2003).

of . . . attack."[46] The defendants' savage treatment of Bosniak women brought global condemnation, and the ICTY's conviction of two Foča suspects of sexual enslavement as a crime against humanity is considered a legal milestone. And so I was curious to see how Serbs in Foča treated this dark chapter in their recent past. Many whom I interviewed asserted that whoever commits war crimes should be punished.[47] Yet the dominant theme of Foča residents' statements was that the Hague Tribunal is biased against Serbs. Thus, my interlocutors seemed to imply, Serb atrocities were not deserving of punishment *to the degree reflected in Hague prosecutions*.

Representing an association of families of Serb soldiers killed during the war, Josip Davidović expressed what he described as the common view in Foča:

> The opinion that rules this town . . . is that all war crimes by all sides should be prosecuted, on all three sides. But we believe that the war crimes against Serbs are not prosecuted in the same volume as in the case of war crimes against Bosniaks and Croats. We also stand on the opinion that The Hague is established to bring Serbs to trial. . . . We also stand on the opinion that The Hague is a political court.[48]

When asked if he thought the Foča defendants who faced judgment in The Hague deserved to be punished, Davidović said "yes" and added: "All those who committed war crimes deserve to be tried . . . Whoever committed crimes should be brought before the face of justice." Yet, like many Bosnian Serbs, he insisted the number of non-Serbs the ICTY has prosecuted is "so minor compared to trials against Serbs. It's almost negligible."[49] As for sentences imposed on the Foča defendants—the same sentences victims from Foča found painfully short[50]—Davidović told me "public opinion" in Foča is that those sentences "are too high."[51]

Noting several of the ICTY's defendants came from "this town," Đoran Kalajdžić, an officer of the Foča chapter of an RS veterans' group, continued: "It's our opinion that the guilt is individual and everyone should be responsible for what he did. So my organization never stood behind those [defendants]. If they have committed war crimes, they should be held responsible." Going farther than Davidović in acknowledging the scale of war crimes committed against Bosniaks, Kalajdžić said: "The truth is the Bosniaks were the major victims. They suffered the most."[52]

---

[46] Prosecutor v. Kunarac et al., Case No. IT-96-23 & IT-96-23/1-A, Appeal Judgment, ¶ 3 (Int'l Crim. Trib. for the Former Yugoslavia June 12, 2002).

[47] I heard this so often I wondered whether it might reflect a partial ICTY "success," measured in terms of norm penetration. Virtually everyone in Bosnia whom I asked about this possibility believed, instead, that the proposition is so fundamental all Bosnians would endorse it whether or not the ICTY existed. Perhaps a more plausible way to interpret the Foča sources' statement is to recognize that their intended emphasis was on the notion that "everyone" who commits war crimes—not just Serbs—should be punished. As well, they may have sought to distance "Serbs" as a community from Serb defendants in The Hague.

[48] Interview with Josip Davidović, President, Association of Families of Fallen Soldiers and Missing and Detained Persons, in Foča, Bosn. & Herz. (July 20, 2009).

[49] As previously noted, two-thirds of the defendants indicted by the ICTY were ethnic Serbs.

[50] *See* Chapter 6.

[51] Interview with Josip Davidović, President, Association of Families of Fallen Soldiers and Missing and Detained Persons, in Foča, Bosn. & Herz. (July 20, 2009).

[52] Interview with Đoren Kalajdžić, Executive Secretary, Association of Republika Srpska Veterans, in Foča, Bosn. & Herz. (July 20, 2009).

Perhaps believing he had conceded too much, Kalajdžić also claimed that the "rate" of suffering was "higher for Serbs,"[53] and justified Serbs' mass execution of Bosniaks in Srebrenica as a "gesture of revenge by one segment of the Serb army for what the Bosnian Army did to Serbs in the first two years of the war"—a common thread in Serb discourses. In the same vein, he added, "it takes two to fight." Like Davidović, Kalajdžić told me, "We Serbs see [the Hague Tribunal] as a political court" that does not treat everyone equally.[54]

I encountered another brand of denialism when I interviewed Ljubiša Simović, president of the Association of Displaced and Refugees in Republika Srpska. When asked about defendants whom the ICTY convicted of horrific crimes in Foča, Simović went on at some length about how "traumatic" it was for the defendants' families when SFOR troops arrested the suspects. Like Davidović and Kalajdžić, Simović said the ICTY focused disproportionately on Serbs. Even so, he said, "It was correct to form this court." "But the way in which it works," he added, "is not OK."[55]

Like the Serbs I interviewed in Foča, Neđeljko Mitrović, president of the Republika Srpska Association of Families of Missing Persons in the RS capital of Banja Luka, affirmed that "whoever committed war crimes deserves to be punished." Indeed, Mitrović told me, "whoever was prosecuted before the ICTY deserves to be." Yet he implicitly rejected the ICTY's central conclusions about the siege of Sarajevo, in which an estimated 11,000 residents were killed.[56] At the time we spoke, two Bosnian Serb commanders, Stanislav Galić and Dragomir Milošević, had been convicted of war crimes in relation to the three-and-a-half year siege. The Tribunal found Bosnian Serb forces deliberately attacked civilians in Sarajevo "while attending funerals, while in ambulances, trams, and buses, and while cycling. They were attacked while tending gardens, or shopping in markets, or clearing rubbish in the city. Children were targeted while playing or walking in the streets."[57] Insisting Sarajevo was a "front-line" in a two-way war, Mitrović dismissed the Serb assault as the "so-called siege." When reminded that Serbs targeted civilians in Sarajevo, Mitrović immediately conceded the point and pivoted to his final redoubt: the ICTY is "one-sided, partial, biased."[58]

Like wartime atrocities in Foča, ethnic cleansing in Prijedor is a litmus test of Serb acknowledgment. As Julian Borger writes, "Prijedor has earned a place in history as a byword for inhumanity."[59] At the outset of war in Bosnia, the region's Serbs proved ruthlessly efficient: in a matter of months, Prijedor's prewar population of more than 50,000 non-Serbs was reduced to 3,000. Thousands were tortured to death or executed outright in 1992, many in detention camps that soon became infamous.[60] It would be impossible for Prijidor residents alive at the time not to know

---

[53] *Id.*

[54] *Id.*

[55] Interview with Ljubiša Simović, President, Association of Displaced and Refugees in Republika Srpska, in Foča, Bosn. & Herz. (July 20, 2009).

[56] BORGER, *supra* note 3, at 66.

[57] Prosecutor v. Galić, Case No. IT-98-29-T, Summary of Judgment, 2 (Int'l Crim. Trib. for the Former Yugoslavia Dec. 5, 2003).

[58] Interview with Neđeljko Mitrović, President, RS Association of Families of Missing Persons, in Banja Luka, Bosn. & Herz. (July 23, 2009).

[59] BORGER, *supra* note 3, at 46.

[60] *Id.* at 47. Addressing killings only, the ICTY website states, conservatively, "It was found that more than 1,500 killings occurred" in Prijedor. ICTY website, *Bridging the Gap in Prijedor, Bosnia*

what happened. As Edin Ramulić points out, "All these people came to mass graves in trucks and were buried with bulldozers. They drove past people's houses along quiet roads. For every one missing person, at least three people know exactly where they are buried—the driver, the digger, and the policeman, plus whoever saw them pass."[61] Even so, by the time of my last research visit to Prijedor (in 2014), denialism was pervasive.

Local sources described two prevalent approaches to the wartime past among Prijedor Serbs: (1) avoiding the subject altogether and (2) justifying Serb atrocities. Goran Zorić routinely encounters the first brand of denial. An ethnic Serb, Zorić now devotes his life to "challeng[ing] the ways we look at dealing with the past."[62] He has made scant headway among other Serbs in Prijedor. When he speaks about war crimes, Zorić told me, "everyone's like, 'Oh, why are you doing this? Ah, no, no, no.'"[63]

Zorić described an episode that, in his view, signified the depth of Serb denialism. In the Fall of 2013, a mass grave containing the bodies of Bosniak and Croat victims was discovered[64] and excavated[65] in the village of Tomašica, near the town of Prijedor. When the grave was opened, Zorić told me, he sensed the situation was "so heavy" that "something [would] have to happen"—that is, that local Serbs would be shaken out of collective denial. "But actually nothing happened."[66] As he recalled, most Prijedor residents who were interviewed in a video about Tomašica "said, 'Oh, it's overblown, it's common, it's not so—it's exaggerated,' and like that."[67]

I asked Ramulić, who was detained in the Trnopolje camp and whose father and brother were tortured and killed in Keraterm,[68] if the ICTY had had any impact on

---

and Herzegovina, http://www.icty.org/en/outreach/bridging-the-gap-with-local-communities/ prijedor (last visited on Dec. 8, 2017). This figure appears to refer only to casualties proved in ICTY cases. The Prijedor-based Izvor Association places "the total number of killed and missing people from Prijedor municipality [at] 3,177 (3,015 Bosniaks, 138 Croats, 12 Albanians, 8 Roma, 1 Czech, 1 Pakistani, 1 Serb, 1 Ukrainian)." Of the total number, Izvor estimates that "2,078 people were killed and around 1,099 . . . missing. Around 31,000 were detained in concentration camps, and 53,000 were deported from Prijedor." Haris Subašić, *The Culture of Denial in Prijedor*, Transconflict (Jan. 29, 2013). In 1994, the UN Commission of Experts reported that, as of June 1993, 52,811 non-Serbs were either killed or deported from Prijedor between 1992 and 1994. Commission of Experts, *Final Report of the Commission of Experts, transmitted by letter dated 24 May 1994 from Chairmen of the Commission of Experts, Established pursuant to Security Council Resolution 780 (1994)*, ¶ 153, U.N. Doc. S/1994/674 (May 27, 1994).

[61] Ed Vulliamy, *Bosnia's Survivors Gather and Grieve as the Soil Endlessly Gives Up Its Dead*, Guardian (Aug. 8, 2015).

[62] Ed Vulliamy, *Young Activists in Bosnia Discuss Transitional Justice and Media at the Site of a Former Camp*, ICTJ website (Aug. 6, 2015), https://www.ictj.org/news/young-activists-bosnia-transitional-justice-media.

[63] Interview with Goran Zorić, Executive Director, KVART, in Sarajevo, Bosn. & Herz. (Sept. 17, 2014). Describing several initiatives to address the past, including a major conference in Sarajevo, Zorić added: "Of course, a lot of people from Prijedor ignored all these things but that's, well, the situation." *Id.*

[64] *Dozens of Bodies Discovered in Bosnian Mass Grave Believed to Be Victims of Genocide Carried Out by Serb Forces*, Daily Mail (Oct. 4, 2013).

[65] *Huge Bosnia Mass Grave Excavated at Tomašica*, BBC News (Nov. 1, 2013).

[66] Interview with Goran Zorić, Executive Director, KVART, in Sarajevo, Bosn. & Herz. (Sept. 17, 2014).

[67] *Id.*

[68] *See* Nidžara Ahmetašević, *Bosnia's Unending War*, New Yorker (Nov. 4, 2015).

acknowledgment by Prijedor Serbs. After all, a significant number of Prijedor suspects were indicted and convicted by the ICTY.[69] Ramulić said he could not discern any such impact so far. Noting he cannot speak to what local Serbs actually believe about "everything that occurred during the war," Ramulić continued: "According to what they do, they had no change."[70] If a survey were taken among the Serb population in Prijedor, Ramulić believes, "98 percent of the people would justify everything that happened in the wartime."[71] He elaborated:

> Some of these justifications would go like this: We did it to prevent what they would have done to us if we had not done it to them. Or, they would say this was like compensation, or repayment for something they [i.e., Bosniaks] did to us elsewhere. Or one of their explanations would be simply fascist ideology, like these [presumably Bosniaks] are like lower creatures, they need to be exterminated.[72]

These and other forms of denial are literally inscribed in official monuments in Prijedor honoring Serb soldiers said to have "courageously died for the fatherland of Republika Srpska" or to have died at the hands of "Muslim extremists in the war of defence and liberation."[73] At the same time, efforts by survivors to memorialize sites of Bosniak suffering, including Omarska, Keraterm, and Trnopolje, are routinely blocked by local authorities on a raft of specious grounds.[74]

2. BOSNIAK CITIZENS

While Serbs have the most to answer for when it comes to wartime atrocities, many Bosniak and Croat citizens have been reluctant to condemn war crimes committed by members of their ethnic group. Aleksandar Trifunović made the point this way after describing "classical denial" among Bosnian Serbs:

> But believe me, this is [the] same whenever you talk. If you try to talk to [someone in] Sarajevo about war crimes against Serbs who live in Sarajevo, you have denial, absolutely. And when you talk with Croats [about] war crimes in [the] Mostar area, [they say] "no, this is not true." This means that denial is [the] main process about dealing with the past.[75]

A common perception is that ICTY judgments have had little impact in changing these views. During interviews many noted that each group tends to approve of verdicts convicting "war criminals from the other ethnic group" and fault the ICTY

---

[69] *Id.* The cases of some Prijedor suspects originally indicted by the ICTY were dismissed when the Prosecutor sought to winnow out relatively weak cases.

[70] Interview with Edin Ramulić, Project Coordinator, Izvor, in Prijedor, Bosn. & Herz. (Sept. 16, 2014).

[71] *Id.*

[72] *Id.*

[73] Haris Subašić, *The Culture of Denial in Prijedor*, TRANSCONFLICT (Jan. 29, 2013).

[74] *See id. See also* BORGER, *supra* note 3, at 330.

[75] Interview with Aleksandar Trifunović, Editor, BUKA, in Banja Luka, Bosn. & Herz. (Sept. 15, 2014).

"when it reaches a verdict from our ethnic group." With respect to the latter, Ivan Lovrenović said, "metaphorically, the ears are stuffed with cotton."[76]

For Bosniaks, "it was always a big problem . . . to accept that" some Bosniak military officials faced prosecution in The Hague, according to Aleksandra Letić. She believes their disappointment results from early expectations the ICTY would provide "an overview of what happened to the country" that would establish Bosniaks were the "ultimate victim."[77] Another source observed that many Bosniaks believe the ICTY indicted nine Bosniak suspects "just for the sake of some kind of artificial equilibrium of . . . crimes."[78] These are, of course, generalizations. Many of the Bosniaks I interviewed readily acknowledged Bosniak soldiers committed war crimes worthy of prosecution.[79]

According to some interlocutors, many (though by no means all) Bosniaks have become more willing over time to acknowledge Bosniak war crimes. The first time I interviewed Dobrila Govedarica (in December 2006), she noted that, apart from intellectuals, there was "no understanding" among Bosniaks that "war crimes could also be committed by Bosniak soldiers."[80] If one raised the issue of war crimes for which Bosniaks were prosecuted before the ICTY, she said, the reaction was often defensive, as Bosniaks feared condemning these crimes "could be seen as equalizing guilt."[81] Several other sources interviewed at that time illustrated Bosniak denialism by describing the warm reception earlier that year of Naser Orić, who had just been convicted in The Hague of war crimes against Serbs and was released because he had been detained for a period exceeding his sentence.[82]

---

[76] Interview with Ivan Lovrenović, then Editor-in-Chief, Dani, in Sarajevo, Bosn. & Herz. (July 17, 2009). Words quoted in the previous sentence are also from my interview with Lovrenović but reflect a perception articulated by many Bosnian sources .

[77] Interview with Aleksandra Letić, Secretary-General, Helsinki Committee for Human Rights in Republika Srpska, in Sarajevo, Bosn. & Herz. (Sept. 8, 2014). Letić served on a task force that drafted a transitional justice strategy for Bosnia, whose work gained little traction among Bosnian politicians. She had expected Bosnian Serbs to oppose a component of the strategy that envisioned establishment of a truth commission. Instead, she recalled, Bosniak victims and the Bosniak government representative on the task force were most opposed to the idea. Letić summarized their reasoning this way: a comprehensive account "'could undermine our role,' which has been carefully, carefully created all the years from 1992, internationally in particular, and that was actually the strength of the Bosniak community." Id.

[78] Interview with Edin Hodžić, Director, Public Law Program, Center for Social Research Analitika, in Sarajevo, Bosn. & Herz. (Sept. 11, 2014).

[79] For example Edin Ramulić believes one of the Tribunal's major achievements was prosecuting certain defendants who would not have been prosecuted without it; when I asked for examples, Ramulić included in his answer "some of the military leaders of Bosniaks." Interview with Edin Ramulić, Project Coordinator, Izvor, in Prijedor, Bosn. & Herz. (Sept. 16, 2014).

[80] Interview with Dobrila Govedarica, Executive Director, Open Society Fund BiH, in Sarajevo, Bosn. & Herz. (Nov. 29, 2006).

[81] Id. Indeed, a number of Bosniaks whom I interviewed expressed concern that the ICTY's prosecution of Bosniak soldiers was an effort to establish a "national balance" among perpetrators. E.g., interview with Mirsad Duratović in Prijedor, Bosn. & Herz. (Dec. 8, 2006). Duratović made clear he believed all war crimes deserved punishment and that widespread atrocities by Serbs did not justify a single violation by Bosniaks. He was nonetheless concerned that the ICTY's approach did not reflect differences of degree and nature between crimes committed by Bosniaks and Serbs.

[82] Orić was convicted at trial in relation to war crimes committed against Serbs as Bosniak armed forces defended Srebrenica. The ICTY Appeals Chamber later reversed his conviction, but the

If the situation in 2006 was far from where it should be, some saw overall progress even then. Journalist Senad Pećanin recalled that in 1997, *Dani* magazine investigated war crimes committed by Bosniaks; most but not all of the victims were "innocent Serbs."[83] Because of their reporting, *Dani* journalists were attacked by the Bosniak leadership. Pećanin recalled, "it was a terrible experience for us[; we] received a lot of threats" and a bomb was thrown into *Dani*'s office. But "things have changed," he said. By the time we spoke, leading Bosniak politicians had acknowledged members of their ethnic group committed crimes (as I note later, there have been further instances since I spoke to Pećanin, including acknowledgment of the crimes reported by *Dani* in 1997). Still, among "ordinary people" within each ethnic group, there was an overriding focus on having "their *own* suffering acknowledged."[84]

During my final set of research interviews (in 2014), Edin Hodžić said it was his impression that, while dynamics similar to those prevailing in 2006 were "still present, . . . black and white versions of reality are no longer dominant."[85] Notably, the 2010 and 2012 BCHR surveys in Bosnia suggest a greater willingness on the part of Bosniaks than Bosnian Serbs to acknowledge certain atrocities committed against Serbs. As previously noted, Federation residents were more likely than residents of Republika Srpska to say they had heard (1) Serb detainees were raped in the Čelebići camp,[86] and (2) "Mudjahedins committed crimes against Serb and Croat civilians in Travnik and its vicinities."[87]

3. CROAT CITIZENS

It is often said that Bosnian Croats see Hague prosecutions of Croat suspects as an attempt "to try and equalize everybody,"[88] if not "demonize Croats' heroes."[89] In a similar vein, Aleksandra Letić described a widespread view among Bosnian Croats that the Hague Tribunal is a "Croat-eating court," which is "biased against the Croatian

---

developments described above occurred before Orić's acquittal. Bosniak leaders' response to Orić's trial verdict and return to Bosnia is described at greater length later in this chapter.

[83] Interview with Senad Pećanin, then Editor, Dani, in Sarajevo, Bosn. & Herz. (Dec. 6, 2006). I believe Pećanin was referring to murderous violence committed by Bosniaks against Serbs during the siege of Sarajevo. The bodies of several dozen slain Serbs were thrown into the Kazani ravine on the outskirts of Sarajevo. *See* Rusmir Smajilhodžić, *Sarajevo's Uncounted and Forgotten Serb Victims*, AGENCE FRANCE-PRESSE (July 8, 2016).

[84] Interview with Senad Pećanin, then Editor, Dani, in Sarajevo, Bosn. & Herz. (Dec. 6, 2006). In the course of research conducted in August 2008, another scholar found that Bosniak interviewees "generally acknowledged that there was suffering on all sides." Janine Natalya Clark, *The Limits of Retributive Justice: Findings of an Empirical Study in Bosnia and Herzegovina*, 7 J. INT'L CRIM. JUST. 463, 477 (2009) [hereinafter Clark, *Limits of Retributive Justice*]. Even so, they "were typically dismissive of crimes committed by their own side," often maintaining that whatever crimes the Bosniak army committed were in response to Serb and Croat attacks. *Id.*

[85] Interview with Edin Hodžić, Director, Public Law Program, Center for Social Research Analitika, in Sarajevo, Bosn. & Herz. (Sept. 11, 2014). Hodžić offered this reflection while recalling Bosnian reactions eight years earlier to the conviction and release from prison of Bosniak army officer Naser Orić.

[86] In 2012, 38 percent of Federation respondents said they had heard this compared to 33 percent of RS respondents. *See* Figure 8.5, *supra*.

[87] In 2012, 52 percent of Federation respondents said they had heard this compared to 39 percent of RS respondents. *See* Figure 8.6, *supra*.

[88] Interview with Emir Hodžić, Jer Me Se Tiče, in Sarajevo, Bosn. & Herz. (Sept. 13, 2014).

[89] *Id.* As indicated in the text, although the quoted words are those of Emir Hodžić, I heard similar views in other interviews.

people."[90] Thus, it is not surprising that ICTY convictions of Croat suspects have apparently done little to inspire acknowledgment of Croat war crimes among many Bosnian Croats.

The experience of Štefica Galić and her late husband, Neđelko, highlight the nature of denialism among many Bosnian Croats, as well as a key factor behind it: social pressure. In 1993, Bosniak residents of Ljubuški, where the couple lived, learned how easily their lifelong neighbors jettisoned the empathy that binds a small community. The town's Croats rounded up Bosniaks, detaining the men in the Heliodrom and expelling women and children. Standing in front of the police station in Ljubuški, Neđelko Galić protested, "People, stop, you can't do that, it's madness, it's criminal!"[91] Speaking out was rare enough among Ljubuški's Croats, but the couple did more than protest. They wrote "letters of guarantee" for local Bosniaks who had been detained,[92] saving an estimated two-thirds of the town's Bosniak population.[93] Recalling that other Croats "raised their voices against us," Štefica Galić described the sudden appearance of posters in which she and her husband were called "enemies of the Croatian people."[94]

Twenty years later, six senior military figures of the Croat region proclaimed during the war, Herceg-Bosna, were convicted of participating in a joint criminal enterprise aimed at forcibly removing Bosniaks and other non-Croats from the territory claimed by the HVO.[95] As their trial was underway, Neđelko Galić posthumously received a "civil courage award"[96] from a Bosnian NGO and was featured in a documentary about the couple's wartime heroism. Far from being celebrated, Štefica Galić encountered "low-level hostility" from many of her neighbors and was physically assaulted by Vera Dedić, an activist in the Ljubuški war veterans' association.[97]

In a "toxic atmosphere of denial,"[98] other residents of Ljubuški were quick to deflect responsibility for Bosnian Croat war crimes. When asked about the expulsion of Bosniaks from Ljubuški, one resident told a reporter she was too young at the time to be able to speak to what happened. But, she said, "I know they live far better lives in Western countries than we do here."[99] Others said it was unfair to single out Ljubuški

---

[90] Interview with Aleksandra Letić, Secretary-General, Helsinki Committee for Human Rights in Republika Srpska, in Sarajevo, Bosn. & Herz. (Sept. 8, 2014). Even so, Letić and others suggested Bosnian Croat elites have been relatively "passive and silent" when it comes to the ICTY. Letić explains their passivity this way: "They were not so much interested in something what is happening in the ICTY . . . somewhere in The Netherlands, but they were much more interested in building their own strength inside of Bosnia and Herzegovina and their relations with Croatia." Id.

[91] Boris Pavelić, *Dangerous Life of Štefica Galić, Ljubuški's Oskar Schindler*, BALKAN TRANSITIONAL JUST. (Aug. 9, 2012).

[92] Interview with Štefica Galić, Editor, Tačno.net, in Mostar, Bosn. & Herz. (Sept. 10, 2014).

[93] Boris Pavelić, *Dangerous Life of Štefica Galić, Ljubuški's Oskar Schindler*, BALKAN TRANSITIONAL JUST. (Aug. 9, 2012).

[94] Interview with Štefica Galić, Editor, Tačno.net, in Mostar, Bosn. & Herz. (Sept. 10, 2014). Galić described the attacks as coming from "the whole neighborhood of Western Hercegovina." Id.

[95] Prosecutor v. Prlić et al., Case No. IT-04-74-T, Trial Judgment (Int'l Crim. Trib. for the Former Yugoslavia May 29, 2013).

[96] Interview with Štefica Galić, Editor, Tačno.net, in Mostar, Bosn. & Herz. (Sept. 10, 2014).

[97] Id.

[98] Boris Pavelić, *Dangerous Life of Štefica Galić, Ljubuški's Oskar Schindler*, BALKAN TRANSITIONAL JUST. (Aug. 9, 2012).

[99] Id.

for criticism because "it was much worse elsewhere."[100] At least in Ljubuški, one resident said, "nobody was killed."[101] Yet according to Štefica Galić, while most non-Croat residents were expelled, six Bosniaks were killed in Ljubuški; the homes of several were burned down, and two large mosques were demolished—hardly trivial offenses.[102]

I asked Galić if any other Croats in Mostar, where she now lives, had challenged Croat denial. She replied, "Not, no, no." Instead, when her story was publicized in the 2012 documentary, "everybody knew this was the truth, but none of them backed me up, none of them." No one would "stand behind me and say, 'this woman is right,' not a single Croat."[103]

* * *

For some survivors, the affirmation in ICTY verdicts that their nightmare really happened, that *this person* was responsible, and that what he did was grievously wrong, was precious in itself—and perhaps all the more so in the face of enduring denial by their neighbors. The late Muharem Murselović, who survived detention in the infamous Omarska camp, told me he was "most satisfied with the realistic reflection of what happened in Prijedor through [the ICTY's] verdicts and sentences." [104] Noting the Tribunal has "extremely rich documentation" concerning ethnic cleansing in Prijedor, Murselović said: "With that documentation, with those verdicts . . . the truth about the situation in Prijedor has been established, and this is the largest, the major achievement of the ICTY."[105]

More typically, however, the gratification survivors derive from the Tribunal's fact-finding is profoundly diminished by daily encounters with denial. Edin Hodžić, who interviewed dozens of Bosnians in 2010 for a United Nations Development Programme study, told me he was struck by how often victims said "they need a different kind of acknowledgment" than what the "judicial paradigm" had been able to deliver. They craved "acknowledgment by [their] neighbors, not by a judicial institution, . . . because that's a very distant form of acknowledgment."[106] What victims "really care to see," Hodžić elaborated, is that their neighbors "acknowledge, . . . regret, and possibly . . . apologize for the harm that was done to our community, to us individually."[107]

---

[100] *Id.*

[101] *Id.*

[102] Interview with Štefica Galić, Editor, Tačno.net, in Mostar, Bosn. & Herz. (Sept. 10, 2014).

[103] *Id.* During a research trip in August 2008, Janine Clark interviewed Bosnian Croats who were unwilling to acknowledge that crimes committed by Bosnian Croats who were convicted in The Hague were worthy of condemnation. Instead, those she interviewed typically blamed Bosniaks for what happened to them. Clark, *Limits of Retributive Justice, supra* note 84, at 477.

[104] Interview with the late Muharem Murselović, then Member, Republika Srpska National Assembly; President, RS Parliamentarians Club for the Party for BiH, in Banja Luka, Bosn. & Herz. (July 15, 2009).

[105] *Id.* Nerma Jelačić, then working as a journalist in Bosnia, suggested Murselović was not unique in this respect. When we spoke in December 2006, Jelačić told me the Tribunal had already had "a huge effect in terms of establishing the historical record of what happened, for example conditions in the Omarska camp," and that this "is important for victims" as well as "for society." Interview with Nerma Jelačić, then Director, BIRN in BiH, in Sarajevo, Bosn. & Herz. (Dec. 1, 2006).

[106] Interview with Edin Hodžić, Director, Public Law Program, Center for Social Research Analitika, in Sarajevo, Bosn. & Herz. (Sept. 11, 2014).

[107] *Id.*

Refik Hodžić describes similar findings in research he undertook in Prijedor. Based on interviews with survivors of notorious detention camps and with families of those killed in 1992, Hodžić writes, "they all agreed on [one thing]: in terms of importance, court justice came a distant second to acknowledgment of their suffering by the authorities and their Serb neighbors."[108]

II. ACCOUNTING FOR DENIALISM

As in Serbia, myriad factors account for fluctuating levels of denialism and acknowledgment in Bosnia. In the first two subsections below, I explore social and psychological dynamics Bosnians believe play an important role in explaining denialism. Later, I introduce additional social science accounts after providing relevant context.

A. Motivated Reasoning, Social Identity, and Historical Memory

Bosnians interviewed for this study attribute the gap between facts established in ICTY rulings and many Bosnians' stated beliefs in part to psychological dynamics. Evoking a variation of the phenomenon of "knowing/not knowing" explored previously,[109] Jasna Bakšić Muftić suggested many Bosnians instinctively resist ICTY judgments that cast a harsh light on their ethnic group: "Sometimes the Hague Tribunal is like a mirror and if you see an ugly face, you reject it. But you know it's true. But officially, you say 'I'm nicer, etc.'"[110]

The dynamic Bakšić Muftić described would come as no surprise to social psychologists. As explored in the previous chapter, as motivated reasoners, people often unconsciously process information in ways that advance their interests. Among the motivations that bias the way people process information is a deeply human desire to maintain a positive self-image. If individuals identify strongly with an ethnic group, maintaining a positive self-image may entail positively assessing their ethnic community.[111] Thus they may be motivated to discount, minimize, or dismiss information, including factual findings in ICTY judgments, that casts a harsh light on their in-group.[112]

---

[108] Refik Hodžić, *Post-Karadžić Bosnia and Herzegovina: The End of the Criminal Justice Era*, ICTJ website (Apr. 11, 2016), https://www.ictj.org/news/karadzic-bosnia-herzegovina-criminal-justice [hereinafter Hodžić, *Post-Karadžić*].

[109] See Chapter 7.

[110] Interview with Jasna Bakšić Muftić, Professor, Faculty of Law, University of Sarajevo, in Sarajevo, Bosn. & Herz. (Nov. 30, 2006).

[111] See Sabina Čehajić-Clancy, *Dealing with Ingroup Committed Atrocities: Moral Responsibility and Group-Based Guilt*, in THE SOCIAL PSYCHOLOGY OF INTRACTABLE CONFLICTS 103, 103 (Eran Halperin & Keren Sharvit eds., 2015) [hereinafter Čehajić-Clancy, *Ingroup Committed Atrocities*]; Sabina Čehajić & Rupert Brown, *Silencing the Past: Effects of Intergroup Contact on Acknowledgment of In-Group Responsibility*, 1 SOC. PSYCHOL. & PERSONALITY SCI. 190, 192 (2010).

[112] Čehajić-Clancy, *supra* note 111, at 104. *See also* Sabina Čehajić-Clancy et al., *Affirmation, Acknowledgment of In-Group Responsibility, Group-Based Guilt, and Support for Reparative Measures*, 101 J. PERSONALITY & SOC. PSYCH. 256, 256 (2011) ("Given that people derive feelings of self-worth and integrity in part from group membership, acknowledging transgressions committed by group members can be highly self-threatening"). As Bar-Tal and others have

Like Bakšić-Muftić, Goran Zorić, whose training is in psychology, linked Serb denial to a human desire to have a positive self-image, while emphasizing the powerful pull of ethnic identity in particular:

We are very emotional when it comes about these identity things. And we are slaves, actually, of our collective identities. We cannot speak about anything in a way that you get out from your identity. . . . And of course, I think it's easier . . . for the person to think good things about himself. . . . It's not easy to say, "OK, but someone did something bad," especially when you have this identity connection where it's in my name, or in our name. It's easier to say, "OK, we are good guys. We never did something bad."[113]

Zorić did not express a firm view about whether Serbs truly know what happened during the war. When I pointed out that many Serbs *had* to know what happened in his hometown of Prijedor, Zorić acknowledged the point but added: "Sometimes I'm really not sure if it's about knowing and hiding it on purpose, on a very conscious level, or is it really believing that Serbian people is a good people and that they are just defending themselves, and could never do some bad things. I'm really not sure about that."[114]

Focusing on young Serbs who neither committed nor silently abetted atrocities, Sevima Sali-Terzić reflected: "Maybe it's easier to be in denial. People don't want to know. It's hard for them, I can understand that, knowing your father maybe did something and it's easier to say 'it didn't happen' than to say 'they are lying.'"[115] In her view, the passage of time has compounded this tendency. Much as Srđan Bogosavljević emphasized many Serbians' desire to "forget" what they once heard about wartime atrocities,[116] Sali-Terzić believes "that the more time passes, people forget—not only forget, try to forget, because it's so difficult to live with those thoughts all over again."[117]

In essence, Bakšić Muftić, Zorić, and Sali-Terzić suggested, Bosnians may reject or repress evidence implicating individuals with whom they closely identify

---

noted, maintaining a positive assessment of the group with which one identifies *despite its harmful behavior* can require marginalization of contradictory information. *See* Bar-Tal et al., *Sociopsychological Analysis of Conflict-Supporting Narratives: A General Framework*, 51 J. PEACE RESEARCH 662, 666 (2014).

[113] Interview with Goran Zorić, Executive Director, KVART, in Sarajevo, Bosn. & Herz. (Sept. 17, 2014).

[114] *Id.*

[115] Interview with Sevima Sali-Terzić, Senior Legal Counsel, Constitutional Court of BiH, in Sarajevo, Bosn. & Herz. (Sept. 9, 2014). While Sali-Terzić may be right about many young adults, Nidžara Ahmetašević told me she has spoken with young Serbs who are curious about what happened during the war but whose parents do not want to discuss the subject. Interview with Nidžara Ahmetašević, Journalist, in Sarajevo, Bosn. & Herz. (Sept. 12, 2014).

[116] *See* Chapter 7.

[117] Interview with Sevima Sali-Terzić, Senior Legal Counsel, Constitutional Court of BiH, in Sarajevo, Bosn. & Herz. (Sept. 9, 2014). Sali-Terzić went on to suggest it is not just individuals closely associated with perpetrators who want to forget about wartime atrocities: "I did no crimes, but I don't want to hear about it anymore. . . . Every time I turn on the news, I hear about new mass rapes, the Hague Tribunal processes, about BiH processes. . . . In my lifetime, I want to have a period to not talk about that." *Id.*

in atrocious crimes because conscious knowledge would, by extension, threaten their self-esteem and well-being. Aleksandar Trifunović believes, as well, that many Serbs resist information about Serb atrocities because it would raise uncomfortable questions about their *own* conduct during the war—more precisely, their silent complicity. Saying "this is a really emotional question," Trifunović continued: "When you're dealing with these bad things, what's happened during the war, you must find that in one moment you were sitting in silence and don't do anything to stop this."[118]

Some see the hand of historical memory, which lays heavy across the former Yugoslavia, at play in many Bosnians' reluctance to acknowledge and condemn crimes committed by members of their own ethnic group. Reflecting on why many Bosnian Croats are unwilling to accept the guilt of Croats convicted by the ICTY, for example, Dobrila Govedarica recalled that Croats have long been blamed for crimes committed in World War II, when Croatia was allied with Nazi Germany. "Finally, they get to a point where the Serbs, who took almost all the credit for being on the right side in World War II, are the most guilty ones." In addition, there is a deep-rooted perception that those who defend themselves—a pervasive Croat perspective on the 1990s conflicts—cannot, by definition, commit a crime. In this setting, there are "strong psychological reasons to resist accepting responsibility."[119]

B. Belief Perseverance: Confirmation Biases

Confirmation biases likely reinforced many Bosnians' resistance to information implicating their in-group in atrocities. As we have seen, people are more likely to believe sources that confirm their established views than information at odds with those beliefs.[120] This may be especially true when it comes to "conflict-supporting narratives" that "were maintained and imparted continuously and intensively to society members"[121] during a war, and are thus likely to have become entrenched in beliefs of many.

Thus it is highly relevant that, when Bosnia emerged from war, widespread denial of wartime atrocities was already well-established. Serb narratives of victimization, widely disseminated by state-controlled media, were integral to the 1990s conflict. The ICTY summarized key themes of Serb propaganda this way: "In articles, announcements, television programmes and public proclamations, Serbs were told that they needed to protect themselves from a fundamentalist Muslim threat and must arm themselves and that the Croats and Muslims were preparing a plan of genocide against them."[122] By the Spring of 1992, "only Serb-controlled television channels and programmes were available in many parts of Bosnia and Herzegovina."[123]

---

[118] Interview with Aleksandar Trifunović, Editor, BUKA, in Banja Luka, Bosn. & Herz. (Sept. 15, 2014).

[119] Interview with Dobrila Govedarica, Executive Director, Open Society Fund BiH, in Sarajevo, Bosn. & Herz. (Nov. 29, 2006).

[120] See Chapter 7 for discussion of confirmation biases.

[121] Bar-Tal et al., *supra* note 112, at 670.

[122] Prosecutor v. Tadić, Case No. IT-94-1-T, Trial Judgment, ¶ 91 (Int'l Crim. Trib. for the Former Yugoslavia May 7, 1997).

[123] *Id.* ¶ 92.

Throughout the conflict, Serb leaders flagrantly inverted the facts, often blaming Serb atrocities on their victims.[124] As Aleksandra Letić recalled, Serbs "were carefully structuring, and carefully prepared to implement, a culture of denial from the early beginning. So from 1992, before the first war crimes were committed, the culture of denial of possible war crimes was already created."[125] As for Bosniaks and Croats, Letić added, media aligned with their wartime leaders prepared their constituencies to believe "anything that happened" in the nature of war crimes by their soldiers "will definitely have a good reason."[126]

Today, the enduring effects of wartime narratives, motivated reasoning, and confirmation biases play out in a context of continuous and rising ethnic contestation. As we have seen and as explored further below, the electoral structure imposed in Dayton has incentived ethnic mobilization.[127] In this setting, the psychological dynamics explored here—in particular, defensive reactions to information implicating members of one's in-group in atrocities—may be even more intense in Bosnia than in Serbia, as identity is infinitely more contested in the former.[128]

* * *

While insights derived from social psychology help explain why ICTY judgments have not radically transformed Bosnians' stated knowledge of what happened during the war, their implications should not be overdrawn. As later sections make clear, the nature and intensity of denial has fluctuated over time in Bosnia, as in Serbia. Thus, however powerful, cognitive biases have not condemned Bosnians to live in perpetual denial. As the next section makes clear, moreover, many citizens privately condemn atrocities they do not publicly acknowledge, suggesting that, for some Bosnians, denialism is more a function of social and political pressures than cognitive biases.

C. Community Pressure and Fear of Speaking Out

In February 2001 the ICTY convicted Bosnian Croat Dario Kordić, who commanded the HVO in the early 1990s, of war crimes committed against Bosniaks in Lašva Valley and sentenced him to serve twenty-five years in prison.[129] Upon his release in June 2014 after serving two-thirds of his sentence,[130] Kordić received a hero's welcome in Zagreb, Croatia.[131] Several months later, Aleksandra Letić told me that, in "closed meetings," Bosnian Croat associations "would say, 'what they did with Kordić

---

[124] *See* Mark Danner, *Bosnia: The Turning Point*, N.Y. REV. BOOKS (Feb. 5, 1998).

[125] Interview with Aleksandra Letić, Secretary-General, Helsinki Committee for Human Rights in Republika Srpska, in Sarajevo, Bosn. & Herz. (Sept. 8, 2014).

[126] *Id.*

[127] See discussion of DPA in Chapter 2.

[128] I am grateful to Eric Witte for this point.

[129] Prosecutor v. Kordić et al., Case No. IT-95-14/2-T, Trial Judgment (Int'l Crim. Trib. for the Former Yugoslavia Feb. 26, 2001).

[130] Kordić was given credit for time served in detention before his conviction. His release in June 2014 meant that he served two-thirds of his twenty-five-year sentence, calculated to have begun running from his date of detention in October 1997. As noted in Chapter 6, this is in line with the Tribunal's consistent practice.

[131] *See* Ina Vukić, *Croatia: Tears and Prayers as Bosnian Croat Dario Kordić Arrives Home from ICTY Prison* (June 7, 2014).

[i.e., celebrating a convicted war criminal] was not okay.' But . . . when they have to say it publicly, they will not do it."[132]

As Letić's observation reflects, many Bosnians feel strong community pressure *not* to condemn atrocities committed by their own ethnic group.[133] For some, this is linked to a belief they have a personal stake in maintaining denial. Noting more than half of Ljubuški's prewar population of 3,000 was no longer there as a result of ethnic cleansing, Štefica Galić said residents who remained (ethnic Croats) "had to know, and they know, they *do* know" what happened.[134] If they knew, I asked, why were they silent? In Galić's assessment, some of her former neighbors were "always nationalists," and were "waiting for this to come." As for the rest, she said:

> I think fear is the core problem. . . . They're afraid of losing everything they have, [and] if they don't stay quiet, they might lose everything. That's why they didn't raise their voices. People were calculating . . . they were making their own calculations—what they could lose, what they can gain. . . . They are simply afraid—what else could it be? You see what happened to me.[135]

Just as Ljubuški's residents must have known their town was ethnically cleansed, I frequently heard it was impossible for Serbs *not* to know what happened in their towns, but most were loath to say so publicly. For example, one of the rare local Serbs who acknowledged Serbs in Prijedor committed ethnic cleansing, Milimir Popović, told me in 2006 that "many [Serbs] talk like this [privately] but won't come out and [do so publicly]."[136] More recently, as Serbs like Goran Zorić have devoted themselves to dispelling denial, other Serbs have openly opposed their efforts. As Emir Hodžić noted, Serbs who "say, 'Yes, it did happen' . . . have been branded as traitors." And "it's very difficult to live in a . . . small community like Prijedor to be branded as a traitor." Few Serbs are "ready to take that on."[137]

Josip Davidović, who decried ICTY sentences of Foča defendants as too harsh, acknowledged his statements (if not his actual beliefs) were shaped by his ethnic belonging. Toward the end of our meeting, Davidović volunteered: "You have to be partial or biased when it is about your people, you have to be partial. This is an unwritten rule, regardless of how much you would like it to be different."[138]

Johanna Mannergren Selimović describes a similar dynamic. A Bosniak whom she interviewed about crimes committed against Serbs in Čelebići "reluctantly acknowledge[ed] that atrocities had in fact been committed there against Bosnian Serb civilians." But when Mannergren Selimović turned off the tape recorder and the two spoke informally over lunch, the same person expressed forthright concern about the Serb victims. In her view, this "revealed a tension between upholding of

[132] Interview with Aleksandra Letić, Secretary-General, Helsinki Committee for Human Rights in Republika Srpska, in Sarajevo, Bosn. & Herz. (Sept. 8, 2014).

[133] The extent and nature of such pressure varies, of course; virtually every Sarajevo elite whom I interviewed readily condemned war crimes by their own as well as other ethnic groups.

[134] Interview with Štefica Galić, Editor, Tačno.net, in Mostar, Bosn. & Herz. (Sept. 10, 2014).

[135] *Id.*

[136] Interview with Milimir Popović in Prijedor, Bosn. & Herz. (Dec. 8, 2006).

[137] Interview with Emir Hodžić, Jer Me Se Tiče, in Sarajevo, Bosn. & Herz. (Sept. 13, 2014).

[138] Interview with Josip Davidović, President, Association of Families of Fallen Soldiers and Missing and Detained Persons, in Foča, Bosn. & Herz. (July 20, 2009).

the narrative of collective innocence [of Bosniaks] and [the source's] own individual and more ambivalent moral position."[139]

To recognize that many Bosnians feel intense pressure *not* to acknowledge atrocities committed by their in-group begs the question, what accounts for that pressure? Several explanations loomed large in my interviews with Bosnians. One emphasizes the influence of political elites (whose motivations may not, it should be emphasized, be the same as those of citizens who follow their lead).[140] Another involves the impact of governance structures forged in Dayton, while a third emphasizes the fundamental importance of Bosnians' daily circumstances. I explore each in the sections that follow.

D. Elite Discourses, the Incentives that Shape Their Content, and Their Impact on Acknowledgment

The past two decades of war crimes trials have done little to dent the denialism of [Bosnia's] leaders.

—CARL THOR DAHLMAN[141]

Much as elite discourses have molded many Serbians' beliefs about wartime atrocities,[142] nationalist discourses in Bosnia have shaped the way many Bosnians understand and speak about wartime atrocities and make sense of ICTY judgments. As a general matter, Mirko Zelenika observed, "those in structures of power . . . definitely have a huge influence on citizens, on the common people."[143] More pointedly, Edin Ramulić said nationalist leaders "pollute [citizens'] minds with lies and ideas."[144] Saying "everything happens here through the channel of political elites and their discourses," Edin Hodžić continued: "So even the influence of the ICTY . . . is mediated by political elites."[145] And, as Mervan Miraščija noted, "politicians . . . use [the ICTY] for their own aims."[146]

This section explores what elites say about the 1990s conflict and the Hague Tribunal. Proverbially, however, their actions often speak louder than their words. As Zelenika accurately observed, political leaders have undermined the ICTY's message in myriad ways: the "authorities . . . were sending the accused to The Hague as if they

---

[139] Johanna Mannergren Selimović, *Perpetrators and Victims: Local Responses to the International Criminal Tribunal for the Former Yugoslavia*, 57 J. GLOBAL & HIST. ANTHROPOLOGY 50, 54–55 (2010).

[140] For example, as the analysis in this chapter suggests, political elites may employ nationalist narratives to secure and maintain political power, while citizens may faithfully repeat those narratives because (1) the narratives bolster their self-esteem, (2) maintaining the party line minimizes conflicts with neighbors, and/or (3) adhering to leaders' discourses ensures continued funding for the groups in which individuals participate.

[141] Carl Thor Dahlman, *Bosnia's War Ended, But Not Its Ethnic Politics*, HUFF. POST (Nov. 19, 2014).

[142] *See* Chapter 7.

[143] Interview with Mirko Zelenika, Acting President, Association of Croat Detainees of BiH, in Mostar, Bosn. & Herz. (Sept. 10, 2014).

[144] Interview with Edin Ramulić, Project Coordinator, Izvor, in Prijedor, Bosn. & Herz. (Sept. 16, 2014).

[145] Interview with Edin Hodžić, Director, Public Law Program, Center for Social Research Analitika, in Sarajevo, Bosn. & Herz. (Sept. 11, 2014).

[146] Interview with Mervan Miraščija, Law Program Coordinator, Open Society Fund BiH, in Sarajevo, Bosn. & Herz. (Nov. 29, 2006).

were heroes."[147] During trials in The Hague, "they were providing the accused with all sorts of support."[148] After convicted war criminals returned home upon the completion of their sentences, public authorities "were hosting these people as heroes."[149]

The views of politicians are widely disseminated in the "mainstream media, . . . a lot of [whose] directors and employees are . . . politically-aligned."[150] Far from offering information that may challenge the narratives of political elites, Emir Hodžić noted, Bosnia's mainstream "media is helping the war-mongering and nationalist rhetoric, it's spreading it."[151] As in Serbia, local media amplify the views not only of political elites,[152] but also those of "very strong nationalistic-oriented intellectuals."[153]

Among other discursive strategies, Jasna Bakšić Muftić noted, some of the most influential elites use "statistics [to demonstrate] how many Serbs, how many Croats" have been prosecuted by the ICTY, presenting their approach as "scientific"[154]—to "prove," in other words, that the Tribunal is biased against their ethnic group. And, as Edin Hodžić noted, Bosnians "tend to be willing to trust people" they perceive to be offering "a so-called scientific approach," typically "people from academia."[155] These individuals "still dominate the public discourse. . . . They're very prominent on the TV, in the media, and so on."[156]

If elite discourses shape citizens' beliefs, a more prosaic dynamic constrains what many citizens *say* they believe. Aleksandra Letić notes that victims associations, a key constituency in Bosnian politics, tend to follow the prevailing discourse of "the political leadership . . . because they're depending financially" on them. According to Letić, victims' associations are "not *always* ideologically" aligned with the leaders they purport to follow, "but sometimes they're financially blackmailed. If you are not supporting [the leaders' positions] you are not going to be financed" by entity governments, the principal source of funding for Bosnian victims' associations.[157] In her words, "the economical factor" behind victims' stated views is "always underestimated."[158]

---

[147] Interview with Mirko Zelenika, Acting President, Association of Croat Detainees of BiH, in Mostar, Bosn. & Herz. (Sept. 10, 2014).

[148] *Id.* On this subject, see Saša Dimovski et al., *How Ex-Yugoslav States Funded War Crimes Defendants*, BALKAN INSIGHT (Dec. 23, 2013).

[149] Interview with Mirko Zelenika, Acting President, Association of Croat Detainees of BiH, in Mostar, Bosn. & Herz. (Sept. 10, 2014). Elsewhere in this chapter, I note two examples: Bosniaks' reception of Naser Orić in 2006, and Croats' reception of Dario Kordić in 2014.

[150] Interview with Emir Hodžić, Jer Me Se Tiče, in Sarajevo, Bosn. & Herz. (Sept. 13, 2014).

[151] *Id.*

[152] A survey conducted in July 2008 found that 85 percent of Bosnians polled relied on media reports and politicians' statements for information about war crimes institutions. Refik Hodžić, *Living the Legacy of Mass Atrocities: Victims' Perspectives on War Crimes Trials*, 8 J. INT'L CRIM. JUST. 113, 115 n.3 (2010) [hereinafter Hodžić, *Living the Legacy*].

[153] Interview with Jasna Bakšić Muftić, Professor, Faculty of Law, University of Sarajevo, in Sarajevo, Bosn. & Herz. (Sept. 17, 2014).

[154] *Id.*

[155] Interview with Edin Hodžić, Director, Public Law Program, Center for Social Research Analitika, in Sarajevo, Bosn. & Herz. (Sept. 11, 2014).

[156] *Id.*

[157] Interview with Aleksandra Letić, Secretary-General, Helsinki Committee for Human Rights in Republika Srpska, in Sarajevo, Bosn. & Herz. (Sept. 8, 2014).

[158] *Id.*

Making a somewhat different point—that Bosnian politicians routinely exploit victims—Nidžara Ahmetašević described a similar dynamic. In many cases, victims associations "cannot even pay like basic administrative costs, they cannot buy paper, you know, . . . or anything they need to have or want to have." Desperate for basic resources and unable to meet the burdensome requirements imposed by international donors, many victims associations accept funding from "politicians."[159]

1. KEY THEMES OF DOMINANT DISCOURSES AND THEIR RESONANCE FOR TARGET AUDIENCES

In a region where historical narratives cast a long shadow, ethnic leaders and many citizens are deeply invested in ensuring the primacy of their account of the 1990s Yugoslav wars. Almost a quarter century after the Bosnia war ended, one of the most highly-contested issues is how to characterize the nature and causes of the conflict, a subject "often used by politicians to stir up ethnic instability."[160] While Bosnians and Croats emphasize Serb aggression, Serb leaders characterize the conflict as a civil war that accompanied the dissolution of the former Yugoslavia.[161] Neđeljko Mitrović, leader of an RS victims association, described his view in terms many Serbs would embrace: "I believe that the war was about whether the former Yugoslav state would remain or dissolve and the decision to outvote Serbs" in the 1992 referendum for independence.[162]

In line with the "civil war" narrative espoused by Mitrović and many other Serbs, Jasna Bakšić Muftić noted, "The first proposition in the [Serb] media . . . is that all parties . . . did something wrong and contributed to . . . the whole war and dissolution of the former Yugoslavia."[163] In this discourse, the tragedy that befell Bosnia was more akin to a "natural disaster" like a tsunami or an "accident" than the intended outcome of calculated policy. Something terrible happened, yet there was no "politics behind it," and no "personal responsibility for that."[164]

Consistent with this narrative, a central tenet of dominant Bosnian Serb discourses is that all sides were equally responsible for wartime atrocities. In the words of Gojko Berić, "Serbs, as is well known, would like to equalize those war crimes, make them relative by using the thesis that all three sides committed crimes in wartime."[165] And this claim, Bakšić Muftić believes, signifies the end of accountability. For if "all are

---

[159] Interview with Nidžara Ahmetašević, Journalist, in Sarajevo, Bosn. & Herz. (Sept. 12, 2014). Ahmetašević explained that many foreign donors require grant applicants to complete complex forms that use "NGO donor language," and "also require you to know one foreign language." She evoked a typical reaction by survivors: "So you want me to survive, like, mass rape, to survive concentration camp, to survive postwar kind of like life without psychological help, doctors or anything, and plus to know all this!" *Id.*

[160] Denis Džidić, *Why There's No "Truth" About the Bosnian War*, BALKAN TRANSITIONAL JUST. (May 12, 2014). Anđelko Kvesić voiced a common Croat account when he told a reporter: "The war, from my position, was a defensive war. I had my home and my line and I defended my home. I went nowhere. Those who attacked me, if they did as I did, then we would not have had this war." *Id.*

[161] *See id.*

[162] *Id.*

[163] Interview with Jasna Bakšić Muftić, Professor, Faculty of Law, University of Sarajevo, in Sarajevo, Bosn. & Herz. (Sept. 17, 2014).

[164] *Id.*

[165] Interview with Gojko Berić, Journalist & Columnist, Oslobođenje, in Sarajevo, Bosn. & Herz. (July 17, 2009).

guilty, ... if you do relativization of everything ..., you lose the main point."[166] Others, including Dženana Karup Druško, believe the fact that Serbs were not decisively defeated in the 1990s war has made it easier for Serb nationalists to justify Serb atrocities as acts of self-defense in a civil war in which all sides committed war crimes.[167]

For reasons developed earlier, it would be natural for many Serbs to embrace the view that all three major ethnic groups were equally responsible for and victimized by wartime atrocities and thereby minimize their in-group's responsibility for such crimes.[168] Jasna Bakšić Muftić seemed to suggest as much:

> I think that [there] is still a very strong, very strong feeling of ethnic justice. They want to see the ethnic justice. Let's say, "OK, our Serbs ... did very bad crimes, ... they [have] to be ... sentenced and etc. *But*, at the same time, what about the Croat, the Bosniak, and etc.? We want to see [them held] responsible for [the] crime[s] they did during the war." And ... I think ... this is the pursuing of the ethnic justice, let's say.[169]

The dynamic Bakšić Muftić described evokes a phenomenon said to be common in intergroup conflicts, which social psychologists have called *competitive victimhood*.[170] Typically, *competitive victimhood* is defined as "a group's motivation and consequent efforts to establish that it has suffered *more* than its adversaries."[171] Among Bosnian Serbs, however, the same dynamic often manifests as a discursive claim that Serbs suffered *as much* as others, effectively equalizing victimhood.[172] The surveys explored earlier reflect the powerful influence of this equalizing narrative among Bosnian Serbs: when asked which side committed and suffered the most war crimes, respondents living in predominantly Serb areas were most likely to say all sides committed equal numbers of war crimes and were equally victimized; the second most frequent responses identified Serbs as the greatest victims and the least responsible wrongdoers among the country's ethnic groups.[173] As previously noted, the equalizing narrative apparently became more entrenched in the period between the

---

[166] Interview with Jasna Bakšić Muftić, Professor, Faculty of Law, University of Sarajevo, in Sarajevo, Bosn. & Herz. (Sept. 17, 2014).

[167] Interview with Dženana Karup Druško, Director, Transitional Justice, Accountability and Remembrance, in Sarajevo, Bosn. & Herz. (Sept. 8, 2014).

[168] I refer in particular to social psychology research showing that people are motivated to process information in a way that preserves their self-esteem—which, in turn, may be tied to their estimation of their in-group. In addition to the discussion of these dynamics in Chapter 7, see *supra* text accompanying notes 110–12.

[169] Interview with Jasna Bakšić Muftić, Professor, Faculty of Law, University of Sarajevo, in Sarajevo, Bosn. & Herz. (Sept. 17, 2014).

[170] *See* Masi Noor et al., *When Suffering Begets Suffering: The Psychology of Competitive Victimhood Between Adversarial Groups in Violent Conflicts*, 16 PERSONALITY & SOC. PSYCHOL. REV. 351 (2012). *See also* Čehajić & Brown, *supra* note 111, at 192. A building block of competitive victimhood is a belief in the *collective* victimhood of one's in-group. A common theme among those who share this belief is "that the rival group continuously inflicted unjust and immoral harm upon them" during a conflict. Daniel Bar-Tal et al., *A Sense of Self-Perceived Collective Victimhood in Intractable Conflicts*, 91 INT'L REV. RED CROSS 229, 230 (2009).

[171] Noor et al., *supra* note 170, at 351 (emphasis added).

[172] *See* Mannergren Selimović, *supra* note 139, at 54 ("Competition for victimhood may lead to the relativization of suffering.").

[173] *See* Figures 8.1 and 8.2, *supra*.

two BCHR survey years. In 2010, 44 percent of respondents in predominantly Serb areas said all three of Bosnia's major ethnic groups bore equal responsibility for war crimes; the percentage rose to 66 percent in 2012.[174]

If many Serbs are subconsciously motivated to believe "all sides suffered equally" because this would bolster their collective self-esteem, this narrative also advances strategic goals, which many Bosnian Serbs have a distinct motivation to support. The equalizing narrative challenges the asserted basis of efforts by some Bosniak survivors and prominent Bosniak leaders, among whom Haris Silajdžić looms large, to revise the constitutional structure imposed in Dayton.[175] As previously noted, although Silajdžić participated in the Dayton negotiations, he has vigorously challenged its ethnic map[176] and sought greater centralization of government authority. Of particular relevance here, those efforts rest on the claim that Serbs committed singular atrocities. Condemning the Serb entity as a product of genocide,[177] Silajdžić pivoted off the ICJ's February 2007 genocide judgment to demand that "the interior structure of Bosnia" be altered.[178] Similarly, in Refik Hodžić's words, "ICTY trials were somehow seen by many as a possible way to win back the territory and the constitutional framework lost in the war."[179]

A corollary of the claim that all sides were equally responsible for war crimes/ suffered equally is that the ICTY has *disproportionately* prosecuted Serbs (as previously noted, two-thirds of those indicted by the Tribunal were ethnic Serbs), and disproportionately acquitted those charged with crimes against Serbs.[180] In the words of Edin Hodžić, Serb discourses have consistently maintained the ICTY "is not a credible institution, it was formed by the West . . . to blame the Serbs."[181] As several Bosnians noted, the ICTY's controversial acquittal of Croatian general Ante Gotovina in November 2012 (addressed in Chapter 6) played into this narrative. Describing the impact of Gotovina's acquittal on Bosnian Serb perceptions, Aleksandar Trifunović said: "On the bottom line, when Serbs in Bosnia think[] about Hague Tribunal, [they] think] 'this is only for Serbs.'"[182] As with other tenets of nationalist narratives, the

---

[174] *See* Figure 8.2, *supra.*

[175] Survivors' and other local actors' efforts to challenge the legal status of Srebrenica are described in Lara J. Nettelfield & Sarah E. Wagner, Srebrenica in the Aftermath of Genocide 120 et seq. (2014).

[176] *See* Chapter 2; *see also* Joanne McEvoy, Power-Sharing Executives: Governing in Bosnia, Macedonia, and Northern Ireland 14 (2015).

[177] *See Fragile Bosnia: The Break-Up Danger*, Economist (Nov. 8, 2008).

[178] When the ICJ judgment was rendered, Silajdžić told *ABC News:* "Bosnia-Herzegovina must . . . purge itself of the remnants of the genocide that permeates throughout Bosnian society. We will achieve this by altering what has been founded on the genocide's outcome—the interior structure of Bosnia and its constitution." Dragana Jovanović, *International Court Clears Serbia of Genocide*, ABC News Online (Feb. 26, 2007), http://abcnews.go.com/International/ Story?id=2906051&page=1. For a fine-grained account of Silajdžić's position, see Nettelfield & Wagner, *supra* note 175, at 126 et seq.

[179] Hodžić, *Post-Karadžić, supra* note 108.

[180] Thus, Gojko Berić noted, Serbs routinely "claim that only Serbs are being prosecuted in The Hague. Which of course is notorious nonsense." Interview with Gojko Berić, Journalist & Columnist, Oslobođenje, in Sarajevo, Bosn. & Herz. (July 17, 2009).

[181] Interview with Edin Hodžić, Director, Public Law Program, Center for Social Research Analitika, in Sarajevo, Bosn. & Herz. (Sept. 11, 2014).

[182] Interview with Aleksandar Trifunović, Editor, BUKA, in Banja Luka, Bosn. & Herz. (Sept. 15, 2014).

media has amplified this claim. Serb attacks on the independence of the Tribunal are "openly" disseminated "in the public media," Nusreta Sivac noted, and with palpable effect. "Even small, simple people now believe this idea, that the ICTY is politically-oriented, that . . . the ICTY was set up only to prosecute representatives of only one ethnic group."[183]

This perspective is hardly conducive to acknowledging Serbs were responsible for the overwhelming majority of wartime atrocities. Instead, as Karup Druško noted, many Serb elites "constantly" cite the number of Serbs prosecuted in The Hague and "are never talking about . . . how many non-Serbs were actually ethnically cleansed and killed during the war."[184] Far from reflecting Serbs' relative responsibility, ICTY charging patterns are said to prove Serbs are "victims of the international community, of international justice."[185]

Yet Serbs do not consistently discredit the Tribunal; rather, they (like politicians from other ethnic groups) instrumentalize it. Prijedor mayor Marko Pavić reportedly cites the fact that the ICTY has not ruled genocide was committed in Prijedor as proof that "ethnic cleansing" there did not amount to genocide.[186] More generally, Edin Hodžić notes, "Elites see [the ICTY] as some kind of a shopping list from which they can pick and choose their arguments and the facts . . . that they like, that speak in their favor."[187]

So far, I have emphasized discursive themes that equalize responsibility for war crimes. Another leitmotif in elite Serb discourses—claims that *justify* Serb atrocities—appeals more directly to Bosnian Serbs' stake in the survival of Republika Srpska (as previously noted, this interest also provides a distinct motivation to embrace the equalizing narrative). Emir Hodžić made the point this way:

> Unfortunately, due to propaganda, due to people like Dodik and Marko Pavić and the official politics of Republika Srpska, . . . war crimes are almost justified as a necessary tool for a kind of final goal, which is the political goal of Republika Srpska, independence of Republika Srpska.[188]

---

[183] Interview with Nusreta Sivac, Former Judge, in Prijedor, Bosn. & Herz. (Sept. 16, 2014).

[184] Interview with Dženana Karup Druško, Director, Transitional Justice, Accountability and Remembrance, in Sarajevo, Bosn. & Herz. (Sept. 8, 2014).

[185] Interview with Jasna Bakšić Muftić, Professor, Faculty of Law, University of Sarajevo, in Sarajevo, Bosn. & Herz. (Sept. 17, 2014).

[186] Emir Hodžić summarized the mayor's stance as, "There's no ruling for genocide, therefore there's no genocide" in Prijedor. Interview with Emir Hodžić, Jer Me Se Tiče, in Sarajevo, Bosn. & Herz. (Sept. 13, 2014). Hodžić described an analogous yet somewhat distinct dynamic in Croat narratives: in his perception, Croats have often discredited the ICTY, saying it was "set up to try and equalize everybody and demonize Croats' heroes." When I asked if this remained the case after the ICTY acquitted Ante Gotovina, the most high-profile ethnic Croat tried before the Tribunal, Hodžić said many Croats saw this outcome as "proving their point." Now Croats could point to Gotovina's acquittal to argue "he should never have been there because he's a hero." *Id.*

[187] Interview with Edin Hodžić, Director, Public Law Program, Center for Social Research Analitika, in Sarajevo, Bosn. & Herz. (Sept. 11, 2014). In a similar vein, Lara Nettelfield writes that Bosnian Serbs have cited the ICTY's verdict in the Čelebići trial, in which non-Serbs were convicted of crimes against Serb victims, "as confirmation that Serbs had suffered equally in the war." LARA J. NETTELFIELD, COURTING DEMOCRACY IN BOSNIA AND HERZEGOVINA: THE HAGUE TRIBUNAL'S IMPACT IN A POSTWAR STATE 182 (2010).

[188] Interview with Emir Hodžić, Jer Me Se Tiče, in Sarajevo, Bosn. & Herz. (Sept. 13, 2014).

A veiled example of this type of discursive claim, which occurred in September 2014, was frequently cited during interviews that month. Campaigning for re-election, Dodik said (as paraphrased by one source), "The day will come soon when we'll have streets in Banja Luka [the capital of Republika Srpska] named after Karadžić and Mladić."[189]

It is easy to see why this framing would resonate with its target audience: 92 percent of Bosnian Serbs live in Republika Srpska. Aleksandar Trifunović characterized the perspective of many RS residents this way: "OK, this [i.e., the fact that war crimes were "in the foundation of the entity"] is bad, but now we are in Republika Srpska, we have our hopes fulfilled."[190]

Another source, who asked that I not identify him, imagined a pathway for Bosnian Serb acknowledgment that resolves the Serb entity's foundational dilemma: the RS leadership would develop a new narrative that separates atrocities committed by wartime Serb leaders on the one hand from "the creation of Republika Srpska" on the other hand. The imagined discourse might go something like this: " 'Yes, the crimes have happened, the leadership was really bad at that time, but the concerns of the people were legitimate, and the struggle of our people . . . was legitimate.'" It is, of course, hardly obvious Bosniak victims would find this approach acceptable, much less compelling. But that is not the point here. Rather, it is to highlight a powerful, context-specific factor behind Serb denial distinct from Serbs' motivation to preserve a positive self-image.

As previously suggested, the persistence of denialist discourses is not the same as their consistency across time. In fact, official Bosnian Serb discourses have changed markedly during the postwar years, an important point I develop later. First, however, I explore motivations behind contemporary leaders' denialist claims and policies.

2. ELITE MOTIVATIONS

As the preceding section suggests, key themes in denialist narratives advance nationalist agendas. Doing so may not, however, be the primary motivation of elites who pedal those narratives with toxic effect. Their primary motivation, many Bosnians believe, is to maintain political power (in this respect they are hardly unique among candidates for political office). Beyond winning the next election, it is widely thought that some politicians, notably including Dodik, use nationalist discourses to distract attention from possible corruption charges.[191]

In line with the first motivation, Bosnian politicians have "instrumentalized" the subject of war crimes with special intensity in advance of elections.[192] Nationalist

---

[189] Id. See also Refik Hodžić, Karadžić's Trial Ends, But His Legacy Lives On, ICTJ website (Oct. 8, 2014), https://www.ictj.org/news/karadzic%E2%80%99s-trial-ends-his-legacy-lives [hereinafter Hodžić, Karadžić's Trial Ends].

[190] Interview with Aleksandar Trifunović, Editor, BUKA, in Banja Luka, Bosn. & Herz. (Sept. 15, 2014).

[191] See, e.g., Rodolf Toe & Srećko Latal, Bosnian Serb Chief Plays Nationalist Card in Elections, BALKAN INSIGHT (Mar. 21, 2016); Ed Vulliamy, Bosnia's Survivors Gather and Grieve as the Soil Endlessly Gives Up Its Dead, GUARDIAN (Aug. 8, 2015).

[192] In interviews many Bosnians used the words "instrumentalize" and "use and misuse" to describe how politicians appeal to victims' interests to advance their own. Nidžara Ahmetašević told me that, while politicians are especially likely to "pull out" victims during pre-election periods, they do so on other occasions when they feel the need to distract attention from political problems. To illustrate, she suggested (while indicating she was simplifying reality) that if a politician is accused

rhetoric is common in municipal as well as national elections. Goran Zorić saw its pernicious effects in his previous work with at-risk youth in Prijedor. Appalled at the poverty of resources available to citizens with urgent social needs, Zorić had an epiphany: government services were shamefully inadequate in no small part because local leaders could get elected simply by pledging to defend "nationalist interests." "Because of that," Zorić said, "they don't have to resolve any kind of problems in Prijedor—social, social protection, health care protection, child protection."[193]

It is not just Serb politicians who instrumentalize victims and the topic of war crimes. Some Croat politicians have managed to "stay in power" by appealing to fears of "atrocities by other ethnic groups," according to Štefica Galić. This happens "especially prior to an election, or when some of the Hague indictees or those who served their sentences are released and come back."[194] Sevima Sali-Terzić and others[195] note that Bosnian politicians of all ethnic groups, including Bosniaks, are prone to manipulate victims in the lead-up to elections, using them as an electoral "tool."[196]

E. A "Hostile Environment" for Acknowledgment

I feel like the entire country is falling apart. Like completely. . . . I feel like I'm just . . . drowning, and I'm waving with my hands, . . . but I don't see the ship coming to pick me up.

—Nidžara Ahmetašević[197]

I believed more in reconciliation in the Balkans in the 1990s than today. . . . Relations across the region are worse than ever and one has to be a true optimist to believe that this peace will hold.

—Snežana Tasić[198]

---

of corruption, he might "go and . . . take a picture with [a] group of victims." Interview with Nidžara Ahmetašević, Journalist, in Sarajevo, Bosn. & Herz. (Sept. 12, 2014). *See also* Sven Milekić et al., *Nationalist Commemorations Threaten Balkan Reconciliation*, Balkan Transitional Just. (Aug. 7, 2015). Speaking in the specific context of Srebrenica survivors' relationship to political parties, Lara Nettelfield and Sarah Wagner sound a cautionary note. Noting "[c]onventional wisdom held that Srebrenica's survivor groups were financed and supported by [a particular political party] and faithfully delivered their votes to it," they write: "Overt political manipulation was, however, impossible to prove, and family associations vehemently rejected their characterization as pawns of forces in the nation's capital." Nettelfield & Wagner, *supra* note 175, at 128.

[193] Interview with Goran Zorić, Executive Director, KVART, in Sarajevo, Bosn. & Herz. (Sept. 17, 2014).

[194] Interview with Štefica Galić, Editor, Tačno.net, in Mostar, Bosn. & Herz. (Sept. 10, 2014).

[195] *E.g.*, interview with Dobrila Govedarica, Executive Director, Open Society Fund BiH, in Sarajevo, Bosn. & Herz. (Nov. 29, 2006).

[196] Interview with Sevima Sali-Terzić, Senior Legal Counsel, Constitutional Court of BiH, in Sarajevo, Bosn. & Herz. (Nov. 30, 2006 & Sept. 9, 2014). In a comment on a draft of this chapter, Edin Hodžić raised the question why political elites still use the *same* rhetoric they used during the war and immediately after it ended to garner votes. He reflected: "Obviously, part of the answer is the fact that more or less the same political parties have been ruling the country since 1990. In the overwhelming inability and reluctance to genuinely distance themselves from the heinous crimes (which is an interesting and very complex phenomenon), they probably see dealing with the past as mostly dealing with themselves, which they then want to avoid at any cost." Comment by Edin Hodžić on draft chapter (provided Sept. 10, 2017).

[197] Interview with Nidžara Ahmetašević, Journalist, in Sarajevo, Bosn. & Herz. (Sept. 12, 2014).

[198] Sven Milekić et al., *Nationalist Commemorations Threaten Balkan Reconciliation*, Balkan Insight (Aug. 7, 2015) (quoting Prijedor resident Snežana Tasić).

Measured against the impact it might have had, the ICTY has been extremely un-lucky when it comes to timing: its most seasoned prosecutors hit their stride at a time when trials in The Hague were far less likely to matter to Bosnians than they once would have. As noted in Chapter 2, Sevima Sali-Terzić and others believe the early years of peace offered a singular chance to "reconsider that part of our his-tory"—that is, the 1990s war. But the early failure of NATO forces to arrest Hague fugitives allowed war criminals to consolidate their influence, and meant top-line fugitives would elude capture for well over a decade. By the time trial proceedings began against Radovan Karadžić and Ratko Mladić, few Bosnians were following Hague proceedings.

In Chapter 6 I described how this has affected victims' subjective experience of Hague justice. Here I am making a distinct point: deteriorating social, political, and economic conditions in Bosnia have radically reduced prospects for acknowledg-ment, no matter how compelling the ICTY's judicial fact-finding. With staggeringly high rates of unemployment and poverty,[199] perennial political crises,[200] and deep ethnic divisions, Goran Zorić said addressing painfully difficult questions about war crimes committed by one's in-group is "not important" for "a majority of the people." Instead, "they are struggling for everyday life—how to survive, how to . . . go to hol-iday, how to save the children from bad things."[201] Making much the same point, Štefica Galić sees little prospect for improvement: "Life is going to get worse . . . and worse, due to the economic situation we have been brought to. We are on our knees, we are in prison."[202]

Deteriorating economic conditions might provide further incentive for incum-bent leaders to sustain wartime narratives, as they can hardly win re-election on the ground they delivered economic prosperity.[203] At the same time, dismal conditions may deplete the psychic reserves citizens need to address unsettling questions about the past.[204]

---

[199] A 2015 study reported: "Only about one in three working-age adults [in Bosnia] has a job (and only one in four has a formal job)." Ellen Goldstein et al., *Three Reasons Why the Economy of Bosnia and Herzegovina Is Off Balance*, BROOKINGS INSTITUTION (Nov. 5, 2015).

[200] *See* Chapter 2.

[201] Interview with Goran Zorić, Executive Director, KVART, in Sarajevo, Bosn. & Herz. (Sept. 17, 2014).

[202] Interview with Štefica Galić, Editor, Tačno.net, in Mostar, Bosn. & Herz. (Sept. 10, 2014).

[203] On this point, see Goran Zorić's previously-quoted point about the poverty of social services in Prijedor.

[204] Several scholars have identified a correlation between economic conditions and the measures a country takes to address human rights violations committed in the recent past. *See, e.g.*, Hun Joon Kim, *Structural Determinants of Human Rights Prosecutions After Democratic Transition*, 49 J. PEACE RESEARCH 305, 315 (2012); TRICIA D. OLSEN ET AL., TRANSITIONAL JUSTICE IN BALANCE: COMPARING PROCESSES, WEIGHING EFFICACY 68–69, 73–77 (2010). But as the authors of the latter study point out, it is not clear what accounts for the correlation. One possibility is that countries with comparatively healthy economies have the institutional capacity to mount trials, which are generally the most expensive transitional justice measure. *See id.* at 77. *See also* JON ELSTER, CLOSING THE BOOKS: TRANSITIONAL JUSTICE IN HISTORICAL PERSPECTIVE 213 (2004) (in situations of political transition, new leaders who face dire economic challenges are prone to forgo costly measures of transitional justice). This consideration does not have significant explan-atory power for Bosnia, however. Despite high levels of unemployment and other indicators of a weak economy, Bosnian courts have mounted extensive war crimes trials. *See* Chapter 9.

Focusing on Bosnia's deteriorating political situation more than its economic straits, Edin Hodžić observed: "It's really hard to expect any kind of significant impact in a hostile environment."[205] "Whatever you achieve in the field of transitional justice," he added, "you lose in everyday political life."[206] Like Hodžić, Svjetlana Nedimović believes many Bosnians have been losing faith in the ICTY because "things were not being set right in the country." In her view, this reflects misplaced expectations: "Disillusionment with the Hague Tribunal was not just a problem of the Hague Tribunal; it was also the problem of how we understood what it was going to do for us. Courts do not set political reality right."[207]

But if Bosnians never should have expected the Tribunal to "fix" their political reality, their country's toxic politics and dire economic conditions are inimical to reckoning with a torturous past. In Nedimović's words, "these issues are so hard that we can deal with them only when we are living a dignified life, which doesn't expose us to pressures that push us into rather polarized corners." So far, it has not been possible for Bosnians to address the past "in a . . . dignified manner where we can respect each other, without cutting each other's throats, metaphorically speaking, just because we are miserable, on so many fronts."[208]

F. The Distinct Effects of Ethnic Division

I believe there will never be a consensus, because the Dayton peace accords
divided the country along ethnic lines.

—MURAT TAHIROVIĆ[209]

Edin Hodžić is steeped in the literature of transitional justice, which he has mined for insights that might explain Bosnia's experience and prospects. Yet he has found little on offer that might help advance acknowledgment in Bosnia. In his words, much of the field's scholarship assumes a context in which citizens are *capable* of forging a unitary vision of the country's past and future—a "resolution," if you will, of a common "tragedy."[210] But in a country as starkly divided as Bosnia, "there's no plausible resolution."[211] In particular, Hodžić noted, the segregation enshrined in Dayton,

---

[205] Interview with Edin Hodžić, Director, Public Law Program, Center for Social Research Analitika, in Sarajevo, Bosn. & Herz. (Sept. 11, 2014).

[206] *Id.*

[207] Interview with Svjetlana Nedimović, Activist, in Sarajevo, Bosn. & Herz. (Sept. 18, 2014).

[208] *Id.*

[209] Denis Džidić, *Why There's No "Truth" About the Bosnian War*, BALKAN TRANSITIONAL JUST. (May 12, 2014) (quoting Murat Tahirović, President, Association of Genocide Survivors and Witnesses).

[210] Interview with Edin Hodžić, Director, Public Law Program, Center for Social Research Analitika, in Sarajevo, Bosn. & Herz. (Sept. 11, 2014). Hodžić was alluding to a notion underpinning some conceptions of transitional justice. As framed by Pierre Hazan, transitional justice "identifies the wrong; then, it invites judicial or extrajudicial institutions to take account of the tragedy before proposing its resolution." PIERRE HAZAN, JUDGING WAR, JUDGING HISTORY: BEHIND TRUTH AND RECONCILIATION 9 (Sarah Meyer De Stadlhofen trans., 2010). *See also* TEITEL, *supra* note 7, at 109–15.

[211] Interview with Edin Hodžić, Director, Public Law Program, Center for Social Research Analitika, in Sarajevo, Bosn. & Herz. (Sept. 11, 2014).

along with the political structures it mandates, have made it all but impossible to bridge incommensurate perspectives among Bosnia's ethnic groups.

To Hodžić's second point, fundamental features of the governance structures enshrined in the DPA incentivize polarization. As noted in Chapter 2, for example, key positions are allocated on an ethnic basis (thus, for example, the Serb member of the three-person presidency must be "from" Republika Srpska), incentivizing politicians to appeal to their own ethnic constituency, and the Dayton constitution's minority veto provisions have often produced paralysis rather than consensus. Eric Witte describes the effects of Dayton's "polarizing electoral logic" this way: "Once one nationalist from one group says something outrageous, there arises a competition among politicians from other ethnic groups to pledge to protect 'their' people—and this usually involves more heated rhetoric that further provokes the other groups." Even though "post-Dayton pre-election polling has consistently shown that Serbs, Croats, and Bosniaks all care most about jobs, the economy, education, etc., every single election has devolved into fear-mongering and nationalism, with voters responding accordingly."[212] Not surprisingly, then, post-conflict Bosnia is, in Edin Hodžić's words, "a total mess of different perspectives, that are really legitimized by the constitutional and political process."[213]

Beyond the polarizing effects of the governance structures imposed by the Dayton constitution, the ethnic segregation it enshrines is antithetical to acknowledgment. Building on previous studies finding that contact improves intergroup relations, Sabina Čehajić and Rupert Brown conducted a study in high schools in two towns in Republika Srpska. Respondents (all of whom were Serb) who had meaningful contact with non-Serbs were significantly more likely to say they were "ready to acknowledge that members of my group have committed atrocities during the war" and were "responsible for" those crimes than respondents who did not report such contact.[214]

Their study offers insights into the pathway through which contact influences acknowledgment: meaningful intergroup contact enhances group members' capacity to "understand the other group's point of view" (i.e., capacity for empathy) and diminishes the likelihood they will see their own group as "the biggest victim" in the war. These perspectives, Čehajić and Brown concluded, make it more likely group members will acknowledge another group's suffering.[215]

---

[212] Email from Eric Witte, Senior Project Manner, National Trials of Grave Crimes, Open Society Justice Initiative, to Diane Orentlicher (Sept. 24, 2017).

[213] Interview with Edin Hodžić, Director, Public Law Program, Center for Social Research Analitika, in Sarajevo, Bosn. & Herz. (Sept. 11, 2014).

[214] Čehajić & Brown, *supra* note 111, at 193. The study authors assessed contact through questions measuring the quantity and quality of respondents' contacts with non-Serbs. Quantity was gauged through the question, "How many friends do you have among members from the other groups in BiH?" Three questions were used to gauge quality, including time spent with non-Serb friends. The study authors found that "contact quality, not mere quantity, seemed to be the more potent correlate of acknowledgment." *Id* at 194. *See also* Sabina Čehajić et al., *Forgive and Forget? Antecedents and Consequences of Intergroup Forgiveness in Bosnia and Herzegovina*, 29 POL. PSYCHOL. 351 (2008).

[215] Čehajić & Brown, *supra* note 111, at 194. *See also* Mirza Ajnadžić & Ajdin Kamber, *Bosnia: Daunting Task of Confronting the Past*, IWPR (Oct. 28, 2011) (quoting Čehajić Clancy saying her research shows people of different ethnic backgrounds who communicate with each other regularly are more willing to reconcile with each other than those who do not).

Physical proximity may also facilitate acknowledgment through other phenomena, including peer pressure. A study conducted in 2000–2002 found that Serbs living in Vukovar, Croatia, where they were a minority, were significantly more likely to acknowledge that Serbs committed war crimes than were Serbs in Prijedor, where Serbs are a majority.[216] The authors of this study speculate that, having chosen to remain in Croatia, the Vukovar Serbs "must admit to the existence of war criminals on their side if they wish to remain as accepted citizens of the state."[217]

Another study, which focused on assessments of the ICTY, also found a strong correlation between respondents' views and their place of residence. The authors of the study, who conducted opinion surveys between 1997 and 2004, found "the diversity of views expressed by members of the same ethnic group often"—though not invariably—"corresponds closely to the views expressed by members of other ethnic groups from the same site."[218] Thus, for example, Serbs in Sarajevo and Vukovar, where Serbs are a minority, expressed views about the ICTY that were closer to those expressed by Sarajevo Bosniaks than to the views of Serbs in Belgrade, where Serbs are a majority.[219] The study authors suggest that what matters most in explaining the responses of Sarajevo and Vukovar Serbs is their exposure to the perspectives of "dominant political groups" in their place of residence.[220]

Other studies suggest a further reason Dayton's geography of separation may undermine acknowledgment: in myriad contexts, tensions between two social groups have been ameliorated and prospects for intergroup forgiveness enhanced when group members see themselves as members of a "common superordinate group."[221] Building on this research, Noor et al. believe "recategorizing separate group identities" (e.g., Serbs, Bosniaks) "into a common, superordinate identity" (e.g., Bosnian citizens) "can serve as an effective strategy for promoting inter-group forgiveness and reconciliation."[222] Against these studies' findings, the ethnic segregation enshrined in Dayton, which reinforces ethnic rather than Bosnian identity, may present one of the most formidable barriers to acknowledgment. Even within that framework, however, Bosnia saw significant progress in respect of official Serb acknowledgment during the early years of the twenty-first century, as explained in Section III.

---

[216] More specifically, the study found that 98.5 percent of Vukovar Serbs were willing to acknowledge Serbs committed war crimes, compared to 52.5 percent of Prijedor Serbs. Miklós Biró et al., *Attitudes Toward Justice and Social Reconstruction in Bosnia and Herzegovina and Croatia*, in My Neighbor, My Enemy: Justice and Community in the Aftermath of Mass Atrocity 194 (Eric Stover & Harvey M. Weinstein eds., 2004).

[217] *Id.* at 195. As the authors of this study acknowledge, however, any attempt to explain these data must be tentative. *Id.* at 194.

[218] Sanja Kutnjak Ivković & John Hagan, Reclaiming Justice: The International Tribunal for the Former Yugoslavia and Local Courts 82 (2011).

[219] In 2004, 71.5 percent of Belgrade Serb respondents rated the ICTY as "not fair." In 2003, 25.9 percent of Sarajevo Serbs chose that response, with 74.1 percent rating the Tribunal as "fair." That same year (2003), 88.1 percent of Sarajevo Croats and 93.4 percent of Sarajevo Bosniaks rated the ICTY as "fair." *Id.* at 76.

[220] *Id.* at 83.

[221] Noor et al., *supra* note 170, at 363.

[222] *Id.* at 364.

G. Absence of Local Truth Commissions?

In light of the persistence of robust denialism despite decades of judicial fact-finding, some have suggested that what Bosnia (or the region) needs is a truth commission.[223] The argument in support of such a body has two principal strands. First, as a criminal court whose job is to establish the guilt or innocence of individual defendants, the ICTY is not capable of establishing a comprehensive truth, much less one citizens will believe across ethnic lines.[224] Second, as a foreign court, the ICTY cannot assume a burden of reckoning with the past that only former Yugoslav citizens can discharge.[225]

Some proponents of this view fault past Tribunal officials, including then Prosecutor Louise Arbour and then president Gabrielle Kirk McDonald, for discouraging an initiative in 1997 to create a truth commission for Bosnia.[226] The initiative was controversial, and may not have gotten off the ground in any event.[227] Many of the same divisions that have neutralized the ICTY's potential contributions to acknowledgment have thwarted successive efforts to launch a Bosnian truth commission[228] and, more generally, to adopt a national strategy on transitional justice developed by a governmental working group in 2011.[229] An initiative to form a regional truth commission, known as RECOM, has failed to gain political traction despite relentless efforts since 2008 by local proponents and the nominal support of several political leaders.[230]

To be sure, it is possible such an initiative would have fared better during the period in which it was first proposed. When we discussed RECOM in 2014, Edin Hodžić noted that, in line with a significant stream of transitional justice scholarship, the most auspicious time to establish a truth commission is generally "as early as possible

---

[223] See, e.g., Clark, *Limits of Retributive Justice*, supra note 84, 479–81. Focusing more on reconciliation than denialism, Ralph Zacklin made this point in a 2004 publication. Ralph Zacklin, *The Failings of Ad Hoc International Tribunals*, 2 J. INT'L CRIM. JUST. 541, 544 (2004).

[224] See Clark, *Limits of Retributive Justice*, supra note 84, at 479.

[225] See id. at 479–80. Clark offers a third argument in support of a truth commission: while criminal trials focus on perpetrators, truth commissions have historically been "more victim-centred." Id. at 480.

[226] Their opposition is described in ERIC STOVER, THE WITNESSES: WAR CRIMES AND THE PROMISE OF JUSTICE IN THE HAGUE 116 (2005), and ELIZABETH NEUFFER, THE KEY TO MY NEIGHBOR'S HOUSE: SEEKING JUSTICE IN BOSNIA AND RWANDA 328 (2002). Arbour and McDonald were concerned that a local commission's work could undermine and partially duplicate the ICTY's own efforts. In 2001, then ICTY president Claude Jorda expressed qualified support for a local truth commission, while cautioning against interfering with the Tribunal's work. See INTERNATIONAL CENTER FOR TRANSITIONAL JUSTICE, BOSNIA AND HERZEGOVINA: SELECTED DEVELOPMENTS IN TRANSITIONAL JUSTICE 7 (2004).

[227] See Nerma Jelačić & Nidžara Ahmetašević, *Truth Commission Divides Bosnia*, BALKAN TRANSITIONAL JUST. (Sept. 18, 2007).

[228] See id.

[229] The draft text of the transitional justice strategy developed by a Working Group of the BiH Ministry for Human Rights and Refugees is available at http://www.mpr.gov.ba/aktuelnosti/propisi/konsultacije/Strategija%20TP%20-%20bosanski%20jezik%20fin%20doc.pdf (last visited Dec. 8, 2017).

[230] Nataša Kandić, one of the leading proponents of this initiative, summarizes the principal arguments in support of RECOM and the obstacles it has encountered in Nataša Kandić, *RECOM: A New Approach to Reconciliation and a Corrective for Criminal Justice*, in 4 F. TRANSITIONAL JUST. 78 (2012).

after the conflict,"[231] before discourses of denial become entrenched. While it is difficult to know whether the Tribunal derailed an otherwise promising initiative, the opposition of its then leaders likely had another effect, reinforcing the notion that "the judicial paradigm would do everything, would do the job of dealing with the past."[232]

III. ICTY IMPACT ON OFFICIAL ACKNOWLEDGMENT

A. Acknowledgment by Serb Leaders and Institutions

That denialism is alarmingly high in Bosnia plainly belies the early expectations of many Bosnians. Yet this tells us relatively little about whether the Tribunal had *any* impact on acknowledgment. To begin, we cannot know whether denialism would have been even more pervasive and extreme if the Tribunal had never been established.[233] Here, I want to explore a more specific possibility: whether, as some Bosnians suggested, the ICTY helped foster progress in acknowledgment during the early years of this century, when Bosnia was a more auspicious setting for this type of impact.

That the first few years of the twenty-first century brought palpable progress is clear to many Bosnians. During my first set of research interviews in 2006, sources in a position to observe broad trends told me it had become relatively rare to hear extreme forms of outright denial. In a similar vein, in a 2005 publication Rachel Kerr noted it was no longer common to hear of violent reprisals against Serbs who forthrightly addressed Serb atrocities, as had happened in 1999, when an independent RS newspaper published details of two episodes of wartime atrocities alleged to have been committed by Serb forces; soon after the account was published, the newspaper's editor lost both legs in a car bomb attack.[234]

This is not to suggest that, during this period, most Bosnian Serbs acknowledged the full extent of Serb responsibility for wartime atrocities and expressed unequivocal remorse. In late 2006 Matias Hellman, then the ICTY's liaison officer in Sarajevo, told me the prevailing Serb discourse was no longer to deny Serbs committed wartime atrocities but instead to suggest the ICTY was biased against Serbs in its case selection, asking questions such as, "Why haven't you dealt with *this* crime against Serb victims?"[235] During the same period, civil society lawyer Mervan Miraščija described the prevailing discourse of Bosnian Serb leaders this way:

> Serbian politicians like Dodik realize they should talk about war crimes as something that was bad. They will say that people who committed them should be

---

[231] Interview with Edin Hodžić, Director, Public Law Program, Center for Social Research Analitika, in Sarajevo, Bosn. & Herz. (Sept. 11, 2014). Hodžić did not explicitly link this point to the position of Arbour and McDonald.

[232] *Id.* Again, Hodžić did not draw a link to the position of Arbour and McDonald when he spoke these words.

[233] Despite high levels of denialism in Serbia after the collapse of the Milošević regime, Mirko Klarin has observed: "It is quite possible, indeed probable that the situation would be even worse without ICTY trials and judgments." Mirko Klarin, *The Impact of the ICTY Trials on Public Opinion in the Former Yugoslavia*, 7 J. INT'L CRIM. JUST. 89, 93 (2009) [hereinafter Klarin, *Impact of ICTY*].

[234] *See* Rachel Kerr, *The Road from Dayton to Brussels? The International Criminal Tribunal for the Former Yugoslavia and the Politics of War Crimes in Bosnia*, 14 EUR. SECURITY 319, 325 (2005).

[235] Interview with Matias Hellman, then ICTY Liaison Officer, in Sarajevo, Bosn. & Herz. (Nov. 29, 2006).

punished. They insist on individualization, but they won't say there were no crimes. They may add, "But Serbs were also victims." But they realize that it's not profitable to deny. That's a change.[236]

Perhaps no development more dramatically demonstrates progress in official Serb acknowledgment during the early years of the twenty-first century than RS authorities' contrasting characterizations of the Srebrenica massacre in 2002 and 2004. In September 2002, Serb authorities published a report that was a study in distancing, distortion, and denial. Issued more than a year after an ICTY Trial Chamber first ruled the Srebrenica massacre a genocide,[237] the report stunned Federation authorities and citizens, as well as the international community.[238] Noting the RS report contains what it "believes to be serious inaccuracies," the International Commission on Missing Persons condemned the distortion.[239] Then High Representative Paddy Ashdown denounced the report's findings as "so far from the truth as to be almost not worth dignifying with a response. It is tendentious, preposterous, and inflammatory."[240] Even the RS government distanced itself from the report in the face of international outrage.[241]

The next two years saw progress that, in retrospect, now seems remarkable. In July 2003, then RS prime minister Dragan Mikerević attended the annual commemoration of the Srebrenica massacre in Potočari, the first time a senior RS official had done

---

[236] Interview with Mervan Miraščija, Law Program Coordinator, Open Society Fund BiH, in Sarajevo, Bosn. & Herz. (Nov. 29, 2006).

[237] Prosecutor v. Krstić, Case No. IT-98-33-T, Trial Judgment, ¶¶ 599, 560, 653 (Int'l Crim. Trib. for the Former Yugoslavia Aug. 2, 2001).

[238] *Time Magazine* summarized the report's key findings and reactions to it:

> Authorities in the Federation Entity of Bosnia and Herzegovina and the international community have severely condemned a report released by authorities in the Republika Srpska claiming the July 1995 massacre of Bosnian Muslims at Srebrenica never happened. Though it is widely accepted that between 7,000 and 8,000 Bosniak men and boys were massacred by Bosnian Serb forces when they took control of Srebrenica in eastern Bosnia between 11 and 15 July 1995, the report offers a completely different story, blaming deaths on "exhaustion," among other things.
>
> The report—conducted in early September by the Republika Srpska's Government Bureau for Relations with the [ICTY]—claims that no more than 2,000 were killed, and that all were armed soldiers of the Bosnian Army and not civilians. Of those 2,000, the new study says that 1,600 were killed in battle or while attempting escape, and 100 died simply because they were "exhausted." The study also claims that it is possible that fewer than 200 members of the Bosnian Army were killed by members of the Bosnian Serb Army in acts of revenge or because they were not aware of the particulars of the Geneva Convention on prisoners of war.

Anes Alić & Dragan Stanimirović, *Imaginary Massacres?*, TIME MAG. (Sept. 11, 2002). Analysts linked the report's emergence to then-upcoming elections. *See id.*

[239] *Id.*

[240] *Id.* Six months later, Bosnia's Human Rights Chamber issued a decision in a case filed by forty-nine immediate relatives of individuals who disappeared during the Srebrenica massacre. The chamber called on RS authorities to, among other measures, conduct an investigation and publish its results by September 2003. While RS authorities apparently did not respond to this decision, their response to the OHR mandate, described on the next page, came the following year.

[241] RS authorities claimed the report had been compiled by a bureau but had not yet been fully assessed and endorsed by the government. Gordana Katana, *Bosnian Serbs Play Down Srebrenica*, IWPR (Sept. 2–7, 2002).

so.[242] While stopping short of calling the massacre a genocide, Mikerević said recent reports "prove that there was a crime here" that had to be addressed. "One needs to learn from one's mistakes," he said, "and there have been a lot of mistakes in our history. The time has come to talk about everything that happened in this area."[243]

The OHR mandated RS to undertake an investigation that would "establish the full truth" about events relating to the Srebrenica massacre; pursuant to that mandate a commission was established in December 2003.[244] The commission issued its report (which it later supplemented) in June 2004.[245] For the first time, RS authorities themselves compiled data on almost 7,800 victims of the Srebrenica massacre and identified thirty-two previously unknown mass graves.[246] The report also acknowledged Serbs "undertook measures to cover up the crime by moving the bodies" to other sites.[247]

Eleven days after the report was released, then RS president Dragan Čavić appeared on RS television. A member of the party of Radovan Karadžić, Čavić acknowledged the commission's report "undoubtedly establishes that in nine days of July 1995 atrocities were committed in the area of Srebrenica."[248] "The participants in this crime," he said, "cannot justify themselves before anyone and with anything."[249] In words Bosnians would long remember and quote often, Čavić condemned the massacre: "I have to say that these nine days of July of the Srebrenica tragedy represent a black page in the history of the Serb people."[250]

Although Čavić stopped short of offering an apology,[251] the RS government expressed one after reviewing the commission's final report. In a statement released in November 2004, the government said it "shares the pain of the families of the Srebrenica victims, is truly sorry and apologizes for the tragedy."[252] In addition, the

---

[242] *See* Beth Kampschror, *RS Prime Minister Attends Srebrenica Anniversary Ceremony*, SETimes. com (July 14, 2003).

[243] *Id.*

[244] Azra Somun, *Reports on the Transitional Justice Experience in Bosnia and Herzegovina*, 1 Int'l J. Rule L., Transitional Just. & Hum. Rts. 56, 60 (2010).

[245] The final report listed 8,371 names of missing or killed persons. *See* Davide Denti, *Sorry for Srebrenica? Public Apologies and Genocide in the Western Balkans*, in Disputed Memory: Emotions and Memory Politics in Central, Eastern and South-Eastern Europe 79 (Tea Sinbœk Andersen et al. eds., 2016). In April 2004, then High Representative Paddy Ashdown discharged two Bosnian Serb officials for obstructing the work of the commission. *See Bosnian Serbs Admit Srebrenica Massacre*, Agence France-Presse (June 11, 2004).

[246] *See Bosnian Serbs Admit to Srebrenica*, BBC News (June 11, 2004). Of these, twenty-eight were "secondary," meaning they contained bodies originally buried somewhere else. *See* Nicholas Wood, *Bosnian Serbs Admit Responsibility for the Massacre of 7,000*, N.Y. Times (June 12, 2004).

[247] Samir Krilić, *Bosnian Serbs Admit to Massacre*, Wash. Post (June 12, 2004).

[248] *Bosnia Herzegovina: President Dragan Čavić Acknowledges Atrocities Against Muslims in Srebrenica in 1995*, Reuters (June 22, 2004).

[249] *Id.*

[250] *Id.* In the lead-up to the report, Čavić indicated his government would (in the words of the *New York Times*) "begin to redress its hard-line stance" on wartime atrocities by Serbs. Čavić said: "After years of prevarication, we will have to finally face up to ourselves and to the dark side of our past. We must have courage to do that." Nicholas Wood, *Bosnian Serbs Admit Responsibility for the Massacre of 7,000*, N.Y. Times (June 12, 2004).

[251] *Bosnia Herzegovina: President Dragan Čavić Acknowledges Atrocities Against Muslims in Srebrenica in 1995*, *supra* note 248.

[252] *Bosnian Serbs Issue Apology for Massacre*, Associated Press (Nov. 11, 2004).

government said, it was determined to "face the truth about the recent tragic conflict in Bosnia-Herzegovina" and "take decisive steps to force all persons who committed war crimes to face justice."[253] "It was through such gestures," a *New York Times* journalist would later recall, "that the schism running through [Bosnian] society appeared to diminish."[254]

At the time, Čavić's and the RS government's statements seemed a milestone on a linear path toward unequivocal Serb acknowledgment. Instead, they would prove to be the apogee of acknowledgment by a Bosnian Serb leader or RS institution (at least as of this writing).[255] While myriad factors account for later regression, two interrelated developments loomed large in the accounts of Bosnians: the radical transformation of Milorad Dodik beginning in 2006, and the retreat of robust international engagement at approximately the same time.[256]

As elucidated in Chapter 2, the collapse of the SDS government elevated Dodik, leader of the Alliance of Independent Social Democrats (SNSD), to the position of RS prime minister in March 2006, and elections in October 2006 returned him to that position, which he held until November 2010, when he became RS president. Once hailed as a relative moderate,[257] in 2001 Dodik criticized the Serb Democratic Party (SDS) founded by Radovan Karadžić for "organizing and perpetrating" crimes in the 1990s war.[258] At that time, Dodik urged, "One should say openly that crimes had been committed under the SDS leadership and they have to be punished. We can expect all the leading party officials . . . to end up at the Tribunal in The Hague."[259] Just five years later, Dodik relied on "radical rhetoric, playing on Bosnian Serb nationalist emotions and threatening the secession of RS from Bosnia," to win the 2006 poll.[260]

By many accounts, the 2006 election convinced Dodik the rhetoric of extreme nationalism pays handsome dividends at the polls. As Dženana Karup Druško put it, Dodik "realized that it was easier to rule Republika Srpska through manipulation and nationalism" than fidelity to core principles of humanity.[261] That same year Čavić lost his bid for re-election to the position of RS president. Noting Dodik is a "clever person," Aleksandar Trifunović said he could "see what happened to Čavić. And of course he [did the] opposite." In Trifunović's words, the lesson Dodik drew was, "If

---

[253] *Id.* While noting limitations in the RS apology (it did not, for example, use the word *genocide*), Davide Denti writes that "its importance can hardly be overstated: for the first time, a Bosnian Serb official institution recognized the scale of the massacre and the Serb involvement, extending apologies for it." Denti, *supra* note 245, at 79–80.

[254] Scott Anderson, *Life in the Valley of Death*, N.Y. Times Mag. (May 28, 2014).

[255] In the words of Dženana Karup Druško, Čavić's gesture seemed to mark "a window of opportunity in terms of reckoning with the past." But, she lamented, the window "was completely blocked" after that. Interview with Dženana Karup Druško, Director, Transitional Justice, Accountability and Remembrance, in Sarajevo, Bosn. & Herz. (Sept. 3, 2014).

[256] *See also Anderson, supra* note 254.

[257] *See* Christiane Amanpour, *Moderate Bosnian Serb Prime Minister Begins Reforms*, CNN World News (Apr. 19, 1998), http://www.cnn.com/WORLD/europe/9804/19/bosnian.serbs/; Tracy Wilkinson, *In a Twist, Serbs Serve as Model*, L.A. Times (Feb. 1, 1998).

[258] *Dodik: SDS Party Leadership Involved in War Crimes*, Sense News Agency (Dec. 8, 2015).

[259] *Id.*

[260] Srećko Latal, *Milorad Dodik: From Pro-US Moderate to Bosnian-Serb Separatist*, Balkan Insight (Sept. 14, 2016).

[261] Interview with Dženana Karup Druško, Director, Transitional Justice, Accountability and Remembrance, in Sarajevo, Bosn. & Herz. (Sept. 8, 2014).

you want to be popular, don't . . . be like Čavić." Dodik instead resolved to "repeat every day" denialist claims, such as Srebrenica was a "big war crime, but this is not genocide."[262] Emir Suljagić has a somewhat different interpretation, but ends up in the same place as Trifunović. In his account, one of Dodik's advisors in the 2006 election "looked at the [poll numbers] and said 'we need to go hard to the right, that's what the people want to hear.' "[263] In any event, the fateful election marked the beginning of "a downward spiral of political stagnation and mounting nationalist rhetoric."[264] Elected president of RS in 2010 and again in 2014, Dodik has grown increasingly strident and destabilizing.[265]

Even so, Čavić's 2004 remarks were not the last time RS authorities expressed remorse. A moment of truth came in February 2007, when the International Court of Justice (ICJ) ruled that Bosnian Serbs committed genocide in Srebrenica.[266] The ICJ's key legal and factual conclusions relied heavily on the ICTY's judgments, including in particular its conclusion in *Krstić* that Bosnian Serbs committed genocide.[267] Two days after the ICJ judgment was issued, the RS government issued a statement "express[ing] its deepest regret for the crimes committed against non-Serbs during the recent war in Bosnia and condemn[ing] all persons who took part in these crimes."[268] In its stated view, it was "essential that a deepest apology be extended to the victims, their families and friends, regardless of their ethnicity."[269] The government pledged, as well, to bring war criminals to justice.[270]

[262] Interview with Aleksandar Trifunović, Editor, BUKA, in Banja Luka, Bosn. & Herz. (Sept. 15, 2014). Čavić, whom Trifunović interviewed two or more years after his June 2004 speech, stood by his remarks in that interview. As Trifunović recalled, Čavić said: "I absolutely understand that people don't like [what I said], but I think somebody *must* say something about this." *Id.*

[263] Interview with Emir Suljagić, Author, in Sarajevo, Bosn. & Herz. (Sept. 11, 2014).

[264] ADAM MOORE, PEACEBUILDING IN PRACTICE: LOCAL EXPERIENCE IN TWO BOSNIAN TOWNS 160 (2013). *See also* Andrew MacDowall, *Dayton Ain't Going Nowhere*, FOREIGN POL'Y (Dec. 12, 2015) (characterizing the decade since 2006 as a "decade of stasis and rising nationalist rhetoric").

[265] *See* MacDowall, *supra* note 264; Eldar Sarajlić, *Bosnian Elections and Recurring Ethnonationalisms: The Ghost of the Nation State*, 2 J. ETHNOPOLITICS & MINORITY ISSUES EUR. 66, 77 (2010).

[266] Application of the Convention on the Prevention and Punishment of the Crime of Genocide (Bosn. & Herz. *v.* Serb. & Montenegro), 2007 I.C.J. 43, ¶ 297 (Feb. 26).

[267] The ruling came in a case brought by Bosnia against the FRY; thus RS authorities were not respondents. But the ICJ assessed Bosnian Serbs' wartime actions as part of its assessment of Belgrade's legal responsibility for crimes committed in Bosnia. The RS leadership had unsuccessfully tried to have the case discontinued. Between June 1999 and October 2000, in a series of letters sent to the Court, then chairman of the presidency of BiH Živko Radišić—himself a Bosnian Serb—and a co-agent he unilaterally appointed (Svetozar Miletić, another Serb), argued the case should be terminated. The RS National Assembly declared during that period that continuation of the case would be "destructive of a vital interest" of Republika Srpska. During the same period, the Bosniak and Croat members of the tripartite Bosnian presidency informed the Court the case should continue. Finally, on October 10, 2000, the Court concluded there had been no discontinuance of the case by BiH. Application of the Convention on the Prevention and Punishment of the Crime of Genocide (Bosn. & Herz. *v.* Serb. & Montenegro), 2007 I.C.J. 43, ¶ 18-24 (Feb. 26). Controversially, on February 23, 2017, the Bosnian government (or at least the part represented by Bakir Izetbegović) asked the ICJ to revise its previous judgment. The ICJ rejected its application.

[268] Merdijana Sadović, *Bosnian Serbs Now Anxious about ICJ Ruling*, IWPR (Mar. 4, 2007).

[269] *Id.*

[270] *RS Issues Apology to Victims of BiH Conflict*, SETIMES (Mar. 1, 2007).

While its response went farther in expressing regret for Serb atrocities than would have been imaginable ten years earlier, the RS government took care to avoid language of responsibility. As well, it stopped short of using the word *genocide*, as indeed it always had. For his part, Dodik was quick to reject the ICJ's finding of genocide and attributed the Srebrenica killings to rogue elements of the Bosnian Serb army.[271] Accordingly, he said, while individuals must be held accountable, neither Serbs nor government institutions should be held responsible.[272]

The second factor often cited to explain the rise in denialist rhetoric since 2006 is the retreat of activist international engagement in Bosnia before local conditions made this appropriate. As noted in Chapter 2, in the early 2000s, two successive High Representatives spearheaded major progress in state-building and, when needed, used their Bonn powers to foster significant improvements in Bosnia's sociopolitical environment. During this period, Dodik reportedly feared that then High Representative Paddy Ashdown might take action that would undercut Dodik's base of support, and even remove him from a position of power.[273] Notably, it was during this period that Čavić and the government of Republika Srpska apologized for the Srebrenica massacre.[274] More recently, however, Dodik has had ample grounds to believe he can defy international opinion without provoking robust action from the High Representative or other international actors.[275]

To the extent there was progress in Serb acknowledgment during the early 2000s, a key question is whether the ICTY played a part. Aleksandra Letić and others believe it did. Letić recalled that, in the relatively auspicious political context of those years, Serb victims' associations evinced a greater openness to acknowledging the crimes for which Serbs had been convicted in The Hague.[276] Noting Serbs' current antipathy to the ICTY, Letić added:

> The attitudes were a bit different in the beginning of 2000 until 2005. So the readiness of the victims' associations to at least listen to the verdicts, and listen to the representatives of the ICTY on what they have done and how they have worked on these cases, the readiness was bigger among the Serb side.[277]

---

[271] *See* Peter Lippman, *International Court of Justice Finds Serbia Innocent of Genocide, But Not Entirely Clean*, WASH. REP. MIDDLE EAST AFF. 30–31 (May–June 2007), http://www.wrmea.com/archives/May-June_2007/0705030.html.

[272] *See* Dragana Jovanović, *International Court Clears Serbia of Genocide*, ABC NEWS ONLINE (Feb. 26, 2007), http://abcnews.go.com/International/Story?id=2906051&page=1.

[273] Email from Eric Witte, Senior Project Manager, National Trials of Grave Crimes, Open Society Justice Initiative, to Diane Orentlicher (Sept. 24, 2017).

[274] While Čavić apparently was moved by conscience to express regret for Srebrenica, then High Representative Ashdown's forward-leaning policies arguably provided a supportive environment. Ashdown enjoyed a close relationship with Čavić. Kurt Bassuener, A Durable Oligarchy: Bosnia and Herzegovina's False Postwar Democratic Transition 27 (unpublished draft) (on file with author).

[275] *See* Chapters 2 and 9.

[276] Notably, then, it was during this period that the ICTY rendered its trial and appeals judgments in *Krstić*, in which the Tribunal first ruled that genocide was committed in Srebrenica. As noted later, several sources said they believe the *Krstić* judgment had a palpable impact on Serb acknowledgment.

[277] Author's interview with Aleksandra Letić, Secretary-General, Helsinki Committee for Human Rights in Republika Srpska, in Sarajevo, Bosn. & Herz. (Sept. 8, 2014).

In earlier research interviews, before Dodik routinely espoused ultranationalist rhetoric, other sources credited the Tribunal with reducing denialism in elite discourses. For example Damir Arnaut, a senior legal advisor to the Bosniak member of the BiH presidency when I interviewed him in 2009, was convinced the ICTY's genocide determination in *Krstić* (by then confirmed on appeal[278]) had a significant impact in this regard. Recognizing the persistence of Serb denialism, Arnaut nonetheless believed *Krstić* changed the dynamic between members of Bosnia's major ethnic groups. While it had been common in 1998–1999 for Serbs to deny there was a genocide in Srebrenica, Arnaut said, now "there is no denial that genocide happened."[279] On the level of daily interactions between Bosniak officials like himself and their Serb counterparts, Arnaut continued, "it helps that there are judicial findings. . . . When you talk about other issues, this elephant isn't in the room" anymore.[280]

Like Arnaut, Ivan Lovrenović thought the *Krstić* judgment had a palpable impact on how Serb politicians spoke about Srebrenica. When I interviewed him in July 2009, Lovrenović attributed their rhetorical change to the *Krstić* ruling's "reminder" that the international community knew what happened and would not allow the issue to fade into obscurity. And yet, Lovrenović continued, "that's when [Serb politicians] intensively started working on discovering victims on their side." Where they had previously been "completely quiet even about their own victims," after *Krstić* they were trying "to equalize [by saying] that Serbs were victims the same as others."[281]

Not long after my interviews with Arnaut and Lovrenović, Dodik's rhetoric of denial intensified. In September 2009, Dodik questioned "well established facts"[282] concerning Serb responsibility for wartime massacres of civilians in Tuzla and Sarajevo, accusing the Bosnian army of staging the attacks to provoke NATO action against Serb forces.[283] The ICTY, as well as the Court of Bosnia and Herzegovina, had by then determined Bosnian Serb forces carried out these attacks.[284] Noting the 1995 Serb

---

[278] Prosecutor v. Krstić, Case No. IT-98-33-A, Appeal Judgment, ¶¶ 21, 23 (Int'l Crim. Trib. for the Former Yugoslavia Apr. 19, 2004).

[279] There were, of course, exceptions. Dodik was at pains to deny the word *genocide* applied to Srebrenica following the ICJ's 2007 judgment.

[280] Interview with Damir Arnaut, then Advisor for Legal and Constitutional Affairs, Cabinet of Haris Silajdžić, in Sarajevo, Bosn. & Herz. (July 16, 2009). In a similar vein, during interviews in December 2006, other Bosnians said the ICTY's work had curbed Serb denial. For example, while recognizing there was not yet a consensus among Bosnia's ethnic groups about "what happened," Sinan Alić was convinced the situation would be far worse "if there were no ICTY" and that it had already "made it harder to deny abuses." Interview with Sinan Alić, then Director, Truth, Justice, and Reconciliation, in Tuzla, Bosn. & Herz. (Dec. 5, 2006).

[281] Interview with Ivan Lovrenović, then Editor-in-Chief, Dani, in Sarajevo, Bosn. & Herz. (July 17, 2009).

[282] Rachel Irwin, *Bosnian Serbs Block Srebrenica Massacre Resolution*, IWPR (Apr. 12, 2010) (quoting Bogdan Ivanišević).

[283] *See* Daria Sito-Sučić, *Bosnian Serb Leader Faces Charges over Massacre Denial*, REUTERS (Sept. 24, 2009); *Envoy Slams Bosnian Serb Leader for Massacre Denial*, AGENCE FRANCE-PRESSE (Sept. 16, 2009); Rachel Irwin, *Bosnian Serbs Block Srebrenica Massacre Resolution*, IWPR (Apr. 12, 2010), https://iwpr.net/global-voices/bosnian-serbs-block-srebrenica-massacre-resolution. This brand of denial is strikingly similar to the narrative Bosnian wartime leader Radovan Karadžić was advancing at roughly the same time during his trial before the ICTY. *See* Marlise Simons, *Indicted Ex-leader of Bosnian Serbs Calls Atrocities "Myths"*, N.Y. TIMES (Mar. 3, 2010).

[284] At the time of Dodik's comment, Bosnian Serb Army commander Novak Đukić had recently been convicted in the Bosnian court of charges stemming from the Tuzla massacre. *See* Daria

mortar attack in Tuzla "was the biggest tragedy in the history" of the town, its mayor denounced the "arrogant and unbelievably cruel statement" of Dodik.[285] In a joint statement, High Representative Valentin Inzko and other diplomats condemned Dodik's statement, saying: "Any attempt to change the established historical record of war crimes is unacceptable and inexcusable."[286]

The following year, Bosnian Serb legislators blocked a declaration that would have condemned the Srebrenica massacre. Their opposition was particularly striking at that moment, as Serbia's parliament had adopted a similar declaration (albeit by a narrow margin and after contentious debate) a week earlier.[287] Ironically, the Bosnian Serbs' stance left Bosnia, the site of Srebrenica, "the only country in the region not to have passed . . . a resolution" condemning the massacre.[288] In successive years, Bosnian Serbs blocked similar resolutions.[289] When they signaled they would do so again on the twentieth anniversary of the genocide, Srebrenica survivor Munira Subašić said what many survivors felt: "Each year we are offended by those who deny the crime. If they are against this resolution then they are proud of the genocide and the criminals."[290]

Dodik and other RS leaders have not merely failed to acknowledge the full scope of the tragedy in Srebrenica. They have aggressively *denied* it, and even celebrated Hague suspects charged with genocide:

- In July 2010, one day after 50,000 people gathered in Potočari in solemn remembrance of the Srebrenica massacre on its fifteenth anniversary, Dodik sent a different message: "Republika Srpska does not deny that a large scale crime occurred in Srebrenica, but by definition it was not genocide as described by the international court in The Hague." Instead, he said: "If a genocide happened then it was committed against Serb people of this region, where women, children and the elderly were killed en masse."[291] Dodik has made similar remarks on other occasions.[292]

Sito-Sučić, *Bosnian Serb Leader Faces Charges over Massacre Denial*, REUTERS (Sept. 24, 2009). The events in Sarajevo challenged by Dodik had already been adjudicated in the ICTY trials of Stanislav Galić and Dragomir Milošević. Prosecutor v. Galić, Case No. IT-98-29-T, Trial Judgment, ¶¶ 582–594 (Int'l Crim. Trib. for the Former Yugoslavia Dec. 5, 2003); Prosecutor v. Milošević, Case No. IT-98-29/1-T, Trial Judgment, ¶¶ 254–267 (Int'l Crim. Trib. for the Former Yugoslavia Dec. 12, 2007).

[285] Daria Sito-Sučić, *Bosnian Serb Leader Faces Charges over Massacre Denial*, REUTERS (Sept. 24, 2009).

[286] *Id.*

[287] Serbia's declaration is discussed in Chapter 7.

[288] Rachel Irwin, *Bosnian Serbs Block Srebrenica Massacre Resolution*, IWPR (Apr. 12, 2010).

[289] *See Srebrenica Genocide Resolution Expected to Fail*, BALKAN TRANSITIONAL JUST. (May 22, 2015).

[290] *Id.*

[291] Scott Anderson, *Life in the Valley of Death*, N.Y. TIMES MAG. (May 28, 2014); *Srebrenica Massacre "Not Genocide"*, SYDNEY MORNING HERALD (July 13, 2010).

[292] A news report about Dodik's visit to Srebrenica in April 2015 implies he made somewhat milder remarks then. While saying "It is true that a crime happened here and I am sorry for all the victims," he also said the massacres had been "politicized." Denis Džidić, *War Crimes: Why "Sorry" Is Never Enough*, BALKAN TRANSITIONAL JUST. (May 22, 2015). In July 2016, the OHR rebuked Dodik for declaring that "genocide never took place in Srebrenica and he would never recognize it as such." OHR, *Dodik's Civilizational Darkness* (July 12, 2016).

- In June 2015, Dodik called the Srebrenica massacre "the greatest deception of the 20th century."[293] *Reuters* characterized this remark as "the strongest yet by Dodik casting doubt on what happened" in Srebrenica.[294]
- In March 2016, days before the ICTY was scheduled to hand down its trial verdict in the case against Radovan Karadžić, Dodik dedicated a student dormitory in Republika Srpska to the wartime leader. Making clear the timing was anything but accidental, Dodik hailed the honoree as "a man who is without doubt one of the founders of the Republika Srpska."[295] Again, the appeal of Dodik's message to Bosnian Serbs should not be confused with the motivation behind it. The ceremony "was seen as an important part of Dodik's campaign to rally Bosnian Serb opinion . . . ahead of local elections" slated for October.[296]
- A few months later, as many solemnly marked the twenty-first anniversary of Srebrenica, Dodik accused Bosniaks of "manipulating the number of victims, starting with the false story about 8,700 dead."[297] Condemning the 2004 RS study as "an imposed report" that RS authorities were forced to "accept under pressure," Dodik called for a new commission to determine "the truth" about Srebrenica.[298] Regardless of what such a body determined, Dodik vowed Republika Srpska would "never recognize genocide in Srebrenica because it did not happen."[299]
- When the ICTY issued its November 2017 trial verdict convicting Ratko Mladić of genocide and other charges, Dodik hailed Mladić as a "true hero and patriot."[300]

---

[293] *Bosnian Serb Leader: Srebrenica Was 20th Century's "Greatest Deception,"* REUTERS (June 25, 2015).

[294] *Id.*

[295] Daria Sito-Sučić, *Bosnian Serbs Honor Karadžić Ahead of the U.N.'s Genocide Verdict,* WASH. POST (Mar. 21, 2016). Dodik described the timing of the dedication as "strongly symbolic," indicating it had been chosen to counter the impending verdict in a trial that was "humiliating for the Serb Republic." *Id.*

[296] Rodolfo Toe & Srećko Latal, *Bosnian Serb Chief Plays Nationalist Card in Elections,* BALKAN TRANSITIONAL JUST. (Mar. 21, 2016). Dodik reportedly "already opened the same dormitory ahead of elections" two years earlier, though it "had remained unfinished." *Id.*

[297] *Srebrenica Genocide Resolution Expected to Fail,* BALKAN TRANSITIONAL JUST. (May 22, 2015).

[298] *Dodik: There Was No Genocide in Srebrenica,* TANJUG (July 11, 2016).

[299] *Id.* Dodik has also vowed RS students would never use textbooks from the Federation "in which it is written that the Serbs committed genocide and held Sarajevo under siege. It's not true and it will not be studied." Danijel Kovačević, *Bosnian Serbs to Ban Lessons on Srebrenica Genocide,* BALKAN TRANSITIONAL JUST. (June 6, 2017). Although Dodik is the most visible RS leader, other Bosnian Serb politicians espouse similar positions. *See, e.g., Srebrenica Mayor Disagrees That Genocide Happened There,* RTV B92 NEWS (Apr. 13, 2017).

[300] *Dodik: Mladić Is a "True Hero and Patriot,"* RFE/RL (Nov. 22, 2017). Dodik offered more measured comments when Mladić was arrested in 2011, saying: "I hope Mladić will have a fair trial in The Hague . . . The institutions of Republika Srpska have never supported or defended anyone who has committed war crimes, whatever their ethnic or religious background." Merdijana Sadović & John MacLeod, *Top War Crimes Suspect Mladić Faces Extradition,* IWPR (May 26, 2011).

In the words of Emir Hodžić, Bosnians are "just flabbergasted" at international in-dulgence of Dodik. Given how "destructive" and "obviously dangerous" he is, Hodžić said Bosnians wonder, "Why is nobody doing anything about this guy?"[301]

B. Acknowledgment by Leaders of Other Ethnic Groups

It would be a perverse distortion to suggest Bosniak leaders bear a burden to acknowl-edge crimes equivalent to those committed by Serbs. Even so, during my first set of re-search interviews in late 2006, several sources noted with concern that Bosniak leaders were slow to condemn war crimes for which Bosniaks were found guilty in The Hague (although wartime Bosniak leader Alija Izetbegović expressed regret for war crimes committed by Bosniaks against Croats and Serbs in May 2000[302]). Many cited Bosniak officials' then recent treatment of Naser Orić, who commanded Bosnian forces in Srebrenica during the war, to illustrate the point. As previously noted, at the time of these interviews Orić had recently been convicted of failing to prevent war crimes against Serbs by soldiers under his command, and was sentenced to serve two years in prison.[303] Since he had already spent three years in detention, Orić was released imme-diately after his trial verdict. When he returned to Bosnia, he was welcomed as a hero. The Bosniak chairman of the Bosnian presidency, Sulejman Tihić, publicly welcomed the trial verdict—a *conviction* on war crimes charges—as a vindication: "Now it can clearly be seen who was defending unarmed civilians and who was committing crimes," Tihić said.[304] As Sevima Sali-Terzić noted, Bosniak citizens followed Tihić's lead: "People celebrated Orić here, they didn't understand he was guilty of anything." Sali-Terzić continued: "As long as someone found guilty of war crimes is celebrated as a hero something is terribly wrong, with politicians and with the people."[305]

Subsequent years saw some progress, though it is not clear whether or to what extent the ICTY contributed to this. When Serbia's parliament adopted a declara-tion condemning the Srebrenica massacre in 2010, Tihić urged Bosnia's parliament to adopt a resolution apologizing for crimes against Serb and Croat victims. But the timing, he concluded, was not auspicious. As noted earlier, during this same period Bosnian Serb legislators blocked a parliamentary declaration condemning the Srebrenica genocide against Bosniaks. Accordingly, Tihić concluded, it was "not realistic at this time to condemn crimes against Serbs, since parliament has not yet taken care of the issue of a declaration on Srebrenica, as a prerequisite for any other kind of declaration."[306]

---

[301] Interview with Emir Hodžić, Jer Me Se Tiče, in Sarajevo, Bosn. & Herz. (Sept. 13, 2014). As previously noted, the Peace Implementation Council (PIC), comprising Western countries that oversee the OHR, has mostly been unwilling in recent years to authorize robust action by the High Representative. The incumbent, Valentin Inzko, has been able to do little more than con-demn denialist statements by Dodik and other RS leaders throughout his tenure.

[302] *See Balkans: When Is It Time to Apologize?*, RFE/RL (Dec. 5, 2003).

[303] Prosecutor v. Orić, Case No. IT-03-68-T, Trial Judgment (Int'l Crim. Trib. for the Former Yugoslavia June 30, 2006). Orić was later acquitted on appeal. Prosecutor v. Orić, Case No. IT-03-68-A, Appeal Judgment (Int'l Crim. Trib. for the Former Yugoslavia July 3, 2008).

[304] *Bosnian Muslim Leader Hails Hague Verdict on Orić*, BBC WORLDWIDE MONITORING (June 30, 2006) (from FoNet News Agency, Belgrade).

[305] Interview with Sevima Sali-Terzić, Senior Legal Counsel, Constitutional Court of BiH, in Sarajevo, Bosn. & Herz. (Nov. 30, 2006).

[306] Ian Bancroft, *The Dynamics of Apology and Forgiveness in the Balkans*, RFE/RL (Apr. 27, 2010).

Later that year, however, Bakir Izetbegović, then newly-elected as the Bosniak member of the three-person presidency, expressed an apology during an interview for "every innocent person killed by the [Bosnian Army]."[307] Tellingly, his remarks were immediately attacked by several Bosniak victims' associations and others, who viewed them as equalizing the crimes of all ethnic groups.[308]

In June 2016 Izetbegović paid respect to Serb victims killed in Sarajevo by Bosniak soldiers, who had dumped the victims' corpses into the Kazani ravine,[309] saying: "I should have come here earlier to make my condolences." Stating "these things should not happen anymore to anybody," Izetbegović expressed the hope that his gesture would "encourage other people to take similar steps."[310] Miladin Vidaković, who heads an association of Sarajevo Serbs, described Izetbegović's visit to Kazani as a "major contribution to reconciliation, peace and tolerance."[311]

Regrettably, episodic progress in acknowledgment has increasingly been overwhelmed by intensifying nationalism. As Refik Hodžić wrote in 2016, "Militant extremism is on the rise in all ethnic groups, actively fanned by hate speech in the media and on social networks."[312]

Turning to Croat leaders, former Croatian presidents Stjepan Mesić and Ivo Josipović have offered a number of apologies for their country's role in 1990s violence.[313] Yet, despite Bosnian Croat wartime leaders' close affiliation with their Croatian patrons, Bosnian Croat political leaders have, at this writing, apparently still not followed suit.[314]

---

[307] See *Chronology of Presidential Apologies for War Crimes in Former Yugoslavia*, DALJE (Apr. 25, 2013), http://arhiva.dalje.com/en-world/chronology-of-presidential-apologies-for-warcrimes-in-formeryugoslavia/465325; *Izetbegović: All Sides Committed Crimes*, website of Esmir Milavić (Nov. 4, 2010), https://esmirmilavic.wordpress.com/2010/11/04/izetbegovic-all-sides-committed-crimes/. The latter source describes Izetbegović's remarks as the "first time that [a] Bosniak politician issued an apology to [the] Serbian side in Bosnia and Herzegovina" (though as previously noted, Alija Izetbegović expressed regret for war crimes committed by Bosniaks in May 2000). Bakir Izetbegović's November 2010 apology may have been prompted by an imminent exchange of apologies by the presidents of Serbia and Croatia. See Denti, *supra* note 245, at 84.

[308] See *Izetbegović: All Sides Committed Crimes*, *supra* note 307.

[309] See Rusmir Smajilhodžić, *Sarajevo's Uncounted and Forgotten Serb Victims*, AGENCE FRANCE-PRESSE (July 9, 2016).

[310] Srđan Kureljusić, *Izetbegović Paid Respect to People Killed at Kazani*, JUST. REP. (June 13, 2016). In another report, Izetbegović's remarks are translated somewhat differently: "It's a personal gesture. I've felt I had to do this for a while. I hope it will inspire others to do something similar." Smajilhodžić, *supra* note 309.

[311] Smajilhodžić, *supra* note 309.

[312] Hodžić, *Post-Karadžić*, *supra* note 108.

[313] As described in Chapter 7, during a 2003 visit to Belgrade Mesić apologized for Croatian war crimes after then president of SaM Svetozar Marović offered an apology for war crimes committed by the FRY. During his presidency, Josipović offered a number of apologies to Croatia's neighbors. See *Chronology of Presidential Apologies for War Crimes in Former Yugoslavia*, DALJE (Apr. 25, 2013), http://arhiva.dalje.com/en-world/chronology-of-presidential-apologies-for-warcrimes-in-formeryugoslavia/465325).

[314] I have been unable to identify any apologies by Bosnian Croat leaders, and sources in Bosnia confirmed for me that there had not been any as of September 2017. In the words of one of them, "None of the Bosnian Croat political leaders have publicly accepted or apologized for the crimes committed by the Croatian military and Croats in general in Bosnia and Herzegovina." Email from Mervan Miraščija, Law Program Coordinator, Open Society Fund BiH, to Diane Orentlicher (Sept. 18, 2017).

IV. COMMUNICATING WITH REGIONAL COMMUNITIES

It was always that problem of communication with the audience, with the public. Like here, you know. That was one of the biggest mistakes ICTY had in the entire history.

—NIDŽARA AHMETAŠEVIĆ [315]

In the view of Aleksandar Trifunović, pernicious manifestations of denial mean the Outreach Programme of the Hague Tribunal "didn't explain" adequately the nature and meaning of its work.[316] Trifunović's critique, shared by many Bosnians and others,[317] raises a host of questions. Among them: Is it reasonable to suppose well-conceived and adequately funded outreach efforts by a distant court could overcome entrenched denial in local communities—or at least make a meaningful difference? Is it even the job of an ICT to concern itself with ensuring its judicial work is meaningfully "understood" by citizens?[318] As a foundation for addressing these questions in the specific context of the ICTY and Bosnia, it will be helpful briefly to describe the Tribunal's evolving approach toward communicating with local audiences.

A. A Remote Court

During its early years, the ICTY made scant effort to communicate with citizens of former Yugoslav countries, and did not even translate its press releases into local languages until 1999. With a few exceptions, moreover, during its early years the Tribunal excluded local citizens from working at the Tribunal. In consequence, the "remoteness of the Hague Tribunal from Bosnia and Herzegovina was a *big* one,"[319] said Branko Todorović, who before he retired played a leading role in educating Serbs "and all others in this country" about the ICTY.

To be sure, during the first two-and-a-half years of the Tribunal's life travel to Bosnia was profoundly constrained by ongoing conflict. But the Tribunal's reticence

---

[315] Interview with Nidžara Ahmetašević, Journalist, in Sarajevo, Bosn. & Herz. (Sept. 12, 2014).

[316] Trifunović believes nothing more starkly demonstrates the irreconcilability of facts established in The Hague and Bosnian beliefs than celebrations organized for Hague convicts when they return home after serving their sentences. In his view, that gap shows the ICTY "didn't explain" itself adequately. But Trifunović does not blame Outreach Programme personnel. Instead, he said, the effort did not have sufficient funding or capacity to organize public discussions in Bosnia comparable to robust programs on transitional justice in post-apartheid South Africa. Interview with Aleksandar Trifunović, Editor, BUKA, in Banja Luka, Bosn. & Herz. (Sept. 15, 2014).

[317] *See, e.g.*, Laurel E. Fletcher & Harvey M. Weinstein, *A World Unto Itself? The Application of International Justice in the Former Yugoslavia, in* MY NEIGHBOR, MY ENEMY: JUSTICE AND COMMUNITY IN THE AFTERMATH OF MASS ATROCITY 29, 40 (Eric Stover & Harvey M. Weinstein eds., 2004); Janine Clark, *Why the ICTY Has Not Contributed to Reconciliation in the Former Yugoslavia*, OSSERVATORIO BALCANI E CAUCASO (Feb. 20, 2013).

[318] For a thoughtful effort to theorize the case for ICT outreach, see Marlies Glasius, *Between "Autistic" Courts and Mob Justice: Theorizing the Call for More "Democratic" International Justice*, 27 MACALESTER INT'L, Article 5, http://digitalcommons.macalester.edu/cgi/viewcontent.cgi?article=1489&context=macintl.

[319] Interview with Branko Todorović, then President, Helsinki Committee for Human Rights in Republika Srpska, in Bijeljina, Bosn. & Herz. (Dec. 5, 2006).

was above all a function of professional culture, reinforced by funding constraints.[320] Recalling his early visits to The Hague, Todorović described the prevailing view of judges this way: "Why do we need to show those people in the Balkans what we are doing, to prove ourselves? What we are doing is right." When trials are finished, "we will have the verdicts. What the reflections of those verdicts will be [in the region] are not our interest. We don't want to be biased."[321] In this setting, Todorović said, "the reflections that were here in Bosnia and Herzegovina were only the ones that could have passed through the manipulations of the media bosses, the politicians here."[322]

By 1998, the ICTY's then president, Gabrielle Kirk McDonald, and then Prosecutor, Louise Arbour, became acutely aware the Tribunal was "absolutely misunderstood" in former Yugoslav states. Anton Nikiforov, who joined the Prosecutor's staff in 1998, recalled that local officials "were knowingly misrepresenting the Tribunal," yet the court had "no capacity to work in the region [and] no capacity to speak in the regional language."[323] Convinced this was undermining its work, Judge McDonald launched the ICTY's Outreach Programme, which became operational in October 1999.[324]

That denialist narratives intensified some years after this program was launched squarely raises the question whether an ICT's outreach efforts *can* significantly counter denialism. As we have seen, local politicians are well placed to subvert information that counters their own discourses, and have done so long after the Tribunal launched its Outreach Programme.[325] For these and other reasons explored in Chapter 7 and here, it would be naïve to suppose outreach efforts can dispel the appeal of elite nationalist discourses.[326] A more significant question is whether they might make a meaningful difference—and how.

---

[320] The ICTY's Outreach Programme has always been extra-budgetary, meaning special funds had to be raised to support its work. The European Union has funded its work.

[321] Interview with Branko Todorović, then President, Helsinki Committee for Human Rights in Republika Srpska, in Bijeljina, Bosn. & Herz. (Dec. 5, 2006). Todorović's characterization has been widely echoed by others, including former ICTY personnel and scholars. *See, e.g.,* Victor Peskin, *Courting Rwanda: The Promises and Pitfalls of the ICTR Outreach Programme,* 3 J. INT'L CRIM. JUST. 950, 953 (2005) (The notion of engagement with former Yugoslavia communities reportedly "did not sit well with some Tribunal officials, who did not regard community outreach or public relations as the responsibility of a court").

[322] Interview with Branko Todorović, then President, Helsinki Committee for Human Rights in Republika Srpska, in Bijeljina, Bosn. & Herz. (Dec. 5, 2006). "In control of all the media," Todorović added, "the criminal political structures" in Republika Srpska were "able to have an immense effect on people's opinions" about the ICTY. *Id.*

[323] Interview with Anton Nikiforov, then Special Advisor for Political Affairs to then Prosecutor Carla del Ponte, in The Hague, Neth. (Mar. 5, 2007). *See also* Anton Nikiforov, *The Need for Outreach, in* OUTREACH: 15 YEARS OF OUTREACH AT THE ICTY 60 (2016).

[324] *See* Lal C. Vohrah & Jon Cina, *The Outreach Programme, in* ESSAYS ON ICTY PROCEDURE AND EVIDENCE IN HONOUR OF GABRIELLE KIRK MCDONALD 554 (Richard May et al eds., 2000); Judge Gabrielle Kirk McDonald, *Introductory Remarks, in* OUTREACH: 15 YEARS OF OUTREACH AT THE ICTY (2016).

[325] More generally, myriad studies confirm that being exposed to information at odds with established beliefs does not necessarily persuade people to believe what they hear. Sometimes, exposure to such information has a "backfire effect," hardening established beliefs. *See* Chapter 7.

[326] *See* Matias Hellman, *Challenges and Limitations of Outreach, in* CONTESTED JUSTICE: THE POLITICS AND PRACTICE OF INTERNATIONAL CRIMINAL COURT INTERVENTIONS 251, 252 (Christian de Vos et al. eds., 2015).

One possibility is that *timely* well-targeted communications can reduce the influence of claims at odds with an ICT's general work or specific rulings by, for example, persuading at least some citizens to question those claims.[327] A key takeaway of social science research concerning belief-formation is that it is considerably more difficult to change entrenched beliefs than to shape new ones.[328] Accordingly, scholars who have studied belief perseverance emphasize the importance of correcting errors "as quickly as possible."[329] While it is challenging in any context to reverse the effects of misinformation, "rapid corrections" are among the best antidotes.[330] At the very least then, Todorović's intuition—that an aggressive outreach program would have been especially effective if launched early—is plausible.

In larger perspective, however challenging it is to counter the effects of denialist discourses, neglecting even to provide accessible information about the Tribunal is an inexcusable lapse in transparency as well as self-defeating, ceding the ground to those determined to distort the ICTY's work. Conversely, once the Tribunal made information more accessible to former Yugoslav residents (by, for example, including local language information on its website), those who were motivated to learn more could do so readily. The downstream effects are, of course, unknowable but could be significant: I have asked relatively young Serb activists how they developed their views about accountability, which were strikingly at odds with dominant discourses in the communities in which they were raised. Typically they responded that, as they began to wonder what really happened during the 1990s conflicts, they went to the ICTY's website to see what they could learn.[331] Thus, while skeptics have grounds to question whether ICTY outreach efforts can make a significant impact on denialism, effective communication can at least help empower local advocates pressing for acknowledgment. And, as the work of several political scientists suggests, one of the principal vehicles through which an ICT can promote social change is by mobilizing local advocacy networks.[332]

---

[327] Espousing such a view in a 2009 publication, Mirko Klarin argued the Tribunal should "at least . . . do all it could to make it more difficult for the local elites to distort and manipulate its message." Klarin, *Impact of ICTY, supra* note 233, at 96.

[328] *See* Chapter 7.

[329] Brendan Nyhan & Jason Reifler, *Countering Misinformation: Tips for Journalists*, COLUMBIA JOURNALISM REV. (Feb. 29, 2012).

[330] *Id.*

[331] The Tribunal's website now has significantly more non-judicial information than during its early years, and its Outreach Programme has produced documentaries designed to provide "insight into some of the ICTY's most significant cases" as well as its "contributions to international law." These have "been seen by hundreds of thousands of people"—infinitely more than the number who have read Hague judgments. *Documentary Production, in* OUTREACH: 15 YEARS OF OUTREACH AT THE ICTY 53 (2016). Other aspects of the Tribunal's expanded communications efforts are summarized in Janine Natalya Clark, *International War Crimes Tribunals and the Challenge of Outreach*, 9 INT'L CRIM. L. REV. 99, 101–02 (2009).

[332] *See* Leslie Vinjamuri, *Deterrence, Democracy, and the Pursuit of International Justice*, 24 ETHICS IN INT'L AFF. 191, 197 (2010). Beth Simmons has developed this argument in a related context. Claiming adherence to human rights treaties can improve a country's human rights record, Simmons argues that this results, in part, from the popular mobilizing effect of a state's treaty commitments. BETH A. SIMMONS, MOBILIZING FOR HUMAN RIGHTS: INTERNATIONAL LAW IN DOMESTIC SETTINGS 15, 135–55 (2009).

B. Bridging the Gap

A program implemented in 2004–2005, Bridging the Gap, was the most robust outreach initiative undertaken by the ICTY. As such, it provides a window into what an effective outreach program can accomplish, as well as the outer limits to its impact—or, at least, of an extremely finite program's impact. Under the program, once a case reached a final conclusion, ICTY officials and staff traveled to the town where adjudicated crimes occurred and met with local citizens and officials to explain how they investigated the crimes, describe the outcome of cases, and respond to questions. Bridging the Gap events were organized in Prijedor, Brčko, Konjic, Foča, and Srebrenica.[333] According to Branko Todorović, who organized these events in partnership with the ICTY, local authorities in three target towns were "strictly against" the programs.[334] Yet the turnout was larger than expected in all five locations. Todorović explained public interest this way: "Simply there is an authentic feeling among people to see what The Hague is doing."[335]

Todorović is convinced that, at least for a while, "seeing what the Hague is doing" had a palpable impact.[336] Local citizens, whose knowledge of the ICTY had long been filtered by political leaders and ethnic media, were finally "able to see the factual truth, not the political truth."[337] Todorović cited an example from Brčko, where it had long been rumored among the Bosniak community that Serbs burned the bodies of Bosniak victims in ovens normally used to cremate animals. An ICTY police investigator explained that Tribunal investigators had looked into this report and described how they were able definitely to establish that Serbs had not burned humans in the *Kafilerija*, the facility where this was rumored to have happened. Todorović believes that if the Tribunal expert had not persuasively put this rumor to rest, "it would always cause hate" in Brčko. Instead, "the book on that was closed."[338]

I heard similar accounts of this episode from Sead Golić, whom I interviewed in Brčko in July 2009,[339] and former ICTY Deputy Prosecutor David Tolbert, who participated in the Brčko program. Johanna Mannergren Selimović describes a very different dynamic at Bridging the Gap events in Srebrenica and Konjic, however. In

---

[333] *See* ICTY, http://www.icty.org/en/outreach/bridging-the-gap-with-local-communities (last visited Dec. 8, 2017). Other programs in which ICTY officials met with Bosnians took place sooner. When we spoke in 2006, Todorović, who helped organize meetings between ICTY officials and local lawyers over several years, said these meetings helped transform an essentially hostile relationship into something closer to a partnership. Interview with Branko Todorović, then President, Helsinki Committee for Human Rights in Republika Srpska, in Bijeljina, Bosn. & Herz. (Dec. 5, 2006).

[334] Todorović told me had to come up with funds for electricity and bathroom doors in the cultural center in Srebrenica because the local mayor doubted the need for such a program. Heating was too expensive, however, "so [the program] was held in a very cold room." Local authorities in Foča and in Konjic refused to support the program, while authorities in Brčko District, which is more ethnically diverse than the other towns, were supportive and cooperative.

[335] Interview with Branko Todorović, then President, Helsinki Committee for Human Rights in Republika Srpska, in Bijeljina, Bosn. & Herz. (Dec. 5, 2006).

[336] *Id.*

[337] *Id.*

[338] *Id.*

[339] Interview with Sead Golić, Association of the Families of Missing, Forcibly Detained and Murdered Bosniaks of Bosnia and Herzegovina, in Brčko, Bosn. & Herz. (July 22, 2009).

her account, both events "became fora for denial in the form of shouts and laughter from the audience when information was presented."[340]

Mannergren Selimović did not attend the Bridging the Gap program in Foča, but Todorović's account of that event contrasts starkly with her description of events in Srebrenica and Konjic.[341] When people gathered for the program in Foča (whose authorities, like those of Srebrenica and Konjic, opposed the program), the air was thick with tension. Todorović described what happened after ICTY participants presented a videotape about their work on war crimes committed in Foča:

> All present could see on a screen the guy who did the raping in Foča. And all of them could hear and see how the prosecutor was asking him, "Did you rape that little girl?" And he said, "Yes, I did." "And you were very well aware at that moment that she was only 12 years old?" And he said, "Yes." At that time he was probably 45 years old. And then the prosecutor repeated his question, saying "You knew that she was 12 at the most, and what else did you tell her?" He told her, "you know I would do many more terrible things to you but I shall not because I have at home a daughter" who is her age, "so I won't." So the prosecutor confirmed, "It's true you have a daughter at home?"
>
> I was in the back rows and there were like 140 people there and [when the technical people changed the tapes] I closed my eyes and you wouldn't believe it, for a moment there was such a silence . . . that you can hear. It's a horrible silence. And it lasted for [a] long [time]. . . . And for me it was the most important moment of the day. Then we had a lunch break, and you could see the change. Now the people . . . are leaving the room, looking down, some were commenting, "You know, we really didn't know this, it is a horrible crime."

Todorović did not expect many residents to return after the lunch break. They did, and remained until the end of the program. Todorović "really think[s] that they left a bit different."[342] Nerma Jelačić had a similar perception, saying "people were genuinely shocked."[343] Todorović believes the events were especially valuable because they countered a dominant theme in nationalist discourses: they helped people understand ICTY defendants from their communities "weren't convicted because they were Bosniak, Serb, or Croat, but because they committed crimes."[344]

---

[340] Mannergren Selimović, *supra* note 139, at 57.

[341] While the differences in their respective accounts might be partly attributable to different experiences in the events each described, it is of course also possible that Todorović's appraisal is partly a function of motivated reasoning, whose impact on beliefs is explored in Chapter 7.

[342] Interview with Branko Todorović, then President, Helsinki Committee for Human Rights in Republika Srpska, in Bijeljina, Bosn. & Herz. (Dec. 5, 2006).

[343] Interview with Nerma Jelačić, then Director, BIRN in BiH, in Sarajevo, Bosn. & Herz. (Dec. 1, 2006). These accounts are striking not least because, when thirteen survivors of wartime rape in Foča returned there to place a plaque commemorating their experience just over a month before the Bridging the Gap program, they were taunted by local residents, who prevented them from mounting the plaque. These women's experience is chronicled in the film *I Came to Testify*, part of a five-part series on Women, War & Peace broadcast on PBS, http://www.pbs.org/wnet/women-war-and-peace/full-episodes/i-came-to-testify/ (last visited Dec. 8, 2017)

[344] Interview with Branko Todorović, then President, Helsinki Committee for Human Rights in Republika Srpska, in Sarajevo, Bosn. & Herz. (July 14, 2009).

It is worth pausing to consider an intriguing, and in some respects challenging, perspective offered by Todorović. In his account of Bridging the Gap events, when faced with compelling evidence of their neighbors' depredations "ordinary people" were able "to make a distance" between themselves and the war criminals found guilty by the ICTY, and to condemn the latter's acts. Todorović recognized some would fault the premise of these citizens' distancing—in his words, that the criminal conduct addressed in the events "has nothing to do with me."[345] After all, this form of self-deception negates the morally compelling claim that, in the aftermath of mass atrocity, "those who participated . . . *by acquiescence* cannot escape their moral responsibility for the violence that shredded the fabric of community."[346]

And yet, Todorović said, if you insist all Serbs are guilty, "you don't give them a chance to change. And if you push a man to the wall, what can he do but say 'yes, yes, I am the same, so what?' "[347] In short, he seemed to suggest, if one's overriding goal is to persuade a critical mass of Serbs who lived through the war to acknowledge and condemn wartime atrocities committed by other Serbs, it might be strategically prudent to abide some measure of self-deception about bystanders' silent complicity.[348]

Recent research suggests there may be other pathways to the same result (that is, lowering psychological barriers to acknowledgment of wrongdoing by members of one's in-group). A study conducted in Bosnia found that bolstering Serb participants' self-esteem in ways *unrelated* to "the past" increased their propensity to acknowledge Serbs' responsibility for victimizing others. This and related studies "demonstrate[ed] that

---

[345] Interview with Branko Todorović, then President, Helsinki Committee for Human Rights in Republika Srpska, in Bijeljina, Bosn. & Herz. (Dec. 5, 2006). Indeed, a common critique of German citizens' contemporaneous reactions to the Nuremberg prosecution of major Nazi war criminals is that they effectively scapegoated the defendants, absolving themselves of responsibility for Nazi policies. *See* Chapter 11.

[346] Laurel E. Fletcher & Harvey M. Weinstein, *Violence and Social Repair: Rethinking the Contribution of Justice to Reconciliation*, 24 HUM. RTS. Q. 573, 626 (2002) [hereinafter Fletcher & Weinstein, *Violence and Social Repair*]. Fletcher and Weinstein argue for education programs that "address the question of community shame." *Id.* This suggestion follows from their critique of initiatives that focus single-mindedly on prosecutions. Because trials focus on individual perpetrators, they obscure "the ways in which bystanders are implicated in the establishment and maintenance of societal structures that facilitate the onset and implementation of mass violence." *Id.* at 580.

[347] Interview with Branko Todorović, then President, Helsinki Committee for Human Rights in Republika Srpska, in Bijeljina, Bosn. & Herz. (Dec. 5, 2006). Jelena Obradović-Wochnik makes a similar point in the context of Serbia. She argues that local NGO strategies for "facing the past" require participants to "speak within set boundaries." Obradović-Wochnik believes those boundaries, which "are usually centred on the singular issue of admitting that 'Serbs' committed war crimes," prevent many Serbians from publicly expressing their complex knowledge of Serb atrocities. Jelena Obradović-Wochnik, *The "Silent Dilemma" of Transitional Justice: Silencing and Coming to Terms with the Past in Serbia*, 7 INT'L J. TRANSITIONAL JUST. 328, 340–41 (2013).

[348] Alyssa Rosenberg made a somewhat similar point in a different context. When the actor Mahershala Ali accepted an award for his performance in *Moonlight*, a movie about a young, gay African American, he spoke about his mother's acceptance of his conversion to Islam at a time when anti-Muslim rhetoric was on the rise in the United States. Rosenberg reflected: "Ali's speech drew a connection between anti-gay sentiment and suspicion of Islam without straining the comparison. That created space for audiences to step back and apply now-familiar opposition to bullying to a new subject, and encouraged listeners to consider that all suspicions of difference might spring from the same well. Ali was able to portray his mother's lack of enthusiasm for his conversion as something she was glad she had overcome without labeling her a bigot." Alyssa Rosenberg, Opinion, *Oscars and the Art of Political Speech*, WASH. POST (Feb. 26, 2017).

self-affirmation can reduce defensiveness about the misdeeds of one's group even when they involve the most extreme forms of victimization including . . . genocidal acts."[349]

To the extent Bridging the Gap programs advanced acknowledgment in the short term, its impact was limited by its finite scope. Due to funding constraints, Bridging the Gap programming ended after five events in 2004–2005. Had the program continued, events would have been convened only in towns that had not yet been the site of such programs;[350] the Tribunal did not plan to return to towns where events had already been organized. Yet the effects of an occasional program, however compelling, can all too easily be eroded by daily discourses of denial. Refik Hodžić, who played a leading role designing the program, noted in 2009 that local residents who had attended Bridging the Gap events had, in the years since, continuously been "exposed to other rhetoric."[351] "Disappointingly," as well, subsequent programs organized by local NGOs "did not manage to gather a multi-ethnic audience as representatives of each group decided to ignore events organized by NGOs regarded as associated with the other group."[352]

C. Reaching Youth

Almir Alić believes educating Bosnian youth "offers *the* greatest potential" for changing the trajectory of denialism; whatever views they may have about the war are more susceptible to change than those of their parents (conversely, youth are especially vulnerable to pernicious influences[353]). As the ICTY's liaison officer based in Sarajevo, Alić worked tirelessly to educate young Bosnians, traveling across the country to speak to students.[354] Describing a three-year project that enabled him to visit almost fifty schools, Alić saw encouraging results. "The impact of that project was visible after one presentation. . . . You can see that [students'] perception of ICTY, of justice, has changed. Those kids are *ready* to think out of [the] box. The problem is nobody offers them this kind of presentation."[355]

---

[349] Čehajić-Clancy, *Ingroup Committed Atrocities, supra* note 111, at 109.

[350] Specifically, the Outreach Programme would have organized Bridging the Gap events in Travnik, Višegrad, Banja Luka, and Sarajevo. Interview with Almir Alić, Liaison Officer, ICTY Registry, in Sarajevo, Bosn. & Herz. (Sept. 12, 2014).

[351] Interview with Refik Hodžić, then Liaison Officer, ICTY, in Sarajevo, Bosn. & Herz. (July 13, 2009). The day before we spoke, a nationalist group had disrupted the annual commemoration of the Srebrenica massacre, "chanting insults" against the Muslim survivors. *Controversial Group in Srebrenica Incident*, RTV B92 News (July 13, 2009). More generally, as I have noted, the years following Bridging the Gap events saw a surge in nationalist rhetoric.

[352] Hodžić, *Living the Legacy supra* note 152, at 127.

[353] *See* Jusuf Žiga et al., Youth Study: Bosnia and Herzegovina 13 (2015). There are several reasons young audiences may be especially receptive to outreach efforts. Among them, as we have seen, it is easier to shape views than change them once they are entrenched. In addition, for those born after the war, information about wartime atrocities does not raise troubling questions about their *own* responsibility, though of course it may raise difficult questions about their parents' wartime conduct.

[354] In light of Bosnia's complex administrative system, Alić had to secure eleven different clearances at different levels before he could even approach a school principal. Each approval was relevant for a single canton only. Interview with Almir Alić, Liaison Officer, Registry, ICTY, in Sarajevo, Bosn. & Herz. (Sept. 12, 2014).

[355] *Id.* As Alić noted, a number of Bosnian NGOs, including the Helsinki Committee for Human Rights in Republika Srpska and the Youth Initiative for Human Rights, now focus on educating

Yet innovative and committed officers like Alić never received the support they would need to have an enduring influence on large numbers of students. More than twenty years after the ICTY was created, with crises in other countries claiming their attention, donors had grown reluctant to sustain even the modest support they provided the Outreach Programme in years past.[356]

D. Communicate What?

Beyond the effects of finite resources, ICTY outreach officers have long been institutionally constrained in their ability to address questions foremost in the minds of local communities. When a complex or controversial judgment is rendered, they are not authorized to explain it, even if they thought they could do so. "The whole institution," Alić explained, "is very strict about the statements because of all this sensitivity, and possibility of manipulation, polarization and everything"[357]—the very conditions the Outreach Programme was designed to counter. The individuals best placed to answer questions about recent judgments are, of course, the judges themselves. As Alić noted, however, "there is this notion . . . that judges should not comment" on judgments . . . . If you want to know more about [the] judgment, you should read it." Yet "people do not read [ICTY] judgments. Nobody."[358]

ICTY judges' reticence is hardly surprising. In most if not all of their native countries, the judiciary's apparent absence from general public discourses is integral to its image as impartial and objective.[359] Yet as I have argued elsewhere, in democratic societies domestic courts engage in a continuous dialogue with citizens as well as other public institutions, which in myriad ways helps sustain their legitimacy.[360] This is not to suggest ICTY judges should engage in wide-ranging forms of social debate—far from it. The point instead is that an effective communications strategy may be uniquely important for an ICT, whose judges do not naturally engage in the kind of ongoing, multilayered dialogue with local citizens that grounds the legitimacy of domestic courts. As an institution detached from local governance, the ICTY is particularly susceptible to misunderstanding.

What, then, should Tribunal personnel—whether judges or outreach officers—communicate? Two former liaison officers, Refik Hodžić and Matias Hellman, believe

---

youth. ICTY outreach officers trained Helsinki Committee activists to make similar school presentations going forward.

[356] *Id.*; interview with Nenad Golčevski, Chief of Outreach, ICTY, and Giorgia Tortora, Chief of Communications, MICT, in The Hague, Neth. (May 28, 2015).

[357] Interview with Almir Alić, Liaison Officer, Registry, ICTY, in Sarajevo, Bosn. & Herz. (Sept. 12, 2014).

[358] *Id.* Edin Hodžić characterizes the Tribunal's approach as "some kind of liberal approach of justice—just deliver justice, and we are here to accept" it. Interview with Edin Hodžić, Director, Public Law Program, Center for Social Research Analitika, in Sarajevo, Bosn. & Herz. (Sept. 11, 2014). In addition to questions about controversial judgments, local citizens often have questions about prosecutorial decisions about whom to prosecute and how. Here, too, outreach officers are constrained in what they can say, as they do not represent the ICTY prosecutor. On the challenges this presents, *see* Hellman, *supra* note 326, at 262.

[359] As Marlies Glasius notes, it is "not taken for granted" that domestic courts have a responsibility "to explain themselves to affected communities." Glasius, *supra* note 318, at 4.

[360] Diane F. Orentlicher, *Whose Justice? Reconciling Universal Jurisdiction with Democratic Principles*, 92 Geo. L.J. 1057, 1093–96 (2004).

it crucially important to answer questions foremost in the minds of the "people of the former Yugoslavia."[361] In their eyes, Hodžić notes, "critical questions" include:

> Why were certain people indicted and others not? What was the philosophy of [the] Tribunal's so-called sentencing policy? How was it possible to quash 1,300-page trial judgments with several pages of an appeal judgment? Why were defendants allowed to get rich by splitting Tribunal-provided fees with their lawyers?[362]

Hellman writes that "failing to engage in substantive discussion on a question that the audience considers important is one of the surest ways to alienate them, and to reduce one's own legitimacy as a court representative."[363] Conversely, certain types of information can go a long way toward alleviating victims' frustrations. As noted in Chapter 6, for example, Mirsad Duratović, who was highly critical of plea agreements, suggested his perspective would change if he knew the details of defendants' cooperation: "It would mean a lot, by all means, yes, if we knew that the defendant's cooperation [with the Prosecutor] led to mass graves or the conviction of others who were even more responsible."[364]

One of the most valuable functions of outreach transcends its contribution to knowledge. The very presence of liaison officers in-country sends a message—that the Tribunal recognizes the central importance of local communities to its project of justice. Against a widespread perception among Bosnians that the Tribunal never adequately recognized survivors as its primary constituency,[365] the presence and engagement of liaison officers serves as a partial corrective.

The ICTY's most effective outreach officers, in Serbia as well as Bosnia, partnered with local NGOs committed to advancing accountability. The importance of this engagement should not be underestimated. If ICTs can never "produce transformative and restorative societal effects" simply through their judicial work,[366] they can bolster domestic advocacy efforts crucial to social transformation. Finally, a fundamental and necessary role of the communications efforts of an ICT is managing expectations—in Hellman's words, promoting "a realistic understanding of [its] mandate."[367]

V. A FOUNDATION FOR FUTURE ACKNOWLEDGMENT?

If we are one day ready to embark on the road of genuine reconciliation based on truth and accountability for the atrocities committed during the Nineties,

---

[361] Refik Hodžić, *Accepting a Difficult Truth: ICTY Is Not Our Court*, BALKAN TRANSITIONAL JUST. (Mar. 6, 2013).

[362] *Id.*

[363] Hellman, *supra* note 326, at 262 n.30.

[364] Interview with Mirsad Duratović in Prijedor, Bosn. & Herz. (Dec. 8, 2006).

[365] *See* Refik Hodžić, *A Long Road Yet to Reconciliation: The Impact of the ICTY on Reconciliation and Victims' Perceptions of Criminal Justice*, in ASSESSING THE LEGACY OF THE ICTY 115, 117 (Richard H. Steinberg ed., 2011).

[366] Hellman, *supra* note 326, at 252.

[367] *Id.* at 270.

the ICTY's work will be our starting point. . . . Just imagine where we start from
if the ICTY had never existed.

—Refik Hodžić[368]

As he launched a national truth commission in 1989, Chile's first post-dictatorship president, Patricio Alwyn, espoused a claim that would soon become sacred canon in the field of transitional justice:

> To close our eyes to what has happened and to ignore it as if it was nothing will infinitely prolong a long-lasting source of pain, division, hate and violence at the heart of our society. Only enlightenment of the truth and a search for justice creates the moral climate indispensable to reconciliation and peace.[369]

Several years later, then U.S. ambassador Madeleine Albright expressed similar faith in the ICTY's capacity to "cleanse the ethnic and religious hatreds and begin the healing process" by rendering the truth.[370] Before long, South Africa's Truth and Reconciliation Commission distilled the new creed in a popular rhyme, "revealing is healing."[371]

Transitional justice theorists and practitioners would soon eschew such facile claims.[372] But it took many Bosnians longer to relinquish the hope that a judicially-authenticated record would dispel denial about wartime atrocities and restore civility and trust.[373] After all, many projected nearly magical powers onto the Hague Tribunal. In Nidžara Ahmetasević's words, "many people here, maybe even I . . . , expected that the Tribunal will erase all the suffering and the pain, and everything bad."[374] Edin Hodžić made much the same point: "We thought here in Bosnia . . . that the judicial paradigm would do everything, would do the job of dealing with the past—that some good things will emerge from the trials on their own, and trials will have a positive impact on other activities." But, Hodžić added, "I don't think that, you know, that was proven in subsequent years."[375]

Many Bosnians who once hoped "the judicial paradigm would . . . do the job of dealing with the past" have revised their expectations without forsaking the Tribunal. In their view, the ICTY established a precious legacy through its meticulous

[368] Refik Hodžić, *Why the ICTY Has Contributed to Reconciliation in the Former Yugoslavia*, Osservatorio Balcani e Caucaso (Feb. 20, 2013).

[369] Hazan, *supra* note 210, at 37–38.

[370] Provisional Verbatim Record, U.N. SCOR, 3,217th mtg., at 12 UN Doc. S/PV.3217 (May 25, 1993).

[371] Hazan, *supra* note 210, at 37.

[372] See, *e.g.*, Teitel, *supra* note 7, ch. 3. Michael Ignatieff published an early and prescient critique of the notion captured in the South African commission's slogan. Ignatieff, *supra* note 8. More recently, David Rieff has argued that in some circumstances, collective remembrance can hinder rather than advance social repair. David Rieff, In Praise of Forgetting: Historical Memory and Its Ironies (2016).

[373] Some, like Edin Ramulić, told me they always thought it wrong to expect the ICTY to "lead to . . . overall general acceptance of truth" among Bosnians. In his view, the job of courts is to prosecute; reckoning with war crimes is the work of "this society." Interview with Edin Ramulić, Project Coordinator, Izvor, in Prijedor, Bosn. & Herz. (Sept. 16, 2014).

[374] Interview with Nidžara Ahmetasević, Journalist, in Sarajevo, Bosn. & Herz. (Sept. 12, 2014).

[375] Interview with Edin Hodžić, Director, Public Law Program, Center for Social Research Analitika, in Sarajevo, Bosn. & Herz. (Sept. 11, 2014).

accumulation of evidence. When I interviewed Emir Suljagić in 2014, he began to say he was now resigned "to knowing [the ICTY] has failed . . . in achieving what it set out to achieve." But he quickly corrected himself, saying: "It didn't fail . . . in everything. In fact, . . . there's a mountain of facts that's been established, you know. It is now a starting point for anything to do with [the] former Yugoslavia, for anything to do with the '90s." And "that's good in and of itself."[376]

Others are convinced the ICTY's findings will, more than the discourses of any contemporary politician, write the history of wartime atrocities. In Dženana Karup Druško's words: "Neither Dodik nor [Serbian leader Aleksandar] Vučić, their statements won't be the ones that are written down in history. It actually will be the statements of the ICTY judgments. The role of the ICTY is invaluable, just priceless. I don't even want to think about what would have happened if the ICTY had not been established."[377] While pained by the persistence of denialism, Nusreta Sivac expressed a similar faith in the Tribunal's long-term impact: "We have to bear in mind in all those verdicts, all those convictions and sentences, they write the history of this country, regardless of the fact that this history is being written in The Netherlands."[378] Noting Bosnian Serbs now "negate" the ICTY, Emir Hodžić, too, believes the Tribunal "will go into a history book."[379]

In the meantime, when Hodžić and his colleagues encounter denialism, they are grateful they can invoke the judgments of an "independent body, that is . . . officially recognized by the international community," which has proved certain facts "beyond all doubt."[380] As Hodžić explained, "We use it to say, 'this is what happened' as a sort of fact, just plain facts."[381]

At the time we spoke, however, the ICTY had become a less stable resource since November 2012, when it began to render controversial verdicts, such as the Appeals Chamber's acquittal of Ante Gotovina.[382] Earlier in the Tribunal's life, when Ahmetašević encountered denial or doubt about wartime atrocities, she would react much the same way Hodžić described: "I could always . . . say, 'OK, there is the ICTY, and they . . . established . . . the facts.'" But, she said, "now I can't after what happened with Gotovina and Stanišić" and other high-profile suspects acquitted in The Hague.

---

[376] Interview with Emir Suljagić, Author, in Sarajevo, Bosn. & Herz. (Sept. 11, 2014). Suljagić made a similar point in a 2009 interview. At first, he said the ICTY had failed to achieve the main goals it set for itself—countering impunity and promoting reconciliation. But when asked if, in light of this, it was a mistake to establish the ICTY, Suljagić (like virtually everyone I interviewed) responded adamantly, "No, no!," and explained that, because of its work there are "adjudicated facts that we can call upon, and that we can point to, that we can try and learn from and build upon which would not have been there had it not been for the Tribunal." In his view, this alone "justified its existence." Interview with Emir Suljagić, then Advisor to the Mayor, in Sarajevo, Bosn. & Herz. (July 14, 2009).

[377] Interview with Dženana Karup Druško, Director, Transitional Justice, Accountability and Remembrance, in Sarajevo, Bosn. & Herz. (Sept. 8, 2014).

[378] Interview with Nusreta Sivac, Former Judge, in Prijedor, Bosn. & Herz. (Sept. 16, 2014).

[379] Interview with Emir Hodžić, Jer Me Se Tiče, in Sarajevo, Bosn. & Herz. (Sept. 13, 2014). Jasna Bakšić Muftić believes that, in the future when the "whole situation in the region [is] relaxed," there will be "no room for the manipulation" of facts established by a "really . . . independent court." Interview with Jasna Bakšić Muftić, Professor, Faculty of Law, University of Sarajevo, in Sarajevo, Bosn. & Herz. (Sept. 17, 2014).

[380] Interview with Emir Hodžić, Jer Me Se Tiče, in Sarajevo, Bosn. & Herz. (Sept. 13, 2014).

[381] Id.

[382] These judgments are described in Chapter 6.

"Because somebody will just tell me . . . about Gotovina. And what to do with that?" Ahmetašević hoped Bosnians might "find a way . . . to deal with these new findings by the ICTY in the future." For now, she lamented, "they took away from me something that I really needed."[383] (Later rulings, described earlier, revived faith in the Tribunal.[384])

Ahmetašević's disappointment in then recent rulings hardly diminished her commitment to working on "issues of . . . facing the past."[385] Instead, she explained, rather than hope the ICTY would somehow foster acknowledgment, "we realized we have to do it by ourselves."[386] Ahmetašević, Hodžić, Zorić, Ramulić, and others are foot soldiers in a new era of grassroots activism that does not rely on the Tribunal to do the work of social change, even as some stand on the factual foundation it has built. The activists do not know where their efforts will take them. For now, in Zorić's words, they are "focused on starting the debate, the public debate, social debate, whatever, . . . on some level that is not emotional."[387]

Emblematic of their efforts is an initiative Hodžić pioneered, White Armband Day. The name evokes a baneful edict issued by Bosnian Serbs as they prepared to ethnically cleanse Prijedor. On May 31, 1992, Serb nationalists ordered non-Serbs in Prijedor to mark their homes with white cloths and wear white armbands when they went out.[388] Twenty years later, Hodžić, Ramulić, Zorić, and four others wore white armbands as they stood in silent remembrance in a public square in Prijedor. The following years, more people joined the annual gathering. At the commemoration in May 2015, Zoran Vučkovac, a Bosnian Serb, was among those who gathered; his remarks epitomized the reaction the organizers hoped to elicit from local Serbs. Speaking in the public square, Vučkovac, who was five years old in 1992, recalled that "one hundred and two children were killed in this city" and said: "They are the litmus test of our humanity."[389]

---

[383] Interview with Nidžara Ahmetašević, Journalist, in Sarajevo, Bosn. & Herz. (Sept. 12, 2014). Although Emir Hodžić said he still relied on the ICTY's factual findings, he worried that its controversial rulings might be turned against him. More specifically, he expressed concern that when he cites an ICTY ruling, someone will counter, "Is that the same court that was discredited due to that ruling, and this, and this, and this, and all those controversies?" Interview with Emir Hodžić, Jer Me Se Tiče, in Sarajevo, Bosn. & Herz. (Sept. 13, 2014).

[384] As previously noted, for example, the May 2013 acquittal of Jovica Stanišić and his codefendant, Franko Simatović was overturned by the ICTY Appeals Chamber. This happened in December 2015, after my interview with Ahmetašević. The Tribunal's November 2017 conviction of Ratko Mladić was a milestone, as well, for many Bosnians.

[385] Interview with Nidžara Ahmetašević, Journalist, in Sarajevo, Bosn. & Herz. (Sept. 12, 2014).

[386] Id.

[387] Interview with Goran Zorić, Executive Director, KVART, in Sarajevo, Bosn. & Herz. (Sept. 17, 2014). The activism I describe here is hardly the first manifestation of grassroots initiatives in Bosnia. As Lara Nettlefield and Sarah Wagner have chronicled, initiatives such as the annual pilgrimage to Srebrenica-Potočari have been crucial components of Bosnian responses to wartime atrocities. NETTLEFIELD & WAGNER, *supra* note 175, at 2–3.

[388] *See* Nidžara Ahmetašević, *Bosnia's Unending War*, NEW YORKER (Nov. 4, 2015); Sead Numanović, *Interview with Refik Hodžić: Karadžić's Ideas Can Defeat Humanity and Vision, Not by the Cult of Victims*, DNEVNI AVAZ (May 28, 2017), http://www.avaz.ba/clanak/294791/refik-hodzic-karadziceve-ideje-mogu-se-poraziti-ljudskoscu-i-vizijom-a-ne-kultom-zrtve.

[389] Ahmetašević, *supra* note 388.

None of these activists suggested their turn to grassroots efforts was inspired by the insights of transitional justice professionals (much the opposite). But their approach accords with the insights of a maturing field. Transitional justice scholars have increasingly recognized and critiqued the field's previous marginalization of civil society[390] and, more generally, of local needs and priorities.[391] At times, the "historically dominant" paradigm of transitional justice "resulted in a 'top-down' approach," of which creating an ICT is a prime example, that downplayed "participatory approach[es] . . . from the grassroots."[392]

In larger perspective, transitional justice experts have long recognized that the field's early preoccupation with criminal prosecutions obscured the need for comprehensive approaches to a legacy of grievous harms.[393] Extending this insight to the role of an ICT, the UN Special Rapporteur on transitional justice has noted such tribunals "work best in conjunction with a variety of other measures, including local initiatives more attentive to social integration and reconstruction and the needs and wishes of those more directly affected by violence."[394] Yet for many years, the ICTY was essentially the only mechanism on offer to address Bosnia's legacy of mass atrocities, detracting attention and energy from other dimensions of social repair. While born in part from disappointed expectations, Bosnia's new generation of grassroots activism reflects a thicker understanding of what it takes to transform a society emerging from mass violence to one in which respect for human dignity is habitual.[395]

---

[390] *See, e.g.,* David Taylor, *The Objectives and Experiences of International Justice at the Grassroots, in* FACING THE PAST: AMENDING HISTORICAL INJUSTICES THROUGH INSTRUMENTS OF TRANSITIONAL JUSTICE 139 (Peter Malcontent ed., 2016); David Backer, *Civil Society and Transitional Justice: Possibilities, Patterns and Prospects,* 2 J. HUM. RTS 297 (2003); Dustin N. Sharp, *Interrogating the Peripheries: The Preoccupations of Fourth Generation Transitional Justice,* 26 HARV. HUM. RTS J. 149 (2013). International relations scholars have long recognized "the important role of individuals and advocacy groups" in generating political momentum for transitional justice programs. Kathryn Sikkink & Hun Joon Kim, *The Justice Cascade: The Origins and Effectiveness of Prosecutions of Human Rights Violations,* 9 ANN. REV. L. SOC. SCI. 269, 277 (2013).

[391] *See, e.g.,* Laurel E. Fletcher et al., *Context, Timing and the Dynamics of Transitional Justice: A Historical Perspective,* 31 HUM. RTS. Q. 163, 210 (2009).

[392] Sharp, *supra* note 390, at 149–50. Transitional justice scholars have more recently foregrounded the key role of civil society initiatives not only at the national level, but locally. *See, e.g.,* Laura J. Arriaza & Naomi Roht-Arriaza, *Weaving a Braid of Histories: Local Post-Armed Conflict Initiatives in Guatemala, in* LOCALIZING TRANSITIONAL JUSTICE: INTERVENTIONS AND PRIORITIES AFTER MASS VIOLENCE 205 (Rosalind Shaw et al. eds., 2010).

[393] *See, e.g.,* Fletcher & Weinstein, *Violence and Social Repair, supra* note 346. On the need for a comprehensive approach, see Diane Orentlicher, *Independent Study on Best Practices, Including Recommendations, to Assist States in Strengthening Their Domestic Capacity to Combat All Aspects of Impunity,* 2 & ¶ 10, U.N. Doc. E/CN.4/2004/88 (Feb. 27, 2004).

[394] Pablo de Greiff, *Report of the Special Rapporteur on the Promotion of Truth, Justice, Reparation and Guarantees of Non-recurrence,* 8 n.8, U.N. Doc. A/HRC/21/46 (Aug. 9, 2012) (citing approvingly an overarching theme in MY NEIGHBOR, MY ENEMY: JUSTICE AND COMMUNITY IN THE AFTERMATH OF MASS ATROCITY (Eric Stover & Harvey M. Weinstein eds., 2004)).

[395] Summarizing his own "lessons learned," Prijedor native Refik Hodžić has written that, if Bosnia is to avoid returning to conflict, it is not necessary to abandon the pursuit of justice for war crimes. What must end, however, is "the dominance of criminal justice as the preferred cure for our broken society." In its place, "collective energy needs to be directed to other means of dismantling" the legacy of ethnic cleansing. Refik Hodžić, *Post-Karadžić, supra* note 108.

PART FIVE

Catalyzing Domestic Prosecutions

9

War Crimes Prosecutions
in Bosnia-Herzegovina

The Hague Tribunal opened the door for national courts to start trials of war criminals . . . This is one of the major achievements of the ICTY.

—Gojko Berić[1]

The vast financial and human resources required by the ICTY diverted the discussion and funding away from building a domestic war crimes capacity in Bosnia.

—Fidelma Donlon[2]

Expressing support for the draft resolution that would formally create the Hague Tribunal, Japan's representative to the UN Security Council acknowledged the need for urgent action. But in a gentle rebuke he suggested, "Perhaps more extensive legal studies could have been undertaken" on various issues, such as "measures to establish a bridge with domestic legal systems."[3] It would take several more years for the Council to address this question in a substantial fashion. Ultimately, the Tribunal would play a key role, along with the Office of the High Representative (OHR)[4] and other actors, in preparing Bosnia to prosecute wartime atrocities. (As the next chapter explores, the ICTY also played a crucial yet quite distinct role catalyzing war

---

[1] Interview with Gojko Berić, Journalist & Columnist, Oslobođenje, in Sarajevo, Bosn. & Herz. (July 17, 2009).
[2] Fidelma Donlon, *Rule of Law: From the International Criminal Tribunal for the Former Yugoslavia to the War Crimes Chamber of Bosnia and Herzegovina*, in Deconstructing the Reconstruction: Human Rights and Rule of Law in Postwar Bosnia and Herzegovina 255, 269 (Dina Francesca Haynes ed., 2008).
[3] U.N. SCOR, 3217 mtg, Maruyama, S/PV.3217 (May 25 1993).
[4] As explained in Chapter 2, the OHR oversees implementation of the Dayton Peace Agreement and operates under the supervision of the Peace Implementation Council (PIC).

crimes trials in Serbia.) This marked a sea change in the ICTY's mission. When the Tribunal was created and for much of its first decade, its officials were more likely to worry about than encourage prosecutions in the Western Balkans.

The institutions that emerged from the Tribunal's transformed mandate, incorporating international actors for a transitional period, are often cited as models for other post-conflict countries, and with good reason.[5] Even so, the Bosnian experience is hardly an unqualified success. Bosnia's perennial dysfunctions have at times hobbled its war crimes institutions, and gains in this sphere have seen periodic setbacks. In this setting, it would be nonsensical to ask whether the ICTY helped launch flawless institutions. This chapter instead explores specific ways in which the Tribunal bolstered Bosnian capacity to render justice for wartime atrocities, highlighting practices worth emulating as well as those that could be improved upon in the practice of other international tribunals.

I. THE ICTY'S EVOLVING RELATIONSHIP WITH BOSNIAN COURTS

A. Primacy

It is now widely accepted that domestic prosecutions for human rights violations are preferable to international trials,[6] provided they can be safely and fairly conducted. Ideally, though not always in practice, victims and other citizens are significantly more likely to *experience* justice rendered by local courts, in their own language and legal tradition, than that dispensed by a distant court.[7] Effective domestic prosecutions can, moreover, help anchor the rule of law in countries that have endured lawless violence, while restoring citizens' trust in their own government. Welcoming the launch of Bosnia's then new war crimes chamber in March 2005, then ICTY president Theodor Meron evoked these and other values:

> [S]uccessfully prosecuting war crimes in Bosnia and Herzegovina is an essential component to showing that justice is being served, promoting reconciliation among Bosnia and Herzegovina's communities, and bringing closure to the families of the victims of the war. I have always felt that war crimes trials

---

[5] *See, e.g.,* Param-Preet Singh, Human Rights Watch, Justice for Atrocity Crimes: Lessons of International Support for Trials Before the State Court of Bosnia and Herzegovina 1 (2012) [hereinafter Justice for Atrocity Crimes]; Human Rights Watch, Soldiers Who Rape, Commanders Who Condone 53–54 (2009); Donlon, *supra* note 2, at 283.

[6] For a summary of literature espousing this view, see Claire Garbett, *Transitional Justice and "National Ownership": An Assessment of the Institutional Development of the War Crimes Chamber of Bosnia and Herzegovina*, 13 Hum. Rts. Rev. 65, 70–71 (2012). This preference is embedded in the statute of the permanent International Criminal Court, which allows the Court to exercise jurisdiction only when a state with jurisdiction is unable or unwilling genuinely to investigate or prosecute atrocity crimes. *See* Rome Statute of the International Criminal Court, art. 17, July 17, 1998, U.N.T.S. 90 (corrected by procès-verbaux of November 10, 1998, July 12, 1999, November 30, 1999, May 8, 2000, January 17, 2001, and January 16, 2002) [hereinafter Rome Statute].

[7] While this is theoretically the case, national war crimes courts can also work in relative obscurity unless they have a robust communications strategy. Six years after Bosnia's war crimes chamber was launched, a survey found that 93 percent of Bosnian participants could not name a war crimes trial conducted by a court in the former Yugoslavia. *See* Garbett, *supra* note 6, at 78.

conducted close to the scene of the crime, and to the families of the victims, have the highest resonance and the greatest impact for reconciliation and deterrence.[8]

Yet ICTY officials did not always espouse this view, nor did the Security Council task the Tribunal to strengthen domestic prosecutions, even as a secondary mandate. In the vernacular of international law, the Tribunal was given "primacy" over national courts: while maintaining concurrent jurisdiction over wartime atrocities, national courts had to defer to the ICTY if it decided to assert jurisdiction in a case.[9] To be sure, in principle the Tribunal's primacy need not have excluded Bosnian courts as partners in the project of rendering justice for wartime atrocities. In his report to the Security Council proposing the Statute of the ICTY, then UN Secretary-General Boutros Boutros-Ghali affirmed the role of national courts: "In establishing [the ICTY], it was not the intention of the Security Council to preclude or prevent the exercise of jurisdiction by national courts with respect to such acts. Indeed national courts should be encouraged to exercise their jurisdiction in accordance with their relevant national laws and procedures."[10] The first ICTY president, the late Italian jurist Antonio Cassese, made much the same point in the Tribunal's first annual report to the UN Security Council and General Assembly, stating the ICTY "does not monopolize criminal jurisdiction over certain categories of offences committed in the former Yugoslavia."[11]

But if Cassese seemed to invite states to exercise jurisdiction, his message was more likely directed to West European countries than former Yugoslav states. Noting "the huge number of potential cases and the fact that *many defendants may find themselves in countries whose authorities are willing and prepared to bring them to justice,*" Cassese said: "it was felt it would be salutary if national courts exercised their jurisdiction under their own legislation or on the strength of the 1949 Geneva Conventions,"[12] which call upon parties to prosecute grave breaches of those conventions even when committed elsewhere if they do not extradite the

---

[8] Theodor Meron, President of the ICTY, Statement Delivered at the Inauguration of the War Crimes Chamber of the State Court of Bosnia and Herzegovina (Mar. 9, 2005). The passage preceding the quoted text implies the ICTY and international community had been committed from the outset to strengthening Bosnia's domestic capacity:

Indeed, from the beginning of its involvement, the international community has sought to increase the capacity of the judicial institutions of Bosnia and Herzegovina to allow those domestic institutions to play a crucial role in the effective and fair prosecution of war criminals consistent with internationally recognized standards of due process and the rule of law.

Id. As explained later, however, the engagement Judge Meron describes came about only when the ICTY began to fashion its completion strategy.

[9] *See* Updated Statute of the International Criminal Tribunal for the Former Yugoslavia, art. 9, Sept. 2009.

[10] U.N. Secretary-General, *Report of the Secretary-General Pursuant to Paragraph 2 of Security Council Resolution 808*, ¶ 64, U.N. Doc. S/255704 (May 3, 1993).

[11] ICTY President, *Report of the International Tribunal for the Prosecution of Persons Responsible for Serious Violations of International Humanitarian Law Committed in the Territory of the Former Yugoslavia Since 1991*, ¶ 20, U.N. Doc. A/49/342-S/1994/1007 (Aug. 29, 1994).

[12] *Id.* ¶ 87 (emphasis added). Two months after this report's publication date, the ICTY Prosecutor filed a deferral request in relation to a Bosnian Serb suspect, Dušan Tadić, against whom German prosecutors had already begun a criminal proceeding. As noted in Chapter 2, Tadić was the first defendant over whom the Tribunal gained custody.

perpetrators for trial in another country.[13] Cassese would later explain the need for primacy in terms that emphasized concerns about the quality of justice in former Yugoslav states:

> In the case of the former Yugoslavia, the ongoing armed conflict [at the time the ICTY was established] and the deep-seated animosity between the various ethnic and religious groups made it unlikely that national courts would be willing or able to conduct fair trials. It was considered that the authorities would have hesitated to bring their own people (Muslims, Croats, and Serbs) to book, whereas, had they initiated proceedings against their adversaries, probably such proceedings would have been highly biased.[14]

In larger perspective, if courts in former Yugoslav countries could in principle prosecute wartime atrocities, states that led efforts to create the ICTY considered it "the principal purveyor of justice over these crimes."[15]

For good reason, courts in Bosnia and other former Yugoslav states were not seen as credible partners during the ICTY's early years. As law professor Jasna Bakšić Muftić noted, "During the communist period . . . we didn't have [an] independent judiciary. And the judiciary was misused in the political elimination of [those whom the state saw as] the political enemy."[16] Already burdened by the legacy of its communist tradition, Bosnia's judiciary was devastated during the 1990s conflict. The Organization for Security and Co-operation in Europe (OSCE) Mission to Bosnia and Herzegovina (BiH) described the conflict's impact this way:

> [The] loss of skilled members of the legal profession and the judiciary, as well as the physical destruction and lack of proper equipment or facilities significantly hampered the ability of the courts to administer justice properly or efficiently. . . . Outdated and inadequate procedural laws contributed to the inefficiency of the system. The loss of many pre-war judges resulted in the judiciary and prosecutors' offices, in different parts of the country, being dominated by the majority ethnicity. New, inexperienced judges and prosecutors were appointed on ethnic and political grounds. The prosecution of war crimes, in particular, ineffectual investigations, excessive and systematic delays in the resolution of trials and dubious decisions, compounded by a lack of public faith in the judicial system, brought into serious question the applicability of the rule of law.[17]

---

[13] *See, e.g.*, Geneva Convention (IV) Relative to the Protection of Civilian Persons in Time of War, art. 146, Aug. 12, 1949, 6 U.S.T. 3516, 75 U.N.T.S. 287.

[14] Antonio Cassese, International Criminal Law 349 (2003).

[15] David Tolbert & Aleksandar Kontić, *The International Criminal Tribunal for the Former Yugoslavia: Transitional Justice, the Transfer of Cases to National Courts, and Lessons for the ICC*, *in* The Emerging Practice of the International Criminal Court 135, 136 (Carsten Stahn & Göran Sluiter eds., 2009).

[16] Interview with Jasna Bakšić Muftić, Professor, School of Law, University of Sarajevo, in Sarajevo, Bosn. & Herz. (Sept. 17, 2014).

[17] Organization for Security and Co-operation in Europe, Mission to Bosnia & Herzegovina, War Crimes Trials Before the Domestic Courts of Bosnia and Herzegovina: Progress and Obstacles 4 (2005) [hereinafter Progress and Obstacles].

Bosnian courts undertook a limited number of war crimes prosecutions even before the conflict ended, but these were strongly criticized by independent observers, as were prosecutions undertaken in the early post-conflict years.[18] Bosnia's Human Rights Chamber later found "[m]any of the trials" conducted in this period to have been unfair.[19]

Far from ending this state of affairs, the Dayton Peace Agreement (DPA) in some respects compounded the challenge of developing an impartial judiciary by establishing a two-entity state with separate legal systems for each entity.[20] Until 2003, war crimes trials were held exclusively before courts in the entities and the Basic Court in Brčko;[21] there was not yet a state-level court that could transcend those courts' structural biases. In this setting war crimes cases were prosecuted before courts largely "packed . . . with individuals of the majority ethnic group"[22] of each entity, though there were also highly "competent, dedicated and honourable judges" among them.[23] Judges and prosecutors encountered particularly intense political pressure in war crimes cases, in which they, as well as witnesses, "feared intimidation or violence if they diligently proceeded with a case or testified."[24]

In the immediate aftermath of Dayton, moreover, ICTY personnel were hard-pressed to undertake basic investigative work, much less contemplate capacity-building efforts. Former prosecutor Alan Tieger, who made his first trip to Bosnian crime scenes in Republika Srpska immediately after the Dayton accord was concluded, described the challenges he and his colleagues faced at that time: "It was all we could do to get into the region with the benefit of essentially military protection and do our utmost, . . . buoyed by the presence of [the NATO Stabilization

---

See also Wolfgang Petritsch (High Representative), *22nd Report by the High Representative for Implementation of the Peace Agreement to the Secretary-General of the United Nations,* ¶ 53 (May 14, 2002) [hereinafter *22nd Report of the High Representative*] ("War crimes prosecutions have suffered due to the inadequacy of the domestic system. . . . [I]n several cases, police have refused to act against high-profile criminals because they know that the offenders will be quickly released and will never be effectively prosecuted. The judicial system of BiH has not merely suffered the ravages and disruption of war and immediate post-war, but also emerged from a communist culture in which there was no separation of powers and no tradition of judicial independence. Furthermore, judges and prosecutors continue to lack the capacity to deal with complex cases. . . . "); Yaël Ronen, Bosnia and Herzegovina: The Interaction Between the ICTY and Domestic Courts in Adjudicating International Crimes 33–34 (DOMAC/8, 2011) [hereinafter DOMAC/8 Report] ("During the war, . . . [j]udges in some regions were sent to concentration camps, some fled and others were removed from office because of their ethnicity. New judges were appointed, . . . [some] without having the requisite, or even any, basic qualifications. In the immediate aftermath of the armed conflict, . . . [t]here were frequent accusations of lack of impartiality, corruption and general incompetence in respect of the judiciary.").

[18] Progress and Obstacles, *supra* note 17, at 4. *See also* Human Rights Watch, Justice at Risk: War Crimes Trials in Croatia, Bosnia and Herzegovina, and Serbia and Montenegro 6 (2004) [hereinafter HRW, Justice at Risk].

[19] Donlon, *supra* note 2, at 255, 262.

[20] *See id.* at 261.

[21] *Id.* at 264.

[22] *Id.*

[23] Email from Shireen Fisher, Former International Judge, BWCC, to Diane Orentlicher (Aug. 30, 2017). Judge Fisher was describing national judges appointed to the then-new war crimes chamber in its early years.

[24] Donlon, *supra* note 2, at 265.

Force], to obtain documents, to manage to see witnesses."[25] Nor, in any case, did many OTP staff speak the local languages.[26]

For a variety of reasons, then, advancing local trials was not an objective, much less a priority, of the ICTY or its sponsors. When the international community and Tribunal addressed local governments on the subject of war crimes, their emphasis was overwhelmingly on ensuring that national authorities arrest those indicted by the ICTY and transfer them to The Hague. Louise Arbour, the Tribunal's second Prosecutor,[27] would later recall "there was only one overwhelming, all-encompassing and . . . life threatening issue for the ICTY as it had been conceived: arrests."[28] In this and other respects, during the Tribunal's early years international efforts to ensure justice focused overwhelmingly on "the international rather than the national justice system."[29]

B. Supervision and Restraint

In 1996, a new role of supervision and restraint was layered onto ICTY primacy. Far from helping empower the Bosnian judiciary to play its part in providing redress for wartime atrocities, the Tribunal was charged with ensuring local courts did not destabilize the fragile peace. The Tribunal's new role arose from the first significant challenge to the DPA: in late January 1996, Federation authorities arrested two senior RS army officers who had taken a wrong turn into Federation territory after misreading a signpost,[30] and brought war crimes charges against them. One of the officers, Lieutenant General Đorđe Đukić, was a close aide to Bosnian Serb Army chief of staff Ratko Mladić, by then a fugitive from The Hague. Although the Federation was legally entitled to arrest suspected war criminals, its action triggered "the most serious" dispute "to arise between the Bosnian Serbs and the Bosnian Government since the signing of the Balkan peace agreement" one month earlier,[31] setting off "a series of arbitrary and retaliatory" arrests and detentions.[32]

The specter of arbitrary arrests was seen as a "threat to Dayton itself," as freedom of movement was fundamental to Dayton's conception of a single, if divided, country.[33] This, in turn, imperiled larger goals, as freedom of movement was seen as "crucial to the success of holding free and fair municipal elections in September 1996,

---

[25] Interview with Alan Tieger, then Senior Trial Attorney, Office of the Prosecutor, ICTY, in The Hague, Neth. (May 26, 2015).

[26] *See* Tolbert & Kontić, *Transfer of Cases*, *supra* note 15, at 138, 138 n.17.

[27] Technically, Justice Arbour was the ICTY's third Prosecutor but, as noted earlier, its first Prosecutor left the job almost immediately after reporting for duty. *See* Chapter 2.

[28] Louise Arbour, *The Crucial Years*, 2 J. INT'L CRIM. JUST. 396, 397 (2004). This period is described in Chapter 2.

[29] Donlon, *supra* note 2, at 267.

[30] *See* Chris Hedges, *Muslim Detention of Bosnian Serbs Threatens Truce*, N.Y. TIMES (Feb. 7, 1996). The Bosnian government arrested several other Bosnian Serbs during the same period, but the arrest of these two men proved especially controversial.

[31] PROGRESS AND OBSTACLES, *supra* note 17, at 5. *See also* Stacey Sullivan, *Bosnian Serb Leaders Halt Contacts with Government; Arrest of 8 Military Men Threatens Fragile Peace*, WASH. POST (Feb. 7, 1996); Chris Hedges, *Muslim Detention of Bosnian Serbs Threatens Truce*, N.Y. TIMES (Feb. 7, 1996).

[32] Janet Manuell & Aleksandar Kontić, *Transitional Justice: The Prosecution of War Crimes in Bosnia and Herzegovina Under the "Rules of the Road"*, 5 Y.B. INT'L HUMANITARIAN L. 331, 333 (2002).

[33] *Id.*

especially as candidates and voters were being encouraged to stand and vote in their pre-conflict constituencies."[34]

In this fraught setting, the Bosnian government asked the ICTY to question the detained Serbs to determine whether they should be indicted.[35] Then ICTY Prosecutor Richard Goldstone sought the Serbs' provisional arrest and transfer to The Hague for questioning and possible indictment.[36] Contemporaneous reports suggested Goldstone's intervention helped defuse the crisis,[37] a view shared by John Shattuck, then the senior human rights official in the Clinton administration,[38] and others.[39] But Richard Holbrooke, the lead negotiator at Dayton, had a different view: since the two Serb officers had been apprehended in a manner that, in his view, violated the DPA, "we would normally have insisted that the Muslims release them immediately." But, Holbrooke wrote, "Justice Goldstone complicated matters considerably; from the International War Crimes Tribunal in The Hague, he issued a warrant for the two men—even though they had not been indicted."[40]

To ensure, in Holbrooke's words, "that we would never again have to struggle with the consequences of a surprise arrest" in Bosnia,[41] in mid-February 1996 the leaders of Bosnia, Serbia, and Croatia agreed that local authorities would not arrest anyone on war crimes charges without first obtaining approval from the ICTY.[42] For the next eight years, if Bosnian authorities wanted to arrest someone suspected of war crimes, they had to submit relevant evidence to the Office of the Prosecutor (OTP), and

---

[34] PROGRESS AND OBSTACLES, *supra* note 17, at 5.

[35] *See* Jack Kelley, *Bosnia Arrests 2 Top Serbs, Seeks Charges*, USA TODAY (Feb. 6, 1996).

[36] *See* Press Release, ICTY, Tribunal's Prosecutor Requests Bosnia to Provisionally Arrest General Đukić and Colonel Krsmanović, CC/PIO/031-E (Feb. 7, 1996). Krsmanović was quickly released for lack of evidence. *See* Press Release, ICTY, Colonel Krsmanović Remanded Back to Bosnia and Herzegovina, CC/PIO/058 (Apr. 3, 1996). The ICTY confirmed an indictment of Đukić in late February 1996. *See* ICTY President, *Report of the International Tribunal for the Prosecution of Serious Violations of International Humanitarian Law Committed in the Territory of the Former Yugoslavia Since 1991*, ¶ 18, U.N. Doc. A/51/292/S/1996/665 (Aug. 16, 1996). By then terminally ill, Đukić was granted provisional release two months later and died the following month. *See* ICTY, CASE INFORMATION SHEET: ĐORĐE ĐUKIĆ, http://www.icty.org/x/cases/djukic/cis/en/cis_djukic_en.pdf (last visited Dec. 10, 2017).

[37] *See, e.g.*, Sullivan, *supra* note 31 (commander of NATO forces in Bosnia, Adm. Leighton W. Smith, Jr., "released a statement saying he was reassured that the Bosnian government would abide by the decision of the war crimes tribunal").

[38] JOHN SHATTUCK, FREEDOM ON FIRE: HUMAN RIGHTS WARS & AMERICA'S RESPONSE 216 (2003) ("Flying the two Serb military officers to the tribunal was clearly preferable to leaving them in the hands of the Bosnians").

[39] *See, e.g.*, Donlon, *supra* note 2, at 263.

[40] RICHARD HOLBROOKE, TO END A WAR 332 (1998).

[41] *Id.* at 334.

[42] This agreement was reached at the first post-Dayton Compliance Summit in Rome. The Agreed Measures, one of the documents comprising the Rome Agreement, provided in pertinent part:

> Persons, other than those already indicted by the International Tribunal, may be arrested and detained for serious violations of international humanitarian law only pursuant to a previously issued order, warrant, or indictment that has been reviewed and deemed consistent with international legal standards by the International Tribunal. Procedures will be developed for expeditious decision by the Tribunal and will be effective immediately upon such action.

> NATO, Rome Statement: Agreed Measures, ¶ 5, Feb. 18, 1996, http://www.nato.int/IFOR/rome/rome2.htm.

could proceed with an arrest only if the OTP determined there was a prima facie case the suspects committed war crimes.[43] Understandably focused on its own cases,[44] the OTP hardly relished the assignment but had little choice in the matter.[45]

To the extent its aim was to help ensure freedom of movement by averting weak indictments,[46] the review undertaken in The Hague—colloquially known as the "Rules of the Road" (RoR) process—was successful. Aleksandar Kontić, a Bosnian lawyer who worked in the OTP's RoR unit, believes that without it "the whole country would go into a, probably not full-blown conflict, but . . . the whole idea of freedom of movement within Bosnia-Herzegovina would be halted completely."[47] Damir Arnaut, too, believes the RoR program "helped *enormously* in making the country more functional and making freedom of movement a reality" in the early years of peace.[48] In larger perspective, Kontić believes the review process helped dispel ethnic tensions surrounding prosecutions in Bosnian courts; without vetting in The Hague, representatives of Bosnia's major ethnic groups could more plausibly argue, "Oh, they [i.e. local courts] are only prosecuting Serbs," or "they are only prosecuting Croats, or Bosniaks."[49]

The RoR program apparently averted thousands of poorly-substantiated war crimes charges: the OTP found sufficient evidence to proceed with charges against roughly one-sixth of the nearly 5,000 suspects whose files it reviewed.[50] Recalling the files she reviewed in the RoR project, Tea Polešćuk told me "it was very much clear" that national prosecutors, "although willing to prosecute alleged war criminals, had no really understanding of how to do it, according to which standards." In her assessment, without the review "many people" could have been inappropriately prosecuted.[51]

---

[43] Tolbert & Kontić, *Transfer of Cases, supra* note 15, at 141. Although the presidents of Bosnia, Serbia, and Croatia signed the Agreed Measures, only Bosnia undertook to abide by the Rules of the Road procedure. *See* Mark S. Ellis, *Bringing Justice to an Embattled Region—Creating and Implementing the Rules of the Road for Bosnia-Herzegovina*, 17 BERKELEY J. INT'L L. 1, 7–8 (1999). The Croatian and Serbian governments maintained their leaders signed the agreement on behalf of Bosnian Croats and Bosnian Serbs, respectively. *See* Manuell & Kontić, *supra* note 32, at 334, 334 n.12.

[44] *See* Tolbert & Kontić, *Transfer of Cases, supra* note 15, at 143.

[45] *See* DOMAC/8 REPORT, *supra* note 17, at 27.

[46] Tolbert & Kontić, *Transfer of Cases, supra* note 15, at 142.

[47] Interview with Aleksandar Kontić, Legal Officer, Office of the Prosecutor, ICTY, in The Hague, Neth. (May 26, 2015).

[48] Interview with Damir Arnaut, then Advisor for Legal and Constitutional Affairs, Cabinet of Haris Silajžić, in Sarajevo, Bosn. & Herz. (July 16, 2009). *See also* Mechtild Lauth, *Ten Years After Dayton: War Crimes Prosecutions in Bosnia and Herzegovina*, 16 HELSINKI MONITOR 253, 257 (2005).

[49] Interview with Aleksandar Kontić, Legal Officer, Office of the Prosecutor, ICTY, in The Hague, Neth. (May 26, 2015).

[50] According to the ICTY's website, under the Rules of the Road procedure "OTP staff reviewed 1,419 files involving 4,985 suspects, and advised local prosecutors whether or not they had enough evidence to proceed. Approval was granted for the prosecution of 848 persons." ICTY website, http://www.icty.org/sid/96 (last visited Dec. 10, 2017). *See also* Alejandro Chehtman, *Developing Bosnia and Herzegovina's Capacity to Process War Crimes Cases: Critical Notes on a "Success Story,"* 9 J. INT'L CRIM. JUST. 547, 556 (2011).

[51] Interview with Tea Polešćuk, Legal Advisor, Office of the Prosecutor, MICT Hague Branch, in The Hague, Neth. (May 27, 2015).

Kontić and former Deputy Prosecutor David Tolbert suggest the process also had a positive, though admittedly limited, effect on domestic prosecutors: "Given the large number of cases reviewed, local prosecutors no doubt did begin to get a better sense of the relevant international standards."[52] Although it did not do so at first, the OTP eventually provided advice on how gaps in local prosecutors' investigations could be filled; "what kind of new . . . leads should be taken in order to have a proper[ly] investigated case," for example.[53] Even so, there was "no real follow up" component to the program, "as the local prosecutor was more or less left on his or her own to pursue the case after receiving the ICTY Prosecutor's imprimatur."[54]

The program's contributions came at a cost, moreover, though perhaps not as great as some have suggested. Strapped for resources and under pressure to expedite its own prosecutions, the Tribunal was hard-pressed to provide timely reviews.[55] Compounding these challenges, Bosnian files arrived, naturally, in the local language, in which few of the staff were fluent, and were "organized in a way that was entirely strange" to the staff.[56] Until native BCS speakers took over reviews, English-speaking attorneys had to work with translators.[57] Thus, assuming local prosecutors were willing and able impartially to pursue war criminals, substantial time was lost as the review process advanced slowly in The Hague.

Domestic prosecutors did not always wait for clearance, however. According to one study, "a significant number of cases were heard by Entity courts in disregard of the RoR procedure."[58] As two RoR veterans recall, moreover, the unit developed

---

[52] Tolbert & Kontić, *Transfer of Cases, supra* note 15, at 145. A *Transitional Justice Guidebook for Bosnia and Herzegovina* prepared by the United Nations Development Programme also credits the RoR program with "raising the professional level of BiH's judicial institutions." U.N. Dev. Program, Transitional Justice Guidebook for Bosnia and Herzegovina: Executive Summary 17 (2009) (Only the Executive Summary is available in English.) Tolbert and Kontić acknowledge the limits of this contribution, writing that the "engagement with local judicial authorities" arising from the RoR program "was sporadic and not driven by a coherent strategy." Thus, they conclude, before 2004 "one could not credibly identify significant contributions of the ICTY to the development of the court systems in the region or even an active engagement with those institutions." Tolbert & Kontić, *Transfer of Cases, supra* note 15, at 145.

[53] Interview with Aleksandar Kontić, Legal Officer, Office of the Prosecutor, ICTY, in The Hague, Neth. (May 26, 2015). Tea Polešćuk made a similar point, noting RoR lawyers did not simply criticize local investigations but provided "suggestion[s] on what evidence should be gathered in order to have an effective prosecution of alleged war criminals." Interview with Tea Polešćuk, Legal Advisor, Office of the Prosecutor, MICT Hague Branch, in The Hague, Neth. (May 27, 2015). *See also* Manuell & Kontić, *supra* note 32, at 338.

[54] David Tolbert, *The International Criminal Court for the Former Yugoslavia: Unforeseen Successes and Foreseeable Shortcomings*, 26 Fletcher F. World Aff. 7, 14 (2002).

[55] In these circumstances, the U.S. Department of State asked the American Bar Association Central and East European Law Initiative (CEELI) to assist the ICTY in reviewing RoR files. Attorneys provided by CEELI and the Coalition for International Justice conducted preliminary reviews for the ICTY in The Hague for one-and-a-half years. *See* Ellis, *supra* note 43, at 19–20. When ABA CEELI funding ended, the program continued with support from various countries. *See* Manuell & Kontić, *supra* note 32, at 335 n.17.

[56] Chehtman, *supra* note 50, at 556.

[57] The RoR project was initially staffed by three English-speaking lawyers from the United States and six language assistants. Two members of the first group of language assistants had been trained as lawyers, so eventually they were hired, along with other BCS-speaking lawyers, to undertake the review themselves rather than translate documents for English-speaking lawyers. Interview with Aleksandar Kontić, Legal Officer, Office of the Prosecutor, ICTY, in The Hague, Neth. (May 26, 2015).

[58] DOMAC/8 Report, *supra* note 17, at 27.

a procedure for reviewing some files—typically involving suspects amenable to immediate arrest—on an urgent basis. In these instances, the OTP could provide a decision within days.[59] Often, however, by the time the OTP approved cases submitted for review, Bosnian prosecutors had to revive stale files.[60]

Some believe the process had a more insidious impact on the Bosnian judiciary, sapping its morale and inhibiting initiative. In a 2005 interview, a Bosnian court official told William Burke-White that some Bosnian prosecutors experienced a "loss of face" having to seek international approval through a process they found "shameful."[61] Burke-White attributes Bosnian prosecutors' desultory record in prosecuting cases approved in The Hague to their low morale.[62] According to a study by the human rights centers of Berkeley University and the University of Sarajevo, the sense of shame engendered by the review process was compounded by the ICTY's poor communication with jurists who submitted files for approval. Based on interviews with thirty-two Bosnian judges and prosecutors in 1999, the study reported:

> ICTY officials failed to keep their Bosnian colleagues informed of the status of the [RoR] investigations, even in response to direct inquiries. . . . A judge reported that after having submitted twenty-five cases and waiting eight months, the ICTY had not responded. Other judges and prosecutors stated that they too had submitted files several years before and had received no communication . . . These professionals viewed the ICTY as unresponsive and detrimental to the ability of Bosnian courts to conduct national war crimes trials.[63]

In the view of Damir Arnaut, however, the "anti-imperialistic instinct" that informed the Berkeley/University of Sarajevo study was misplaced. Arnaut insisted: "Some of these [judges] are incompetent. These courts were trying to do war crimes cases and they just couldn't do it."[64] Tarik Jusić, too, noted national courts were "inefficient,

---

[59] Manuell & Kontić, *supra* note 32, at 336.

[60] Many of those cases were not, in any case, sufficiently developed for trial. Reflecting on the value of the cleared files for domestic prosecutions, David Schwendiman, then head of the Special Department for War Crimes in Bosnia's State Prosecutor's office, wrote: "The ICTY Rules of the Road files have not proven to be reliable except as starting points for [essentially new] domestic investigations. They do not translate immediately into prosecutable cases, partly because they are old, but mostly because they were and are incomplete." David Schwendiman, Background and Introduction 20 (July 2009) (unpublished paper) (on file with author).

[61] William W. Burke-White, *The Domestic Influence of International Criminal Tribunals: The International Criminal Tribunal for the Former Yugoslavia and the Creation of the State Court of Bosnia & Herzegovina*, 46 COLUM. J. TRANSNAT'L L. 279, 314 (2007–2008) (quoting Biljana Potparić-Lipa, then Registrar, Court of BiH). *See also* Paul R. Williams & Patricia Taft, *The Role of Justice in the Former Yugoslavia: Antidote or Placebo for Coercive Appeasement?*, 35 CASE W. RES. J. INT'L L. 219, 253–54 (2003); Chehtman, *supra* note 50, at 556.

[62] Burke-White, *supra* note 61, at 314. A 2002 publication stated that less than 10 percent of suspects cleared for prosecution by the OTP had been prosecuted in Bosnia. Manuell & Kontić, *supra* note 32, at 339.

[63] Laurel E. Fletcher & Harvey M. Weinstein, *Justice, Accountability and Social Reconstruction: An Interview Study of Bosnian Judges and Prosecutors*, 18 BERKELEY J. INT'L L. 36 (2000) [hereinafter *Interview Study*].

[64] Interview with Damir Arnaut, then Advisor for Legal and Constitutional Affairs, Cabinet of Haris Silajdžić, in Sarajevo, Bosn. & Herz. (July 16, 2009).

corrupt and they submitted to political pressure."[65] Consistent with their assessment, Polešćuk, who served in the RoR unit from 1997 to 2002, recalled that many files submitted for review were "completely insufficient," while Bosnia lacked basic resources, including prosecutors, to conduct effective war crimes prosecutions during the eight years of the project.[66]

When I interviewed Jovan Spaić, a representative of the Bosnian Serb government, in 2009, he offered various explanations for why investigating judges in Republika Sprska did *not* aggressively pursue war crimes cases during the 1990s, none of which hinted at the demoralizing effects of the RoR program. In Spaić's view, "It would be hard to expect . . . judges to operate so soon after the war when everything was so unstable, people were moving; it would have been hard to make witnesses come."[67] As Arnaut implied, moreover, the perceptions of Bosnian jurists who participated in the Berkeley/University of Sarajevo survey should be placed in context, as some had cause to be defensive. As the survey report recognizes, Bosnian judges felt "beleaguered" as a result of well-founded criticism by international actors as well as "pressure from those within, particularly politicians and criminal elements who act with impunity."[68] Indeed, Vehid Šehić told me he resigned from his position as a judge in the District Court of Tuzla in 1994 because the judiciary worked in a debilitating "political climate" inimical to war crimes prosecutions.[69] When asked if she thought the RoR process had inhibited domestic war crimes prosecutions, Judge Mira Smajlović, who had served as a war crimes judge for six years when I interviewed her in 2014, rejected the notion out of hand. In the immediate aftermath of the war, she said, "there was no will to prosecute war crimes because in both entities there was a perception that these [perpetrators] were heroes."[70] In short, it is hardly obvious Bosnian prosecutors would have mounted credible war crimes prosecutions but for the RoR program.[71]

The more substantial questions are whether the international community could have done more sooner to prepare the Bosnian judiciary to mount credible war crimes prosecutions—here the answer is surely yes, assuming relevant actors possessed the necessary bandwidth and resources—and whether the RoR program contributed to donors' failure to address deficiencies in Bosnia's courts sooner. I return to the first question later in this chapter. As for the second, Fidelma Donlon, a former official in

---

[65] Interview with Tarik Jusić, then Program Director, Mediacenter Sarajevo, in Sarajevo, Bosn. & Herz. (Dec. 6, 2006).

[66] Interview with Tea Polešćuk, Legal Advisor, Office of the Prosecutor, MICT Hague Branch, in The Hague, Neth. (May 27, 2015).

[67] Interview with Jovan Spaić, then Director, Republika Srpska Center for War Crimes Investigations, in Banja Luka, Bosn. & Herz. (July 15, 2009).

[68] *Interview Study*, *supra* note 63, at 39.

[69] Interview with Vehid Šehić, President, Citizens Forum of Tuzla, in Tuzla, Bosn. & Herz. (July 15, 2009).

[70] Interview with Mira Smajlović, Judge, BWCC, in Sarajevo, Bosn. & Herz. (Sept. 9, 2014).

[71] As another study notes, "it would be imprudent to attribute the paucity of cases in the Entities entirely to the slowness of the RoR process. The small number of cases adjudicated in FBiH from 1997 until 2001 and the absolute absence of cases in RS from 1998 until 2003 may also indicate a lack of sufficient determination among prosecutors, police and courts to see the cases through." DOMAC/8 Report, *supra* note 17, at 52–53. In addition, the small number of prosecutions for war crimes during the period the RoR project operated may be misleading, as "war-related crimes have often been prosecuted as ordinary crimes." *Id.* at 53.

the OHR and later deputy registrar in the Bosnian war crimes chamber, believes the RoR program induced unwarranted complacency about Bosnia's judiciary:

> [M]any diplomats misconstrued the Rules of the Road agreement as a mechanism to ensure fair trials in national courts rather than one to prevent arbitrary arrests. Frequently, this misconception caused people to believe that there were procedures in place to address problems with national trials, when in fact there were not.[72]

C. Creating a Partner

After years of stagnation, Bosnia's courts became the focus of international reform initiatives, spearheaded by the OHR, in the early 2000s. These efforts were far-reaching, entailing the replacement of an inquisitorial with an adversarial criminal procedure as well as comprehensive vetting of the country's judges and prosecutors.[73] Of high importance to the OHR, judicial reforms included creating a state-level court, which then High Representative Wolfgang Petritsch used his Bonn powers to create in November 2000,[74] and a state prosecutor's office, created by an August 2002 decision of Petritsch's immediate successor, Lord Paddy Ashdown.[75] By 2002–2003 the reforms included significant steps toward establishing a specialized war crimes chamber within the new Court of Bosnia and Herzegovina (Court of BiH).[76]

Impetus for Bosnia's War Crimes Chamber (BWCC) came from The Hague, marking a watershed in the Tribunal's relationship with local judiciaries. The shift was driven more by pragmatic calculation than enlightened vision: pressed in the late 1990s to devise a strategy for completing their work expeditiously, ICTY officials concluded they could do so only by sending some of their cases to national courts. As the site of the most extensive wartime atrocities, Bosnia and Herzegovina became the focus of their efforts to find a credible domestic partner. But if the ICTY initially saw Bosnia's war crimes institutions as a means to fulfill its own needs, it would later see their work as integral to its legacy.

1. IMPETUS FOR CHANGE: THE ICTY'S EXIT STRATEGY

The ICTY faced demands for results as soon as it had a Prosecutor in place,[77] and pressure intensified several years into its work. In a 1999 study commissioned by the UN General Assembly, a group of experts cited "[m]ajor concerns" about the

---

[72] Donlon, *supra* note 2, at 266.

[73] The vetting process is described in CASPAR FITHEN, INTERNATIONAL CENTER FOR TRANSITIONAL JUSTICE, THE LEGACY OF FOUR VETTING PROGRAMS: AN EMPIRICAL REVIEW 5–10 (2009).

[74] Wolfgang Petritsch (High Representative), Office of the High Representative, *Decision Establishing the BiH State Court* (Nov. 12, 2000). The Bonn powers are described in Chapter 2.

[75] Paddy Ashdown (High Representative), Office of the High Representative, *Decision Enacting the Law on the Prosecutor's Office of Bosnia and Herzegovina* (Aug. 6, 2002).

[76] The Criminal Division of the Court of BiH has three sections, dealing with distinct types of criminal offenses. Section I adjudicates war crimes, crimes against humanity, and genocide; Section II deals with "Organized Crime, Economic Crime and Corruption," and Section III handles "General Crime." *See* Court of Bosn. & Herz. website, http://www.sudbih.gov.ba/stranica/40/pregled (last visited Dec. 10, 2017).

[77] As noted in Chapter 2, going into his first budget meeting at UN Headquarters soon after becoming ICTY Prosecutor in 1994, Richard Goldstone was "informed ahead of time that at least

slow pace of proceedings before the ICTY and its sister court, the International Criminal Tribunal for Rwanda (ICTR), as well as the two tribunals' costs.[78] While its recommendations focused on streamlining the tribunals' procedures, the study provided "a little nudge" for ICTY judges to begin "thinking ahead towards formulating a completion or exit strategy."[79] Anticipating they would soon be pressed to wind up their work, key Tribunal officials seized the initiative to shape their own plan.[80]

Transferring certain cases not yet tried in The Hague to domestic courts—a subject addressed only briefly in the experts' study[81]—was a key element of the strategy devised by ICTY officials and adopted by the UN Security Council.[82] Specifically, transferring cases of comparatively low-level suspects[83] would free up the Hague Tribunal to focus on high-level suspects "in line with the spirit of the mission it received from the Security Council."[84]

While these considerations were of paramount importance to the Security Council and donor governments,[85] Tribunal prosecutors saw other benefits to strengthening domestic capacity in war crimes cases. At the time the strategy took shape, then ICTY Prosecutor Carla del Ponte planned to continue issuing new indictments for another two years, potentially indicting another 100 suspects.[86] Ironically, then, the prospect of transferring lower-level suspects to domestic courts would not only allow

---

one indictment had to be issued before the . . . meeting in order to demonstrate that the system was working and that the tribunal was worthy of financial support." RICHARD J. GOLDSTONE, FOR HUMANITY: REFLECTIONS OF A WAR CRIMES INVESTIGATOR 105 (2000).

[78] The experts asked "pointedly . . . why, after almost seven years and expenditures totaling $400 million, only 15 ICTY and ICTR trials have been completed." Jerome Ackerman, Chairman of the Expert Group, *Report of the Expert Group to Conduct a Review of the Effective Operation and Functioning of the International Tribunal for the Former Yugoslavia and the International Criminal Tribunal for Rwanda*, U.N. Doc. S/2000/597, Annex I, 19–20, ¶ 35 [hereinafter *Report of the Expert Group*].

[79] Michael Bohlander, *Last Exit Bosnia—Transferring War Crimes Prosecution from the International Tribunal to Domestic Courts*, 14 CRIM. L.F. 59, 61 (2003).

[80] The terrorist attack of September 11, 2001, may have intensified pressure on the Tribunal to wrap up its work, as international attention shifted elsewhere. See DOMAC/8, *supra* note 17, at 39.

[81] *Report of the Expert Group, supra* note 78, at 40, ¶ 101.

[82] *See, e.g.*, President of the Security Council, Statement Before the 4582nd Meeting of the Security Council, U.N. Doc. S/PRST/2002/21 (July 23, 2002); S.C. Res. 1503 (Aug. 28, 2003); S.C. Res. 1534 (Mar. 26, 2004). Another key element was the appointment of ad litem judges, which enabled the ICTY to conduct more trials simultaneously.

[83] In a 2002 report, senior ICTY officials explained that indictees transferred to national courts would be "those who, though in a sufficiently high-level position of authority to be indicted by the Prosecutor of the [ICTY], may be tried by national courts provided certain conditions have been satisfied." ICTY President, Prosecutor & Registrar, *Report on the Judicial Status of the International Criminal Tribunal for the Former Yugoslavia and the Prospects for Referring Certain Cases to National Courts*, ¶ 32, U.N. Doc. S/2002/678 (June 19, 2002) (citation omitted) [hereinafter *Judicial Status Report*].

[84] *Id.* ¶ 2.

[85] The administration of then U.S. president George W. Bush pressed for the ICTY and ICTR to wind up their work as quickly as possible. See Bohlander, *supra* note 79, at 65 (quoting 2002 testimony of a U.S. official before a congressional committee). See also Colum Lynch, *U.S. Seeks End to War Crimes Tribunals by 2008*, WASH. POST (Feb. 1, 2003).

[86] *Judicial Status Report, supra* note 83, ¶ 16. The ICTY Prosecutor suggested that, of this number, "50 possible intermediary-level accused" could be transferred to national courts. *Id.* ¶ 17. These transfers would be in addition to several individuals already detained by the Tribunal. *Id.* ¶ 31. In the event, only six ICTY indictments involving ten defendants would actually be transferred to Bosnia.

the Tribunal to complete its current cases, but also initiate new ones. In addition, ICTY prosecutors had gathered a wealth of evidence implicating individuals whom they would not be able to charge themselves; they relished the possibility it could now be used by a viable partner in Bosnia.[87]

Regional developments made the prospect of transferring cases to former Yugoslav states increasingly plausible. Introducing the idea of "relocating" some ICTY cases to domestic courts in late 2001, then ICTY president Claude Jorda noted:

> The political upheavals recently witnessed in the Balkans have gradually changed the perception of the International Tribunal held by the States from the region. However, must these upheavals not also lead us to change our own view as to the ability of these States to try some of the war criminals in their territory?[88]

In a report the following year, the ICTY's president, Prosecutor, and Registrar said "the gradual restoration of democratic institutions in the countries of the former Yugoslavia," along with other developments, made the prospect of referring cases to national courts "increasingly likely."[89] As framed in the report, the overarching case for doing so bore scant relation to the values Meron would cite four years later, when Bosnia's war crimes chamber was launched.[90] Instead, the report concluded: "The main purpose of implementing the Tribunal's completion strategy and referring cases . . . to the courts of Bosnia and Herzegovina is to complete the [ICTY's] first instance trials by around 2008."[91]

2. Joint Planning for the Future War Crimes Chamber

The ICTY would not be in a position to transfer cases until its judges were satisfied national courts could "fully . . . conform to internationally recognised standards of human rights and due process in the trials of referred persons."[92] The Tribunal's

---

[87] Interview with Clint Williamson, Former Trial Attorney, Office of the Prosecutor, ICTY, in Washington, D.C., United States (Aug. 12, 2009).

[88] Press Release, ICTY, Address by His Excellency, Judge Claude Jorda, President of the International Criminal Tribunal for the former Yugoslavia, to the U.N. Security Council (Nov. 27, 2001). Jorda did not specify the nature of the "upheavals" he mentioned, but they doubtless included the collapse of the Milošević regime in Serbia in October 2000, which eventually led to the former Serbian leader's transfer to the ICTY in late June 2001. See Chapter 3. By the time of Jorda's remarks, Croatian wartime leader Franjo Tudman, a hardline nationalist, had passed away (Tudman died in December 1999). In February 2000, Stjepan Mesić, who had been highly critical of Tudman's nationalist policies, was elected president of Croatia. In Bosnia, 2001 saw the formation of a ten-party coalition of non-nationalist parties, which enjoyed relative success in general elections. See Adis Merdžanović, Democracy by Decree: Prospects and Limits of Imposed Consociational Democracy in Bosnia and Herzegovina 284–86 (2015).

[89] *Judicial Status Report, supra* note 83, ¶ 2.

[90] *See supra* text accompanying note 8.

[91] *Judicial Status Report, supra* note 83, ¶ 75.

[92] *Id.* ¶ 32. *See also* Alison Freebairn & Nerma Jelačić, *Bringing War Crimes Justice Back Home*, IWPR (Nov. 26, 2004) (quoting ICTY spokesperson saying "there must be cast-iron guarantees that there will be a fair trial" in Bosnia before the Tribunal can transfer cases there). This is not the only reason Bosnia's war crimes institutions would need to satisfy international standards. The Bosnian constitution provides that "the rights and freedoms set forth in the European Convention for the Protection of Human Rights and Fundamental Freedoms and its Protocols shall apply directly in Bosnia and Herzegovina" and "shall have priority over all other law."

Prosecutor strongly preferred to transfer cases involving crimes committed in Bosnia—the majority of the OTP's docket—to Bosnian courts.[93] But in 2002, ICTY officials believed Bosnia's judiciary "display[ed] shortcomings too great for it to constitute a sufficiently solid judicial foundation to try cases referred by the Tribunal."[94] So they intensified efforts to ensure the Bosnian judiciary could competently try transferred cases.[95]

Their efforts linked up with the ambitious judicial reform process by then underway, spearheaded by the OHR.[96] While the Tribunal was intent on finding "a trustworthy domestic court" to which it could transfer cases,[97] the OHR was engaged in broader efforts to modernize Bosnia's judiciary while assuring its independence, integrity, competence, and ethnic balance.[98] And while the ICTY focused on war crimes prosecutions, a key preoccupation of the High Representative was to empower Bosnia's judiciary to tackle organized crime—a pervasive and formidable challenge.[99]

The High Representative hoped, as well, that state-level institutions would help knit Bosnia's fractured entities into a unified country.[100] The Bosnian constitution, adopted in Dayton, allocates few powers to the Bosnian state,[101] and establishes only

---

General Framework Agreement for Peace in Bosnia and Herzegovina, Bosn. & Herz.-Croat.-Rep. Yugo., Annex 4, art. II (2), Dec. 14, 1995, 35 I.L.M. 75 [hereinafter BiH Constitution].

[93] Interview with David Tolbert, then Deputy Prosecutor, Office of the Prosecutor, ICTY, in The Hague, Neth. (Mar. 5, 2007). Indeed, the section of the ICTY's 2002 report addressing the transfer of cases to national courts dealt only "with the possibility of referring cases to the courts of Bosnia as the Prosecutor believes that it is the only country that may now be considered for the referral process." *Judicial Status Report, supra* note 83, ¶ 45. *See also id.* ¶ 17.

[94] *Judicial Status Report, supra* note 83, ¶ 49. *See also* Assessments of the President & Prosecutor of the ICTY, transmitted by Letter dated 21 May 2004 from the President of the International Tribunal for the Prosecution of Persons Responsible for Serious Violations of International Humanitarian Law Committed in the Territory of the Former Yugoslavia since 1991, addressed to the President of the Security Council, ¶ 29, U.N. Doc. S/2004/420 (May 24, 2004).

[95] These efforts are described in ICTY President, *Report of the International Tribunal for the Prosecution of Serious Violations of International Humanitarian Law Committed on the Territory of the Former Yugoslavia Since 1991*, ¶¶ 18–21, U.N. Doc. A/57/379-S/2002/985 (Sept. 4, 2002). In 2001, the Tribunal asked the OHR and Bosnian presidency to explore options that would enable the ICTY to transfer cases to the Bosnian judiciary. *See* Donlon, *supra* note 2, at 272.

[96] *See supra* text accompanying notes 73–75. *See also 22nd Report of the High Representative, supra* note 17, ¶¶ 54–55; PROGRESS AND OBSTACLES, *supra* note 17, at 9. These initiatives were undertaken during the period of robust state-building efforts during the tenures of High Representatives Petritsch and Ashdown, respectively, which are noted in Chapter 2.

[97] Consultants' Report to the OHR, *The Future of Domestic War Crimes Prosecutions in Bosnia and Herzegovina* 5 (May 2002).

[98] *See* PROGRESS AND OBSTACLES, *supra* note 17, at 9; Burke-White, *supra* note 61, at 288. Previous, unsuccessful reform efforts are described in INTERNATIONAL CRISIS GROUP, BALKANS REP. 127, COURTING DISASTER: THE MISRULE OF LAW IN BOSNIA AND HERZEGOVINA (Mar. 25, 2002) [hereinafter COURTING DISASTER].

[99] *See* Sebastian van de Vliet, *Addressing Corruption and Organized Crime in the Context of Re-establishing the Rule of Law, in* DECONSTRUCTING THE RECONSTRUCTION: HUMAN RIGHTS AND RULE OF LAW IN POSTWAR BOSNIA AND HERZEGOVINA 203, 229–30 (Dina Francesca Haynes ed., 2008); Donlon, *supra* note 2, at 275–76; Burke-White, *supra* note 61, at 331. The problem has persisted long after the OHR prioritized efforts to combat organized crime. *See* Katarina Panić, *Bosnian Serb Corruption Battle Leaves Big Fish Untouched*, BALKAN INSIGHT (June 11, 2015).

[100] Conversation with Fidelma Donlon, in Bogotá, Colombia (Nov. 24, 2014).

[101] *See* Yaël Ronen, *The Impact of the ICTY on Atrocity-Related Prosecutions in the Courts of Bosnia and Herzegovina*, 3 PENN STATE J. L. & INT'L AFF. 113, 118 (2014) [hereinafter Ronen, *Impact of ICTY*].

one state-level court, the Constitutional Court.[102] Accordingly, a key plank of the High Representative's judicial reform strategy was to create the new Court of BiH[103] and ensure enactment of a national criminal code and code of criminal procedure.[104] In 2000, the Court of BiH and in 2002 the Prosecutor's Office of BiH (POBiH) were established as state-level institutions with national competence over certain categories of crimes.[105]

By late 2001, discussions among ICTY, OHR, and other actors focused on developing a specialized war crimes chamber within the state court that could receive cases transferred from the ICTY, and also play a filtering role for war crimes cases instituted before local courts in Bosnia.[106] Their deliberations were informed in part by a May 2002 report of four consultants, one of whom was a former ICTY judge and another of whom previously served as Chief of Investigations at the Tribunal.[107] Unsurprisingly, the experts affirmed the need to ensure the multiethnic composition of the new chamber and prosecution office. They also believed international participation was needed at all levels of the state court proceedings, but "only . . . for such a period of time as necessary to develop standards to a level consistent with those expected by the international and national community"; in their stated view, five years would be sufficient.[108] In mid-2002, ICTY officials laid out criteria to ensure Bosnian courts could try cases "in accordance with the principles laid down in the [ICTY's] Statute."[109] As the experts' report foreshadowed, "this would involve," among other

---

[102] BiH Constitution, *supra* note 92, art. VI.

[103] The need for a state court was identified by the Peace Implementation Council as early as 1998, though legislation to create the court was not adopted until November 2000. *See* Donlon, *supra* note 2, at 268.

[104] Then High Representative Petritsch imposed the Law on the State Court of BiH on November 12, 2000, after the Bosnian parliament failed to adopt the law. Wolfgang Petritsch (High Representative), Office of the High Representative, *Decision Establishing the BiH State Court* (Nov. 12, 2000). *See also* Donlon, *supra* note 2, at 268–69. Upon challenge by RS parliamentarians, the Constitutional Court of Bosnia upheld the OHR's power to do so in September 2001. *See* COURTING DISASTER, *supra* note 98, at 25. The law on the state court was endorsed by Bosnia's Parliamentary Assembly in July 2002. In light of delays enacting state-level criminal legislation, resulting in part from the lengthy process of forming a new government following the 2002 elections, then High Representative Paddy Ashdown enacted a new Criminal Code and Criminal Procedure Code of BiH on January 24, 2003; both entered into force on March 1, 2003. *See* Donlon, *supra* at note 2, at 278; PROGRESS AND OBSTACLES, *supra* note 17, at 9.

[105] ORGANIZATION FOR SECURITY AND CO-OPERATION IN EUROPE, MISSION TO BOSNIA & HERZEGOVINA, DELIVERING JUSTICE IN BOSNIA AND HERZEGOVINA: AN OVERVIEW OF WAR CRIMES PROCESSING FROM 2005 TO 2010, at 13 (May 2011) [hereinafter DELIVERING JUSTICE].

[106] In August 2001, then ICTY Prosecutor Carla del Ponte proposed to Bosnian authorities that they consider establishing an international court based in Bosnia. *Judicial Status Report, supra* note 83, ¶ 59. The OHR, however, "suggested focusing on the yet to be established Court of BiH." Donlon, *supra* note 2, at 272. The OHR believed public confidence in Bosnia's ability to hold fair trials for "these most terrible crimes" would be integral to public confidence in "their own state." Beth Kampschror, *Bosnia to Try Its War criminals, But Is New Court up to the Job?,* CHRISTIAN SCI. MONITOR (Dec. 23, 2003) (quoting spokesman for then High Representative Paddy Ashdown).

[107] Their report is analyzed in Bohlander, *supra* note 79.

[108] *Id.* at 73.

[109] *Judicial Status Report, supra* note 83, ¶ 70.

measures, "sending international judges to serve in the courts responsible for trying cases referred by the Tribunal."[110]

Upon receiving a mandate to go forward from the Peace Implementation Council, the ICTY and OHR formed joint working groups to develop the legal framework for transferring indicted cases to the Court of BiH,[111] whose core elements would reflect the consultants' and ICTY officials' recommendations. The new chamber would at first include both international and national judges.[112] A Special Department for War Crimes (SDWC), also initially staffed by international as well as national prosecutors, would be created within the POBiH.[113] Crucial to the chamber's design, international judges and prosecutors would be phased out after five years[114]—an approach that, on its face, properly emphasized domestic ownership but whose implementation would later hobble the war crimes institutions.

The planners' vision soon became a UN mandate. In August 2003, the Security Council adopted Resolution 1503, which "reaffirm[ed] in the strongest terms" a previous statement by the Council's president endorsing

> the ICTY's strategy for completing investigations by the end of 2004, all trial activities at first instance by the end of 2008, and all of its work in 2010 . . . by concentrating on the prosecution and trial of the most senior leaders suspected of being most responsible for crimes within the ICTY's jurisdiction and *transferring cases involving those who may not bear this level of responsibility to competent national jurisdictions, as appropriate, as well as the strengthening of the capacity of such jurisdictions.*[115]

The Council focused on ensuring the Bosnian judiciary could receive cases from the Hague. Noting "an essential prerequisite to achieving" the goals of the completion strategy "is the expeditious establishment . . . and early functioning of a special chamber within the State Court of Bosnia . . . and the subsequent referral by the ICTY of cases of lower- or intermediate-rank accused to the Chamber,"[116] Resolution 1503 called on donors to support efforts to create the war crimes chamber.[117]

Bosnia's parliament adopted legislation establishing the BWCC—officially named Section I of the Court of BiH—as well as the SDWC in December 2004, while some laws relevant to their work had already been imposed by then High Representative Paddy Ashdown in January 2003.[118] A task force proposed reforms to Bosnia's Criminal Code (BiH CC), which the parliament adopted, making it possible to prosecute the full

---

[110] *Id.*

[111] *See* Tolbert & Kontić, *Transfer of Cases, supra* note 15, at 146–47.

[112] *See* Donlon, *supra* note 2, at 277.

[113] *See id.* at 280.

[114] *Id.* at 280–81.

[115] S.C. Res. 1503, preambular ¶ 7 (Aug. 28, 2003) (emphasis added).

[116] *Id.* preambular ¶ 11.

[117] *Id.* ¶ 5. *See also* S.C. Res. 1534, ¶¶ 4, 9, 10 (Mar. 24, 2004).

[118] *See* Donlon, *supra* note 2, at 278, 281; interview with Mechtild Lauth, then Senior Legal Counsel, The Registry, War Crimes and Organized Crime, Court of BiH, in Sarajevo, Bosn. & Herz. (June 12, 2007); David Schwendiman, *Prosecuting Atrocity Crimes in National Courts: Looking Back on 2009 in Bosnia and Herzegovina*, 8 Nw. J. Int'l Hum. Rts. 269, 278 (2010) [hereinafter Schwendiman, *Prosecuting Atrocity Crimes*].

range of offenses subject to ICTY jurisdiction.[119] A Law on the Transfer of Cases, which addressed the ICTY's preconditions for transferring indictments, was also introduced before the Bosnian parliament in June 2004 and adopted by the end of the year along with other key laws.[120] As elaborated later, although the impetus for these laws came from external actors, Bosnian nationals took the lead in drafting them.

Meanwhile, ICTY judges amended Rule 11*bis* of the Tribunal's Rules of Procedure and Evidence to establish procedures for transferring ICTY cases.[121] Under the amended rule, the president of the ICTY could constitute a Referral Bench to determine whether to transfer an indictment already confirmed but in respect of which trial has not yet begun in The Hague.[122] Along with other guidelines, the rule stipulates the Referral Bench must be "satisfied that the accused will receive a fair trial" before it could approve a referral.[123]

The war crimes chamber was finally launched on March 9, 2005, two years after the Court of BiH began operating. Even before then, the ICTY Prosecutor informed the BiH presidency the OTP was no longer in a position to review war crimes cases and that the PoBiH should assume authority for such cases effective October 1, 2004.[124] Thus the "supervision and restraint" phase of the Tribunal's relationship with Bosnia's judiciary ended before the new arrangement was up and running.

---

[119] *See* Schwendiman, *Prosecuting Atrocity Crimes, supra* note 118, at 276.

[120] Interview with Mechtild Lauth, then Senior Legal Counsel, the Registry, War Crimes and Organized Crime, Court of BiH, in Sarajevo, Bosn. & Herz. (June 12, 2007).

[121] Key amendments were adopted on July 28, 2004. *See* Alison Freebairn & Nerma Jelačić, *Bringing War Crimes Justice Back Home*, IWPR (Nov. 26, 2004). Previously, Rule 11*bis* made it possible to suspend an ICTY indictment in the event of proceedings before national courts, but provided for referrals in narrower circumstances than those contemplated in the amended rule. *See Judicial Status Report, supra* note 83, ¶¶ 37–38.

[122] Amended Rule 11*bis* provides that judges on the Referral Bench must, "in accordance with Security Council resolution 1534 (2004), consider the gravity of the crimes charged and the level of responsibility of the accused." Rules of Procedure and Evidence, Int'l Crim. Trib. for the Former Yugoslavia, U.N. Doc. IT/32/Rev.49, Rule 11*bis* (C) (May 22, 2013) (as amended Sept. 30, 2002; July 28, 2004; and Feb. 11, 2005) (internal citation omitted) [hereinafter ICTY RPE].

[123] *Id.* Rule 11*bis* (B) (as amended Sept. 30, 2002; July 28, 2004; Feb. 11, 2005).

Rule 11*bis* does not express a preference for transferring cases to a particular country, but instead provides that a referral bench shall determine whether to transfer a case "to the authorities of a State":

> (i) in whose territory the crime was committed; or
> (ii) in which the accused was arrested; or
> (iii) having jurisdiction and being willing and adequately prepared to accept such a case[.]

Id. Rule 11*bis*(A) (amended as of May 22, 2013). In line with its long-standing desire to transfer cases to Bosnia, the OTP argued early on that these criteria reflect a ranked hierarchy, giving greatest weight to the state in which crimes were committed in the event more than one state wished to prosecute a transferred case. *See, e.g.,* Prosecutor v. Mejakić et al., Decision on Prosecutor's Motion for Referral of Case Pursuant to Rule 11*bis*, ¶ 33 (Int'l Crim. Trib. for the Former Yugoslavia July 20, 2005). ICTY judges rejected this claim, while nonetheless assessing which state has the greater nexus to the case, *see id.* ¶¶ 40, 42, which in practice favored Bosnia in a majority of transferred cases.

[124] *See* PROGRESS AND OBSTACLES, *supra* note 17, at 5; Carla del Ponte, ICTY Prosecutor, Office of the Prosecutor of the ICTY and War Crimes Chamber of BH Court—Way Forward and Challenges, Address at the BIRN Conference in Sarajevo (Nov. 10, 2005). The OHR had already taken the position that "sensitive Rules of the Road cases would . . . be dealt with by the [BWCC]." *See* Donlon, *supra* note 2, at 277.

3. Bosnian Engagement in Launching the War Crimes Institutions; Local Reactions

In light of the ICTY's and OHR's prominent roles in launching Bosnia's war crimes institutions, it is easy to overlook the leadership of Bosnians in this endeavor; indeed, much of the literature on this development has obscured their contributions. Yet Bosnian legal professionals, including officials from the Court of BiH, the POBiH, and the Ministry of Justice, were deeply engaged in drafting legislation that would govern the work of the war crimes institutions.[125] As judge Melika Murtezić would later recall, "from the beginning and through the entire development of the [BWCC], the national staff was really involved. . . . The team that drafted the law on the court, the criminal procedure code and the criminal code was composed by national staff, national legal experts."[126] Biljana Potparić-Lipa, who later served as Registrar of the BWCC, served as secretary of the task force that prepared the first draft of these foundational laws, while two other Bosnians co-chaired the task force.[127]

Individuals familiar with the jurists' work extol their legal achievement. Noting the task force was given just thirty days to produce key legal texts governing the BWCC's work, Shireen Fisher, who served as an international judge in the chamber from 2005 to 2008, described the enormity of the task they had to complete: task force members sought to "harmonize the former Yugoslavia code and the . . . statutes from war crimes tribunals," from Nuremberg and Tokyo to the ICTY and ICTR.[128] "And that's an astounding thing to try to do, especially since the Yugoslavian code is civil and the Nuremberg/ICTY statutes are much more common law."[129]

Bosnians also played central roles in building the new institutions once they were launched. Patricia Whalen, who served as an international judge on the BWCC from 2007 through 2012, emphasizes "It was really their court, and we were more invited guests."[130] Bosnian nationals provided the energy and commitment that would be needed to secure the success of such an ambitious project. Judge Fisher recalled:

> Bosnians who had been children or teenagers during the war and fled . . . came back to work on the court. It was the court that pulled them back. Because they . . . *really* wanted it to work. I mean, the energy and the enthusiasm—the optimism was just inspiring.[131]

---

[125] For a brief account of the task force established to deal with a range of matters relating to the creation of the new institutions, see Lauth, *supra* note 48, at 258.

[126] Interview with Melika Murtezić, Judge, Municipal Court in Sarajevo, in Washington, D.C., United States (May 30, 2016). Judge Whalen made much the same point, noting Bosnian "nationals were at the table right from the beginning" in creating the legal framework for Bosnia's war crimes institutions. Judge Patricia Whalen, Remarks at the Conference on Prosecuting Serious International Crimes: Exploring the Intersections between International and Domestic Justice Efforts, Sponsored by the War Crimes Research Office, Washington College of Law, Washington, D.C., United States (Mar. 30, 2016).

[127] Interview with Shireen Fisher, Former International Judge, BWCC, in Washington, D.C., United States (May 29, 2016).

[128] *Id.*

[129] *Id.*

[130] Interview with Patricia Whalen, Former International Judge, BWCC, in Washington, D.C., United States (May 29, 2016).

[131] Interview with Shireen Fisher, Former International Judge, BWCC, in Washington, D.C., United States (May 29, 2016).

If the new institutions were to thrive, they would also need a supportive political environment. How, then, did political elites and others react when ICTY officials first proposed "relocating" some of the Tribunal's cases to Bosnia? The country's predominantly Muslim government welcomed the initiative, if somewhat warily. Following then-ICTY President Jorda's remarks suggesting local courts might now be ready to "try some of the war criminals in their territory," a Bosnian representative stated:

> We are aware that many more suspected war criminals in the region have to be prosecuted either by the ICTY or by the authorized national courts. The Government of Bosnia and Herzegovina welcomes the ICTY initiative to process some of the cases by the local judiciary structures under the auspices of the ICTY, suggesting that the Court of Bosnia and Herzegovina, which was established by the High Representative's decision, should be the first institution in the country for delegating such a task. . . . The position of the Government of Bosnia and Herzegovina is that *the prosecution and trial of the indicted war criminals in the region should continue to be a United Nations responsibility*, especially in light of the universal importance of the ICTY mandate after the tragic events of 11 September.[132]

But if the ICTY's proposal aroused some anxiety, Bosniak officials soon came to embrace the BWCC.[133] Many saw the strength of autonomous RS institutions as an enduring legacy of wartime atrocities, and state-level judicial institutions could help restore a measure of unified governance. Once the ICTY Referral Bench approved 11*bis* transfers to Bosnia, moreover, its decisions "provided a clear mark of international legitimation for the BiH judiciary."[134] Some officials reportedly welcomed domestic institutions in part because they were "an alternative to the ICTY, frustration with which was growing."[135] Finally, some felt a moral imperative, as well as sovereign right, to address atrocities of the immediate past in domestic courts. In the words of Potparić-Lipa, "The victims are citizens of Bosnia & Herzegovina. We have a moral, ethical and legal right to prosecute ourselves."[136]

Some RS leaders opposed the BWCC, in part because they saw the Court of BiH, in which it was embedded, as an unconstitutional threat to Serb autonomy,[137] and

---

[132] Representative of Bosnia-Herzegovina, U.N. SCOR, 56th Sess., 4429th mtg. at 18, U.N. Doc. S/PV.4429 (Nov. 27, 2001) (emphasis added).

[133] See Ronen, *Impact of ICTY, supra* note 101, at 129–30.

[134] Burke-White, *supra* note 61, at 328. Burke-White quotes then Assistant Minister of Justice Mustafa Bisić saying, in a 2005 interview, that "the referral of cases gives the State Court new clout. It is now seen as a real court." *Id.* Following a conference to raise funds for the BWCC in October 2003, leaders of political parties voiced a range of views. Rasim Kadić, then president of the Bosnian Liberal Democratic Party, voiced concerns that ethnic divisions in Bosnia would make it difficult for the chamber to earn public confidence. In contrast, Ivo Komšić, then president of the Bosnian Social Democratic Union, believed the court would be able to handle the cases of the "many small and anonymous people" who committed wartime atrocities. *Financing Local Justice*, TOL BALKAN RECONSTRUCTION REP. (Nov. 3, 2003).

[135] DOMAC/8 REPORT, *supra* note 17, at 64. *See also* Burke-White, *supra* note 61, at 331.

[136] Burke-White, *supra* note 61, at 331.

[137] As previously noted, RS parliamentarians challenged the Court of BiH; its constitutionality was upheld by Bosnia's Constitutional Court in September 2001. *See* COURTING DISASTER, *supra* note 98, at 25.

in part because they believed the chamber would be biased against ethnic Serbs.[138] In addition, the "close involvement of so many internationals" reportedly "enraged Bosnian Serb politicians."[139] Not long after the war crimes institutions began operating, RS leaders publicly challenged their performance, which they claimed showed an anti-Serb bias.[140] Initially, however, Serb opposition was tempered by a desire on the part of some RS officials to prevent "ethnically-charged cases from landing on their own doorsteps."[141]

Civil society, including victims groups and legal professionals, were not widely consulted about the proposed war crimes institutions.[142] But "setting up a highly specialized, all-Bosnian institution was not a controversial step" for most of them, according to the International Center for Transitional Justice.[143] Understandably, however, "Serb associations of former camp inmates vigorously objected to the choice of the building where the Court of BiH is seated," which had been used as a detention facility for Serbs during the war.[144]

A few years after it began operating, the BWCC had earned the admiration and pride of many civil society actors. When I interviewed her in 2009, journalist Nidžara Ahmetašević described the chamber as one of "the strongest state institution[s] we have," which was playing an important role in Bosnians' process of reckoning with wartime atrocities.[145] Yet the transfer of cases from The Hague to Sarajevo—the prime impetus for the BWCC's creation—disappointed some victims, who had hoped to see those responsible for their suffering prosecuted in The Hague. According to Mirko Zelenika, who served for sixteen years as president of the Association of Croat Detainees in Bosnia and Herzegovina, between May 1995 and October 1998 ICTY investigators interviewed "hundreds" of Croat victims over the course of twenty-two visits to Mostar. The investigators, Zelenika recalled, anticipated the OTP would indict some fifteen suspects for the crimes they were investigating; instead, most of the cases were transferred to the SDWC.[146] Even so, representatives of other victims associations made clear that, with the ICTY no longer able to bring charges, they were grateful state institutions could continue processing war crimes cases long after the Hague Tribunal stopped issuing indictments.[147]

---

[138] *See* Ronen, *Impact of ICTY, supra* note 101, at 130.

[139] Alison Freebairn & Nerma Jelačić, *Bringing War Crimes Justice Back Home*, IWPR (Nov. 26, 2004).

[140] *See* Maja Milavić, *Court Faces "Political" Smears*, JUST. REP. (Sept. 8, 2006).

[141] Ronen, *Impact of ICTY, supra* note 101, at 130.

[142] BOGDAN IVANIŠEVIĆ, INTERNATIONAL CENTER FOR TRANSITIONAL JUSTICE, THE WAR CRIMES CHAMBER IN BOSNIA AND HERZEGOVINA: FROM HYBRID TO DOMESTIC COURT 6 (2008) [hereinafter FROM HYBRID TO DOMESTIC].

[143] *Id.* at 7.

[144] *Id.* at 33–34. *See also* Janine Natalya Clark, *The State Court of Bosnia and Herzegovina: A Path to Reconciliation?*, 13 CONTEMP. JUST. REV. 371, 378 (2010).

[145] Interview with Nidžara Ahmetašević, then Editor, BIRN in BiH, in Sarajevo, Bosn. & Herz. (July 13, 2009). As an example of the latter, Ahmetašević noted a "strong judgment for genocide" issued by the BWCC against eleven defendants, and said: "It's a huge thing. It's a historical thing." *Id.*

[146] Interview with Mirko Zelenika, then President, Association of Croat Detainees in Bosnia and Herzegovina, in Mostar, Bosn. & Herz. (Sept. 10, 2014).

[147] *E.g.*, interview with Edin Ramulić, Project Coordinator, Izvor, in Prijedor, Bosn. & Herz. (Sept. 16, 2014).

II. THE ICTY'S IMPRINT ON BOSNIA'S WAR CRIMES INSTITUTIONS

Designed to complete the Tribunal's unfinished work in accordance with standards prescribed by its judges, the BWCC reflects the ICTY's influence in myriad ways. Noting the chamber is sometimes seen as a "mini-ICTY," BWCC Judge Mira Smajlović summarized the Hague Tribunal's influence this way:

> In general I would say that the ICTY influenced this court in [three] ways. One is institutionally. The model of operation of this court is based on the model adopted by the ICTY ... We are following the [ICTY's] case law as well. Another way the ICTY influenced the Court of BiH is best practices. We follow the ICTY's best practices to a large extent.[148]

The rest of this chapter briefly elaborates upon each type of influence Judge Smajlović noted.[149] Its principal focus, however, is on how the Tribunal has affected Bosnian jurists' capacity to render justice for atrocious crimes in a divided country, where few issues are more contested that than that of responsibility for wartime atrocities.

A. Impact on the BWCC's Independence, Impartiality, and Adherence to Fair Process

1. MONITORING CASES TRANSFERRED FROM THE ICTY TO THE BWCC

A "core part of the strategy" devised by the architects of the BWCC "was for the new court to begin with cases transferred pursuant [to] Rule 11*bis*, thus allowing it to build its capacity under the eye of the ICTY."[150] To this end, the Tribunal's amended Rule 11*bis* enabled the Prosecutor to designate observers to monitor cases originating in an ICTY indictment.[151] At the request of the Prosecutor and on her behalf, the Organization for Security and Co-operation in Europe (OSCE) Mission to Bosnia monitored cases transferred pursuant to Rule 11*bis*.[152]

Rule 11*bis* empowered the Tribunal to recall a transferred case if local proceedings fell short of international standards.[153] It was virtually inconceivable the ICTY would

---

[148] The moniker "mini-ICTY" is not always meant as a compliment, particularly when used by RS leaders. Noting this, Judge Smajlović added: "I would see it as a compliment to be a mini-ICTY, an honor to work for such an institution." Interview with Mira Smajlović, Judge, BWCC, in Sarajevo, Bosn. & Herz. (Sept. 9, 2014).

[149] "Briefly" because earlier sections have already addressed the first and third types of impact cited by Judge Smajlović, while other studies have extensively explored the ICTY's impact on the BWCC's case law in greater depth than is useful here.

[150] Tolbert & Kontić, *Transfer of Cases, supra* note 15, at 147. *But see* Donlon, *supra* note 2, at 277 (although the question of how to prioritize among broad *categories* of cases arose during negotiations between the OHR and ICTY, ultimately they decided there should be no prioritization as between Rule 11*bis* and other cases). Transfers to Bosnia of 11*bis* cases occurred between 2005 and 2007. The last 11*bis* transfer to Bosnia, involving the case against Milorad Trbić, occurred on June 11, 2007.

[151] ICTY RPE, *supra* note 122, Rule 11*bis* (D)(iv) (as amended on Sept. 30, 2002).

[152] Organization for Security and Co-operation in Europe, *Decision No. 673, Cooperation Between the Organization for Security and Cooperation in Europe and the International Criminal Tribunal for the Former Yugoslavia*, PC.DEC/673 (May 19, 2005).

[153] ICTY RPE, *supra* note 122, Rule 11*bis* (F)–(G) (as amended on Sept. 30, 2002).

do so; the whole point of the transfers was to reduce its docket. Even so, then HJPC president Branko Perić told me, "judges and prosecutors [were] well aware of the Hague's ability to take back cases," which "motivated [them] to show that they [were] just as capable of trying cases as the ICTY."[154]

The OSCE mission's early, detailed, and public critiques of BWCC proceedings addressed systemic concerns early on. Judge Mira Smajlović described the BWCC planning process and the early years of OSCE monitoring as "certainly a beneficial experience for us."[155] "Weaknesses were identified" early on, and necessary steps were taken to address them. Then, national judges "were able to apply these good practices we developed" in later cases.[156] The monitoring process was hardly perfect, however. At times, according to BWCC veterans, the inexperience of young monitors was clear, as they seized upon apparent procedural anomalies that a more seasoned lawyer would realize made good judicial sense. Nor is it easy to separate the impact of the monitoring process from that of international judges, who likely played a more significant role in sensitizing their colleagues to international standards.

With the conclusion of the OSCE monitoring process at the end of 2009 and withdrawal of international judges three years later, it has been difficult to sustain some elements of progress achieved in the BWCC's early years. Its approach to transparency is a sobering case in point. In two early cases involving allegations of systematic rape, the chamber excluded the public from almost the entire proceedings. Following criticism by OSCE monitors, the chamber was more judicious in its use of closed sessions.[157] OSCE mission staff believe standards for witness protection developed by the ICTY provided important guidance as the BWCC adjusted its approach in the direction of greater transparency,[158] and that their monitoring reports "may

---

[154] Interview with Branko Perić, then President, HJPC, in Sarajevo, Bosn. & Herz. (Dec. 4, 2006). The OSCE monitoring mission staff believe that, while it was understood the recall authority would not be used lightly, the fact that it was possible, "coupled with the notable international and public interest in these transferred cases, certainly made all actors (particularly the justice authorities, the political ones, and the international community) very conscious of the fact that Rule 11*bis* cases were perceived as a test case for the capacity of the national judiciary to deal with war crimes fairly and effectively." Email from Pipina Katsaris, then Legal Adviser-Head of the Rule 11*bis* Monitoring Project and Capacity Building and Legacy Implementation Project, Human Rights Department, OSCE Mission to BiH, to Diane Orentlicher (Sept. 30, 2009). The same point was made during interviews in Bosnia in September 2014. Not everyone agrees, however. Two former international judges on the BWCC believe the prospect of a recall was truly inconceivable (not just virtually so), and therefore did not significantly shape the work of the chamber. Interview with Patricia Whalen & Shireen Fisher, Former International Judges, BWCC, in Washington, D.C., United States (May 29, 2016).

[155] Interview with Mira Smajlović, Judge, BWCC, in Sarajevo, Bosn. & Herz. (Sept. 9, 2014).

[156] *Id.*

[157] *See* Diane F. Orentlicher, Open Society Justice Initiative & International Center for Transitional Justice, That Someone Guilty Be Punished: The Impact of the ICTY in Bosnia 120 (2010). For expressions of concern about these practices, see From Hybrid to Domestic, *supra* note 142, at 19; Param-Preet Singh, Human Rights Watch, Narrowing the Impunity Gap: Trials Before Bosnia's War Crimes Chamber 30–35 (2007); Organization for Security and Co-operation in Europe, Mission to Bosn. & Herz., Second OSCE Report, Case of Radovan Stanković Transferred to the State Court Pursuant to Rule 11*bis* (2006). *See also Anger at Secrecy Surrounding Foča Rape Cases*, Just. Rep. (Mar. 8, 2006).

[158] Interview with Staff, OSCE Mission to BiH, in Sarajevo, Bosn. & Herz. (June 8, 2007).

have contributed to the fact that trial panels [as of 2007] attempted to close proceedings as little as possible."[159]

After the public monitoring function of the mission ended, however, the BWCC became even less transparent than during its early years—in some respects, astonishingly so. In early 2012, the Court of BiH adopted a decision to anonymize court documents.[160] Going forward, instead of providing the names of defendants and places where crimes were committed, verdicts and other key documents would use only initials for defendants, locations of atrocities, and other key information.[161] Illustrating the implications, journalist Anisa Sućeska-Vekić said that, if the BWCC convicted Radovan Karadžić of genocide in relation to Srebrenica, its verdict would read "R.K., sentenced for genocide in XXX year. . . ."[162] Meanwhile, the POBiH decided to stop publishing indictments on its website.[163] Victims and others decried the new approach (later modified)[164] as an infringement of their internationally-protected right to know the truth about grave violations of human rights and a breach of Bosnia's duty to remember the truth. In the words of Bakira Hasečić, president of the Association of Women Victims of War, "We must speak openly about war crimes. If a victim wants to testify publicly, why should a court limit that right? We must end the cycle of silence."[165]

The ICTY bore no apparent responsibility for this development,[166] but troubling trends in the domestic war crimes institutions inevitably shape public perceptions of

[159] Pipina Th. Katsaris, *The Domestic Side of the ICTY Completion Strategy: Focus on Bosnia and Herzegovina*, 78 REVUE INTERNATIONALE DE DROIT PÉNAL 183, 201 (2007). *See also* ORGANIZATION FOR SECURITY AND CO-OPERATION IN EUROPE, MISSION TO BOSN. & HERZ., THE PROCESSING OF ICTY RULE 11BIS CASES IN BOSNIA AND HERZEGOVINA: REFLECTIONS ON FINDINGS FROM FIVE YEARS OF OSCE MONITORING 19 (2010).

[160] *See* Denis Džidić, *Bosnia to End Controversial Anonymised Verdicts*, BALKAN INSIGHT (Mar. 17, 2014).

[161] *Anonymization "Threat" to Bosnian Justice Criticized*, JUST. REP. (Dec. 25, 2012). The decision was based on the Court's interpretation of a 2012 opinion of Bosnia's Agency for the Protection of Personal Data, *see id.*, which was established pursuant to an opinion of the European Union. Despite the reported basis of the agency's decision, the European Commission "was shocked" by the agency's approach, according to Anisa Sućeska-Vekić. Interview with Anisa Sućeska-Vekić, then Director, BIRN in BiH, in Sarajevo, Bosn. & Herz. (Sept. 17, 2014).

[162] Interview with Anisa Sućeska-Vekić, then Director, BIRN in BiH, in Sarajevo, Bosn. & Herz. (Sept. 17, 2014).

[163] *Id. See also* Denis Džidić, *Bosnian Court Accused of War Crimes Censorship*, BALKAN TRANSITIONAL JUST. (June 26, 2013).

[164] In December 2012, the state court's press officer said the court understood it had made a mistake. Interview with Anisa Sućeska-Vekić, then Director, BIRN in BiH, in Sarajevo, Bosn. & Herz. (Sept. 17, 2014); *see also Non-selective Anonymization Tarnishes Bosnian Court*, JUST. REP. (undated). Further developments are noted in note 166.

[165] Denis Džidić, *Bosnian Court Accused of War Crimes Censorship*, BALKAN TRANSITIONAL JUST. (June 26, 2013).

[166] Instead, a range of domestic actors—from the Court of BiH and State Prosecutor to the Bosnian Parliament and HJPC—share responsibility. According to Anisa Sućeska-Vekić, by forwarding the 2012 opinion of the Agency for the Protection of Privacy Data (*see supra* note 162) to courts and to prosecutors, the HJPC in effect made the opinion binding on them. "Legally, when the HJPC is sending you something, it's obligatory for [the judicial recipients]," Sućeska-Vekić explained. The President of the Court and prosecutors concluded the HJPC "was silently requesting them to do it"—that is, to act in accordance with the agency's opinion. *Id.* Meanwhile, in June 2013 the Bosnian parliament amended the country's Freedom of Access to Information Law, limiting public access to previously public documents. Apparently the European Commission, learning of this development, asked Bosnian authorities to change the law and practice. In May 2014, it was

the Tribunal. As Sućeska-Vekić noted, the Hague Tribunal "is now seen [in Bosnia] through the lens of how the Court of Bosnia-Herzegovina is" performing.[167] After all, the BWCC is the "legacy of the ICTY."[168]

2. Enhancing Judicial Independence and Perceptions of Impartiality through Hybridity

If external monitoring helped assure fair process in the BWCC's early years, a more substantial safeguard was implanted in the fledgling chamber through the participation of international judges. As previously noted, ICTY officials and others believed the participation of foreign jurists would help ensure confidence in the chamber's impartiality while, ideally, providing a bridge between local legal tradition and global standards.[169] Like the OSCE mission's 11*bis* monitoring effort, this safeguard was transitional: as previously noted, it was envisaged that the foreign jurists would participate for only five years, during which they would gradually be phased out.

Integrating foreign judges and prosecutors was challenging. But as a bulwark against political pressures, the hybrid model was a success while it lasted. The participation of foreign jurists boosted public confidence in the fledgling court,[170] no small achievement in a country as polarized as Bosnia. As former BWCC judge Patricia Whalen notes, through their "very presence" the international judges were a human "firewall between [the national judges] and the controversies of the day."[171] As for international prosecutors, Human Rights Watch found they "played a key role in investigating and prosecuting serious cases that would have likely remained unaddressed because of their sensitivity."[172]

But the hybrid design had a serious flaw: while it made sense to plan for the eventual withdrawal of foreign jurists, the timeline for doing so proved too short and the process for extending their mandate too rigid. As the December 2009 deadline for phasing out remaining international personnel approached, the need for their continued participation became glaringly clear. With respect to the BWCC, the key issue was not the professionalism of Bosnian judges; by December 2008,

---

reported that the Court of BiH had changed its Rulebook on accessing information, accepting recommendations "arising from the structural dialogue between BiH and the European Union" held the previous year. Under the revised Rulebook, cases of special interest to the public, including war crimes cases, would not be anonymized. Amer Jahić, *Bosnian State Court Abolishes Anonymisation of Verdicts*, JUST. REP. (May 6, 2014). But the practice reportedly continued when I visited Bosnia in September 2014. Interview with Anisa Sućeska-Vekić, then Director, BIRN in BiH, in Sarajevo, Bosn. & Herz. (Sept. 17, 2014). More recently, however, names of defendants have been available on the POBiH website and in BWCC verdicts.

[167] Interview with Anisa Sućeska-Vekić, then Director, BIRN in BiH, in Sarajevo, Bosn. & Herz. (Sept. 17, 2014).

[168] *Id.*

[169] Speaking to the first consideration, a Tribunal spokesperson said: "In terms of perception of fair handling and ethnic bias, that's why internationals have been brought on board initially, to try to diminish these concerns." Alison Freebairn & Nerma Jelačić, *Bringing War Crimes Justice Back Home*, BOSNIAN INSTITUTE (Dec. 21, 2004).

[170] This point has been made repeatedly in my research trips to Bosnia. *See also* Ronen, *Impact of ICTY, supra* note 101, at 132.

[171] Telephone interview with Patricia Whalen, Former International Judge, BWCC (Mar. 25, 2016). Judges on the BWCC and other close observers made similar points confidentially. As one BWCC judge put it, the international judges "stiffened our spines."

[172] JUSTICE FOR ATROCITY CRIMES, *supra* note 5, at 1.

an external assessment found national judges were "generally perceived to be good professional judges [who] presided over fair trials and appeals."[173] Nor were there significant concerns about the independence and impartiality of national judges on the BWCC.[174] Instead, the chamber came under mounting pressure from resurgent nationalists as the end of the mandate of international judges approached.

To understand the nature of this pressure, it is useful to recall the broader context in which the fate of international judges was addressed in 2009. As recounted in Chapter 2, RS president Milorad Dodik, once a relative moderate, has routinely challenged state institutions, Bosnian unity, and the OHR since 2006. Although hardly the sole target of Dodik's attacks, the BWCC has long been one of them. In September 2006, for example, Dodik questioned "the fairness of the prosecution's work," threatening to withdraw RS authority for state-level war crimes institutions if they continued to prosecute more Serbs than individuals belonging to other ethnic groups.[175]

By 2009 Bosnia was in the throes of a paralyzing "political crisis,"[176] centering on a conflict between Dodik and his supporters on the one hand and High Representative Valentin Inzko on the other.[177] In this setting, Dodik continued to direct rhetorical fire at the Court of BiH, claiming the "internationals" were "controlling judicial institutions in Bosnia [that were] being used against Serbs and certain politicians who do not conform to them."[178]

Dodik's challenge was of a piece with his broader opposition to state institutions, which he routinely cast as a threat to RS autonomy. But by many accounts, his opposition to foreign jurists was prompted above all by self-interest: in 2009, Dodik was facing charges before the state court's specialized chamber on organized crime, which included international personnel. Like the foreign jurists participating in the BWCC and SDWC, their mandate was set to expire in December 2009.[179] Dodik reportedly reckoned his legal fate would be much improved with international prosecutors and judges out of the picture.[180] As one analyst wrote, Dodik "apparently

---

[173] David Tolbert & Aleksandar Kontić, Final Report of the International Criminal Law Services (ICLS) Experts on the Sustainable Transition of the Registry and International Donor Support to the Court of Bosnia and Herzegovina and the Prosecutor's Office of Bosnia and Herzegovina in 2009, ¶ 123 (2008) [hereinafter ICLS Report]. See also ICTJ Warns Bosnian War Crimes Chamber's Early Success at Risk, Bosnia Daily (Oct. 15, 2008).

[174] The 2008 ICLS report concluded "there is no doubt that both national and international judges are independent and without bias." ICLS Report, supra note 173, ¶ 125.

[175] Maja Milavić, Court Faces "Political" Smears, Just. Rep. (Sept. 8, 2006).

[176] Bodo Weber, West's Last Chance to Get Serious on Bosnia, Balkan Insight (Dec. 1, 2009).

[177] See International Crisis Group, Bosnia's Dual Crisis 3 (2009) [hereinafter Dual Crisis]; Kurt Bassuener & Bodo Weber, Balkan Tango: The EU's Disjointed Policies Compound Bosnia's Paralysis, 2 IP Global Edition 19, 21 (2010) [hereinafter Bassuener & Weber, Balkan Tango]. In May and June 2009, Inzko forced Republika Srpska to retract "largely symbolic declarations critical of allegedly improper transfers of competencies from the entities to the state," provoking a fierce backlash from Dodik. Dual Crisis, supra, at 3. The crisis was heightened in September 2009, when Inzko used his Bonn powers to impose eight laws. See id. at 2.

[178] Velma Šarić, Bosnia: Future of International Judges and Prosecutors in Doubt, IWPR (Sept. 16, 2009).

[179] See Weber, supra note 176; Erna Mačkić, Decision Close on Bosnia's International Judges and Prosecutors, Just. Rep. (Sept. 16, 2009).

[180] E.g., interview with Anisa Sućeska-Vekić, then Director, BIRN in BiH, in Sarajevo, Bosn. & Herz. (Sept. 17, 2014). See also Bassuener & Weber, Balkan Tango, supra note 177; Kurt Bassuener &

felt the need to destroy the state's post-Dayton institutions in order to escape prosecution" for corruption.[181]

In another view, expressed by then SDWC prosecutor Irisa Čevra, the motivations behind RS attacks on war crimes institutions are "always twofold."[182] As Čevra sees it, political figures in RS have a "genuine interest" in attacking the organized crime court, but at the same time "are preserving this hatred in Republika Srpska as a way . . . for winning elections."[183] "Relentless" attacks on the state war crimes institutions are, she believes, integral to the latter.[184]

Whatever their motivations, the attacks were debilitating. Reviewing the BWCC's first ten years, the OSCE Mission to BiH concluded that the "prolonged campaign of de-legitimization[,] particularly in 2009," had undermined public confidence in the war crimes institutions.[185] Another study reported the attacks placed "considerable additional pressure on [BWCC] judges, as their decisions are attributed [by some] to bias regardless of the fact that the decision is fully justified, based on the relevant evidence fairly evaluated."[186] In this setting, while praising the achievements of Bosnia's war crimes institutions, then ICTY president Patrick Robinson voiced concern about the looming expiration of the mandates of international judges and prosecutors, who were "still critical to protecting the integrity of the judiciary" in Bosnia.[187]

Extending their mandates would require an amendment to Bosnian law.[188] Although Bosniak and Croat delegates supported the extension (as did the Bosnian president of the Court of BiH, the Prosecutor of BiH and Bosniak victims), RS opposition thwarted parliamentary action.[189] Thus it would fall to the High Representative, if anyone, to extend the jurists' mandate. On December 14, 2009, the day their mandate was set to expire, Inzko extended their terms for three years.[190] By then, it was

---

Bodo Weber, "Are We There Yet?" International Impatience vs. a Long-Term Strategy for a Viable Bosnia 5 (2010) [hereinafter Bassuener & Weber, Are We There Yet?].

[181] Weber, *supra* note 176. *See also* Mačkić, *supra* note 179 (quoting Bosniak political figures stating those opposed to extending the mandate of international judges were "afraid of eventual trials against them, in particular before the Organized Crime and Corruption Section;" Dodik wanted to abolish "all courts and prosecutors, 'so that his own case was never tried' ").

[182] Interview with Irisa Čevra, then Assistant to the Deputy Prosecutor, SDWC, in Sarajevo, Bosn. & Herz. (Sept. 18, 2014).

[183] *Id.*

[184] *Id.*

[185] Delivering Justice, *supra* note 105, at 86. Almost 60 percent of Bosnian respondents in a survey conducted in July 2008 said they did not have faith in the Court of BiH to prosecute war crimes fairly and produce a just result. *See id.* at 90.

[186] ICLS Report, *supra* note 173, ¶ 125. The withdrawal of international prosecutors, who were handling complex cases within the SDWC, raised similar and also distinct concerns, the latter principally relating to continuity of work on cases. *See* Mačkić, *supra* note 179. ICTY Prosecutor Serge Brammertz likewise emphasized the disruptive effect of losing international personnel, stating: "Unless the issue is resolved as a matter of urgency, ongoing war-crimes trials and investigations might be endangered." Marima Husejnović, *Bosnia Judicial Institutions Await Final Decision*, Balkan Insight (Dec. 11, 2009).

[187] Velma Šarić, *Bosnia: Future of International Judges and Prosecutors in Doubt*, IWPR (Sept. 16, 2009).

[188] Mačkić, *supra* note 179.

[189] *Id.*; Velma Šarić, *Bosnia: Future of International Judges and Prosecutors in Doubt*, IWPR (Sept. 16, 2009).

[190] *See* Valentin Inzko (High Representative), Office of the High Representative, *Decision Enacting the Law on Amendments to the Law on Court of Bosnia and Herzegovina* (Dec. 14, 2009); Valentin Inzko (High Representative), Office of the High Representative, *Decision Enacting the Law on*

too late to prevent all of the remaining international jurists from leaving: with no guarantee their mandates would be extended, three of the six remaining international judges had left the BWCC and were not replaced.[191] The SDWC was left with only one "experienced international prosecutor,"[192] as a result of which "[m]any international staff members in the [SDWC] found it necessary to leave" as well.[193] Why, then, did Inzko wait so long to extend their mandate?

His authority to act was held captive to the "Butmir process," an initiative of the United States and European Union aimed at securing agreement to constitutional reform and an end to the OHR mandate.[194] The effort was a spectacular failure, but while talks were underway in late 2009 the PIC prevented Inzko from extending the foreign jurists' mandates until the last possible moment.[195] (In the words of a former international judge, European negotiators "threw the [BWCC] under the bus."[196]) Beyond its deleterious effect on the chamber, the Butmir process further weakened the High Representative, who was sidelined so publicly that the "entire process seemed calculated to portray the OHR as an irrelevance or an impediment to progress."[197]

When authorization to extend the foreign jurists' mandate finally came, it was compromised in a manner sure to embolden Dodik further. PIC ambassadors "opted for a *lex Dodik*: they decided to extend only international judges and prosecutors" working on war crimes, voting against extending senior personnel in the organized crime institutions that could prosecute Dodik for corruption.[198] Even so, Dodik and other RS leaders protested Inzko's decision to extend the mandates of foreign war crimes jurists.[199]

Amendments to the Law on Prosecutor's Office of Bosnia and Herzegovina (Dec. 14, 2009); *OHR Extends International Judges' Mandate*, BALKAN INSIGHT (Dec. 16, 2009). Inzko did not, however, extend the mandate of BWCC international judges sitting on first-instance panels beyond what was required to complete cases in progress. Schwendiman, *Prosecuting Atrocity Crimes, supra* note 118, at 280; Mačkić, *supra* note 179.

[191] Interview with Patricia Whalen, Former International Judge, BWCC, in Washington, D.C., United States (May 29, 2016). Another source writes that four international judges remained. Olga Martin-Ortega, *Prosecuting War Crimes at Home: Lessons from the War Crimes Chamber in the State Court of Bosnia and Herzegovina*, 12 INT'L CRIM. L. REV. 589, 596 (2012).

[192] Schwendiman, *Prosecuting Atrocity Crimes, supra* note 118, at 280.

[193] *Id.*

[194] *See* DUAL CRISIS, *supra* note 177, at 3.

[195] *See* Bassuener & Weber, ARE WE THERE YET?, *supra* note 180, at 5.

[196] Interview with Shireen Fisher, Former International Judge, BWCC, in Washington, D.C., United States (May 29, 2016). In a similar vein, Judge Whalen explained the delay in authorizing Inzko to act as an "EU-driven political decision to . . . appease Dodik at the time." Interview with Patricia Whalen, Former International Judge, BWCC, in Washington, D.C., United States (May 29, 2016).

[197] Kurt Bassuener, A Durable Oligarchy: Bosnia and Herzegovina's False Postwar Democratic Transition 40 (draft manuscript) (on file with author); *see also* JOANNE MCEVOY, POWER-SHARING EXECUTIVES: GOVERNING IN BOSNIA, MACEDONIA, AND NORTHERN IRELAND 141 (2015).

[198] Bassuener & Weber, *Balkan Tango, supra* note 177, at 22. Lara Nettelfield characterizes this as "a blatant attempt to appease Milorad Dodik," which "reflected the fears of [PIC] member states that a decision to impose an extension for all foreign personnel would trigger severe backlash in RS." LARA J. NETTELFIELD, COURTING DEMOCRACY IN BOSNIA AND HERZEGOVINA: THE HAGUE TRIBUNAL'S IMPACT IN A POSTWAR STATE 267 (2010).

[199] *See Inzko Extended the Stay of Internationals*, HUM. RTS. HOUSE NETWORK (Dec. 15, 2009); *OHR Extends International Judges' Mandate*, BALKAN INSIGHT (Dec. 16, 2009). Inzko stated that

In December 2012, in accordance with the terms of Inzko's December 2009 eleventh-hour reprieve, the mandates of remaining international judges and prosecutors expired. The costs of their premature withdrawal have been profound.[200] As then SDWC lawyer Irisa Čevra observed, while embedded in the BWCC and SDWC, the foreign jurists "helped us . . . to preserve this like sense of impartiality. And they actually protected us from political biases." When their mandates ended, "they just left us exposed to any sort of political pressure. And Dodik was really relentless in that."[201] In 2014, I asked Nidžara Ahmetašević, who previously described the BWCC as one of "the strongest state institution[s] we have," if she still saw it this way. Ahmetašević replied:

> It was. It was really until the international community decided that their job is done, and until the local politicians decided, "OK, now our job is starting again." And then they start manipulating with the trials, playing with the way they wanted to do that. The judges became unsecure, the prosecutors are also unsecure about what to do.[202]

Pressure grew even more intense after I interviewed Čevra and Ahmetašević. In July 2015, the RS assembly voted to hold a referendum on the Court of BiH because of what Dodik claimed was its encroachment on RS authority and its anti-Serb bias,[203] though Dodik later put the plan on hold.[204]

The contours of the crisis surrounding extension of the foreign jurists' mandate are peculiar to Bosnia. But the episode holds wider lessons for countries in which hybrid courts are established.[205] Most important, in fraught settings where international judges and prosecutors can play a useful, perhaps vital, role, it is foolhardy to set a rigid deadline for their exit without regard to prevailing conditions. Instead, the need to extend their mandate in light of relevant criteria, such as continued threats to judicial independence, should be anticipated.

---

international judges and prosecutors would stay on in the organized crime section as advisors. *OHR Extends International Judges' Mandate, supra.*

[200] *See* Martin-Ortega, *supra* note 191, at 618 (RS allegations of BWCC bias "have been constant from the start of the [chamber's] work, and since the winding down of the presence of the internationals it has increased"). By the end of June 2014, two international experts who served as advisors to national war crimes judges left as well. One was a former international judge on the BWCC, Patricia Whalen. Interview with Biljana Potparić, then Registrar, Court of BiH, in Sarajevo, Bosn. & Herz. (Sept. 11, 2014); interview with Mervan Miraščija, Law Program Coordinator, Open Society Fund BiH, in Sarajevo, Bosn. & Herz. (Sept. 8, 2014).

[201] Interview with Irisa Čevra, then Assistant to the Deputy Prosecutor, SDWC, in Sarajevo, Bosn. & Herz. (Sept. 18, 2014).

[202] Interview with Nidžara Ahmetašević, Journalist, in Sarajevo, Bosn. & Herz. (Sept. 12, 2014).

[203] Elvira M. Jukić & Srećko Latal, *Bosnian Serb Referendum Meets Chorus of Condemnation*, Balkan Insight (July 17, 2015); Denis Džidić, *Bosnian State Court Rejects Anti-Serb Bias Claims*, Balkan Insight (Oct. 22, 2015); *Bosnia's Serbs Vote for Referendum on National Court*, BBC News (July 16, 2015).

[204] Danijel Kovačević, *Bosnian Serb Leader Puts Justice Referendum on Hold*, Balkan Insight (Sept. 20, 2017).

[205] Hybrid courts have been created to address atrocities and acts of terrorism committed in Cambodia, East Timor, Kosovo, Lebanon, and Sierra Leone and have been planned or considered for the Central African Republic (which enacted legislation for such a court in 2015), the Democratic Republic of the Congo, Colombia, North Korea, South Sudan, Sri Lanka, Libya,

There are, to be sure, sound reasons to establish a timeline for transitioning to a fully national court. As former BWCC judge Shireen Fisher notes, the deadline for phasing out international judges provided a strong incentive to meet key targets in a timely fashion.[206] "The incredible thing and the part that worked out really well," she notes, was that, over the course of the BWCC's first five years, key departments in the registry and in judicial support were "transitioning from having leadership in internationals to leadership in nationals. They met each and every transition milestone. They knew that they had a short window, so they hired terrific people" who did a "fantastic" job.[207] It is, moreover, almost unthinkable that donor states would assume an open-ended commitment to sponsor international judges.[208]

When rigidly enforced, however, a deadline for withdrawing international actors can compromise fragile courts, allowing spoilers like Dodik to exploit their heightened vulnerability during the lame duck period of foreign jurists' service and after the foreigners depart. Accordingly, Judge Fisher argues, despite the value of the original deadline for phasing out international judges, in retrospect it would have been better to link their removal to "a political benchmark and a professional benchmark in terms of how much more . . . needed to be done . . . with some degree of safety."[209]

Bosnia's experience holds another important lesson, Judge Whalen believes: external actors must take care to ensure they do not obscure the crucial roles played by national actors in launching and building local war crimes institutions. Whalen recalls that, throughout the time she served on the BWCC: "All you ever heard about was the OHR, the ICTY, the OHR, the ICTY, blah, blah, blah, blah, blah, blah, blah." Without detracting from their contributions, she continued, "there were a lot of [Bosnian nationals] at the table that never got recognized."[210] Yet the misleading

---

and Burundi. *See* Beth Van Schaack, *The Building Blocks of Hybrid Justice*, 44 DENVER J. INT'L L. & POL'Y 169 (2016).

[206] Interview with Shireen Fisher, Former International Judge, BWCC, in Washington, D.C., United States (May 29, 2016).

[207] *Id.* When the BWCC was launched, three-judge panels comprised one national and two international judges, one of whom presided; later, the composition remained the same but the national judge presided; in 2008, the ratio shifted: panels were composed of one international and two national judges, one of whom presided. Ultimately, the panels were composed solely of Bosnian judges.

[208] A source who was involved in establishing Bosnia's war crimes institutions explained that states that helped finance the BWCC, already experiencing donor fatigue, insisted on the five-year transition period. The OHR realized international personnel might be needed for a longer period but tailored its plans to accommodate the outer limits of donor states' support.

[209] Interview with Shireen Fisher, Former International Judge, BWCC, in Washington, D.C., United States (May 29, 2016). Human Rights Watch reached a similar conclusion in its assessment of lessons learned from the Bosnia experience:

> Rather than setting an arbitrary deadline, policymakers, donors and national authorities in other country situations developing an exit strategy for international staff would do well to consider establishing benchmarks linked to progress in handling cases and to the development of an institutional framework. The achievement of those benchmarks would then trigger the phasing out of international staff.

JUSTICE FOR ATROCITY CRIMES, *supra* note 5, at 3.

[210] Judge Patricia Whalen, Remarks at the Conference on Prosecuting Serious International Crimes: Exploring the Intersections Between International and Domestic Justice Efforts, Sponsored by the War Crimes Research Office, Washington College of Law, Washington, DC (Mar. 30, 2016).

perception that the BWCC was a foreign institution "became a weapon that was used against [it]."[211]

Whalen believes, as well, that the BWCC's experience highlights the importance of effective communication—a skill that does not come naturally to most judges in most countries but was essential in the charged environment surrounding the chamber's work. Recalling "there was a lot of propaganda right from the very beginning to destroy and attack the integrity" of the BWCC, Whalen observed: "And I don't think the court itself was very good at responding to those kinds of attacks or myths out there."[212] Judge Fisher agrees; in her view, the BWCC needed to embrace "outreach" as "part of [its] culture, . . . explaining, explaining, explaining."[213] Civil society leader Branko Todorović made much the same point ten years earlier. When RS leaders began attacking the BWCC, Todorović feared the chamber's lack of transparency played into their hands. In his words: "There is no longer cooperation with the media, non-governmental organisations and simple citizens. Because of this lack of information, people have the feeling that these institutions do not serve justice any more, which immediately gives politicians the opportunity to politicize information and use it for their purposes."[214]

There is, of course, no way to know whether a robust communications strategy would have neutralized RS attacks. But Judge Fisher believes it "could have minimized" their toxic impact if begun early. After all, she noted, when the BWCC was launched, "Dodik wasn't [yet] Dodik."[215] (As noted earlier, Dodik was a relative moderate until 2006.)

B. Impact on Prosecutions: Transfer of Evidence

The mountains of dossiers ICTY transferred to local jurisdictions has given them the basis to continue prosecuting direct perpetrators for years to come.
—REFIK HODŽIĆ[216]

If the ICTY's principal impact on the BWCC arose from decisions taken before the chamber was launched, it has influenced the SDWC through continuous engagement in its work. Evidence-sharing initiatives have formed a particularly productive context for engagement.

---

[211] *Id.*

[212] Interview with Judge Patricia Whalen, Former International Judge, BWCC, in Washington, D.C., United States (May 29, 2016).

[213] Interview with Shireen Fisher, Former International Judge, BWCC, in Washington, D.C., United States (May 29, 2016). Efforts were, in fact, made to ensure effective outreach as preparations were made to launch the new court. *See* Alison Freebairn & Nerma Jelačić, *Bringing War Crimes Justice Back Home*, IWPR (Nov. 26, 2004). These did not, however, prove effective.

[214] Maja Milavić, *Court Faces "Political" Smears*, JUST. REP. (Sept. 8, 2006).

[215] Interview with Shireen Fisher, Former International Judge, BWCC, in Washington, D.C, United States (May 29, 2016). Human Rights Watch has made a similar point. Noting growing attacks by several "vocal and influential politicians" had significantly eroded public confidence in the SDWC and BWCC, the organization concluded that "[i]nitial weaknesses in the outreach and communications strategies left the SDWC and the court ill-equipped to effectively address these misperceptions." JUSTICE FOR ATROCITY CRIMES, *supra* note 5, at 3.

[216] Refik Hodžić, *Why the ICTY Has Contributed to Reconciliation in the Former Yugoslavia*, OSSERVATORIO BALCANI E CAUCASO (Feb. 20, 2013).

1. 11*BIS* CASES

At first, evidence-sharing between The Hague and Sarajevo revolved around 11*bis* transfers, each of which brought a wealth of evidence, developed by OTP staff, to the SDWC.[217] The first Prosecutor of BiH, Marinko Jurčević, told me the SDWC's prosecution of one of its first 11*bis* cases was "based only on Hague evidence."[218] Still, most of the cases transferred under Rule 11*bis* required further preparation. Then SDWC head David Schwendiman told me it was wrong to assume 11*bis* cases generally arrived "trial ready." Although Hague prosecutors had "done everything they could to get everything to us," in some cases "nothing had been done for awhile" by the time they were transferred.[219]

At first, moreover, transferring evidence from The Hague to Sarajevo was hardly a seamless process. To the consternation of BWCC judges and SDWC personnel, two suspects were transferred to the Court of BiH before evidence supporting their indictments arrived.[220] Branko Perić dryly recalled the dilemma facing Bosnian prosecutors when I interviewed him in late 2006: "We have an indicted guy but the documentation is still in their archives. It was senseless [for the SDWC] to charge him" until supporting evidence arrived from The Hague.[221] According to SDWC personnel, this happened "only once or twice."[222]

Despite these and other teething problems,[223] ICTY evidence proved immensely useful in the first BWCC cases. When I interviewed local prosecutors in 2009,[224] they had high praise for the contributions of their counterparts in The Hague. Then Prosecutor Milorad Barašin told me: "It's indisputable that the Hague Tribunal gave us major support in setting up this institution and getting cases going."[225] Barašin characterized cooperation with the Hague Tribunal as "great," adding:

> And really, whatever we asked in accordance with [the law] we have received. Above all, I have to compliment them on their efficiency. Always they have been available, especially the prosecutorial office of the Hague Tribunal.[226]

---

[217] As previously noted, 11*bis* transfers involved cases that had already been indicted but not yet prosecuted in The Hague.

[218] Interview with Marinko Jurčević, then Prosecutor of BiH, in Sarajevo, Bosn. & Herz. (Dec. 4, 2006). *See also* Chehtman, *supra* note 50, at 558.

[219] Interview with David Schwendiman, then Deputy Chief Prosecutor, State Court of BiH, and Head, SDWC, in Sarajevo, Bosn. & Herz. (July 14, 2009).

[220] Interview with Shireen Fisher, Former International Judge, BWCC, in Washington, D.C, United States (May 29, 2016).

[221] Interview with Branko Perić, then President, HJPC, in Sarajevo, Bosn. & Herz. (Dec. 4, 2006).

[222] Interview with Toby Cadman & David Schwendiman, SDWC, in Sarajevo, Bosn. & Herz. (June 12, 2007).

[223] Some are noted in ORENTLICHER, *supra* note 157, at 121; other early challenges are described in Martin-Ortega, *supra* note 191, at 602–03.

[224] At that time, all but one of the Rule 11*bis* first instance trials conducted before the BWCC had been completed. *See* David Schwendiman, Background and Introduction 14–15 (unpublished paper July 2009) (on file with author).

[225] Interview with Milorad Barašin, then Prosecutor of BiH, in Sarajevo, Bosn. & Herz. (July 14, 2009).

[226] *Id.*

2. Evidence-Sharing in Category II and Other Cases

A second category of cases prosecuted by the SDWC grew out of investigations carried out by the OTP that did not lead to indictments by the end of 2004, when the Tribunal had to conclude investigations. Known as "Category II" cases in recognition of the fact that "Rule 11*bis* cases were the first priority" under the ICTY's completion strategy, this grouping technically comprised collections of material relating to crimes,[227] such as those committed in a particular municipality, rather than formalized "cases." In practice, many Category II files made clear whom the OTP was likely to indict had it been able to continue issuing indictments.[228]

ICTY prosecutors transferred thirteen Category II files implicating thirty-eight suspects to Sarajevo[229] in the hope their investigatory work would not "simply be left on the proverbial wayside."[230] In an effort to narrow the gap between raw evidence in Category II files and criminal cases, the OTP Transition Team—created in 2004[231] to coordinate with local prosecutors on both 11*bis* and Category II transfers—prepared "a summary of the 'case' outlining the principal factual and legal issues and an accompanying analysis."[232] Beyond this, the OTP deepened its engagement with domestic prosecutors with a view to ensuring they could make full use of the vast and unique evidence gathered by ICTY investigators through initiatives described later.

It would be hard to overstate the breadth and depth of the Tribunal's archives, which are by far the most extensive and authoritative repository of evidence of wartime atrocities in the former Yugoslavia. By mid-2015, more than twenty years after OTP investigators had acquired access to all of Bosnian territory, the Tribunal had amassed 9.3 million documents. Its archives also include thousands of physical records—artifacts, audio and visual records, and other material.[233]

The archives are not just an evidentiary gold mine for domestic prosecutors, though they are surely that: they are essential to the SDWC's work. The ICTY

---

[227] Tolbert & Kontić, *Transfer of Cases, supra* note 15, at 157.

[228] An OTP official described the state of at least some Category II files transferred to Bosnia this way: "Basically we had investigated all the way up to indictment, but we just didn't issue the indictment, or didn't put it in for confirmation for the issuance of the indictment." Interview with Bob Reid, Chief of Operations, Office of the Prosecutor, ICTY, in The Hague, Neth. (May 28, 2015).

[229] Various sources provide somewhat different figures. This one comes from Serge Brammertz, *Report of Serge Brammertz, Prosecutor of the International Tribunal for the Former Yugoslavia, provided to the Security Council under paragraph 6 of Security Council resolution 1534 (2004),* Annex II, ¶ 57, U.N. Doc. S/2012/354 (May 23, 2012).

[230] Tolbert & Kontić, *Transfer of Cases, supra* note 15, at 157.

[231] When the Transition Team was established, most of the OTP staff who had previously worked on the Rules of the Road project "moved over" to the new team. *Id.* at 145. The Transition Team was formally ended at the end of 2014, Interview with Aleksandar Kontić, Legal Officer, Office of the Prosecutor, ICTY, in The Hague, Neth. (May 26, 2015), but many of its functions were taken over by the MICT.

[232] Tolbert & Kontić, *Transfer of Cases, supra* note 15, at 158.

[233] Interview with Jules Albers, Head of Evidence Unit, Office of the Prosecutor, ICTY, in The Hague, Neth. (May 26, 2015); interview with Lada Šoljan, Legal Officer, Office of the Prosecutor, ICTY, in The Hague, Neth. (May 27, 2015); interview with Bob Reid, Chief of Operations, Office of the Prosecutor, ICTY, in The Hague, Neth. (May 28, 2015). According to Albers, the ICTY possessed almost 10,000 audio visual items, and more than 13,000 audio items when I visited the Tribunal in May 2015.

acquired a vast trove of documents "authored by the parties to the conflict"[234] them-selves through sweeping search and seizure operations. Undertaken in collaboration with NATO forces then operating in Bosnia, these operations began in Prijedor in December 1997 and expanded to other Bosnian municipalities in 1998, eventually enabling the ICTY to acquire military records of all three of Bosnia's major ethnic groups.[235] No measure of local investigative skill could compensate for this evidence, now available only through access to Tribunal archives.

Explaining the significance of this evidence for the SDWC, Irisa Čevra, then Special Assistant to the Deputy Prosecutor, told me: "It was invaluable, invaluable to our cases." In her assessment, without ICTY evidence "our indictments would be defi-cient or they wouldn't have covered the scope of crimes that have been committed."[236] Documents seized from police stations and other municipal authorities included crucial information, such as "who was detained, who was in charge, patrolling, the lists of military units, list of police officers, everything." As Čevra explained, "every-thing" includes records disclosing

> members of the police—whether they were working during that period, whether they received [a] salary during that period, and also . . . daily dispatches. It is the same for the police and military structures, they were ac-tually reporting every day, sending orders and reporting on execution of these orders. And . . . also [the] movement of police, [the] movement of military structures.

In short, Čevra said: "You can see that it's indispensable."[237]

Mira Smajlović, who had been a judge in two cases involving the Srebrenica mas-sacre when I interviewed her in 2014, said ICTY evidence would also be "invaluable for future cases,"[238] bearing in mind the "inexorable effects of the crime itself." If these "neutral investigators" had not gathered evidence soon after the massacre, she said, it would have been infinitely more difficult for the BWCC, which began oper-ating a decade later, to secure vital evidence.[239]

3. EXPANDING ACCESS TO ICTY ARCHIVES AND WITNESSES

Over time, the ICTY adopted measures progressively facilitating local jurists' access to its archives. Some were devised primarily with a view to easing the workload of

---

[234] Interview with Bob Reid, Chief of Operations, Office of the Prosecutor, ICTY, in The Hague, Neth. (May 28, 2015).

[235] Id.

[236] Interview with Irisa Čevra, then Assistant to the Deputy Chief Prosecutor, SDWC, in Sarajevo, Bosn. & Herz. (Sept. 11, 2014). In Čevra's words: "[Y]ou have to take into account that [the NATO Stabilization Force] and the ICTY, during the strongest mandate of the international community," were responsible for "a lot of seizures of documentation here in Bosnia that we could never have accessed [on our own]," as "a lot of the seized documents . . . ended up in The Hague." Id.

[237] Id.

[238] Interview with Mira Smajlović, Judge, BWCC, in Sarajevo, Bosn. & Herz. (Sept. 9, 2014).

[239] Id. As David Luban has noted, an often-overlooked byproduct of ICTs' work is that they provide incentive for the collection of evidence that would likely be degraded, if not destroyed, without their work. See David Luban, *Demystifying Political Violence: Some Bequests of ICTY and ICTR*, 110 AJIL UNBOUND 251, 252 (2016).

ICTY staff: the transfer of 11*bis* and Category II cases generated additional requests for assistance (RFAs) from Bosnia and elsewhere, placing surging demands on OTP personnel.[240] But the new measures also reflected Tribunal officials' growing commitment to help Yugoslav legal professionals play their part in providing justice for wartime atrocities.

These efforts began modestly in September 2005, when the OTP granted SDWC personnel remote access to the Electronic Disclosure Suite (EDS), an electronic archive of OTP evidence.[241] While valuable, such access does not obviate the need for significant interaction with the ICTY. Remote access enables users to research non-confidential ICTY material only.[242] Only ICTY and MICT employees have access to the OTP's confidential database, but they can and do conduct searches of those databases in response to RFAs.[243] Moreover, nonconfidential evidence accessed by SDWC staff in Sarajevo often generates requests that require further action by Tribunal judges or other personnel.[244]

---

[240] Aleksandar Kontić recalled the OTP received around forty or fifty RFAs from former Yugoslav countries in 2008, and "then in 2009 I believe we had like almost 200 requests for assistance." Interview with Aleksandar Kontić, Legal Officer, Office of the Prosecutor, ICTY, in The Hague, Neth. (May 26, 2015). The MICT, which assumed responsibility for processing most RFAs in July 2013, had received over 500 RFAs, most from the former Yugoslavia and a majority of those from Bosnia, by May 2015. Interview with Mathias Marcussan, Senior Legal Officer & Officer in Charge for the OTP, MICT Hague Branch, in The Hague, Neth. (May 27, 2015). Speaking at a conference in June 2017, Prosecutor Brammertz said domestic prosecutors had by then used more than 120,000 pages from the Tribunal's database. Emina Dizdarević, *Hague Tribunal Shares Lessons of War Crime Probes*, BALKAN TRANSITIONAL JUST. (June 23, 2017).

[241] Memorandum of Understanding between the Office of the Prosecutor of the International Criminal Tribunal for the Former Yugoslavia and the Special Department for War Crimes of the Prosecutor's Office of Bosnia and Herzegovina, arts. 2(1) and 3(1). *See also* Kate Gibson & Cainneh Lussiaà-Berdou, *Disclosure of Evidence*, in PRINCIPLES OF EVIDENCE IN INTERNATIONAL CRIMINAL JUSTICE 314 n.35 (Karim A.A. Kahn et al. eds., 2010). Initially provided to the SDWC, EDS access was later extended to judicial chambers and defense counsel in Bosnia, the latter via the Odsjek Krivične Odbrane (OKO), a criminal defense unit attached to the Court of BiH Registry. Interview with Kevin Hughes, Legal Advisor to the Prosecutor, Office of the Prosecutor, ICTY, in The Hague, Neth. (May 26, 2015). More recently, EDS access was extended to war crimes prosecutors in district and cantonal courts. *Id. See also* Press Release, OSCE Mission to Bosn. & Herz., OSCE and EU Support Training of Judges and Prosecutors in BiH on Use of ICTY Evidence (June 27, 2013).

[242] There are distinct levels of access even to nonconfidential material. According to the OTP's computer information systems coordinator, "all defense teams have access to the [OTP's] general collection," and "each team also has access to their own [case-specific] suite," which includes material not available in the general collection. Interview with Sandra Vukša, Computer Information Systems Coordinator, Office of the Prosecutor, ICTY, in The Hague, Neth. (May 26, 2015).

[243] Interview with Mathias Marcussen, Senior Legal Officer, Officer in Charge, Office of the Prosecutor, MICT Hague Branch, in The Hague, Neth. (May 27, 2015).

[244] If an SDWC attorney finds in the EDS a redacted witness statement that is highly relevant to one of her cases, she can rely on the statement as evidence in court only if she can obtain the unredacted statement and/or secure access to the witness. If the witness statement is subject to judicially-mandated protective measures, the SDWC would need to utilize a relatively formal procedure, which is cumbersome and time-consuming, to seek a modification of those measures. Only an ICTY/MICT judge or chamber could grant such a request. Aleksandar Kontić estimated that judicial decisions about authorizing a variation of protective measures depend on the witness's consent "in 99 percent of the cases," and that roughly half the witnesses contacted consent. Interview with Aleksandar Kontić, Legal Officer, Office of the Prosecutor, ICTY, in The Hague, Neth. (May 26, 2015).

For awhile, the need for further action by Tribunal personnel entailed frequent travel by domestic prosecutors to The Hague and, in consequence, mounting costs. Soon after Serge Brammertz became ICTY Prosecutor in 2008, he and regional prosecutors devised a solution: war crimes prosecutors' offices from Bosnia, Serbia, and Croatia would each send a member of its staff to The Hague to serve as a "liaison prosecutor"[245] for a rotation of six months or longer.[246] These lawyers would expedite their domestic colleagues' requests, including those seeking evidence developed in connection with Category II files.[247] Funded by the European Union, the liaison prosecutors program was launched in July 2009.[248]

The program simultaneously expedites the work of the SDWC and deepens collaboration between the Hague and Sarajevo.[249] Explaining dynamics behind the latter,

---

Even if there are no judicially-ordered protective measures, a statement might be confidential because the witness told the ICTY investigator who interviewed her that her name and other identifying information could be shared with other judicial systems only with the witness's permission. If a Bosnian prosecutor wants to see the unredacted statement or interview the witness, she would have to ask the OTP to contact the witness on her behalf. Interview with Tea Polešćuk, Legal Advisor, Office of the Prosecutor, MICT Hague Branch, in The Hague, Neth. (May 27, 2015). At some point, the ICTY began including in signed written statements a question asking if the witness consented to sharing her statement with other judicial authorities. If the witness said yes, the OTP could share her statement without further consent; if she said no, the OTP would have to locate the witness and request her consent. Interview with Tomasz Blaszcyk, Investigator, Office of the Prosecutor, MICT Hague Branch, in The Hague, Neth. (May 27, 2015).

The OTP would also have to follow up on requested information provided on a strictly confidential basis for lead purposes only in accordance with Rule 70 of the ICTY's Rules of Procedure and Evidence. When it receives such a request, the OTP contacts the provider and asks for its consent to provide the material to the requesting authority. Kontić estimates that the provider consents to 98 percent of these requests. Interview with Aleksandar Kontić, Legal Officer, Office of the Prosecutor, ICTY, in The Hague, Neth. (May 26, 2015).

[245] Some of the "liaison prosecutors" are not actually prosecutors, but instead serve as legal officers or associates in a domestic prosecutor's office.

[246] Brammertz told me that, when he attended his first annual meeting of regional war crimes prosecutors after taking office as Prosecutor, he asked, "What can we do to make your life easier?" The regional prosecutors responded that they were incurring substantial financial costs "sending every week or every month investigators and prosecutors . . . to The Hague." Brammertz asked if it would be useful, then, to base one of the local prosecutors' staff members in the ICTY, and the local prosecutors' response was enthusiastic. Interview with Serge Brammertz, Prosecutor, ICTY, in The Hague, Neth. (May 27, 2015).

[247] Interview with Irisa Čevra, then Assistant to the Deputy Prosecutor, SDWC, in Sarajevo, Bosn. & Herz. (Sept. 11, 2014).

[248] See Press Release, ICTY, Office of the Prosecutor of the ICTY Welcomes Liaison Prosecutors from Bosnia and Herzegovina, Croatia and Serbia to the Tribunal (July 1, 2009). The program ended when the EU stopped funding it at the end of 2016, but was restarted in 2017, now with liaison prosecutors based in the MICT OTP. Email from Kevin Hughes, Legal Advisor to the Prosecutor, Office of the Prosecutor, ICTY, to Diane Orentlicher (July 17, 2017).

[249] As Bosnia's first liaison prosecutor put it, the project "served just to accelerate and facilitate the exchange of information [and] evidence" between the OTP and SDWC. Interview with Irisa Čevra, then Assistant to the Deputy Prosecutor, SDWC, in Sarajevo, Bosn. & Herz. (Sept. 11, 2014). Before the project was established, SDWC prosecutors seeking information not available on the EDS "were obliged to write like a formal . . . request for international assistance. It was so formal, and it took some time; you know, several months" to receive a response. Now, local prosecutors can send an email to the liaison prosecutor from their office, who can often secure a response from the OTP "within a day" in urgent matters. Id. With intimate knowledge of the kind of information her colleagues would need to strengthen their cases as well as the ICTY's resources, moreover, Čevra was able to initiate search requests beyond those received from her colleagues during her rotation as a liaison prosecutor.

MICT OTP Legal Advisor Tea Polešćuk noted that regional prosecutors sometimes phrase RFAs in terms that may not be efficient for purposes of searching an ICTY database. She and her colleagues work with the relevant liaison officer to "try to set up search criteria jointly so that we both know what they are really looking for. It's quite easy to do that if someone is a floor below you, and you pick up the phone."[250] Meanwhile, the liaison officers, who receive intensive training on how to use ICTY databases when they begin their rotations in The Hague, can share their expertise with colleagues at home by, for example, explaining why their search requests are framed too broadly to yield productive results.[251]

C. Processing Category II Cases: Renewed Oversight by the OTP

With a shrinking caseload in The Hague, Brammertz (who has served as Prosecutor of the MICT since February 2016 as well as Prosecutor of the ICTY) has devoted growing attention to local war crimes prosecutions. The Prosecutor explained the shift this way in a 2016 report to the UN Security Council: "As the Tribunal nears the completion of its mandate, the Office of the Prosecutor remains committed to promoting effective war crimes prosecutions in the former Yugoslavia through on-going dialogue with counterparts and efforts to build capacity in the national justice sectors."[252]

For several years, that dialogue entailed increasingly critical monitoring of SDWC progress. In contrast to the OTP's mandated oversight of Bosnian indictments from 1996 to 2004, when the RoR program was in effect, the new oversight emerged with no formal mandate and in an organic fashion, prompted by mounting concerns about sluggish progress in Sarajevo. While these concerns had largely abated when I completed this book, it is worth considering how Brammertz and other key actors responded when they emerged, as the experience holds wider lessons about the fragility of progress in post-conflict settings and the role of external actors in addressing challenges as they arise.

For the first few years after the OTP completed its transfer of Category II files, Brammertz asked the SDWC to brief him on the status of its Category II investigations each time he visited Sarajevo. He received the same reply on every visit: the SDWC was making progress. Increasingly concerned, Brammertz asked if he could review the SDWC's case files. Recognizing the SDWC had no obligation to agree, Brammertz was "quite pleased" that they did so.[253] What Brammertz and his staff discovered was that, in some Category II cases, "especially the more complicated ones, almost nothing had been done for two, three, or four years."[254] Starting in mid-2012, Brammertz's completion strategy reports to the UN Security Council

---

[250] Interview with Tea Polešćuk, Legal Advisor, Office of the Prosecutor, MICT Hague Branch, in The Hague, Neth. (May 27, 2015).

[251] Interview with Mathias Marcussen, Senior Legal Officer, Officer in Charge, Office of the Prosecutor, MICT Hague Branch, in The Hague, Neth. (May 27, 2015).

[252] Serge Brammertz, *Report of Serge Brammertz, Prosecutor of the International Tribunal for the Former Yugoslavia, provided to the Security Council under paragraph 6 of Security Council resolution 1534 (2004)*, ¶ 24, U.N. Doc. S/2016/454, Annex II (May 17, 2016).

[253] Interview with Serge Brammertz, Prosecutor, ICTY, in The Hague, Neth. (May 27, 2015).

[254] *Id.*

became increasingly critical of Bosnian prosecutors for their sluggish pace in processing these cases.[255]

Myriad factors, some more readily addressed than others, accounted for the problems Brammertz flagged in his reports. The political sensitivity of some cases may have been a factor, though it did not appear to be the most important.[256] Also relevant, in the assessment of Irisa Čevra, was the legal complexity and novelty of issues raised by some Category II cases.[257] But in her view, these challenges were readily "solvable."[258] A further factor was insufficient staffing relative to the enormity of the SDWC's work.[259] While significant, this was by no means the sole or even most important reason for slow progress on Category II cases. According to OTP Chief of Operations Bob Reid, "The Category II cases that we gave [Bosnia concerning certain municipalities], . . . basically we had investigated all the way up to indictment . . . So there wasn't a lot of work that needed to be done."[260]

More significant was the convergence of three factors—the dearth of specialized skills among many SDWC prosecutors, the effects of a quota system governing their work, and above all weak leadership by the Prosecutor of BiH. To the first point, Čevra recounted a conversation between SDWC staff and Brammertz in the Fall of 2014 in which, as she recalled, the latter said: "I'm coming here for many years, just waiting for you . . . to start working on Category II cases. For a number of years I believed that political pressure is one of the key obstacles to progress in [these] cases. Now,

---

[255] See Serge Brammertz, *Report of Serge Brammertz, Prosecutor of the International Tribunal for the Former Yugoslavia, provided to the Security Council under paragraph 6 of Security Council resolution 1534 (2004)*, Annex II, ¶¶ 57–58, U.N. Doc. S/2012/354 (May 23, 2012). Previous reports expressed concern about slow progress overall; now, the Prosecutor's reports included specific criticism about Category II cases. In his November 2014 and May 2015 completion strategy reports, Brammertz cited "only limited progress" in the investigation and prosecution of Category II cases. Serge Brammertz, *Report of Serge Brammertz, Prosecutor of the International Tribunal for the Former Yugoslavia, provided to the Security Council under paragraph 6 of Security Council resolution 1534 (2004)*, Annex II, ¶ 43, U.N. Doc. S/2014/827 (Nov. 19, 2014) [hereinafter 2014 Report of Serge Brammertz]; Serge Brammertz, *Report of Serge Brammertz, Prosecutor of the International Tribunal for the Former Yugoslavia, provided to the Security Council under paragraph 6 of Security Council resolution 1534 (2004)*, Annex II, ¶ 46, U.N. Doc. S/2015/342 (May 15, 2015).

[256] Irisa Čevra noted that Category II files implicated, among others, individuals who "were members of the [political party founded by Radovan Karadžić], for example, political parties," and prosecuting them could be "politically sensitive." Interview with Irisa Čevra, then Assistant to the Deputy Chief Prosecutor, SDWC, in Sarajevo, Bosn. & Herz. (Sept. 18, 2014).

[257] For example, Čevra noted, "Our legal system and the court [do] not have an answer" to the question of how legally to prosecute some of the wartime suspects "in their political capacity." Interview with Irisa Čevra, then Assistant to the Deputy Chief Prosecutor, SDWC, in Sarajevo, Bosn. & Herz. (Sept. 11, 2014). Čevra noted that the office had issued an indictment against a member of the crisis staff in Kluj who "was like a political figure, and that indictment was rejected on legal grounds." *Id.*

[258] Interview with Irisa Čevra, then Assistant to the Deputy Chief Prosecutor, SDWC, in Sarajevo, Bosn. & Herz. (Sept. 18, 2014).

[259] The SDWC typically had a three-person team (a prosecutor, his or her legal officer, and "maybe" an investigator) working on each Category II case, Čevra said in a 2014 interview. In contrast, "at the ICTY you had like 30 or 40 persons committed to one case . . . of the same complexity." Interview with Irisa Čevra, then Assistant to the Deputy Chief Prosecutor, SDWC, in Sarajevo, Bosn. & Herz. (Sept. 11, 2014).

[260] Interview with Bob Reid, Chief of Operations, Office of the Prosecutor, ICTY, in The Hague, Neth. (May 28, 2015).

I think that it is incompetence."[261] When I asked how her office responded, Čevra said: "Well, we basically all agreed with him that it is incompetence. We don't know how to deal with those cases."[262]

To address its backlog, not only on Category II investigations but on thousands of other potential cases, the SDWC doubled the size of its prosecution staff in 2014 with funding from the EU.[263] But few of the new hires had experience in war crimes cases.[264] Although they attended an intensive eight-day training program, which included training in "ICTY practice," Čevra believes the new staff lacked the foundational knowledge they needed to benefit from the program. As she noted, "This is [a] completely new area to them, and this is [a] highly specialized area."[265]

Crucially important, as well, Bosnian prosecutors had to meet an annual quota of five completed cases per year.[266] When applied to SDWC prosecutors, this requirement—since modified for war crimes prosecutors—was a powerful disincentive to pursue complex cases against senior officials.[267] As Čevra explained, "it's easier to do less complex cases, and prosecutors . . . just tend to do these cases to satisfy their . . . annual quotas."[268] Čevra estimated that 95 percent of SDWC cases were against direct perpetrators rather than senior officials, whose prosecution is more legally challenging.[269]

Of particular concern to Brammertz, SDWC prosecutors were bringing separate cases against suspects whom the OTP would have charged in a single case,[270] an approach for which the quota system provided strong incentive. For example, in one Category II case involving six accused, some of whom were military and

---

[261] Interview with Irisa Čevra, then Assistant to the Deputy Chief Prosecutor, SDWC, in Sarajevo, Bosn. & Herz. (Sept. 18, 2014).

[262] *Id.*

[263] At the beginning of 2014 the SDWC employed nineteen prosecutors. The European Union "gave a specialized grant to hire [the new] prosecutors," and as of September 2014, they had "38 working in the state prosecution." Interview with Denis Džidić, Journalist, in Sarajevo, Bosn. & Herz. (Sept. 17, 2014). *See also* Denis Džidić, *Bosnia Doubles Number of War Crimes Indictees*, BALKAN TRANSITIONAL JUST. (Nov. 3, 2014) (with the hiring of new prosecutors funded by the EU, Bosnia's chief prosecutor expected a steep rise in the number of war crimes indictments). A 2016 report said that thirty-five prosecutors were then working in the SDWC. JOANNA KORNER, PROCESSING OF WAR CRIMES AT THE STATE LEVEL IN BOSNIA AND HERZEGOVINA ¶ 37 (June 2016) [hereinafter KORNER REPORT].

[264] Interview with Irisa Čevra, then Assistant to the Deputy Chief Prosecutor, SDWC, in Sarajevo, Bosn. & Herz. (Sept. 18, 2014).

[265] *Id. See also* KORNER REPORT, *supra* note 263 ¶¶ 37–38.

[266] For this purpose, closing an investigation without issuing an indictment counted as completing a case. Interview with Denis Džidić, Journalist, in Sarajevo, Bosn. & Herz. (Sept. 17, 2014).

[267] In July 2016, the HJPC adopted a new Rulebook on Orientation Measures for the Prosecutors in Bosnia and Herzegovina, Official Gazette of BiH No. 64/16 (July 7, 2016), which lowered the number of prosecutorial decisions SDWC prosecutors must take to satisfy their annual quota. Under the new rule, those prosecutors must take four such decisions, which could include issuing an indictment, suspending an investigation, or deciding not to carry out an investigation. *Id.* art. 21(2).

[268] Interview with Irisa Čevra, then Assistant to the Deputy Chief Prosecutor, SDWC, in Sarajevo, Bosn. & Herz. (Sept. 18, 2014). Čevra continued: "It's easier to raise like three indictments for less complex cases than, you know, to spend a year or two on more complex cases. And serious work, you know, on [a] very complex case requires at least one to two years of dedicated work." *Id.*

[269] *Id.* This estimate is, of course, relevant as of September 2014, when I interviewed Čevra.

[270] Interview with Serge Brammertz, Prosecutor, ICTY, in The Hague, Neth. (May 27, 2015).

others police personnel, the SDWC brought charges in five separate cases for which three prosecutors had responsibility.[271] For Brammertz, a key problem was that the resulting prosecutions obscured the context in which atrocities occurred.[272] A series of "smaller cases" cannot illuminate collaboration among the "different elements"— police, military, and political actors—that operated in concert to produce mass atrocities the way a consolidated trial might.[273] Summarizing the SDWC's approach in 2014, Margriet Prins, then head of the ICTY's liaison office in Sarajevo, told me: "It's all against individuals, never against the whole structure, and that's what we would be looking for. And that hasn't happened at all."[274]

The practice of splitting up Category II files compounded an already formidable challenge: Bosnian prosecutors have long faced a chronic backlog in processing war crimes cases.[275] In December 2008, Bosnia's Council of Ministers adopted a National Strategy for War Crimes (NSWC), which set December 2015 as the deadline for prosecuting "the most complex and top priority war crimes cases," and 2023 as the deadline for completing other war crimes cases.[276] At the heart of the strategy was a concept similar to the ICTY's relationship of primacy vis-à-vis domestic courts: Much as the ICTY once decided which cases it would retain and which it would transfer to national courts, the SDWC would keep only the most "complex" cases for prosecution before the BWCC and transfer the rest to entity-level prosecutors. Implementation of the NSWC has been vexed, and the pace of prosecutions has fallen far below what was required to meet the strategy's deadlines.[277] In this setting, the practice of fracturing Category II files thwarted the already challenging goals set by the NSWC. As a Bosnian Justice Ministry source noted:

> This practice [i.e., splitting Category II files into several small cases] consumes the human and material resources of the state prosecution on prosecuting cases which, by their nature, should be referred to the entities' judiciary in the

---

[271] Id.

[272] Id.

[273] Id.

[274] Interview with Margriet Prins, ICTY Liaison Officer, in Sarajevo, Bosn. & Herz. (Sept. 12, 2014).

[275] See Denis Džidić, War Crimes Strategy Faces Credibility Crisis, JUST. REP. (July 27, 2009).

[276] COUNCIL OF MINISTERS OF BOSN. & HERZ., NATIONAL WAR CRIMES STRATEGY 4, 28 (2008) (copy on file with author). BiH authorities have been working on a revised strategy with new deadlines for the completion of cases. See AMNESTY INTERNATIONAL, "WE NEED SUPPORT, NOT PITY": LAST CHANCE FOR JUSTICE FOR BOSNIA'S WARTIME RAPE SURVIVORS 22 (2017) [hereinafter AI, SUPPORT NOT PITY].

[277] In his May 2017 completion strategy report, Brammertz wrote that "approximately 1,200 cases involving 5,000 suspects still need to be processed" by Bosnian authorities. Serge Brammertz, Progress Report of the Prosecutor of the International Residual Mechanism for Criminal Tribunals, Serge Brammertz, for the Period from 16 November 2016 to 15 May 2017, Annex II, ¶ 48, U.N. Doc. S/2017/434 (May 17, 2017) [hereinafter 2017 Report of Serge Brammertz]. Brammertz cited somewhat different figures at a conference one month after the date of this report. See Emina Dizdarević, Hague Tribunal Shares Lessons of War Crime Probes, BALKAN TRANSITIONAL JUST. (June 23, 2017) (SDWC's database indicates there were 642 ongoing cases in which perpetrators have been identified, 612 against unknown perpetrators, 1,669 cases covering a specific event, and "[b]esides that, . . . more than 300 most complex war-crime cases").

investigation phase, but also the resources of the state court which conducts separate procedures for one event, instead of speeding up the process.[278]

It is fair to ask whether the SDWC's failure to prosecute Category II cases in line with the OTP and Justice Ministry's vision is a failure of justice. While many believe war crimes prosecutors should prioritize the architects of mass atrocity[279] and develop a rich historical record, victims often find greatest satisfaction in trials of direct perpetrators, regardless of whether they implicate senior leaders or help construct a narrative of systemic criminality. But the SDWC's practice of "splitting cases" has been problematic from the perspective of survivors, not just the OTP and the Justice Ministry. Beyond the problems already noted, witnesses may be called to testify about traumatic events in several trials that could have been consolidated in one.[280]

As indicated, a third and, it is now clear, crucial factor was weak leadership on the part of Bosnia's Chief Prosecutor. An independent report by British judge Joanna Korner suggested that Goran Salihović, who served in this position from 2013 until his suspension in 2016,[281] was doing little to counter the natural effects of the quota system. To the contrary: "The view expressed by the [BWCC] judges was that the [Chief Prosecutor] was simply obsessed by making statistics look good and was therefore concentrating on the simpler cases at the expense of the higher level perpetrators."[282] Prosecutors interviewed by Judge Korner agreed.[283] More generally, Korner concluded, Salihović provided little if any strategic direction to the SDWC.[284] Nor did leadership issues begin with Salihović's tenure; until the appointment of Salihović's successor, Acting Prosecutor Gordana Tadić, the POBiH suffered from a succession of vexed leaders, with each transition disrupting implementation of any strategy the outgoing Prosecutor may have tried to implement.[285]

---

[278] Marija Tausan, *Huge War Crimes Case Backlog Overwhelms Bosnia*, BALKAN TRANSITIONAL JUST. (Oct. 23, 2015) (quoting unnamed Justice Ministry source).

[279] For a more nuanced discussion of criteria for prioritizing prosecutions, see Pablo de Greiff (Special Rapporteur), *Report of the Special Rapporteur on the promotion of truth, justice, reparation and guarantees of non-recurrence*, U.N. Doc. A/HRC/27/56 (Aug. 27, 2014).

[280] *See* KORNER REPORT, *supra* note 263, ¶ 73.

[281] Salihović was suspended amidst allegations that he had "used his influence to ensure that several investigations" into Milorad Dodik's conduct were closed. Srđan Kureljusić, *Bosnian Chief Prosecutor Investigated for Abuse of Office*, BALKAN INSIGHT (Aug. 10, 2016). Salihović claims he was suspended because he opened an investigation against Dodik relating to the September 2016 referendum mentioned earlier. Daria Sito-Sučić, *Bosnia Chief Prosecutor Cries Foul After Suspension*, REUTERS (Sept. 28, 2016).

[282] *See* KORNER REPORT, *supra* note 263, ¶ 34.

[283] *Id.* ¶¶ 118, 121.

[284] *See id.* ¶ 51 ("There is apparently no office policy on prioritisation of cases," which "is left to individual prosecutors to decide").

[285] Interview with Bob Reid, Chief of Operations, Office of the Prosecutor, ICTY, in The Hague, Neth. (May 28, 2015). Salihović's predecessor, Milorad Barašin, was dismissed from the position of Prosecutor of BiH in July 2011 under the cloud of corruption charges. None of Bosnia's state prosecutors has completed his six-year term. Erna Mačkić, *Bosnia's New Chief Prosecutor Undergoes Stormy Start*, BALKAN TRANSITIONAL JUST. (Nov. 21, 2016). Denis Džidić, who has closely followed and reported on Bosnia's war crimes institutions, placed the problems associated with Salihović's tenure in a wider context when we spoke in 2014:

> Obviously there's an issue of political will ... These are not ... complicated cases of command responsibility. They really are not. There's evidently a question of political will. There's also a lack of any real substantive pressure from lawmakers, from anyone, from the

The suspension of Salihović in 2016 amidst charges he had abused his office[286] opened the way to significant improvement in the SDWC's performance. Brammertz forged a close partnership with the Acting Chief Prosecutor, Gordana Tadić, who previously served as Head of the SDWC, and has reported significant progress under her stewardship.[287] Although a daunting backlog of cases remained, Brammertz praised the POBiH for taking "important steps towards meeting the public's expectations for expeditious and effective justice for war crimes" in his November 2016 report, as well as Tadić's "strong commitment to continuing reforms and improvements in her Office."[288] Reporting sustained progress in his May 2017 report, Brammertz praised the POBiH for notable progress in investigating and prosecuting "appropriate complex cases."[289] Against the SDWC's previous practice of splitting cases and charging direct perpetrators, by mid-2017 it was bringing "many high- and mid-level cases" involving several defendants and large crime bases. Moreover the quality of indictments had also improved.[290] By all accounts, Gordana Tadić "deserves much of the recognition and credit" for the SDWC's improved performance.[291]

Yet even a strong leader can be constrained by political pressure. And as previously noted, pressures directed at Bosnia's war crimes institutions, including the POBiH during Tadić's tenure, have intensified in recent years. When the SDWC arrested ten former members of the HVO from Orašje for war crimes committed there, it faced intense pressure from Bosnian Croats as well as the Croatian government. Crucially, however, the OTP and other external actors quickly mobilized to express strong support for the POBiH.[292] This seemed a turning point, as the POBiH and its staff reportedly realized that, if they brought a well-founded case that attracted political pressure, international actors would rally to their defense.

While the details are peculiar to Bosnia, the challenges the SDWC confronted are not unusual in a country emerging from vicious conflict. In these settings, it is prudent to anticipate profound challenges over an extended period. What is unusual is that a range of actors, Bosnian and international, mobilized effective efforts to address the problems Brammertz flagged in successive reports.

HJPC, to really do it faster. And you know this is kind of the norm now. And, you know, if everyone's doing one indictment a year, why would you be crazy and do extra work, you know? So we're seeing a little bit of both, you know—just old fashioned laziness, without a really good manager, and on the other side really a lack of political will [on the part of the] prosecutors themselves.

Interview with Denis Džidić, Journalist, in Sarajevo, Bosn. & Herz. (Sept. 17, 2014).

[286] *See supra* note 281.

[287] *See, e.g.*, Serge Brammertz, *Progress Report of the Prosecutor of the International Residual Mechanism for Criminal Tribunals, Serge Brammertz, for the period from 16 May to 15 November 2016*, Annex II, ¶¶ 39–40, U.N. Doc. S/2016/975 (Nov. 17, 2016).

[288] *Id.*

[289] *2017 Report of Serge Brammertz, supra* note 277, ¶ 47.

[290] Email from Kevin Hughes, Legal Advisor to the Prosecutor, Office of the Prosecutor, ICTY, to Diane Orentlicher (July 14, 2017).

[291] *Id.*

[292] *See* Vedran Pavlić, *ICTY Prosecutor Brammertz Criticizes Croatia's Reaction to Arrests in Bosnia*, TOTAL CROATIA NEWS (Nov. 6, 2016).

D. Capacity-Building Initiatives

While the OTP has developed a robust commitment to capacity-building, the Tribunal devotes scant programmatic resources to efforts in this sphere. Instead, a raft of other organizations, including the OSCE Mission to Bosnia, the United Nations Development Programme (UNDP), the International Committee of the Red Cross (ICRC), the European Commission, the Council of Europe, and others have led efforts to provide training and related programs to Bosnian jurists,[293] with ICTY participation in some of them.

By widespread acknowledgment, myriad training programs organized in the early years of the BWCC and SDWC did not reflect an effective strategy for capacity-building.[294] While it is beyond the scope of this book to assess programs in which other institutions played leading roles, it is relevant to note that ICTY participation did not invariably enhance those programs. At times, the nature of its engagement exacerbated local perceptions of Hague arrogance. When, for example, Bosnian judges on the BWCC sought the participation of ICTY judges in training programs they had organized for themselves, the Tribunal instead "sent legal officers." As a former international judge on the chamber recalled, this "was interpreted correctly as a *real* insult" to the Bosnian jurists.[295]

The ICTY, in partnership with other organizations, has taken steps to address some of the early training programs' deficiencies[296] and participated in several

---

[293] Interview with Dubravka Piotrovski, then Staff Attorney, American Bar Association CEELI, in Sarajevo, Bosn. & Herz. (Nov. 29, 2006); Chehtman, *supra* note 50, at 551 n.19.

[294] Former SDWC head David Schwendiman expressed a widely-held view when he observed in late 2009:

> [T]he value of what has been done and the extent to which what has been done in conferences and other sessions has actually helped prepare anyone for anything is . . . questionable. It is the source of a great deal of waste [of] time and energy for the participants and for the people who put on the conferences and training programs. Most, I have found, have been ill-conceived . . . , measuring success by attendance rather than what was actually delivered or received that had value either in enlarging the participants' necessary knowledge base or imparting skills that would help them use the knowledge they have effectively. . . . Very little careful thought or meaningful thought goes into determining what needs to be done from a professional development point of view and very little meaningful thought goes into planning or preparing or arranging professional development programs or measuring their results.

> Email from David Schwendiman, Former Head, SDWC, to Diane Orentlicher (Oct. 5, 2009). For a more comprehensive assessment of problems associated with early training initiatives, see Chehtman, *supra* note 50, at 550–54.

[295] Interview with Shireen Fisher, Former International Judge, BWCC, in Washington, D.C., United States (May 29, 2016). *See also* Chehtman, *supra* note 50, at 552.

[296] In May 2008 the ICTY, in partnership with the OSCE Office for Democratic Institutions and Human Rights and the UN Interregional Crime and Justice Research Institute (UNICRI), undertook an in-depth assessment of outstanding judicial needs and evaluated the effectiveness of past efforts to strengthen domestic capacity to prosecute war crimes cases. *See* Patrick Robinson, *Assessment and Report of Judge Patrick Robinson, President of the International Criminal Tribunal for the Former Yugoslavia, provided to the Security Council pursuant to paragraph 6 of Council resolution 1534 (2004), covering the period from 15 May to 15 November 2009*, Annex I, ¶ 63, U.N. Doc. S/2009/589 (Nov. 13, 2009). In May 2009 the ICTY published a comprehensive guide to its "developed practices," including operational procedures in areas such as investigations, judgment drafting, management of the Detention Unit, and legal aid policies. ICTY & UNICRI, *ICTY Manual on Developed Practices* (June 2009).

initiatives designed to correct previous missteps.[297] The most substantial program implemented primarily in The Hague is an EU-funded Visiting Young Professionals (VYP) program, which was launched in 2009 along with the liaison prosecutors project described earlier.[298]

1. Visiting Young Professionals

The VYP program brings young professionals from former Yugoslav countries to the OTP for approximately six months with a view to "invest[ing] in the future capacity of the countries in the former Yugoslavia to deal effectively with complex war crimes cases."[299] In contrast to liaison prosecutors, whose function within the OTP is to expedite RFAs submitted by their national colleagues, professionals selected for the VYP program assist the Hague Prosecutor on ICTY/MICT cases, working under the direct supervision of OTP lawyers.[300] In addition to "learning by doing," VYP participants attend lectures by ICTY/MICT personnel covering a range of topics, such as how to conduct effective investigations; the doctrine of joint criminal enterprise; legal writing; the history of the conflict in the former Yugoslavia; and military analysis.[301]

Program participants whom I interviewed had high praise for these lectures, saying they learned an enormous amount about substantive international criminal law and professional skills. In addition, they said, their exposure to ICTY evidence provided a crucial perspective on their own countries' experience. As a visiting professional from Croatia put it, "we get to see things that we knew about, but from a different standpoint."[302] Alluding to the ethnic-based narratives that prevail in the former Yugoslavia, a VYP from Serbia added: "We get an opportunity to form our own opinion based on the material that we see here, not peoples' stories, which is a very important thing, actually."[303]

In terms of capacity-building, the most valuable component of the program comes from the VYPs' incorporation in OTP teams. When I interviewed VYPs in May 2015, the only case then still in trial was that of Ratko Mladić, the wartime military leader of Bosnian Serbs. Most of the young professionals had an opportunity to assist prosecutors in this trial, which one described as "the biggest case in the history of international criminal law"—an incomparable training ground for a junior or aspiring war crimes prosecutor.

---

[297] The ICTY Registry managed the ICTY component of several initiatives, but in the Tribunal's later years, its contributions to capacity-building increasingly shifted to the OTP.

[298] This program ended when EU funding expired at the end of 2015, but the EU agreed to restart the program for a further two-year period beginning in 2017. *2017 Report of Serge Brammertz*, *supra* note 277, ¶¶ 15–16; email from Kevin Hughes, Legal Advisor to the Prosecutor, Office of the Prosecutor, ICTY, to Diane Orentlicher (July 17, 2017).

[299] ICTY website, http://www.icty.org/sid/10292 (last visited Sept. 4, 2015).

[300] *See id.*

[301] Interview with Lana Šahman (Bosnia-Herzegovina); Branislav Vučinić (Bosnia-Herzegovina); Miki Vidaković (Serbia); Ante Družak (Croatia); and Ivana Ivanković (Croatia), then Visiting Young Professionals, Office of the Prosecutor, ICTY, in The Hague, Neth. (May 27, 2015).

[302] Interview with Ante Družak, then Visiting Young Professional from Croatia, in The Hague, Neth. (May 27, 2015).

[303] Interview with Miki Vidaković, then Visiting Young Professional from Serbia, in The Hague, Neth. (May 27, 2015).

Participating in the program does not assure one will prosecute war crimes upon returning home, however (though a significant number of participants do). The two Bosnian professionals in the cohort I interviewed came from the SDWC in Bosnia, to which they planned to return; one of the Croatian participants came from the war crimes section of the county state's attorney office in Osijek, Croatia, and planned to return there. Two others (one from Serbia and one from Croatia) did not yet work primarily on war crimes issues in their home countries, but hoped their experience at the ICTY would improve their prospects for appointment to a position in this area.

Would the program be more effective if participation were limited to individuals guaranteed to return home to a position prosecuting war crimes? In the view of Brammertz, one reason not to do so is precisely because participation enhances individuals' prospects for securing a position as war crimes prosecutor in his or her country, even if it does not assure such a placement. As noted in Chapter 10, however, even with these credentials VYPs may not have significant prospects of employment as a war crimes prosecutor without external support. As a pathway to a job involving war crimes cases, then, the VYP and similar programs work best when linked to a funded or otherwise guaranteed position in a relevant institution.

Yet Brammertz believes the program has benefits that transcend its principal objective: it enables young professionals from the former Yugoslavia to see for themselves "that this is just a normal and relatively well-functioning organization."[304] Brammertz elaborated:

> Because this is the reaction I got from many when I see them a week before they are leaving—they are saying, "well, we did not imagine that there will be so many international dedicated people just trying to do as good as they can." Because with all those conspiracy theories, . . . some people think that we are receiving from the Americans or whomever instructions about what to do or not to do in all decisions, and once they're coming here, they totally change their opinion on the functioning, and on the professionalism, of the institution.[305]

Michelle Jarvis, Brammertz's senior legal advisor, added: "It's a more general investment in the next generation, in trying to strengthen it in many different ways, and as the Prosecutor said, we really have noticed this added benefit of changing attitudes toward the work that we do and they see that we are just normal people with no political objective; [that] we really are just trying to make the cases work."[306]

2. Capacity-Building through the Participation of International Judges

As previously noted, the architects of the BWCC believed international judges would bolster the fledgling chamber's independence and impartiality, as well as public confidence in it. They had a second expectation as well—that foreign jurists would enhance Bosnian judges' capacity to try complex war crimes cases. Not surprisingly, in

---

[304] Interview with Serge Brammertz, Prosecutor, ICTY, in The Hague, Neth. (May 27, 2015).
[305] Id.
[306] Interview with Michelle Jarvis, Senior Legal Advisor to the Prosecutor, ICTY, in The Hague, Neth. (May 27, 2015).

practice the foreign judges' contributions "really depend[ed] on the judge."[307] Some brought extraordinary expertise and commitment to their work; others lacked both.

Among those with relevant substantive expertise was Judge Almiro Rodrigues, who served on the BWCC from April 2005 until April 2009, and had previously served as a judge on the ICTY.[308] Branko Perić, then president of the HJPC, told me Bosnian judges conveyed "how helpful Judge Rodrigues was for them" as they first confronted the myriad challenges associated with trying complex war crimes cases.[309] But he contrasted Rodrigues's contributions with those of other foreign judges, who were in much "the same position as domestic judges" when it came to expertise in international humanitarian law (IHL).[310] Meddžida Kreso, who served as president of the Court of BiH until 2017, also noted the mixed qualifications of foreign judges. On the one hand, she praised the contribution of some in "strengthening the rule of law and [introducing] international norms and standards in war crimes trials, where they have brought high standards.[311] But, she said, "I can't say all were good or that they all gave an equal contribution. . . . There were those who did not leave a significant mark."[312] Similar concerns have routinely arisen in respect of other hybrid tribunals, highlighting the vital importance of rigorous recruitment practices to ensure appointment of qualified jurists.

This is not to suggest expertise in IHL is the only relevant qualification, as the BWCC's experience underscores. As a former international judge observed, Bosnian judges, who had been trained in a largely civil law system, faced a "huge sea change" when judicial reforms adopted in 2003 moved Bosnia toward a more adversarial system.[313] In this setting, a crucial contribution of judges from countries with adversarial criminal law systems was helping their Bosnian colleagues master the complexities of adversarial procedures. But expertise in this area, as in IHL, was hardly uniform. Some of the BWCC's foreign judges had previously presided over

---

[307] Interview with Melika Murtezić, Judge, Municipal Court in Sarajevo, in Washington, D.C., United States (May 30, 2016). Judge Murtezić was a legal officer in the BWCC before she became a judge.

[308] At least three other BWCC judges previously worked in the ICTY OTP. Former ICTY personnel were also employed by other components of Bosnia's war crimes institutions in their early years. For example, Michael Th. Johnson was Chief of Prosecutions at the ICTY before becoming the first Registrar of the Court of BiH. Lucia Dighiero, who had previously worked in the ICTY's Victims and Witnesses Section, became the first director of the Witness and Victim Support Section of the Court of BiH. For a brief account of how Dighiero's Hague experience shaped her work in Sarajevo, see ORENTLICHER, supra note 157, at 126.

[309] Interview with Branko Perić, then President, HJPC, in Sarajevo, Bosn. & Herz. (Dec. 4, 2006). In similar terms, Sevima Sali-Terzić told me that, after several years of hybrid justice, it was all too obvious that international judges were not necessarily "real experts" in IHL. Interview with Sevima Sali-Terzić, Senior Legal Counsel, Constitutional Court of BiH, in Sarajevo, Bosn. & Herz. (Nov. 30, 2006). See also Ronen, Impact of ICTY, supra note 101, at 133; ICLS REPORT, supra note 173, ¶¶ 91–92.

[310] Interview with Branko Perić, then President, HJPC, in Sarajevo, Bosn. & Herz. (Dec. 4, 2006). See also Chehtman, supra note 50, at 566.

[311] Marija Tausan, Bosnia Calls Time on Foreign Judges, BALKAN TRANSITIONAL JUST. (Mar. 26, 2012).

[312] Id.

[313] Judge Patricia Whalen, Lessons Learned from External Engagement in Domestic or Hybrid Justice Efforts, Remarks at the Conference on Prosecuting Serious International Crimes: Exploring the Intersections Between International and Domestic Justice Efforts, Sponsored by the War Crimes Research Office, Washington College of Law, Washington, D.C., March 30, 2016.

civil law proceedings, "leaving them ill-equipped to manage the newly-introduced adversarial elements" in Bosnia's criminal trials.[314]

As a result of changes in procedures for recruiting international judges, qualifications of candidates improved.[315] In addition, BWCC judges asserted greater control over training programs, establishing their own priorities rather than responding to those of donors. In 2006, then international judge Shireen Fisher launched a Judicial College, initially as "a forum for bringing together perspectives of the national and international judges" outside the context of specific cases.[316] Cantonal and District Court judges interested in war crimes adjudication were also invited to participate; some of those who did were later appointed to the Court of BiH.[317]

3. CAPACITY-BUILDING THROUGH THE PARTICIPATION OF INTERNATIONAL PROSECUTORS

As previously indicated, the participation of international prosecutors in the SDWC during its early years helped the office successfully prosecute complex 11*bis* cases and bolstered its independence. For a variety of reasons, however, their participation did not have a profound impact on capacity-building. To begin, language barriers limited opportunities for Bosnian prosecutors to learn by collaborating with foreign colleagues in the SDWC or OTP prosecutors. David Schwendiman, who led the SDWC from May 2007 through 2009, recalled he "had terrible trouble because most of the information" in the ICTY's files were in English,[318] in which neither of the Bosnians who worked on 11*bis* cases was fluent.[319] In part for this reason, international prosecutors took the lead in four out of six 11*bis* cases transferred to Bosnia.[320] This addressed an immediate challenge but diminished opportunities for capacity-building: as the fledgling SDWC prepared 11*bis* cases for trial, few Bosnian prosecutors could interact with their more experienced counterparts in The Hague.[321]

Irisa Čevra believes "cultural" factors also inhibited interactions between Bosnian and OTP prosecutors: Bosnian lawyers were less inclined than international prosecutors to reach out for assistance from OTP personnel, from whom the

---

[314] JUSTICE FOR ATROCITY CRIMES, *supra* note 5, at 12. Some foreign judges lacked any previous judicial experience. *Id.* In addition to expertise in international humanitarian law and experience in adversarial criminal procedures, court management skills were vitally important for the young court.

[315] *See id.*

[316] Email from Shireen Fisher, Former International Judge, BWCC, to Diane Orentlicher (Aug. 30, 2017).

[317] JUSTICE FOR ATROCITY CRIMES, *supra* note 5, at 14. The college usually convenes once a year, during which "some important legal issues are discussed" and training is provided that is "really specific for the judges of Bosnia and Herzegovina." Interview with Melika Murtezić, Judge, Municipal Court in Sarajevo, in Washington, D.C., United States (May 30, 2016). Growing out of the Judicial College, the chamber established a Judicial Education Committee, chaired by an international judge, to assess the chamber's training priorities and coordinate responsive programs. *See* JUSTICE FOR ATROCITIES, *supra* note 5, at 13.

[318] Interview with David Schwendiman, then Head, SDWC, in Sarajevo, Bosn. & Herz. (July 14, 2009).

[319] *Id.*, as clarified by email from David Schwendiman to Diane Orentlicher (Oct. 5, 2009).

[320] FROM HYBRID TO DOMESTIC, *supra* note 142, at 11–12; interview with Toby Cadman & David Schwendiman, SDWC, in Sarajevo, Bosn. & Herz. (June 12, 2007).

[321] Studies assessing different vehicles for transferring knowledge from ICTY practitioners to their regional counterparts have found collaboration in the context of specific cases is more effective than general discussions aimed at sharing experience. *See, e.g.*, Chehtman, *supra* note 50, at 553.

local prosecutors could have become "more knowledgeable."[322] Accordingly, when international prosecutors were phased out, the SDWC "lost that momentum" to learn, if indirectly, from more experienced war crimes prosecutors in The Hague.[323] Many Bosnian prosecutors were in any case reluctant to "learn from" international prosecutors, whom the former saw as "imposing something on them."[324]

E. Impact through Case Law

Beyond the ICTY's direct influence on Bosnian criminal law and procedure as described earlier in this chapter, the BWCC's jurisprudence has been significantly influenced by ICTY case law. As Yaël Ronen has noted, while BWCC judges consult and cite decisions of other international and hybrid courts, the ICTY "is the international legal source that has had the most pronounced impact" on the chamber's jurisprudence.[325] Its influence is evident in BWCC judgments' application of such doctrines as command responsibility and joint criminal enterprise, both of which, when applicable, can establish the criminal responsibility of individuals for crimes directly perpetrated by others,[326] as well as the domestic chamber's case law concerning elements of crimes and procedural matters.

To recognize this influence is not to assume a domestic court inevitably works best when its case law tracks the jurisprudence of an international tribunal. Indeed, BWCC judges note they have not slavishly followed ICTY case law but instead canvass all relevant sources and assess their value.[327] Later, I explore the problems that can arise from domestic application of international law and practice. On the whole, however, ICTY case law has enriched the BWCC's jurisprudence, as the latter's approach to crimes of sexual violence exemplifies.

1. PROSECUTING SEXUAL VIOLENCE CRIMES

As noted in Chapter 2, alarming levels of rape during the Bosnian conflict galvanized global and Bosnian advocates to press for gender justice in The Hague. As these advocates recognized, the fact that rape was prevalent during the conflict hardly assured it would figure in ICTY indictments; although widely committed in previous wars, crimes of sexual violence had been largely absent from the charge lists of postwar war crimes tribunals and, when they were included, were downplayed at trial.[328] In some respects, the activists' efforts were "remarkably successful."[329] Along with the International Criminal Tribunal for Rwanda (ICTR) and Special Court for Sierra Leone, the ICTY produced pathbreaking decisions highlighting gender-based

---

[322] Interview with Irisa Čevra, then Assistant to the Deputy Prosecutor, SDWC, in Sarajevo, Bosn. & Herz. (Sept. 18, 2014).

[323] *Id.*

[324] *Id.*

[325] DOMAC/8 REPORT, *supra* note 17, at 42.

[326] *See id.* at 44–47; Ronen, *Impact of ICTY, supra* note 101, at 153–54. On the ICTY's early influence on the BWCC's jurisprudence, see FROM HYBRID TO DOMESTIC, *supra* note 142, at 25.

[327] *E.g.*, interview with Shireen Fisher, Former International Judge, BWCC, in Washington, D.C., United States (May 29, 2016).

[328] *See* United Nations, *Sexual Violence and Armed Conflict: United Nations Response* 3–4 (2000), http://www.un.org/womenwatch/daw/public/cover.pdf.

[329] Janet Halley, *Rape at Rome: Feminist Interventions in the Criminalization of Sex-Related Violence in Positive International Criminal Law*, 30 MICH. J. INT'L L. 1,15 (2008).

violence, bringing these crimes out of the shadows to which they had been relegated at Nuremberg.[330]

Along with advances in substantive law, the ICTY introduced a crucial innovation in the procedural law governing prosecution of sexual assault. The Rules of Procedure and Evidence adopted by the ICTY's first cohort of judges included Rule 96, which: (1) provides that corroboration of the sexual assault victim's testimony is not required for conviction, thereby bringing sexual violence prosecutions in line with those of other serious crimes; (2) does not allow the defense of consent if the circumstances of the alleged assault were inherently coercive (e.g., the victim "has been subjected to or threatened with or has had reason to fear violence, duress, detention or psychological oppression"); and (3) does not allow the victim's prior sexual conduct to be admitted into evidence, thus eliminating a tactic that, in national prosecutions, has all too often been used to blame rape survivors and shame them in court.

In myriad ways, the jurisprudence of the BWCC reflects these developments. During my first research visit to Bosnia in November 2006, University of Sarajevo professor Jasna Bakšić Muftić reflected on the significance of the BWCC's recognition of rape as an international crime, a legacy of ICTY and ICTR jurisprudence. In her words, "what is important is that it is now part of our jurisprudence. . . . This is really important."[331] A review of the BWCC's gender jurisprudence published ten years later found "compelling examples of ICTY jurisprudence positively influencing the adjudication of sexual violence crimes" in Bosnia.[332] During that period, a significant number of indictments issued by the SDWC included charges of sexual violence.[333]

Beyond the ICTY's direct influence on BWCC case law, the ad hoc tribunals' jurisprudence had a powerful influence indirectly, via the Rome Statute of the International Criminal Court ("Rome Statute"), to which Bosnia became a party in 2002. Global advocates secured advances beyond those reflected in ICTY jurisprudence at the 1998 diplomatic conference that produced the Rome Statute. For example, where the ICTY Statute explicitly recognizes rape as a crime against humanity when other elements are established,[334] the Rome Statute more broadly recognizes "[r]ape, sexual slavery,

---

[330] For an overview of the tribunals' major innovations in this area, see Kelly D. Askin, *A Decade of the Development of Gender Crimes in International Courts and Tribunals: 1993 to 2003*, 3 HUM. RTS. BRIEF 16 (2004).

[331] Interview with Jasna Bakšić Muftić, Professor, University of Sarajevo, in Sarajevo, Bosn. & Herz, (Nov. 30, 2006).

[332] Serge Brammertz et al., *Using the OTP's Experience with Sexual Violence Prosecutions as a Springboard for Building National Capacity*, in PROSECUTING CONFLICT-RELATED SEXUAL VIOLENCE AT THE ICTY 335, 368 (Serge Brammertz & Michelle Jarvis eds., 2016).

[333] *Over 500 Indicted for War Crimes, in Bosnia*, BALKAN TRANSITIONAL JUST. (Oct. 6, 2015). A study published in May 2017 reported that cases involving sexual violence "currently represent approximately 30% of all completed war crimes cases." AI, SUPPORT NOT PITY, *supra* note 276, at 24.

[334] The ICTY Statute defines crimes against humanity subject to the Tribunal's jurisdiction in pertinent part as follows:

> The International Tribunal shall have the power to prosecute persons responsible for the following crimes when committed in armed conflict, whether international or internal in character, and directed against any civilian population:
>
> . . .
> (c) enslavement;
> . . .
> (g) rape;
> (h) persecutions on political, racial and religious grounds . . .

Statute of the International Criminal Tribunal for the former Yugoslavia, art. 5.

enforced prostitution, forced pregnancy, enforced sterilization, or any other form of sexual violence of comparable gravity" as a crime against humanity when other elements are satisfied.[335] Building on the ICTY's landmark convictions for the crime against humanity of "enslavement" in circumstances involving sexual slavery,[336] the Rome Statute explicitly includes "sexual slavery" in its enumeration of crimes against humanity.[337] And while the ICTY Statute recognizes persecution on "political, racial and religious grounds" as a potential crime against humanity, the Rome Statute explicitly includes gender as a basis of the crime against humanity of persecution.[338] The 2003 BiH Criminal Code (BiH CC) largely follows the Rome Statute definition of crimes against humanity,[339] thereby indirectly incorporating the gender jurisprudence of the ICTY and ICTR and further advances codified in the ICC's statute.

In other respects, however, until it was amended in 2015, the BiH CC made it more difficult to prosecute rape before the BWCC than the ICTY. The ICTY and ICTR had made clear that the threat or use of force is not invariably required to sustain a rape charge,[340] recognizing the inherently coercive circumstances in which wartime victims were sexually assaulted. In contrast, as originally adopted the 2003 code defined rape to require "coercing another by force or by threat of immediate attack upon his life or limb, or the life or limb of a person close to him,"[341] an approach

---

[335] Article 7(1) of the Rome Statute defines crimes against humanity subject to the ICC's jurisdiction as follows:

    1. For the purpose of this Statute, "crime against humanity" means any of the following acts when committed as part of a widespread or systematic attack directed against any civilian population, with knowledge of the attack:

      . . .

      (c) Enslavement;

      . . .

      (g) Rape, sexual slavery, enforced prostitution, forced pregnancy, enforced sterilization, or any other form of sexual violence of comparable gravity;

      (h) Persecution against any identifiable group or collectivity on political, racial, national, ethnic, cultural, religious, gender as defined in paragraph 3, or other grounds that are universally recognized as impermissible under international law, in connection with any act referred to in this paragraph or any crime within the jurisdiction of the Court . . .

Rome Statute, *supra* note 6, art. 7(1).

    Paragraph 3 of the Rome Statute, incorporated by reference in paragraph 1(h), provides: "For the purpose of this Statute, it is understood that the term 'gender' refers to the two sexes, male and female, within the context of society. The term 'gender' does not indicate any meaning different from the above."

[336] Prosecutor v. Kunarac et al., Case No. IT-96-23-T & IT-96-23/1-T, Trial Judgment, ¶ 745 (Int'l Crim. Trib. for the Former Yugoslavia Feb. 22, 2001) (finding Dragoljub Kunarac guilty of enslavement); *id.* ¶ 782 (finding Radomir Kovač guilty of enslavement).

[337] *See supra* note 335.

[338] *See id.*

[339] *See* KRIVIČNI ZAKON [Z. KRIM.] [CRIMINAL CODE], art. 172(1(h) (Official Gazette of Bosnia and Herzegovina (3/03, 32/03, 37/03, 54/04, 61/04, 30/05, 53/06, 32/07, 8/10, 57/14, 22/15) (Bosn. & Herz.) [hereinafter BiH CC]. The BiH CC also includes sexual slavery in its definition of 172(1) (g).

[340] *See, e.g.*, Prosecutor v. Kunarac, Case Nos. IT-96-23 & IT-96-23/1-A, Appeal Judgment, ¶¶ 128–129 (Int'l Crim. Trib. for the Former Yugoslavia Mar. 22, 2006); Prosecutor v. Akayesu, Case No. ICTR-96-4-T, Trial Judgment, ¶ 598 (Sept. 2, 1998); and Prosecutor v. Furundžija, Case No. IT-95-17/1-T, Trial Judgment, ¶ 185 (Int'l Crim. Trib. for the Former Yugoslavia Dec. 10, 1998).

[341] BiH CC, *supra* note 339, arts. 172(1)(g), 173.

that drew wide criticism.[342] In May 2015 Bosnia's parliament amended the code to eliminate the requirement that crimes of sexual violence be perpetrated by force or the threat of force.[343] In the meantime, in at least one case the BWCC found support in ICTY case law for interpreting the previous requirement of "force" to be satisfied through evidence of coercive circumstances.[344]

Since this brief section emphasizes the salutary influence of ICTY gender jurisprudence on BWCC case law, I would be remiss if I failed to note the Bosnian chamber has made original contributions to global jurisprudence in this sphere. Notably, for example, the BWCC is believed to be the first court worldwide to find defendants guilty of *gender-based persecution* as a crime against humanity.[345]

2. *Maktouf-Damjanović*: A Cautionary Tale

While ICTY jurisprudence has generally enriched the BWCC's case law, the chamber experienced a serious setback arising from the Bosnian judiciary's efforts to adhere to international sentencing standards, as exemplified in the practice of the ICTY and other international criminal courts. While the significance of this highly idiosyncratic episode should not be overstated, it offers a useful reminder: incorporating international approaches into domestic practice is not invariably appropriate, and may carry risks.

At the outset of its work, the BWCC had to resolve the question whether it should apply the war crimes provisions of the 2003 BiH CC, which were drafted with a view to harmonizing Bosnian and international criminal law, or those of the 1976 Criminal Code of the former Socialist Federal Republic of Yugoslavia (1976 SFRY CC), which was in effect in Bosnia during the 1990s conflict.[346] This question has several dimensions, but the one that became particularly problematic involves the sentencing provisions of the two codes. The 1976 SFRY CC specifies that war crimes are punishable "by imprisonment for not less than five years or by the death penalty,"[347] but permits courts to impose twenty years' imprisonment as an alternative

---

[342] *See, e.g.,* Organization for Security and Co-operation in Europe, Mission to Bosn. & Herz., Combating Impunity for Conflict-Related Sexual Violence in Bosnia and Herzegovina: Progress and Challenges 29 (2014) [hereinafter Combating Impunity for Sexual Violence]; Amnesty International, "Whose Justice?": The Women of Bosnia and Herzegovina Are Still Waiting 21–22 (2009); Angela J. Edman, *Crimes of Sexual Violence in the War Crimes Chamber of the State Court of Bosnia and Herzegovina: Successes and Challenges,* 16 Hum. Rts. Brief 21, 21–22 (2008).

[343] *See* BiH CC, *supra* note 339, arts. 172(1)(g), 173(1)(e).

[344] Brammertz et al., *supra* note 332, at 368.

[345] Combating Impunity for Sexual Violence, *supra* note 342, at 6, 59–61. In another milestone, in June 2015 a Bosnian Serb soldier convicted of wartime rape and sentenced to eight years' imprisonment was also ordered to pay €15,000 to the victim. *See* Julian Borger, *Bosnia Rape Victims May Claim Compensation for the First Time,* Guardian (June 30, 2015). Bosnian courts have built on this precedent, awarding compensation in several other cases, but victims have faced challenges recovering the compensation awarded to them. *See* AI, Support Not Pity, *supra* note 276, at 39.

[346] An overview of the Court of BiH's approach to sentencing is provided in the Case of Maktouf and Damjanović v. Bosnia and Herzegovina, Eur. Ct. H.R., App. Nos. 2312/08 & 34179/08, Judgment ¶ 29 (2013). Here as elsewhere I use the phrase "war crimes" as shorthand for war crimes, crimes against humanity, and genocide.

[347] 1976 SFRY Krivični Zakon [Z. Kriv.] [Criminal Code], art. 142(1) (Official Gazette of the Socialist Fed. Rep. Yugoslavia, 44/76, 36/77, 56/77, 34/84, 37/84, 74/87, 57/89, 3/90, 38/90 and 45/90).

to the death penalty,[348] effectively specifying a range of five to twenty years in prison or the death penalty for war crimes. Someone convicted for aiding and abetting the commission of war crimes could be sentenced to as little as one year. In contrast, the 2003 BiH CC prescribes a range of ten (reducible to five in light of extraordinary mitigating factors) to forty-five years for war crimes, with no possibility of the death penalty.[349]

In deciding which law to apply, the BWCC was constrained by the *lex mitior* provision of Article 7(1) of the European Convention on Human Rights (ECHR), as incorporated in Bosnian law,[350] which provides that courts may not impose a "heavier penalty" than the one applicable when the crime in question was committed. The implications of this rule were anything but clear, as there were plausible arguments on both sides of the broad question of which code imposed heavier penalties. Those favoring application of the 2003 BiH CC emphasized its abolition of the death penalty. Those favoring application of the 1976 SFRY CC saw this argument as specious, as the death penalty had been suspended in Dayton. Once capital punishment was removed from the 1976 code, they argued, the five (reducible to one)-to-twenty year sentencing range of the 1976 code was patently more lenient than the 2003 law's range of ten (reducible to five)-to-forty-five years.

Fatefully, in its first verdict, a trial panel of the BWCC concluded it should apply the sentencing provisions of the 2003 BiH CC, and sentenced Abduladhim Maktouf to five years in prison for aiding and abetting war crimes committed in Central Bosnia in 1993.[351] Mindful of the *lex mitior* rule and acknowledging that the 1976 code's minimum sentence is lower than that specified in the 2003 code, the panel nonetheless concluded the 2003 law is more lenient because it excludes the death penalty.[352] A panel of the BWCC's appellate division reached a similar conclusion,[353] in part "because it is evident that there is no heavier penalty than capital punishment."[354] More important to its reasoning, the appellate panel interpreted the ECHR as excluding application of the *lex mitior* rule to crimes under international law, adding this "is fully justified" considering the maximum prison sentence allowed under the 1976 code "could not achieve the general purpose of punishment given the gravity of these criminal offenses and their consequences, in particular if we consider the cases referred by the ICTY to the Court of Bosnia and Herzegovina."[355]

---

[348] *Id.* art. 38(2).

[349] BiH CC, *supra* note 339, art. 173 read in conjunction with art. 42(2).

[350] As previously noted, the Constitution of BiH imposed in the DPA makes the European Convention on Human Rights legally binding in Bosnia. *See supra* note 92.

[351] Sud Bosne i Hercegovine, Odjel I za Ratne Zločine [Court of Bosnia and Herzegovina, Section I for War Crimes] July 1, 2005, K-127/04.

[352] *Id.* at 26.

[353] The trial verdict was quashed by an appellate panel in November 2005. Sud Bosne I Hercegovine, Apelaciono Odjelenje [Court of Bosnia and Herzegovina, App. Div.] Nov. 24, 2005, KPŽ 32/05. Following retrial before the appellate panel, that panel concluded that, "in the concrete case" of Maktouf, the 2003 code "has to be applied." Sud Bosne I Hercegovine, Apelaciono Odjelenje [The Court of Bosnia and Herzegovina, App. Div.] Apr. 4, 2006, KPŽ 32/05.

[354] Sud Bosne I Hercegovine, Apelaciono Odjelenje [Court of Bosnia and Herzegovina, App. Div.] Apr. 4, 2006, KPŽ 32/05.

[355] *Id.* Although the appeal chamber's reasoning is somewhat cryptic, its interpretation seems to follow from the structure of Article 7 of the ECHR. Paragraph 1 of Article 7 prohibits holding someone guilty for conduct that was not criminal under national or international law when

Maktouf appealed to the Constitutional Court of BiH, which found no violation of the ECHR.[356]

Maktouf complained to the European Court of Human Rights (ECtHR), as did another individual who had been sentenced by the BWCC under the 2003 BiH CC, Goran Damjanović. In a somewhat surprising ruling, the Grand Chamber of the ECtHR ruled Bosnia had violated Article 7 of the ECHR.[357] Its judgment emphasized the narrowness of its holding, making clear it was limited to the specific facts of the two applicants' cases (for Maktouf, the key fact being that he was in principle eligible to be sentenced to as little as one year in prison under the 1976 SFRY CC).[358]

But the Bosnian Constitutional Court's initial response transformed a setback into a crisis. Soon after the Grand Chamber issued its judgment, the Constitutional Court quashed sentences imposed under the 2003 law as well as the underlying convictions in ten cases without making the kind of case-specific determination undertaken by the European Court.[359] In response, the BWCC ordered the defendants' release pending retrial.[360] Soon, fourteen men convicted by the chamber, half of whom had been found guilty of genocide, were released rather than recharged and detained pending retrial.[361]

The releases were devastating for survivors. Munira Subašić, president of the Mothers of Srebrenica Association, denounced the decision to release men convicted of genocide as "shameful."[362] Two UN human rights mandate holders weighed in, stating Bosnian courts' failure to remand duly convicted criminals to custody had

---

committed, and then sets forth the *lex mitior* rule. The second paragraph provides a caveat: "This Article shall not prejudice the trial and punishment of any person for any act or omission which, at the time when it was committed, was criminal according to the general principles of law recognised by civilised nations." It appears the BWCC appeal chamber interpreted this language as applicable to the *lex mitior* rule as well as to the prohibition of punishment for conduct that was not outlawed at the time it was committed.

[356] Ustavni sud Bosne i Hercegovine [Constitutional Court of Bosnia and Herzegovina] Mar. 30, 2007, AP 1785/06.

[357] Case of Maktouf and Damjanović v. Bosnia and Herzegovina, Eur. Ct. H.R., App. Nos. 2312/08 & 34179/08, Judgment (2013). The ruling was somewhat unexpected because the Court had previously indicated, albeit in dictum, that the *lex mitior* rule did not apply to international crimes. *See* Francesco de Sanctis, *Reconciling Justice and Legality: A Quest for Fair Punishment in Cases on Bosnian Atrocity Crimes*, 12 J. INT'L CRIM. JUST. 847, 863–64 (2014)

[358] Case of Maktouf and Damjanović v. Bosnia and Herzegovina, Eur. Ct. H.R., App. Nos. 2312/08 & 34179/08, Judgment, ¶ 65 (2013).

[359] *See, e.g.,* Ustavni sud Bosne i Hercegovine [Constitutional Court of Bosnia and Herzegovina] Sept. 27, 2013, AP 325/08, 1.

[360] Sud Bosne i Hercegovine, Odjel I za Ratne Zločine [Court of Bosnia and Herzegovina, Section I for War Crimes] Oct. 11, 2013, S1 1 K 013419 13 Kvl. *See also* De Sanctis, *supra* note 357, at 864. Apparently the BWCC reasoned that Bosnian criminal procedure did not make provision for depriving a suspect of his liberty if his sentence was quashed. *See id.* A press account published in early October 2015 reported that the Court of BiH had overturned twenty-three second-instance verdicts following the European Court's ruling. *Over 500 Indicted for War Crimes in Bosnia*, BALKAN TRANSITIONAL JUST. (Oct. 7, 2015).

[361] Letter from Meddžida Kreso, President of Court of BiH, to Ministry for Human Rights and Refugees, May 28, 2014, responding to a joint letter by several UN special rapporteurs (on file with author). *See also* De Sanctis, *supra* note 357, at 863–64; Valerie Hopkins, *Justice Undone: Why Is Bosnia Releasing People Convicted of Genocide?*, FOREIGN POL'Y (Nov. 27, 2013) (both describing release of ten prisoners pursuant to the first six decisions of the Constitutional Court following the European Court's ruling).

[362] Hopkins, *supra* note 361.

placed victims in "fear for their lives and the safety of their families in the context of the release and return of the defendants to their communities," particularly in Srebrenica.[363] After individuals convicted by the BWCC were released in almost twenty cases, the Constitutional Court finally reversed itself in two judgments rendered on November 6, 2014, putting an end to the controversial releases.[364]

As the crisis played out, there was no small measure of finger-pointing about who bore responsibility for pressing Bosnia to use the 2003 code. Some pointed out that the OSCE Mission to BiH had urged the SDWC as well as entity prosecutors to apply the 2003 code in war crimes cases.[365] In the words of the OSCE mission, the 2003 code "represents an improvement in addressing" atrocity crimes over the SFRY code "because it acknowledges the developments in international criminal law recognized by the Statute and the case-law of the [ICTY] as well as by the Statute of the [ICC]."[366]

In confidential conversations soon after the crisis erupted, former OHR personnel suggested the ICTY had pushed for application of the 2003 BiH CC. While the OTP had, in fact, argued that the 2003 BiH CC should apply to cases transferred from The Hague pursuant to 11*bis,* the ICTY's Referral Bench rejected this position, ruling it was for Bosnia's state court to decide which code it would apply.[367] Bosnian judges made their own determinations on this question, grounded in relevant legal principles and informed by discussions with each other, not with external actors.[368] Even so, as Francesco de Sanctis notes, "it seems likely that the [BWCC's] flexible approach to the principle of legality was influenced by [the ICTY's] example."[369]

III. STRENGTHENING DOMESTIC PARTNERS: THE QUESTION OF TIMING

While substantial, the concerns noted in this chapter should not obscure a fundamental fact: Bosnia's war crimes institutions are "in all senses . . . in a much stronger

---

[363] Letter from Pablo de Greiff, Special Rapporteur on the promotion of truth, justice, reparation and guarantees of non-recurrence, and Ariel Dulitzky, Chair-Rapporteur of the Working Group on Enforced or Involuntary Disappearances, to Miloš Prica, Bosnian Ambassador and Permanent Representative in Geneva, 7 (Apr. 1, 2014) (on file with author).

[364] *See* Ustavni sud Bosne i Hercegovine [Constitutional Court of Bosnia and Herzegovina] Nov. 6, 2014, AP 1751/11; Ustavni sud Bosne i Hercegovine, Nov. 6, 2014, AP 1240/11. *See also* Denis Džidić & Marija Tausan, *Bosnia Blocks Controversial War Crimes Convict Releases,* BALKAN INSIGHT (Jan. 16, 2015). Since 2014, the Constitutional Court has held that reversing decisions in part based on application of law does not affect the current detention of the defendants, a matter left to the lower courts. *See* Ustavni sud Bosne i Hercegovine, Nov. 10, 2015, AP 3939/12.

[365] *See* Case of Maktouf and Damjanović v. Bosnia and Herzegovina, Eur. Ct. H.R., App. Nos. 2312/08 & 34179/08, Judgment, 30-33 (2013) (citing OSCE, UN Human Rights Committee and Venice Commission).

[366] ORGANIZATION FOR SECURITY AND CO-OPERATION IN EUROPE, MISSION TO BOSN. & HERZ., MOVING TOWARDS A HARMONIZED APPLICATION OF THE LAW APPLICABLE IN WAR CRIMES CASES BEFORE COURTS IN BOSNIA AND HERZEGOVINA 8 (2008).

[367] *See, e.g.,* Prosecutor v. Mejakić et al., Case No. IT-02-65-PT, Decision on Prosecutor's Motion for Referral of Case Pursuant to Rule 11*bis,* ¶¶ 48, 63 (Int'l Crim. Trib. for the Former Yugoslavia July 20, 2005).

[368] Former BWCC judge Shireen Fisher notes "there was no outside pressure" on the BWCC as its judges deliberated about which code to apply in sentencing suspects. Interview with Shireen Fisher, Former International Judge, BWCC, in Washington, D.C., United States (May 29, 2016).

[369] De Sanctis, *supra* note 357, at 860.

position than" they were and would have been were it not for the ICTY.[370] If they survive the threats posed by resurgent nationalism, the BWCC and SDWC will almost certainly be seen in the future, as they are today, as one of the ICTY's most important legacies in Bosnia. In light of this, a crucial question is whether the international community could have prepared Bosnian courts to prosecute war crimes cases earlier—and how questions of timing may have been influenced by donor states' commitment to the ICTY.

A. Launching State-Level Institutions

In retrospect there is little doubt more should have been done sooner to strengthen Bosnia's judicial capacity in general, and its capacity to prosecute war crimes cases in particular. Before I elaborate, it is useful to recall that, historically, the two matters were connected: as previously explained, the BWCC and SDWC were grafted onto the Court of BiH and POBiH, respectively, at the very time the OHR was creating the state institutions. For that reason, Meddžida Kreso, then president of the Court of BiH, insisted it was "impossible to transfer cases [from the ICTY] sooner" than actually happened, citing the absence of the legal framework and institutions needed to support the BWCC.[371] But her observation begs the question whether comprehensive judicial reform could have occurred sooner. More to this point, Dobrila Govedarica noted: "There was no clear strategy" about judicial reform for years. In consequence, "a lot of time was wasted."[372] And the time that was lost, Edin Ramulić noted, comprised "very important years."[373]

The costs of delay were incalculable. Reflecting on the international community's failure to prioritize judicial reform in the early postwar years, former High Representative Paddy Ashdown lamented the impact on Bosnia's endemic corruption:

It was only in 2002, seven years after the war ended, that the international community finally decided to make the establishment of the rule of law its first priority. By this time, however, corruption had seeped into the very marrow and bone of Bosnian society from the lowest to the highest level. The Bosnian state in many of its aspects had become little more than an organised conspiracy to rob from its citizens. . . . So when we made the rule of law our first priority in 2002, we discovered that we had not only to clean up the judiciary, and the prosecutorial service, but also rewrite the criminal and economic codes so as to make it easier for the forces of the law to do their jobs, establish new courts, . . . and consider a whole new programme for improving Bosnia's penal institutions. Only when

---

[370] Interview with Serge Brammertz, Prosecutor, ICTY, in The Hague, Neth. (May 27, 2015).
[371] Interview with Meddžida Kreso, Judge and then President, Court of BiH, in Sarajevo, Bosn. & Herz. (Dec. 4, 2006). Branko Perić made the same point, saying he did not believe "domestic courts were capable of handling war crimes cases before January 1, 2005." Interview with Branko Perić, then President, HJPC, in Sarajevo, Bosn. & Herz. (Dec. 4, 2006).
[372] Interview with Dobrila Govedarica, Executive Director, Open Society Fund BiH, in Sarajevo, Bosn. & Herz. (Nov. 30, 2006).
[373] Interview with Edin Ramulić, Project Coordinator, Izvor, in Prijedor, Bosn. & Herz. (Dec. 8, 2006).

we had done this could we begin . . . the long, long process of decapitating the networks of organised crime . . .[374]

Even if broader judicial reform programs had been launched earlier, some doubt whether viable war crimes institutions could have been created sooner than they were. Several sources stressed the very conditions that, in their view, made it necessary to create an international tribunal and, for a time, to subject Bosnian indictments to screening in The Hague. In a 2006 interview, for example, I asked civil society leader Tarik Jusić whether he thought the BWCC could have been established sooner, as some believed. He called this view "absurd," adding: "That it actually works and there are no bombs are amazing. Ten years ago this would have been unimaginable."[375] In 2009, I asked then Prosecutor of BiH Milorad Barašin whether he agreed with an assessment identifying 1998 as a year of lost opportunity to begin bolstering domestic capacity to prosecute war crimes. He emphatically disagreed, saying "it was not possible at all" in view of the prevailing security situation and absence of local political will at the time. "Even today everybody is trying to destroy this court," he said. "If it had been established sooner, it would never be operational."[376]

Mirsad Tokača draws much the opposite conclusion from the political pressure to which Barašin alluded. In his view, the BWCC should have been established "immediately after [the] war," when it would have been easier to protect the chamber from the "terrible political pressure" to which it is now routinely exposed.[377] Bosnia's first postwar state prosecutor, Marinko Jurčević, likewise believes Bosnia should have taken on the work of war crimes prosecutions "as soon as the war was over."[378] In his view, both Bosnia and "the international community failed the exam because in 1995 they did not recognize the importance of war crimes processing."[379]

To the extent, as Barašin suggested, the absence of political will in Bosnia made it impossible to establish the BWCC and SDWC sooner, Damir Arnaut drew a different conclusion from the same premise: even when the state institutions were launched, it was impossible to achieve this "through the will of political elites" in Bosnia; instead, they were created by OHR fiat. Since this action was not taken by Bosnian political leaders, Arnaut reasoned, "it's not clear why the High Representative couldn't have done this sooner." Indeed, he noted, in some respects conditions were "riskier in 2004" than when NATO forces were in Bosnia "in force in the 1990s."[380] "The question," Arnaut concluded, "is whether you could convince governments to give money for the project sooner."[381]

---

[374] PADDY ASHDOWN, SWORDS AND PLOWSHARES: BRINGING PEACE TO THE 21ST CENTURY 77–78 (2007).

[375] Interview with Tarik Jusić, then Program Director, Mediacentar Sarajevo, in Sarajevo, Bosn. & Herz. (Dec. 6, 2006).

[376] Interview with Milorad Barašin, then Prosecutor of BiH, in Sarajevo, Bosn. & Herz. (July 14, 2009).

[377] Interview with Mirsad Tokača, President, Research and Documentation Center (Sarajevo), in Sarajevo, Bosn. & Herz. (Sept. 11, 2014).

[378] Nidžara Ahmetašević & Mirna Mekić, *The Future of War Crimes Trials*, JUST. REP. (Nov. 13, 2006).

[379] *Id.*

[380] Interview with Damir Arnaut, then Advisor for Legal and Constitutional Affairs, Cabinet of Haris Silajdžić, in Sarajevo, Bosn. & Herz. (July 16, 2009). Although the state court and prosecutor's office were created by the High Representative, the parliament adopted legislation establishing the war crimes bodies. *See* Donlon, *supra* note 2, at 281.

[381] *Id.* Although laws establishing Bosnia's war crimes institutions were adopted in 2004, they did not become fully operational until 2005.

This may well be the crucial question, and the answer is, "probably not"—notably, for reasons that involve the ICTY. As Arnaut noted, the Tribunal "was just beginning to do its work" in the late 1990s, as it finally began to secure custody of suspects.[382] In this setting, governments may have regarded efforts to build a domestic war crimes court as a "ploy to get around the ICTY" just when it was finally becoming effective.[383] Making a distinct but related point, Mirsad Tokača faulted the PIC, OHR, and other international actors who "ignored [Bosnian war crimes prosecutions] for a long time," saying "everything will be realized by the ICTY."[384] This mindset was natural yet shortsighted in the early postwar years, when the international community had a long list of urgent priorities in Bosnia—among them, securing the return of refugees and addressing housing needs. Particularly with the ICTY already at work, judicial reform in Bosnia simply "wasn't on the list" of those priorities.[385]

Donor states' financial commitment to the Hague Tribunal almost certainly played a role as well. Fidelma Donlon, former head of the OHR's Criminal Institutions and Prosecutorial Reform Unit and former deputy registrar of the Court of BiH, evoked the underlying dynamic: "Arguably, the vast financial and human resources required by the ICTY diverted the discussion and funding away from building a domestic war crimes trials capacity in Bosnia, and only when the international community's attention turned toward winding down the ICTY, did the need for a domestic process become more urgent."[386] (Arguably, as well, the ICTY eventually "was of crucial importance in helping to secure funding for the Court of BiH," if belatedly, "by presenting it as a necessary tool for the success of its Completion Strategy."[387])

While some Bosnians are not convinced the BWCC and SDWC could have been established sooner than they were, others lament the costs of time lost in launching the two. When I interviewed Nerma Jelačić in December 2006, she asked: "What if you had created it in 2000? Imagine where you would be in 2006." Where you would be, Jelačić said, is "farther along in ending impunity."[388] In her view, the costs of extended impunity were substantial: "The passage of time has allowed some beliefs to become more concrete," making it "harder to change attitudes" by the time the new institutions were launched.[389] Like Jelačić, Nidžara Ahmetašević believes

---

[382] This context is described in Chapter 2.

[383] Interview with Damir Arnaut, then Advisor for Legal and Constitutional Affairs, Cabinet of Haris Silajdžić, in Sarajevo, Bosn. & Herz. (July 16, 2009).

[384] Interview with Mirsad Tokača, Director, Research and Documentation Center (Sarajevo), in Sarajevo, Bosn. & Herz. (Dec. 6, 2006).

[385] Interview with Edin Ramulić, Project Coordinator, Izvor, in Prijedor, Bosn. & Herz. (July 23, 2009).

[386] Donlon, *supra* note 2, at 270. *See also id.* at 267 (many donors considered their "substantial investment in the Tribunal . . . to fulfil their obligation to bring the perpetrators of the wartime atrocities to justice"). Donlon believes the Peace Implementation Council's 1998 meeting, in which it addressed the need for judicial reform but failed to address war crimes prosecutions in particular, was a lost opportunity to "comprehensively audit the work of the national authorities in relation to war crimes cases and develop a strategy to combat impunity." *Id.* at 267–68.

[387] Chehtman, *supra* note 50, at 559. *See also* Martin-Ortega, *supra* note 191, at 601 (the conception of Bosnia's state-level war crimes institutions as part of the ICTY's completion strategy "has meant that a significant amount of resources have gone to capacity building and information sharing").

[388] Interview with Nerma Jelačić, then Editor, BIRN in BiH, in Sarajevo, Bosn. & Herz. (Dec. 1, 2006).

[389] *Id.*

planning for the war crimes chamber could and should have begun sooner. Had this happened, Bosnia could have gone farther, sooner, in "fac[ing] the past," which Ahmetašević reckoned to be "the only way for us . . . to look to the future."[390]

It is, of course, impossible to know whether domestic war crimes prosecutions would have had the impact Jelačić and Ahmetašević suppose if they had begun sooner.[391] But other deleterious effects are less speculative. As Melika Murtezić pointed out in a 2016 interview, Bosnia's war crimes institutions were confronting "the problem of witnesses dying. . . . Many of the witnesses were available ten years ago, but we are not sure they will [be] in ten years."[392] Vehid Šehić made much the same point when I interviewed him seven years earlier, noting "time is not an ally," as many witnesses had already died while others were growing increasingly reluctant to testify before the BWCC. "It's not that they don't want to see justice satisfied," Šehić said. "They do. [But] this situation is taking way too long."[393]

Wolfgang Schomburg, who served as an ICTY judge from 2001 to 2007, draws a lesson from the Bosnia experience—now obvious, but hardly so when the BWCC was planned. Noting "the ICTY is only one wheel in the entire machinery" of transitional justice, he said "one of the most important lessons to be learned . . . in the future, when establishing an international tribunal, is that you must take care to ensure that a functioning judiciary worth its name be established at the same time in the area, i.e. capacity building from the outset."[394]

B. Completing the Completion Strategy

Like many I interviewed, civil society leader Dobrila Govedarica identified the ICTY's role in launching Bosnia's war crimes institutions as one of its signal achievements. Even so, Govedarica noted in November 2006, the Tribunal's impact in this sphere was "limited to the state court. We now have the problem of how to apply it to lower courts."[395] Even if it operated at maximum efficiency, the SDWC could prosecute a small fraction of wartime atrocities committed in Bosnia. The rest would be prosecuted in Bosnia, if at all, by entity-level prosecutors. For years, however, international efforts to strengthen Bosnian capacity to prosecute war crimes focused on state-level institutions, creating what many perceived as "double standards for justice" in Bosnia.[396]

---

[390] Interview with Nidžara Ahmetašević, then Editor, BIRN in BiH, in Sarajevo, Bosn. & Herz. (July 13, 2009).

[391] Some of the factors accounting for the ICTY's limited impact on beliefs about wartime atrocities, explored in Chapters 7 and 8, might also limit the belief-shaping impact of domestic war crimes courts.

[392] Interview with Melika Murtezić, Judge, Municipal Court in Sarajevo, in Washington, D.C., United States (May 30, 2016).

[393] Interview with Vehid Šehić, President, Citizens Forum of Tuzla, in Tuzla, Bosn. & Herz. (July 15, 2009).

[394] Interview with Wolfgang Schomburg, then Judge, ICTY, in The Hague, Neth. (Mar. 5, 2007). See also Donlon, supra note 2, at 283 (a lesson to be drawn from the Bosnian experience is that "national long-term strategic plans to combat impunity in a post-conflict environment" should be developed and implemented "as soon as is practicable after the conflict").

[395] Interview with Dobrila Govedarica, Executive Director, Open Society Fund BiH, in Sarajevo, Bosn. & Herz. (Nov. 30, 2006).

[396] Interview with Branko Perić, then President, HJPC, in Sarajevo, Bosn. & Herz. (Dec. 4, 2006).

In recent years, a range of governments and organizations, including the OSCE Mission to Bosnia, the EU, and UNDP, have sponsored initiatives to improve the capacity of entity prosecutors and courts[397] to process war crimes cases.[398] That they were not launched earlier compounded Bosnia's chronic backlog in processing war crimes cases. Meanwhile, the passage of time is hardly conducive to successful prosecutions before entity-level courts. In words reminiscent of Judge Šehić's reflections about the impact of lost time on the BWCC, a war crimes prosecutor in the cantonal prosecutor's office in Sarajevo observed: "Witnesses die, evidence about victims disappears, and there is no crime without a victim."[399]

As explained earlier, the decision to create the BWCC and SDWC was informed by systemic weaknesses in Bosnia's judiciary, then comprising entity-level courts. Thus there are grounds to doubt those courts could have been adequately prepared to handle war crimes cases at the same time the BWCC and SDWC were launched. Even so, BWCC veteran Patricia Whalen makes a compelling case that "efforts should have been made to build up" the entity courts early on, as "that would have created trust" in the judiciary on the part of local citizens. And, she noted, having "excellent municipal [and] cantonal court judges . . . does everybody well."[400]

IV. CONCLUDING OBSERVATIONS

ICTs raise a perennially vexing question, for which there is still no generally-accepted answer (there are a multitude): What good can a finite number of prosecutions by an international court achieve in the aftermath of mass atrocities? The ICTY's relationship with Bosnia's judiciary offers a critically important, if partial, answer. Leveraging its work to catalyze domestic capacity can enlarge and sustain an ICT's contributions, whether conceived in terms of preventing future atrocities, honoring victims' need for and right to justice, reaffirming moral commitments radically ruptured in the recent past, or removing perpetrators from victims' communities. Summing up this dimension of the Tribunal's legacy, Edin Hodžić observed that it is through Bosnia's domestic war crimes institutions that "the impact of [the] ICTY really is continuing to be significant."[401]

As the Bosnian experience highlights, the potential contributions of an ICT in this sphere are not self-executing. They require a clear strategy and concerted commitment. The Serbian experience, explored in the next chapter, shows this need not entail the same level of engagement the ICTY had in designing and monitoring Bosnia's war crimes institutions. Yet in countries emerging from cataclysmic violence, ongoing international engagement will assuredly be necessary over a sustained period, as fledgling institutions face inevitable pressures and setbacks.

---

[397] I use the phrase "entity courts" here as shorthand for courts and prosecutors' offices operating in Bosnia's two entities (the Federation and RS) as well as in the Brčko District.

[398] *See, e.g.*, Press Release, OSCE and EU support training of judges and prosecutors in BiH on use of ICTY evidence (June 27, 2013).

[399] Aida Alić & Merima Husejnović, *Sarajevo: A Year Without a War Crimes Indictment*, JUST. REP. (Dec. 19, 2007).

[400] Interview with Patricia Whalen, Former International Judge, BWCC, in Washington, D.C., United States (May 29, 2016).

[401] Interview with Edin Hodžić, Director, Public Law Program, Center for Social Research Analitika, in Sarajevo, Bosn. & Herz. (Sept. 11, 2014).

10

War Crimes Prosecutions in Serbia

> *The very existence of the Tribunal and its work gave rise to the creation of domestic . . . war crimes trials in the region, which are also one of the tools for getting the truth closer to the people and making them accept the notion of responsibility for war crimes by [members of] your own nation.*
>
> —IVAN JOVANOVIĆ[1]

In 2001, Jelena Pejić persuasively wrote that, in light of the "very low esteem in which the ICTY is held" in Serbia, it could not provide an "impetus to domestic prosecutions for crimes under international and domestic law."[2] Yet Serbia launched a dedicated war crimes court and prosecutor's office two years later. While the new institutions were launched with minimal ICTY involvement, the Hague Tribunal provided crucial impetus.

The way this came about is instructive, showing how an ICT can stimulate domestic war crimes prosecutions without even trying. So, too, is the Tribunal's response to Serbia's initiative, seizing an opportunity it did not foresee but whose potential it recognized and bolstered. Its approach is well worth attention in particular by officers of the International Criminal Court (ICC), whose statute contemplates a partnership with local courts.[3] The experience explored here provides a rich case

---

[1] Interview with Ivan Jovanović, Attorney, in Belgrade, Serb. (June 9, 2014).

[2] Jelena Pejić, *The Yugoslav Truth and Reconciliation Commission: A Shaky Start*, 25 FORDHAM INT'L L. REV. 1, 3–4 (2001).

[3] Pursuant to the principle of complementarity, the ICC can exercise jurisdiction only when national courts with jurisdiction are unable or unwilling genuinely to investigate or prosecute crimes over which the Court has subject matter jurisdiction. Rome Statute of the International Criminal Court, preamble, arts. 1, 17, July 17, 1998, 2187 U.N.T.S. 90. Some of the Court's proponents have promoted the concept of "positive complementarity," pursuant to which the ICC catalyzes domestic prosecutions. *See* René Urueña, *Prosecutorial Politics: The ICC's Influence in Colombian Peace Processes, 2003–2017*, 111 AM. J. INT'L L. 104, 105 (2017).

Some Kind of Justice. Diane Orentlicher.
© Diane Orentlicher 2018. Published 2018 by Oxford University Press.

study, as well, of the role third parties can play in advancing domestic processes of accountability during fragile and incomplete political transitions. As this chapter elucidates, at critical times external actors helped widen the space in which domestic actors could pursue accountability, while providing resources no ICT could offer.

Yet the record of Serbia's war crimes institutions is decidedly mixed, as one might expect in a country fitfully advancing beyond Milošević-era political perspectives. Following a period of notable progress in their early years, those institutions became less effective as Serbia's political leadership grew increasingly hostile to their work. As I finalized this book, influential actors, notably including the European Union, had not yet used the leverage they possessed to address these threats adequately, though it remained well within their reach to do so.

I. WAR CRIMES PROSECUTIONS IN SERBIA BEFORE 2003

A. The Milošević Era

Serbia's record of prosecuting war crimes during and immediately after the Milošević era provides a baseline for assessing the ICTY's impact. Dušan Protić, who served as deputy minister of justice in the Đinđić government, aptly summarized Milošević-era war crimes prosecutions this way: "[T]hese were not success stories, they didn't meet the expectations of anyone involved."[4]

The FRY's criminal law enabled national courts to prosecute war crimes throughout the 1990s conflicts,[5] but only one war crimes trial of ethnic Serbs, in the so-called *Yellow Wasps* case, was instituted and concluded during the Milošević era.[6] It was hardly a model of accountability. Instead, as Eric Gordy has written, the prosecution was a calculated effort to obscure Serbian responsibility for the defendants' crimes:

> [T]he principal suspect, Dušan Vučković, had been dismissed from the army in 1982 with a diagnosis of alcoholism and severe psychological illness, meaning that (1) a rhetorical wall was constructed between the [Serbian] military and the crimes, and (2) a ground was established . . . for any observer to trace the crimes to an individual condition rather than a political setting. Vučković was in fact charged with only a small portion of the offenses to which he had confessed, and the role of the Serbian Radical Party . . . , which organized his paramilitary formation, was never raised.[7]

---

[4] Interview with Dušan Protić, Former Deputy Minister of Justice, Serbia, in Belgrade, Serb. (Nov. 23, 2006). *See also* HUMANITARIAN LAW CENTER, TRANSITIONAL JUSTICE REPORT: SERBIA, MONTENEGRO AND KOSOVO, 1999–2005, at 31 (2006) [hereinafter HLC, 2006 REPORT].

[5] Relevant Serbian criminal law provisions are summarized in KEREN MICHAELI, THE IMPACT OF THE INTERNATIONAL CRIMINAL TRIBUNAL FOR YUGOSLAVIA ON WAR CRIME INVESTIGATIONS AND PROSECUTIONS IN SERBIA, DOMAC/13, at 22 (2011) [hereinafter DOMAC/13 REPORT].

[6] The sibling defendants, Dušan and Vojin Vučković, belonged to a Serb paramilitary formation in Bosnia known as the Yellow Wasps. Their trial began in the District Court of Šabac in 1994. ORGANIZATION FOR SECURITY AND CO-OPERATION IN EUROPE, MISSION TO SERB. & MONTENEGRO, WAR CRIMES BEFORE DOMESTIC COURTS 8 (2003) [hereinafter OSCE MISSION TO SAM, WAR CRIMES BEFORE DOMESTIC COURTS]. The OSCE Report dates this trial to 1996, which is the year the verdict was reached. Two other prosecutions of ethnic Serbs were initiated in 1999 but were not concluded until 2002 and 2003, respectively.

[7] ERIC GORDY, GUILT, RESPONSIBILITY, AND DENIAL: THE PAST AT STAKE IN POST-MILOSEVIC SERBIA 49 (2013).

The trial struck Deputy War Crimes Prosecutor Bruno Vekarić as pre-scripted, and both the prosecutor and court hewed closely to the script: "You had on one side [a] prosecutor [who] indicted people and on other hand you had a court and ... it was like a match, you know—all people on the case [were] on the same side."[8]

Particularly by the late 1990s, there was no shortage of Serb suspects to be prosecuted if Serbian prosecutors wanted to do so. As recounted in Chapter 2, Serb perpetrators enjoyed de facto impunity in Bosnia until July 1997, when NATO forces deployed there began arresting ICTY fugitives. Measured by new arrests in Bosnia, NATO's newly robust approach was a success. Before long, however, in the words of an ICTY official, "we became victims of our own success, and anybody who thought they could have been indicted fled to Serbia."[9]

While Milošević-era courts fully tried just one war crimes case involving Serb defendants, the same period saw a "large number of dubious convictions on terrorism charges, principally against Kosovo Albanians,"[10] and FRY courts launched at least twenty-six war crimes investigations of ethnic Croats in 1992 alone.[11] Summarizing this period, one study concluded "the domestic response to the mass atrocities of the Yugoslav and Kosovo wars under Milošević [was] negligible. Aside from one show trial aimed at appeasing the international community, and a host of dubious trials against Albanians for terrorism, no real attempt [was] made to adjudicate war crimes perpetrators."[12]

The FRY courts' performance in war crimes cases epitomized a more far-reaching subordination of justice under Milošević. During the 1990s "cases carrying special significance to Serbia's elite were allocated to certain 'suitable' judges in order to ensure a desired outcome."[13] By the time the Milošević government collapsed, the judiciary had been deeply compromised by years of operating under executive pressure. The president of the Supreme Court of Serbia, Leposava Karamarković, captured the regime's corrosive impact this way in a 2001 speech:

> For decades in this country the principle of utilitarianism dominated instead of the principle of legality, and it reached its shameful height during the previous regime.... In pursuing its goals, the oligarchy ... expressed contempt for the law and for legal form, and recognized it only to the extent that it was useful. That led to the worst possible consequence for the legal system of any country—the legal system collapsed [and] fell apart.... The masters of manipulation brought fear into the courtroom, ordering up not only trials but sentences as well.... Few judges ... managed to remain upright.... [S]ome of

---

[8] Interview with Bruno Vekarić, Deputy War Crimes Prosecutor, in Belgrade, Serb. (July 10, 2012). See also HLC, 2006 REPORT, supra note 4, at 31 ("the brothers Vučković and their counsel had both the trial chamber and the prosecutor on their side while no one represented the victims.... [T]he trial very quickly degenerated into a farce ... ").

[9] Interview with Bob Reid, Chief of Operations, Office of the Prosecutor, ICTY, in The Hague, Neth. (May 28, 2015).

[10] GORDY, supra note 7, at 53. Before NATO's engagement in the Kosovo conflict, some 2,000 Kosovo Albanians were arrested and approximately 200 were tried for terrorism and subversive activities. DOMAC/13 REPORT, supra note 5, at 29. After the NATO campaign, over 600 Kosovo Albanians were tried in Serbia. Id. at 30.

[11] DOMAC/13 REPORT, supra note 5, at 27.

[12] Id. at 62. The "show trial" cited here was the prosecution of the Vučković brothers in Šabac.

[13] Id. at 26.

the responsibility for their current state is borne by the judges themselves, who
did not react when in the dissolution of Yugoslavia cities were destroyed, people
were killed and shocking ethnic cleansing was carried out.[14]

Thus an intensive and long-term effort would be needed to prepare Serbia's judiciary
to undertake credible war crimes prosecutions in the post-Milošević era.[15]

B. Early Post-Milošević Era Prosecutions

Six years would pass after the Vučković brothers were found guilty before Serbian
courts would convict a Serb suspect of war crimes, this time in relation to the murder
of two Kosovo Albanian civilians during the 1999 Kosovo conflict.[16] Conducted in
the immediate aftermath of the Milošević era, the trial highlighted its enduring impact. According to the Humanitarian Law Center (HLC), the defendant, a former
Yugoslav army reservist, "was tried amid cheers that he was a hero and that he had
fought in Kosovo for Serbia and for the Serb people."[17] Even the prosecutor "insisted
that the court make allowances for the defendant's courageous conduct during the
war in Kosovo."[18] That the prosecution took place at all was in no small part due to
external actors, who pressed for progress in addressing war crimes.[19]

By late 2003, only a handful of Serbs had been prosecuted for war crimes and related
offenses,[20] and the suspects were all "ordinary soldiers or lower-ranking officers."[21] In
January 2004, an ICTY spokesman summarized Serbia's record this way:

So far, of the handful of war crimes trials held [in Serbia] over the past decade,
none whatsoever have included senior leaders. Some observers have concluded

---

[14] GORDY, *supra* note 7, at 53–54 (quoting Leposava Karamarković).

[15] A range of external actors became engaged in assessing Serbia's judicial system and providing
input on its plans to develop dedicated war crimes institutions. Foremost among these was the
Organization for Security and Co-operation in Europe (OSCE) Mission to Serbia and Montenegro.
According to Mark Ellis, "the OSCE determined that one of its main priorities in 2003 would be to
assist the Serbian Government in creating the capacity for the national judiciary to conduct war
crimes trials." Mark S. Ellis, *Coming to Terms with Its Past—Serbia's New Court for the Prosecution
of War Crimes*, 22 BERKELEY J. INT'L L. 165, 166 (2004). The International Bar Association also
assembled a group of international experts to provide comments and recommendations on draft
legislation. *See id.* at 166–67. The U.S. government funded a multimillion dollar program to
develop Serbia's capacity to institute war crimes trials. *See id.* at 169 n.20.

[16] On July 8, 2002, the District Court in Prokuplje convicted Ivan Nikolić, a former reservist in the
Yugoslav army, of killing two Albanian civilians in Kosovo in April 1999 and sentenced him to
eight years in prison. *See* OSCE MISSION TO SaM, WAR CRIMES BEFORE DOMESTIC COURTS,
supra note 6, at 8; HLC, 2006 REPORT, *supra* note 4, at 31 n.81; *Ex-reservist Is Convicted at War
Crimes Trial in Serbia*, WASH. POST (July 9, 2002). Nikolić was tried in a "hostile atmosphere,"
in which "the judge, the prosecutor and witnesses . . . all received death threats." Bojan Tončić,
Regional Report—Serbia: "Token" War Crimes Trial, IWPR (Apr. 30, 2005).

[17] HLC, 2006 REPORT, *supra* note 4, at 31 n.82.

[18] *Id.* (emphasis omitted).

[19] Tončić, *supra* note 16 (although this report is dated Apr. 30, 2005, it appears to report on a July
2002 verdict).

[20] *See* OSCE MISSION TO SaM, WAR CRIMES BEFORE DOMESTIC COURTS, *supra* note 6, at 8–10;
DOMAC/13 REPORT, *supra* note 5, at 64.

[21] OSCE MISSION TO SaM, WAR CRIMES BEFORE DOMESTIC COURTS, *supra* note 6, at 47.

that there appears to be a policy of exclusively trying low-level perpetrators, thus promoting a culture of impunity for the military and political leadership.[22]

Serbs convicted of war crimes generally received short sentences, moreover.[23]

Prosecutions instituted after the 2000 political transition nonetheless reflected modest progress.[24] One, before the Belgrade District Court, involved the kidnapping of sixteen Bosniaks from Sjeverin and their torture and murder in Višegrad, both in Bosnia. The other, against a former member of the Scorpions unit of Serbia's Ministry of the Interior, involved the murder of fourteen Kosovo Albanian civilians and the severe wounding of five children in Podujevo, Kosovo in March 1999.[25] According to the HLC, these were the first war crimes trials in Serbia in which victims and their families provided testimony and which ended with the court imposing the maximum penalty of twenty years (in the *Sjeverin* case, against three of the four defendants).[26]

In both cases, however, it was "clear that . . . there was enough evidence to institute proceedings against the defendants' superiors, but the prosecutors took no action in this connection whatever."[27] As will be seen, despite significant progress in the years after these trials were conducted, senior Serbian suspects remained beyond the reach of Serbian justice.

II. SERBIA'S WAR CRIMES INSTITUTIONS

Efforts to develop a dedicated war crimes chamber and prosecutor's office, along with similar institutions to address organized crime, began during the stewardship of Serbian prime minister Zoran Đinđić and culminated soon after his March 2003 assassination.[28] On July 1, 2003, the Serbian parliament adopted a Law on Organisation and Competence of Government Authorities in War Crimes Proceedings,[29] which established a new Serbian War Crimes Chamber (SWCC) as a specialized component of the Belgrade District Court;[30] the Office of the War Crimes Prosecutor (OWCP);[31] a War Crimes Investigation Service (WCIS), located in Serbia's Ministry of the Interior;[32] and a special detention unit for war

---

[22] INTERNATIONAL CENTER FOR TRANSITIONAL JUSTICE, SERBIA AND MONTENEGRO: SELECTED DEVELOPMENTS IN TRANSITIONAL JUSTICE 5 (2004) [hereinafter ICTJ, SELECTED DEVELOPMENTS] (quoting Jim Landale).

[23] Interview with Ivan Jovanović, then National Legal Advisor, OSCE Mission to Serbia, in Belgrade, Serb. (Nov. 22, 2006).

[24] *See* HLC, 2006 REPORT, *supra* note 4, at 31–32.

[25] *Id. See also War Crimes Trial Begins*, WASH. POST (Oct. 10, 2002).

[26] HLC, 2006 REPORT, *supra* note 4, at 31–32.

[27] *Id.* at 32.

[28] Đinđić's assassination and its aftermath are described in Chapter 3.

[29] Law on Organisation and Competence of Government Authorities in War Crimes Proceedings, *Official Gazette of the Republic of Serbia*, No. 67/2003, July 1, 2003 [hereinafter 2003 Law on War Crimes]. This law entered into force on July 9, 2003.

[30] *Id.* art. 10. The English translation of this provision uses the phrase "War Crimes Panel," but I use the phrase "War Crimes Chamber" because it is more commonly used in English-language literature about the chamber.

[31] *Id.* art. 4.

[32] *Id.* art. 8. A precursor to this unit was created in 2001 following the discovery of mass graves in Serbia. *See* HUMANITARIAN LAW CENTER, TEN YEARS OF WAR CRIMES PROSECUTIONS IN SERBIA: CONTOURS OF JUSTICE 31 (2014) [hereinafter HLC, TEN YEARS].

crimes.[33] The 2003 law gave the SWCC, OWCP, and WCIS exclusive responsibility for investigating, prosecuting, and trying all new war crimes cases.[34]

On July 23, 2003, the National Assembly elected Vladimir Vukčević, at that time Deputy Public Prosecutor of the Republic of Serbia, as War Crimes Prosecutor, a post he would hold until his term expired at the end of 2015.[35] The SWCC began operating in October 2003[36] and started its first trial in March 2004.

A. The ICTY's Role in the Establishment of Serbia's War Crimes Institutions

In striking contrast to its purposeful role in launching Bosnia's war crimes institutions,[37] the ICTY played a minor part in preparations for the SWCC and OWCP.[38] Indeed, its engagement was so marginal, Vukčević told me he did not believe "the Hague Tribunal had anything to do with the establishment of [his] office."[39] Instead, he credited Serbia's political transition: "After the democratic changes in our country," he explained, "the new democratic authorities wanted to do away with both organized crime and war crimes."[40]

Everyone I interviewed about the origins of Serbia's war crimes institutions shared Vukčević's view that the political transition at the end of 2000 was critical. But almost everyone else insisted those institutions "wouldn't exist but for the ICTY,"[41] "at least

---

[33] 2003 Law on War Crimes, *supra* note 29, art. 12. That same day, the Serbian parliament adopted legislation establishing a specialized chamber and prosecutor for Organized Crime. Law on Organisation and Competence of Government Authorities in Suppression of Organised Crime, Official Gazette of the Republic of Serbia, No. 42/02, July 1, 2003. As part of a general reform of the Serbian judiciary, in 2010 the SWCC of the Belgrade District Court became the War Crimes Department (WCD) of the Belgrade Higher Court, and appeals from its judgments would now be heard by a Department for War Crimes in the Belgrade Court of Appeal. DOMAC/13 REPORT, *supra* note 5, at 84–85; HLC, TEN YEARS, *supra* note 32, at 36. The Belgrade Court of Appeal is one of four appellate courts in Serbia. The others are in Novi Sad, Niš, and Kragujevac. Appeals from the SWCC's first instance verdicts previously were heard by the Supreme Court of Serbia.

[34] Other Serbian courts would complete any war crimes cases they had already begun. 2003 Law on War Crimes, supra note 29, art. 21. The law addresses war crimes and genocide cases but does not explicitly recognize crimes against humanity. Some Serbian advocates argue Serbia's War Crimes Prosecutor has a sufficient basis in customary international law to bring crimes against humanity charges, but this view is not widely accepted in Serbia.

[35] *See* Republic of Serbia Office of the War Crimes Prosecutor, http://www.tuzilastvorz.org.rs/html_trz/o_nama_eng.htm (last visited Sept. 24, 2017).

[36] ICTJ, SELECTED DEVELOPMENTS, *supra* note 22, at 5.

[37] *See* Chapter 9.

[38] In 2003, Tribunal officials participated in an experts' roundtable organized by the OSCE Mission to Serbia and Montenegro to discuss a draft law establishing the new war crimes institutions and provided detailed comments on the draft. Interview with Ivan Jovanović, then National Legal Advisor, OSCE Mission to Serbia, in Belgrade, Serb. (Nov. 22, 2006); email from Ivan Jovanović to Diane Orentlicher (May 7, 2008). *See also* DOMAC/13 REPORT, *supra* note 5, at 85–86. Even this limited participation came at the initiative of the OSCE Mission to Serbia, not Tribunal officials. *See id.* at 87.

[39] Interview with Vladimir Vukčević, then War Crimes Prosecutor, in Belgrade, Serb. (Nov. 21, 2006).

[40] *Id.* By "new democratic authorities" Vukčević meant the Đinđić government, which initiated plans to create the SWCC and OWCP. As noted below, by the time the OWCP was launched (after Đinđić's assassination), its relationship with the government had become antagonistic.

[41] Interview with Nataša Kandić, then Executive Director, Humanitarian Law Center, in Belgrade, Serb. (Nov. 27, 2006).

not at this point."[42] Branko Rakić, who helped Slobodan Milošević defend himself in The Hague, offered inadvertent support for this view. Rakić told me the international community should have helped Serbia develop its own war crimes institutions rather than launch the Hague Tribunal. When I asked Rakić to explain the scenario he had in mind—how would his proposal have worked in 1993, when the ICTY was created?—he replied:

> In 1993, perhaps it was too early to do that. What I am speaking would have come later but . . . well anyway, if you start from the . . . presumption that the authorities in 1993 had criminal intentions and things like that, the existence of a court wouldn't have helped anyway, so.[43]

Summarizing her understanding of the ICTY's influence on Serbia's war crimes institutions, journalist Antonela Riha said: "That's the main impact of The Hague. If it didn't exist, there would be no war crimes chamber."[44]

If, as Vukčević claimed, Serbia's war crimes institutions owe their existence to the change in government, how could their creation be the Tribunal's "main impact" in Serbia? As explained by Dušan Protić, the ICTY enabled reformists in the coalition government that succeeded Milošević to realize their aspirations despite the contested political space in which they operated.[45] According to Protić, who was a senior justice official in the Đinđić government, two principal considerations motivated that government to address wartime atrocities. First, "we really thought that this was a shame, something we have to bring to the surface."[46] Second, the new government believed "addressing this problem" would help advance Serbia's "integration in the West,"[47] a high priority of Đinđić.[48]

---

[42] Interview with Radmila Nakarada, then Associate Professor, Faculty of Political Sciences, University of Belgrade, in Belgrade, Serb. (Nov. 24, 2006). Ljiljana Smajlović said she thought "there would have been a war crimes chamber here" even if Milošević had not been transferred to The Hague, but also said: "Watching those proceedings [in The Hague] maybe made the war crimes chamber more acceptable here." Interview with Ljiljana Smajlović, Journalist, in Belgrade, Serb. (Nov. 24, 2006).

[43] Interview with Branko Rakić, Professor, Faculty of Law, University of Belgrade, in Belgrade, Serb. (July 11, 2012). Rakić went on to clarify that he did not personally believe "the state policy of Serbia was a criminal one, and that is, let's say, the central point of my attitude." *Id.*

[44] Interview with Antonela Riha, Journalist, in Belgrade, Serb. (Nov. 27, 2006).

[45] As elaborated in Chapter 3, the reformist Serbian prime minister Đinđić was in a coalition with the nationalist president of the FRY, Vojislav Koštunica.

[46] Interview with Dušan Protić, Former Deputy Minister of Justice, Serbia, in Belgrade, Serb. (Nov. 23, 2006). *See also* MLADEN OSTOJIĆ, BETWEEN JUSTICE AND STABILITY: THE POLITICS OF WAR CRIMES PROSECUTIONS IN POST-MILOŠEVIĆ SERBIA 169 (2014) (the emergence of Serbia's war crimes institutions "is primarily attributable to the resolve of the reformist political elites whose endeavor benefited from foreign support").

[47] Interview with Dušan Protić, Former Deputy Minister of Justice, Serbia, in Belgrade, Serb. (Nov. 23, 2006).

[48] Indeed, Serbia faced significant pressure from Western states to develop credible war crimes prosecutions. *See* Ellis, *supra* note 15, at 169; DOMAC/13 REPORT, *supra* note 5, at 62. Several sources indicated that this initiative provided the first post-Milošević government a chance to repair Serbia's standing in the international community. Filip Švarm made the point this way: "Setting up the special court showed that we're also part of the international community." Interview with Filip Švarm, Journalist, in Belgrade, Serb. (Nov. 24, 2006). Ivan Jovanović noted, "The new government saw domestic trials as an opportunity to change [Serbia's] image in the

But when the government entered office, Protić continued, "we were all aware that our judicial system is fragile and not capable of dealing with these issues." The solution on which they settled was to create "specialized judicial institutions to deal with these crimes, . . . to focus the capacity we had toward one point."[49] Serbia's minister of justice, Vladan Batić, initiated plans for specialized courts to deal with organized crime as well as war crimes.[50] In this setting, Protić recalled, the government saw the ICTY as "very useful" in helping create a political space for Serbia to deal with "the burden of war crimes in all its dimensions."[51]

In the view of Ivan Jovanović, who led the War Crimes Trials program of the Organization for Security and Co-operation in Europe (OSCE) Mission to Serbia, the Đinđić government's initiative reflected "good-faith plans for laying down the foundation for a better society not based on lies" about wartime atrocities. There was "a genuine willingness to establish the truth, to bring Serbian perpetrators to justice before Serbian courts, to reach a higher level of self-responsibility and self-criticism through war crimes prosecutions."[52] But, Jovanović noted, there was not a "sufficient shift of political elites" to enable the government to implement this plan during Đinđić's tenure.[53]

A confluence of other factors made it possible to establish the war crimes bodies even in the face of continuing opposition from nationalists. The March 2003 assassination of Đinđić provided impetus to adopt legislation, originating in his government, establishing specialized institutions to prosecute war crimes and organized crime.[54] Even in this expanded political space, strong encouragement from outside actors was needed to ensure passage of the legislation.[55] Indeed, opposition from powerful sectors of government and the public persisted. Describing the environment in which he took office, Vukčević told a reporter:

At that time there was no political will and consensus for the prosecution of war crimes, that is for sure; the contrary was the case: there was resistance, the public

---

international community and to empower the judiciary to do so." Interview with Ivan Jovanović, then National Legal Advisor, OSCE Mission to Serbia, in Belgrade, Serb. (Nov. 22, 2006).

[49] Interview with Dušan Protić, Former Deputy Minister of Justice, Serbia, in Belgrade, Serb. (Nov. 23, 2006).

[50] Interview with Ivan Jovanović, then National Legal Advisor, OSCE Mission to Serbia, in Belgrade, Serb. (Nov. 22, 2006).

[51] Interview with Dušan Protić, Former Minister of Justice, in Belgrade, Serb. (Nov. 23, 2006).

[52] Interview with Ivan Jovanović, then National Legal Advisor, OSCE Mission to Serbia, in Belgrade, Serb. (Nov. 22, 2006).

[53] *Id.*

[54] Interview with Dušan Protić, Former Minister of Justice, Serbia, in Belgrade, Serb. (Nov. 23, 2006). The legislation was adopted during the short-lived period of reform following Đinđić's assassination. *See* Chapter 3.

[55] According to several sources, in the wake of the Đinđić assassination, the U.S. government and OSCE Mission to Serbia encouraged the Serbian government to introduce a law on war crimes as well as one on organized crime. *E.g.*, interview with Bruno Vekarić, Deputy War Crimes Prosecutor, in Belgrade, Serb. (Nov. 21, 2006). The HLC attributed the new war crimes institutions in large part to international pressure: "Under the International Community's pressure and in direct relation to the state's obligation to respond to the war crimes committed in the recent past with legal instruments, the state of Serbia adopted laws, which were the basis for establishment of special institutions for prosecution of war crimes." Press Release, Humanitarian Law Center, War Crimes Trials in Serbia (July 26, 2006) (on file with author).

opinion was still thinking that the Serbs were attacked, that we led a defensive war and that all those who took part in it were patriots.[56]

In this setting, some sectors of government otherwise disinclined to prosecute Serbs came to accept local war crimes institutions for reasons relating to the Hague Tribunal. With the ICTY poised to implement its completion strategy, a key component of which was transferring cases to local courts,[57] they hoped the Tribunal would send cases against Serb suspects to Serbia.[58]

Anti-Hague sentiment also made domestic prosecutions more palatable to the public than would have been the case if the ICTY did not exist. As then Serbian minister of justice Vladan Batić noted, Serbians "have a bitter taste in their mouth when you mention that court. They see it as a place of selective justice."[59] A public opinion survey taken in late 2004 disclosed that, while only 57 percent of Serbian respondents believed national courts were ready to prosecute war crimes cases,[60] 71 percent believed it would be better to institute such prosecutions in Serbian courts than in The Hague.[61]

If anti-Hague sentiment helped clear the way for domestic trials, it also produced a crisis for Vukčević early in his tenure. The episode is worth briefly recounting, as it illustrates the constrained space for accountability in Serbia's incomplete political transition and the crucial role outside actors played in holding that space open against new pressures.

In early March 2004, former FRY president Vojislav Koštunica, no fan of war crimes prosecutions, became prime minister of Serbia. In his first press conference as minister of justice in the Koštunica cabinet, Zoran Stojković sent a shot across the bow, saying he thought the special chambers for war crimes and organized crime should be abolished.[62] But the new government's antipathy toward domestic war crimes institutions was trumped by its desire to keep Serbian officials from facing justice in The Hague. Vukčević came under intense pressure when he refused to espouse the government's position that four Serbian generals indicted by the ICTY in October 2003 should be tried in Serbia. In the face of his refusal, Stojković sought Vukčević's ouster.[63] Recalling Stojković's stance, Deputy War Crimes Prosecutor Bruno Vekarić

---

[56] *Confidence Is the Key to Cooperation*, Interview by Tatjana Tagirov with Vladimir Vukčević, in JUSTICE IN TRANSITION 56 (special ed. Sept. 2006) [hereinafter *Confidence Is the Key to Cooperation*].

[57] This development is described in Chapter 9.

[58] The reformists in the coalition government also advocated transfers from The Hague to Belgrade, perhaps hoping to ensure the support of their nationalist coalition partners for domestic war crimes institutions. *See* Fredrik Dahl, *Serbia Says Ready to Prosecute War Crimes*, REUTERS (July 17, 2003) (quoting then minister of justice Vladan Batić saying, "I hope that The Hague will give us a certain number of cases").

[59] *Id.*

[60] Of this total, 24 percent responded "absolutely yes" when asked whether Serbia's courts were ready to prosecute war crimes, while 33 percent responded "mostly yes." OSCE MISSION TO SERB., BELGRADE CENTRE FOR HUM. RTS., & STRATEGIC MARKETING RESEARCH, *Public Opinion in Serbia: Views on Domestic War Crimes Judicial Authorities and the Hague Tribunal*, 48 (Dec. 2006).

[61] *Id.* at 48–49.

[62] Terry Carter, *Playing by the Rule of Law*, A.B.A J. (Oct. 29, 2005).

[63] Interview with Vladimir Vukčević, then War Crimes Prosecutor, in Belgrade, Serb. (Nov. 21, 2006).

told me: "His wish was to destroy this office."[64] In line with the government's position, Serbia's parliament scheduled a session to consider Vukčević's removal.[65]

Vukčević told me that, at that moment, he needed "international support, because here I encountered a great deal of resistance by the Executive Branch."[66] Vukčević credits international support—from the ICTY and, even more importantly, from the U.S. embassy in Belgrade—with averting his ouster.[67] Sandra Orlović recalls that, when foreign embassies opposed the bid to oust Vukčević, "everything stopped."[68]

While Vukčević would come to prize his partnership with the OTP, the Tribunal's principal impact on him early on was to inspire him, as a matter of "professional pride," to prove Serbia could capably prosecute war criminals itself.[69] In his view, the fact that war crimes associated with Serbia were prosecuted before an international court placed his country in the same column as war-ravaged countries whose judiciaries he reckoned to be far less developed than Serbia's.[70] Now, Vukčević could "show that local courts can handle these cases."[71] By his own account, this was a key reason Vukčević agreed to serve as War Crimes Prosecutor.[72]

This is not to suggest Vukčević's sole motivation was to redeem Serbian pride. People who worked with him say Vukčević truly believes war criminals should be prosecuted—that it is a "false pride to say that what happened in [Serbians'] name was good if it's a war crime."[73] Bob Reid, chief of operations in the ICTY Office of the Prosecutor (OTP), recalled a conversation he had with Vukčević in which the latter explained why he had prosecuted "so many Serbs" (in the view of Serbian nationalists): "You've just got to face facts. We were in three wars, so we've probably committed more crimes than the others *could* have."[74]

Beyond providing an incentive for domestic prosecutions, one of the ICTY's most significant contributions came from the model of judicial reckoning it embodied. Deputy War Crimes Prosecutor Bruno Vekarić made the point this way:

> The Hague Tribunal was the necessity of the moment during Milošević [because there was no will to prosecute war crimes in Serbian courts]. I do believe

---

[64] Interview with Bruno Vekarić, Deputy War Crimes Prosecutor, in Belgrade, Serb. (July 10, 2012).

[65] Interview with Sandra Orlović, then Executive Director, Humanitarian Law Center, in Belgrade, Serb. (June 10, 2014).

[66] Interview with Vladimir Vukčević, then War Crimes Prosecutor, in Belgrade, Serb. (Nov. 21, 2006).

[67] *Id.* Deputy War Crimes Prosecutor Bruno Vekarić credits delegations from "the White House and the EU" for intervening with Koštunica to prevent Vukčević's ouster during this period. OSTOJIĆ, *supra* note 46, at 173.

[68] Interview with Sandra Orlović, then Executive Director, Humanitarian Law Center, in Belgrade, Serb. (June 10, 2014).

[69] Confidential interview.

[70] Interview with Vladimir Vukčević, then War Crimes Prosecutor, in Belgrade, Serb. (Nov. 21, 2006). See also *Confidence Is the Key to Cooperation, supra* note 56, at 56–57.

[71] Interview with Vladimir Vukčević, then War Crimes Prosecutor, in Belgrade, Serb. (Nov. 21, 2006).

[72] See *Confidence Is the Key to Cooperation, supra* note 56, at 56–57.

[73] Confidential interview. Another confidential source told me Vukčević views war criminals as "human garbage who should be behind bars."

[74] Interview with Bob Reid, Chief of Operations, Office of the Prosecutor, ICTY, in The Hague, Neth. (May 28, 2015). Reid believes this conversation occurred in 2014.

it was exactly through the Hague Tribunal that the process of facing the past was initiated in the states of the former Yugoslavia.[75]

In the words of Judge Siniša Važić, who served as the SWCC's first president, the Hague Tribunal was "the embryo" for the domestic chamber. "Everyone learned from [the ICTY both] as an idea and as know how."[76]

B. From International to Transitional Justice . . . ?

Serbians who supported the ICTY believed it morally imperative to prosecute those responsible for wartime depredations, and were convinced there would be no justice without the Tribunal.[77] Unsurprisingly, then, these citizens generally welcomed the creation of domestic war crimes institutions, though some worried Vukčević would not prosecute senior Serb suspects or a sufficient number of cases.[78]

Indeed, they believed credible prosecutions in Serbia could advance goals the ICTY could not achieve. Belgrade District Court Judge Radmila Dragičević-Dičić hoped that, by bringing justice "closer to the people," the fledgling SWCC would enable Serbians to "see victims from Bosnia here."[79] This was impossible in cases tried in The Hague, she said, and not just because of physical distance: "People don't see victims, they see politics in The Hague."[80] Others said they hoped Serbian war crimes prosecutions would help dispel neighboring countries' deep mistrust of Serbia, an enduring legacy of the 1990s wars. For example, Filip Švarm expressed the belief—and surely his hope—that when Croatian, Bosniak, and Kosovo Albanian victims testified and found justice in Serbian courts, this would "contribute[] to reconciliation."[81]

Nataša Kandić, who represented victims from other former Yugoslav countries in early trials before the SWCC,[82] believed Serbian prosecutions could advance a core goal of transitional justice measures—"recognition of victims and their dignity."[83]

---

[75] Interview with Bruno Vekarić, Deputy War Crimes Prosecutor, in Belgrade, Serb. (Nov. 21, 2006).

[76] Interview with Siniša Važić, then President, SWCC, in Belgrade, Serb. (Nov. 21, 2006). Another study reached similar conclusions:

> [T]he very existence of the ICTY and the work it had done were at the heart of the necessity to take on war crimes trials. Indeed, all those interviewed by DOMAC [in May 2008], specifically Serbian judges, prosecutors and NGO representatives, stated that without the ICTY, at least as a concept, there would not have been domestic prosecutions of war crimes in Serbia.

DOMAC/13 Report, *supra* note 5, at 68.

[77] *See* Chapter 5.

[78] *See* Dahl, *supra* note 58.

[79] Interview with Radmila Dragičević-Dičić, Judge, Belgrade District Court, in Belgrade, Serb. (Nov. 21, 2006).

[80] *Id.*

[81] Interview with Filip Švarm, Journalist, in Belgrade, Serb. (Nov. 24, 2006).

[82] Under the 2010 Criminal Procedure Code, it is no longer possible for non-lawyers such as Kandić to represent victims in court.

[83] Interview with Nataša Kandić, then Executive Director, Humanitarian Law Center, in Belgrade, Serb. (Nov. 27, 2006). The United Nations Special Rapporteur on transitional justice has emphasized the central importance of recognition of victims as a proximate goal of transitional justice measures. *See, e.g.*, Pablo de Greiff, Report of the Special Rapporteur on the promotion of truth, justice, reparation and guarantees of non-recurrence, ¶¶ 29–31, U.N. Doc. A/HRC/21/46 (Aug. 9, 2012).

She explained: "All Bosniaks know what happened, but if you want to show them that the families of victims are important, it means that Serbian society—the state and its institutions—should invite the victims [to testify in Serbian courts], to restore their dignity."[84] At the same time, Kandić hoped Serbians' exposure to victims of Serb crimes would advance a national reckoning with wartime atrocities. In her words, it is "important that our society face the victims, the 'others,' because we're only talking here about Serbs as victims. Through the trials, it's an opportunity to show [Serbians] what we did to others."[85]

Several years after Serbia's war crimes institutions were launched, some saw another value in their work. Trials before the SWCC had helped normalize the prosecution of war crimes[86]—no small achievement in a country where discourses of denial were still robust.[87] This is not to suggest Serbia's war crimes institutions enjoyed enthusiastic or reliable support from the government and society—far from it. Even so, the public saw prosecution of Serb war crimes suspects as being far more legitimate in Belgrade than The Hague.[88]

As we shall see, troubling trends in recent years have undermined domestic institutions' capacity to advance the goals articulated by Kandić, Švarm, and Dragičević-Dičić. Even so, after closely observing Serbia's war crimes institutions for over a decade, Ivan Jovanović had become more convinced than ever that

> domestic trials . . . are in a better position, and have better potential, to generate more . . . public acceptance than any international or foreign court. It's simply a natural, psychological mechanism. And when I'm saying national courts, that means if [a] court *of your own nation* convicts somebody from your nation, it's much easier for you to accept such a conviction. . . . And it's a natural . . . human tendency to more easily accept criticism coming from your own family than from the outside.[89]

Still, Jovanović noted, this does not mean "post-conflict situations can and should always be handled by domestic or hybrid courts, because simply these courts, . . . in most of the imaginable scenarios, would not be able—and I'm not speaking only about this region but I speak about the whole world— . . . to handle all the cases" meriting prosecution in light of the political pressures to which they are vulnerable.[90]

---

[84] Interview with Nataša Kandić, then Executive Director, Humanitarian Law Center, in Belgrade, Serb. (Nov. 27, 2006).

[85] *Id.*

[86] *E.g.*, interview with Ana Miljanić, Playwright and then Director, Center for Cultural Decontamination, in Belgrade, Serb. (Nov. 22, 2006); interview with Radmila Dragičević-Dičić, Judge, Belgrade District Court, in Belgrade, Serb. (Nov. 21, 2006). As I elaborate later, however, this was true only with respect to low-level perpetrators.

[87] *See* Chapter 7.

[88] *E.g.*, interviews with Dejan Anastasijević, Journalist, in Belgrade, Serb. (Nov. 20, 2006); and Jovan Nicić & Mato Meyer, United Nations Development Programme, in Belgrade, Serb. (Nov. 20, 2006).

[89] Interview with Ivan Jovanović, Attorney, in Belgrade, Serb. (June 9, 2014).

[90] *Id.*

C. The ICTY's Impact on the Operation of the SWCC and OWCP

If the Hague Tribunal did not set out to catalyze Serbian prosecutions, its leadership embraced opportunities to bolster the OWCP and SWCC once they were launched.[91] In particular, Serge Brammertz, who took up the post of ICTY Prosecutor in January 2008, became deeply invested in the success of the new institutions, forging a dense network of connections between his office and the OWCP.

As elaborated below, the Tribunal made significant contributions to capacity-building in Serbia through a range of activities. Its principal contributions came through: (1) transferring evidence to Serbian prosecutors,[92] (2) participating in training programs for Serbian war crimes prosecutors and judges, and (3) bringing Serbian war crimes prosecutors and other young professionals to The Hague to participate in internship and other programs.[93]

1. HAGUE EVIDENCE IN SERBIAN CASES
a. 11*bis* and Category II Transfers
One of the ICTY's most important contributions to Serbian war crimes prosecutions has been its facilitation of access to evidence. In contrast to the Bosnian experience described earlier, so-called 11*bis* transfers did not provide a significant vehicle for transferring evidence to Serbia.[94] The ICTY transferred only one 11*bis* case to Serbia,[95] which was hardly likely to lead to prosecution: the Tribunal had already granted provisional release to the suspect on mental health grounds, and he was later judged unfit to stand trial in Serbia.

Even so, as a well-informed source noted in the OWCP's early years, this should not detract from "what . . . happened: the transfer of a wealth of information from non-indicted cases."[96] The source was referring to "Category II" transfers—the

---

91 The ICTY has also engaged with the WCIS and the witness protection unit, both of which operate within Serbia's ministry of the interior. Nevertheless, a 2011 report concluded that the ICTY's contributions to these bodies had been unable "to overcome problems related to their limited capacity" and other factors. DOMAC/13 REPORT, *supra* note 5, at 90.

92 Domestic defense counsel can also obtain ICTY evidence, but the procedure is different than for the OWCP.

93 In nature if not in scale, the last set of initiatives mirror the ICTY's evidence-sharing and capacity-building efforts in Bosnia, which are described in greater depth in Chapter 9. For example, Serbia's OWCP has a liaison prosecutor in The Hague whose sole function is to respond to requests for information from his or her colleagues in Belgrade and, conversely, to facilitate OTP requests for information from Serbia. Interviews with Svetislav Rabrenović, Assistant Prosecutor, OWCP, in Belgrade, Serb. (June 12, 2014); Snežana Stanojković, then Deputy War Crimes Prosecutor, OWCP, in Belgrade, Serb. (June 12, 2014); Jelena Vladisavljev, Investigator, OWCP, in Belgrade, Serb. (June 12, 2014); and Novak Vučo, Investigator, OWCP, in Belgrade, Serb. (June 12, 2014).

94 The origin and nature of 11*bis* transfers are explained in Chapter 9.

95 *See* Prosecutor v. Kovačević, Case No. IT-01-42/2-I, Decision on Referral of Case Pursuant to Rule 11*bis* (Int'l Crim. Trib. for the Former Yugoslavia Nov. 17, 2006). The ICTY's failure to transfer other 11*bis* cases to Serbia reflects, among other considerations, its general preference for transferring cases to the state in whose territory the crimes charged by the Hague prosecutor were committed. Interview with David Tolbert, then Deputy Prosecutor, ICTY, in The Hague, Neth. (Mar. 5, 2007). In practice, this preference led the ICTY to transfer most of its 11*bis* cases to Bosnia and Herzegovina; it transferred only one such case involving two suspects to Croatia.

96 Confidential interview.

transmission of evidence developed by ICTY investigators that did not lead to an indictment by the Tribunal.[97] Although the Hague Tribunal transferred only two Category II files to Serbia, each generated several prosecutions in Serbia. One file, which was transferred in 2003, involved a massacre of Croat victims by Serb perpetrators in Croatia.[98] While the ICTY tried the three most senior suspects in this massacre,[99] which occurred near Vukovar, Croatia, other defendants associated with this crime have been prosecuted in several cases in Serbia, including in the first trial before the SWCC.[100] The second Category II transfer, which took place in 2004, provided evidence that has been used in at least three prosecutions before the SWCC.[101]

This is not to suggest the OWCP simply received Category II evidence from the Hague and then coasted into court with fully prepared cases. While acknowledging the ICTY's contributions, Vukčević emphasized his office's ability to take investigative work well beyond that undertaken by the OTP.[102] Even so, an assessment of the first ten years of Serbia's war crimes institutions found that Category II transfers "proved extremely effective, since the case materials were almost complete and could quickly be transformed into viable cases" in Serbia.[103]

Nor should the ICTY's contributions obscure the important role Serbian NGOs played in supporting the fledgling OWCP, including by providing evidence. In particular, the Belgrade-based HLC played a vital role in the office's early cases by persuading skeptical victims from neighboring countries to provide testimony,[104] while the OSCE Mission to Serbia has played a leading role in organizing training and other capacity-building programs.

---

[97] Category II transfers are described in Chapter 9.

[98] *See* ICTJ, Selected Developments, *supra* note 22, at 6.

[99] For an overview of these proceedings, see ICTY case information sheet for "Vukovar III" case, http://www.icty.org/x/cases/mrksic/cis/en/cis_mrksic_al_en.pdf (last visited September 29, 2017).

[100] The SWCC convicted thirteen defendants and acquitted five at the conclusion of the first of these cases. *See 193 Years in Prison for Ovčara Massacre*, Dalje (Mar. 12, 2009). For discussion of Serbian prosecutions stemming from the Ovčara massacre, *see* OSCE Mission to Serb., War Crimes Proceedings in Serbia (2003–2014), at 32 (2015) [hereinafter OSCE, 2015 Report].

[101] *See* OSCE, 2015 Report, *supra* note 100, at 32.

[102] For example, the OTP identified four suspects in what became the first SWCC *Zvornik* case before transferring its evidence to Serbia; Vukčević's office identified four more suspects, and later expanded its investigation to include hundreds of potential victims. Interviews with Vladimir Vukčević, then War Crimes Prosecutor, in Belgrade, Serb. (Nov. 21, 2006); Bruno Vekarić, Deputy War Crimes Prosecutor, in Belgrade, Serb. (Nov. 28, 2006); and Nataša Kandić, then Executive Director, Humanitarian Law Center, in Belgrade, Serb. (Nov. 27, 2006).

[103] OSCE 2015 Report, *supra* note 100, at 32.

[104] As Human Rights Watch has noted, without HLC's intervention, "it is doubtful victims living outside Serbia would [have been] prepared to cooperate" with the SWCC. Human Rights Watch, Unfinished Business: Serbia's War Crimes Chamber 7 (2007) [hereinafter HRW, Unfinished Business]. *See also* Humanitarian Law Center, Victim/Witness Counselling and Legal Representation: A Model of Support—Project Implementation Report (2007) [hereinafter HLC, Model of Support]; Humanitarian Law Center, Participation of the Humanitarian Law Center in War Crimes Prosecutions in Serbia 1–2 (2012) [hereinafter HLC, Participation]. In light of the OWCP's and SWCC's disappointing performance in later years, however, victims and witnesses from other countries are now far less willing to participate in Serbian war crimes trials. Email from Sandra Orlović, then Director, Humanitarian Law Center, to Diane Orentlicher (July 12, 2016); *Sandra Orlović, Prosecution of War Crimes in Serbia Will Sink Even Lower*, Danas (June 16, 2016) [hereinafter *Orlović Interview*]; Humanitarian Law

Still, ICTY evidence enabled the OWCP to overcome formidable evidentiary challenges in its early years.[105] Some came from Serbian police investigators' reluctance to provide effective assistance.[106] Sources interviewed in late 2006 indicated the WCIS had not taken initiative in war crimes investigations, instead responding to specific requests from the War Crimes Prosecutor without going a step beyond the literal confines of his requests.[107] Its reticence is not surprising: its first leader held a senior position in Kosovo during the conflict there, and its second was even more directly implicated in war crimes.[108] More generally, the HLC reports, Serbian police were "not willing to share [their] data on war crimes perpetrators with prosecutors, primarily because most of them belonged to the police."[109] As Ivan Jovanović noted, "There's a tendency to focus on courts, but they're just at the end of a chain of responsibility which starts with the police. The police are a weak if not the weakest link in the chain.[110]

By late 2006, the situation seemed to be "changing for the better" according to Jovanović[111] and others.[112] When interviewed again in June 2007, Jovanović said the war crimes prosecutor had established "better control" over the WCIS, and the unit was also showing greater initiative.[113]

CENTER, REPORT ON WAR CRIMES TRIALS IN SERBIA DURING 2016, at 9 (2017) [hereinafter HLC, 2017 REPORT].

[105] Interview with Nataša Kandić, then Executive Director, Humanitarian Law Center, in Belgrade, Serb. (Nov. 27, 2006). A report published in November 2011 concluded the "use of ICTY materials in war crimes cases in Serbia . . . has been crucial to the OWCP's work thus far, and according to most persons interviewed . . . , including persons from the OWCP, judges and NGOs members [sic], has been the most important contribution of the ICTY to Serbia's war crimes proceedings." DOMAC/13 REPORT, supra note 5, at 93.

[106] Legislation establishing Serbia's war crimes institutions placed the WCIS within the interior ministry rather than under the OWCP's direct authority, though the unit was legally required to "act on requests of the Prosecutor for War Crimes." 2003 Law on War Crimes, supra note 29, art. 8.

[107] E.g., interview with Ivan Jovanović, then National Legal Advisor, OSCE Mission to Serbia, in Belgrade, Serb. (Nov. 22, 2006).

[108] HRW, UNFINISHED BUSINESS, supra note 104, at 27. Both were transferred or retired in the face of protests over their human rights disqualifications. See Serbian Government Sacks Head of War Crimes Department, BBC MONITORING EUR. (Feb. 8, 2006), cited in DANAS (Feb. 8, 2006).

[109] HLC, MODEL OF SUPPORT, supra note 104, at 26–27.

[110] Interview with Ivan Jovanović, then National Legal Advisor, OSCE Mission to Serbia, in Belgrade, Serb. (Nov. 22, 2006). See also HLC, 2006 REPORT, supra note 4, at 26; HLC, MODEL OF SUPPORT, supra note 104, at 1. During the same period, the president of the SWCC described "police support" as the "biggest challenge for the court." He emphasized the small number of officers detailed to investigate war crimes rather than their natural disposition to protect their colleagues. Interview with Siniša Važić, then President, SWCC, in Belgrade, Serb. (Nov. 21, 2006).

[111] Interview with Ivan Jovanović, then National Legal Advisor, OSCE Mission to Serbia, in Belgrade, Serb. (Nov. 22, 2006).

[112] See HRW, UNFINISHED BUSINESS, supra note 104, at 27–28; BOGDAN IVANIŠEVIĆ, INTERNATIONAL CENTER FOR TRANSITIONAL JUSTICE, AGAINST THE CURRENT—WAR CRIMES PROSECUTIONS IN SERBIA 12 (2007) [hereinafter ICTJ, AGAINST THE CURRENT]. The WCIS's contributions remained limited, however, due to the combined effects of capacity limitations, legal restrictions on its ability to interview witnesses outside Serbia, and the sensitivity of investigating potential suspects within the police itself. See AMNESTY INTERNATIONAL, SERBIA: ENDING IMPUNITY FOR CRIMES UNDER INTERNATIONAL LAW 11 (2014) [hereinafter AI, ENDING IMPUNITY].

[113] Interview with Ivan Jovanović, then National Legal Advisor, OSCE Mission to Serbia, in Belgrade, Serb. (June 6, 2007). According to a deputy war crimes prosecutor interviewed in April 2007, the unit "provided solid assistance in amassing evidence on a major war crime in Kosovo." ICTJ, AGAINST THE CURRENT, supra note 112, at 12. These gains were further entrenched in a new Criminal Procedure Code, which vested lead responsibility for investigations

Other investigative challenges stemmed from enduring tensions between Serbia and neighboring countries. Three years into his tenure as war crimes prosecutor, Vukčević pointed out that, until recently, Serbian authorities had no access to evidence in neighboring countries.[114] In this setting, evidence obtained by ICTY investigators could prove indispensable.[115]

Category II transfers may have had a deeper impact on the fledgling OWCP than their tangible contributions to trial evidence. Nataša Kandić, who worked intensively on ICTY and SWCC prosecutions, believes dossiers provided by the OTP bolstered the resolve of Serbian prosecutors when they began their sensitive work. In her view, local prosecutors "were afraid, but faced with documentation from The Hague, they said [to themselves] 'it's horrible what Serbs did to others'" and marshaled the courage to pursue prosecutions.[116]

b. Remote Access to OTP Databases and Requests for Assistance

As in Bosnia, the OTP progressively enhanced Serbian jurists' access to ICTY evidence. In 2006, the OWCP was given remote access to the Electronic Disclosure Suite (EDS), the electronic archive of ICTY material.[117] OWCP investigator Jelena

---

in the prosecutor rather than investigative judges, as had previously been the case. According to Deputy War Crimes Prosecutor Bruno Vekarić, as a result of the legislative change the OWCP "had to form joint investigative teams with the police"; he requested that the teams be staffed with new police who were "completely uncompromised." Interview with Bruno Vekarić, Deputy War Crimes Prosecutor, in Belgrade, Serb. (June 10, 2014). His request was granted, and Vekarić characterized the new officers as "fantastic." When I interviewed OWCP investigator Novak Vučo in 2012, he characterized his working relationship with the WCIS as "really good," adding: "They're really professional, they're really making an effort to add something." Interview with Novak Vučo, Investigator, OWCP, in Belgrade, Serb. (July 12, 2012). Even so, a comprehensive assessment of Serbia's war crimes institutions published in 2014 identified several concerns relating to the WCIS-OWCP working relationship. HLC, TEN YEARS, *supra* note 32, at 34–35. Another report suggests bureaucratic arrangements may have disincentived the most experienced police from working in the WCIS. According to the report, published in 2015, no WCIS employees had "been promoted within the police ranks, and they are rarely invited for trainings and seminars organized by" the ministry of interior. For these and other reasons, "experienced police officers with a reputation for high professional standards are reluctant to work in the WCIS," which "can lead to a decrease in [the unit's] efficiency." OSCE 2015 REPORT, *supra* note 100, at 50. In its most recent report on war crimes cases in Serbia, the HLC was unable to include an assessment of the WCIS "as a result of the lack of publicly available information on their work." HLC, 2017 REPORT, *supra* note 104, at 7.

[114] In February 2005, the OWCP concluded a memorandum of agreement with the Croatian attorney general's office to establish a basis for cooperating in addressing serious crimes, and concluded a similar memorandum in April 2005 with the Bosnian prosecutor's office. These agreements were later strengthened by others, discussed below. Despite these agreements, the OWCP's access to crime sites in neighboring countries remained limited long after the 1990s conflicts ended. *See* OSCE, 2015 REPORT, *supra* note 100, at 30.

[115] As the OWCP's website points out in relation to its Kosovo investigations, "the ICTY investigators, being close to the sites of incidents, had access to relevant information/materials at the time of their investigations, and were therefore able to collect evidence and interrogate first-hand witnesses of the crimes." Republic of Serb. Office of the War Crimes Prosecutor, http://www.tuzilastvorz.org.rs/html_trz/saradnja_eng.htm (last visited Dec. 12, 2017).

[116] Interview with Nataša Kandić, then Executive Director, Humanitarian Law Center, in Belgrade, Serb. (Nov. 27, 2006).

[117] Memorandum of Understanding on Access to Documents through the Electronic Disclosure Suite between the Office of the Prosecutor of the Int'l Criminal Tribunal for the former Yugoslavia and the Office of the War Crimes Prosecutor of the Republic of Serbia (July 19, 2006).

Vladisavljev described the importance of the Tribunal's database for early cases before the SWCC: one such case was "based on" documentation found on ICTY databases, while the prosecutor in another early case "got all [the] documentation" he needed, "at least for the beginning" of the case, by searching ICTY databases.[118] Another OWCP investigator, Novak Vučo, expressed frustration with the limits of EDS access, but nonetheless acknowledged its value in generating leads. Like their counterparts in Bosnia, Serbian prosecutors can access only nonconfidential material, such as redacted testimony of protected witnesses, through the EDS. This limitation can be significant. In Vučo's words, "you are always restricted. . . . Whenever you find a statement which is suitable for our cases here it is redacted in 90 percent of the cases."[119] Asked how useful ICTY evidence is in light of the limitations he described, Vučo replied:

> From one to five?: Three. . . . They can be useful sometimes; . . . it can be even better in the preliminary procedure, they can be really important. We received some really [helpful] documents. OK, 3.5. They're really useful [in providing initial leads], sometimes crucial.[120]

When an EDS search turns up a redacted witness statement that could be useful in one of their cases, OWCP staff can use the applicable ICTY procedure to seek an unredacted version and even access to the witness. If, for example, a statement was redacted because the witness received a promise of confidentiality from the OTP, the OWCP can ask that office to contact the witness on its behalf.[121] The OTP's engagement can be invaluable. Noting the OWCP might seek access to witnesses who provided statements in the 1990s, MICT investigator Tomasz Blaszczyk said: "my job is to find them and talk to them" about their willingness to allow their unredacted statements to be provided or to be contacted by the OWCP.[122] Once he locates such a witness, Blaszczyk straddles the delicate line between advancing OWCP cases and scrupulously respecting the needs and wishes of each witness: "Of course I'm not going to push him, but then I ask him whether . . . you just need some time, whether you can sleep with it; I will call you later on, or whatever, [in] a few days."[123]

Inevitably in light of their searing experience of Serb-perpetrated atrocities, many "Muslim victims are very reluctant" to share their statements or disclose their identities to Serbian prosecutors, Blaszczyk said.[124] Although the result may

---

[118] Interview with Jelena Vladisavljev, Investigator, OWCP, in Belgrade, Serb. (June 12, 2014).

[119] Interview with Novak Vučo, Investigator, OWCP, in Belgrade, Serb. (June 12, 2014).

[120] *Id.*

[121] If a witness is subject to judicially-ordered protective measures, the OWCP must seek authorization from an ICTY chamber or judge to modify those measures. The relevant procedure is cumbersome, and the outcome depends on the consent of the protected witness "in 99 percent of the cases," according to an OTP source. In his estimate, roughly half of the protected witnesses consent. Interview with Aleksandar Kontić, Legal Officer, Office of the Prosecutor, ICTY, in The Hague, Neth. (May 26, 2015). But the rate may be significantly lower when requests come from Serbia. According to Vučo, "in most of the cases" in which the OWCP seeks a modification of an ICTY protective order, the "witness says no." Interview with Nowak Vučo, Investigator, OWCP, in Belgrade, Serb. (June 12, 2014).

[122] Interview with Tomasz Blaszczyk, Investigator, MICT Hague Branch, in The Hague, Neth. (May 27, 2015).

[123] *Id.*

[124] *Id.*

be frustrating for OWCP personnel, they understand witnesses' reticence. When I asked Vučo why witnesses who had testified in The Hague would decline to be contacted by the OWCP, he replied: "Mostly they're intimidated," and added:

> They are usually from the non-Serbian ethnicity . . . and when you meet them . . . —I am talking from my own [experience]—when you have Serbian perpetrators, non-Serbian victim and then somebody calls him and says, "OK, are you willing to testify in front of the Serbian court?", and he is, like, "Please, I don't want to have nothing to do with it." You can change the Serbian to Croatian or Bosniak, it's the same.[125]

Beyond their specific apprehensions about testifying in a Serbian court, many ICTY witnesses are reluctant to engage with yet another judicial procedure. As Blaszczyk put it:

> We have to understand that . . . they're just fed up sometimes, just, they testified in the Tribunal several times and they met with the Tribunal investigators several times, and they're fed up with this issue. It's coming up always, this war crime [issue]. And still, [the] atmosphere in the region is not good.[126]

In short, Tribunal assistance is no guarantee witnesses who have spoken to OTP investigators will cooperate with Serbian prosecutors. But intermediaries such as Blaszczyk have enabled the OWCP to interview some of them.[127]

c. Liaison Prosecutors Program

Like their counterparts in Bosnia's Special Department for War Crimes, OWCP staff have participated in the OTP liaison prosecutors project described in Chapter 9. I asked Jelena Vladisavljev, then on her second rotation as a liaison prosecutor, what information she could obtain in this capacity that she could not access via the EDS or through formal requests for assistance (RFAs). Noting liaison officers can use some ICTY databases they cannot access from Belgrade, Vladisavljev went on to emphasize the program's broader benefits: "I think that the most *important* thing is that we have the opportunity to consult with people who are dealing with those cases here."[128]

Through "day to day communication, everyday cooperation" with ICTY prosecutors, Vladisavljev could ensure her Serbian colleagues' requests were processed "faster, more efficient[ly]." At least as important, being in The Hague enabled Vladisavljev to discover crucial evidence her office would not otherwise have known to request. According to Vladisavljev, during her rotation "many, many documents" had been introduced in an ICTY trial that was invaluable evidence for

---

[125] Interview with Novak Vučo, Investigator, OWCP, in Belgrade, Serb. (June 12, 2014).

[126] Interview with Tomasz Blaszczyk, Investigator, MICT Hague Branch, in The Hague, Neth. (May 27, 2015).

[127] After speaking with Blaszczyk, four or five witnesses in the Srebrenica case, described later in this chapter, were willing to speak to Serbian prosecutors, and were "willing to go to Belgrade to give evidence." Interview with Bob Reid, Chief of Operations, Office of the Prosecutor, ICTY, in The Hague, Neth. (May 28, 2015). As elaborated later, this case has recently seen setbacks.

[128] Interview with Jelena Vladisavljev, Investigator/Advisor, OWCP, then Serbian Liaison Prosecutor, Office of the Prosecutor, ICTY, in The Hague, Neth. (May 27, 2015).

a major OWCP case. Perhaps Vladisavljev and her colleagues would have learned about this evidence "in a year, in two years." But by spending time in The Hague, she became aware of it in a timely fashion.[129]

As Vladisavljev's comments suggest, ICTY evidence remained vital to Serbian prosecutions long after the early years of the OWCP's work. In June 2014, I asked then Deputy War Crimes Prosecutor Snežana Stanojković (now War Crimes Prosecutor), who had also done a rotation as a liaison prosecutor, whether the OWCP, by then more than a decade old, still received useful evidence from The Hague. Without hesitating, she said ICTY evidence remained "the most important and the most relevant and significant" aspect of her office's relationship with the Tribunal. When asked if she anticipated ICTY evidence would become comparatively less useful over time as other sources of evidence became more readily available, Stanojković replied: "No, it won't become *less* useful."[130]

Along with other forms of collaboration, information-sharing between Belgrade and The Hague fostered what many described as "a partnership" between the ICTY and its Serbian counterpart, at least during the tenure of Vučković.[131] During my first set of interviews for this study, the prosecutor, president, and other officials at the SWCC and OWCP extolled the "great cooperation" between Belgrade and The Hague, and judges and OWCP staff did the same during interviews through 2015.[132] The corridors of the OWCP bore witness to the relationship that emerged with The Hague: among the photographs that lined its walls, images of longtime War Crimes Prosecutor Vukčević with the ICTY Prosecutor figured prominently.[133]

2. Sharing "Know How"

Beyond its direct and indirect contributions through evidence-sharing initiatives, the ICTY shaped Serbia's war crimes institutions through its transmission of "know how," in the words of the SWCC's first president, Siniša Važić.[134] This occurred in large part by modeling state-of-the-art procedures and, secondarily, through the participation of ICTY personnel in various capacity-building initiatives.

---

[129] *Id.*

[130] Interview with Snežana Stanojković, then Deputy War Crimes Prosecutor, in Belgrade, Serb. (June 12, 2014). This is not to say Serbian war crimes institutions have taken full advantage of ICTY evidence, including facts established in Tribunal judgments. In its assessment of the first ten years of those institutions, the HLC noted the OWCP and SWCC "often use ICTY evidence," but in some cases, domestic courts failed to use evidence that had been "used before the ICTY [even though it had] great evidential value . . . for trials in Serbia." HLC, Ten Years, *supra* note 32, at 48.

[131] *E.g.*, interview with Nataša Kandić, then Executive Director, Humanitarian Law Center, in Belgrade, Serb. (Nov. 27, 2006).

[132] *E.g.*, interviews with Bruno Vekarić, Deputy War Crimes Prosecutor, in Belgrade, Serb. (July 10, 2012 & June 12, 2014). In the later of these two interviews, Vekarić spoke of his office's "excellent cooperation" with ICTY Prosecutor Serge Brammertz.

[133] The OWCP's participation in Serbia's efforts to apprehend ICTY fugitives—the focus of Chapter 3—deepened the relationship between the two prosecutors' offices during Vukčević's tenure. When I mentioned to Serge Brammertz the manifestly warm and high regard in which the OWCP held him, he reflected: "I think that those years working together on the fugitives meant that we spent a lot of time together—a lot of professional time, but also more moments where you relax, and you have lunch together," fostering a productive working relationship in other realms as well. Interview with Serge Brammertz, Prosecutor, ICTY, in The Hague, Neth. (May 27, 2015).

[134] Interview with Siniša Važić, then President, SWCC, in Belgrade, Serb. (Nov. 21, 2006).

a. Modeling Procedures

Despite the ICTY's peripheral role in launching Serbia's war crimes institutions, many of the SWCC's procedural innovations were consciously modeled on those used in The Hague. As Judge Važić put it, when Serbia adopted legislation establishing its war crimes institutions "we took a lot of provisions" from the ICTY,[135] and sought to emulate the "skills, knowledge and technical gadgets" of ICTY judges and facilities.[136]

Some of the innovations inspired by the ICTY center on the role of victims, including legislation authorizing the use of video links so that witnesses who are afraid or unable to testify in Serbia can bear witness from afar.[137] In addition, the SWCC "got the idea to establish" a witness support unit (WSU) from a conference in Sarajevo organized by the ICTY's Victim and Witness Support Unit (VWSU).[138] Describing this unit in 2006, then-SWCC spokeswoman Ivana Ramić told me: "We have very good cooperation with the VWSU of the ICTY,"[139] which, along with the OSCE Mission to Serbia, provided training to WSU personnel.[140] According to Judge Tatjana Vuković, who, like Važić, previously served as president of the SWCC, the chamber "established the rule similar to the Hague that our [witness support] unit calls [witnesses]" fifteen days after they testify to find out how they are doing, in recognition that providing testimony can be "very stressful."[141] ICTY personnel also provided training for SWCC judges on judicial techniques concerning "how to treat the victims," according to Judge Radmila Dragičević-Dičić.[142]

To recognize the imprint of the ICTY in this sphere is not to suggest the SWCC has consistently used best practices, however. In 2012, Amnesty International reported the Serbian WSU unit "is under-resourced, lacks the necessary infrastructure," and "fails to provide support before and after proceedings, providing support only when the victim reaches the courtroom."[143] In a 2013 assessment, the HLC wrote that, due to a lack of professional qualifications for WSU personnel, "victims who are expected to testify do not receive adequate assistance and are often exposed to secondary victimization."[144]

Key legal provisions governing the work of the Witness Protection Unit (WPU), which is charged with protecting particularly sensitive witnesses, also were "inspired

---

[135] *Id.*

[136] *Id.*

[137] *Id.* These facilities were funded by the U.S. government.

[138] Interview with Ivana Ramić, then Spokeswoman, SWCC, in Belgrade, Serb. (Nov. 21, 2006). The SWCC's unit was established with funding from the U.S. government. *Id.*

[139] *Id.*

[140] HRW, UNFINISHED BUSINESS, *supra* note 104, at 8.

[141] Interview with Tatjana Vuković, Judge, Belgrade Court of Appeal, in Belgrade, Serb. (June 10, 2014). The Criminal Procedure Code adopted in 2012 changed the unit's mandate somewhat. Previously, the WSU could provide assistance during investigations. Under the new code, it is formally authorized to provide assistance only immediately before, during, and after the trial. This change reflected the transfer of investigative competency from investigating judges to prosecutors. HLC, TEN YEARS, *supra* note 32, at 59.

[142] Interview with Radmila Dragičević-Dičić, Judge, Belgrade District Court, in Belgrade, Serb. (Nov. 21, 2006).

[143] AI, ENDING IMPUNITY, *supra* note 112, at 29.

[144] HUMANITARIAN LAW CENTER, REPORT ON WAR CRIMES TRIALS IN SERBIA IN 2012, at 9–10 (2013) [hereinafter HLC, 2013 REPORT]. In a more recent report, the HLC raised concerns about the impact on witnesses of a new procedure for reimbursing their travel expenses. HLC, 2017 REPORT, *supra* note 104, at 9–10.

by the rules of the ICTY."[145] As with the WSU, however, this hardly assured the WPU's effectiveness. Located within the police unit of the ministry of the interior, the WPU is staffed by police officers, some of whom reportedly were involved in war crimes themselves.[146] Its employees have at times threatened rather than protected insider witnesses (former members of the armed forces summoned to testify in WCC/WCD trials) and their families. One such witness, Zoran Rašković, said WPU members had threatened his parents and called him "garbage" for testifying about crimes committed by fellow members of the paramilitary unit in which he fought in Kosovo; Rašković found it safer to leave the "protection" program than to remain in it.[147] Faced with threats from the WPU, some witnesses have decided to change their testimony or not to testify at all.[148]

These practices were condemned by numerous organizations, including the Council of Europe, European Commission, European Parliament, HLC, OSCE Mission to Serbia, and Amnesty International,[149] before significant action was taken in June 2014. That month, the government dismissed Miloš Perović, who had headed the WPU since 2008.[150] While his dismissal was seen as progress, other flaws in the WPU's operation—such as the absence of a vetting system to ensure the unit is not staffed by individuals implicated in war crimes—remained to be addressed.[151] These and other concerns are substantial, and remind us that borrowing legal practices from the ICTY is hardly a panacea for entrenched flaws in the administration of justice.

By equal measure, the Tribunal influenced judicial process in Serbia in ways that transcend the value of specific procedures. Sources interviewed in late 2006 noted that ICTY trials had raised public expectations of fair process in Serbia (although, it should be noted, some later proceedings, notably that of Vojislav Šešelj, have highlighted flaws in the Tribunal's own procedures).[152] While often critical of the ICTY, journalist Ljiljana Smajlović said it "taught the public what defendants are entitled to [and] this is a positive impact."[153] Having grown accustomed to procedural

---

[145] DOMAC/13 Report, *supra* note 5, at 82.

[146] *See* Marija Ristić, *Serbia's War Crimes Witness Protection Unit "Failing"*, Balkan Transitional Just. (Nov. 29, 2013).

[147] *Id. See also* Marija Ristić, *Zoran Rašković—The Jackal Who Repented*, Balkan Transitional Just. (May 17, 2013).

[148] *See* Humanitarian Law Center, *Statement: The Belated Dismissal of Miloš Perović Is Insufficient* (June 10, 2014); Rep. by Thomas Hammarberg, Comm'r for Human Rights of the Council of Eur., following his visit to Serbia on 12–15 June 2011, ¶¶ 21–22, CommDH(2011) 29 (Sept. 22, 2011).

[149] *See, e.g.,* Jean-Charles Gardetto (Rapporteur on Committee on Legal Affairs and Human Rights), *The Protection of Witnesses as a Cornerstone for Justice and Reconciliation in the Balkans*, ¶¶ 118–119, Eur. Parl. Doc. (2010); Eur. Comm'n, Serbia: 2013 Progress Report 12 (2013); HLC, Participation, *supra* note 104, at 7–8; AI, Ending Impunity, *supra* note 112, at 33–38.

[150] Marija Ristić, *Serbia Sacks Police Witness Protection Unit Chief*, Balkan Transitional Just. (June 9, 2014).

[151] *See* Humanitarian Law Center, *Statement: The Belated Dismissal of Miloš Perović Is Insufficient* (June 10, 2014). Four years after condemning patterns of intimidation in 2011, the Council of Europe expressed continuing concern about Serbia's failure to undertake effective investigations into reports of witness intimidation, most of which "relate to the witnesses in war crimes proceedings against members of the Serbia police who participated in the Kosovo war." Marija Ristić, *End War Crimes Impunity, Council of Europe Tells Serbia*, Balkan Insight (July 8, 2015).

[152] The vexed trial of Šešelj is discussed in Chapter 6.

[153] Interview with Ljiljana Smajlović, Journalist, in Belgrade, Serb. (Nov. 24, 2006).

guarantees she observed while covering the Milošević trial in particular, Smajlović said she was "flabbergasted by the different quality" of Serbian courts when she observed a high-profile case back home, and described ICTY proceedings as "a civic education."[154]

This aspect of the ICTY's influence extended beyond Serbia's war crimes chamber. Judge Sonja Prostan noted that procedural innovations inspired by the ICTY, ranging from witness-protection measures to status conferences aimed at improving the efficiency of trial proceedings, were "implemented in the new criminal procedure code" of Serbia.[155]

b. Capacity-Building: Training and Exchange Programs

Despite its fiscal and mandate-related limits, the Tribunal has contributed to capacity-building efforts that must, of necessity, be led by others. ICTY officials have participated in myriad training programs for Serbian judges, prosecutors, and defense counsel,[156] as well as peer-to-peer exchanges, mostly organized and funded by third parties.[157]

Nataša Kandić, who organized early judicial training programs for SWCC judges in The Hague, believes Serbian judges took home a lesson in judicial independence. "Before," she said, "it was usual to see judges and prosecutors discussing cases. Now you don't see that"—a change she attributes to Serbian judges observing, during visits to the ICTY, "how far judges are from prosecutors."[158]

Studies suggest peer-to-peer encounters can be particularly useful when they offer an opportunity to work through a specific judicial or prosecutorial challenge,[159] and Serbian war crimes judges and prosecutors have initiated visits to The Hague to do just that.[160] Judge Vuković provided an example of an exchange she found especially useful. She and ICTY judge Alphons Orie, who had presided over the trial of a senior Bosnian Serb political figure, Momčilo Krajišnik, discussed "the responsibility of a civil[ian] commander" who exercises some measure of command over military units. At the time of their exchange, Judge Vuković was dealing with this issue in the *Zvornik II* case, one of whose defendants, Branko Grujić, was the mayor of Zvornik. According to Vuković, the exchange "very much" helped her work through an issue that had proved vexing—the responsibility of a civilian leader who did not

---

[154] *Id.*

[155] Interview with Sonja Prostan, then Judge, Second Municipal Court of Belgrade, in Belgrade, Serb. (June 7, 2007).

[156] Organizations that have sponsored training programs include, in addition to the OSCE Mission to Serbia, the United Nations Development Programme, the Humanitarian Law Center, and the U.S. government.

[157] When I interviewed her in 2014, Judge Tatjana Vuković said she had participated in "many, many meetings and conferences" with ICTY judges and had been to The Hague "at least four times." Interview with Tatjana Vuković, Judge, Belgrade Court of Appeal, in Belgrade, Serb. (June 10, 2014). Judge Važić told me every judge in the chamber had visited the ICTY two or three times by late 2006. Interview with Siniša Važić, then President, SWCC, in Belgrade, Serb. (Nov. 21, 2006).

[158] Interview with Nataša Kandić, then Executive Director, Humanitarian Law Center, in Belgrade, Serb. (Nov. 27, 2006).

[159] *See* Alejandro Chehtman, *Developing Bosnia and Herzegovina's Capacity to Process War Crimes Cases: Critical Notes on a "Success Story,"* 9 J. INT'L CRIM. JUST. 547, 553 (2011).

[160] Comment by Ivan Jovanović on draft chapter (provided June 11, 2017).

have de jure responsibility for war crimes committed by armed forces.[161] After a five-year trial, on November 22, 2010, the Higher Court WCD (as the SWCC had been renamed) convicted Grujić and his codefendant for their respective roles in the abduction, inhumane treatment, and murder of hundreds of Muslim men.[162]

c. Capacity-Building: Visiting Young Professionals
Among the most effective capacity-building initiatives are programs that enable Serbian professionals to gain hands-on experience prosecuting war crimes by working in the OTP. The principal program of this kind is the Visiting Young Professionals (VYP) project described in Chapter 9.[163] In 2007 the Belgrade-based NGO Youth Initiative for Human Rights (YIHR) developed a similar program for young professionals from Serbia, Montenegro, and Kosovo.[164] Under this Swiss-funded program, selected interns spent three to eight months at the ICTY followed by a two- to three-month internship at a national war crimes court or prosecutor's office or with an NGO that works on war crimes issues.

OWCP staff who participated in these programs spoke with palpable enthusiasm about their experiences. Jelena Vladisavljev, who participated in the VYP program in the first half of 2010, described it as a "great experience," adding: "I was in love with my job. I was totally delighted to be there, really, and I was very excited to be part of something like that."[165] Her participation was life-changing; after completing the VYP program, Vladisavljev was placed as an intern with the OWCP and, upon completing her internship, was offered a full-time position.[166] Vladisavljev not only received intense on-the-job training, but also made "tremendously important" contributions to the OTP's work, in the words of an ICTY prosecutor whom she

---

[161] Interview with Tatjana Vuković, Judge, Belgrade Court of Appeal, in Belgrade, Serb. (June 10, 2014). *See also* DOMAC/13, *supra* note 5, at 89 (interactions between Serbian and ICTY judges have led to acknowledgment of ICTY case law in, and similarity of structure of, judgments in Serbia).

[162] As in other areas, the ICTY's influence was no guarantee the results would be an unqualified success: the HLC criticized several aspects of the *Zvornik II* judgment, such as the six-year sentence given Grujić. *See* Humanitarian Law Center, *Statement: Judgment for War Crimes in Zvornik Municipality Failed to Bring Justice for Victims or the Accused* (Dec. 8, 2010). Others have expressed disappointment because the verdict did not explicitly apply the principle of command responsibility to Grujić's codefendant, Branko Popović, instead finding him guilty for "aiding and abetting by omission." *See* AI, Ending Impunity, *supra* note 112, at 22. Despite its concerns, the HLC has faulted the OWCP for not following this precedent, which it characterized as "bridging the gap that exists given the [OWCP's] unwillingness to bring indictments on the basis of the command responsibility doctrine." HLC, 2013 Report, *supra* note 144, at 6–7.

[163] As noted in Chapter 9, during six-month internships in The Hague, participants are integrated into OTP teams, in which they are treated as professional staff.

[164] *See* ICTY website, http://www.icty.org/en/press/serbian-students-begin-internship (last visited Dec. 12, 2017).

[165] Interview with Jelena Vladisavljev, Investigator, OWCP, in Belgrade, Serb. (June 12, 2014).

[166] It should be noted, however, that placements were often possible only with the help of outside funding. In 2010, the ICTY and partner organizations launched a time-limited project, funded by the EU, aimed at enhancing local capacity. One component of this initiative was a fifteen-month project in which thirty young professionals were given six-month training internships with the OTP, after which they were placed for six months in judicial institutions in Serbia, Bosnia, and Croatia. A majority of those placed in Serbian institutions were offered positions in their host institutions when their internships ended. *Project Beneficiaries Celebrate Success of WCJP*, 5 War Crimes Just. Project (2011).

assisted.[167] Her colleagues at the OWCP just as clearly value her work; during a 2012 interview, Deputy War Crimes Prosecutor Bruno Vekarić described Vladisavljev (at that time in the Hague doing a rotation as the OWCP liaison officer) as "really, really good . . . she's a really good investigator."[168]

Novak Vučo believes his eight-month internship with the OTP, during which he performed the work of a legal assistant, provided "the crucial credential" for him to get his job at the OWCP, as his time in The Hague made him one of the few Serbians with experience "in actually prosecuting the crimes against international humanitarian law."[169] Like Vadisavljev, Vučo's principal training in The Hague consisted of learning by doing (he received additional training in international humanitarian law through a program sponsored by the OSCE Mission to Serbia,[170] which sponsored his initial placement at the OWCP).

Miki Vidaković, who participated in the VYP program in 2015, told me he hoped his on-the-job training in the OTP would help him secure a permanent position in the OWCP (as of June 2017, this had not happened). In the meantime, participation provided a lesson in impartial justice and regional collaboration. In his words, VYP participants "get an opportunity to form our own opinion [about what happened during the 1990s conflicts] based on the material that we see here, not on peoples' stories, which is a very important thing actually."[171] Before coming to The Hague, he explained, his understanding of the war was shaped by "narratives we hear at home."[172] Now, it was based on meticulously documented facts. Through his collaboration with his Bosnian and Croatian colleagues, moreover, Vidaković had "learned a lot about ways to communicate with members of Croat and Bosnian communities"—no small achievement, he reflected, for someone who "grew up in a Serbian environment."[173]

III. PROGRESS AND CONSTRAINTS

It is not the task of this chapter to provide an in-depth appraisal of Serbia's war crimes institutions. Some measure of assessment is useful, however, in illuminating the circumstances and ways in which ICTs and other actors can help advance local initiatives, as well as contextual conditions that limit their contributions.

Serbians interviewed for this study and others who have assessed Serbia's war crimes institutions have implicitly used several criteria to evaluate their performance, which also guide this account. These include: (1) the professionalism of judges; (2) the number of cases and individuals prosecuted on war crimes charges; (3) the ranks of accused prosecuted; (4) closely related to the third category, the degree to

---

[167] Interview with Douglas Stringer, Senior Trial Attorney, Office of the Prosecutor, ICTY, in The Hague, Neth. (May 28, 2015).

[168] Interview with Bruno Vekarić, Deputy War Crimes Prosecutor, in Belgrade, Serb. (July 10, 2012).

[169] Interview with Novak Vučo, Investigator, OWCP, in Belgrade, Serb. (July 12, 2012). Vučo's internship at the ICTY, which lasted from November 2008 until July 2009, was sponsored by the YIHR.

[170] Some ICTY staff participated in one of the training sessions.

[171] Interview with Miki Vidaković, Visiting Young Professional from Serbia, Office of the Prosecutor, ICTY, in The Hague, Neth. (May 27, 2015).

[172] *Id.*

[173] *Id.*

which indictments and judgments have forthrightly recognized links between direct perpetrators of war crimes and Serbian state institutions; and, finally, (5) the degree to which domestic prosecutions have advanced regional reconciliation.

A. Professionalism of Judges

With the exception of the OSCE Mission to Serbia, no organization has tracked the performance of Serbia's war crimes chamber and prosecutor more closely than the Belgrade-based HLC. In a preliminary assessment published in 2006, the organization wrote that SWCC "judges have so far manifested a high level of professionalism and considerably improved the quality of war crimes prosecutions compared with the previous period."[174] That same year, the HLC praised SWCC judges for "their clear impartiality, professionalism, and commitment to the law."[175] In its final assessment for 2006, the organization wrote that SWCC judges

> are loyal to the law and show utmost respect for both victims' rights and rights of the accused. In the course of all war crimes trials to date as well as the current trials known to the public . . . the judges were guided by facts and evidence trying to shed light on the context behind the events and thus complete the picture of the responsibility or innocence of the accused.[176]

When I first interviewed her about Serbia's war crimes institutions in late 2006, the HLC's founding director, Nataša Kandić, described trials before the SWCC as "probably the best in the region."[177] Kandić would soon find significant fault in more than a few of its judgments.[178] Even so, in a May 2008 interview, Kandić still considered Serbia's war crimes trials "the best in the region."[179] In subsequent years, HLC reports have, while faulting aspects of some judges' performance, frequently noted the professional manner in which war crimes proceedings were conducted.[180]

But the organization's concerns are significant and have intensified in recent years. Among other concerns, the HLC has criticized Serbian judges' failure to use options at their disposal to protect vulnerable witnesses in a number of cases[181] and expressed mounting concern about the war crimes institutions' lack of transparency. Only the Department for War Crimes of the Belgrade Court of Appeal and OWCP

---

[174] HLC, 2006 Report, *supra* note 4, at 26. *See also* Press Release, Humanitarian Law Center, War Crimes Trials in Serbia (July 26, 2006) (on file with author) (trials before the SWCC "are being administered in technically impeccable conditions").

[175] Press Release, Humanitarian Law Center, War Crimes Trials in Serbia (July 26, 2006) (on file with author).

[176] Humanitarian Law Center, *Political Elites in Serbia Show No Responsibility for Legacy of the Past* (Dec. 11, 2006).

[177] Interview with Nataša Kandić, then Executive Director, Humanitarian Law Center, in Belgrade, Serb. (Nov. 27, 2006).

[178] *See* Diane F. Orentlicher, Open Society Justice Initiative, Shrinking the Space for Denial: The Impact of the ICTY in Serbia 55–56 (2008).

[179] DOMAC/13 Report, *supra* note 5, at 88 n.448.

[180] *E.g.*, Humanitarian Law Center., Report on War Crimes Trials in Serbia 2013, at 12 (2014) [hereinafter HLC, 2014 Report]. These assessments are notable in light of the organization's deservedly harsh critique of Serbian courts during the Milošević era, as described earlier.

[181] *See* HLC, Ten Years, *supra* note 32, at 65.

publish judgments and indictments, respectively, whereas the WCD of the Higher Court in Belgrade, where first instance trials are conducted, does not even post information about trial schedules.[182] Much like Bosnia's war crimes chamber,[183] moreover, both the first instance and appellate war crimes departments began redacting crucial information from verdicts in 2012.[184] Judgments are so highly redacted, the HLC wrote in a 2017 report, as to be "entirely unreadable . . . , with victims denied a symbolic recognition of their suffering, and the general public . . . denied the right to know the truth about past crimes."[185]

It became increasingly difficult, moreover, for the HLC to sustain positive assessments of *individual* war crimes judges. Beginning in 2013, judges who had obtained years of experience in war crimes cases were transferred to other judicial departments.[186] Compounding the resulting loss of expertise, newly-appointed judges were no longer receiving the kind of training provided to Serbia's first generation of war crimes judges by international organizations.[187] Reflecting on the state of Serbia's war crimes institutions as she prepared to step down as HLC director in June 2016, Sandra Orlović told a reporter that "judges who now sit in [war crimes] cases are far from demonstrating the high standards established by the judges during the first six or seven years" of their work.[188] Among the contributing factors, she said, was "the fact that judges who have neither experience in these cases nor professional training for such a complicated area of law are appointed to chambers."[189]

In its assessment of war crimes cases during 2016, the HLC identified another (perhaps related) trend: "Unwarranted delays . . . have become the hallmark of war crimes cases in Serbia."[190] Courts contributed to those delays through lengthy periods between hearings, averaging forty-seven days between hearings in first-instance

---

[182] HLC, 2017 REPORT, *supra* note 104, at 13. Although the first instance chamber never posted its decisions, the HLC was able to obtain judgments and post them on its website. But the anonymization process described below diminished its role as a vehicle for public access. Comment by Ivan Jovanović on draft chapter (provided June 11, 2017).

[183] *See* Chapter 9.

[184] In a 2014 report, the HLC described this trend as follows: "Access to judgments handed down in war crimes cases by the Higher Court Department and the Appeal Court Department was restricted in 2012 and 2013 by the process of anonymization (redaction by way of blackouts and editing) of their written judgments. In some cases, courts would redact even the names of the defendants, their attorneys, the names of judges, witnesses, experts and even whole paragraphs and pages of a judgment." HLC, TEN YEARS, *supra* note 32, at 47. According to Ivan Jovanović, after 2014, appellate judgments in war crimes cases became less anonymized (though names of defendants, victims, and witnesses were still redacted). But these judgments do not include the rich details set forth in first instance verdicts. Comment by Ivan Jovanović on draft chapter (provided June 11, 2017).

[185] HLC, 2017 REPORT, *supra* note 104, at 13.

[186] HLC, TEN YEARS, *supra* note 32, at 38; HUMANITARIAN LAW CENTER, REPORT ON WAR CRIMES TRIALS IN SERBIA DURING 2014 AND 2015, at 18–20 (2016) [hereinafter HLC, 2016 REPORT].

[187] Sandra Orlović, Remarks at the Conference on Prosecuting Serious International Crimes: Exploring the Intersections Between International and Domestic Justice Efforts, Washington College of Law, American University, Washington, D.C. (Mar. 30, 2016). Serbia itself does not provide specialized training to its war crimes judges. *See* HLC, TEN YEARS, *supra* note 32, at 38.

[188] *Orlović Interview*, *supra* note 104.

[189] *Id.* HLC reports have faulted judgments at both the first- and second-instance levels. *See, e.g.*, HLC, 2017 REPORT, *supra* note 104, at 110–15.

[190] HLC, 2017 REPORT, *supra* note 104, at 8.

cases.[191] This alone, the organization suggested, undermined one of the paramount goals its founding leader hoped domestic trials would advance—recognition of victims harmed by Serb atrocities:

> As the years pass, defendants die and witnesses lose trust in the Serbian judiciary and refuse to testify at repeated trials. Over the reporting period [i.e., 2016], many victim-witnesses declined to testify again owing to weariness, the desire to avoid re-traumatization from repeating their testimony . . . , and also because they have lost faith in the procedures and institutions. . . . Additionally, the excessive length of proceedings and their repetition sends a negative and discouraging message to future witnesses and victims—that it would be difficult, if not impossible, for them to receive justice from Serbian institutions.[192]

B. Prosecution Rates

With the launch of its war crimes institutions in 2003, Serbia saw a marked uptick in prosecutions of Serb defendants compared to prior years. In its first few years, the OWCP brought as many indictments as FRY and SaM prosecutors had issued against Serb suspects during the previous dozen years—an admittedly easy record to surpass.[193] By July 9, 2014, the OWCP reported it had indicted 170 suspects,[194] more than the 161 defendants indicted by the ICTY prosecutor during roughly the same period.

Yet institutions that monitor Serbia's war crimes institutions have been uniformly and increasingly troubled by the small number of cases prosecuted relative to the large number of potential war crimes suspects subject to Serbia's jurisdiction.[195] If the OWCP faithfully fulfilled its mandate, one would expect the rate of indictments to rise as the office gained experience and its evidentiary base deepened. Instead, as Ivan Jovanović noted in mid-2014, "there is a slow-down, a noticeable slow down" in the rate of new indictments issued by the OWCP.[196] In 2015, the OSCE Mission to Serbia

---

[191] *Id.* In the organization's view, proceedings were "being deliberately delayed." *Id.*

[192] *Id.* at 9. The reference to victim-witnesses "testifying again" refers to their need to testify at a retrial of defendants following reversal of the initial first-instance verdict due to errors in the judgment.

[193] *See* Ambassador Hans Ola Urstand (Head of the OSCE Mission to Serbia and Montenegro), Report to the Permanent Council, at 4 (Feb. 27, 2006).

[194] Republic of Serb. Office of the War Crimes Prosecutor, http://www.tuzilastvorz.org.rs/html_trz/saradnja_eng.htm (visited July 9, 2017). The OSCE Mission to Serbia uses a somewhat lower figure: "From the start of its operations in November 2003 until the end of 2014, the WCPO filed 60 indictments charging 162 defendants with war crimes." OSCE, 2015 REPORT, *supra* note 100, at 41. The discrepancy might stem from the fact that the mission's figures exclude indictments that were not subsequently confirmed by a court, as well as indictments of individuals charged with providing assistance to ICTY fugitives. *See id.* at 41 n.99.

[195] By one estimate, at least 3,000 people suspected of committing serious crimes in Croatia, Bosnia, and Kosovo were in Serbia in 2016. *Orlović Interview, supra* note 104.

[196] Interview with Ivan Jovanović, Attorney, in Belgrade, Serb. (June 9, 2014). *See also* HLC, 2014 REPORT, *supra* note 180, at 4. According to the HLC's report on war crimes trials in 2012, the OWCP indicted only seven individuals that year, the lowest number for any year since its establishment. HLC, 2013 REPORT, *supra* note 144, at 5. In remarks presented in December 2017, a member of the HLC's leadership team stated that the OWCP had issued only eight indictments in the previous three years, compared to fifteen in 2011. *The International Tribunal and Beyond: Pursuing Justice for Atrocities in the Western Balkans: J. Briefing Tom Lantos Hum.*

reported that this trend, which began in 2010, had continued through the period covered by the study.[197] As she prepared to step down as head of the HLC in mid-2016, Sandra Orlović ruefully assessed that, based on the number of suspects prosecuted annually, "Serbia has become an oasis of impunity for war crimes in the past four to five years."[198] By the end of the year, the OWCP had brought only seven indictments, each against a single suspect, in 2016. All seven involved cases transferred to Serbia from Bosnia, where prosecutors had already undertaken investigations.[199]

The record for completed war crimes trials was just as lackluster. Between 2003 and 2014, only 162 defendants had been tried in forty-nine cases, and just twenty-seven war crimes trials had resulted in a final verdict.[200] In its 2015 review, the OSCE Mission to Serbia reported the OWCP had "effectively generated [an average of 2.58] investigations per year that resulted in trials, and . . . each [OWCP] prosecutor generated approximately one new investigation resulting in a trial every three years."[201]

Judge Siniša Važić was hard-pressed to explain the slowdown in OWCP indictments when I interviewed him in 2014. He added: "To be honest, . . . judges in [the] War Crimes Department [of the Appellate Court,] we are dealing with those cases, war crimes cases, but also we [are dealing with] other cases, appellate cases that come from the low-level courts. But [the] war crimes prosecutors are dealing *only* with war crimes cases, nothing else."[202]

The decline in prosecutions would be less troubling if the OWCP had been taking on increasingly complex cases. Instead, the office was generally bringing charges in "very small cases."[203] In mid-2014, then HLC executive director Orlović summarized recent trends this way:

> In the last few years, it's very visible that they are focusing on the cases which are not so complex, with one, two, three accused, where one, two, three victims

---

Rts. Comm. & Comm. on Security and Cooperation in Europe, 115th Cong. (2017) (statement of Nemanja Stjepanović, Humanitarian Law Center).

[197] Marija Ristić, OSCE: Serbia Faltering on War Crime Prosecutions, BALKAN TRANSITIONAL JUST. (Oct. 27, 2015).

[198] Orlović Interview, supra note 104.

[199] HLC, 2017 REPORT, supra note 104, at 16. See also Filip Rudić, Serbia Failing to Prosecute War Crimes, HLC Says, BALKAN TRANSITIONAL JUST. (May 18, 2017).

[200] Ristić, supra note 197.

[201] OSCE, 2015 REPORT, supra note 100, at 42. The office's performance is even more desultory than these figures suggest: the OSCE statistics include cases in which Serbian authorities received substantial evidence from the ICTY, Bosnia, and Croatia. Id.

[202] Interview with Siniša Važić, Judge, Belgrade Court of Appeal, in Belgrade, Serb. (June 13, 2014). Several caveats must be added to Judge Važić's observation that the OWCP is devoted solely to prosecuting war criminals: under pressure to apprehend ICTY fugitives, in 2006 Serbia appointed an Action Team to work on securing the arrest of remaining fugitives; Vladimir Vučkević headed the team, whose other members included four of his deputies. OSCE, 2015 REPORT, supra note 100, at 31. But this function came to an end with the arrest of the last remaining fugitive in July 2011. Since 2007, the OWCP has had another mandate, also resulting from ICTY pressure—to prosecute those who harbored ICTY fugitives. See id. at 48; HLC, TEN YEARS, supra note 32, at 19. In the assessment of the OSCE mission, the latter mandate is "relatively undemanding," as the four cases prosecuted by the OWCP were resolved through guilty pleas. OSCE, 2015 REPORT, supra, at 48. Finally, the OWCP has jurisdiction over war crimes committed during World War II. See HLC, TEN YEARS, supra, at 19–20.

[203] Interview with Sandra Orlović, then Executive Director, Humanitarian Law Center, in Belgrade, Serb. (June 10, 2014). See also HLC, TEN YEARS, supra note 32, at 17.

were killed. So there are no major cases with 50, 100 victims killed or forcibly disappeared. And at the same time, knowing that at least in Kosovo you have at least five or ten cases where at least 100 victims were killed in one event, then, you know, the frustration increases because of their lack of more activities in bringing such cases to court.[204]

To be sure, the OWCP was devoting some attention to relatively complex cases, discussed below, which had not yet resulted in indictments when I interviewed Orlović.[205] But this cannot account for overall charging patterns. Journalist Marija Ristić, who covers war crimes cases, notes it can actually be more challenging to prosecute smaller cases, for which only "one or two witnesses" may be available.[206] In her view, the declining rate of indictments, as well as the OWCP's general pattern of targeting of lower-level perpetrators, was "due to lack of political support" by the government, by then led by "reformed" nationalists.[207]

Though he shared these concerns, Ivan Jovanović noted, correctly, that Serbia's troubling record was hardly unusual in countries emerging from a protracted period of wholesale violence:

When making an account of [the OWCP's] success or failure so far, . . . I always say that they're probably the most successful national prosecution office in the history of mankind when it comes to war crimes prosecutions . . . because first, the competition is really not big, there are just a few countries that they compete with, and then they definitely prosecuted the highest number of individuals of their own ethnicity for crimes in inter-ethnic wars, which I would count when you judge about national war crimes trials. It's always easy to prosecute those [nationals] of "hostile" . . . nations [or perpetrators from prior regimes]. So it's all relative when you compare Serbia's record to other post-conflict countries.[208]

"But," Jovanović added, "if we take into account other objective criteria, such as the crime base, the [large] number of incidents they can investigate and [individuals they can] prosecute . . . and so on and so on, I think that they could have done more."[209]

---

[204] Interview with Sandra Orlović, then Executive Director, Humanitarian Law Center, in Belgrade, Serb. (June 10, 2014).

[205] Without commenting on the cases' complexity, the OSCE Mission to Serbia reported in 2015 that the OWCP had twenty-three cases "formally at the investigation stage" at that time. OSCE, 2015 REPORT, *supra* note 100, at 40. More than 1,000 additional cases were then "at the pre-investigation stage." *Id.* at 41.

[206] Interview with Marija Ristić, Journalist, in Belgrade, Serb. (June 13, 2014).

[207] *Id.* As noted in Chapter 3, elections in 2012 produced the first such government.

[208] Interview with Ivan Jovanović, Attorney, in Belgrade, Serb. (June 9, 2014). By Jovanović's count, 87 percent of those whom the OWCP had accused of war crimes by June 2017 were ethnic Serbs. Comment by Ivan Jovanović on draft chapter (provided June 11, 2017). *See also* OSCE, 2015 REPORT, *supra* note 100, at 17 (by the end of 2014, 86 percent of war crimes defendants were "former members of Serbian forces").

[209] Interview with Ivan Jovanović, Attorney, in Belgrade, Serb. (June 9, 2014).

C. Ranks of Indictees; Political Pressure on the OWCP

We are ready to try every perpetrator of a war crime, regardless of his place in the chain of command.

—Vladimir Vukčević[210]

Whether human rights trials target senior officials has long been seen as a litmus test for a country's successful political transition following a period of wholesale violations of basic rights. Among other reasons, prosecuting high-ranking suspects may not be *possible* if remnants of a prior regime remain powerful. Nor, of course, may a successor government with strong links to that regime be inclined to prosecute its senior officials.[211] Set against these considerations, the OWCP's failure to indict high-ranking Serb officers, and the paucity of indictments against even mid-ranking Serb officers,[212] highlights the incomplete nature of Serbia's democratic transition. In fact, recent years have seen a reversal of previous progress.

Noting concerns when we spoke in 2014 about the OWCP's failure to indict high-ranking suspects, Ivan Jovanović emphasized the pattern' persistence over time:

And I mean it's been the case since their establishment, but only now after ten years, eleven years, of their work, we can draw a solid and well-based conclusion that this is obviously a pattern of their work.[213]

Although a long-standing pattern, the average rank of suspects indicted by the OWCP *declined* after 2009.[214]

What accounts for Serbian prosecutors' failure to indict senior suspects? One factor, though possibly the least important, relates to legal challenges. Without proof of a direct order—a prosecutor's dream but difficult to obtain[215]—a key path under international criminal law for convicting superior officers has been through the doctrine of command responsibility.[216] But there has been debate about the degree

---

[210] *Serbia Able to Try Generals, Says War Crimes Prosecutor*, B92 News (Nov. 14, 2003).

[211] Empirical research suggests prosecutions of relatively high-ranking rights violators "have a stronger deterrent effect" than those of lower-ranking officials. Hun Joon Kim & Kathryn Sikkink, *How Do Human Rights Prosecutions Improve Human Rights After Transition?*, 7 Interdisc. J. Hum. Rts. L. 69, 71 (2013). Joon Kim and Sikkink believe a key reason is that high-level prosecutions are more visible than those of lower-ranking suspects, and thus are more likely to communicate norms of individual accountability through publicity and media attention. *Id.* at 85–86.

[212] *See* HLC, 2014 Report, *supra* note 180, at 5. For this purpose, the HLC defines "high-ranking officer" as an officer holding the rank of "major, colonel or general." *Id.*

[213] Interview with Ivan Jovanović, Attorney, in Belgrade, Serb. (June 9, 2014).

[214] A report assessing the OWCP's first decade found that none of the defendants prosecuted by the OWCP "held 'high-ranking' positions at the time of the offences" for which they were charged, while less than 10 percent held positions of medium rank. OSCE, 2015 Report, *supra* note 100, at 45. Most of the indictments of mid-ranking suspects took place before 2009; all of the "defendants indicted in 2011, 2012 and 2014 were low ranking ones." *Id.*

[215] As Ivan Jovanović noted, "there [is] almost no written evidence [of such orders], and then you're relying on witnesses, and the witnesses are often unwilling to testify" against suspects who may have given orders to commit war crimes. Interview with Ivan Jovanović, Attorney, in Belgrade, Serb. (June 9, 2014).

[216] Article 7(3) of the Statute of the ICTY adopts this version of the doctrine:

The fact that any of the acts referred to in [provisions of the Statute defining crimes subject to the ICTY's jurisdiction] was committed by a subordinate does not relieve his superior of

to which, under Serbian law, individuals can be criminally prosecuted under this doctrine, and the OWCP and Serbian judges have taken a conservative approach to this question.[217] Even so, the OWCP signaled it had found a way forward when it announced in 2014 that it had begun an investigation of General Dragan Živanović, former commander of the 125th motorized brigade of the Yugoslav Army, on suspicion he failed to prevent war crimes against civilians in several towns in Kosovo, while noting that a final determination about prosecution would depend on the evidence (in the event, the OWCP decided not to bring charges).[218]

Far more important in accounting for the OWCP's failure to indict senior suspects are institutional constraints and related political pressures. With respect to the first, the OWCP has faced long-running resistance from military intelligence, which has failed to produce documents that may be necessary to establish Serb commanders' criminal responsibility.[219] Its motivation, in the view of Ivan Jovanović, may be

to protect the reputation of the army and the higher army officers as a matter of principle. As soon as a crime does not appear as an individual act of a "bad apple" acting on his own, but, instead, suggests a higher level of responsibility and some organisation and plan behind it, it switches on a red alarm in the army circles.[220]

In a striking instance of institutional veto, when the HLC published a report implicating defense minister Ljubiša Diković in war crimes, the ministry of defense classified his unit's wartime file as "secret."[221]

---

criminal responsibility if he knew or had reason to know that the subordinate was about to commit such acts or had done so and the superior failed to take the necessary and reasonable measures to prevent such acts or to punish the perpetrators thereof.

[217] See OSCE, 2015 REPORT, supra note 100, at 63–64; HLC, 2014 REPORT, supra note 180, at 5. Nevertheless, as will be seen, the OWCP has sought the extradition of senior officials from Bosnia and other neighboring countries for alleged crimes against Serbs.

[218] See Gordana Andrić, Serbia Investigates General over Kosovo War Crimes, BALKAN TRANSITIONAL JUST. (Aug. 5, 2014); Probe Against Serbian General Is Only the First, Prosecutor Says, SETIMES (Aug. 14, 2014). This was the first time the OWCP is known to have investigated a Serbian military official of this rank. HLC, 2016 REPORT, supra note 186, at 10. Ivan Jovanović explained the OWCP's legal theory for charging Živanović based on his leadership position: "It [would] not [involve the] direct application of international law, but a charge based on commission by omission of a duty (failure to prevent and sup[p]ress [war crimes committed by subordinates]) under the domestic law, with the duty to act coming from international law command responsibility rules." Email from Ivan Jovanović, Attorney, to Diane Orentlicher (Aug. 21, 2014). On the the OWCP's decision not to bring charges against Živanović, see Marija Ristić, Serbia Ends Probe of Army General for Kosovo Atrocities, BALKAN TRANSITIONAL JUST. (Nov. 27, 2017).

[219] Vukčević seemed to confirm this when he told a reporter some of the OWCP's investigations had been compromised by the police. Vukčević continued: "Information was leaking, cases were compromised, some things we requested were never done." Marija Ristić, Serbia's War Crimes Crusader Leaves the Battlefield, BALKAN INSIGHT (Jan. 15, 2015). See also Orlović Interview, supra note 104 (HLC director states that ministry of interior and ministry of defense were obstructing OWCP access to crucial archives, in violation of Serbian law). Typically, military intelligence personnel do not flatly refuse to provide documents; instead, they reportedly say they cannot find the documents; they may have been destroyed during the 1999 NATO intervention, when Serbia's ministry of defense was bombed; etc. Confidential interview.

[220] Email from Ivan Jovanović, Attorney, to Diane Orentlicher (Aug. 21, 2014).

[221] Ristić, supra note 151.

Political pressure, often implicit and sometimes overt, has been by far the most important factor behind the OWCP's failure to indict high-level suspects from the earliest years of its work. As already noted, in March 2004 Zoran Stojković used his first news conference as minister of justice to say the war crimes chamber should be abolished. Recalling the pressure he experienced that year, in 2005 Vukčević told a reporter: "I have been under pressure to make this a puppet show. . . . Late last year they wanted me out because I don't listen to instructions."[222] When I interviewed him in late 2006, Vukčević acknowledged there was a "kind of obstacle we would meet if we made cases against the most senior officials—we would be exposed to great pressures by the public."[223] As Vukčević's term drew to an end eight years later, his office still faced considerable pressure. The only question, as Orlović put it then, is "what is the level of the influence" of political pressure on its work.[224]

The level has been substantial, increasingly so since 2012. The election that year of a "reformed" nationalist government, discussed further below, is only one reason. By the end of that year, the ICTY's performance also became a contributing factor: soon after an ICTY trial chamber acquitted former Kosovo Liberation Army officer Ramush Haradinaj of charges relating to atrocities against Serbs in late November 2012, just days after the Tribunal's appeals chamber reversed the conviction of two senior Croatian generals for attacks against Croatian Serbs, Vukčević was summoned to appear before a parliamentary committee.[225] The acquittals, which effectively ended any possibility the ICTY would establish the guilt of senior Croatian or Kosovo Albanian suspects for crimes against Serbs, provoked a furious backlash in Serbia. At that moment the parliamentary committee channeled the nation's fury against its own war crimes prosecutor.

Orlović described the episode as a "very, very aggressive move towards the war crimes prosecutor['s] office," and understandably so. Committee members pressed Vukčević about what his office had done to prevent Haradinaj's acquittal, and suggested "that [OWCP personnel] were actually accomplices in [his] acquittal."[226] In fact, Vukčević had been highly and publicly critical of the ICTY Prosecutor's handling of *Haradinaj*,[227] provoking a rare rebuke from The Hague.[228] But this hardly mattered. The chairman of the parliamentary committee said "nothing could

---

[222] Carter, *supra* note 62.

[223] The only examples he provided were ICTY suspects, such as the Serbian Radical Party's founding leader Vojislav Šešelj and Bosnian Serb general Ratko Mladić. Vukčević speculated: "We would probably have 5,000 people demonstrating" if Šešelj, then on trial in The Hague, were prosecuted before the SWCC. Vukčević insisted he could surmount political pressures with respect to other suspects. Interview with Vladimir Vukčević, then War Crimes Prosecutor, in Belgrade, Serb. (Nov. 21, 2006).

[224] Interview with Sandra Orlović, then Executive Director, Humanitarian Law Center, in Belgrade, Serb. (June 10, 2014).

[225] *See Committee on Kosovo Debates Belgrade-Priština Agreements*, B92 NEWS (Dec. 12, 2012).

[226] Interview with Sandra Orlović, then Executive Director, Humanitarian Law Center, in Belgrade, Serb. (June 10, 2014).

[227] *Hague Tribunal "Responsible for Deaths of Witnesses,"* TANJUG (Nov. 28, 2012).

[228] *Hague Tribunal Reacts to Serbian Prosecutor's Statement*, TANJUG (Nov. 28, 2012). Years later, the OWCP pursued a 2004 arrest warrant against Haradinaj even after he became prime minister of Kosovo. *See* Maja Živanović, *Serbia Still Seeking Arrest of Kosovo PM Haradinaj*, BALKAN TRANSITIONAL JUST. (Sept. 12, 2017).

persuade him that the Serbian War Crimes Prosecution was not partially responsible for Haradinaj's acquittal."[229]

The parliamentary grilling heightened concerns within the OWCP about how its work would be affected by the election earlier that year of a government led by former officials of an ultranationalist party. As noted in Chapter 3, in May 2012 Boris Tadić, whose government had been supportive of the OWCP, lost his bid for re-election, and his rival in past elections, Tomislav Nikolić, was elected president. Once a leading member of the Serbian Radical Party, Nikolić split from the Radicals in 2008 and formed his own party, the Serbian Progressive Party (SNS), positioning himself as pro-European integration. But Nikolić's stance toward war crimes prosecutions were well known; as the *New York Times* reported, "[i]n the past, Mr. Nikolić has presided over rallies feting war criminals, including Ratko Mladić."[230] Further consolidating the country's nationalist drift, two months after Nikolić was elected president the wartime spokesman for Milošević's party, Ivica Dačić, became prime minister.[231]

The new government's minister of justice, Nikola Selaković, who has significant influence over the budget of the OWCP, provided further cause for concern. Soon after Vukčević's public lashing in parliament, Selaković visited The Hague, where he reportedly "spent an entire working day talking with members of the 'Serbian community'" detained while on trial at the ICTY. One Serbian suspect "gave him a pie, another offered juice, and . . . Ratko Mladić . . . served him chocolate."[232] In the view of Orlović, Selaković's conduct sent an unmistakable message to the OWCP:

> [Selaković] was putting his impressions from [his] meetings with these detainees on Twitter, and giving public statements on how he was impressed with them, that they are patriots, what their messages were. . . . And I can also say and argue that this behavior of the minister of justice is also a form of . . . political pressure on the war crimes prosecutor, because this is a clear message . . . in terms of values and the . . . notion of what is the priority for this government . . . when [the] minister of justice goes to visit and . . . is overwhelmed with the possibility to meet and speak with Ratko Mladić, and at the same time he didn't visit [the] war crimes prosecutor or even the war crimes chamber—I think it's [a] clear message.[233]

Selaković's disdain for the OWCP had a tangible impact on its functioning. In June 2014, Vekarić told me that, due to Selaković's "very negative view" of the OWCP, the office's "capacities are being restricted all the time."[234] At that time, the OWCP had

[229] *Committee on Kosovo Debates Belgrade-Priština Agreements*, B92 News (Dec. 12, 2012) (apparently paraphrasing the chairman's comment).

[230] Dan Bilefsky, *Nationalist Wins Serbian Presidency, Clouding Ties to the West*, N.Y. Times (May 20, 2012).

[231] Dan Bilefsky, *Next Premier of Serbia Is from Party of Milošević*, N.Y. Times (July 26, 2012).

[232] Slobodan Georgijev, *Delicacies and Denial at The Hague*, Balkan Transitional Just. (Jan. 25, 2013).

[233] Interview with Sandra Orlović, then Executive Director, Humanitarian Law Center, in Belgrade, Serb. (June 10, 2014). In what was seen as a deliberate snub, Selaković did not make even a brief appearance at the OWCP's tenth anniversary celebration in 2013. *Id.*

[234] Interview with Bruno Vekarić, Deputy War Crimes Prosecutor, in Belgrade, Serb. (June 12, 2014).

not yet been authorized to fill two vacancies for deputy prosecutor positions[235]—a major gap in the allotted team of eight deputy war crimes prosecutors[236]—and there was "a lot of discussion" about reducing the war crimes prosecutors' salaries.[237]

Before long, pressure on the OWCP became increasingly visible—and perilous. When Serbian authorities arrested five Serb suspects in the Štrpci case in December 2014, Selaković publicly urged the OWCP to investigate crimes against Serbian victims as well.[238] Around the same time, two members of parliament from the ruling coalition filed espionage and other charges against Vukčević and other prosecutors, alleging they shared sensitive information with U.S. embassy officials. One of the lawmakers, Milovan Drecun, disputed the election of Deputy War Crimes Prosecutor Vekarić to his position. Both Vukčević and Vekarić received threats, some directed against members of their families.[239] Even before then, OWCP sources acknowledged they felt direct pressure not to pursue specific cases. In mid-2014, Vekarić told me Vukčević's security detail had recently been reinforced as a result of an investigation then underway, potentially reaching into senior levels of a government ministry.[240]

Political pressure continued to mount in early 2015. In January, the HLC released a publication implicating General Ljubiša Diković, chief of staff of Serbia's armed forces, in war crimes in Kosovo more than fifteen years earlier, as well as in a cover-up operation.[241] Soon after, Aleksandar Vučić, by then prime minister, lashed out,

---

[235] A report published in 2015 indicated these two positions still had not been filled by the time of publication. OSCE, 2015 REPORT, *supra* note 100, at 48. A more recent report states that four deputy prosecutors and four assistant prosecutors were supposed to be appointed by the end of 2016 but this had not happened at the time of the report's publication. HLC, 2017 REPORT, *supra* note 104, at 20.

[236] The allotted number of deputy war crimes prosecutors has changed somewhat over time. This figure is relevant at least as of 2014. *See* HLC, TEN YEARS, *supra* note 32, at 13.

[237] *Id.* These prosecutors have been paid at a higher rate than most prosecutors in light of the additional complexity and risks associated with their work. *Id.* According to Vekarić, the minister of justice "has a decisive role in determining the number of deputy prosecutors and other members of the War Crimes Prosecutor's staff." He offered the following examples:

This Office is financed from the Republic's budget, which is created by the Ministry of Finance and subject to the opinion provided by the Ministry of Justice.

The War Crimes Prosecutor renders a ruling on the systematization of positions at the War Crimes Prosecutor's Office. The Prosecutor's ruling is then approved by the Justice Minister.

Salaries at this Office have been defined by the Act on the Competence of State Authorities in War Crimes Proceedings. Any amendments to this Act, which may also affect the size of salaries, can be initiated by the Ministry of Justice.

Email from Bruno Vekarić, Deputy War Crimes Prosecutor, to Diane Orentlicher (June 13, 2014).

[238] Marija Ristić & Milka Domanović, *Serbia, Bosnia Arrest 15 in War Crimes Swoop*, BALKAN TRANSITIONAL JUST. (Dec. 5, 2014). This case involves a massacre of twenty non-Serb victims who were forced off a train in Štrpci, a small town in eastern Bosnia, in February 1993.

[239] *Serb War Crimes Prosecutor: "We Stirred Up a Hornet's Nest,"* ASSOCIATED PRESS (Jan. 8, 2015).

[240] Interview with Bruno Vekarić, Deputy War Crimes Prosecutor, in Belgrade, Serb. (June 12, 2014). According to then HLC executive director Sandra Orlović, in the course of her organization's research for a report assessing the first ten years of the OWCP's work, sources in the prosecutor's office "were saying . . . to us that they had some very direct political pressure on them in dealing with some prosecutions. . . . They said that openly to us." Interview with Sandra Orlović, then Executive Director, Humanitarian Law Center, in Belgrade, Serb. (June 10, 2014).

[241] HUMANITARIAN LAW CENTER, DOSSIER: RUDNICA (2015). This was not the first time the HLC had implicated Diković. After publishing a previous report implicating him in Kosovo war crimes, Diković sued then HLC executive director Nataša Kandić. *See* Milan Antonijević, *A*

denouncing "attacks on the Serbian Army"[242] as "the continuation of the campaign against an institution which has the highest public support in Serbia."[243] Vučić said he was personally convinced "Diković is no criminal," adding: "It is up to the institutions to do their job, and the institutions will show if this is true or not."[244]

In this setting, it took no small measure of courage for Vukčević to announce—as he did in February 2015—that he was investigating Diković and others in connection with the execution of forty-five civilians in the Drenica region of Kosovo in 1999, whose bodies were exhumed from a recently-discovered mass grave in Rudnica, Serbia.[245] The next day, then president Nikolić met with Diković, making sure the press covered the encounter.[246] Lest anyone mistake his message, Nikolić extolled Diković as "an honourable officer of the Serbian army"[247] and denounced those who "want to cause instability . . . by any means and return [Serbia] to chaos."[248] On February 15, Nikolić awarded Diković the Order of the White Eagle with Swords, First Class, for his contributions to the country.[249] More ominously, the president warned that Vukčević had "better think about what he is digging up in Serbia."[250] Ostensibly affirming "every prosecutor . . . has complete autonomy in Serbia," Nikolić added: "but no independence."[251]

At that moment, Vukčević had just survived a parliamentary maneuver to force his early retirement. In accordance with legislation adopted in the Summer of 2014, in mid-January 2015 the government announced Vukčević would retire when he reached his sixty-fifth birthday, then rapidly approaching.[252] The 2014 law, adopted on an expedited basis and quickly dubbed "Lex Vukčević," lowered the mandatory retirement age for Serbian prosecutors to sixty-five.[253] In Vukčević's assessment, the decision was linked to the OWCP's investigation of sensitive cases that could implicate senior officials.[254] In his words, "We stirred up a hornet's

Serbian Guide to Ruining Reputations, BALKAN INSIGHT (Jan. 20, 2015); Antonela Riha, *Serbia's Leaders Find New "Enemies Within"*, BALKAN INSIGHT (Feb. 23, 2015). In March 2016, the First Basic Court in Belgrade partially granted Diković's claim for damages, awarding 550,000 dinars. In August 2016, the Court of Appeal upheld the decision. For a more in-depth account of this troubling precedent, see HLC, 2017 REPORT, *supra* note 104, at 31–34.

[242] Marija Ristić, *Serbia Leaders Condemn Army Chief War Crimes Claim*, BALKAN TRANSITIONAL JUST. (Jan. 30, 2015).

[243] *PM Sees "Campaign" Against Serbian Army*, TANJUG (Jan. 30, 2015).

[244] *Id.*

[245] *See* Riha, *supra* note 241; Ivana Nikolić & Petrit Collaku, *Serbia Probes Suspected Kosovo War Mass Grave*, BALKAN TRANSITIONAL JUST. (Nov. 16, 2015).

[246] *See* Riha, *supra* note 241.

[247] *Id.*

[248] Ristić, *supra* note 242.

[249] Riha, *supra* note 241.

[250] *Id.*

[251] *Id. See also Serbia Opposition Party Accuses President of Violating Constitution*, B92 NEWS (Feb. 18, 2015). Diković had not been indicted as of late 2017.

[252] Ristić, *supra* note 219.

[253] Email from Ivan Jovanović, Attorney, to Diane Orentlicher (Jan. 22, 2015) (on file with author); Antonijević, *supra* note 241.

[254] Ristić, *supra* note 219; Antonijević, *supra* note 241. Serbian lawyer Ivan Jovanović is not confident Vukčević's new focus on relatively senior suspects was the sole impetus for "Lex Vukčević," noting:

> Vukčević and his office are generally disliked by the people currently in power because they have prosecuted such [a] high percentage of Serbs. In addition, many from the prosecution service and the judiciary would like to see their end for that "patriotic" reason too,

nest."[255] Apparently in response to pressure from the international community,[256] Vukčević got a temporary reprieve: he would be allowed to complete his term as War Crimes Prosecutor, serving until the end of 2015.[257] As he prepared to retire, Vukčević attributed the fragility of Serbia's war crimes institutions to "constant pressure on our work."[258]

It would take a year and a half for the government to appoint Vukčević's successor. In mid-May 2017, Serbia's National Assembly elected Snežana Stanojković, former Deputy Prosecutor, as the new Prosecutor for War Crimes.[259] Based on her candidacy statement, observers expected the OWCP to focus under Stanojković's leadership on crimes against Serbs.[260]

D. Judicialization of Denial: Obscuring Links between Crimes and the State

Related to concerns about the OWCP's failure to indict high-level suspects, NGOs and others have faulted the office, and at times Serbian courts,[261] for obscuring links between direct perpetrators and Serbian state institutions.[262] On a number of occasions, according to former HLC director Sandra Orlović, the evidence presented at trial so clearly implicated suspects more senior than those charged, the presiding

---

> but also, if not more, because of a simple professional jealousy: the war crimes people have double salaries for the job the rest of the prosecution does not particularly revere.

Email from Ivan Jovanović, Attorney, to Diane Orentlicher (Jan. 22, 2015).

[255] Ristić, *supra* note 219.

[256] Skype interview with Sandra Orlović, then Executive Director, Humanitarian Law Center (Jan. 23, 2015). Orlović believes the interventions that spared Vukčević from imminent retirement came from European governments, the United States, and ICTY Prosecutor Serge Brammertz. *Id.*

[257] On January 21, 2015, the government introduced in parliament an amendment to the 2003 Law on War Crimes, *supra* note 29, that would exempt the War Crimes Prosecutor from the recently adopted provision on retirement of prosecutors so he could serve out his six-year term. Email from Ivan Jovanović, Attorney, to Diane Orentlicher (Jan. 22, 2015).

[258] Marija Ristić, *OSCE: Serbia Faltering on War Crime Prosecutions*, Balkan Transitional Just. (Oct. 27, 2015).

[259] Filip Rudić, *Serbia Selects New Chief War Crimes Prosecutor*, Balkan Transitional Just. (May 15, 2017).

[260] *Id.*

[261] An early example involved the April 2007 verdict in a case instituted after the broadcast of a video showing Serbs shooting Muslim victims near Srebrenica (*see* Chapter 7). Although relatives testified the victims were in Srebrenica until the genocide there in July 1995, when they were bussed to a nearby town to be executed, the presiding judge said it was not clear they had come from Srebrenica or were victims of the massacre there. *See* Nicholas Wood, *Serbian Court Convicts 4 in Srebrenica Massacre*, N.Y. Times (Apr. 11, 2007); Dejan Anastasijević, *The Price of Speaking Out in Serbia*, Time Mag. (Apr. 17, 2007). Writing "the most disappointing thing about the verdict was the efforts of the judge . . . to absolve the Serbian government," Anastasijević reported that the judge "described the [executioners] as an 'irregular volunteer unit' and insisted that they had no relationship with any branch of government in Serbia, despite ample evidence that they had been an integral part of Milošević's security forces." *Id.*

[262] *See* Documenta, Humanitarian Law Center & Research and Documentation Center, Transitional Justice in Post-Yugoslav Countries: Report for 2006, at 14; ICTJ, Against the Current, *supra* note 112, at 10–11; Press Release, Humanitarian Law Center, War Crimes Trials in Serbia (July 26, 2006) (on file with author); HLC, 2014 Report, *supra* note 180, at 13.

judge commented from the bench about those *missing* from the indictment.[263] For example, pronouncing judgment in the *Lovas* case, presiding judge Olivera Anđelković said:

> We have heard in this courtroom the full names of some other actors involved in the events in question, some of them even appeared before us as witnesses, so the prosecutor should fulfill the promise he gave in his closing argument and look into their criminal responsibility as well, if we are to ensure fairness both to the victims and the accused.[264]

E. Regional Reverberations

As previously noted, Serbian civil society advocates hoped the OWCP's work would advance regional reconciliation. Several early cases seemed to vindicate their faith in the reparative potential of Serbian prosecutions. In recent years, however, a series of controversial indictments have stoked regional tensions.

A conviction rendered by the WCD of the Belgrade Higher Court in February 2014 exemplifies the former. That month, the WCD convicted nine former members of the Jackals, a notorious Serbian paramilitary group, of killing more than 120 ethnic Albanian civilians in western Kosovo.[265] Hailing the "demolition of myths" achieved through the verdict, Dušan Janjić, director of the Belgrade-based Forum for Ethnic Relations, thought the routine rendering of similar verdicts would improve Serbia's fraught relationship with Kosovo:

> Two positive trends will emerge once this becomes the praxis of the rule of law. The first is the public's confidence in institutions and the rule of law. The second is a change to the hard prejudice about what happened in the war in Serbia, which will allow Serbs to start to view Kosovo from the perspective of economic cooperation, as a neighbor.[266]

Commenting on the same verdict, Bekim Blakaj, executive director of HLC-Kosovo, said victims' relatives would value the "public and legal admission that harm has been caused to these families." Noting Serbians are increasingly "admitting the crimes committed against Albanians," Blakaj told a reporter: "this creates a kind of empathy and solidarity with the victims."[267]

But the reverse is also true: when victims' hopes are raised and then frustrated, "this [affects] the credibility of the entire . . . structure."[268] At least for awhile, victims' hopes in the Jackals' case have been thwarted: a year after the first instance verdict

---

[263] Interview with Sandra Orlović, then Executive Director, Humanitarian Law Center, in Belgrade, Serb. (June 10, 2014).

[264] HLC, 2013 REPORT, *supra* note 144, at 60.

[265] Their indictment in 2010 was widely seen as a watershed in Serbia's "resolve to deal with its wartime past." *Serbia Indicts Nine Men in Kosovo Killings*, REUTERS (Sept. 12, 2010).

[266] Safet Kabashaj & Ivana Jovanović, *War Crimes Verdicts Improve Kosovo-Serbia Relations, Experts Say*, SETIMES (Mar. 6, 2014).

[267] *Id.*

[268] Caroline Tosh & Aleksandar Roknić, *Politicians Stymie Belgrade War Crimes Trials*, GROUND REPORT (Apr. 29, 2008) (quoting Ivan Jovanović).

was rendered, the Department for War Crimes in the Belgrade Court of Appeal annulled it.[269] To be sure, this is not fatal to successful prosecution on retrial, and the primary grounds for annulment in this case "are not unusual when war crimes verdicts are annulled" in Serbia.[270] But the prospects for justice were hardly encouraging: some of the freed suspects "managed to abscond" while awaiting retrial,[271] and key survivors have refused to testify at the new trial, saying they no longer wanted to participate in "farcical" proceedings.[272]

Meanwhile, Serbian prosecutors advanced on another front, taking action they hoped would "be very important in the process of reconciliation in the region."[273] In March 2015, Serbian authorities arrested eight men suspected of participation in the Srebrenica massacre—a milestone for Serbia, which had never previously tried Serbs for this atrocity.[274] To its credit, the OWCP described its action in the idiom of reparation and remorse. In the words of Deputy War Crimes Prosecutor Bruno Vekarić, "It is very important that Serbia take a clear stance toward Srebrenica through the judicial process. We have sent a clear message that the Srebrenica victims, perpetrators or even potential war crimes will not be forgotten."[275]

The arrests, a result of collaboration between Bosnian and Serbian authorities, were widely hailed as a watershed both in regional cooperation and Serbian willingness to address Srebrenica. But early hopes dissipated as the trial date was postponed on at least two occasions. The trial finally began in February 2017, but proceedings were abruptly terminated in mid-July 2017 for a reason one commentator has described as "almost amazing for its banality and inaccuracy":[276] the suspects were indicted during the prolonged period in which the job of War Crimes Prosecutor remained unfilled; the appellate court therefore held the charges "formally nonexistent."[277] After a flurry of legal appeals, a new trial began in November 2017.[278]

---

[269] *Ukinuta Presuda "Šakalima" za Zločine na Kosovu, Biće Novog Suđenja*, BLIC (Mar. 31, 2015), http://www.blic.rs/vesti/hronika/ukinuta-presuda-sakalima-za-zlocine-na-kosovu-bice-novog-sudenja/xczfl8y.

[270] Ivan Jovanović, *Kosovo Massacres Trial: Understanding the Acquittal*, BALKAN TRANSITIONAL JUST. (May 14, 2015). Jovanović went on to note, however, that some of the appeals court's findings are "not convincing." *Id.*

[271] Marija Ristić, *Will Serbia Ever Try Generals for Kosovo Crimes?*, BALKAN TRANSITIONAL JUST. (Aug. 8, 2016).

[272] *Id.* The retrial began in June 2015. A report released in mid-2017 stated, "the end of the retrial is not in sight." HLC, 2017 REPORT, *supra* note 104, at 75.

[273] Alan Cowell, *Serbia Arrests Eight Suspected in 1995 Srebrenica Massacre*, N.Y. TIMES (Mar. 19, 2015).

[274] The OWCP concluded a plea agreement with another suspect in a Srebrenica-related case in the face of a request from the Office of the Prosecutor of Bosnia seeking the suspect's extradition. The Higher Court in Belgrade accepted the plea agreement in January 2016. *See* HUMANITARIAN LAW CENTER, THROUGH ACCESSION TOWARDS JUSTICE 5 (2017).

[275] Cowell, *supra* note 273.

[276] Alfredo Sasso, *The Kravica Case and the Judicial Cooperation in the Former Yugoslavia*, OSSERVATORIO BALCANI E CAUCASO (July 31, 2017). The HLC places greater fault on the OWCP. Noting that the Law on Public Prosecution requires Serbia's Public Prosecutor to appoint an acting public prosecutor if a public prosecutor position becomes vacant, the organization states this "never occurred" following Vukčević's retirement. HUMANITARIAN LAW CENTER, THROUGH ACCESSION TOWARDS JUSTICE 7 (2017).

[277] Sasso, *supra* note 276.

[278] Filip Rudić, *Landmark Srebrenica Trial Starts Over in Serbia*, BALKAN TRANSITIONAL JUST. (Nov. 14, 2017). Another case that had seemed a milestone in regional cooperation has also

Whatever trust non-Serb victims had begun to invest in Serbian justice was depleted in the face of these setbacks. Early hopes that war crimes prosecutions in Belgrade would contribute to reconciliation had become unsustainable. This was not, however, solely a function of OWCP passivity or incompetence: a series of controversial indictments against Bosniak, Kosovo Albanian, and Croat figures roiled regional relations.

The pattern dates to May 2007, when Serbian authorities arrested Ilija Jurišić, former head of public security in Tuzla, Bosnia, at an airport in Belgrade. In September 2009, the SWCC convicted Jurišić of war crimes in connection with a 1992 attack on a retreating Yugoslav National Army (JNA) convoy in Tuzla, provoking protests by Bosnian authorities.[279] Jurišić's protracted legal saga was a long-running irritant in Serbian-Bosnian relations: in October 2010, the appellate court quashed his conviction, finding insufficient evidence to support the accusations, but in 2013 Jurišić was convicted again by the WCD.[280] By then, he had returned to Bosnia, where he received a hero's welcome.[281] The prosecution finally ended in March 2016, when a Serbian appeal court ruled there was no evidence proving Jurišić ordered the attack on the retreating JNA convoy.[282]

In the meantime, the OWCP pursued another case that stoked tensions with Bosnia: in February 2009, an SWCC investigative judge opened an investigation of nineteen former Bosnian officials, alleging they were criminally responsible for attacking a convoy of retreating JNA troops in Dobrovoljačka Street in Sarajevo in May 1992, the day after the JNA seized Bosnia's wartime president, Alija Izetbegović, in the early days of the Bosnia conflict.[283] Among those charged was Ejup Ganić, who served as Bosnia's acting president while Izetbegović was held captive. The Bosniak and Croat members of Bosnia's presidency vigorously denounced the judicial move, but at that time there seemed scant possibility Serbia could arrest Ganić.[284] A little over a year later, however, Ganić was arrested by British police at Heathrow airport at the request of Serbia, provoking outrage in Bosnia.[285] A British court ultimately

---

stalled. In 2015, Serbia and Bosnia carried out a joint operation to arrest suspects in the notorious 1993 Štrpci massacre (*see supra* note 238). See Marija Ristić, *Serbia Charges Ex-policemen with Srebrenica Killings*, BALKAN TRANSITIONAL JUST. (Sept. 10, 2015). As Bosnia moved forward in its case against 10 suspects arrested in the same operation, proceedings against the other hit a wall in Serbia. In October 2017, the Belgrade Appeal Court dismissed charges against the five because the indictment was not filed by the authorized prosecutor. Filip Rudić, *Serbian Court Dismisses Štrpci Train Massacre Charges*, BALKAN TRANSITIONAL JUST. (Oct. 9, 2017).

[279] Bojana Barlovac, *Belgrade Court Overturns Jurišić Verdict*, BALKAN TRANSITIONAL JUST. (Oct. 11, 2010).

[280] Maja Tuljković, *Ilija Jurišić Sentenced to 12 Years in Jail*, INDEP. BALKAN NEWS AGENCY (Dec. 2, 2013).

[281] *See Jurišić Given Hero's Welcome in BiH*, SETimes (Oct. 12, 2010).

[282] Marija Ristić, *Serbia Acquits Bosnian Policeman of Yugoslav Army Attack*, BALKAN TRANSITIONAL JUST. (Mar. 7, 2016).

[283] Aleksandar Vasović & Daria Sito-Sučić, *Serbia Charges 19 Bosnian Officials with War Crimes*, REUTERS (Feb. 26, 2009); *Bosnian Ire over Serbian Warrants*, AGENCE FRANCE-PRESSE (Feb. 27, 2009).

[284] *See Bosnian Ire over Serbian Warrants*, AGENCE FRANCE-PRESSE (Feb. 27, 2009).

[285] Sylvia Hui, *Ejup Ganić, Ex-Bosnian Leader, Arrested at London Airport*, HUFF. POST (May 1, 2010).

denied Serbia's extradition request, finding its attempt to extradite Ganić "abusive" and "politically motivated."[286]

When I asked Deputy War Crimes Prosecutor Bruno Vekarić about this episode, he at first offered a desultory defense: the *Ganić* case was a holdover from the Milošević period, which the OWCP was obliged to "check." But Vekarić acknowledged that, in his personal opinion, Serbia's pursuit of Ganić was ill-advised.[287] In his view, the conclusion of a protocol between Bosnia and Serbia[288]—then still pending but subsequently signed—would go a long way toward averting the kind of tensions *Ganić* and other cases had generated.

The protocol to which Vekarić referred, finally concluded on January 31, 2013, after years of delay,[289] sought to avoid "parallel investigations"—situations in which both Serbian and Bosnian prosecutors were investigating the same individuals—and to overcome a barrier to prosecution that often doomed both countries' investigations: each country's law bars it from extraditing its own nationals.[290] In light of this prohibition, if, for example, Bosnia wanted to prosecute Serb suspects residing in Serbia who possessed Serbian nationality for crimes committed in Bosnia, Serbia legally could not extradite the suspect. If Bosnia did not share with

---

[286] Explaining his ruling, the British judge said:

> These proceedings are brought and are being used for political purposes and as such amount to an abuse of process of this court.
>
> . . .
>
> In the absence of any additional significant evidence, there would appear to be only two possible explanations, that of incompetence by the Serbian prosecutors or a motive for prosecuting which is based upon politics, race or religion.
>
> From the evidence I have received from [the Serbian deputy prosecutor] I am satisfied that the War Crimes Prosecutor's Office is far from incompetent.

Ex Bosnian Leader Ejup Ganić's Extradition Blocked, BBC News (July 27, 2010). Serbia's then president, Boris Tadić, sought to repair the rift with Bosnia triggered by Ganić's arrest by saying he did not object to Bosnian jurisdiction over the Ganić matter. *See Serbia and Its Neighbors: Patching Things Up*, Economist (Apr. 3, 2010). A year after Ganić's arrest, a retired Bosnian army general, Jovan Divjak, was arrested at the Vienna airport at the request of Serbian authorities, triggering a new round of protests in Sarajevo while eliciting praise from some Bosnian Serb politicians. *See* Dražen Remiković, *Bosnian Serb Officials Welcome Arrest of General Divjak*, Balkan Transitional Just. (Mar. 11, 2009). Born in Belgrade and ethnically Serb (though he refuses to identify himself by ethnicity), Divjak was one of the rare Serbs who fought with the Bosnian Army during the war. Rusmir Smajil Hodžić & Nicolas Gaudichet, *For Serb Defender of Sarajevo, Mladić's Forces Have Won*, Agence France-Presse (Nov. 19, 2017). The OWCP sought to prosecute Divjak, like Ganić, in connection with the May 1992 Dobrovoljačka Street episode. *See* Marija Arnautović, *Divjak Arrest Exposes Balkan Prosecutors' Failings*, IWPR (Mar. 15, 2011). Later, local authorities in the Bosnian town of Trebinje, located in Republika Srpska, submitted war crimes charges against Divjak to the state Prosecutor's Office. *See Divjak Faces War Crime Charges in Bosnia*, Balkan Transitional Just. (May 25, 2017).

[287] Interview with Bruno Vekarić, Deputy War Crimes Prosecutor, in Belgrade, Serb. (July 10, 2012).

[288] Protocol of the Prosecutor's Office of Bosnia and Herzegovina and the Office of the War Crimes Prosecutor of the Republic of Serbia on Cooperation in Prosecution of Perpetrators of War Crimes, Crimes against Humanity and Genocide, Jan. 31, 2013.

[289] *See Serbia, Bosnia Sign War Crimes Protocol*, Agence France-Presse (Jan. 31, 2013). The European Commission hosted the signing ceremony.

[290] According to Ivan Jovanović, in Serbia this prohibition can be legally superseded by treaty. Comment on draft chapter by Ivan Jovanović, Attorney (provided June 11, 2017).

the OWCP evidence its own prosecutors had developed implicating the suspects, Serbian prosecutors might not have sufficient evidence to proceed against them.[291]

Implementation of the 2013 protocol has been vexed, however. A key tenet of the protocol was that, within three months of its signing, each country would notify the other of any investigations underway that involved war crimes allegedly committed by nationals of the other. Despite this undertaking, nine months after Serbia should have notified Bosnia of any pending war crimes investigations against its nationals, the OWCP announced it was pursuing a case against former Bosniak military commander Naser Orić and four other Bosnian servicemen for crimes committed in Eastern Bosnia.[292] The OWCP acknowledged it had been investigating Orić, who had been tried and ultimately acquitted in a trial before the ICTY, since October 2011.[293] The case had powerful emotional resonance for Bosniaks: Orić commanded the Bosniak army's defense of Srebrenica during the 1990s war.

In the view of then HLC director Sandra Orlović, the OWCP's move "ruined [the] sense of good faith around the protocol of cooperation" with Bosnia, adding: "So now everybody can think, 'how many cases do they have still in their drawers against Bosnian citizens?'"[294] The Bosniak member of Bosnia's presidency denounced the move, saying: "If Serbia wants to improve relations with Bosnia after everything that occurred in this country, it should do more to help. Serbia hopes to become an EU member. If so, it should reconsider its actions towards Bosnian citizens."[295]

Despite this flare-up, as a result of the 2013 protocol the Serbian and Bosnian prosecutors' offices were "exchanging information" in "about 35 cases" as of June 2014.[296] Emerging trust between the two offices was once again shaken, however, when, at the request of Serbia's justice ministry, Switzerland arrested Orić on June 10, 2015.[297] Coming a month before the twentieth anniversary of the Srebrenica

---

[291] The 2013 protocol was not the first agreement between Bosnia and Serbia aimed at alleviating this challenge; in 2005 the two countries signed an agreement facilitating the exchange of evidence in war crimes cases. See "No Results" from Serbia-Bosnia War Crimes Deal, BALKAN TRANSITIONAL JUST. (Feb. 20, 2014). But Bosnia resisted signing the protocol for years, insisting atrocities committed in Bosnia should be tried there, not in neighboring countries where suspects had sought impunity. See Merima Husejnović et al., Bosnia Holds Back on Prosecution Agreement, BALKAN INSIGHT (Sept. 22, 2006). Nor was the problem of parallel investigations unique to Serbia and Bosnia. But Serbia had made greater headway resolving this issue with Croatia, concluding a robust agreement with Zagreb years before it concluded the 2013 protocol with Bosnia. See Husejnović et al., supra. After it concluded the 2013 protocol with Serbia, Bosnia concluded a similar protocol with Croatia. See Bosnia, Croatia Join Forces to Try War Crime Suspects, AGENCE FRANCE-PRESSE (June 3, 2013).

[292] See Marija Ristić & Denis Džidić, Serbia Probes Bosnian Army Commander Naser Orić, BALKAN TRANSITIONAL JUST. (Jan. 29, 2014).

[293] See id. See also discussion of Orić in Chapter 8.

[294] Interview with Sandra Orlović, then Executive Director, Humanitarian Law Center, in Belgrade, Serb. (June 10, 2014).

[295] Serbia to Prosecute Bosnian War Hero Naser Orić, WORLD BULL. (Jan. 31, 2014).

[296] Interview with Bruno Vekarić, Deputy War Crimes Prosecutor, in Belgrade, Serb. (June 12, 2014). See also Denis Džidić, Serbia-Bosnia War Crimes Protocol Generates Indictments, BALKAN TRANSITIONAL JUST. (Apr. 7, 2014).

[297] Ivana Nikolić, Serbia Seeks Extradition of Bosniak Ex-commander Orić, BALKAN INSIGHT (June 22, 2015). Around the same time, then former (now current) Kosovo prime minister Ramush Haradinaj, who, like Orić, had been acquitted of war crimes charges by the ICTY, was briefly detained in Slovenia on a Serbian war crimes warrant. Una Hajdari, 40 Kosovo Ex-guerrillas Still Wanted by Serbia, BALKAN TRANSITIONAL JUST. (June 22, 2015). As noted earlier, Serbian authorities made another attempt to secure Haradinaj's extradition in 2017. See supra note 228.

genocide, the arrest aggravated already high tensions between Serbia and Bosnia around the anniversary.[298]

Swiss authorities extradited Orić to Bosnia, where he was also under investigation for war crimes.[299] A month later, Bosnian prosecutors charged him with killing three Serb prisoners of war in 1999.[300] Orić's acquittal in October 2017 set off a new round of recriminations. Aleksandar Vučić, by then president of Serbia, denounced the verdict on the asserted ground that it proved Serbs' lives were not considered to be "worth as much as other lives."[301]

IV. CONCLUDING OBSERVATIONS

The ICTY helped catalyze a serious, if plainly incomplete, process of judicial reckoning in Serbia, which would not have taken place without the Hague Tribunal. To its credit, the OTP recognized and seized the opportunity that emerged in Serbia. In limited but meaningful ways, the OTP bolstered the professionalism and independence of its Serbian partner, the OWCP, during the extended tenure of its first leader. Serbian lawyers' participation in the ICTY's Visiting Young Professionals and Liaison Prosecutors programs, both funded by the European Union and administered by the OTP, helped seed a new generation of professionals committed to principles of impartial justice. Most of the Serbian alumni of these programs whom I interviewed were inspired by their experience in The Hague and, to the extent one can glean from interviews, gained a sophisticated grasp of complex law and procedures during their internships. Thus one of the most practically useful lessons learned from the Serbia experience is that, if an ICT catalyzes domestic proceedings, relevant actors—not just the relevant Tribunal, but also states and international organizations—should be prepared to support those efforts through what will inevitably be challenging periods.

The domestic institutions have always operated in a constrained environment, and have come under heightened pressure during the era of "reformed" nationalist leadership. Serbia's government has, in the words of the HLC, "actively engaged in creating a social environment where the prosecution of those responsible for war crimes, especially those who held medium or high ranks, has become virtually impossible."[302] To be sure, recent reversals are not unusual. Looking to experience in other post-conflict settings, transitional justice processes are anything but "neat and straightforward" but instead are "complex and messy."[303] Progress is often followed by setbacks, which, in turn, might be followed by further advances.

---

[298] See Elvira M. Jukić & Srečko Latal, *Naser Orić Arrest Threatens Srebrenica Anniversary*, BALKAN TRANSITIONAL JUST. (June 24, 2015).

[299] Denis Džidić, *Switzerland to Extradite Naser Orić to Bosnia*, JUSTICE REP. (June 25, 2015).

[300] See Erna Mačkić, *Bosniak Commander Orić "Ordered Burning of Village,"* BALKAN INSIGHT (Apr. 5, 2016).

[301] Admir Muslimović & Filip Rudić, *Serbs Express Outrage at Naser Orić Verdict*, BALKAN TRANSITIONAL JUST. (Oct. 9, 2017). While my focus here is on Bosnian-Serbian relations, Serbia has also provoked tensions with Croatia through its efforts to prosecute Croatian suspects. *See* Sven Milekić & Saša Dragojlo, *Croatia Stalls Serbia's EU Negotiations*, BALKAN TRANSITIONAL JUST. (Apr. 7, 2016).

[302] HLC, 2017 REPORT, *supra* note 104, at 22.

[303] Rachel Kerr, *Transitional Justice in Post-Conflict Contexts: Opportunities and Challenges*, in INTERNATIONAL CENTER FOR TRANSITIONAL JUSTICE, JUSTICE MOSAICS: HOW CONTEXT SHAPES TRANSITIONAL JUSTICE IN FRACTURED SOCIETIES 116, 125–26 (Roger Dutie & Paul Seils

Yet complacency is by no means warranted. In the justified view of many Serbian advocates, key international actors have not used their full potential to support Serbia's fledgling war crimes institutions. Many believe the institution with unique influence during the past decade, the European Union, has squandered much of its potential to advance Serbia's home-grown process of accountability.[304] Of course, external pressure is no substitute for national leaders' commitment to accountability. But it can, if deftly managed, enlarge the space in which domestic actors like the OWCP can advance justice. In time, what began as a modest enterprise can take root, deepen into a habit of accountability, mold public expectations and deepen a society's moral commitments.

---

eds., 2017). *See also* Harvey M. Weinstein et al., *Stay the Hand of Justice: Whose Priorities Take Priority?, in* LOCALIZING TRANSITIONAL JUSTICE: INTERVENTIONS AND PRIORITIES AFTER MASS VIOLENCE 27, 36 (Rosalind Shaw & Lars Waldorf eds., 2010).

[304] Even governments that support Serbia's war crimes institutions have largely overlooked what one leading advocate calls "auxiliary" issues crucial to their success, such as vetting Serbia's security services. Sandra Orlović, Remarks at the Conference on Prosecuting Serious International Crimes: Exploring the Intersections Between International and Domestic Justice Efforts, Washington College of Law, American University, Washington, D.C., Mar. 30, 2016. The HLC's 2017 report on war crimes cases provides a disturbing account of the Serbian government's cynical approach to satisfying EU obligations for Chapter 23 of the accession process. *See* HLC, 2017 REPORT, *supra* note 104, at 20–22, 29–30.

PART SIX

Concluding Observations

Looking Ahead

11

The Afterlife of a Tribunal

A theme running through previous chapters is that the ICTY's influence in Bosnia and Serbia changed profoundly across the decades of its work. This chapter proceeds from the premise that the Tribunal's local influence will last significantly longer than its formal lifetime.[1] Indeed, its local reverberations will continue to unfold, and assuredly change, well beyond our sight lines.

Domestic war crimes institutions catalyzed and fortified by the ICTY will continue operating for some years. For many survivors, the possibility they might still find justice, now in domestic courts, by itself abundantly justifies the Tribunal's existence. Yet this legacy is fragile, as Bosnian and Serbian war crimes institutions remain vulnerable to political pressure.[2] At times of special peril, outside engagement has ensured their relative independence. Going forward, however, it will become increasingly challenging to sustain the attention and commitment of external actors.

Beyond the satisfaction survivors may yet derive from local trials, the wider impact of Bosnia's and Serbia's war crimes institutions is unknowable. But an intriguing body of research has found a striking correlation between domestic prosecutions for

---

[1] As previously noted, the official closing of the ICTY at the end of 2017 is something of a sleight of hand, as the MICT (the residual mechanism for the ICTY and ICTR), will continue to carry on essential functions. In fact, the retrial trial of Jovica Stanišić and Franko Simatović, whose case is discussed in Chapter 6, began before the MICT on June 13, 2017. *See* MICT, Case Information Sheet: Jovica Stanišić and Franko Simatović, http://www.unmict.org/sites/default/files/cases/public-information/cis-stanisic-simatovic-en.pdf (last visited on Dec. 4, 2017).

[2] *See* Chapters 9 and 10.

Some Kind of Justice. Diane Orentlicher.
© Diane Orentlicher 2018. Published 2018 by Oxford University Press.

past atrocities and heightened enjoyment of human rights over time, despite periodic and significant setbacks in many countries.[3] While this suggests local war crimes trials in Bosnia and Serbia might have a salutary long-term effect, their record to date may also signify limits to their likely contribution in this sphere: the most significant improvements in countries' human rights records have been associated with prosecutions of senior suspects.[4] Yet as we have seen, Serbia's War Crimes Prosecutor has yet to bring charges against senior Serb suspects, while Bosnia's Chief Prosecutor has only recently moved in this direction. Moreover, none of the countries included in comparative studies of domestic trials' long-term impact has faced the unique challenges of Bosnia's ethnic divisions. It is hard to imagine a scenario in which Bosnia's war crimes institutions help entrench a culture of respect for human rights until effective measures are taken to address the radically destabilizing developments chronicled in Chapters 2, 8, and 9.

As the ICTY's formal life drew to a close in 2017, conditions in Bosnia and Serbia offered scant grounds for optimism in another sphere this book has explored: leaders and citizens of both Bosnia and Serbia seemed far from acknowledging the full scope of atrocities committed by members of their own ethnic group and condemning them without equivocation. Instead, both countries saw heightened levels of denialism. By the time of my final research interviews, no one in either country suggested he or she expected to see a robust national or regional process of "dealing with the past" in the near term or, indeed, in his or her lifetime.

Yet many still hoped such a reckoning would take place in the future, and drew particular inspiration from the German experience.[5] Civil society advocates in both Bosnia and Serbia expressed the hope that, much as Germany eventually became a "model penitent,"[6] their own societies would someday forthrightly confront the calculated violence of the 1990s. The very fact that it took German society decades to embrace a robust reckoning with the malevolence of the Third Reich encouraged them to hope their countries may yet be willing to confront their wartime past.[7]

---

[3] *See, e.g.,* Kathryn Sikkink, The Justice Cascade: How Human Rights Prosecutions Are Changing World Politics 150–52, 183–85 (2011); Kathryn Sikkink & Hun Joon Kim, *The Justice Cascade: The Origins and Effectiveness of Prosecutions of Human Rights Violations,* 9 Ann. Rev. L. & Soc. Sci. 269, 279–80 (2013) [hereinafter Sikkink & Kim, *Justice Cascade*]. Another stream of scholarship has found that countries that addressed past violations of human rights with both amnesties and prosecutions on average experienced greater improvements in human rights than countries that used either amnesties or prosecutions alone. *See* Tricia D. Olsen et al., *Conclusion: Amnesty in the Age of Accountability, in* Amnesty in the Age of Human Rights Accountability: Comparative and International Perspectives 336, 344–45 (Francesca Lessa & Leigh A. Payne eds., 2012); Tricia D. Olsen et al., Transitional Justice in Balance: Comparing Processes, Weighing Efficacy 146 (2010).

[4] *See* Hun Joon Kim & Kathryn Sikkink, *How Do Human Rights Prosecutions Improve Human Rights After Transition?,* 7 Interdisc. J. Hum. Rts. L. 71, 85–86 (2012–2013). *See also* Sikkink & Kim, *Justice Cascade, supra* note 3, at 281–82.

[5] When used in a postwar context, references to "German," "Germans," and "Germany" in this chapter refer to the Federal Republic of Germany and its citizens before and after reunification, and thus do not include the German Democratic Republic.

[6] Thomas U. Berger, War, Guilt, and World Politics After World War II, at 36 (2012).

[7] Even so, several Bosnian sources noted what they consider a significant dissimilarity between their country and Germany: in contrast to World War II, there was no outright victor at the end of the Bosnian war. In their view, this made it less likely a common narrative about atrocities committed in the 1990s would emerge in Bosnia. *E.g.,* interview with Dženana Karup Druško, Director, Transitional Justice, Accountability and Remembrance, in Sarajevo, Bosn. & Herz.

For some, this hope rests in part on a notion to which international lawyers have long been attracted—that Germany's "impressive achievements in facing its own past"[8] are due, in meaningful part, to the Allied nations' prosecution of Nazi war criminals in Nuremberg.[9] As we have seen, some Bosnian and Serbian advocates believe that, if and when their own countries are ready to face the past, they will build on and benefit from the factual foundation meticulously established by the ICTY, much as Germany has built on the facts laid bare in Nuremberg.[10]

The discussion that follows briefly explores relevant aspects of the German experience in light of these expectations.[11] To the extent it draws comparisons to developments explored in previous chapters, it focuses on those in Serbia. The reason is not because the similarities are striking—indeed, I do not mean to suggest anything like an equivalency between postwar Germany and post-Milošević Serbia. Rather, Bosnia's ethnic divisions, cemented in the dysfunctional structures of Dayton, so deeply complicate and compromise questions of acknowledgment that any effort to extrapolate insights from the German experience are infinitely more complex in respect of Bosnia.

As Anna Sauerbrey noted when comparing German and U.S. responses to neo-Nazis in their societies, "In a way, it is pointless to compare political cultures. Each is unique and deeply rooted in each country's history."[12] Even so, it is useful to consider the German experience for several distinct reasons, each modest yet instructive. First, in line with the views of accountability advocates who look to Germany for inspiration, its experience at the very least shows that the influence of an ICT *can* evolve long after it wraps up its work, even if there is no assurance the ICTY will have a significant downstream impact in Bosnia or Serbia. As well, the German experience—in particular, postwar Germany's general aversion to confronting its moral responsibility for the Holocaust—places some of the more disturbing patterns chronicled in Chapter 7 (as well as 8) in perspective, reminding us that pervasive denialism does not necessarily portend perennial denial. Third, even historically-specific aspects of Germany's evolution are instructive (while some point to factors that may merit attention in comparative research): They remind

---

(Sept. 8, 2014). For Svjetlana Nedimović, Germany is a model not because it reached a "settled" orientation toward the past but rather because its government and society recognize the need for continuous vigilance against extremist tendencies. Interview with Svjetlana Nedimović, Activist, in Sarajevo, Bosn. & Herz. (Sept. 18, 2014).

[8] Belinda Cooper, Nuremberg's Misunderstood Influence on Post-WW II Germany, Remarks at Conference on the Occasion of IntLawGrrls! 10th Birthday, University of Georgia School of Law, Athens, Ga., Mar. 3, 2017.

[9] Thane Rosenbaum makes the claim this way: "Nuremberg forced the Germans to confront the full enormity and vast evil of their crimes." Thane Rosenbaum, *The Romance of Nuremberg and the Tease of Moral Justice*, 27 Cardozo L. Rev. 1731, 1733 (2006). This claim is typically associated with the 1945–1946 trial of major war criminals before the International Military Tribunal (IMT), organized by the United States, France, United Kingdom, and Soviet Union. Some accounts of the impact of "Nuremberg" in Germany encompass, as well, the twelve "Subsequent Proceedings" conducted before U.S. military tribunals in Nuremberg over a two-year period.

[10] See the concluding sections of Chapters 7 and 8.

[11] It is, of course, impossible to offer anything approaching a full account of this extraordinarily complex subject (nor, in any case, is there consensus among historians about key elements of Germany's trajectory).

[12] Anna Sauerbrey, Opinion, *How Germany Deals with Neo-Nazis*, N.Y. Times (Aug. 23, 2017).

us that a society's readiness to face the past turns on the interplay of a multitude of factors. At times the account that follows notes developments in Germany that may well have no parallels in Serbia's future precisely to highlight this general point, not to suggest Serbia must follow a similar trajectory if it is to reckon forthrightly with the Milošević era.

Two further preliminary points should be noted. First, while much of the following discussion focuses on denialism (as defined in Chapter 5), we would do well to remember this phenomenon is not the prevailing orientation of all societies in which fundamental moral commitments were breached wholesale. Many countries have undertaken robust measures of retrospective justice in the immediate aftermath of a political transition;[13] indeed, the widespread use of such measures in Latin America gave rise to the field of transitional justice.

Second, while the following discussion is ultimately concerned with the potential long-term impact of the ICTY on acknowledgment, this is not to suggest its overall work will have been a failure if the denialism explored in previous chapters persists for the foreseeable future. It bears repeating that the Tribunal was explicitly mandated to provide justice for grievous atrocities, not to dispel denial about them. As survivors of ethnic cleansing repeatedly emphasized in interviews, even though many of their expectations of Hague justice were gravely disappointed, they are grateful the Tribunal was created precisely because it provided "a little piece of justice."[14] Painfully aware the Tribunal had not dispelled denialism in their own lifetimes, they nonetheless considered this contribution invaluable.

I. POSTWAR GERMANY: TRANSITIONAL DENIAL

While there are myriad dissimilarities between them, the German and Serbian experiences with international justice share a common expectation. As elucidated in previous chapters, Serbian supporters of Hague justice hoped that, by laying bare the nature and extent of atrocities committed by Serbian-sponsored forces, the ICTY would stimulate a process of collective moral reckoning.[15] In a similar spirit, the architects of the International Military Tribunal (IMT, or "Nuremberg tribunal")[16] conceived of that court, as well as follow-on proceedings undertaken by occupation powers, in part as a pedagogical exercise whose "chief immediate target was the

---

[13] In two countries that undertook relatively robust prosecutions of military officials responsible for human rights violations in the immediate past, Argentina in the 1980s and Greece in the 1970s, "public opinion overwhelmingly supported prosecution and punishment of those [who were] guilty." SAMUEL P. HUNTINGTON, THE THIRD WAVE: DEMOCRATIZATION IN THE LATE TWENTIETH CENTURY 219 (1991).

[14] Interview with Kada Hotić, Vice President, Association of Mothers of Srebrenica and Žepa Enclaves, in Sarajevo, Bosn. & Herz. (July 24, 2009). See generally Chapter 6.

[15] See Chapters 5 and 7.

[16] The United States was the driving force behind the IMT and the follow-on prosecutions of Nazi war criminals. In Gary Bass's words, "Nuremberg was largely an American creation." GARY JONATHAN BASS, STAY THE HAND OF VENGEANCE: THE POLITICS OF WAR CRIMES TRIBUNALS 150 (2000). Yet the idea of prosecutions was controversial even within the U.S. government and among the American public. See id. at 150–73; NORBERT FREI, ADENAUER'S GERMANY AND THE NAZI PAST: THE POLITICS OF AMNESTY AND INTEGRATION 97–98 (Joel Golb trans., 2002); Elizabeth Borgwardt, Re-examining Nuremberg as a New Deal Institution: Politics, Culture and the Limits of Law in Generating Human Rights Norms, 23 BERKELEY J. INT'L L. 401, 414 et seq. (2005).

German populace."[17] More particularly, they hoped the IMT would "bring home to the German people the wrongdoing done in their name"[18] and thereby "inculcate a sense of responsibility" for Nazi crimes.[19]

For a brief period roughly coinciding with the trial of leading Nazi figures before the IMT, the Allies' pedagogical aims seemed to have been realized. Soon after the trial began, according to public opinion surveys administered by American occupation forces, 67 percent of the German public said they had learned new facts about war crimes; by the end of the year-long trial, the percentage grew to 85 percent.[20] Notably, as well, surveys registered strong German support for the international trial,[21] as clear majorities believed their former leaders deserved punishment.[22]

Yet, setting aside questions about the extent to which U.S.-administered surveys captured the complexity of German beliefs,[23] contemporaneous support for the IMT trial should not be confused with a general disposition by Germans to confront their own political or moral responsibility for Hitler's monstrosities. To the contrary,

---

[17] Donald Bloxham, *The Nuremberg Trials and the Occupation of Germany*, 27 Cardozo L. Rev. 1599, 1599 (2005–2006). While a key objective, this was not the only aim or motivation of those who pressed for war crimes trials and led the prosecution effort. *See* David Cohen, Transitional Justice in Divided Germany after 1945, at 3 (2006), https://www.ocf.berkeley.edu/~changmin/Papers/cohen-trans-justice-germany.pdf. A key impetus for the trials was strong public demand for punishment among the Allied nations. *See* Berger, *supra* note 6, at 43. As well, the chief U.S. prosecutor thought a conviction on the charge of crimes against peace "would make an enormous contribution to the future development of international law and order." In this sense, the IMT was "directed at the remote future, at future generations of mankind." Judith N. Shklar, Legalism: Law, Morals, and Political Trials 170 (1986).

[18] Errol P. Mendes, Peace and Justice at the International Criminal Court: A Court of Last Resort 5 (2010) (quoting U.S. war secretary Henry L. Stimson).

[19] Bloxham, *supra* note 17, at 1600. *See also id.* at 1599; Susanne Karstedt, *The Nuremberg Tribunal and German Society: International Justice and Local Judgment in Post-Conflict Reconstruction*, in The Legacy of Nuremberg: Civilising Influence or Institutionalised Vengeance? 13, 17 (David A. Blumenthal & Timothy L.H. McCormack eds., 2008) [hereinafter Karstedt, *Nuremberg and German Society*].

[20] *See* Susanne Karstedt, *Coming to Terms with the Past in Germany After 1945 and 1989: Public Judgments on Procedures and Justice*, 20 L. & Pol'y 15, 24 (1998) [hereinafter Karstedt, *Coming to Terms*].

[21] *See* Frei, *supra* note 16, at 98.

[22] Bloxham, *supra* note 17, at 1602. *See also* Jörg Friedrich, *Nuremberg and the Germans*, in War Crimes: The Legacy of Nuremberg 87, 89 (Belinda Cooper ed., 1999) (summarizing contemporaneous German views toward the IMT as, "The men responsible for leading them into this desperate situation deserved the worst"). An overwhelming majority of Germans rated the IMT proceeding as "fair" from the beginning through the end of the trial. *See* Karstedt, *Coming to Terms*, *supra* note 20, at 23–24; Karstedt, *Nuremberg and German Society*, *supra* note 19, at 19. By the end of the trial, 78 percent of those living in the U.S.-occupied zone said they regarded the proceedings as fair. Gunnar Theissen, Between Acknowledgment and Ignorance: How White South Africans Have Dealt with the Apartheid Past 3 (in ch. 2) (Brandon Hamber et al. eds., 1997). This is striking not least because the Nazis' chief propagandist, Joseph Goebbels, had prepared the German public to believe any postwar justice meted out by the Allies would be vengeful. *See* Frei, *supra* note 16, at 93.

[23] *See* Berger, *supra* note 6, at 44 n.26. American occupation forces steered the German press toward coverage of the IMT "that was both extensively documentary and affirmative in nature." Frei, *supra* note 16, at 98. "For this reason," Norbert Frei has noted, public opinion, captured in contemporaneous surveys, "was at first strongly dominated by published opinion." *Id. See also* Christoph Burchard, *The Nuremberg Trial and Its Impact on Germany*, 4 J. Int'l Crim. Just. 800, 811 (2006) ("in the years immediately after the war it was simply *not considered appropriate* to criticize the trial" of major war criminals in Nuremberg (emphasis in original)).

with only twenty-one defendants in the dock, Germans could readily confine moral condemnation to a finite group.[24] Ten months into the trial, 91 percent of German respondents agreed that "Hitler and his government were criminals and misled the German people," who considered *themselves* victims of the Nazi regime.[25] As Tony Judt observed:

> Precisely because the personal guilt of the Nazi leadership . . . was so fully and carefully established, many Germans felt licensed to believe that the rest of the nation was innocent, that Germans in the collective were as much passive victims of Nazism as anyone else.[26]

It soon became clear a majority of citizens had scant interest in a more far-reaching process of reckoning, and that their general revulsion at the criminality laid bare in Nuremberg did not signify a fundamental reorientation toward the immediate past. To the first point, prosecutions of Nazi war criminals conducted by Allied powers immediately after the IMT trial "were greeted mainly with rejection and protest" from the beginning.[27] Although the guilt of those tried in the American zone "was proven beyond a reasonable doubt, the public simply chose not to believe it."[28] At the level of political leadership, postwar Germany's first chancellor, Konrad Adenauer, used his inaugural speech in September 1949 to call for an end to the denazification process and consideration of an amnesty for most who had been purged.[29] By then, Germany had already embarked on what would be an extended period of "vital forgetting"[30] (though, it should be noted, National Socialism was never wholly absent from Germany's public sphere).

Germans quickly revised even their appraisal of the IMT's fairness: while only 4 percent rated the trial unfair in October 1946, a few years later close to a third of Germans surveyed said they found it unjust.[31] Their altered assessment corresponded to growing rejection of the principles for which the Nuremberg trial stood. Just over a year after the IMT trial concluded, 37 percent of those surveyed said "the

---

[24] The Allied Powers indicted twenty-four individuals, but one, Robert Ley, committed suicide before the trial began and another, Gustav Krupp von Bohlen und Halbach, was declared medically unfit to stand trial. A third, Martin Bormann, was tried and convicted in absentia. It was later determined that Bormann had already died before the trial began.

[25] Karstedt, *Coming to Terms, supra* note 20, at 24; Karstedt, *Nuremberg and German Society, supra* note 19, at 24.

[26] TONY JUDT, POSTWAR: A HISTORY OF EUROPE SINCE 1945, at 54 (2005). *See also id.* at 809; Bloxham, *supra* note 17, at 1601–03; BERGER, *supra* note 6, at 47; Karstedt, *Nuremberg and German Society, supra* note 19, at 24.

[27] FREI, *supra* note 16, at 94.

[28] Friedrich, *supra* note 22, at 92. Instead, Friedrich writes, "The wedge of criminal guilt that was meant to be a wedge between the public and the defendants turned out to form a link between them." *Id.*

[29] BERGER, *supra* note 6, at 51.

[30] Fritz Stern, *Foreword* to NORBERT FREI, ADENAUER'S GERMANY AND THE NAZI PAST: THE POLITICS OF AMNESTY AND INTEGRATION, at vii, xiv (Joel Golb trans., 2002) (quoting Dolf Sternberger).

[31] FREI, *supra* note 16, at 98; THEISSEN, *supra* note 22, at 4. German views about the IMT were complex, however. The first government of the Federal Republic of Germany apparently was grateful the Allies relieved it of the politically sensitive task of prosecuting war criminals. *See* Karstedt, *Nuremberg and German Society, supra* note 19, at 21.

extermination of the Jews and Poles and other non-Aryans was necessary for the security of Germans."[32] In a poll taken six years later, the same percentage said it was better for German territory to have no Jews, while 25 percent acknowledged holding a "good opinion" of Hitler.[33] By the early 1950s, "the Nuremberg principles were increasingly rejected socially, politically, and judicially."[34]

The confluence of myriad factors produced a virtual end to the ambitious Allied project of postwar prosecutions and denazification in relatively short order.[35] Among them were Germany's new geostrategic importance to Western countries as the Cold War emerged,[36] flaws in the "victors' justice" of Nuremberg and occupation forces' denazification programs,[37] a more generalized resentment of Allied occupation,[38] and the emergence of a robust campaign by "a formidable portion of Germany's old elite" against the continuation of war crimes trials.[39]

Other factors seem arrestingly similar to dynamics that partially account for high levels of denialism in Serbia, yet are difficult to disentangle from historically-specific circumstances of postwar Germany. Reflecting on the early postwar years, German lawyer Juergen Baumann wrote, in words reminiscent of accounts of many Serbians' propensity to "forget" Serb atrocities:[40]

For years, most German citizens made all possible efforts to forget what happened in twelve ill-fated years. They made their gaps in memory systematic, and developed the handling of these generous gaps to perfection . . . Of collective responsibility, a responsibility of the German people (not collective guilt), nobody wanted to know.[41]

---

[32] Judt, *supra* note 26, at 58.

[33] *Id.*

[34] Burchard, *supra* note 23, at 810.

[35] During the first four years of Adenauer's government, the *Bundestag* passed a series of laws exempting specific categories of persons from prosecution for acts committed during the Nazi era. See Berger, *supra* note 6, at 51. In 1951, U.S. high commissioner John McCloy reduced the sentences of or pardoned many previously convicted of war crimes. See Burchard, *supra* note 23, at 812. By the mid-1950s, "[l]ittle was . . . left of the moral sweep implicit in [the Allies'] decision to expiate crimes of the 'Third Reich' according to principles of elementary law." Frei, *supra* note 16, at 230. Even so, for years to come, "outside pressure" would continue to be a "significant factor [in keeping] a lid on any flareups of Nazism within Germany (which did happen now and again)." Comment by Belinda Cooper on draft chapter (provided Sept. 29, 2017).

[36] See Frei, *supra* note 16, at 230; Judt, *supra* note 26, at 808. Initially opposed to the government's efforts to reverse some effects of denazification, U.S. occupation powers gradually eased up in the face of their own pressing priorities. See Berger, *supra* note 6, at 51–52. Thomas Berger cites in particular "the need to prevent Germany from falling under Soviet control," which meant appeasing Adenauer to some extent, and a felt need to rehabilitate the German officer corps to ensure Germany could become "an effective member of the Western military alliance." *Id.* at 52.

[37] See Berger, *supra* note 6, at 44–48; Theissen, *supra* note 22, at 4–5; Burchard, *supra* note 23, at 805–06.

[38] See Bloxham, *supra* note 17, at 1603.

[39] Frei, *supra* note 16, at 94. See also Berger, *supra* note 6, at 49. Much as lawyers who served as defense counsel in The Hague have played a key role discrediting the ICTY in Serbia, *see* Chapter 7, former defense counsel in Nuremberg played a central role, along with law professors, in retrospectively challenging the legitimacy of the IMT in Germany. See Burchard, *supra* note 23, at 802.

[40] I refer here to the insights of Srđan Bogosavljević and Svetlana Logar quoted in Chapter 7.

[41] Burchard, *supra* note 23, at 812 (quoting Juergen Baumann).

The pattern Baumann described may well result, at least in part, from the kind of motivated reasoning explored in Chapter 7—that is, a human propensity to reject or deflect information that threatens one's individual or collective self-esteem. Indeed, a productive line of comparative research would consider whether societies are more likely to engage in a far-reaching reckoning with depredations of the *immediate* past if most of its citizens justifiably consider themselves "blameless" in the sense that they not only did not commit crimes, but opposed the regime responsible for them.

If psychological dynamics played a part in most Germans' resistance to self-critical reflection, situational factors were also important. Many felt keenly the extent to which Germans had been victims of savage wartime atrocities, particularly at the hands of the Soviets.[42] This, combined with the fact that the Allies did not seriously consider prosecuting their own war crimes and the presence of a Soviet judge in Nuremberg, diminished the pedagogical potential of Nuremberg.[43] With much of Germany in ruins, moreover, by the end of 1945 "most of the German population felt brutalized, was cold and hungry, and faced a bleak future."[44] A majority "felt that they had other, more pressing, concerns than pursuing questions of guilt or innocence."[45]

In this setting, it would be an understatement to say Germany's first postwar government did not face a popular clamor to initiate a project of national soul-searching. To the contrary, political figures were acutely mindful of the voting power of former Nazis.[46] Ironically, then, postwar prosecutions "put an extraordinary amount of documentation . . . on record (notably concerning the [Nazi] project to exterminate Europe's Jews), at the very moment when Germans . . . were most disposed to forget as fast as they could."[47]

If postwar Germany was not yet ready to face the past, what was Nuremberg's near- and long-term impact on German beliefs? There is no consensus among scholars who have considered this question, with one notable exception: there is

---

[42] *See* BERGER, *supra* note 6, at 52–53; *see also* Jeffrey K. Olick & Daniel Levy, *Collective Memory and Cultural Constraint: Holocaust Myth and Rationality in German Politics*, 62 AM. SOC. REV. 921, 928 (1997). For a vivid account of the devastation Germans experienced, particularly in the wake of Allied bombing, which intensified in the final half-year of the war, see Robert G. Moeller, *The Third Reich in Post-War German Memory*, *in* NAZI GERMANY (Jane Caplan ed., 2008).

[43] *See* BERGER, *supra* note 6, at 46. These perspectives are somewhat similar to Serbian critiques of the ICTY: as noted throughout this book, the perception that crimes against Serb victims have not received adequate attention has intensified Serbs' antipathy toward the Hague Tribunal. This ground for suspicion of Hague justice was, moreover, reinforced by a perception that the ICTY protected the interests of Western states in certain judgments. *See* Chapter 6. Despite these parallels, while a majority of Serbians rejected the ICTY from the outset of its work, "Germans accepted and embraced victors' justice" at Nuremberg, at least contemporaneously. Karstedt, *Nuremberg and German Society*, supra note 19, at 25.

[44] BERGER, *supra* note 6, at 41.

[45] *Id. See also* Olick & Levy, *supra* note 42, at 928. Although the circumstantial bases for these sentiments were unique to postwar Germany, the general phenomena are reminiscent of several dynamics underlying Serbian denialism. As previously elucidated, these include: (1) a widespread sense of Serbian victimization, (2) a belief, fueled by wartime narratives of the Milošević government, that the ICTY was created by Western powers as an anti-Serb institution, and (3) Serbian citizens' preoccupation with daily struggles to make ends meet.

[46] *See* JUDT, *supra* note 26, at 53; BERGER, *supra* note 6, at 49. As noted in Chapter 3, a similar dynamic was at play in post-Milošević Serbia: the continued strength of nationalist parties operated as a political constraint on leaders who may have wished to condemn wartime atrocities in a more forthright manner.

[47] JUDT, supra note 26, at 54.

broad agreement that "the judicial reckoning" at Nuremberg had "inestimable long-term value."[48] In Norbert Frei's words, "Without the trials, the criminal dimensions of Nazi rule and the Nazi military campaigns might have remained obscure for a long time."[49] Indeed, evidence amassed by the Allies with a view to prosecution "provided the foundation for . . . historical research on the Nazi regime and its crimes" for decades to come.[50]

Scholarly opinion is divided, however, on the near-term impact of Nuremberg. On one view, the trial of Nazi leaders may have *compounded* Germans' reluctance to face the past.[51] Frei suggests "the enlightening impact of the trials—their central role in exposing the atrocities for perpetuity—also comprised the deeper ground for the massive collective resistance [of Germans] that faced the Allies."[52] Despite Allied efforts to individualize responsibility, German society felt the strong undertow of collective responsibility in the Allies' imposed reckoning with Nazi crimes.[53] Social science literature explored in Chapter 7 suggests a possible reason why postwar prosecutions did not stimulate a wider moral reckoning: to the extent they invite a target audience to reflect on its own or its in-group's moral failings, trials may trigger a host of psychological defenses.[54]

If this was the case in the early years of postwar Germany, the brevity of the IMT trial, and the relatively short duration of subsequent proceedings mounted by occupation forces, might be seen as a virtue. Following the approach of other writers, Tony Judt made the arresting claim that, without the "collective amnesia" that fell across much of postwar Europe, the continent's "astonishing post-war recovery would not have been possible."[55] To be sure, Judt's claim was specific to "a continent covered with rubble"[56] and focused on broader dimensions of recovery than the moral reconstruction of societies that had abetted radical evil.

Even so, it invites reflection on a discomfiting question: whether, in countries still heavily populated by (politically-influential) individuals who may be implicated in wartime atrocities, either as bystanders or perpetrators, a period of "transitional silence" may ultimately facilitate a robust reckoning with an odious past. If this were the case, a principal reason would be that citizens who were adults during a period of calamitous rule may be especially inclined to "forget" the past,[57] and thereby avoid deeply unsettling questions about their own moral responsibility. In this context,

---

[48] FREI, *supra* note 16, at 231.

[49] *Id.*

[50] Cohen, *supra* note 17, at 3.

[51] *See* JUDT, *supra* note 26, at 57.

[52] FREI, *supra* note 16, at 231.

[53] In Frei's words, "What was at stake was the question of the guilt and responsibility of an entire nation." *Id. See also* Cooper, *supra* note 8, at 2 (postwar trials "backfired: Germans resisted trials that implicated their own complicity").

[54] At worst, they might produce a "backfire effect," further entrenching the kind of denialist beliefs many proponents of international justice hoped prosecutions would dispel. *See* Chapter 7.

[55] JUDT, *supra* note 26, at 61. At a conference commemorating the fiftieth anniversary of the Nazis' ascension to power, the philosopher Hermann Lübbe argued that postwar Germans needed to maintain "a 'certain silence (*gewisse Stille*)' around memories of Nazi Socialism." Moeller, *supra* note 42, at 260.

[56] JUDT, *supra* note 26, at 62.

[57] Again, I use the word "forget" here to invoke the insights of Srđan Bogosavljević and Svetlana Logar about the psychology of denialism in Serbia. *See* Chapter 7.

"imposed justice"[58] could provoke a "backfire effect," further entrenching denialist beliefs.[59] To the extent an ICT's work keeps the issue of wartime atrocities in the public space, its prolongation over time arguably sustains narratives of denial, which, in turn, could infect the views of the next generation.[60]

Yet this is by no means the only plausible account of the dynamics at play in countries, such as postwar Germany and post-Milošević Serbia, in which many citizens have cause to resist the moral implications of retrospective justice. With respect to the former, many scholars believe Germany's prolonged silence about the Holocaust hardly facilitated its eventually robust reckoning. Instead, they believe Germany's protracted "forget[ting] about the past" reinforced undemocratic beliefs and anti-Semitic views.[61] Belinda Cooper notes that, beyond the harm it causes survivors, silence "imprints institutions with bad traits that may be hard to get rid of later."[62] Robert Moeller succinctly summarizes the view of many historians (though not his own): "more memory, not less, would have been beneficial to the development of civic culture and a sense of political responsibility among Germans after the experience of the Third Reich."[63]

The views of several Serbians and Bosnians on a somewhat related question broadly correspond to this perspective. During research visits to Serbia and Bosnia, I asked individuals who once hoped the ICTY would advance acknowledgment what they thought about the view, expressed by some scholars, that the ICTY has exacerbated denialism and, more generally, ethnic tensions.[64] Typical of responses

---

[58] Interview with Branko Rakić, Professor, Faculty of Law, University of Belgrade, in Belgrade, Serb. (July 11, 2012).

[59] I build here on the analysis set forth in Chapter 7, which explores social science research indicating that (1) as motivated reasoners, people are prone to disbelieve information that casts their in-group in a negative light; and (2) new information at odds with established beliefs may, in some circumstances, have a backfire effect, further entrenching them.

[60] In a forthcoming publication, Marko Milanović offers a version of this claim, suggesting the protracted silence of German society about its wartime past facilitated a "disruption of transgenerational transmission" of wartime perspectives, enabling a new generation of Germans to emerge "utterly ignorant of the Third Reich." Marko Milanović, *Courting Failure: When Are International Criminal Courts Likely to Be Believed by Local Audiences?, in* THE OXFORD HANDBOOK OF INTERNATIONAL CRIMINAL LAW (Kevin Jon Heller et al. eds., forthcoming 2017).

In a related vein, several scholars have speculated about potentially beneficial effects of amnesties for past violations of human rights when followed by prosecutions. By way of background, some studies suggest that countries that addressed past violations of human rights with both amnesties and prosecutions experienced greater improvements in human rights than countries that used either amnesties or prosecutions alone. *See supra* note 3. A possible reason amnesties might, when followed by trials, increase prospects for improved human rights conditions is that they placate spoilers, effectively buying time before prosecutions are instituted. *See* Olsen et al., *supra* note 3, at 344–45; Sikkink & Kim, *Justice Cascade, supra* note 3, at 282. Once conditions have stabilized, this line of speculation runs, prosecutions advance human rights by deterring violations and strengthening the rule of law.

[61] THEISSEN, *supra* note 22, at 19.

[62] Comment by Belinda Cooper on draft chapter (provided Sept. 29, 2017).

[63] Moeller, *supra* note 42, at 260–61.

[64] *See, e.g.,* Janine Natalya Clark, *Why the ICTY Has Not Contributed to Reconciliation in the Former Yugoslavia,* OSSERVATORIO BALCANI E CAUCASO (Feb. 20, 2013); Janine Natalya Clark, *Justice Far from Reconciliation,* OSSERVATORIO BALCANI E CAUCASO (Mar. 5, 2013). The principal evidence offered in support of this claim has been characteristic responses to ICTY verdicts. If, for example, the Tribunal exonerates a suspect, political leaders belonging to his or her ethnic group typically hail the verdict, while individuals and leaders belonging to the same ethnic group as the victims of his or her alleged crimes protest.

to this question was that of Ivan Jovanović, who said there is some truth to the view that "frustrations caused by certain verdicts may further . . . lead people to this feeling of self-victimization." Jovanović believes this is especially true among Serbs when an ethnic Serb is convicted in The Hague "because . . . there is high number of convictions of Serbs whereas . . . very few convictions of crimes against Serbs." Yet Jovanović is convinced that, without the ICTY's work, "people in Serbia would hardly know anything about Srebrenica." Although there still is "relativization" about the massacre, Jovanović continued, "people are aware, and they do accept that some terrible crimes were committed by Serbs in Srebrenica," which he attributes to the ICTY.[65]

Others, such as Edin Hodžić, reject the notion the ICTY has caused *any* harm socially. When I asked Hodžić what he thought of the claim that the ICTY has heightened ethnic tensions, he replied: "I don't see negative aspects, there's nothing." Instead, Hodžić placed blame for tensions squarely on local politicians, saying: "It's not that, you know, that justice did harm, it's that the politicians and political elites did a lot of harm enough."[66]

As Hodžić intimated and others noted, there is little reason to suppose former Yugoslav states would have avoided divisive discourses about the past had it not been for the ICTY. Although this book's focus has been on the Tribunal, survivors of ethnic cleansing have demanded recognition of their suffering through myriad and continuous interventions,[67] while political elites have exploited a raft of opportunities to perpetuate wartime narratives. For example, leaders of each major ethnic group and country have mobilized around anniversaries of wartime victories and defeats, perennially reviving interethnic and inter-state tensions.[68] In short, it is by no means obvious the region would have experienced an extended period of "transitional silence" had the ICTY not kept the issue of wartime atrocities in the foreground of public consciousness.[69] In the view of Jovanović and others, the Tribunal advanced acknowledgment farther than would have been the case without its work. As I have repeatedly emphasized, moreover, trials that speculatively may seem inimical to acknowledgment have unambiguously been of central importance to victims.

II. DELAYED NORM DIFFUSION?

By the late 1980s if not sooner, the dominant view in Germany's political discourse was "defined by the acknowledgment of the centrality of the Holocaust and of

---

[65] Interview with Ivan Jovanović, Attorney, in Belgrade, Serb. (June 9, 2014).

[66] Interview with Edin Hodžić, Director, Public Law Program, Center for Social Research Analitika, in Sarajevo, Bosn. & Herz. (Sept. 11, 2014).

[67] For a rich account of Srebrenica survivors' local interventions, see LARA J. NETTELFIELD & SARAH E. WAGNER, SREBRENICA IN THE AFTERMATH OF GENOCIDE (2014).

[68] See, e.g., Vedran Pavlić, Tensions Between Croatia and Serbia to Rise Again?, TOTAL CROATIA NEWS (July 16, 2017).

[69] In a relatively early effort to measure the effect of the ICTY's work on societal peace in Bosnia, James Meernik found that, "more often than not, ethnic groups responded with increased hostility toward one another after an arrest" of a high profile suspect or issuance of a notable judgment. On the whole, however, "ICTY actions exercised little effect on societal peace" one way or the other. James Meernik, Justice and Peace? How the International Criminal Tribunal Affects Societal Peace in Bosnia, 42 J. PEACE RES. 271, 287 (2005).

German crimes against humanity."[70] As previously noted, some attribute Germany's eventual emergence as a model penitent at least in part to Nuremberg, presumably through a process of delayed norm diffusion.[71]

Yet there is no consensus about whether or how the IMT trial and follow-on proceedings shaped Germany's ultimately far-reaching process of addressing the past beyond their role in generating an extraordinary trove of documentation. At one end of the spectrum of scholarly opinion, Devan Pendas believes the eventual transformation of German attitudes has "to be attributed mainly to factors outside the realm of law."[72] On the other end, scholars such as Susanne Karstedt believe Nuremberg provided a normative foundation for Germany's delayed reckoning, even if German society was able fully to benefit from its contribution only over an extended period and with the advent of other facilitative developments.[73]

There is, however, wide agreement on circumstances that advanced German society's evolution from generalized amnesia to far-reaching retrospection, whether by unlocking Nuremberg's latent potential or by fostering processes largely independent of the historic trial. Of crucial importance was generational change.[74] In Germany, its impact may have been especially pronounced because the first generation of Germans too young to be implicated in National Socialism—and thus psychologically more able than their parents to condemn its crimes—came of age during the 1960s, a time of global youth rebellion.[75] Notably, the generation who

---

[70] Moeller, *supra* note 42, at 266.

[71] For present purposes the word *norms* refers to "collective expectations for the proper behavior of [certain] actors," which in turn "influence the behavior . . . of states." Thomas Risse & Kathryn Sikkink, *The Socialization of International Human Rights Norms into Domestic Practices: Introduction* to THE POWER OF HUMAN RIGHTS: INTERNATIONAL NORMS AND DOMESTIC CHANGE 1, 7 (Thomas Risse et al. eds., 1999). "Norm diffusion" occurs when the adoption of a norm and/or practice consistent with that norm by some makes it more likely others will adopt the norm/practice. *See* Hun Joon Kim, *Structural Determinants of Human Rights Prosecutions After Democratic Transition*, 49 J. PEACE RES. 305, 308 (2012). Scholars have identified a phenomenon of diffusion *among* states of the norm that grave violations of human rights should be prosecuted. *See, e.g.,* Ellen Lutz & Kathryn Sikkink, *The Justice Cascade: The Evolution and Impact of Foreign Human Rights Trials in Latin America*, 2 CHI. J. INT'L L. 2 (2001); Sikkink & Kim, *Justice Cascade, supra* note 3. In this section, I consider whether the IMT contributed, albeit over an extended period and within a single country, to a general acceptance of the view that Nazi crimes were an abomination and deserved to be punished.

[72] Devan O. Pendas, *The Fate of Nuremberg: The Legacy and Impact of the Subsequent Nuremberg Trials in Postwar Germany, in* REASSESSING THE NUREMBERG MILITARY TRIBUNALS: TRANSITIONAL JUSTICE, TRIAL NARRATIVES, AND HISTORIOGRAPHY 249, 270 (Kim C. Priemel & Alexa Stiller eds., 2014); *see also* Cooper, *supra* note 8, at 1. Pendas's conclusion was offered in a publication focusing more on the Subsequent Proceedings than the IMT, but apparently embraces both.

[73] *See* Karstedt, *Nuremberg and German Society, supra* note 19, at 33.

[74] *See* Pendas, *supra* note 72, at 270; JUDT, *supra* note 26, at 416–17; BERGER, *supra* note 6, at 60–61; Cohen, *supra* note 17, at 16; THEISSEN, *supra* note 22, at 7–8.

[75] *See* BERGER, *supra* note 6, at 60; *see also* JUDT, *supra* note 26, at 417. Generational change may have been a particularly important factor in light of the enormity of Nazi evil. Olick and Levy suggest that public discussion about the past "was possible only because it fit with the younger generation's rejection of their parents' entire world." Olick & Levy, *supra* note 42, at 929. Indeed, "conflict between the generations in West Germany was much greater" than in other West European countries. Detlef Siegfried, *"Don't Trust Anyone Older than 30?" Voices of Conflict and Consensus Between Generations in 1960s West Germany*, 40 J. CONTEMP. HIST. 727, 728 (2005).

were adults during the rise of National Socialism and implementation of the Final Solution did not, on the whole, publicly condemn itself.[76]

Among other key factors were external pressure, which helped ensure that the *Bundestag* extend the statute of limitations for prosecuting crimes against humanity;[77] domestic leadership, notably during the tenure of Willy Brandt, "who succeeded brilliantly in making the theme of facing up to the past a central element of his diplomatic campaign to normalize relations with the East European nations" in the 1970s;[78] and powerful economic growth from the 1950s on.[79] Also important, by the 1970s Germany's school curricula "changed radically to include the history of racial discrimination and persecution, as well as the holocaust."[80] In troubling contrast, school curricula in Bosnia and Serbia perpetuate the dominant narratives of students' ethnic communities.

As important and perhaps necessary as these developments were, on many accounts German society as a whole did not embrace its contemporary orientation toward the past until 1979.[81] That year, the broadcast on German television of a four-part fictionalized miniseries, *Holocaust*, galvanized public opinion.[82] Before it was aired, 64 percent of those surveyed agreed one should draw a line with the Nazi past and opposed a then-pending measure to extend the statute of limitations for prosecuting Nazi crimes. After the series was broadcast, only 46 percent believed it was time to leave the past behind; the extension was adopted.[83] Some thirty-four years after the war ended, a "tipping point had been reached where the broader collective memory of the society had shifted in favor of greater contrition."[84]

Another frequently-cited factor merits particular note here. Many scholars trace the onset of Germany's protracted process of reorientation toward the past to a series of trials of Nazi war criminals beginning with Israel's prosecution of Adolf Eichmann in 1961, which "thoroughly and forever changed the way Germans could look back at their past."[85] Where the IMT proceedings drew attention to the defendants, these trials exposed German citizens to the victims of Nazi atrocities.[86] As influential as the Eichmann proceedings were, it was a 1963-65 trial in Frankfurt of former officers

---

[76] Many did, however, struggle with their responsibility privately. Detlef Siegfried notes that, when rebellious youth rebuked their parents' generation in harsh terms, adults mostly reacted "less unforgivingly than one might have expected." The reason, he suggests, is that their "more or less clear awareness of their implication with the nazi past reinforced their widespread inclination to follow the example of the young generation, who for many Germans epitomized their hope of being set free from the nazi past." Siegried, *supra* note 75, at 743.

[77] *See* BERGER, *supra* note 6, at 62.

[78] *See id.* at 62–63.

[79] *See* THEISSEN, *supra* note 22, at 19 ("The West German economic miracle strongly boosted the acceptance of the new political order and its values").

[80] *Id.* at 17.

[81] *But see id.* at 10 ("The perception that Nazi ideas were basically evil only started to prevail in 1977, when a broad majority of 72% opposed the myth that National Socialism was a good idea").

[82] *See* Pendas, *supra* note 72, at 271; BERGER, *supra* note 6, at 64–65; JUDT, *supra* note 26, at 811; Moeller, *supra* note 42, at 265.

[83] *See* BERGER, *supra* note 6, at 64–65.

[84] *Id.* at 65. *But see* THEISSEN, *supra* note 22, at 18 (suggesting the impact of the series on German attitudes was relatively short-lived).

[85] Karstedt, *Nuremberg and German Society*, *supra* note 19, at 29. *See also* Moeller, *supra* note 42, at 265. Tony Judt cites a 1958 trial in Ulm as the first "trigger for German self-interrogation." JUDT, *supra* note 26, at 810. *See also* Cohen, *supra* note 17, at 16.

[86] Karstedt, *Nuremberg and German Society*, *supra* note 19, at 29–30.

and guards in Auschwitz that many consider a "watershed" for German society.[87] Graphically illuminating the reality of death camps, this proceeding "became a defining moment for the identity of the younger generation, who were not directly involved, and it allegedly shaped the students' movement in Germany."[88]

That many scholars attribute a turning point in German public opinion to highly-visible war crimes trials offers an important counterpoint to broad claims that such prosecutions are likely to entrench denialism. In Germany, periodic trials may have helped the German public to advance, albeit incrementally, toward acknowledgment and condemnation of Nazi crimes.[89] Moreover historians' recognition of the impact of these trials bolsters the view of some legal scholars that Nuremberg ultimately had a significant normative influence on German society, even if it took the intervention of other factors to realize its potential in this sphere. As Susanne Karstedt notes, the Eichmann, Aushwitz, and other national trials "evoked the model of the Nuremberg Tribunal." In her assessment, this "showed that the IMT had left its mark"[90]—more particularly, that Nuremberg had a "civilizing influence" on Germany society, even if it "took several decades and developed at a slow pace."[91] If the precise relationship between contemporary German penitence and Nuremberg is unsettled, it is clear "the German public as a whole today views the Nuremberg trials" positively;[92] indeed, German lawyers are now among the most enthusiastic proponents of international justice.[93] In short, German society has generally embraced the normative model and message of Nuremberg.

That this happened in Germany, of course, hardly ensures that Serbia will eventually overcome contemporary denialism, forthrightly reckon with wartime atrocities, and retrospectively embrace the ICTY as a symbol of fundamental precepts of humanity. The German experience does, however, remind us that developments now unforeseeable can profoundly alter an ICT's influence long after its daily work has come to an end.

---

[87] *Id.* at 30. *See also* JUDT, *supra* note 26, at 416.

[88] Karstedt, *Nuremberg and German Society*, *supra* note 19, at 31. *See also* IAN BURUMA, THE WAGES OF GUILT: MEMORIES OF WAR IN GERMANY AND JAPAN 148 (2015) (the impact on most Germans of the Auschwitz and a later German trial focusing on the Majdanek concentration camp was greater than the impact of the IMT).

[89] *See* Cohen, *supra* note 17, at 17 (suggesting these trials "sensationally prodded the German public to yet again 'rediscover' their past").

[90] Karstedt, *Nuremberg and German Society*, *supra* note 19, at 30.

[91] *Id.* at 33.

[92] Bloxham, *supra* note 17, at 1600.

[93] *Id.*

Epilogue

The first 15 months of the Tribunal's afterlife were eventful. Notably, two of the most important verdicts in the history of the ICTY were issued after it ceased to exist. The court handling its leftover work, the International Residual Mechanism for Criminal Tribunals (MICT), issued final verdicts in one of the ICTY's most vexed prosecutions and one of its landmark cases. Both improved upon flawed trial judgments, burnishing the Tribunal's legal legacy.

On April 11, 2018, a MICT Appeals Chamber, with Judge Theodor Meron presiding, reversed an ICTY Trial Chamber's wholesale acquittal of Serbian firebrand Vojislav Šešelj, convicting him of three counts of crimes against humanity and sentencing him to 10 years' imprisonment.[1] The ruling bore the mark of political compromise: Having spent 11 years in jail, Šešelj would not have to serve more time in prison, sparing the MICT a debilitating confrontation over his return to custody.

Yet the ruling also provided a necessary if incomplete corrective. Two years earlier, Šešelj's "catastrophically mismanaged trial"[2] had produced a massively misguided verdict.[3] At times, the Trial Chamber used reasoning "so far-fetched," the *Economist* wrote, "that it defies belief."[4] Even as the Appeals Chamber sustained Šešelj's previous acquittal on most counts, it took pains to nullify egregious conclusions in the trial judgment.[5]

Almost a year later, an Appeals Chamber delivered its judgment in the *Karadžić* case. However it ruled, the verdict would be historic. For as the *New York Times* reported, the trial of Karadžić "was the most important in the ... history of the United Nations tribunal, and was widely seen as a test of whether the modern international criminal justice system could impose accountability on wartime leaders."[6]

In the lead-up to final judgment, many expected the court to convict Karadžić of grave crimes, as an acquittal would entail a radical revision of ICTY precedent. To be sure, some Bosnians still hoped the Appeals Chamber would rule that genocide had

---

[1] Prosecutor v. Šešelj, Case No. MICT-16-99, Appeal Judgment (Int'l Residual Mech. for Crim. Tribs. Apr. 11, 2018) [hereinafter Šešelj Appeal Judgment].

[2] Eric Gordy, *Šešelj Verdict: A Compromised Court Compromises*, Balkan Transitional Just., Apr. 12, 2018.

[3] *See supra* at 188.

[4] *Vojislav Šešelj's Acquittal Is a Victory for Advocates of Ethnic Cleansing*, Economist, Mar. 31, 2016.

[5] *See, e.g.*, Šešelj Appeal Judgment, *supra* note 1, ¶¶ 71, 130.

[6] Marlise Simons, *Radovan Karadžić Sentenced to Life for Bosnian War Crimes*, N.Y. Times, Mar. 20, 2019.

444 Epilogue

been committed not only in Srebrenica but also elsewhere in Bosnia.[7] Yet they scarcely supposed this would happen. The more substantial question was how the chamber would sentence Karadžić.

This was no small matter. Survivors had been dismayed when an ICTY Trial Chamber sentenced Karadžić to 40 years in prison,[8] sparing him the life sentence already imposed on defendants who were hardly less culpable.

When the moment of final judgment arrived, the Appeals Chamber sustained virtually all of the convictions set forth in the trial verdict, finding Karadžić guilty of genocide (in relation to Srebrenica), crimes against humanity, and war crimes.[9] Reading the chamber's judgment in open court, it took roughly an hour for Presiding Judge Vagn Prüsse Joensen to reach the sentencing verdict. When he did, Joensen asked the defendant to stand. In a quietly dramatic moment, Karadžić rose to hear that he would spend the rest of his life in prison.[10]

Victims in the public gallery erupted in cheers. Murat Tahirović, president of a Bosnian survivors' association, welcomed the sentence, saying: "Total justice is not possible but it is satisfaction for the victims."[11]

Beyond the courtroom, survivors found little to celebrate. To no one's surprise, the judgment drew ethnically divided reactions among regional politicians. In Bosnia, Bosniak and Croat leaders hailed the verdict as milestone in Bosnian history, while Serb leaders denounced it as further evidence that the Hague Tribunal is "biased, selective and was established [to proclaim] Serbs and their leaders the sole perpetrators."[12]

This was by no means the only sign of intense polarization on the subject of wartime atrocities. Since the first edition of this book was published, denialism continued to dominate the political space in Bosnia and Serbia. The political rehabilitation of convicted war criminals, now in Serbia after serving sentences imposed in The Hague, continued.[13] In Bosnia, nationalist leaders pursued an openly revisionist agenda. In a new low, in August 2018, the parliament of Republika Srpska (RS) voted to annul a watershed achievement in Serb acknowledgement—the pathbreaking 2004 report of an RS commission documenting Serb responsibility for the Srebrenica massacre.[14]

---

[7] The background to this point is discussed *supra* at 167-70.

[8] *See supra* at 135, 169 & n.311.

[9] Prosecutor v. Karadžić, Case No. MICT-13-55-A, Appeal Judgment (Int'l Residual Mech. for Crim. Tribs. Mar. 20, 2019). The Appeals Chamber overturned a small number of the Trial Chamber's convictions, but these were "*de minimis* in nature compared to the extraordinary gravity of the crimes for which Karadžić remains convicted." *Id.*, ¶ 776.

[10] The Appeals Chamber found that the 40-year sentence previously imposed was "unreasonable and plainly unjust," denigrating "the extraordinary gravity of Karadžić's responsibility." *Id.*, ¶ 773.

[11] Denis Džidić, *Radovan Karadžić Sentenced to Life in Prison*, BALKAN TRANSITIONAL JUST., Mar. 20, 2019. That said, "many Bosniaks" were upset by the chamber's failure to find genocide outside Srebrenica, according to Ivan Jovanović. But, he added, "that would certainly not turn them against the ICTY." Email from Ivan Jovanović, Attorney, to Diane Orentlicher (May 13, 2019).

[12] *Bosnians Ethnically Divided Over Karadžić Life Sentence*, BALKANS TRANSITIONAL JUST., Mar. 20, 2019 (quoting Neđeljko Čubrilović)

[13] See HUMANITARIAN LAW CENTER, REPORT ON WAR CRIMES TRIALS IN SERBIA 10-11 (May 2019). An earlier instance of this trend is noted *supra* at 77 n.131.

[14] See *Bosnian Serb Lawmakers Reject 2004 Srebrenica Report, Call for New Probe*, RFE/RL's BALKAN SERVICE, Aug. 15, 2018; Alfredo Sasso, *Srebrenica, Revisionist Siege*, OSSERVATORIO BALCANI E CAUCASO, Mar. 1, 2019. The 2004 report is discussed *supra* at 299.

In the face of rising nationalism in Bosnia and Serbia, it is all too easy to suggest, as some have, that the ICTY/MICT "failed" to alter political narratives. Yet this presumes it is the Tribunal's job to transform polarized polities. It is not.

The truth is more complex. The Hague Tribunal provided a meticulously developed factual foundation for Bosnians, Serbians, and other citizens of former Yugoslav states to learn about the nature and scale of wartime atrocities, and to reckon with the agonizingly difficult questions of responsibility for them. Whether they do so is a matter well beyond the Tribunal's writ, turning on factors largely beyond its control.

In the past, influential outside actors played a constructive role in this sphere. Regrettably, they no longer do so. Preoccupied with internal problems, the European Union has lately squandered much of its influence in the Western Balkans.[15] The U.S. government, whose president traffics in hate speech untethered from fact,[16] was hardly in a position to discourage denialist discourses elsewhere.

In this setting, the moral satisfaction victims derived from the *Karadžić* verdict highlights the distinct contribution an international criminal court can offer. If it could not transform polarized politics, the Hague Tribunal accomplished something uniquely precious: it delivered justice.

Diane Orentlicher
May 31, 2019

---

[15] *See* Adnan Huskić, *The Reluctant West Is Needed in the Balkans*, Balkan Insight, Sept. 7, 2018.

[16] *See* Nancy LeTourneau, *Trump's Hate Speech Makes the Threat of Violence More Real*, Wash. Monthly, Mar. 18, 2019.

Bibliography

Nidžara Ahmetašević, *Bosnia's Unending War*, NEW YORKER (Nov. 4, 2015).

Payam Akhavan, *Justice in the Hague, Peace in the Former Yugoslavia? A Commentary on the United Nations War Crimes Tribunal*, 20 HUM. RTS. Q. 737 (1998).

José E. Alvarez, *Crimes of States/Crimes of Hate: Lessons from Rwanda*, 24 YALE J. INT'L L. 365 (1999).

Diane Marie Amann, *Group Mentality, Expressivism, and Genocide*, 2 INT'L CRIM. L. REV. 93 (2002).

AMNESTY INTERNATIONAL, SERBIA AND MONTENEGRO: ALLEGED TORTURE DURING "OPERATION SABRE" (2003).

AMNESTY INTERNATIONAL, BOSNIA AND HERZEGOVINA: "WHOSE JUSTICE?": THE WOMEN OF BOSNIA AND HERZEGOVINA ARE STILL WAITING (2009).

AMNESTY INTERNATIONAL, SERBIA: ENDING IMPUNITY FOR CRIMES UNDER INTERNATIONAL LAW (2014).

AMNESTY INTERNATIONAL, "WE NEED SUPPORT, NOT PITY": LAST CHANCE FOR JUSTICE FOR BOSNIA'S WARTIME RAPE SURVIVORS (2017).

Louise Arbour, *The Crucial Years*, 2 J. INT'L CRIM. JUST. 396 (2004).

HANNAH ARENDT, EICHMANN IN JERUSALEM: A REPORT ON THE BANALITY OF EVIL (Penguin Classics 14th ed. 1994) (1963).

JUDITH ARMATTA, TWILIGHT OF IMPUNITY: THE WAR CRIMES TRIAL OF SLOBODAN MILOŠEVIĆ (2010).

Laura J. Arriaza & Naomi Roht-Arriaza, *Weaving a Braid of Histories: Local Post-Armed Conflict Initiatives in Guatemala*, in LOCALIZING TRANSITIONAL JUSTICE: INTERVENTIONS AND PRIORITIES AFTER MASS VIOLENCE (Rosalind Shaw et al. eds., 2010).

Donna E. Arzt, *Views on the Ground: The Local Perception of International Criminal Tribunals in the Former Yugoslavia and Sierra Leone*, ANNALS AM. ACAD. POL. & SOC. SCI. 226 (2006).

PADDY ASHDOWN, SWORDS AND PLOWSHARES: BRINGING PEACE TO THE 21ST CENTURY (2007).

Kelly D. Askin, *Prosecuting Wartime Rape and Other Gender-Related Crimes under International Law: Extraordinary Advances, Enduring Obstacles*, 21 BERKELEY J. INT'L L. 288 (2003).

Kelly D. Askin, *A Decade of the Development of Gender Crimes in International Courts and Tribunals: 1993 to 2003*, 11 HUM. RTS. BRIEF 16 (2004).

Kelly Askin, *International Criminal Tribunals and Victim-Witnesses, in* INTERNATIONAL WAR CRIMES TRIALS: MAKING A DIFFERENCE? (Steven R. Ratner & James L. Bischoff eds., 2004.

Klaus Bachmann, *Framing the Trial of the Century: Influences of, and on, International Media, in* THE MILOŠEVIĆ TRIAL: AN AUTOPSY (Timothy William Waters ed., 2011).

David Backer, *Civil Society and Transitional Justice: Possibilities, Patterns and Prospects*, 2 J. HUM. RTS. 297 (2003).

Mirko Bagaric & John Morss, *International Sentencing Law: In Search of a Justification and Coherent Framework*, 6 INT'L CRIM. L. REV. 191 (2006).

PATRICK BALL ET AL., THE BOSNIAN BOOK OF DEAD: ASSESSMENT OF THE DATABASE (2007).

Tim Banning, *The "Bonn Powers" of the High Representative in Bosnia Herzegovina: Tracing a Legal Figment*, 6 GOETTINGEN J. INT'L L. 259 (2014).

Elazar Barkan & Alexander Karn, *Group Apology as an Ethical Imperative, in* TAKING WRONGS SERIOUSLY: APOLOGIES AND RECONCILIATION (Elazar Barkan & Alexander Karn eds., 2006).

Bar-Tal et al., *A Sense of Self-Perceived Collective Victimhood in Intractable Conflicts*, 91 INT'L REV. RED CROSS (2009).

Bar-Tal et al., *Sociopsychological Analysis of Conflict-Supporting Narratives: A General Framework*, 51 J. PEACE RES. 662 (2014).

GARY JONATHAN BASS, STAY THE HAND OF VENGEANCE: THE POLITICS OF WAR CRIMES TRIBUNALS (2000).

M. Cherif Bassiouni, *The United Nations Commission of Experts Established Pursuant to Security Council Resolution 780 (1992)*, 88 AM. J. INT'L L. 784 (1994).

KURT BASSUENER & BODO WEBER, DEMOCRATIZATION POLICY CENTER, "ARE WE THERE YET?"; INTERNATIONAL IMPATIENCE VS. A LONG-TERM STRATEGY FOR A VIABLE BOSNIA 3 (2010).

Kurt Bassuener & Bodo Weber, *Balkan Tango: The EU's Disjointed Policies Compound Bosnia's Paralysis*, 2 IP GLOBAL EDITION 19 (2010).

JUERGAN BAUMANN, DER AUFSTAND DES SCHLECHTEN GEWISSENS (1965).

BELGRADE CENTRE FOR HUMAN RIGHTS & STRATEGIC MARKETING RESEARCH, PUBLIC OPINION IN SERBIA: ATTITUDES TOWARDS THE ICTY (Aug. 2004).

BELGRADE CENTRE FOR HUMAN RIGHTS, OSCE MISSION TO SERBIA & STRATEGIC MARKETING RESEARCH, PUBLIC OPINION IN SERBIA: VIEWS ON DOMESTIC WAR CRIMES, JUDICIAL AUTHORITIES AND THE HAGUE TRIBUNAL (Dec. 2006).

ROBERTO BELLONI, STATE BUILDING AND INTERNATIONAL INTERVENTION IN BOSNIA (2007).

THOMAS U. BERGER, WAR, GUILT, AND WORLD POLITICS AFTER WORLD WAR II (2012).

Florian Bieber, *Popular Mobilization in the 1990s: Nationalism, Democracy and the Slow Decline of the Milošević Regime, in* NEW PERSPECTIVES ON YUGOSLAVIA: KEY ISSUES AND CONTROVERSIES 161 (Dejan Djokić & James Ker-Lindsay eds., 2011).

Florian Bieber & Sören Keil, *Power Sharing Revisited: Lessons Learned in the Balkans?*, 34 REV. CENT. & EAST EUR. L. 337 (2009).

Miklós Biró et al., *Attitudes Toward Justice and Social Reconstruction in Bosnia and Herzegovina and Croatia, in* MY NEIGHBOR, MY ENEMY: JUSTICE AND COMMUNITY IN THE AFTERMATH OF MASS ATROCITY 183 (Eric Stover & Harvey M. Weinstein eds., 2004).

Donald Bloxham, *The Nuremberg Trials and the Occupation of Germany*, 27 CARDOZO L. REV. 1599 (2006).

Gideon Boas & Timothy L.H. McCormack, *Learning the Lessons of the Milošević Trial*, 9 Y.B. INT'L HUMANITARIAN L. 65 (2006).

Michael Bohlander, *Last Exit Bosnia—Transferring War Crimes Prosecution from the International Tribunal to Domestic Courts*, 14 CRIM. L.F. 59 (2003).

SISSELA BOK, SECRETS: ON THE ETHICS OF CONCEALMENT AND REVELATION (1982).

JULIAN BORGER, THE BUTCHER'S TRAIL: HOW THE SEARCH FOR BALKAN WAR CRIMINALS BECAME THE WORLD'S MOST SUCCESSFUL MANHUNT (2016).

Elizabeth Borgwardt, *Re-examining Nuremberg as a New Deal Institution: Politics, Culture and the Limits of Law in Generating Human Rights Norms*, 23 BERKELEY J. INT'L L. 401 (2005).

Serge Brammertz et al., *Using the OTP's Experience with Sexual Violence Prosecutions as a Springboard for Building National Capacity*, in PROSECUTING CONFLICT-RELATED SEXUAL VIOLENCE AT THE ICTY 335 (Serge Brammertz & Michelle Jarvis eds., 2016).

Kris Brown & Fionnuala Ní Aoláin, *Through the Looking Glass: Transitional Justice Futures Through the Lens of Nationalism, Feminism and Transformative Change*, 9 INT'L J. TRANSITIONAL JUST. 127 (2014).

Rupert Brown & Sabina Čehajić, *Dealing with the Past and Facing the Future: Mediators of the Effects of Collective Guilt and Shame in Bosnia and Herzegovina*, 38 EUR. J. SOC. PSYCHOL. 669 (2008).

Christoph Burchard, *The Nuremberg Trial and Its Impact on Germany*, 4 J. INT'L CRIM. JUST. 800 (2006).

William W. Burke-White, *The Domestic Influence of International Criminal Tribunals: The International Criminal Tribunal for the Former Yugoslavia and the Creation of the State Court of Bosnia & Herzegovina*, 46 COLUM. J. TRANSNAT'L L. 279 (2007–2008).

IAN BURUMA, THE WAGES OF GUILT: MEMORIES OF WAR IN GERMANY AND JAPAN (2015).

Kevin M. Carlsmith et al., *Why Do We Punish? Deterrence and Just Deserts as Motives for Punishment*, 83 J. PERSONALITY & SOC. PSYCHOL. 284 (2002).

Antonio Cassese, *The ICTY: A Living and Vital Reality*, 2 J. INT'L CRIM. JUST. 585 (2004).

ANTONIO CASSESE, INTERNATIONAL CRIMINAL LAW (2003).

Antonio Cassese, *Reflections on International Criminal Justice*, 61 MOD. L. REV. 1 (1998).

Sabina Čehajić et al., *Forgive and Forget? Antecedents and Consequences of Intergroup Forgiveness in Bosnia and Herzegovina*, 29 POL. PSYCHOL. 351 (2008).

Sabina Čehajić & Rupert Brown, *Not in My Name: A Social Psychological Study of Antecedents and Consequences of Acknowledgment of Ingroup Atrocities*, 3 GENOCIDE STUD. & PREVENTION 195 (2008).

Sabina Čehajić & Rupert Brown, *Silencing the Past: Effects of Intergroup Contact on Acknowledgment of In-Group Responsibility*, 1 SOC. PSYCHOL. & PERSONALITY SCI. 190 (2010).

Sabina Čehajić-Clancy et al., *Affirmation, Acknowledgment of In-Group Responsibility, Group-Based Guilt, and Support for Reparative Measures*, 101 J. PERSONALITY & SOC. PSYCHOL. 256 (2011).

Sabina Čehajić-Clancy, *Dealing with Ingroup Committed Atrocities: Moral Responsibility and Group-Based Guilt*, in THE SOCIAL PSYCHOLOGY OF INTRACTABLE CONFLICTS 103 (Eran E. Halperin & Keren Sharvit eds., 2015).

Eugene Cerruti, *Self-Representation in the International Arena: Removing a False Right of Spectacle*, 40 GEO. J. INT'L L. 919 (2009).

Alejandro Chehtman, *Developing Bosnia and Herzegovina's Capacity to Process War Crimes Cases: Critical Notes on a "Success Story,"* 9 J. INT'L CRIM. JUST. 547 (2011).

Jonathan H. Choi, *Early Release in International Criminal Law*, 123 YALE L.J. 1784 (2014).

Dennis Chong & James N. Druckman, *Framing Theory*, 10 ANN. REV. POL. SCI. 103 (2007).

KRISTEN CIBELLI & TAMY GUBEREK, JUSTICE UNKNOWN, JUSTICE UNSATISFIED? (2000).

MIRNA CICIONI, PRIMO LEVI: BRIDGES OF KNOWLEDGE (1995).

Janine Natalya Clark, *International War Crimes Tribunals and the Challenge of Outreach*, 9 INT'L CRIM. L. REV. 99 (2009).

Janine Natalya Clark, *Judging the ICTY: Has It Achieved Its Objectives?*, 9 SOUTHEAST EUR. & BLACK SEA STUD. 123 (2009).

Janine Natalya Clark, *Plea Bargaining at the ICTY: Guilty Pleas and Reconciliation*, 20 EUR. J. INT'L L. 415 (2009).

Janine Natalya Clark, *The Limits of Retributive Justice: Findings of an Empirical Study in Bosnia and Hercegovina*, 7 J. INT'L CRIM. JUST. 463 (2009).

Janine Natalya Clark, *The State Court of Bosnia and Herzegovina: A Path to Reconciliation?*, 13 CONTEMP. JUST. REV. 371 (2010).

Janine Natalya Clark, *The Impact Question: The ICTY and the Restoration and Maintenance of Peace*, in THE LEGACY OF THE INTERNATIONAL CRIMINAL TRIBUNAL FOR THE FORMER YUGOSLAVIA 55 (Bert Swart et al. eds., 2011).

Janine Natalya Clark, *Courting Controversy: The ICTY's Acquittal of Croatian Generals Gotovina and Markač*, 11 J. INT'L CRIM. JUST. 399 (2013).

JANINE NATALYA CLARK, INTERNATIONAL TRIALS AND RECONCILIATION: ASSESSING THE IMPACT OF THE INTERNATIONAL CRIMINAL TRIBUNAL FOR THE FORMER YUGOSLAVIA (2014).

Jennifer J. Clark, *Zero to Life: Sentencing Appeals at the International Criminal Tribunals for the Former Yugoslavia and Rwanda*, 96 GEO. L.J. 1685 (2008).

STANLEY COHEN, STATES OF DENIAL: KNOWING ABOUT ATROCITIES AND SUFFERING (2001).

Nancy Amoury Combs, *Regulation of Defence Counsel: An Evolution Towards Restriction and Legitimacy*, in THE LEGACY OF THE INTERNATIONAL CRIMINAL TRIBUNAL FOR THE FORMER YUGOSLAVIA 296 (Bert Swart et al. eds., 2001).

Nancy Amoury Combs, *Copping a Plea to Genocide: The Plea Bargaining of International Crimes*, 151 U. PA. L. REV. 1 (2002).

Nancy Amoury Combs, *Procuring Guilty Pleas for International Crimes: The Limited Influence of Sentence Discounts*, 59 VANDERBILT L. REV. 67 (2006).

Claudio Cordone, *Bosnia and Herzegovina: The Creeping Protectorate*, in HONORING HUMAN RIGHTS UNDER INTERNATIONAL MANDATES: LESSONS FROM BOSNIA, KOSOVO, AND EAST TIMOR 63 (Alice H. Henkin ed., 2003).

IVO H. DAALDER, GETTING TO DAYTON: THE MAKING OF AMERICA'S BOSNIA POLICY (2000).

Mirjan Damaška, *Assignment of Counsel and Perceptions of Fairness*, 3 J. INT'L CRIM. JUST. 3 (2005).

Mirjan Damaška, *What Is the Point of International Criminal Justice?*, 3 CHI.-KENT L. REV. 329 (2008).

Roman David, *International Criminal Tribunals and the Perception of Justice: The Effect of the ICTY in Croatia*, 8 INT'L J. TRANSITIONAL JUST. 476 (2014).

Erica Dawson et al., *Motivated Reasoning and Performance on the Wason Selection Task*, 28 PERSONALITY & SOC. PSYCHOL. BULL. 1379 (2002).

Pablo de Greiff, *Deliberative Democracy and Punishment*, 5 BUFF. CRIM. L. REV. 373 (2002).

Pablo de Greiff, *DDR and Reparations: Establishing Links Between Peace and Justice Instruments*, in BUILDING A FUTURE ON PEACE AND JUSTICE 321 (Kai Ambos et al. eds., 2009).

Pablo de Greiff, *Some Thoughts on the Development and Present State of Transitional Justice*, 5 ZEITSCHRIFT FÜR MENSCHENRECHTE (J. HUM. RTS.) 98 (2011).

Margaret M. deGuzman, *Choosing to Prosecute: Expressive Selection at the International Criminal Court*, 33 MICH. J. INT'L L. 265 (2012).

Isabelle Delpla, *In the Midst of Injustice: The ICTY from the Perspective of Some Victim Associations*, in THE NEW BOSNIAN MOSAIC: IDENTITIES, MEMORIES AND MORAL CLAIMS IN A POST-WAR SOCIETY 211 (Xavier Bougarel et al. eds., 2007).

BOGDAN DENITCH, ETHNIC NATIONALISM: THE TRAGIC DEATH OF YUGOSLAVIA (1994).

Davide Denti, *Sorry for Srebrenica? Public Apologies and Genocide in the Western Balkans*, in DISPUTED MEMORY: EMOTIONS AND MEMORY POLITICS IN CENTRAL, EASTERN AND SOUTH-EASTERN EUROPE (Tea Sindbœk Andersen et al. eds., 2016).

Nenad Dimitrijević, *Serbia After the Criminal Past: What Went Wrong and What Should Be Done*, 2 INT'L J. TRANSITIONAL JUST. 5 (2008).

Vojin Dimitrijević, *Serbia: Towards European Integration with the Burden of the Past?*, in THE VIOLENT DISSOLUTION OF YUGOSLAVIA: CAUSES, DYNAMICS AND EFFECTS 211 (Miroslav Hadžić ed., 2004).

Fidelma Donlon, *Rule of Law: From the International Criminal Tribunal for the Former Yugoslavia to the War Crimes Chamber of Bosnia and Herzegovina*, in DECONSTRUCTING THE RECONSTRUCTION: HUMAN RIGHTS AND RULE OF LAW IN POSTWAR BOSNIA AND HERZEGOVINA 257 (Dina Francesca Haynes ed., 2008).

Ivan Đorđević, *The Current Security Situation in Serbia: Challenges Following the Assassination of Prime Minister Đinđić*, 2 Q.J. 39 (2003).

DOCUMENTA, HUMANITARIAN LAW CENTER & RESEARCH AND DOCUMENTATION CENTER, TRANSITIONAL JUSTICE IN POST-YUGOSLAV COUNTRIES: REPORT FOR 2006 (2006).

LAWRENCE DOUGLAS, THE MEMORY OF JUDGMENT: MAKING LAW AND HISTORY IN THE TRIALS OF THE HOLOCAUST (2001).

Jasna Dragović-Soso, *Apologising for Srebrenica: The Declaration of the Serbian Parliament, the European Union and the Politics of Compromise*, 28 EAST EUR. POL. 173 (2012).

James N. Druckman, *The Implications of Framing Effects for Citizen Competence*, 23 POL. BEHAV. 225 (2001).

James N. Druckman & Kjersten R. Nelson, *Framing and Deliberation: How Citizens' Conversations Limit Elite Influence*, 47 AM. J. POL. SCI. 729 (2003).

James N. Druckman, *What's It All About?: Framing in Political Science*, in PERSPECTIVES ON FRAMING 279 (Gideon Keren ed., 2010).

MARK A. DRUMBL, ATROCITY, PUNISHMENT AND INTERNATIONAL LAW (2007).

Angela J. Edman, *Crimes of Sexual Violence in the War Crimes Chamber of the State Court of Bosnia and Herzegovina: Successes and Challenges*, 16 HUM. RTS. BRIEF 21 (2008).

Andrew J. Elliot & Patricia G. Devine, *On the Motivational Nature of Cognitive Dissonance: Dissonance as Psychological Discomfort*, 67 J. PERSONALITY & SOC. PSYCHOL. 382 (1994).

Mark S. Ellis, *Bringing Justice to an Embattled Region—Creating and Implementing the "Rules of the Road" for Bosnia-Herzegovina*, 17 BERKELEY J. INT'L L. 1 (1999).

Mark S. Ellis, *Coming to Terms with Its Past—Serbia's New Court for the Prosecution of War Crimes*, 22 BERKELEY J. INT'L L. 165 (2004).

JON ELSTER, CLOSING THE BOOKS: TRANSITIONAL JUSTICE IN HISTORICAL PERSPECTIVE (2004).

Stefan Engert, *Germany—Israel: A Prototypical Political Apology and Reconciliation Process*, in APOLOGY AND RECONCILIATION IN INTERNATIONAL RELATIONS: THE IMPORTANCE OF BEING SORRY 29 (Christopher Daase et al. eds., 2016).

Rebecca Everly, *Assessing the Accountability of the High Representative*, in DECONSTRUCTING THE RECONSTRUCTION: HUMAN RIGHTS AND RULE OF LAW IN POSTWAR BOSNIA AND HERZEGOVINA 103 (Dina Francesca Haynes ed., 2008).

Joel Feinberg, *The Expressive Function of Punishment*, in DOING AND DESERVING: ESSAYS IN THE THEORY OF RESPONSIBILITY 95 (1970).

LEON FESTINGER, A THEORY OF COGNITIVE DISSONANCE (1957).

CASPAR FITHEN, INTERNATIONAL CENTER FOR TRANSITIONAL JUSTICE, THE LEGACY OF FOUR VETTING PROGRAMS: AN EMPIRICAL REVIEW (2009).

Laurel E. Fletcher & Harvey M. Weinstein, *Justice, Accountability and Social Reconstruction: An Interview Study of Bosnian Judges and Prosecutors*, 18 BERKELEY J. INT'L L. 102 (2000).

Laurel E. Fletcher & Harvey M. Weinstein, *Violence and Social Repair: Rethinking the Contribution of Justice to Reconciliation*, 24 HUM. RTS. Q. 573 (2002).

Laurel E. Fletcher & Harvey M. Weinstein, *A World Unto Itself? The Application of International Justice in the Former Yugoslavia*, in MY NEIGHBOR, MY ENEMY: JUSTICE AND COMMUNITY IN THE AFTERMATH OF MASS ATROCITY 29 (Eric Stover & Harvey M. Weinstein eds., 2004).

Laurel E. Fletcher et al., *Context, Timing and the Dynamics of Transitional Justice: A Historical Perspective*, 31 HUM. RTS. Q. 163 (2009).

Stuart Ford, *A Social Psychology Model of the Perceived Legitimacy of International Criminal Courts: Implications for the Success of Transitional Justice Mechanisms*, 45 VAND. J. TRANSNAT'L L. 405 (2012).

Stuart Ford, *Complexity and Efficiency at International Criminal Courts*, 29 EMORY INT'L L. REV. 1 (2014).

Stuart Ford, *A Hierarchy of the Goals of International Criminal Courts*, 27 MINNESOTA J. INT'L L. (forthcoming 2017).

NORBERT FREI, ADENAUER'S GERMANY AND THE NAZI PAST: THE POLITICS OF AMNESTY AND INTEGRATION (Joel Golb trans., 2002).

Jörg Friedrich, *Nuremberg and the Germans*, in WAR CRIMES: THE LEGACY OF NUREMBERG 87 (Belinda Cooper ed., 1999).

GALLUP BALKAN MONITOR, INSIGHTS AND PERCEPTIONS: VOICES OF THE BALKANS (2008).

Claire Garbett, *Transitional Justice and "National Ownership": An Assessment of the Institutional Development of the War Crimes Chamber of Bosnia and Herzegovina*, 13 HUM. RTS. REV. 65 (2012).

Jemima García-Godos & Chandra Lekha Sriram, *Introduction* to TRANSITIONAL JUSTICE AND PEACEBUILDING ON THE GROUND: VICTIMS AND EX-COMBATANTS (Chandra Lekha Sriram et al. eds., 2013).

Kate Gibson & Cainnech Lussiaà-Berdou, *Disclosure of Evidence*, in PRINCIPLES OF EVIDENCE IN INTERNATIONAL CRIMINAL JUSTICE 306 (Karim A.A. Kahn et al. eds., 2010).

Demis E. Glasford et al., *Intragroup Dissonance: Responses to Ingroup Violation of Personal Values*, 44 J. EXPERIMENTAL SOC. PSYCHOL. 1057 (2008).

Marlies Glasius, *Between "Autistic" Courts and Mob Justice: Theorizing the Call for More "Democratic" International Justice*, 27 MACALESTER INT'L 2 (2011).

MISHA GLENNY, THE FALL OF YUGOSLAVIA: THE THIRD BALKAN WAR (3d ed. 1996).

Ellen Goldstein et al., Three Reasons Why the Economy of Bosnia and Herzegovina Is Off Balance (2015).

Richard J. Goldstone, *The International Tribunal for the Former Yugoslavia: A Case Study in Security Council Action*, 6 Duke J. Comp & Int'l L. 5 (1995).

Richard J. Goldstone, For Humanity: Reflections of a War Crimes Investigator (2000).

Eric Gordy, Guilt, Responsibility and Denial: The Past at Stake in Post-Milošević Serbia (2013).

Patrick Gosling et al., *Denial of Responsibility: A New Mode of Dissonance Reduction*, 90 J. Personality & Soc. Psychol. 722 (2006).

Kent Greenawalt, *Punishment*, in Criminal Law: Cases and Materials 39 (Joshua Dressler & Stephen P. Garvey eds., 7th ed. 2007).

Dejan Guzina & Branka Marijan, *Local Uses of International Criminal Justice in Bosnia-Herzegovina: Transcending Divisions or Building Parallel Worlds?*, 7 Stud. Soc. Just. 245 (2013).

John Hagan, Justice in the Balkans: Prosecuting War Crimes in the Hague Tribunal (2003).

Janet Halley, *Rape at Rome: Feminist Interventions in the Criminalization of Sex-Related Violence in Positive International Criminal Law*, 30 Mich. J. Int'l L. 1 (2008).

Mark B. Harmon & Fergal Gaynor, *Ordinary Sentences for Extraordinary Crimes*, 5 J. Int'l Crim. Just. 683 (2007).

Priscilla B. Hayner, Unspeakable Truths: Transitional Justice and the Challenge of Truth Commissions (2d ed. 2011).

Pierre Hazan, Justice in a Time of War: The True Story Behind the International Criminal Tribunal for the Former Yugoslavia (2004).

Pierre Hazan, Judging War, Judging History: Behind Truth and Reconciliation (Sarah Meyer De Stadelhofen trans., 2010).

Matias Hellman, *Challenges and Limitations of Outreach*, in Contested Justice: The Politics and Practice of International Criminal Court Interventions 251 (Christian de Vos et al. eds., 2015).

Refik Hodžić, *Living the Legacy of Mass Atrocities: Victims' Perspectives on War Crimes Trials*, 8 J. Int'l Crim. Just. 113 (2010).

Refik Hodžić, *A Long Road Yet to Reconciliation: The Impact of the ICTY on Reconciliation and Victims' Perceptions of Criminal Justice*, in Assessing the Legacy of the ICTY 115 (Richard H. Steinberg ed., 2011).

Barbora Holá et al., *International Sentencing Facts and Figures: Sentencing Practice at the ICTY and ICTR*, 9 J. Int'l Crim. Just. 411 (2011).

Barbora Holá, *Sentencing of International Crimes at the ICTY and ICTR: Consistency of Sentencing Case Law*, 4 Amsterdam L.F. 3 (2012).

Barbora Holá & Joris van Wijk, *Life After Conviction at International Criminal Tribunals*, 12 J. Int'l Crim. Just. 109 (2014).

Richard Holbrooke, To End a War (1998).

Michel-André Horelt, *Serbia-Croatia, Bosnia and Herzegovina: Different Apology Packages, Different Successes*, in Apology and Reconciliation in International Relations: The Importance of Being Sorry 168 (Christopher Daase et al. eds., 2016).

Human Rights Watch, Serbia: Emergency Should Not Trump Basic Rights (2003).

Human Rights Watch, Weighing the Evidence: Lessons from the Milošević Trial (2006).

Human Rights Watch, Unfinished Business: Serbia's War Crimes Chamber (2007).

Human Rights Watch, Soldiers Who Rape, Commanders Who Condone (2009).

Human Rights Watch, Selling Justice Short: Why Accountability Matters for Peace (2009).

Humanitarian Law Center, Transitional Justice Report: Serbia, Montenegro and Kosovo, 1999–2005 (2006).

Humanitarian Law Center, Victim/Witness Counselling and Legal Representation: A Model of Support—Project implementation Report (2007).

Humanitarian Law Center, Participation of the Humanitarian Law Center in War Crimes Prosecutions in Serbia (2012).

Humanitarian Law Center, Report on War Crimes Trials in Serbia in 2012 (2013).

Humanitarian Law Center, Report on War Crimes Trials in Serbia 2013 (2014).

Humanitarian Law Center, Ten Years of War Crimes Prosecutions in Serbia: Contours of Justice (2014).

Humanitarian Law Center, Dossier: Runica (2015) and "Through Accession Toward Justice (2017).

Humanitarian Law Center, Report on War Crimes Trials in Serbia 2013 (2014).

Humanitarian Law Center, Report on War Crimes Trials in Serbia During 2016 (2017).

Samuel P. Huntington, The Third Wave: Democratization in the Late Twentieth Century (1991).

Zora Neale Hurston, Their Eyes Were Watching God (Modern Classics 2013 ed., Harper Perennial) (1937).

Michael Ignatieff, *Articles of Faith*, 5 Index on Censorship 110 (1996).

International Center for Transitional Justice, Bosnia and Herzegovina: Selected Developments in Transitional Justice (2004).

International Center for Transitional Justice, Justice Mosaics: How Context Shapes Transitional Justice in Fractured Societies (Roger Duthie & Paul Seils eds., 2017).

International Crisis Group, ICG Bosnia Project Rep. 33, Minority Return or Mass Relocation? (1998).

International Crisis Group, ICG Balkans Rep. 103, War Criminals in Bosnia's Republika Srpska: Who Are the People in Your Neighbourhood? (2000).

International Crisis Group, Balkan Rep. 127, Courting Disaster: The Misrule of Law in Bosnia and Herzegovina (2002).

International Crisis Group, Eur. Rep. 154, Serbia's U-Turn (2004).

International Crisis Group, Eur. Briefing 46, Serbia's New Government: Turning from Europe (2007).

International Crisis Group, Eur. Rep. 198, Bosnia's Incomplete Transition: Between Dayton and Europe (2009).

International Crisis Group, Eur. Briefing 57, Bosnia's Dual Crisis (2009).

Emory University International Humanitarian Law Clinic, Operational Law Experts Roundtable on the *Gotovina* Judgment: Military Operations, Battlefield Reality and the Judgment's Impact on Effective Implementation and Enforcement of International Humanitarian Law (2012).

Bogdan Ivanišević, Human Rights Watch, Softly-Softly Approach on War Crimes Doesn't Help Democracy in Serbia (2004).

Bogdan Ivanišević & Jennifer Trahan, Human Rights Watch, Justice at Risk: War Crimes Trials in Croatia, Bosnia and Herzegovina, and Serbia and Montenegro (2004).

Bogdan Ivanišević, International Center for Transitional Justice, Against the Current—War Crimes Prosecutions in Serbia (2007).

Bogdan Ivani]ević, International Center for Transitional Justice, The War Crimes Chamber in Bosnia and Herzegovina: From Hybrid to Domestic Court (2008).

Sanja Kutnjak Ivković, *Justice by the International Criminal Tribunal for the Former Yugoslavia*, 37 Stan. J. Int'l L. 255 (2001).

Sanja Kutnjak Ivković & John Hagan, *The Politics of Punishment and the Siege of Sarajevo: Toward a Conflict Theory of Perceived International (In)justice*, 40 L. & Soc'y Rev. 369 (2006).

Sanja Kutnjak Ivković & John Hagan, Reclaiming Justice: The International Tribunal for the Former Yugoslavia and Local Courts (2011).

Michelle Jarvis & Kate Vigneswaran, *Challenges to Successful Outcomes in Sexual Violence Cases, in* Prosecuting Conflict-Related Sexual Violence at the ICTY 33 (Serge Brammertz & Michelle Jarvis eds., 2016).

Karl Jaspers, The Question of German Guilt (E.B. Ashton trans., 2000) (1947).

Ivan Jovanović, *From History to Courtroom and Back: What Can Historiography Obtain from Judgments for Crimes in the Wars in the Former Yugoslavia, in* Forum for Transitional Justice (2017).

Tim Judah, The Serbs (3d ed., 2009).

Tony Judt, Postwar: A History of Europe Since 1945 (2005).

Dan M. Kahan, *Foreward: Neutral Principles, Motivated Cognition, and Some Problems for Constitutional Law*, 125 Harv. L. Rev. 1 (2011).

Daniel Kahneman, Thinking Fast, Thinking Slow (2011).

Nataša Kandić, *The ICTY Trials and Transitional Justice in Former Yugoslavia*, 38 Cornell Int'l L. J. 789 (2005).

Nataša Kandić, *RECOM: A New Approach to Reconciliation and a Corrective for Criminal Justice, in* 4 F. Transitional Just. 8 (2012).

Susanne Karstedt, *Coming to Terms with the Past in Germany After 1945 and 1989: Public Judgments on Procedures and Justice*, 20 L. & Pol'y 15 (1998).

Susanne Karstedt, *The Nuremberg Tribunal and German Society: International Justice and Local Judgment in Post-Conflict Reconstruction, in* The Legacy of Nuremberg: Civilising Influence or Institutionalised Vengeance? (David A. Blumenthal & Timothy L.H. McCormack eds., 2008).

Pipina Th. Katsaris, *The Domestic Side of the ICTY Completion Strategy, Focus on Bosnia and Herzegovina*, 78 Revue Internationale de Droit Pénal 183 (2007).

Rachel Kerr, *The Road from Dayton to Brussels? The International Criminal Tribunal for the Former Yugoslavia and the Politics of War Crimes in Bosnia*, 14 Eur. Security 319 (2005).

Rachel Kerr, *Transitional Justice in Post-Conflict Contexts: Opportunities and Challenges, in* Justice Mosaics: How Context Shapes Transitional Justice in Fractured Societies (Roger Dutie & Paul Seils eds., 2017).

Hun Joon Kim, *Structural Determinants of Human Rights Prosecutions After Democratic Transition*, 49 J. Peace Res. 305 (2012).

Hun Joon Kim & Kathryn Sikkink, *How Do Human Rights Prosecutions Improve Human Rights After Transition?*, 7 Interdisc. J. Hum. Rts. L. 69 (2012–2013).

Julie Kim, Cong. Res. Serv., Serbia: 2004 Presidential Elections (2004).

Johanna Kirchhoff & Sabina Čehajić-Clancy, *Intergroup Apologies: Does It Matter What They Say?*, 20 J. PEACE PSYCHOL. 430 (2014).

Mirko Klarin, *Nuremberg Now!*, BORBA (May 16, 1991), *reprinted in* ICTY, THE PATH TO THE HAGUE: SELECTED DOCUMENTS ON THE ORIGINS OF THE ICTY 43 (2001).

Mirko Klarin, *The Impact of the ICTY Trials on Public Opinion in the Former Yugoslavia*, 7 J. INT'L CRIM. JUST. 89 (2009).

JOANNA KORNER, PROCESSING OF WAR CRIMES AT THE STATE LEVEL IN BOSNIA AND HERZEGOVINA (2016).

Denisa Kostovicova, *Airing Crimes, Marginalizing Victims: Political Expectations and Transitional Justice in Kosovo, in* THE MILOŠEVIĆ TRIAL: AN AUTOPSY 249 (Timothy William Waters ed., 2013).

RADHA KUMAR, DIVIDE AND FAIL?: BOSNIA IN THE ANNALS OF PARTITION (1997).

Ziva Kunda, *The Case for Motivated Reasoning*, 108 PSYCHOL. BULL. 480 (1990).

CHRISTOPHER K. LAMONT, INTERNATIONAL CRIMINAL JUSTICE AND THE POLITICS OF COMPLIANCE (2010).

Mechtild Lauth, *Ten Years After Dayton: War Crimes Prosecutions in Bosnia and Herzegovina*, 16 HELSINKI MONITOR 253 (2005).

Sandra Lavenex & Frank Schimmelfennig, *Relations with the Wider Europe*, 46 J. COMMON MKT. STUD. 145 (2008).

Colin Wayne Leach et al., *Moral Immemorial: The Rarity of Self-Criticism for Previous Generations' Genocide or Mass Violence*, 69 J. SOC. ISSUES 34 (2013).

Colin Wayne Leach & Atilla Cidam, *When Is Shame Linked to Constructive Approach Orientation? A Meta-analysis*, 109 J. PERSONALITY & SOC. PSYCHOL. 983 (2015).

Nicolas Lemay-Hébert, *Coerced Transitions in Timor-Leste and Kosovo: Managing Competing Objectives of Institution-Building and Local Empowerment*, 19 DEMOCRATIZATION 465 (2012).

Arendt Lijphart, *Consociational Democracy*, 4 WORLD POL. 207 (1969).

ARENDT LIJPHART, DEMOCRACY IN PLURAL SOCIETIES: A COMPARATIVE EXPLORATION (1977).

Charles G. Lord et al., *Biased Assimilation and Attitude Polarization: The Effects of Prior Theories on Subsequently Considered Evidence*, 37 J. PERSONALITY & SOC. PSYCHOL. 2098 (1979).

David Luban, *Fairness to Rightness: Jurisdiction, Legality, and the Legitimacy of International Criminal Law, in* THE PHILOSOPHY OF INTERNATIONAL LAW 569 (Samantha Besson & John Tasioulas eds., 2010).

David Luban, *Demystifying Political Violence: Some Bequests of ICTY and ICTR*, 110 AJIL UNBOUND 251 (2016).

Alf Lüdtke, *Review Article: "Coming to Terms with the Past": Illusions of Remembering, Ways of Forgetting Nazism in West Germany*, 65 J. MOD. HIST. 542 (1993).

Ellen Lutz & Kathryn Sikkink, *The Justice Cascade: The Evolution and Impact of Foreign Human Rights Trials in Latin America*, 2 CHI. J. INT'L L. 2 (2001).

NOEL MALCOLM, BOSNIA: A SHORT HISTORY (1994).

Peter Malcontent, *Introduction to* FACING THE PAST: AMENDING HISTORICAL INJUSTICES THROUGH INSTRUMENTS OF TRANSITIONAL JUSTICE (Peter Malcontent ed., 2016).

Jean A. Manas, *The Impossible Trade-Off: "Peace" Versus "Justice" in Settling Yugoslavia's Wars, in* THE WORLD AND YUGOSLAVIA'S WARS 42 (Richard H. Ullman ed., 1996).

Janet Manuell & Aleksandar Kontić, *Transitional Justice: The Prosecution of War Crimes in Bosnia and Herzegovina Under the 'Rules of the Road'*, 5 Y.B. INT'L HUMANITARIAN L. 331 (2002).

Michael R. Marrus, *Official Apologies and the Quest for Historical Justice*, 3 J. HUM. RTS. 75 (2007).

Olga Martin-Ortega, *Prosecuting War Crimes at Home: Lessons from the War Crimes Chamber in the State Court of Bosnia and Herzegovina*, 12 INT'L CRIM. L. REV. 589 (2012).

David C. Matz & Wendy Wood, *Cognitive Dissonance in Groups: The Consequences of Disagreement*, 88 J. PERSONALITY & SOC. PSYCHOL. 22 (2005).

Judge Gabrielle Kirk McDonald, *Introductory Remarks*, in OUTREACH: 15 YEARS OF OUTREACH AT THE ICTY (2016).

JOANNE MCEVOY, POWER-SHARING EXECUTIVES: GOVERNING IN BOSNIA, MACEDONIA, AND NORTHERN IRELAND (2015).

James Meernik, *Justice and Peace? How the International Criminal Tribunal Affects Societal Peace in Bosnia*, 42 J. PEACE RES. 271 (2005).

James Meernik & José Raul Guerrero, *Can International Criminal Justice Advance Ethnic Reconciliation? The ICTY and Ethnic Relations in Bosnia-Herzegovina*, 14 SOUTHEAST EUR. & BLACK SEA STUD 383 (2014).

ERROL P. MENDES, PEACE AND JUSTICE AT THE INTERNATIONAL CRIMINAL COURT: A COURT OF LAST RESORT (2010).

ADIS MERDŽANOVIĆ, DEMOCRACY BY DECREE: PROSPECTS AND LIMITS OF IMPOSED CONSOCIATIONAL DEMOCRACY IN BOSNIA AND HERZEGOVINA (2015).

JULIE MERTUS & OLJA HOČEVAR VAN WELY, WOMEN'S PARTICIPATION IN THE INTERNATIONAL CRIMINAL TRIBUNAL FOR THE FORMER YUGOSLAVIA (ICTY): TRANSITIONAL JUSTICE FOR BOSNIA AND HERZEGOVINA (2004).

KEREN MICHAELI, THE IMPACT OF THE INTERNATIONAL CRIMINAL TRIBUNAL FOR YUGOSLAVIA ON WAR CRIME INVESTIGATIONS AND PROSECUTIONS IN SERBIA (2011).

Marko Milanović, *The Impact of the ICTY on the Former Yugoslavia: An Anticipatory Postmortem*, 110 AM. J. INT'L L. 233 (2016).

Marko Milanović, *Courting Failure: When Are International Criminal Courts Likely to Be Believed by Local Audiences?*, in THE OXFORD HANDBOOK OF INTERNATIONAL CRIMINAL LAW (Kevin Jon Heller et al. eds., forthcoming 2017).

MARTHA MINOW, BETWEEN VENGEANCE AND FORGIVENESS: FACING HISTORY AFTER GENOCIDE AND MASS VIOLENCE (1998).

Anca M. Miron et al., *Motivated Shifting of Justice Standards*, 36 PERSONALITY & SOC. PSYCHOL. BULL. 768 (2010).

GABRIELA MISCHKOWSKI & GORANA MLINAREVIĆ, MEDICA MONDIALE, ". . . AND THAT IT DOES NOT HAPPEN TO ANYONE ANYWHERE IN THE WORLD": THE TROUBLE WITH RAPE TRIALS—VIEWS OF WITNESSES, PROSECUTORS AND JUDGES ON PROSECUTING SEXUALISED VIOLENCE DURING THE WAR IN THE FORMER YUGOSLAVIA (2009).

Lepa Mladjenović, *The ICTY: The Validation of the Experiences of Survivors*, in INTERNATIONAL WAR CRIMES TRIALS: MAKING A DIFFERENCE? (Steven R. Ratner & James L. Bischoff eds., 2004).

Robert G. Moeller, *The Third Reich in Post-War German Memory*, in NAZI GERMANY 246 (Jane Caplan ed., 2008).

ADAM MOORE, PEACEBUILDING IN PRACTICE: LOCAL EXPERIENCE IN TWO BOSNIAN TOWNS (2013).

Gregory L. Naarden, *Non-prosecutorial Sanctions for Grave Violations of International Humanitarian Law: Wartime Conduct of Bosnian Police Officials*, 97 AM. J. INT'L L. 342 (2003).

Radmila Nakarada, *Case Note: Acquittal of Gotovina and Markač: A Blow to the Serbian and Croatian Reconciliation Process*, 29 MERKOURIOS 102 (2013).

Aryeh Neier, War Crimes: Brutality, Genocide,Terror and the Struggle for Justice (1998).

Lara J. Nettelfield, Courting Democracy in Bosnia and Herzegovina: The Hague Tribunal's Impact in a Postwar State (2010).

Lara J. Nettelfield & Sarah E. Wagner, Srebrenica in the Aftermath of Genocide (2014).

Elizabeth Neuffer, The Key to My Neighbor's House: Seeking Justice in Bosnia and Rwanda (2001).

Anton Nikiforov, The Need for Outreach, in Outreach: 15 Years of Outreach at the ICTY 60 (2016).

Masi Noor et al., When Suffering Begets Suffering: The Psychology of Competitive Victimhood Between Adversarial Groups in Violent Conflicts, 16 Personality & Soc. Psychol. Rev. 351 (2012).

Brendan Nyhan & Jason Reifler, When Corrections Fail: The Persistence of Political Misperceptions, 32 Pol. Behav. 303 (2010).

Brendan Nyhan & Jason Reifler, Countering Misinformation: Tips for Journalists, Colum. Journalism Rev. (Feb. 29, 2012).

Jelena Obradović-Wochnik, Knowledge, Acknowledgement and Denial in Serbia's Responses to the Srebrenica Massacre, 17 J. Contemp. Eur. Stud. 61 (2009).

Jelena Obradović-Wochnik, Strategies of Denial: Resistance to ICTY Cooperation in Serbia, in War Crimes, Conditionality and EU Integration in the Western Balkans 30 (Judy Blatt & Jelena Obradovic-Wochnik eds., 2009).

Jelena Obradović, Ethnic Conflict and War Crimes in the Balkans: The Narratives of Denial in Post-Conflict Serbia (2013).

Jelena Obradović-Wochnik, The "Silent Dilemma" of Transitional Justice: Silencing and Coming to Terms with the Past in Serbia, 7 Int'l J. Transitional Just. 328 (2013).

Jens David Ohlin, Proportional Sentences at the ICTY, in The Legacy of the International Criminal Tribunal for the Former Yugoslavia 322 (Bert Swart et al. eds., 2011).

Jeffrey K. Olick & Daniel Levy, Collective Memory and Cultural Constraint: Holocaust Myth and Rationality in German Politics, 62 Am. Soc. Rev. 921 (1997).

Tricia D. Olsen et al., Transitional Justice in Balance: Comparing Processes, Weighing Efficacy (2010).

Tricia D. Olsen et al., Conclusion: Amnesty in the Age of Accountability, in Amnesty in the Age of Human Rights Accountability: Comparative and International Perspectives 336 (Francesca Lessa & Leigh A. Payne eds., 2012).

Diane F. Orentlicher, Settling Accounts: The Duty to Prosecute Human Rights Violations of a Prior Regime, 100 Yale L. J. 2537 (1991).

Diane F. Orentlicher, Separation Anxiety: International Responses to Ethno-Separatist Claims, 23 Yale J. Int'l L. 1 (1998).

Diane Orentlicher, Independent Study on Best Practices, Including Recommendations, to Assist States in Strengthening Their Domestic Capacity to Combat All Aspects of Impunity, U.N. Doc. E/CN.4/2004/88 (Feb. 27, 2004).

Diane F. Orentlicher, Whose Justice? Reconciling Universal Jurisdiction with Democratic Principles, 92 Geo. L.J. 1057 (2004).

Diane F. Orentlicher, Open Society Justice Initiative, Shrinking the Space for Denial: The Impact of the ICTY in Serbia (2008).

Diane F. Orentlicher, Open Society Justice Initiative & International Center for Transitional Justice, That Someone Guilty Be Punished: The Impact of the ICTY in Bosnia (2010).

Diane Orentlicher, Review Essay: *From Viability to Impact: Evolving Metrics for Assessing the International Criminal Tribunal for the Former Yugoslavia*, 7 Int'l J. Transitional Just. 536 (2013).

Organization for Security and Co-operation in Europe, Mission to Bosn. & Herz., War Crimes Trials Before the Domestic Courts of Bosnia and Herzegovina: Progress and Obstacles (2005).

Organization for Security and Co-operation in Europe, Mission to Bosn. & Herz., Moving Towards a Harmonized Application of the Law Applicable in War Crimes Cases Before Courts in Bosnia and Herzegovina (2008).

Organization for Security and Co-operation in Europe, Mission to Bosn. & Herz., The Processing of ICTY Rule 11bis Cases in Bosnia and Herzegovina: Reflections on Findings from Five Years of OSCE Monitoring (2010).

Organization for Security and Co-operation in Europe, Mission to Bosn. & Herz., Delivering Justice in Bosnia and Herzegovina: An Overview of War Crimes Processing from 2005 to 2010 (May 2011).

Organization for Security and Co-operation in Europe, Mission to Bosn. & Herz., Combating Impunity for Conflict-Related Sexual Violence in Bosnia and Herzegovina: Progress and Challenges (2014).

Organization for Security and Co-operation in Europe, Mission to Serb., Views on War Crimes, the ICTY, and the National War Crimes Judiciary (2009).

Organization for Security and Co-operation in Europe, Mission to Serb., Belgrade Centre for Human Rights & Ipsos Pub. Affairs, Attitudes Towards War Crimes Issues, ICTY and the National Judiciary (2011).

Organization for Security and Co-operation in Europe, Mission to Serb., War Crimes Proceedings in Serbia 2003–2014 (2015).

Mladen Ostojić, Between Justice and Stability: The Politics of War Crimes Prosecutions in Post-Milošević Serbia (2014).

Zoran Pajić & Dragan M. Popović, Facing the Past and Access to Justice from a Public Perspective (2011).

Jelena Pejić, *The Yugoslav Truth and Reconciliation Commission: A Shaky Start*, 25 Fordham Int'l L. J. 1 (2001).

Devan O. Pendas, *The Fate of Nuremberg: The Legacy and Impact of the Subsequent Nuremberg Trials in Postwar Germany*, *in* Reassessing the Nuremberg Military Tribunals: Transitional Justice, Trial Narratives, and Historiography 249 (Kim C. Priemel & Alexa Stiller eds., 2014).

Victor Peskin, *Courting Rwanda: The Promises and Pitfalls of the ICTR Outreach Programme*, 3 J. Int'l Crim. Just. 950 (2005).

Victor Peskin, International Justice in Rwanda and the Balkans: Virtual Trials and the Struggle for State Cooperation (2008).

Carla del Ponte in collaboration with Chuck Sudetić, Madame Prosecutor: Confrontations with Humanity's Worst Criminals and the Culture of Impunity (2008).

Kim C. Priemel & Alex Stiller, *Introduction* to Reassessing the Nuremberg Military Tribunals: Transitional Justice, Trial Narratives, and Historiography 1 (Kim C. Priemel & Alexa Stiller eds., 2014).

Stefan Priesner et al., *Transitional Justice in Bosnia and Herzegovina: Findings of a Public Survey*, 2 LOCAL-GLOBAL JUSTICE: IDENTITY, SECURITY, COMMUNITY 119 (2006).

NIKOLAS M. RAJKOVIĆ, THE POLITICS OF INTERNATIONAL LAW AND COMPLIANCE: SERBIA, CROATIA AND THE HAGUE TRIBUNAL (2012).

SABRINA P. RAMET, THE THREE YUGOSLAVIAS: STATE-BUILDING AND LEGITIMATION, 1918–2005 (2006).

Sabrina P. Ramet, *The Denial Syndrome and Its Consequences: Serbian Political Culture Since 2000*, 40 COMMUNIST & POST-COMMUNIST STUD. 41 (2007).

David P. Redlawsk et al., *The Affective Tipping Point: Do Motivated Reasoners Ever "Get It"?*, 31 POL. PSYCHOL. 563 (2010).

DAVID RIEFF, IN PRAISE OF FORGETTING: HISTORICAL MEMORY AND ITS IRONIES (2016).

Thomas Risse & Kathryn Sikkink, *The Socialization of International Human Rights Norms into Domestic Practices: Introduction* to THE POWER OF HUMAN RIGHTS: INTERNATIONAL NORMS AND DOMESTIC CHANGE (Thomas Risse et al. eds., 1999).

Adam Roberts, *NATO's "Humanitarian War" over Kosovo*, 41 SURVIVAL 102 (1999).

YAËL RONEN, BOSNIA AND HERZEGOVINA: THE INTERACTION BETWEEN THE ICTY AND DOMESTIC COURTS IN ADJUDICATING INTERNATIONAL CRIMES (2011).

Yaël Ronen, *The Impact of the ICTY on Atrocity-Related Prosecutions in the Courts of Bosnia and Herzegovina*, 3 PENN ST. J. L. & INT'L AFF. 113 (2014).

Thane Rosenbaum, *The Romance of Nuremberg and the Tease of Moral Justice*, 27 CARDOZO L. REV. 1731 (2006).

Susana SáCouto & Katherine Cleary, *The Importance of Effective Investigation of Sexual Violence and Gender-Based Crimes at the International Criminal Court*, 17 AM. U. J. GENDER, SOC. POL'Y & L. 337 (2009).

Leila Nadya Sadat, *Can the ICTY Šainović and Perišić Cases Be Reconciled?*, 108 AM. J. INT'L L. 475 (2014).

Francesco de Sanctis, *Reconciling Justice and Legality: A Quest for Fair Punishment in Cases on Bosnian Atrocity Crimes*, 12 J. INT'L CRIM. JUST. 847 (2014).

Eldar Sarajlić, *Bosnian Elections and Recurring Ethnonationalisms: The Ghost of the Nation State*, 2 J. ETHNOPOLITICS & MINORITY ISSUES EUR. 66 (2010).

Dan Saxon, *Exporting Justice: Perceptions of the ICTY Among the Serbian, Croatian, and Muslim Communities in the Former Yugoslavia*, 4 J. HUM. RTS. 559 (2005).

Beth Van Schaack, *The Building Blocks of Hybrid Justice*, 44 DENVER J. INT'L L. & POL'Y 101 (2016).

William A. Schabas, *Selecting Situations and Cases*, in THE LAW AND PRACTICE OF THE INTERNATIONAL CRIMINAL COURT 376 (Carsten Stahn ed., 2015).

Michael Scharf, *Self-Representation Versus Assignment of Defence Counsel Before International Criminal Tribunals*, 4 J. INT'L CRIM. JUST. 31 (2006).

Michael Scharf, *The Tools for Enforcing International Criminal Justice in the New Millennium: Lessons from the Yugoslav Tribunal*, 4 DEPAUL L. REV. 925 (2000).

DAVID SCHEFFER, ALL THE MISSING SOULS: A PERSONAL HISTORY OF THE WAR CRIMES TRIBUNALS (2012).

David Schwendiman, *Prosecuting Atrocity Crimes in National Courts: Looking Back on 2009 in Bosnia and Herzegovina*, 8 NW. J. INT'L HUM. RTS. 269 (2010).

Johanna Mannergren Selimović, *Perpetrators and Victims: Local Responses to the International Criminal Tribunal for the Former Yugoslavia*, 57 J. GLOBAL & HIST. ANTHROPOLOGY 50 (2010).

Yuval Shany, *The Legitimacy Paradox of Self-Representation*, *in* THE MILOŠEVIĆ TRIAL: AN AUTOPSY 174 (Timothy William Waters ed., 2013).

Yuval Shany, *Two Sides of the Same Coin? Judging Milošević and Serbia Before the ICTY and ICJ*, *in* THE MILOŠEVIĆ TRIAL: AN AUTOPSY 441 (Timothy William Waters ed., 2013).

IAN SHAPIRO, DEMOCRACY'S PLACE (1996).

Dustin N. Sharp, *Interrogating the Peripheries: The Preoccupations of Fourth Generation Transitional Justice*, 26 HARV. HUM. RTS. J. 149 (2013).

JOHN SHATTUCK, FREEDOM ON FIRE: HUMAN RIGHTS WARS & AMERICA'S RESPONSE (2003).

Emily Shaw, *The Role of Social Identity in Resistance to International Criminal Law: The Case of Serbia and the ICTY* (Berkeley Program in Soviet and Post-Soviet Studies Working Paper Series, 2003).

JUDITH N. SHKLAR, LEGALISM: LAW, MORALS, AND POLITICAL TRIALS (1986).

Detlef Siegfried, *"Don't Trust Anyone Older than 30?" Voices of Conflict and Consensus Between Generations in 1960s West Germany*, 40 J. CONTEMP. HIST. 727 (2005).

KATHRYN SIKKINK, THE JUSTICE CASCADE: HOW HUMAN RIGHTS PROSECUTIONS ARE CHANGING WORLD POLITICS (2011).

Kathryn Sikkink & Hun Joon Kim, *The Justice Cascade: The Origins and Effectiveness of Prosecutions of Human Rights Violations*, 9 ANN. REV. L. SOC. SCI. 269 (2013).

LAURA SILBER & ALLAN LITTLE, YUGOSLAVIA: DEATH OF A NATION (1995).

BETH A. SIMMONS, MOBILIZING FOR HUMAN RIGHTS: INTERNATIONAL LAW IN DOMESTIC SETTINGS (2009).

Eileen Simpson, *Stop to The Hague: Internal Versus External Factors Suppressing the Advancement of the Rule of Law in Serbia*, 36 GEO. J. INT'L L. 1255 (2005).

PARAM-PREET SINGH, HUMAN RIGHTS WATCH, NARROWING THE IMPUNITY GAP: TRIALS BEFORE BOSNIA'S WAR CRIMES CHAMBER (2007).

PARAM-PREET SINGH, HUMAN RIGHTS WATCH, JUSTICE FOR ATROCITY CRIMES: LESSONS OF INTERNATIONAL SUPPORT FOR TRIALS BEFORE THE STATE COURT OF BOSNIA AND HERZEGOVINA (2012).

Robert Sloane, *The Expressive Capacity of International Punishment* (Colum. Public L. & Legal Theory, Working Paper 06100, 2006).

Robert D. Sloane, *The Expressive Capacity of Punishment: The Limits of the National Law Analogy and the Potential of International Criminal Law*, 34 STAN. J. INT'L L. 39 (2007).

Göran Sluiter, *Compromising the Authority of International Justice: How Vojislav Šešelj Runs His Trial*, 5 J. INT'L CRIM. JUST. 529 (2007).

SMMRI ON BEHALF OF B92, PERCEPTION OF TRUTH IN SERBIA (2001).

Jack Snyder & Leslie Vinjamuri, *Trials and Errors: Principle and Pragmatism in Strategies of International Justice*, 28 INT'L SECURITY 5 (2003–2004).

Gary D. Solis, *The Gotovina Acquittal: A Sound Appellate Course Correction*, 215 MIL. L. REV. 78 (2013).

Azra Somun, *Reports on the Transitional Justice Experience in Bosnia and Herzegovina*, 1 INT'L J. RULE L., TRANSITIONAL JUST. & HUM. RTS. 56 (2010).

Marlene Spoerri & Mladen Jokšić, *The Ethics of a Justice Imposed: Ratko Mladić's Arrest and the Costs of Conditionality*, CARNEGIE COUNCIL ETHICS INT'L AFF. (June 2, 2011).

CHRIS STEPHEN, JUDGMENT DAY: THE TRIAL OF SLOBODAN MILOŠEVIĆ (2003).

Izabela Steflja, *Identity Crisis in Post-Conflict Societies: The ICTY's Role in Defensive Nationalism Among the Serbs*, 22 GLOBAL CHANGE, PEACE & SECURITY 231 (2010).

Fritz Stern, *Foreward* to ADENAUER'S GERMANY AND THE NAZI PAST: THE POLITICS OF AMNESTY AND INTEGRATION, at vii (Joel Gold trans., 2002).

ERIC STOVER, THE WITNESSES: WAR CRIMES AND THE PROMISE OF JUSTICE IN THE HAGUE (2005).

JELENA SUBOTIĆ, HIJACKED JUSTICE: DEALING WITH THE PAST IN THE BALKANS (2009).

Jelena Subotić, *Legitimacy, Scope, and Conflicting Claims on the ICTY: In the Aftermath of Gotovina, Haradinaj, and* Perišić, 13 J. HUM. RTS. 170 (2014).

Mark A. Summers, *The Surprising Acquittals in the* Gotovina *and* Perišić *Cases*, 13 RICH. J. GLOBAL L. & BUS. 649 (2015).

Cass R. Sunstein, *What's Available? Social Influences and Behavioral Economics*, 97 NW. U. L. REV. 1295 (2003).

CASS R. SUNSTEIN & REID HASTIE, WISER: GETTING BEYOND GROUPTHINK TO MAKE GROUPS SMARTER (2015).

Charles S. Taber & Milton Lodge, *Motivated Skepticism in the Evaluation of Political Beliefs*, 50 AM. J. POL. SCI. 755 (2006).

HENRI TAJFAL, HUMAN GROUPS AND SOCIAL CATEGORIES: STUDIES IN SOCIAL PSYCHOLOGY (1981).

NICHOLAS TAVUCHIS, MEA CULPA: A SOCIOLOGY OF APOLOGY AND RECONCILIATION (1991).

David Taylor, *The Objectives and Experiences of International Justice at the Grassroots, in* FACING THE PAST: AMENDING HISTORICAL INJUSTICES THROUGH INSTRUMENTS OF TRANSITIONAL JUSTICE (Peter Malcontent ed., 2016).

Telford Taylor, *Opening Argument in Medical Trial, in* I TRIALS OF WAR CRIMINALS BEFORE THE NUERNBERG MILITARY TRIBUNALS UNDER CONTROL COUNCIL LAW No. 10 27 (1948).

RUTI G. TEITEL, TRANSITIONAL JUSTICE (2000).

Ruti G. Teitel, *Transitional Justice Genealogy*, 16 HARV. HUM. RTS. J. 69 (2003).

Ruti Teitel, *The Transitional Apology, in* TAKING WRONGS SERIOUSLY: APOLOGIES AND RECONCILIATION (Elazar Barkan & Alexander Karn eds., 2006).

THE LEGACY OF THE INTERNATIONAL CRIMINAL TRIBUNAL FOR THE FORMER YUGOSLAVIA (Bert Swart et al. eds., 2011).

GUNNAR THEISSEN, BETWEEN ACKNOWLEDGEMENT AND IGNORANCE: HOW WHITE SOUTH AFRICANS HAVE DEALT WITH THE APARTHEID PAST (Hamber et al. eds., 1996).

Oskar N.T. Thoms et al., *The Effects of Transitional Justice Mechanisms* (Ctr. Int'l Pol'y Stud., Working Paper, 2008).

Alan Tieger, *Remorse and Mitigation in the International Criminal Tribunal for the Former Yugoslavia*, 16 LEIDEN J. INT'L L. 777 (2003).

GERARD TOAL & CARL T. DAHLMAN, BOSNIA REMADE: ETHNIC CLEANSING AND ITS REVERSAL (2011).

David Tolbert, *The International Criminal Court for the Former Yugoslavia: Unforeseen Successes and Foreseeable Shortcomings*, 26 FLETCHER F. WORLD AFF. 7 (2002).

DAVID TOLBERT & ALEKSANDAR KONTIĆ, FINAL REPORT OF THE INTERNATIONAL CRIMINAL LAW SERVICES (ICLS) EXPERTS ON THE SUSTAINABLE TRANSITION OF THE REGISTRY AND INTERNATIONAL DONOR SUPPORT TO THE COURT OF BOSNIA AND HERZEGOVINA AND THE PROSECUTOR'S OFFICE OF BOSNIA AND HERZEGOVINA IN 2009 (2008).

DAVID TOLBERT & ALEKSANDAR KONTIĆ, *THE INTERNATIONAL CRIMINAL TRIBUNAL FOR THE FORMER YUGOSLAVIA: TRANSITIONAL JUSTICE, THE TRANSFER OF CASES TO NATIONAL COURTS, AND LESSONS FOR THE ICC, IN* THE EMERGING PRACTICE

OF THE INTERNATIONAL CRIMINAL COURT (CARSTEN STAHN & GÖRAN SLUITER EDS., 2009).

Stefan Trechsel, *Rights in Criminal Proceedings Under the ECHR and the ICTY Statute—A Precarious Comparison, in* THE LEGACY OF THE INTERNATIONAL CRIMINAL TRIBUNAL FOR THE FORMER YUGOSLAVIA (Bert Swart et al. eds., 2011).

NEVENKA TROMP, PROSECUTING SLOBODAN MILOŠEVIĆ: THE UNFINISHED TRIAL (2016).

Amos Tversky & Daniel Kahneman, *Judgment Under Uncertainty: Heuristics and Biases,* 185 SCI. 1124 (1974).

U.S. INSTITUTE OF PEACE, SPECIAL REPORT 128, SERBIA AT THE CROSSROADS AGAIN (2004).

Álvaro de Vasconcelos, *Preface to* WAR CRIMES, CONDITIONALITY, AND EU INTEGRATION IN THE WESTERN BALKANS (Judy Blatt & Jelena Obradović-Wochnik eds., 2009).

Leslie Vinjamuri, *Deterrence, Democracy, and the Pursuit of International Justice,* 24 ETHICS & INT'L AFF. 191 (2010).

Sebastian van de Vliet, *Addressing Corruption and Organized Crime in the Context of Re-establishing the Rule of Law, in* DECONSTRUCTING THE RECONSTRUCTION: HUMAN RIGHTS AND RULE OF LAW IN POSTWAR BOSNIA AND HERZEGOVINA (Dina Francesca Haynes ed., 2008).

Lal C. Vohrah & Jon Cina, *The Outreach Programme, in* ESSAYS ON ICTY PROCEDURE AND EVIDENCE IN HONOUR OF GABRIELLE KIRK MCDONALD (Richard May et al. eds., 2000).

PATRICIA M. WALD, OPEN SOCIETY JUSTICE INITIATIVE, TYRANTS ON TRIAL: KEEPING ORDER IN THE COURTROOM (2009).

Timothy William Waters, *Preface to* THE MILOŠEVIĆ TRIAL: AN AUTOPSY (Timothy William Waters ed., 2013).

Timothy William Waters, *The Context, Contested: Histories of Yugoslavia and Its Violent Dissolution, in* THE MILOŠEVIĆ TRIAL: AN AUTOPSY 3 (Timothy William Waters ed., 2013).

Harvey M. Weinstein et al., *Stay the Hand of Justice: Whose Priorities Take Priority?, in* LOCALIZING TRANSITIONAL JUSTICE: INTERVENTIONS AND PRIORITIES AFTER MASS VIOLENCE (Rosalind Shaw & Lars Waldorf eds., 2010).

Thomas G. Weiss, *Collective Spinelessness: U.N. Actions in the Former Yugoslavia, in* THE WORLD AND YUGOSLAVIA'S WARS 59 (Richard H. Ullman ed., 1996).

Marc Weller, *The International Response to the Dissolution of the Socialist Federal Republic of Yugoslavia,* 86 AM. J. INT'L L. 569 (1992).

LAWRENCE WESCHLER, A MIRACLE, A UNIVERSE: SETTLING ACCOUNTS WITH TORTURERS (1991).

ISABELLE WESSELINGH & ARNAUD VAULERIN, RAW MEMORY: PRIJEDOR, LABORATORY OF ETHNIC CLEANSING (2005).

Alex Whiting, *In International Criminal Prosecutions, Justice Delayed Can Be Justice Delivered,* 50 HARV. INT'L L.J. 323 (2009).

Alex Whiting, *The ICTY as a Laboratory of International Criminal Procedure, in* THE LEGACY OF THE INTERNATIONAL CRIMINAL TRIBUNAL FOR THE FORMER YUGOSLAVIA (Bert Swart et al. eds., 2011).

Paul R. Williams & Patricia Taft, *The Role of Justice in the Former Yugoslavia: Antidote or Placebo for Coercive Appeasement?,* 35 CASE W. RES. J. INT'L L. 219 (2003).

Clint Williamson, *Real Justice, in Time: The Initial Indictment of Milošević, in* THE MILOŠEVIĆ TRIAL: AN AUTOPSY 77 (Timothy William Waters ed., 2013).

David Wippman, *The Costs of International Justice,* 100 AM. J. INT'L L. 861 (2006).

STEVEN WOEHREL, CONG. RES. SERV., CONDITIONS ON U.S. AID TO SERBIA (2008).

Ralph Zacklin, *The Failings of Ad Hoc International Tribunals*, 2 J. INT'L CRIM. JUST. 541 (2004).

Alexander Zahar, *Civilizing Civil War: Writing Morality as Law at the ICTY*, *in* THE LEGACY OF THE INTERNATIONAL CRIMINAL TRIBUNAL FOR THE FORMER YUGOSLAVIA (Bert Swart et al. eds., 2011).

Alexander Zahar, *Legal Aid, Self-Representation, and the Crisis at the Hague Tribunal*, 19 CRIM. L.F. 241 (2008).

José Zalaquett, *Confronting Human Rights Violations Committed by Former Governments: Principles Applicable and Political Constraints*, *in* STATE CRIMES: PUNISHMENT OR PARDON (1989).

JUSUF ŽIGA ET AL., YOUTH STUDY: BOSNIA AND HERZEGOVINA (2015).

WARREN ZIMMERMANN, ORIGINS OF A CATASTROPHE: YUGOSLAVIA AND ITS DESTROYERS—AMERICA'S LAST AMBASSADOR TELLS WHAT HAPPENED AND WHY (1996).

Index

acknowledgement. *See also* denial and
denialism; Germany, Federal
Republic of; public opinion
surveys in Bosnia and Serbia; and
Nuremberg tribunal and trial
 by Bosniak citizens of Bosniak war
crimes, 93, 275–76, 276n84
 by Bosniak leaders of war crimes, 306–07
 by Bosnian Croat citizens of Croat war
crimes, 93, 262
 by Bosnian Serb citizens of Serb war
crimes, 93, 101–02, 262, 273, 319
 by Bosnian Serb leaders and institutions
of Serb war crimes, 297–301
 conceptions of, among Bosnians who
supported the ICTY, 99–103,
259–60, 278–79
 conceptions of, among Serbians who
supported the ICTY, 5–6,
118–121, 193–94
 possible influence of ICTY on, 10,
236–38, 241, 244–45, 257,
297–303
 by Serbian citizens of Serb war crimes,
238–40
 by Serbian and SaM leaders and
institutions, including apologies
and other gestures of remorse,
for Serb war crimes, 246–55
Adenauer, Konrad, 434, 435nn35–36
Ahmetašević, Nidžara, 39, 97–100, 138, 145,
151, 161, 163, 169–70, 280n115,
286, 286n159, 290n192, 291, 308,
317–19, 343, 351, 379–80

Albright, Madeleine, 1, 20n33, 33, 42, 146,
259, 317
Alić, Almir, 314–15, 314nn354–55
Alić, Izudin, 99
Alić, Sinan, 96, 303n280
Alliance of Independent Social Democrats
(SNSD), 52, 300
Amnesty International, 23, 402–03
Anastasijević, Dejan, 10n32, 63, 69, 72n97,
116–18, 119n51, 418n261
Antonetti, Jean-Claude, 163, 163nn272–73
Arbour, Louise, 30n94, 32n104, 42, 296,
296n226, 309, 328, 328n27
Arendt, Hannah, 94
Arnaut, Damir, 20–21, 154, 303, 330, 332–33,
378–79
arrests and other transfers of ICTY
fugitives, policies and practices.
See also Implementation Force,
and Stabilization Force
 of Federation of BiH authorities, 34–35,
35n125, 328–30
 of Serbian authorities, 61–62, 64–68,
67n60, 73–78, 80, 83–85
 of Republika Srpska authorities, 35–36,
35n125, 43–44, 75, 80, 80n158
Ashdown, Paddy, 47, 47n218, 50–51, 51n243,
54, 298, 299n245, 302, 302n274,
334, 337n96, 338n104, 377–78

Bakšić Muftić, Jasna, 23n51, 25, 39, 94, 97–98,
106–07, 140, 148n158, 157, 162,
166, 170–72, 184, 259, 279–80,
285–87, 289, 318n379, 326, 371

Some Kind of Justice. Diane Orentlicher.
© Diane Orentlicher 2018. Published 2018 by Oxford University Press.

CPSIA information can be obtained
at www.ICGtesting.com
Printed in the USA
BVHW040718200919
558724BV00008B/3/P